DOCTRINAL
NEW TESTAMENT
COMMENTARY

Volume II
ACTS — PHILIPPIANS

DOCTRINAL NEW TESTAMENT COMMENTARY

Volume II

ACTS – PHILIPPIANS

By

Bruce R. McConkie

Bookcraft
Salt Lake City, Utah

Copyright © 1971 by

Bookcraft, Inc.

LIBRARY OF CONGRESS CATALOG CARD NUMBER 65-29174

16 17 18 19 20   89 88 87 86 85

ISBN 0-88494-216-3

Lithographed in the United States of America
PUBLISHERS PRESS
Salt Lake City, Utah

Preface

Peter said: "Our beloved brother Paul . . . hath written . . . in all his epistles . . . some things hard to be understood."

And the same is true of James and John, of Jude and Luke, and of Peter himself — all have written deep, difficult doctrine.

Through latter-day revelation we are now able to understand and interpret the doctrines of salvation as recorded by these inspired authors.

Volume II of this *Doctrinal New Testament Commentary* deals with doctrine, with "the words of eternal life," with the gospel teachings which must be known and obeyed if men are to gain peace in this life and inherit immortal glory in the world to come.

And what wondrous doctrine the New Testament doth contain — pure, sound, perfect doctrine; doctrine which makes known the mysteries of the kingdom; doctrine which enables men to make their callings and elections sure; doctrine which leads to joint heirship with Christ, which admits true believers to the General Assembly and Church of the Firstborn in the realms of the exalted.

And thanks be to God that he hath given us the Book of Mormon, the Doctrine and Covenants, the Pearl of Great Price, and the inspired teachings of latter-day prophets to guide and direct gospel students in learning the true and hidden teachings of the New Testament. Abundant use of all these materials has been made in the interpretations and explanations in this *Doctrinal New Testament Commentary*.

This work is not a church publication; I alone am responsible for the interpretations and views set forth.

As with Volume I of this same work, I am greatly indebted to Velma Harvey, my very able and conscientious secretary, for assisting with much of the technical detail of preparation and publication.

—Bruce R. McConkie

Salt Lake City, Utah
December 1, 1970

ABBREVIATIONS

Scriptural references are abbreviated in a standard self-identifying way. Other books are cited by author and title, except the following:

Commentary I — Bruce R. McConkie, *Doctrinal New Testament Commentary*, Volume I, The Gospels

Dummelow — J. R. Dummelow, *The One Volume Bible Commentary*

I. V. — Joseph Smith, *Inspired Version of Bible*, First Edition

Jamieson — Robert Jamieson, A. R. Fausset, and David Brown, *Commentary on the Whole Bible*

Mormon Doctrine — Bruce R. McConkie, *Mormon Doctrine*, Second Edition

Teachings — Joseph Fielding Smith, *Teachings of the Prophet Joseph Smith*

Index — Scriptural Passages

DOCTRINAL NEW TESTAMENT COMMENTARY

INDEX — SCRIPTURAL PASSAGES

11

DOCTRINAL NEW TESTAMENT COMMENTARY

12

INDEX — SCRIPTURAL PASSAGES

DOCTRINAL NEW TESTAMENT COMMENTARY

INDEX — SCRIPTURAL PASSAGES

INDEX — SCRIPTURAL PASSAGES

17

DOCTRINAL NEW TESTAMENT COMMENTARY

The Acts of the Apostles

Acts shows forth the operation of the Holy Spirit in the true Church.

Among Biblical books it ranks first in telling how the Church and kingdom of God on earth operates when Jesus the King is not personally resident on planet earth.

During our Lord's personal ministry, the Holy Ghost bore record of the Father and the Son to selected saints on special occasions. But the gift of the Holy Ghost — the right to the constant companionship of that member of the Godhead — was not poured out on church members generally until Pentecost.

Thereafter the faithful saints — not the apostles and leaders only, but all those who had overcome the world, who had cleansed and perfected their lives, who had gained the companionship of the Holy Ghost — all these began to see visions, entertain angels, prophesy with power, receive revelations, heal the sick, commune with God, and enjoy all of the signs which Jesus said would identify that very gospel which he himself taught.

Acts tells how the spiritual gifts multiplied until they were enjoyed by the apostles and by whole congregations of the faithful. Peter and Paul raise the dead. Angels minister to Jew and Gentile alike. Miracles of healing multiply. Thousands receive the gift of tongues. Revelation and prophecy is everywhere. Visions abound. Stephen sees the Father and the Son; the daughters of Philip prophesy, as do Agabus and nameless hosts of others. And the Lord himself comes again and again and again. But above all, the spirit of testimony and the power of sanctification are everywhere encountered.

Amid the spiritual display, Acts recounts the facts relative to church organization, missionary journeys, and the general spread of truth in a pagan world. It tells of the persecutions, stonings, trials, and impositions heaped upon those who center their hearts on Christ and strive to overcome the world.

And the doctrines of salvation — how many of these are spoken of in plainness and perfection: the Second Coming, the plan of salvation, the atonement of Christ, the restoration of the gospel in latter-days, revelation, prophecy, gifts of the Spirit, miracles, healings, the latter-day gathering of Israel, the resurrection, apostasy from the truth, and so forth.

But Acts is more than a book of spiritual superlatives; it is also an account of righteous men and their weaknesses and bickerings, their jealousies and foibles, their failures and successes.

The meridian saints are not perfect. Paul contends with Silas, corrects Peter, and rejects Mark as a missionary companion. And then with that dogged determination — without which he could not have withstood the Ephesians nor spoken boldly to Felix and Agrippa — he goes to Jerusalem, to bonds and imprisonment, in spite of prophetic counsel relative to the trials ahead. James, the Lord's brother, temporizes on the keeping of the Law of Moses, even a quarter of a century after that law was fulfilled, and hosts of Jewish converts mingle Mosaic practices with the newly found freedom of the gospel. All this is recorded by Luke, the faithful scribe.

Thus Acts is a book for weak mortals. It shows the spiritual heights they can ascend — imperfect, jealous, and stubborn though they may be. It shows that though a man may unwisely call down the curses of heaven upon hypocritical Ananias of the Sanhedrin, yet he can continue so steadfastly in grace that the next day the Lord Jesus will stand by him to give comfort and guidance.

Acts does in reality record how the Holy Spirit operates in the true Church; it is indeed the book which tells how God directs his earthly kingdom; it does in fact show forth the whole splendorous array of gospel gifts; but it is also the record which assures weak members of the Church that even they can have the Holy Spirit from whom gifts and graces flow, that even they can keep the faith and go on with Peter and Paul to eternal glory.

KINGDOM TO BE RESTORED TO ISRAEL

ACTS 1:1-8.

1 The former treatise have I made, O Theophilus, of all that Jesus began both to do and teach.

2 Until the day in which he was taken up, after that he through the Holy Ghost had given commandments unto the apostles whom he had chosen:

3 To whom also he shewed himself alive after his passion by many infallible proofs, being seen of them forty days, and speaking of the things pertaining to the kingdom of God:

4 And, being assembled together with *them*, commanded them that they should not depart from Jerusalem, but wait for the promise of the Father, which, *saith he*, ye have heard of me.

5 For John truly baptized with water; but ye shall be baptized with the Holy Ghost not many days hence.

6 When they therefore were come together, they asked of him, saying, Lord, wilt thou at this time restore again the kingdom to Israel?

7 And he said unto them, It is not for you to know the times or the seasons, which the Father hath put in his own power.

8 But ye shall receive power, after that the Holy Ghost is come upon you: and ye shall be witnesses unto me both in Jerusalem, and in all Judea, and in Samaria, and unto the uttermost part of the earth.

I.V. ACTS 1:3-4.

3 To whom also he **showed** himself alive after his **sufferings** by many infallible proofs, being seen of them forty days, and speaking of the things pertaining to the kingdom of God;

4 And, **being with them when they were assembled together,** commanded them that they should not depart from Jerusalem, but wait for the promise of the Father, which, saith he, ye have heard of me.

1. Luke, the beloved physician and missionary associate of Paul, first wrote his Gospel, telling of our Lord's mortal ministry, and second this book of Acts, which summarizes portions of the ministries of Peter and Paul. Both accounts are addressed to Theophilus, a prominent personage of the period, who, since Luke's writings are addressed to Gentile or Roman readers, may have been a distinguished citizen of Rome.

2. He through the Holy Ghost had given commandments]
The Holy Ghost is Christ's minister; he speaks and acts in the place and stead of the Son; his mission is to testify of Jesus, to reveal the mind and will of the Lord, to say what Christ would say if personally present. So complete, whole, and total is this commission and power that the Holy Ghost speaks in the first person as though he were Christ. (Moses 5:9.) In most instances when God's prophets and apostles say: "Thus saith Christ the Lord," they are announcing Christ's words as revealed to them by the power of the Holy Ghost.

3. His passion] "Our Lord's sufferings — the pain, torture, crown of thorns, scourging, and final crucifixion — which he endured between the night of the Last Supper and his death on the cross are collectively spoken of as the *Passion of Christ.*" (*Mormon Doctrine*, 2nd ed., p. 555.)

Seen of them forty days] At intervals during this period the Immortal Lord appeared, walked, conversed, ate with, and touched the Twelve and hundreds (perhaps thousands) of his mortal disciples. (*Commentary I*, pp. 839-873.)

Speaking of the things pertaining to the kingdom of God] The kingdom of God on earth is the Church of Jesus Christ; they are one and the same. The kingdom of God in heaven is the celestial world, the kingdom where God and Christ and saved beings dwell and reign. (*Mormon Doctrine*, 2nd ed., pp. 415-417.) Thus after his resurrection, Jesus was simply continuing and expanding the same teachings given before he broke the bands of death, teachings which revealed how to govern the Church on earth and attain membership in the Eternal Church in heaven.

4. The promise of the Father] This promise was twofold: 1. They would receive the gift of the Holy Ghost; and 2. They would receive a holy and sacred endowment, one reserved for the faithful, and of such a nature as to prepare them in all things to work out their salvation. See *Commentary I*, p. 859.

5. Ye shall be baptized with the Holy Ghost] 'Ye shall be filled with the Holy Ghost; ye shall actually receive and enjoy the companionship of that member of the Godhead; ye shall be immersed, as it were, in the Spirit.' It is one thing to receive the gift of the Holy Ghost, meaning the *right* to the constant companionship of the Holy Spirit based on faithfulness, and another actually to enjoy the witness and presence of that member of the Godhead. Every member of the Church receives the gift at baptism; those who so live as to receive guidance and direction from the Holy Ghost are the ones who are born again, who are immersed in the Spirit, who are in the full sense baptized with the Holy Ghost.

Thus, President Joseph F. Smith says: "The presentation or 'gift' of the Holy Ghost simply confers upon a man the right to receive at any time, when he is worthy of it and desires it, the power and light of truth of the Holy Ghost, although he may often be left to his own spirit and judgment. . . . It does not follow that a man who has received the presentation or gift of the Holy Ghost shall always receive the recognition and witness and presence of the Holy Ghost himself, or he may receive all these, and yet the Holy Ghost not tarry with him, but visit him from time to time." (Joseph F. Smith, *Gospel Doctrine*, 5th ed., pp. 60-61.)

6-8. For thousands of years nearly every prophet who ministered on earth had spoken of a glorious day when the kingdom would be restored to Israel both temporally and spiritually. And now, though the promised Messiah and Redeemer of Israel had in fact come, though the very Son of God himself had ministered among them, the great question in every heart remained unanswered: Was this the promised day?

Implicit in the apostles' inspired query was a plea for answers to such questions as these:

Is this the day when all nations shall flow to the Lord's house in the tops of the mountains? (Isa. 2:1-5.)

Will Israel now assemble from all nations unto the ensign the Lord shall raise? (Isa. 5:26-30.)

Has the time come for the Lord to set his hand the second time to recover the remnant of his people, to assemble the outcasts of Israel and gather together the dispersed of Judah from the four corners of the earth? (Isa. 11:10-16.)

Is this the promised hour when God shall bring the children of Israel from the land of the north, and from all the lands whither he has driven them, so they shall inherit again the lands given to their fathers? (Jer. 16:14-21; 23:1-8.)

What of the new covenant God promised to make with gathered Israel? Is he now ready to plead with them face to face so all shall know him from the least to the greatest? (Jer. 31:31-37; Ezek. 20:33-44.)

At long last, is Israel to live again as a people, as a nation, as God's covenant race, as a kingdom of priests — all as foretold over and over again by nearly all of the ancient prophets?

It was as though the apostles said to the Lord: 'We know thou hast given us thy Church which is the kingdom of God on earth. We have the keys of the kingdom and can control and regulate, as seemeth good unto thee, all things in this spiritual kingdom. But what of the promises made to Israel? When will they be fulfilled? When is the great day of gathering to occur, the day when that once favored nation will be gathered in from her long dispersion? Tell us, Lord, what of the gathering and the promised political kingdom that of necessity must then be created? Will we play a part in that great work? Is it for our day?'

From the resurrected God of Israel the answer came: 'No, not now, be patient; all that my holy prophets have spoken shall be fulfilled in due time; but it is not for your day; even the time and the season is not now to be revealed. But go ye forth and bear testimony of me and be ye witnesses of my resurrection in all the world as I have commanded you.'

Thus, with an endorsement of the past and a promise for the future, did Jesus place the capstone on his earthly ministry. He thus approved all that his prophets had said concerning the restoration of the kingdom to Israel in the latter-days, and he thus renewed the assurance that there would be yet another glorious gospel dispensation in a day subsequent to New Testament times.

This passage teaches the doctrine of the restoration in latter-days and of revelation for a day after the apostolic era. The very kingdom set up of old with the same laws, officers, and subjects or citizens was to be reestablished. And to accomplish this end revelation of necessity would be required — revelation to identify the subjects who were of Israel, revelation to make known the laws by which the kingdom would be governed, and revelation to appoint and empower the officers who would administer the affairs of the kingdom.

Without latter-day revelation how can the kingdom be restored to Israel? Unless God speaks again, how can the identity of scattered Israel be known? Until he names the date, who will know when to assemble? And where will they go? Who will prepare the way? Around what standard shall they rally? Who will raise the promised ensign to the nations? What kind of a kingdom will it be? Where shall the capital city be built? Will the kingdom have legislators, judges, administrators? If so, how shall they be chosen? Truly the plans and promises and purposes of the God of Israel can only be brought to pass by revelation.

And thanks be to God, the day of restoration has now dawned, the age of revelation is upon us, the gathering of Israel has started, the ecclesiastical kingdom has already been established anew, and the full political kingdom will soon be set up, when the King of Israel returns to reign personally on the earth for a thousand years.

This is the day when God is fulfilling the covenants "that he has covenanted with all the house of Israel, . . . by the mouth of his holy prophets, even from the beginning down, from generation to generation." The time has now come when Israel "shall be restored to the true church and fold of God; when they shall be gathered home to the lands of their inheritance, and shall be established in all their lands of promise." (2 Ne. 9:1-2.) The promises contained in the Tenth Article of Faith — promises of a literal gathering of Israel, of the restoration of the ten tribes, of the building of Zion on the American continent, of the personal millennial reign of Israel's King — are in process of or soon will be fulfilled.

To give power to mortal man to accomplish such an earth-wide and mighty movement as the gathering in of the lost sheep of Israel, Moses the prophet came to Joseph Smith and Oliver Cowdery on April 3, 1836, in the Kirtland Temple, and conferred upon them the keys of the gathering of Israel and the leading of the ten tribes from the land of the north. (D. & C. 110:11.) These keys have and will continue with The Church of Jesus Christ of Latter-day Saints; they consist of the power to direct and govern the promised gathering.

Already "the ten thousands of Ephraim, and . . . the thousands of Manasseh" have been pushed together from "the ends of the earth." (Deut. 33:13-17.) Already there has been some political preparation for the future return of the Jews, an event which shall finally occur when they accept Christ. (2 Ne. 10:7-9.) And in due course the one who holds the keys shall direct the return of the ten tribes from the land of the north. With "their rich treasures" they shall come to their American Zion to "be crowned with glory" by "the children of Ephraim," who already have assembled at the Lord's house in the tops of the mountains. (D. & C. 133:26-35.) And finally, in a millennial setting, the full political kingdom shall be restored. Then shall "the kingdom and dominion, and the greatness of the kingdom under the whole heaven, . . . be given to the people of the saints of the most High"; then shall the kingdom be "an everlasting kingdom"; and then "all dominions shall serve and obey" Christ the King of Israel. (Dan. 7:27.)

How evident it is that the true Church and kingdom of God on earth must know the doctrine of the gathering of Israel, and must have the power to do the mighty work involved, the work which will build up and establish, in all its glory and perfection, the long-desired government. Where this knowledge and power is, there the true Church of Christ is found; and where these things are not, there the true Church of Christ is not.

See *Commentary I*, pp. 648-649; *Mormon Doctrine*, 2nd ed., pp. 305-307; Acts 7:1-36; 13:42-49; 25:23-27; Rom. 11:25-36.

8. Ye shall receive power, after that the Holy Ghost is come upon you] No man can be a minister of Christ until he receives the Holy Ghost, and this follows the laying on of hands by a legal administrator who has power from God to confer so great a gift. Without the Holy Ghost no man can know what the Lord wants him to do or say. By the power of the Holy Ghost the Lord's ministers preach the gospel, administer the affairs of the Church, perform the ordinances of salvation, work miracles, and do all things necessary for the salvation of their fellowmen. Without the power of the Holy Ghost, none of these things can be done, nor should they be attempted. Hence, we have such divine directives as this: "If ye receive not the Spirit ye shall not teach." (D. & C. 42:14.)

In Samaria, and unto the uttermost part of the earth] To whom were the apostles sent? During his mortal ministry Jesus had limited their teachings to the house of Israel. (Matt. 10:1-6.) After his resurrection he removed the restriction and commanded them to go "into all the world, and preach the gospel to every creature." (Mark 16:14-20.) Here he renews that divine decree. See *Commentary I*, pp. 865-872.

JESUS ASCENDETH INTO HEAVEN

ACTS 1:9-14.

9 And when he had spoken these things, while they beheld, he was taken up; and a cloud received him out of their sight.

10 And while they looked stedfastly toward heaven as he went up, behold, two men stood by them in white apparel;

11 Which also said, Ye men of Galilee, why stand ye gazing up into heaven? this same Jesus, which is taken up from you into heaven, shall so come in like manner as ye have seen him go into heaven.

12 Then returned they unto Jerusalem from the mount called Olivet, which is from Jerusalem a sabbath day's journey.

13 And when they were come in, they went up into an upper room, where abode both Peter, and James, and John, and Andrew, Philip, and Thomas, Bartholomew, and Matthew, James *the son* of Alphaeus, and Simon Zelotes, and Judas *the brother* of James.

14 These all continued with one accord in prayer and supplication, with the women, and Mary the mother of Jesus, and with his brethren.

It is now the appointed time. Jesus is to return to his Father. But why not just vanish, as he did after breaking bread with the Emmaus Road disciples? (Luke 24:1-35.) Why not go away in secret? Why create this dramatic scene?

In his Ascension, as in all else, our Lord chose to dramatize and teach a gospel truth in such a way that it could not be misunderstood. Here he is teaching the literal nature of his Second Coming. He stands on the Mount of Olivet and ascends visibly; angels attend; they reveal that his going establishes the pattern for his return. Thus that Jesus whom the apostles knew intimately, whose immortal body they had felt and handled, that same resurrected personage who had eaten fish and an honeycomb before them now ascends personally, literally as they behold. And so shall he come again, on the Mount of Olivet, literally, personally, in the flesh, as a glorified Man, as a personage of tabernacle. See *Commentary I*, pp. 660-663; 1 Thess. 5:1-11; Rev. 14:1-5.

9. While they beheld] They were witnesses to the end; as their hands had felt the nail marks in his hands and feet (Luke 24:36-43), so now their eyes saw him ascend. It was all literal and personal, not imaginary or spiritual.

10. Two men] Angels, holy beings who not only are of the same race as men, but are in fact men, men in a different stage of existence than are mortals, but men who are the offspring of the same Father. See Acts 10:1-8.

12. The mount called Olivet] The Mount of Olives, "the olive-orchard" — hallowed spot! On this Mount is the Garden called Gethsemane where Jesus in agony took upon himself the sins of the world (*Commentary I*, pp. 772-777); here he now ascends in triumphant glory; and here he shall return in that same glory to begin his reign as Israel's King. (D. & C. 133:19-20.) **A sabbath day's journey]** Six furlongs or 3/4ths of a mile.

14. One accord] As the Christian dispensation got under way, the leading brethren and sisters of the Church were united in that perfect faith and love which made them disciples in very deed.

Mary the mother of Jesus] This is the last Biblical reference to our Lord's mother; all that is subsequently supposed to have

28

happened to her is based solely on the traditions and imaginations of those whose interests it serves. See *Commentary I*, pp. 80-85; *Mormon Doctrine*, 2nd ed., p. 471.

His brethren] During the mortal life of Jesus, his brethren, Mary's other sons, apparently did not believe in his divine Sonship. (Mark 6:3-4; John 7:3-9.) Now, forty days later, they are numbered with the disciples. See *Commentary I*, pp. 436-438; 865-872. Paul tells us that James, one of his brothers, subsequently became an apostle. (Gal. 1:19.)

APOSTLES CHOOSE SUCCESSOR TO JUDAS

ACTS 1:15-26.

15 And in those days Peter stood up in the midst of the disciples, and said, (the number of names together were about an hundred and twenty,)

16 Men *and* brethren, this scripture must needs have been fulfilled, which the Holy Ghost by the mouth of David spake before concerning Judas, which was guide to them that took Jesus.

17 For he was numbered with us, and had obtained part of this ministry.

18 Now this man purchased a field with the reward of iniquity; and falling headlong, he burst asunder in the midst, and all his bowels gushed out.

19 And it was known unto all the dwellers at Jerusalem; insomuch as that field is called in their proper tongue, Aceldama, that is to say, The field of blood.

20 For it is written in the book of Psalms, Let his habitation be desolate, and let no man dwell therein: and his bishoprick let another take.

21 Wherefore of these men which have companied with us all the time that the Lord Jesus went in and out among us,

22 Beginning from the baptism of John, unto that same day that he was taken up from us, must one be ordained to be a witness with us of his resurrection.

23 And they appointed two, Joseph called Barsabas, who was surnamed Justus, and Matthias.

24 And they prayed, and said, Thou, Lord, which knowest the hearts of all *men,* shew whether of these two thou hast chosen,

25 That he may take part of this ministry and apostleship, from which Judas by transgression fell, that he might go to his own place.

26 And they gave forth their lots; and the lot fell upon Matthias; and he was numbered with the eleven apostles.

How are apostles chosen to fill vacancies in the Council of the Twelve? With the suicide of Judas, such was the problem facing the remaining witnesses in that apostolic quorum. In choosing the original Twelve, Jesus had spent all night in prayer, learning his Father's will; only then had he chosen those whom he ordained apostles and to whom he gave the keys of his earthly kingdom. (*Commentary I,* pp. 209-211; 424-426.) Now Peter and the others, guided by the Spirit — as they frequently had been, though the gift of the Holy Ghost itself had not yet been given — made the selection and set the pattern for the future. As with all who are called to service in the kingdom, first, God revealed his will, and, then, the people voted to approve the heaven-named choice. God spoke and the saints sustained the voice from heaven. (D. & C. 20:65-67.)

Such also is the pattern followed today. "I give unto you my servant Brigham Young to be a president over the Twelve traveling council," the Lord said, "Which Twelve hold the keys to open up the authority of my kingdom upon the four corners of the earth, and after that to send my word to every creature." Then after naming others whom he had chosen, the Lord said: "A commandment I give unto you, that you should . . . approve of those names which I have mentioned, or else disapprove of them at my general conference." (D. & C. 124:127-128, 144.)

15. Peter stood up] Peter took the lead. But why not John, who was especially beloved by Jesus, or James, or Matthew? Simply because there is an order in the kingdom. Peter, James, and John were the First Presidency of the Church (D. & C. 81:1-2), and Peter was the presiding high priest and senior apostle of God on earth. In the very nature of things, the initiative, the directing prerogative, the final say as to what the Lord himself thought rested with the presiding head of the earthly kingdom.

16. The Holy Ghost by the mouth of David spake] The Psalms are inspired; they are scripture (D. & C. 68:1-4); David is thus a prophet. (Acts 2:29-30.) See *Commentary I,* pp. 251-253.

18-19. See *Commentary I,* pp. 797-798.

20. On separate occasions David, moved upon by the Spirit, had said (first, with reference to those who oppose the Lord and fight the truth): "Let their habitation be desolate; and let none dwell in their tents" (Psalm 69:25), and then (with seeming reference to one of his enemies): "Let his days be few; and let another take his office." (Psalm 109:8.) Peter joined these two statements and applied them to Judas. Thus, as is so often found in holy writ, seemingly slight and inconsequential statements turn out to contain hidden and vital teachings. How hard it would be to give true meaning to scriptures without the interpreting power of the Holy Spirit.

His bishoprick] His overseership, his ministry, his apostleship, or as our present translation renders David's original prophecy, "his office." (Psalm 109:8.)

21-22. For the meridian dispensation, the great apostolic testimony was: 'Jesus is the Lord. He ministered among us as God's Son, as the promised Messiah, as the Redeemer of Israel. And now he is risen from the dead; he has come forth in glorious immortality. And we know it because we felt the nail marks in his hands and feet and thrust our hands into his spear-pierced side. We know he has a tangible body because we handled his resurrected flesh and saw him eat fish and an honeycomb.'

Consequently, the new apostle must be chosen from among those who were present when the Holy Ghost descended upon Jesus after his baptism in Jordan, from those who had seen his miracles, believed his teachings, knelt in the upper room, and worshiped the risen Lord on the mountain in Galilee.

23. They appointed two] Two of their number, Barsabbas and Mathias, had apostolic stature, either of whom in their judgmen might have been chosen.

24. They prayed] They asked the Father, in the name of Christ, to tell which of the two he had chosen. This pattern for working out a problem to the best of one's mortal capacity and, then, asking God if the solution is correct, and also asking him to give such other direction as may be needed, is the standard, revealed procedure for solving problems and gaining direction from on high. It is the way, for instance, that Joseph Smith translated the Book of Mormon. (D. & C. 8 and 9.)

25. To his own place] Hell. Peter might with propriety have quoted from the same Psalm in which it is written that another would take Judas' bishopric, such prophecies as the following: "Let Satan stand at his right hand. When he shall be judged, let him be condemned: and let his prayer become sin. . . . Let there be none to extend mercy unto him. . . . As he loved cursing, so let it come unto him." (Psalm 109:6-17.)

26. If they cast lots, it was an instance in which the Lord chose the result. More probably, however, 'they gave forth their votes,' presumably "sustaining votes" to uphold him whom God had chosen to serve in the holy apostleship.

SPIRIT POURED OUT ON DAY OF PENTECOST

ACTS 2:1-21.

1 And when the day of Pentecost was fully come, they were all with one accord in one place.

2 And suddenly there came a sound from heaven as of a rushing mighty wind, and it filled all the house where they were sitting.

3 And there appeared unto them cloven tongues like as of fire, and it sat upon each of them.

4 And they were all filled with the Holy Ghost, and began to speak with other tongues, as the Spirit gave them utterance.

5 And there were dwelling at Jerusalem Jews, devout men, out of every nation under heaven.

6 Now when this was noised abroad, the multitude came together, and were confounded, because that every man heard them speak in his own language.

7 And they were all amazed and marvelled, saying one to another, Behold, are not all these which speak Galileans?

8 And how hear we every man in our own tongue, wherein we were born?

9 Parthians, and Medes, and Elamites, and the dwellers in Mesopotamia, and in Judea, and Cappadocia, in Pontus, and Asia.

10 Phrygia, and Pamphylia, in Egypt, and in the parts of Libya about Cyrene, and strangers of Rome, Jews and proselytes,

11 Cretes and Arabians, we do hear them speak in our tongues the wonderful works of God.

12 And they were all amazed, and were in doubt, saying one to another, What meaneth this?

13 Others mocking said, These men are full of new wine.

14 But Peter, standing up with the eleven, lifted up his voice, and said unto them, Ye men of Judea, and all *ye* that dwell at Jerusalem, be this known unto you, and hearken to my words:

15 For these are not drunken, as ye suppose, seeing it is *but* the third hour of the day.

16 But this is that which was spoken by the prophet Joel;

17 And it shall come to pass in the last days, saith God, I will pour out my Spirit upon all flesh: and your sons and your daughters shall prophesy, and your young men shall see visions, and your old men shall dream dreams:

18 And on my servants and on my handmaidens I will pour out in those days of my Spirit; and they shall prophesy:

19 And I will shew wonders in heaven above, and signs in the earth beneath; blood, and fire, and vapour of smoke:

20 The sun shall be turned into darkness, and the moon into blood, before that great and notable day of the Lord come:

21 And it shall come to pass, *that* whosoever shall call on the name of the Lord shall be saved.

"They shall speak with new tongues." (Mark 16:17.) So said Jesus of those who would believe his gospel. And now amid this Pentecostal outpouring of divine grace, the purpose of this gift of the Spirit is dramatically set forth. It is to preach the gospel, to make known God's saving truths, and to do it under faith-promoting and testimony-inspiring circumstances. Peter and the others spoke and people of all languages and tongues understood, thus showing forth the power of God and foreshadowing the apostolic ministry which would take the gospel to all nations, kindreds, tongues, and people.

In speaking of the purpose of the gift of tongues, Joseph Smith said: "The gift of tongues by the power of the Holy Ghost in the Church, is for the benefit of the servants of God to preach to unbelievers, as on the day of Pentecost." (*Teachings*, p. 195.) Also: "Be not so curious about tongues, do not speak in tongues except there be an interpreter present; the ultimate design of tongues is to speak to foreigners, and if persons are very anxious to display their intelligence, let them speak to such in their own tongues [that is in the tongues of the foreigners]." (*Teachings*, pp. 247-248.) See 1 Cor. 14:6-28.

"Pentecostal outpourings of the Spirit have occurred many times in many dispensations. One of these great latter-day Pentecostal periods was in connection with the dedication of the Kirtland Temple. For a period of weeks, the visions of eternity were opened to many, angels visited in the congregations of the saints, the Lord himself was seen by many, and tongues and prophecy were multiplied. (*History of the Church*, vol. 2, pp. 379-436.) On Sunday, March 27, 1836, in the dedicatory service itself, an almost exact repetition of the events of the New Testament day of Pentecost took place. 'Brother George A. Smith arose and began to prophesy,' the Prophet recorded, 'when a noise was heard like the sound of a rushing mighty wind, which filled the Temple, and all the congregation simultaneously arose, being moved upon by an invisible power; many began to speak in tongues and prophesy; others saw glorious visions; and I beheld the Temple was filled with angels, which fact I declared to the congregation. The people of the neighborhood came running together (hearing an unusual sound within, and seeing a bright light like a pillar of fire resting upon the Temple), and were astonished at what was taking place.' (*History of the Church*, vol. 2, p. 428.)" (*Mormon Doctrine*, 2nd ed., pp. 181-182.)

1. Day of Pentecost] "In ancient Israel 'the feast of weeks' (Ex. 34:22; Deut. 16:10), or 'the feast of harvest' (Ex. 23:16), or 'the day of the firstfruits' (Num. 28:26), was celebrated 50 days after the Passover. This occasion, from the Greek word Pentekoste (meaning 50th) was known as the day of Pentecost." (*Mormon Doctrine*, 2nd ed., p. 181.) Appropriately on this harvest-centered holiday the great apostolic harvest of souls began in full measure.

2-4. Some spiritual manifestations are so foreign to the experience of mankind generally that there is no way of describing them in words. They can only be felt and understood by the power of the Holy Ghost. (3 Ne. 17:15-25; 19:31-36.)

3. Cloven tongues like as of fire] This same visible appearance of heaven-sent fire has been manifest to the Lord's saints on other special occasions. In the revealed, dedicatory prayer of the Kirtland Temple, the Prophet petitioned: "Let the anointing of thy ministers be sealed upon them with power from on high. Let

34

it be fulfilled upon them, as upon those on the day of Pentecost; let the gift of tongues be poured out upon thy people, even cloven tongues as of fire, and the interpretation thereof. And let thy house be filled, as with a rushing mighty wind, with thy glory." (D. & C. 109:35-37.) As part of the dedicatory services this petition was granted.

After the baptism of the Nephite Twelve, "the Holy Ghost did fall upon them, and they were filled with the Holy Ghost and with fire. And behold, they were encircled about as if it were by fire; and it came down from heaven, and the multitude did witness it, and did bear record; and angels did come down out of heaven and did minister unto them." (3 Ne. 19:13-14; Hela. 5:22-24, 43-45.)

12-13. Miraculous manifestations commonly bring forth one or the other of the reactions here seen. Men either mock, deride, and disbelieve, or they make inquiry, investigate, and seek to learn the truth.

16-21. Speaking, not particularly of Peter's day, but primarily of the age of restoration before the Second Coming, the Prophet Joel said: "And it shall come to pass afterward, that I will pour out my spirit upon all flesh; and your sons and your daughters shall prophesy, your old men shall dream dreams, your young men shall see visions: And also upon the servants and upon the handmaids in those days will I pour out my spirit. And I will shew wonders in the heavens and in the earth, blood, and fire, and pillars of smoke. The sun shall be turned into darkness, and the moon into blood, before the great and the terrible day of the Lord come. And it shall come to pass, that whosoever shall call on the name of the Lord shall be delivered: for in mount Zion and in Jerusalem shall be deliverance, as the Lord hath said, and in the remnant whom the Lord shall call." (Joel 2:28-32.)

When Moroni came to Joseph Smith during the night of September 21 and 22, 1823, he quoted these same verses and "said that this was not yet fulfilled, but was soon to be." (Jos. Smith 2:41.) Peter's application to his day of a yet-to-be fulfilled prophecy was proper because the passage teaches there would be visions, dreams, revelations, and spiritual outpourings among God's people.

35

There was thus a partial and incomplete fulfilment in Peter's day, with the great pre-millennial manifestations being reserved for the appointed time.

17. I will pour out of my Spirit] The Spirit to be poured out in abundant measure upon all flesh in the last days is not the Holy Ghost but the Light of Christ. The gift of the Holy Ghost is reserved for the saints; he is the Spirit whom the world cannot receive. (John 14:17.) The Light of Christ is the Spirit that proceeds forth from the presence of God to fill the immensity of space. (D. & C. 88:7-13.) This Spirit has been shed forth in greater measure in modern times than ever before in earth's history. (Joseph Fielding Smith, *Doctrines of Salvation*, vol. 1, pp. 174-183.) See Jas. 1:17-21.

Visions and revelations come, however, by the power of the Holy Ghost, and the Light of Christ, the all-pervading, universally present Spirit, is the vehicle used by the Holy Ghost to operate and function in all the world. That is, the Holy Ghost uses the Light of Christ to manifest his power and make available his gifts to all men everywhere at one and the same time.

"President Joseph F. Smith has expressed it thus: 'The Holy Ghost as a personage of Spirit can no more be omnipresent in person than can the Father or the Son, but by his intelligence, his knowledge, his power and influence, over and through the laws of nature, he is and can be omnipresent throughout all the works of God.' Thus when it becomes necessary to speak to us, he is able to do so by acting through the other Spirit, that is, through the Light of Christ." (Joseph Fielding Smith, *Doctrines of Salvation*, vol. 1, p. 40.)

19-20. See *Commentary I*, pp. 677-678.

21. In that dread day when the desolations and wonders are shown forth which shall usher in the Second Coming, there will be no safety and no deliverance except by the power of faith. If the heavens should rain atomic bombs, for instance, what safety could the saints find except through divine guidance?

PETER TESTIFIES OF JESUS' RESURRECTION

ACTS 2:22-36.

22 Ye men of Israel, hear these words; Jesus of Nazareth, a man approved of God among you by miracles and wonders and signs, which God did by him in the midst of you, as ye yourselves also know:

23 Him, being delivered by the determinate counsel and foreknowledge of God, ye have taken, and by wicked hands have crucified and slain:

24 Whom God hath raised up, having loosed the pains of death: because it was not possible that he should be holden of it.

25 For David speaketh concerning him, I foresaw the Lord always before my face, for he is on my right hand, that I should not be moved:

26 Therefore did my heart rejoice, and my tongue was glad; moreover also my flesh shall rest in hope:

27 Because thou wilt not leave my soul in hell, neither wilt thou suffer thine Holy One to see corruption.

28 Thou hast made known to me the ways of life; thou shalt make me full of joy with thy countenance.

29 Men *and* brethren, let me freely speak unto you of the patriarch David, that he is both dead and buried, and his sepulchre is with us unto this day.

30 Therefore being a prophet, and knowing that God had sworn with an oath to him, that of the fruit of his loins, according to the flesh, he would raise up Christ to sit on his throne;

31 He seeing this before spake of the resurrection of Christ, that his soul was not left in hell, neither his flesh did see corruption.

32 This Jesus hath God raised up, whereof we all are witnesses.

33 Therefore being by the right hand of God exalted, and having received of the Father the promise of the Holy Ghost, he hath shed for this, which ye now see and hear.

34 For David is not ascended into the heavens: but he saith himself, The Lord said unto my Lord, Sit thou on my right hand,

35 Until I make thy foes thy footstool.

36 Therefore let all the house of Israel know assuredly, that God hath made that same Jesus, whom ye have crucified, both Lord and Christ.

I.V. ACTS 2:27.

27 Because thou wilt not leave my soul in **prison,** neither wilt thou suffer thine Holy One to see corruption.

Teaching and testimony are mingled in perfect measure by Peter as he here bears witness of the divine Sonship of Jesus. As though setting a pattern for all inspired preachers, Peter: 1. *Reasons* that Jesus was approved of God because of the miracles he performed; 2. *Announces* that God had directed and foreordained the mortal ministry of his Son; 3. *Quotes* prophetic utterances foretelling the divine Sonship and resurrection of Christ; 4. *Explains* what these Messianic prophecies mean; and 5. *Bears testimony* that they are fulfilled in and through Jesus and his ministry.

22. Jesus performed miracles by the power of God, which he could not have done unless God was with him and approved of his ministry. (John 9:30-33.) His crowning teaching was: "I am the Son of God." (John 10:36.) Therefore, his miracles proved his divine Sonship, for God would not have endowed him with healing power if he were a false teacher.

23. There was no element of chance in the sufferings and death of our Lord. It was the counsel, program, and plan of God that Jesus should be crucified for the sins of the world. "I came into the world to do the will of my Father, because my Father sent me. And my Father sent me that I might be lifted up upon the cross." (3 Ne. 27:13-14.)

24. Jesus inherited from his Father the power of immortality, the power to live forever, or, after voluntarily giving up his life, the power to take it again in immortality. And thus death could have no power over him. See *Commentary I*, pp. 486-487.

25-31. As preserved for us in the King James Version of the Bible, David's Messianic utterance was: "I have set the Lord always before me: because he is at my right hand, I shall not be moved. Therefore my heart is glad, and my glory rejoiceth: my flesh also shall rest in hope. For thou wilt not leave my soul in hell; neither wilt thou suffer thine Holy One to see corruption. Thou wilt shew me the path of life: in thy presence is fulness of joy; at thy right hand there are pleasures for evermore." (Psalm 16:8-11.)

Either Peter had a better translation from which to quote, or (which is probable) he gave an inspired, interpreting analysis of what David's words meant. In any event, the passage teaches plainly that the Lord Jehovah, born as the Seed of David, would die, be resurrected, and reign eternally on the throne of David. See 1 Cor. 15:1-11.

27. Wilt not leave my soul in hell] 29. His sepulchre is with us] 30. Being a prophet] 34. David is not ascended into the heavens] David's story is one of the saddest in all the history of God's dealings with men. A man after the Lord's own heart — a mighty and valiant king, prophet, and patriarch — he fell into sin and lost his hope of eternal life. Peter here confirms David's prophetic powers, but announces that Israel's great king had not been resurrected as were all the holy prophets. The saints, those who had lived a celestial law from Adam to Christ, were with the Lord in his resurrection. (*Commentary I*, pp. 847-848.)

Though David was not one of these, he received the promise that his soul would not be left in hell, that is, he would not be a son of perdition, he would not be cast out eternally with the devil and his angels. Rather, when death and hell deliver up the dead which are in them, he shall come forth from the grave and receive that inheritance which he merits. See Rev. 20:11-15.

David could not gain a remission of his sins in this life. "A murderer for instance, one that sheds innocent blood, cannot have forgiveness," Joseph Smith said, meaning that such a person cannot come into the Church through baptism and become an heir of the celestial kingdom. "David sought repentance at the hand of God carefully with tears, for the murder of Uriah," the Prophet continued, "but he could only get it through hell: he got a promise that his soul should not be left in hell." (*Teachings*, p. 339.) Thus it is that the revelation says that Israel's once favored king "hath fallen from his exaltation, and received his portion." (D. & C. 132:39.)

32. We all are witnesses] See *Commentary I*, pp. 855-856.

36. Jesus, whom ye have crucified] Who crucified Christ? Peter here lays the blame on the Jews as a people and as a nation — not on Pilate who passed the sentence, not on the Roman soldiers who drive the nails — but on Caiaphas, the Sanhedrin, the priests, and the Jewish mob which chanted, "Crucify him, crucify him." (Luke 23:21.)

Jacob, brother to faithful Nephi, prophesied "that Christ . . . should come among the Jews, among those who are the more wicked part of the world; and they shall crucify him — for thus it behooveth our God, and there is none other nation on earth that would crucify their God. For should the mighty miracles be wrought among other nations they would repent, and know that he be their God. But because of priestcrafts and iniquities, they at Jerusalem will stiffen their necks against him, that he be crucified." (2 Ne. 10:3-5.)

But this does not mean that he was crucified by those Jews who as Nephites dwelt on the American continent (D. & C. 19:27), or by the apostles who also were Jews, or by the Jews who came before or who lived after his day. The generality of the Jews of Jesus' day rejected him and the generality of the Jews who remain at his Second Coming will accept him. Responsibility for sin, though described as attaching to a nation as such, when the dominant element of its society support the action, is nonetheless still a personal and individual thing. Every man will be rewarded or condemned for what he as an individual does.

PETER TELLS HOW TO GAIN SALVATION

ACTS 2:37-40.

37 Now when they heard *this*, they were pricked in their heart, and said unto Peter and to the rest of the apostles, Men *and* brethren, what shall we do?

38 Then Peter said unto them, Repent, and be baptized every one of you in the name of Jesus Christ for the remission of sins, and ye shall receive the gift of the Holy Ghost.

39 For the promise is unto you, and to your children, and to all that are afar off, *even* as many as the Lord our God shall call.

40 And with many other words did he testify and exhort, saying, Save yourselves from this untoward generation.

PETER TELLS HOW TO GAIN SALVATION

If any man then living had a revealed knowledge of what men must do to be saved in the kingdom of God, it was Peter, the Lord's chief apostolic minister. And Peter did not say men are saved through Christ's atonement without more; he did not say it is sufficient to confess the Lord Jesus with the lips; he did not say that men are justified by faith alone without the works of righteousness; he did not say it is enough to go around doing good and living in harmony with a high standard of Christian ethics; he did not say that all roads lead to Rome, that the only baptism which counts is that of the Spirit, or any of the other ten thousand conflicting concepts now current in a confused and faltering Christendom.

But Peter, while and as moved upon by the Holy Ghost, and thus pouring forth the mind and will of the Lord, taught that, based on the atonement, accountable men must:

1. Have faith in the Lord Jesus Christ, a faith in the revealed knowledge of the kind of beings he and his Father are;

2. Repent of all their sins, signifying this by turning to righteousness;

3. Be baptized by immersion in water under the hands of a legal administrator who has power from God to bind on earth and have it sealed eternally in the heavens;

4. Receive the gift of the Holy Ghost, also as conferred by one authorized by the Almighty so to act; and

5. Endure to the end of one's mortal probation, thus keeping the commandments after baptism.

This plan of salvation is eternal in nature; it has been in force in all ages. It was first revealed to Adam and has been given anew in each gospel dispensation. (Moses 6:51-68; 3 Ne. 27:19-21; D. & C. 20:29; Fourth Article of Faith.) See Acts 18:24-28; 19:1-7; 1 Pet. 1:1-16; 3:18-22; 4:1-6; Heb. 2:10-18.

38-39. The same commission given to Peter, to invite men to come unto Christ and be saved by conformity to his gospel, has been conferred anew upon men in modern times. To his latter-day witnesses the Lord says: "I give unto you a commandment that ye

41

go among this people, and say unto them, like unto mine apostle of old, whose name was Peter: Believe on the name of the Lord Jesus, who was on the earth, and is to come, the beginning and the end; Repent and be baptized in the name of Jesus Christ, according to the holy commandment, for the remission of sins; And whoso doeth this shall receive the gift of the Holy Ghost, by the laying on of the hands of the elders of the church." (D. & C. 49:11-14.)

38. The gift of the Holy Ghost] See Acts 10:46-48; *Commentary I*, pp. 752-755; 856-857.

39. All men in all ages may receive the promised gift of the Holy Ghost by compliance with those laws upon which its receipt is predicated.

40. This untoward generation] This rebellious generation which refuses to change its ungodly course. In somewhat the same vein, latter-day revelation speaks of "this unbelieving and stiffnecked generation." (D. & C. 5:8.)

AFTER BAPTISM WHAT?

ACTS 2:41-47.

41 Then they that gladly received his word were baptized: and the same day there were added *unto them* about three thousand souls.

42 And they continued stedfastly in the apostles' doctrine and fellowship, and in breaking of bread, and in prayers.

43 And fear came upon every soul: and many wonders and signs were done by the apostles.

44 And all that believed were together, and had all things common;

45 And sold their possessions and goods, and parted them to all *men*, as every man had need.

46 And they, continuing daily with one accord in the temple, and breaking bread from house to house, did eat their meat with gladness and singleness of heart,

47 Praising God, and having favour with all the people. And the Lord added to the church daily such as should be saved.

42

Baptism — and consequent membership in the Church — is the beginning, not the end, of that spiritual progression which leads to salvation. Baptism opens the door, places the repentant soul on the strait and narrow path, and starts him off in a course of godliness and virtue. Until a person makes the covenant of baptism he has no hope nor promise of eternal reward.

"The gate by which ye should enter is repentance and baptism by water," Nephi says, "and then cometh a remission of your sins by fire and by the Holy Ghost. And then are ye in this straight and narrow path which leads to eternal life; yea, ye have entered in by the gate." (2 Ne. 31:17-18.)

After baptism the saints must work out their salvation (Philip. 2:12), and as they do so their salvation becomes nearer than when they first believed and were baptized. (Rom. 13:11.) The process of working out one's salvation is the process of going forward on the strait and narrow path, of keeping the commandments after baptism, of working the works of righteousness, of enduring to the end.

Nephi propounds this question: "After ye have gotten into this straight and narrow path, I would ask if all is done?" to which he answers, "Nay," and counsels instead: "Ye must press forward with a steadfastness in Christ, having a perfect brightness of hope, and a love of God and of all men. Wherefore, if ye shall press forward, feasting upon the word of Christ, and endure to the end, behold, thus saith the Father: Ye shall have eternal life." (2 Ne. 31:19-20; D. & C. 59:23.)

41. Three thousand souls] There were one hundred and twenty brethren present when the successor to Judas was chosen. (Acts 1:15.) Jesus himself had chosen and commissioned both apostles and seventies. (*Commentary I*, pp. 323-328; 430-434.) More than five hundred brethren saw the risen Lord, probably when he appeared on the mountain in Galilee. (1 Cor. 15:6.) Thus there could have been many priesthood bearers available to perform these three thousand baptisms.

42. Apostles' doctrine] To believe in Christ and obey the laws and ordinances of his gospel. **Fellowship]** See Rom. 15:1-7. **Break-**

ing of bread] The sacrament of the Lord's Supper. See 1 Cor. 11:20-34. **43. Wonders and signs]** See Acts 5:12-16. **44-45.** See Acts 4:32-37.

46. Eat their meat with gladness and singleness of heart] So complete was their devotion and so total their consecration that even their mundane affairs were conducted with an eye single to the glory of God. "Eat thy bread with joy, and drink thy wine with a merry heart; *for God now accepteth thy works.*" (Eccles. 9:7.)

47. Such as should be saved] That is, such as by faith and repentance, by baptism of water and of the Spirit, and by covenanting to endure in righteousness to the end, were beginning to work out their salvation.

PETER HEALS MAN LAME FROM BIRTH

ACTS 3:1-16.

1 Now Peter and John went up together into the temple at the hour of prayer, *being* the ninth *hour.*

2 And a certain man lame from his mother's womb was carried, whom they laid daily at the gate of the temple which is called Beautiful, to ask alms of them that entered into the temple;

3 Who seeing Peter and John about to go into the temple asked an alms.

4 And Peter, fastening his eyes upon him with John, said, Look on us.

5 And he gave heed unto them, expecting to receive something of them.

6 Then Peter said, Silver and gold have I none; but such as I have give I thee: In the name of Jesus Christ of Nazareth rise up and walk.

7 And he took him by the right hand, and lifted *him* up: and immediately his feet and ankle bones received strength.

8 And he leaping up stood, and walked, and entered with them into the temple, walking, and leaping, and praising God.

9 And all the people saw him walking and praising God:

10 And they knew that it was he which sat for alms at the Beautiful gate of the temple: and they were filled with wonder and amazement at that which had happened unto him.

11 And as the lame man which was healed held Peter and John, all the people ran together unto them in the porch that is called Solomon's, greatly wondering.

12 And when Peter saw *it*, he answered unto the people, Ye men of Israel, why marvel ye at this? or why look ye so earnestly on us, as though by our own power or holiness we had made this man to walk?

13 The God of Abraham, and of Isaac, and of Jacob, the God of our fathers, hath glorified his Son Jesus; whom *ye* delivered up, and denied him in the presence of Pilate, when he was determined to let *him* go.

14 But ye denied the Holy One and the Just, and desired a murderer to be granted unto you;

15 And killed the Prince of life, whom God hath raised from the dead; whereof we are witnesses.

16 And his name through faith in his name hath made this man strong, whom ye see and know: yea, the faith which is by him hath given him this perfect soundness in the presence of you all.

I.V. ACTS 3:1, 16.

1 Now Peter and John went up together into the temple **at the ninth hour, for prayer.**

16 **And this man,** through faith in his name, **hath been made strong,** whom ye see and know; yea, the faith which is **in** him hath given him this perfect soundness in the presence of you all.

Jesus set the pattern; Peter walked in the steps of his Master. To gain an audience for one of his greatest public proclamations of his own divine Sonship, Jesus healed "a man which was blind from birth." (John 9 and 10; *Commentary I*, pp. 477-492.) Peter's healing of the "man lame from his mother's womb" had a similar effect. A multitude assembled, to whom, in solemn and compelling words, Peter then bore testimony that salvation centered in and came because of Christ, and that there was a coming day of restoration.

To generate faith in the blind man, Jesus anointed the unseeing eyes with clay made with spittle and sent the man to wash in the pool of Siloam. To accomplish the same end in the soul of the cripple, Peter said with majestic simplicity, "Look on us," that is, 'Exercise your faith in that which we, as ministers of Christ, are about to do in his name and power.'

45

The gift of healing has two aspects. "To some it is given to have faith to be healed; And to others it is given to have faith to heal." (D. & C. 46:19-20.) The instant case is primarily one of "faith to heal." The general pattern is for healings to happen because people have "faith to be healed," but on special occasions, especially when there is need, as part of the Lord's program, to dramatize and testify of the divinity of his work, the Lord's servants perform healings which are primarily by virtue of their own faith. Ordinarily a man who has the gift of healing so acts as to instil faith and confidence in the one to be healed so that the actual blessing comes because of the joint and united faith of both parties. See *Commentary I*, pp. 157-159; Acts 5:12-16.

1. Peter and John went to the temple, at the hour of prayer, to preach the gospel, not to engage in ritualistic Jewish prayers. As ministers of a new dispensation, they would no longer consider themselves bound by the requirements of the Mosaic dispensation which had ended.

2. Alms] See 2 Cor. 9:1-15; *Commentary I*, pp. 232-233.

6. Peter did not ask the Lord to heal the cripple; he did not pray to God to pour out his grace and healing virtue upon the lame man. Instead — acting in the Lord's name and by virtue of a delegation of priestly authority already received — he himself commanded the miracle to occur. Peter was the Lord's servant, his representative and agent; he stood in the place and stead of Christ, doing what the Master would have done if personally present. The illustration here seen of the relationship of Master and servant, of Principal and agent, of the Lord and his representative, is the same as is involved in the ordinance of administration to the sick. See Jas. 5:12-20.

13. The God of Abraham, and of Isaac, and of Jacob] This exalted name-title can be applied, in the broad sense in which Peter is now speaking, to both the Father and the Son. However, since all of the dealings of the Father with Israel were through the Son, Christ himself became and was in a more particular and pointed sense the God of Israel, the God of Abraham, Isaac, and Jacob. See 1 Cor. 10:1-4.

AGE OF RESTORATION BEGINS
BEFORE SECOND COMING

ACTS 3:17-24.

17 And now, brethren, I wot that through ignorance ye did *it,* as *did* also your rulers.

18 But those things, which God before had shewed by the mouth of all his prophets, that Christ should suffer, he hath so fulfilled.

19 Repent ye therefore, and be converted, that your sins may be blotted out, when the times of refreshing shall come from the presence of the Lord;

20 And he shall send Jesus Christ, which before was preached unto you:

21 Whom the heaven must receive until the times of restitution of all things, which God hath spoken by the mouth of all his holy prophets since the world began.

22 For Moses truly said unto the fathers, A prophet shall the Lord your God raise up unto you of your brethren, like unto me; him shall ye hear in all things whatsover he shall say unto you.

23 And it shall come to pass, *that* every soul, which will not hear that prophet, shall be destroyed from among the people.

24 Yea, and all the prophets from Samuel and those that follow after, as many as have spoken, have likewise foretold of these days.

I.V. ACTS 3:17, 20.

17 And now, brethren, I **know** that through ignorance ye **have done this,** as also your rulers.

20 And he shall send Jesus Christ, **whom ye have crucified,** which before was preached unto you;

Peter and the other apostles had learned from the Lord, as he ascended before them on the Mount of Olivet, that the restoration of the kingdom to Israel would take place at a future day, a day subsequent to New Testament times. (Acts 1:1-8.) Now the Holy Ghost, speaking by the mouth of Peter, reveals that not only Israel but all things are to be restored in a day to come. This prophetic pronouncement puts in perspective the teachings and hopes of all the prophets. It opens the door to an understanding of their statements about the restoration of the gospel in latter-days, the gathering of scattered Israel, the Second Coming,

47

Messiah's millennial reign, and the return of the earth itself to its paradisiacal glory. See Rev. 14:6-7.

17. Jesus' murderers acted in ignorance only in the sense that they did not know he was the Son of God. But even this was an ignorance born of rebellion, born of a refusal to believe the Messianic prophecies, born of a deliberate election to close their eyes to the teachings and miracles which testified of his divinity.

18. **Christ should suffer]** Israel had expected a triumphant, temporal King, but the Messianic prophecies spoke of a suffering, reviled, and rejected Redeemer. (Ps. 22; Isa. 50:6; 53:1-12.)

19. **Repent ye therefore, and be converted]** Joseph Smith says that Peter is here addressing the murderers who crucified Christ and that this is the reason Peter "did not" invite them to repent and be baptized for the remission of sins, but rather counseled them to repent and be converted in the hope their sins would be blotted out at the Second Coming. "They could not be baptized for the remission of sins," the Prophet said, "for they had shed innocent blood." (*Teachings*, p. 339.) Speaking of this verse, Joseph Smith also said: "Remission of sins by baptism was not to be preached to murderers. . . . There is no forgiveness for murderers; they will have to wait until the times of redemption shall come, and that in hell." (Franklin D. Richards and James A. Little, *A Compendium*, p. 288, 2nd ed.)

That your sins may be blotted out] Not that they shall be forgiven and be heirs of salvation, as are those whose sins are washed away by baptism; but after they have paid the utmost farthing, they shall rise to some degree of reward in one of the lesser mansions.

The times of refreshing] Joseph Smith says this has "reference to the time when Christ should come; then, and not till then, would their sins be blotted out. Why? Because they were murderers, and no murderer hath eternal life." (*Teachings*, p. 188.) It "has the same meaning as the one in the Tenth Article of Faith which records that 'the earth will be renewed and receive its paradisiacal glory.' This occurrence is 'the regeneration' which shall take place 'when the Son of man shall sit in the throne of his glory.' (Matt.

19:28.) It is also 'the day of transfiguration . . . When the earth shall be transfigured.' (D. & C. 63:20-21.)

"This earth was created in a new or paradisiacal state; then, incident to Adam's transgression, it fell to its present telestial state. At the Second Coming of our Lord, it will be renewed, regenerated, refreshed, transfigured, become again a new earth, a paradisiacal earth. Its millennial status will be a return to its pristine state of beauty and glory, the state that existed before the fall." (*Mormon Doctrine*, 2nd ed., pp. 795-796.)

20. He shall send Jesus Christ] The Second Coming of the Son of Man; he shall be sent again by his Father, this time in glory and triumph to reign on earth a thousand years.

21. Whom the heaven must receive until] Christ must and shall retain heaven as his dwelling place until the time appointed for him to return and reign personally on earth. In the providences of the Father, the Second Coming cannot be until "the times of restitution."

The times of restitution] The age or era of restoration. "It is that period in the earth's history known as the dispensation of the fulness of times, for in that era all things are to be restored. (Eph. 1:10.)

"It should be noted that Peter does not say that all things must be restored before Christ comes, but that the age, era, period, or times in the earth's history in which restoration is to take place must itself commence. That era did begin in the spring of 1820, but all things will not be revealed until after Christ comes. (D. & C. 101:32-34.)" (*Mormon Doctrine*, 2nd ed., p. 796.)

Of all things] What will be restored? All things! Visions, revelations, miracles, and gifts of the Spirit; apostles, prophets, seventies, evangelists, and judges in Israel; doctrines, ordinances, rites, and knowledge; priesthood, keys, and powers; the fulness of the gospel; Israel as a kingdom and a people; and even the earth itself "will be renewed and receive its paradisiacal glory." (Tenth Article of Faith.)

22-23. See Acts 7:37-40. When Moroni came to Joseph Smith during the night of September 21 and 22, he quoted Acts 3:22-23 and "said that that prophet was Christ; but the day had not yet come when 'they who would not hear his voice should be cut off from among the people,' but soon would come." (Jos. Smith 2:40.)

23. In the Book of Mormon account this verse, found in Jesus' language, reads: "Verily I say unto you, yea, and all the prophets from Samuel and those that follow after, as many as have spoken, have testified of me." (3 Ne. 20:24.)

23. Destroyed from among the people] At the Second Coming, the vineyard shall be burned and the wicked consumed. (2 Thess: 1:1-12; Mal. 4:1; D. & C. 101:24.)

WHO ARE CHILDREN OF THE COVENANT?

ACTS 3:25-26.

25 Ye are the children of the prophets, and of the covenant which God made with our fathers, saying unto Abraham, And in thy seed shall all the kindreds of the earth be blessed.

26 Unto you first God, having raised up his Son Jesus, sent him to bless you, in turning away every one of you from his iniquities.

Jesus told the Nephite kinsmen of these Jews almost the same thing spoken here by Peter. To these American Hebrews the resurrected Lord said: "And behold, ye are the children of the prophets; and ye are of the house of Israel; and ye are of the covenant which the Father made with your fathers, saying unto Abraham: And in thy seed shall all the kindreds of the earth be blessed. The Father having raised me up unto you first, and sent me to bless you in turning away every one of you from his iniquities; and this because ye are the children of the covenant — And after that ye were blessed then fulfilleth the Father the covenant which he made with Abraham, saying: In thy seed shall all the kindreds of the earth be blessed — unto the pouring out of the Holy Ghost through me upon the Gentiles, which blessing upon the Gentiles shall make them mighty above all, unto the scattering of my people, O house of Israel." (3 Ne. 20:25-27.)

Who then are the children of the covenant? "According to the terms of the covenant which God made with Abraham, all of the literal seed of that great prophet are entitled to receive the gospel, the priesthood, and all of the ordinances of salvation and exaltation. (Abra. 2:9-11; D. & C. 86:8-11.) When any of those descendants do receive all of these things, 'They become the sons of Moses and of Aaron and the seed of Abraham, and the church and kingdom, and the elect of God.' (D. & C. 84:34.) They are then children of the covenant, that is, they are inheritors of the fulness of the blessings appertaining to the new and everlasting covenant which is the gospel. 'Ye are the children of the covenant' (3 Ne. 20:24-27), our Lord told the Nephites among whom he ministered, a distinction which the faithful saints of this dispensation also enjoy. Rebellious descendants of Abraham are not his children in the special sense that is intended by the designation children of the covenant. (John 8:33-59.)" (*Mormon Doctrine*, 2nd ed., p. 126.)

25. Children of the prophets] "Those who follow in the footsteps of the prophets, who believe as they believed and live as they lived, are the children of the prophets. (D & C. 84:33-34.) They are children in the sense of being followers or disciples, and they may also be their literal seed. (3 Ne. 20:25-27; Acts 3:25.) However, the rebellious literal seed cut themselves off from the blessings of their fathers, and they become the children of the devil rather than the children of the prophets. (John 8:33-59.)" (*Mormon Doctrine*, 2nd ed., p. 127.)

In thy seed] See Gal. 3:1-25.

26. Christ came so that men could free themselves from their iniquities by accepting the terms and conditions of his atoning sacrifice. And this great blessing — out of which salvation comes — was "first" for "the children of the covenant," and thereafter to "all the kindreds of the earth," for because of Christ the Holy Ghost would be poured out upon "the Gentiles" also. (3 Ne. 20:26-27.)

SALVATION COMES BECAUSE OF CHRIST

ACTS 4:1-12.

1 And as they spake unto the people, the priests, and the captain of the temple, and the Sadducees, came upon them,

2 Being grieved that they taught the people, and preached

through Jesus the resurrection from the dead.

3 And they laid hands on them, and put *them* in hold unto the next day: for it was now eventide.

4 Howbeit many of them which heard the word believed; and the number of the men was about five thousand.

5 And it came to pass on the morrow, that their rulers, and elders, and scribes,

6 And Annas the high priest, and Caiaphas, and John, and Alexander, and as many as were of the kindred of the high priests, were gathered together at Jerusalem.

7 And when they had set them in the midst, they asked, By what power, or by what name, have ye done this?

8 Then Peter, filled with the Holy Ghost, said unto them, Ye rulers of the people, and elders of Israel,

9 If we this day be examined of the good deed done to the impotent man, by what means he is made whole;

10 Be it known unto you all, and to all the people of Israel, that by the name of Jesus Christ of Nazareth, whom ye crucified, whom God raised from the dead, *even* by him doth this man stand here before you whole.

11 This is the stone which was set at nought of you builders, which is become the head of the corner.

12 Neither is there salvation in any other: for there is none other name under heaven given among men, whereby we must be saved.

Salvation centers in Christ. He is the Firstborn of the Father, the one who in pre-existence progressed until he became "like unto God." (Abra. 3:24.) He is the Creator of all things, "the Lamb slain from the foundation of the world" (Rev. 13:8), the Savior and Redeemer. He is the Only Begotten, the Son of God, the one person born into the world with the power of immortality, that is, with the power to work out the infinite and eternal atonement.

Christ is the resurrection and the life, meaning that immortality and eternal life come because of him. If he had not ransomed men from the effects of the Fall, there would be no resurrection, no eternal glory, no salvation of any kind or degree. Had it not been for his atoning sacrifice, all mankind would have been lost forever — lost temporally, lost spiritually, and damned eternally as sons of perdition. (2 Ne. 9:6-9.)

1. As they spake] Peter and John both spoke, preaching Christ and proclaiming the message of salvation. **The captain of the temple]** "A priest next in dignity to the high priest, having under him a body of priests and Levites, who maintained order in the Temple." (*Dummelow*, p. 823.) **Sadducees]** See *Commentary I*, p. 119.

5. Their rulers] The Sanhedrin met in formal session to hear the "heresy" heralded by these disciples of Him whom this very Council had but a few weeks before condemned as worthy of death.

7. By what name] See Philip. 2:9-11.

8. Filled with the Holy Ghost] Moved upon by the power of the Holy Ghost, so that he spoke forth the mind and will of the Lord.

11. See 1 Pet. 2:4-10.

12. This same truth was spoken by the angel to King Benjamin in these words: "There shall be no other name given nor any other way nor means whereby salvation can come unto the children of men, only in and through the name of Christ, the Lord Omnipotent." (Mosiah 3:17.)

SADDUCEES STRIVE TO SILENCE APOSTLES

ACTS 4:13-22.

13 Now when they saw the boldness of Peter and John, and perceived that they were unlearned and ignorant men, they marvelled; and they took knowledge of them, that they had been with Jesus.

14 And beholding the man which was healed standing with them, they could say nothing against it.

15 But when they had commanded them to go aside out of the council, they conferred among themselves,

16 Saying, What shall we do to these men? for that indeed a notable miracle hath been done by them *is* manifest to all them that dwell in Jerusalem; and we cannot deny *it*.

17 But that it spread no further among the people, let us straitly threaten them, that they speak henceforth to no man in this name.

18 And they called them, and

commanded them not to speak at all nor teach in the name of Jesus.

19 But Peter and John answered and said unto them, Whether it be right in the sight of God to hearken unto you more than unto God, judge ye.

20 For we cannot but speak the things which we have seen and heard.

21 So when they had further threatened them, they let them go, finding nothing how they might punish them, because of the people: for all *men* glorified God for that which was done.

22 For the man was above forty years old, on whom this miracle of healing was shewed.

If Jesus came forth from the grave, there is no salvation in Saducean doctrine, for it falsely denies the resurrection. Similarly, if Joseph Smith received revelation and enjoyed the gifts of the Spirit, there can be no salvation in sectarian philosophies which falsely deny these things. What, in wisdom, should be the approach to either of these problems?

Honest truth seekers respond by investigating to find out whether there is a resurrection, whether revelation still continues, whether the gifts of the Spirit are still poured out upon the faithful. But the response of these Satan-led Sadducees was to seek to silence the apostles, lest their sect be overthrown by this bold testimony that Jesus had risen from the dead; and it is the same with those today who crusade against the message of the restoration; they contend against those who claim revelation and spiritual gifts rather than make an impartial investigation to learn if such actually exist in this day.

13. Unlearned and ignorant men] Men who had not been trained for the ministry in the schools of the day. "I call upon the weak things of the world," the Lord says, "those who are unlearned and despised, to thrash the nations by the power of my Spirit." (D. & C. 35:13.)

18-21. If Satan could, he would sponsor laws in all nations to forbid the preaching of the true gospel. If he could enact legislation requiring false worship, such would be his course. What would be the proper response of God's servants in such cases? Peter and John here refused to be silenced. Daniel chose the lion's den rather than pray to Darius (Dan. 6), and the three Hebrew children faced the fiery furnace without fear rather than worship the golden image of Nebuchadnezzar. (Dan. 3.) In other words, the Lord's true servants elect to put first in their lives the things of God's kingdom; they choose to do what is right and let the consequence follow — with the full expectancy, that if the Lord wills it, they shall be preserved no matter what the eventuality.

20. See Acts 10:36-43.

SAINTS GLORY IN THE TESTIMONY OF JESUS

ACTS 4:23-31.

23 And being let go, they went to their own company, and reported all that the chief priests and elders had said unto them.

24 And when they heard that, they lifted up their voice to God with one accord, and said, Lord, thou *art* God, which hast made heaven, and earth, and the sea, and all that in them is:

25 Who by the mouth of thy servant David hast said, Why did the heathen rage, and the people imagine vain things?

26 The kings of the earth stood up, and the rulers were gathered together against the Lord, and against his Christ.

27 For of a truth against thy holy child Jesus, whom thou hast anointed, both Herod, and Pontius Pilate, with the Gentiles, and the people of Israel, were gathered together,

28 For to do whatsoever thy hand and thy counsel determined before to be done.

29 And now, Lord, behold their threatenings: and grant unto thy servants, that with all boldness they may speak thy word,

30 By stretching forth thine hand to heal; and that signs and wonders may be done by the name of thy holy child Jesus.

31 And when they had prayed, the place was shaken where they were assembled together; and they were all filled with the Holy Ghost, and they spake the word of God with boldness.

23. Their own company] The assemblage of the saints; hundreds, even thousands, may have been present.

24-30. In the very nature of things, almost by instinct, true saints immediately thank God for deliverance from perilous circumstances, for his preserving care over them, for all his blessings. Hearts centered on God and his righteous causes have no trouble in acknowledging his hand in all things and in thanking him for the multitude of blessings and graces which he pours out upon them. See 2 Cor. 10:1-18; 11:1-11. The expressions of thanksgiving here recorded would be but a summarizing digest of the prayers and sermons given on this occasion of rejoicing.

25-26. David said: "Why do the heathen rage, and the people imagine a vain thing? The kings of the earth set themselves, and the rulers take counsel together, against the Lord, and against his anointed." (Ps. 2:1-2.) In quoting this Messianic utterance, the saints gave an interpreting, paraphasing translation, thus illustrating how scriptures can and should be understood by the power of the Spirit.

28. Christ's ministry was foreordained. "He came into the world, even Jesus, to be crucified for the world, and to bear the sins of the world, and to sanctify the world, and to cleanse it from all unrighteousness." (D. & C. 76:41; 3 Ne. 27:13-14.)

29-30. The true gospel is always taught with power; healings, signs, and wonders always attend; unless these are present, the gospel taught is not the pure doctrine of Christ.

31. The place was shaken] A visible, physical manifestation of the power of God, similar, perhaps, to the shaking of the prison walls when, just before the Christian Era, Nephi and Lehi were imprisoned by the Lamanites. (Hela. 5:20-33.)

SAINTS PRACTICE UNITED ORDER

ACTS 4:32-37.

32 And the multitude of them that believed were of one heart and of one soul: neither said any *of them* that ought of the things which he possessed was his own; but they had all things common.

33 And with great power gave the apostles witness of the resur-rection of the Lord Jesus: and great grace was upon them all.

34 Neither w a s there any among them that lacked: for as many as were possessors of lands or houses sold them, and brought the prices of the things that were sold,

35 And laid *them* down at the apostles' feet: and distribution was

made unto every man according as he had need.

36 And Joses, who by the apostles was surnamed Barnabas, (which is, being interpreted, The son of consolation,) a Levite, *and* of the country of Cyprus,

37 Having land, sold *it*, and brought the money, and laid *it* at the apostles' feet.

In the early part of both this and the meridian dispensations, the saints attempted to live the full law of consecration. That is, they consecrated their temporal means and spiritual abilities to the Lord's work. All of their talents, strength, time, properties, and monies were made available for use in the establishment of the Lord's earthly Church and kingdom. In this dispensation the organizational arrangement whereunder the principles of consecration operated was the United Order. The New Testament contains only passing allusions of how the system operated in that day. See 2 Cor. 8:1-24; 9:1-15; 1 Tim. 5:1-18.

As practiced in this dispensation, the saints conveyed to the Lord's agent all of their property. "They were then given stewardships to use for their own maintenance, with all surpluses reverting back to the Lord's storehouses. Because of greed, avarice, and the worldly circumstances in which they found themselves, the saints did not achieve great success in the practice of this law, and in due course the Lord withdrew from them the privilege of so conducting their temporal affairs." (*Mormon Doctrine*, 2nd ed., p. 158.) Either the Lord withdrew from the primitive saints whatever United Order they had or the practice was lost as the dark era of universal apostasy fell upon the earth.

33. See Acts 10:36-43.

LIARS ARE DAMNED

ACTS 5:1-11.

1 But a certain man named Ananias, with Sapphira his wife, sold a possession,

2 And kept back *part* of the price, his wife also being privy *to* *it*, and brought a certain part, and laid *it* at the apostles' feet.

3 But Peter said, Ananias, why hath Satan filled thine heart to lie to the Holy Ghost, and to keep back *part* of the price of the land?

4 Whiles it remained, was it not thine own? and after it was sold, was it not in thine own power? why hast thou conceived this thing in thine heart? thou has not lied unto men, but unto God.

5 And Ananias hearing these words fell down, and gave up the ghost: and great fear came on all them that heard these things.

6 And the young men arose, wound him up, and carried *him out*, and buried *him*.

7 And it was about the space of three hours after, when his wife, not knowing what was done, came in.

8 And Peter answered unto her, Tell me whether ye sold the land for so much? And she said, Yea, for so much.

9 Then Peter said unto her, How is it that ye have agreed together to tempt the Spirit of the Lord? behold, the feet of them which have buried thy husband *are* at the door, and shall carry thee out.

10 Then fell she down straightway at his feet, and yielded up the ghost: and the young men came in, and found her dead, and, carrying *her* forth, buried *her* by her husband.

11 And great fear came upon all the church, and upon as many as heard these things.

Why did the Lord slay Ananias and Sapphira? Their crime was lying; they conspired together to deceive their church leaders; and the Lord made them an example of how serious the offense, how severe the penalty — for lying. In ancient Israel Achan was similarly punished for stealing. (Josh. 7.)

True, the death penalty is not imposed on all liars and all thieves, but these scriptural accounts of such penalties being justly imposed, stand as a warning of how such sins are viewed by the Lord. In effect the lesson to learn from Ananias is that unrepentant liars will be damned. What, then, of the part tithe-payer who tells his bishop the sum given the Church is a full tithing? Or of the immoral couple who, conspiring together, assert their purity in order to get a temple recommend? Or of church members who deny sins of any sort which would keep them from receiving temple blessings, priesthood ordinations, or positions of leadership?

"Thou shalt not lie," the Lord says, for "he that lieth and will not repent shall be cast out." (D. & C. 42:21.) "Wo unto the liar, for he shall be thrust down to hell." (2 Ne. 9:34.) Liars suffer the second death (D. & C. 63:17; Rev. 21:8), and receive a final inheritance in the telestial kingdom. (D. & C. 76:103.)

3. Lie to the Holy Ghost] 4. Lied unto . . . God] To *tell* a lie to the Lord's servant is to lie to God, although no one can lie to the Lord in the sense of deceiving him, for he knows the thoughts and intents of the heart.

APOSTLES CONTINUE MIRACLES OF JESUS

ACTS 5:12-16.

12 And by the hands of the apostles were many signs and wonders wrought among the people; (and they were all with one accord in Solomon's porch.

13 And of the rest durst no man join himself to them: but the people magnified them.

14 And believers were the more added to the Lord, multitudes both of men and women.)

15 Insomuch that they brought forth the sick into the streets, and laid *them* on beds and couches,

that at the least the shadow of Peter passing by might overshadow some of them.

16 There came also a multitude *out* of the cities round about unto Jerusalem, bringing sick folks, and them which were vexed with unclean spirits: and they were healed every one.

I.V. ACTS 5:13.

13 And of the **rulers** durst no man join himself to them; but the people magnified them.

"These signs shall follow them that believe." (Mark 16:17.) This is the everlasting, eternal, immutable decree of the Almighty. Where there are apostles and prophets, there will be gifts and signs; where there is faith, there will be miracles; where the true saints are, God's power is manifest — and where these wonders are not found, there the saving truth is not. See *Commentary I*, pp. 870-871; Acts 3:1-16; 16:22-40; Heb. 11:1-3.

15. The shadow of Peter] So confident and sure were the people that the healing power of God rested with the apostles, that any contact, however slight, sufficed to bring miracles to pass. It was as when the woman touched the border of Jesus' garment (Luke 8:43-48), or the sick had contact with handkerchiefs used by Paul (Acts 19:11-12), or the dead man revived through touching the bones of Elisha. (2 Kings 13:20-21.)

ANGEL DELIVERS APOSTLES FROM PRISON

ACTS 5:17-26.

17 Then the high priest rose up, and all they that were with him, (which is sect of the Sadducees,) and were filled with indignation,

18 And laid their hands on the apostles, and put them in the common prison.

19 But the angel of the Lord by night opened the prison doors, and brought them forth, and said,

20 Go, stand and speak in the temple to the people all the words of this life.

21 And when they heard that, they entered into the temple early in the morning, and taught. But the high priest came, and they that were with him, and called the council together, and all the senate of the children of Israel, and sent to the prison to have them bought.

22 But when the officers came, and found them not in the prison, they returned, and told,

23 Saying, The prison truly found we shut with all safety, and the keepers standing without before the doors: but when we had opened, we found no man within.

24 Now when the high priest and the captain of the temple and the chief priests heard these things, they doubted of them whereunto this would grow.

25 Then came one and told them, saying, Behold, the men whom ye put in prison are standing in the temple, and teaching the people.

26 Then went the captain with the officers, and brought them without violence: for they feared the people, lest they should have been stoned.

What are prisons to the Lord? Oftimes his servants are imprisoned and he allows it. Jeremiah suffered in the dungeons of his day. (Jer. 37:14-17.) John the Baptist sealed his testimony with his blood in Herod's prison. (Matt. 14:3-12.) But when the Lord's servants, on their Master's errand, have done all they can, and have suffered to the full for the testimony of Jesus, then it oftimes suits the divine will to deliver them by power. And so an angel freed Peter (Acts 12:3-11), and the power of God released Alma and Amulek (Alma 14:22-29), and Nephi and Lehi. (Hela. 5:22-33.)

20. The words of this life] "The words of eternal life in this world." (Moses 6:59.)

APOSTLES TESTIFY OF CHRIST

ACTS 5:27-32.

27 And when they had brought them, they set *them* before the council: and the high priest asked them,

28 Saying, Did not we straitly command you that ye should not teach in this name? and, behold, ye have filled Jerusalem with your doctrine, and intend to bring this man's blood upon us.

29 Then Peter and the *other* apostles answered and said, We ought to obey God rather than men.

30 The God of our fathers raised up Jesus, whom ye slew and hanged on a tree.

31 Him hath God exalted with his right hand *to be* a Prince and a Saviour, for to give repentance to Israel, and forgiveness of sins.

32 And we are his witnesses of these things; and *so is* also the Holy Ghost, whom God hath given to them that obey him.

28. Filled Jerusalem with your doctrine] How successful were the apostles? How large was the Church? Jesus' ministry lasted some three and a half years. Great multitudes followed him everywhere; hundreds of thousands heard him teach. At Bethsaida he fed five thousand men of Israel, "beside women and children" (*Commentary I*, pp. 340-345), and shortly thereafter a multitude of mingled nationalities which included four thousand men, "beside women and children," was similarly provided with temporal food. (*Commentary I*, pp. 374-376.) The apostles and seventies were engaged in missionary work during much of this period, leading to the assumption that many thousands accepted the gospel while Jesus was yet with them.

On the day of Pentecost three thousand new converts were baptized, and thereafter "the Lord added to the church daily such as should be saved." (Acts 2:41-47.) After Peter and John healed the man lame from birth, five thousand men came into the fold, for "all men glorified God for that which was done." (Acts 4:1-22.) And following the taking of Ananias and Sapphira the record says, "Believers were the more added to the Lord, multitudes both of men and women." (Acts 5:1-16.)

This man's blood upon us] How shortly before, lead by these very rulers, had the frenzied mob chanted: "His blood be on us, and on our children." (Matt. 27:25.)

29. See Acts 4:13-22.

30. The God of our fathers] In this instance, Peter means Elohim, the Father; normally, the expression would mean Christ himself, for our Lord is the Lord Omnipotent, the Creator of all things from the beginning, the Almighty Jehovah, the God of Israel. Compare Acts 3:13.

Jesus, whom ye slew] See Acts 2:36. **Hanged on a tree]** Hanged on a dead tree, the cross. Peter is here choosing language expressive of Jewish contempt and hatred for Christ, for their law decreed, "Cursed is every one that hangeth on a tree." (Gal. 3:13; Deut. 21:23.)

31. Christ came to bring salvation. Men are saved because they are given the power to repent and gain forgiveness, for no unclean thing can enter into the Father's kingdom. (3 Ne. 27:19-21.)

32. See Acts 10:36-43.

PERSECUTION IS NOT OF GOD

ACTS 5:33-42.

33 When they heard *that*, they were cut *to the heart*, and took counsel to slay them.

34 Then stood there upon one in the council, a Pharisee, named Gamaliel, a doctor of the law, had in reputation among all the peo-

ple, and commanded to put the apostles forth a little space;

35 And said unto them, Ye men of Israel, take heed to yourselves what ye intend to do as touching these men.

36 For before these days rose up Theudas, boasting himself to be somebody; to whom a number

of men, about four hundred, joined themselves: who was slain; and all, as many as obeyed him, were scattered, and brought to nought.

37 After this man rose up Judas of Galilee in the days of the taxing, and drew away much people after him: he also perished; and all, *even* as many as obeyed him, were dispersed.

38 And now I say unto you, Refrain from these men, and let them alone: for if this counsel or this work be of men, it will come to nought:

39 But if it be of God, ye cannot overthrow it; lest haply ye be found even to fight against God.

40 And to him they agreed:

and when they had called the apostles, and beaten *them*, they commanded that they should not speak in the name of Jesus, and let them go.

41 And they departed from the presence of the council, rejoicing that they were counted worthy to suffer shame for his name.

42 And daily in the temple, and in every house, they ceased not to teach and preach Jesus Christ.

I.V. ACTS 5:39.

39 But if it be of God, ye cannot overthrow it; **be careful, therefore,** lest ye be found even to fight against God.

Persecution is the tool of Satan to harass, hinder, and destroy, if possible, the cause of righteousness. The spiritually weak, the lukewarm disciples, those who have not given themselves wholly to the Cause of Christ are purged from the Church by persecution. See *Commentary I*, pp. 328-332; Acts 17:1-14; 21:27-39.

Conversely, tolerance is of God and abounds in the hearts of those who love the truth and believe in the true doctrine of agency. "We claim the privilege of worshiping Almighty God according to the dictates of our own conscience, and allow all men the same privilege, let them worship how, where, or what they may." (Eleventh Article of Faith.)

Persecution says: 'I have no sure testimony of my own religion, and so I must destroy this other faith, lest it turn out to be true and thus overcome my own sect.'

Tolerance replies: 'I have the truth and know that truth will prevail. Why should I contend against others and their views? Such true principles as they possess shall prevail and all else will vanish away in due course, for truth only is eternal.'

63

34. Gamaliel] "St. Paul's teacher (Acts 22:3), grandson of Hillel and son of Rabbi Simeon, was by far the most influential rabbi of the time. He was the first of the seven teachers who received the title Rabban (higher than Rab or Rabbi). Gamaliel's moderation on this occasion is to be explained, (1) by his hostility to the Sadducees, whom he would not allow to win a decisive triumph over a sect which had much in common with the Pharisees; (2) by the favourable impression which the Apostles' preaching and miracles had made upon him. He was not a convert, but thought that something was to be said for the new teaching. Subsequent developments, particularly the preaching of Stephen, probably alienated him, as it did the other Pharisees." (*Dummelow*, p. 825.)

38-39. May we be so bold as to suggest that this is the same standard by which members of The Church of Jesus Christ of Latter-day Saints would like to be judged. In this dispensation of the fulness of times, the Lord's saints have been driven from New York to Ohio, from Ohio to Missouri, from Missouri to Illinois, and finally from the confines of the United States itself. Murder, arson, rapine, false imprisonment, many stripes, and almost all that has gone with Satan's persecutions in ages past has been poured out upon the Latter-day Saints. To some degree this persecution still continues. Why? Is it because some religionists fear the truth and are afraid this new and peculiar gospel will prevail? How much more Christ-like it would be for every religionist to say of his fellowmen who seek God in a course different from his own: 'Let them alone. If their cause is of God, it shall prosper; if it is not, time and the inevitable spread of truth will topple it and all false systems.'

APOSTLES CHOOSE SEVEN TO ASSIST THEM

ACTS 6:1-6.

1 And in those days, when the number of the disciples was multiplied, there arose a murmuring of the Grecians against the Hebrews, because their widows were neglected in the daily ministration.

2 Then the twelve called the multitude of the disciples *unto*

them, and said, It is not reason that we should leave the word of God, and serve tables.

3 Wherefore, brethren, look ye out among you seven men of honest report, full of the Holy Ghost and wisdom, whom we may appoint over this business.

4 But we will give ourselves continually to prayer, and to the ministry of the word.

5 And the saying pleased the whole multitude: and they chose Stephen, a man full of faith and of the Holy Ghost, and Philip, and Prochorus, and Nicanor, and Timon, and Parmenas, and Nicolas a proselyte of Antioch:

6 Whom they set before the apostles: and when they had prayed, they laid *their* hands on them.

God's command to his people in every age is: "Organize yourselves." (D. & C. 88:119.) Moses chose seventy men to aid him in judging and regulating Israel. (Num. 11:14-30.) Here the ancient apostles select seven brethren to aid them in administering the affairs of whatever system of United Order was then in operation. The work assigned them fell within the realm of those temporal matters normally handled by the Aaronic Priesthood, thus leaving the apostles free to handle the more difficult matters of their Melchizedek ministry.

Two of these seven gained scriptural recognition for their subsequent valiant ministries. Stephen's preaching won him a martyr's crown. (Acts 6:8-15; 7:1-60.) And Philip won many souls to the Christian faith in the city of Samaria and elsewhere. (Acts 8:5-40.)

2-4. Church leaders must delegate responsibility or perish under a mountain of administrative detail that no mortal man can bear. Here the apostles in effect choose to magnify their callings as ministers of the word rather than attempt to carry on the day to day regulation of the programs of the Church.

3. The apostles made the appointments; the delegation of authority came from them; but nominations came from the church members. In principle this is the same as a bishop recommending a young man to serve as a missionary with the actual call coming from the President of the Church. Those who receive the inspiration from the Spirit to call people to church service can and should

65

receive recommendation and counsel from those in positions to give it. Since all who are called to service in the Church become the servants and representatives of the Lord, they must be "full of the Holy Ghost," and as a consequence be able to receive the inspiration to do their work in the way the Lord wants it done.

6. Those called to positions of presidency and administration are ordained and set apart by the laying on of hands; the ordinance thus performed endows the church member with the needed power and authority to perform the assigned work. Compare Acts 8:14-17.

STEPHEN TRANSFIGURED BEFORE THE SANHEDRIN

ACTS 6:7-15.

7 And the word of God increased; and the number of the disciples multiplied in Jerusalem greatly; and a great company of the priests were obedient to the faith.

8 And Stephen, full of faith and power, did great wonders and miracles among the people.

9 Then there arose certain of the synagogue, which is called *the synagogue* of the Libertines, and Cyrenians, and Alexandrians, and of them of Cilicia and of Asia, disputing with Stephen.

10 And they were not able to resist the wisdom and the spirit by which he spake.

11 Then they suborned men, which said, We have heard him speak blasphemous words against Moses, and *against* God.

12 And they stirred up the people, and the elders, and the scribes, and came upon *him*, and caught him, and brought *him* to the council,

13 And set up false witnesses, which said, This man ceaseth not to speak blasphemous w o r d s against this holy place, and the law:

14 For we have heard him say, that this Jesus of Nazareth shall destroy this place, and shall change the customs which Moses delivered us.

15 And all that sat in the council, looking stedfastly on him, saw his face as it had been the face of an angel.

I.V. ACTS 6:9.

9 And there arose certain of the synagogue, who are called Libertines, and also Cyrenians, and Alexandrians, and of them of Cilicia, and of Asia, disputing with Stephen.

7. Disciples multiplied] See Acts 5:27-32.

8-15. Preaching, miracles, and mighty displays of divine favor, were not limited to the apostles. Stephen, called to do more than "serve tables," stepped forth as a mighty preacher of righteousness and a worker of signs and wonders. But miracles alone do not convert. Though the Council knew of the miracles and saw Stephen's face shine with transfiguring radiance, yet, spiritually diseased as they were, they rejected his Spirit-born witness of Christ and of salvation. How true is our Lord's declaration: "If they hear not Moses and the prophets, neither will they be persuaded, though one rose from the dead." (Luke 16:31.)

11. They suborned men] **13. False witnesses]** Such had worked in ridding them, as they supposed, of the Master, how better could they dispose of the disciple! (Matt. 26:59-61.) For that matter, how could they, or anyone, fight the truth except with falsehood?

12. The council] The Sanhedrin.

13-14. Jesus had prophesied the complete destruction of their temple. (Matt. 24:1-2.) He had come to change not only the customs given by Moses, but to fulfil and transcend the whole law revealed through him. And in so teaching, Stephen was but echoing the precepts of his Lord. The false witnesses, thus, were guilty because they twisted, wrested, and perverted Stephen's teachings — a practice common among those who oppose true and revealed religion.

15. Stephen was transfigured before them, visible witness thus being given that God was with him. In a lesser degree, it was with Stephen as it had been with Moses, the skin of whose face shown visibly after he had communed with the Lord for forty days on the mountain. (Ex. 34:29-35.)

STEPHEN PREACHETH ABOUT ISRAEL

ACTS 7:1-36.

1 Then said the high priest, Are these things so?

2 And he said, Men, brethren, and fathers, hearken; The God of glory appeared unto our father Abraham, when he was in Meso-

potamia, before he dwelt in Charran,

3 And said unto him, Get thee out of thy country, and from thy kindred, and come into the land which I shall shew thee.

4 Then came he out of the land of the Chaldeans, and dwelt in Charran: and from thence, when his father was dead, he removed him into this land, wherein ye now dwell.

5 And he gave him none inheritance in it, no, not *so much as* to set his foot on: yet he promised that he would give it to him for a possession, and to his seed after him, when *as yet* he had no child.

6 And God spake on this wise, That his seed should sojourn in a strange land; and that they should bring them into bondage, and entreat *them* evil four hundred years.

7 And the nation to whom they shall be in bondage will I judge, said God: and after that shall they come forth, and serve me in this place.

8 And he gave him the covenant of circumcision: and so *Abraham* begat Isaac, and circumcised him the eighth day; and Isaac *begat* Jacob; and Jacob *begat* the twelve patriarchs.

9 And the patriarchs, moved with envy, sold Joseph into Egypt: but God was with him,

10 And delivered him out of all his afflictions, and gave him favour and wisdom in the sight of Pharaoh king of Egypt; and he made him governor over Egypt and all his house.

11 Now there came a dearth over all the land of Egypt and Chanaan, and great affliction: and our fathers found no sustenance.

12 But when Jacob heard that there was corn in Egypt, he sent out our fathers first.

13 And at the second *time* Joseph was made known to his brethren; and Joseph's kindred was made known unto Pharaoh.

14 Then sent Joseph, and called his father Jacob to *him*, and all his kindred, threescore and fifteen souls.

15 So Jacob went down into Egypt, and died, he, and our fathers,

16 And were carried over into Sychem, and laid in the sepulchre that Abraham bought for a sum of money of the sons of Emmor *the father* of Sychem.

17 But when the time of the promise drew nigh, which God had sworn to Abraham, the people grew and multiplied in Egypt.

18 Till another king arose, which knew not Joseph.

19 The same dealt subtilely with our kindred, and evil entreated our fathers, so that they cast out their young children, to the end they might not live.

20 In which time Moses was born, and was exceeding fair, and nourished up in his father's house three months:

21 And when he was cast out, Pharaoh's daughter took him up and nourished him for her own son.

22 And Moses was learned in all the wisdom of the Egyptians, and was mighty in words and in deeds.

23 And when he was full forty years old, it came into his heart to visit his brethren the children of Israel.

24 And seeing one *of* them suffer wrong, he defended *him*, and avenged him that was oppressed, and smote the Egyptian:

25 For he supposed his brethren would have understood how that God by his hand would deliver them: but they understood not.

26 And the next day he shewed himself unto them as they strove, and would have set them at one again, saying, Sirs, ye are brethren; why do ye wrong one to another?

27 But he that did his neighbour wrong thrust him away, saying, Who made thee a ruler and a judge over us?

28 Wilt thou kill me, as thou diddest the Egyptian yesterday?

29 Then fled Moses at this saying, and was a stranger in the land of Madian, where he begat two sons.

30 And when forty years were expired, there appeared to him in the wilderness of mount Sina an angel of the Lord in a flame of fire in a bush.

31 When Moses saw *it*, he wondered at the sight: and as he drew near to behold *it*, the voice of the Lord came unto him,

32 *Saying,* I *am* the God of thy fathers, the God of Abraham, and the God of Isaac, and the God of Jacob. Then Moses trembled, and durst not behold.

33 Then said the Lord to him, Put off thy shoes from thy feet: for the place where thou standest is holy ground.

34 I have seen, I have seen the affliction of my people which is in Egypt, and I have heard their groaning, and am come down to deliver them. And now come, I will send thee into Egypt.

35 This Moses whom they refused, saying, Who made thee a ruler and a judge? the same did God send *to be* a ruler and a deliverer by the hand of the angel which appeared to him in the bush.

36 He brought them out, after that he had shewed wonders and signs in the land of Egypt, and in the Red sea, and in the wilderness forty years.

Stephen's defense before the Sanhedrin is a masterful one. He is charged with speaking "blasphemous words against Moses, and against God," against "this holy place" (the temple), and against "the law." (Vs. 11, 13.) His reply: 'I have spoken the truth. The whole history of Israel points toward the coming of Christ. Moses and all the prophets foretold his mortal ministry and divine Sonship. But you unbelieving scribes and rulers are following in the footsteps of your rebellious fathers who rejected the word of God which came in their day.'

The manner in which Stephen handles his problem illustrates how one dispensation ties into the next, and how the events occurring and the prophesies made in one age lay the foundation for what is to transpire in a subsequent era. Out of Abraham and the patriarchal dispensation, the nation and history of Israel grew; and out of the history of Israel and the prophecies of her holy men, came Jesus and his saving ministry.

A similar approach in offering salvation to men is often made by the Lord's servants in this day. Standing before Christian people, who suppose they believe what transpired in the meridian of time, modern witnesses of Christ recite the events of Jesus' and Paul's ministries, and the historical data relative to the apostasy; then they show how the restoration of the gospel grows naturally out of these, and how if men believe the testimonies of the previous dispensations, they will accept those of the present one.

2. Before he dwelt in Charran] The Old Testament does not say that God appeared to Abraham in Ur of Chaldea (in Mesopotamia) before he moved to Haran (Charran), though such is implied in Gen. 15:7, Josh. 24:2-3, and Neh. 9:7. But from the Book of Abraham, as translated by Joseph Smith in modern times, we learn that Stephen knew whereof he spoke (Abra. 1:16-19), he and the ancient Jews undoubtedly having scriptural accounts not now found in our Old Testament.

3. This promise as found in Genesis appears to have been made by God while Abraham was in Haran. (Gen. 12:1-4.) The Book of Abraham, however, confirms that Stephen is correct, and that the promise was given in Ur of the Chaldees before Abraham and his kindred dwelt in Haran. (Abra. 2:1-5.)

4. According to the chronology in Genesis, Terah lived sixty years after Abraham left Haran (Gen. 11:26, 32; 12:4), which is contrary to what Stephen here recites. From the Book of Abraham we learn that Abraham was sixty-two and not seventy-five years of age when he left Haran (Gen. 12:4; Abra. 2:14), showing at least that much of an error in the Old Testament account. Presumably, in this as in other historical statements, Stephen and not Genesis gives the true account.

5. Abraham's inheritance in Canaan, for himself and his seed after him, was to be an eternal inheritance, one that would endure in time and in eternity. This promise is the hope of Israel, the hope that the meek shall inherit the earth, first during the millennial era and finally in that same immortal state when the earth becomes a celestial sphere. (*Mormon Doctrine*, 2nd ed., pp. 366-368.) The principle is the same as when the Lord spoke to his Latter-day Saints of their "land of promise" in these words: "I will give it unto you for the land of your inheritance, if you seek it with all your hearts. And this shall be my covenant with you, ye shall have it for the land of your inheritance, and for the inheritance of your children forever, while the earth shall stand, and ye shall possess it again in eternity, no more to pass away." (D. & C. 38:19-20.)

6. Four hundred years] Gen. 15:13 agrees; Ex. 12:40 and Gal. 3:17 say four hundred and thirty years.

8. Circumcision] See Acts 15:1-35.

22. Moses . . . was mighty in words] Though not eloquent to begin with, Moses apparently acquired this talent. When he received his call to deliver Israel, Moses said to the Lord: "I am not eloquent, . . . but I am slow of speech, and of a slow tongue." The Lord replied: "I will be with thy mouth, and teach thee what thou shalt say." In addition to this the Lord made Aaron a spokesman for Moses. (Ex. 4:10-16.)

30-34. Both God and an angel spoke to Moses "in a flame of fire out of the midst of a bush." Exodus 3 and 4 preserve a partial account of the glorious events which transpired there. From latter-day revelation we also know that the Lord said unto Moses on that occasion: "Call upon God in the name of mine Only Begotten, and worship me." (Moses 1:17.)

33. To aid his children in developing those feelings of awe, respect, and godly fear which increase reverence, the Lord commands removal of shoes, kneeling in prayer, abstaining from laughter, and similar things, at appropriate times and places.

MOSES STANDS AS PROTOTYPE OF CHRIST

ACTS 7:37-40.

37 This is that Moses, which said unto the children of Israel, A prophet shall the Lord your God raise up unto you of your brethren, like unto me; him shall ye hear.

38 This is he, that was in the church in the wilderness with the angel which spake to him in the mount Sina, and *with* our fathers: who received the lively oracles to give unto us:

39 To whom our fathers would not obey, but thrust *him* from them, and in their hearts turned back again into Egypt,

40 Saying unto Aaron, Make us gods to go before us: for *as for* this Moses, which brought us out of the land of Egypt, we wot not what is become of him.

When God said to Moses, "Thou art in the similitude of mine Only Begotten" (Moses 1:6), he singled Israel's greatest prophet out as the one prophet, above all others, whose words, life, and ministry would bear record of the Messiah. Indeed, Moses and Christ are companion prophets, with the life and ministry of Moses prefiguring that of the Messiah. Moses was the mediator of the old covenant, Christ of the new. Moses gave Israel manna from heaven, Christ was the bread of life. Moses controlled the waters of the Red Sea, Jesus those of the Sea of Galilee. Moses as lawgiver to Israel revealed the preparatory gospel, our Lord as Lawgiver to the world restored the fulness of the gospel. And so on through the major matters of their ministries, Moses' work prefigured that of the Master, making that ancient prophet a prototype of the Messiah himself. See Acts 3:22-24.

37. As preserved in the Old Testament, Moses' great Messianic prophecy included these promises: "The Lord thy God will raise up unto thee a Prophet from the midst of thee, of thy brethren, like unto me; unto him ye shall hearken; . . . I will raise them up a Prophet from among their brethren, like unto thee, and will put my words in his mouth; and he shall speak unto them all that I shall command him. And it shall come to pass, that whosoever will not hearken unto my words which he shall speak in my name, I will require it of him." (Deut. 18:15, 18-19.)

The perfect interpretation of this prophecy is found in these words of Jesus to the Nephites: "Behold, I am he of whom Moses spake, saying: A prophet shall the Lord your God raise up unto you of your brethren, like unto me; him shall ye hear in all things whatsoever he shall say unto you. And it shall come to pass that every soul who will not hear that prophet shall be cut off from among the people." (3 Ne. 20:23.)

38. The church in the wilderness] That is, the congregation of Israel at Mt. Sinai was the Church of Christ in that day. This usage of terms accords with that found in the Book of Mormon. Nephi spoke of those in Jerusalem in his day as "brethren of the church" (1 Ne. 4:26), and there are nearly two hundred references to the Church in the Book of Mormon during the period prior to the ministry of Christ among the Nephites. (*Mormon Doctrine*, 2nd ed., pp. 133-134.)

Lively oracles] These are the living words of life, the revelations, the inspired truths received by prophets and presented by them to the people. The First Presidency, for instance, are appointed "to receive the oracles for the whole church." (D. & C. 124:126.) Oracles are lively or living because God's word goes forth with power, and the promises in it are always fulfilled.

STEPHEN TESTIFIES OF APOSTASY IN ISRAEL

ACTS 7:41-53.

41 And they made a calf in those days, and offered sacrifice unto the idol, and rejoiced in the works of their own hands.

42 Then God turned, and gave them up to worship the host of heaven; as it is written in the book of the prophets, O ye house of Israel, have ye offered to me slain beasts and sacrifices *by the*

73

space of forty years in the wilderness?

43 Yea, ye took up the tabernacle of Moloch, and the star of your god Remphan, figures which ye made to worship them: and I will carry you away beyond Babylon.

44 Our fathers had the tabernacle of witness in the wilderness, as he had appointed, speaking unto Moses that he should make it according to the fashion that he had seen.

45 Which also our fathers that came after brought in with Jesus into the possession of the Gentiles, whom God drave out before the face of our fathers, unto the days of David;

46 Who found favour before God, and desired to find a tabernacle for the God of Jacob.

47 But Solomon built him an house.

48 Howbeit the most High dwelleth not in temples made with hands; as saith the prophet,

49 Heaven *is* my throne, and earth *is* my footstool: what house will ye build me? saith the Lord: or what *is* the place of my rest?

50 Hath not my hand made all these things?

51 Ye stiffnecked and uncircumcised in heart and ears, ye do always resist the Holy Ghost: as your fathers *did*, so *do* ye.

52 Which of the prophets have not your fathers persecuted? and they have slain them which showed before of the coming of the Just One; of whom ye have been now the betrayers and murderers:

53 Who have received the law by the disposition of angels, and have not kept *it*.

I.V. ACTS 7:44.

44 Our fathers had the tabernacle of witness in the wilderness, as he had appointed, speaking unto Moses, that he should make it according to the **pattern** that he had seen.

Ancient Israel rejected Moses; meridian Israel crucified their Messiah — and the one rebellious group is as the other. So specifies Stephen's arraignment of those who are soon to shed his innocent blood. In principle he is saying what the Master himself once said: "Had ye believed Moses, ye would have believed me." (John 5:46.)

40-43. Israel bowed before a golden calf, offered sacrifice to an idol, worshiped the planets, and carried the tabernacle of Moloch — all of which was part of the false religious systems of the Egyptians and the Ammorites. Their rebellion against the true religion revealed through Moses was a type of their later rejection of Jesus.

44. Tabernacle of witness] 46. A tabernacle for the God of Jacob] 47. An house] Temples made with hands] True temples are part of true religion; where they exist, there is the true Church of God; and where they are not found, true religion has been lost. Stephen here proves the apostasy of Israel by showing they had carried "the tabernacle of Moloch" rather than the true tabernacle (temple) which God had given them.

"Holy sanctuaries wherein sacred ordinances, rites, and ceremonies are performed which pertain to salvation and exaltation in the kingdom of God are called temples. They are the most sacred places of worship on earth; each one is literally a House of the Lord, a house of the great Creator, a house where he and his Spirit may dwell, to which he may come, or send his messengers, to confer priesthood and keys and to give revelation to his people.

"From the days of Adam to the present, whenever the Lord has had a people on earth, temples and temple ordinances have been a crowning feature of their worship. 'My people are always commanded to build' temples, the Lord says, 'for the glory, honor, and endowment' of all the saints. (D. & C. 124:39-40.) These temples have been costly and elaborate buildings whenever the abilities of the people have permitted such; nothing is too good for the Lord, and no sacrifice is too great to make in his service. But in the days of poverty, or when the number of true believers has been small, the Lord has used mountains, groves, and wilderness locations for temple purposes. Endowments, for instance, following the latter-day exodus, were first given on Ensign peak. (*Doctrines of Salvation*, vol. 2, pp. 231-257.)

"Our knowledge of holy sanctuaries which existed before the day of Moses is slight. We do know that as soon as Moses led Israel out of Egyptian bondage detailed instructions were received to build and use a portable temple or tabernacle, not for general assembly and meetings, but for the performance of holy ordinances.

75

It appears that initially there was in ancient Israel a provisional tabernacle (Ex. 33:7-11); that thereafter the people donated of their riches and the tabernacle of the congregation was built (Ex. chapters 25 to 31 and 35 to 40); that this tabernacle was set up at various places in Israel after they entered their promised land (Josh. 18:1-3; Judges 18:31; 21:2; 1 Sam. 1:3, 24; 4; 7:1-2; 21:1-6; 1 Chron. 21:28-30; 2 Chron. 1:3-6); that while the tabernacle was at Gibeon, David erected another tabernacle, in his own city, to house the Ark of the Covenant (1 Sam. 4:10-22; 5; 6; 7:1-2); that with the material collected by David, Solomon built the great temple in Jerusalem (1 Chron. 22:5-19; 1 Kings 5:13-18; 2 Chron., chapters 3 to 7); that Cyrus of Persia sponsored the return of captive Judah from Babylonian bondage to rebuild the temple, a structure called the temple of Zerubbabel (Ezra 1:1-4); and that the so-called temple of Herod, the temple in Jerusalem at the time of our Lord's ministry, was in process of being rebuilt at that time. (John 2:20.)" (*Mormon Doctrine*, 2nd ed., pp. 779-781.)

45. Jesus] Joshua, who took the portable temple into their promised land.

48-50. The great Creator, by whom all things are, dwelleth not in temples made by the hands of his creatures; but he is worshiped by them in his temples, which holy houses he visits occasionally, and in which sacred spots his Spirit may always be found by the faithful.

51. Resist the Holy Ghost] Resist the sure witness of the truth; refuse to open their hearts to the testimony offered by the Spirit to all men. The Holy Ghost is a Revelator whose commission is to bear record of the Father and the Son and of all truth. "By the power of the Holy Ghost ye may know the truth of all things." (Moro. 10:5.)

52. See *Commentary I*, pp. 620-622. **The betrayers and murderers]** See Acts 2:36.

53. Whenever a dispensation of the gospel is given to men, it is "declared by holy angels sent forth from the presence of God, and by his own voice, and by the gift of the Holy Ghost." (Moses

5:58.) What Stephen is here saying is that "the law," which is the "preparatory gospel" (D. & C. 84:26-27), also was dispensed to Israel by angelic ministration.

STEPHEN SEES THE FATHER AND THE SON

ACTS 7:54-60; 8:1a.

54 When they heard these things, they were cut to the heart, and they gnashed on him with *their* teeth.

55 But he, being full of the Holy Ghost, looked up stedfastly into heaven, and saw the glory of God, and Jesus standing on the right hand of God.

56 And said, Behold, I see the heavens opened, and the Son of man standing on the right hand of God.

57 Then they cried out with a loud voice, and stopped their ears, and ran upon him with one accord,

58 And cast *him* out of the city, and stoned *him:* and the witnesses laid down their clothes at a young man's feet, whose name was Saul.

59 And they stoned Stephen, calling upon *God*, and saying, Lord Jesus, receive my spirit.

60 And he kneeled down, and cried with a loud voice, Lord, lay not this sin to their charge. And when he had said this, he fell asleep.

1a And Saul was consenting unto his death.

I.V. ACTS 7:59.

59 And they stoned Stephen; **and he,** calling upon God, **said,** Lord Jesus, receive my spirit.

Who or what is God? Is he the incomprehensible, uncreated, immaterial spirit nothingness described in the creeds of Christendom, or a personal Being in whose image man is created? Is he the laws and forces of nature, or an exalted and perfected Man?

And how can finite man come to a knowledge of the Infinite? Can he find God in the laboratory? Or in the creeds written by contending religionists who haggled and quarreled over every word?

The fact is — God stands revealed or he remains forever unknown. It is not reason or research which makes known the mystery of godliness. In one brief glimpse of heaven and its chief inhabitants, Stephen learned more about God and his glory than could be acquired through eons of research by uninspired philosophers. While the Holy Ghost rested upon him, Stephen saw the Father and the Son — beholding them as glorified, exalted Men, which fact he then announced as he was moved upon by the Spirit.

54. Gnashed on him with their teeth] A figurative expression meaning their attitude toward him and their assault upon him were as though they were wild beasts attacking with bared fangs.

55-56. To Joseph Smith and Sidney Rigdon a similar vision was vouchsafed. "The Lord touched the eyes of our understandings and they were opened," the Prophet wrote, "and the glory of the Lord shone round about. And we beheld the glory of the Son, on the right hand of the Father." (D. & C. 76:19-20.)

55. Being full of the Holy Ghost] Being overshadowed by the power of the Holy Ghost so that the influence of that spirit member of the Godhead filled his being. See Acts 10:46-48; *Commentary I*, pp. 752-756, 856-857.

56. I see . . . God] See Heb. 12:11-17. **The Son of Man]** In the pure Adamic language, the name of Elohim, the Father, is *Man of Holiness* (signifying that God is a Holy Man), and the name of Christ, the Son, is *Son of Man of Holiness* or *Son of Man*. (*Mormon Doctrine*, 2nd ed., pp. 467; 742-743; Moses 6:57.)

57-60. " 'After a man has been condemned to be stoned, they bring him good strong wine, and give him to drink, that he may not feel too great horror of a violent death. Then come the witnesses, and bind his hands and feet, and lead him to the place of stoning. Then the witnesses take a great stone, large enough to cause death, and lay it upon his heart all together, lest one should act before another, according to Dt. 17:7, "The hand of the witnesses shall be first against him": then all the Israelites can overwhelm him with stones' (Talmud). The execution of Stephen was tumultuous and illegal, for, (1) there was no formal sentence pronounced by the court, (2) the Roman authorities were not consulted about the death sentence." (*Dummelow*, p. 828.)

58. Saul] See Acts 9:19b-31.

59-60. To whom did Stephen pray? Sectarian commentators say he prayed to Jesus and not to the Father, and they accordingly claim this instance as justification for the apostate practice of addressing prayers to the Son. From the day of Adam, through all ages, however, the true order of prayer has been to "call upon God in the name of the Son." (Moses 5:8.) The only scriptural instances in which prayers were addressed directly to the Son were when — and because! — that Holy Being, as a resurrected personage, was standing before the petitioners. (3 Ne. 19:18-36.)

SAUL PERSECUTES THE CHURCH

ACTS 8:1b-4.

1b And at that time there was a great persecution against the church which was at Jerusalem; and they were all scattered abroad throughout the regions of Judea and Samaria, except the apostles.

2 And devout men carried Stephen *to his burial,* and made great lamentation over him.

3 As for Saul, he made havoc of the church, entering into every house, and haling men and women, committed *them* to prison.

4 Therefore they that were scattered abroad went every where preaching the word.

1. Persecution] See Acts 5:33-42. **The church which was at Jerusalem]** Jerusalem was the headquarters of the Church; it was there the General Authorities convened to plan and direct the affairs of the growing kingdom; it was there Satan had such great influence with those whose hands still dripped with the blood of Him whose Church it was.

2. Great lamentation] "Thou shalt live together in love, insomuch that thou shalt weep for the loss of them that die." (D. & C. 42:45.)

3. Saul] See Acts 9:19b-31. Let us give Saul — noble and strong minded man that he was — full credit for sincerity of purpose, for devotion to what he esteemed to be his duty, for dedication to a cause, for devoutness of a sort, for zeal which inspired others. But what of it? What value is sincerity without truth? Or devotion and dedication to a false cause? Satan is zealous on his own errand. False religious zeal profiteth nothing. It is not sincerity but truth which leads to salvation. The Aztecs, in the sincerity of their souls, slew thousands of victims as human sacrifices. Korihor, the Anti-Christ, believed his false doctrines and was smitten of the Lord despite his sincerity. Millions today believe the false doctrine of transubstantiation, but their sincere views add no saving grace to a concept that is not true. It is truth, pure, diamond, unadulterated truth that counts in the pursuit of salvation.

4. God did not decree the scattering of his saints as a means of sending them on missions, but valiant members of the kingdom always and everywhere comply with their baptismal covenant "to stand as witnesses" of Christ "at all times and in all things, and in all places . . . even until death." (Mosiah 18:9.)

PHILIP WORKS MIRACLES, CONVERTS SIMON

ACTS 8:5-13.

5 Then Philip went down to the city of Samaria, and preached Christ unto them.

6 And the people with one accord gave heed unto those things which Philip spake, hearing and seeing the miracles which he did.

7 For unclean spirits, crying with loud voice, came out of many that were possessed *with them:* and many taken with palsies, and that were lame, were healed.

8 And there was great joy in that city.

9 But there was a certain man, called Simon, which beforetime in the same city used sorcery, and bewitched the people of Samaria,

giving out that himself was some great one:

10 To whom they all gave heed, from the least to the greatest, saying, This man is the great power of God.

11 And to him they had regard, because that of long time he had bewitched them with sorceries.

12 But when they believed Philip preaching the things concerning the kingdom of God, and the name of Jesus Christ, they were baptized, both men and women.

13 Then Simon himself believed also: and when he was baptized, he continued with Philip, and wondered, beholding the miracles and signs which were done.

5-8. Philip — saintly, valiant, a powerful preacher, a mighty worker of miracles — held only the Aaronic Priesthood! Peter and John must yet come from Jerusalem to Samaria to confer the Holy Ghost upon his baptized converts. (Acts 8:14-17.) And yet Philip, magnifying his calling, casts out devils, commands the lame to leap and the sick to rise from their beds of affliction. Miracles are wrought by the power of faith, and a righteous man need not hold the Melchizedek Priesthood to have power and influence with his Creator. As Joseph Smith said, "If a priest understands his duty, his calling, and ministry, and preaches by the Holy Ghost, his enjoyment is as great as if he were one of the Presidency." (*Teachings*, p. 112.)

Miracles of themselves do not convert men to the truth. The Jews were witnesses of Jesus' mighty works and yet they chose to remain outside the pale of his saving grace. But miracles may so impress the sincere investigator as to cause him to take the steps that lead to faith.

"Signs flow from faith. They may incidentally have the effect of strengthening the faith of those who are already spiritually inclined, but their chief purpose is not to convert people to the truth, but to reward and bless those already converted. 'Faith cometh not by signs, but signs follow those that believe,' the Lord says. 'Yea, signs come by faith, not by the will of men, nor as they please, but by the will of God. Yet, signs come by faith, unto mighty works, for without faith no man pleaseth God; and with whom God is angry he is not well pleased; wherefore, unto such he showeth no signs, only in wrath unto their condemnation.' (D. & C. 63:9-11.)

"Faith that is based on signs alone is weak and ineffective. It continually demands added and greater signs to keep it alive, and those relying on such visible supernatural guidance soon begin 'to be less and less astonished at a sign or a wonder from heaven' until they are in danger of disbelieving all they have 'heard and seen.' (3 Ne. 2:1.) Thus belief based on supernatural experiences is less to be desired than that which stands on its own feet. 'Blessed are they that have not seen, and yet have believed.' (John 20:29.)" (*Mormon Doctrine*, 2nd ed., pp. 713-714.)

81

9. Sorcery] See Acts 16:16-21; 19:13-20. "Use of power gained from the assistance or control of evil spirits is called *sorcery*. Frequently this power is used in divination, necromancy, and witchcraft. In effect a sorcerer worships Satan rather than God and uses such power as Satan can give him in a vain attempt to imitate the power of God.

"Sorcery has been a sinful evil in all ages. It was present in the courts of Pharaoh (Ex. 7:11) and of Nebuchadnezzar. (Dan. 2:2.) Israel's prophets inveighed against it. (Isa. 47; 57:3; Jer. 27:9.) Apostate Nephites revelled in its mysteries. (Alma 1:32; Morm. 1:19.) Peter and John fought its evils in their ministries (Acts 8:9-11; 13:6-8), and its power is prevailing with great success over much of the earth today. (Rev. 9:20-21.) . . .

"But at the Second Coming of the Lord sorcerers will be destroyed (Mal. 3:5; 3 Ne. 24:5); they shall be cast into that hell which is prepared for them (D. & C. 63:17; Rev. 21:8); and finally, having paid the utmost farthing for their crimes, they shall be debased with a telestial inheritance in eternity. (D. & C. 76:103; Rev. 22:15.)" (*Mormon Doctrine*, 2nd ed., p. 747.)

13. Miracles and signs] Proofs of the true Church. See *Commentary I*, pp. 870-871.

APOSTLES CONFER THE GIFT OF THE HOLY GHOST

ACTS 8:14-17.

14 Now when the apostles which were at Jerusalem heard that Samaria had received the word of God, they sent unto them Peter and John:

15 Who, when they were come down, prayed for them, that they might receive the Holy Ghost:

16 (For as yet he was fallen upon none of them: only they were baptized in the name of the Lord Jesus.)

17 Then laid they *their* hands on them, and they received the Holy Ghost.

14-16. To gain celestial salvation a man must be born of water and of the Spirit. (John 3:5.) John's baptism in water merely prepared the way for Christ's baptism of fire and of the Holy Ghost. (Matt. 3:11.) Sin and dross are burned out of the human soul as though by fire when a man becomes a new creature of the Holy Ghost, and until this cleansing takes place the candidate is not qualified for an inheritance with spotless beings in celestial glory. "You might as well baptize a bag of sand," the Prophet said, "as a man, if not done in view of the remission of sins and getting of the Holy Ghost. Baptism by water is but half a baptism, and is good for nothing without the other half — that is, the baptism of the Holy Ghost." (*Teachings*, p. 314.)

17. See Acts 10:44-48. The gift of the Holy Ghost is conferred upon a worthy recipient by the laying on of hands. A man may receive a flash of revelation from the Holy Ghost without submitting to the ordinance which God has ordained. He may, for instance, learn "by the power of the Holy Ghost" that the Book of Mormon is true. (Moro. 10:4-5.) But he can never walk in the continuing light and revelation sent forth by that member of the Godhead until he receives the special anointing under the hands of a legal administrator whose right it is to speak for God and authoritatively open the door to the receipt of his holy gifts.

"There are certain key words and signs belonging to the priesthood," Joseph Smith taught, "which must be observed in order to obtain the blessing." He named one of these as "the laying on of hands," and said, "We cannot obtain the blessing by pursuing any other course except the way marked out by the Lord. What if we should attempt to get the gift of the Holy Ghost through any other means except the signs or way which God hath appointed — would we obtain it? Certainly not; all other means would fail." (*Teachings*, p. 198-199.)

One of the evidences of the great apostasy is that in the main the churches of Christendom do not so much as claim the power to give a present bestowal of the Holy Ghost, to say nothing of having that divine Being respond to such a conferral.

SIMON SEEKS TO BUY THE GIFT OF THE HOLY GHOST

ACTS 8:18-25.

18 And when Simon saw that through laying on of the apostles' hands the Holy Ghost was given, he offered them money,

19 Saying, Give me also this power, that on whomsoever I lay

hands, he may receive the Holy Ghost.

20 But Peter said unto him, Thy money perish with thee, because thou hast thought that the gift of God may be purchased with money.

21 Thou hast neither part nor lot in this matter: for thy heart is not right in the sight of God.

22 Repent therefore of this thy wickedness, and pray God, if perhaps the thought of thine heart may be forgiven thee.

23 For I perceive that thou art in the gall of bitterness, and *in* the bond of iniquity.

24 Then answered Simon, and said, Pray ye to the Lord for me, that none of these things which ye have spoken come upon me.

25 And they, when they had testified and preached the word of the Lord, returned to Jerusalem, and preached the gospel in many villages of the Samaritans.

18-19. What visible manifestation is apparent to an observer when the gift of the Holy Ghost is given to a new convert? Apparently in this instance some dramatic sign was shown forth, as tongues or prophecy. But whatever may have happened here was unusual and miraculous in nature and beyond what normally occurs.

On this point, the Prophet Joseph Smith said that the "Holy Ghost has no other effect than pure intelligence. It is more powerful in expanding the mind, enlightening the understanding, and storing the intellect with present knowledge, of a man who is of the literal seed of Abraham, than one that is a Gentile, though it may not have half as much visible effect upon the body; for as the Holy Ghost falls upon one of the literal seed of Abraham, it is calm and serene; and his whole soul and body are only exercised by the pure spirit of intelligence; while the effect of the Holy Ghost upon a Gentile, is to purge out the old blood, and make him actually of the seed of Abraham. That man that has none of the blood of Abraham (naturally) must have a new creation by the Holy Ghost. In such a case, there may be more of a powerful effect upon the body, and visible to the eye, than upon an Israelite, while the Israelite at first might be far before the Gentile in pure intelligence." (*Teachings*, pp. 149-150; 242-244.)

To receive the Holy Ghost is to hear the still small voice, to have the Holy Spirit speak, quietly and peacefully, to the spirit within one. (D. & C. 8:2-3.) The serene and outwardly unobservable receipt of the Spirit is dramatized in the experience of Elijah. When that valiant prophet went up on Mount Horeb to commune with Deity, there was "a great and strong wind" which "rent the mountains, and brake in pieces the rocks." Thereafter came an earthquake and then a fire, but the Lord was not found in any of these. Finally Elijah heard "a still small voice," the voice of the Spirit coming into his mind, and he then knew, by revelation from the Holy Ghost, what God would have him do. (1 Kings 19:8-12.)

Enos (Enos 1-19), Joseph Smith (D. & C. 85:6), and prophets and saints without number have heard this voice and had truth manifest unto them. The Lamanites, on one occasion, received the companionship of the Spirit and knew it not, so serene and calm was the whispering of that Holy Spirit to their souls. (3 Ne. 9:20.)

20. The Gospel is free (Rev. 22:17; 2 Ne. 9:50), its powers come to the righteous, and its offices to those whom God calls, by revelation, to serve for appointed seasons. On the other hand: "Simony is the practice of buying church offices and various other forms of ecclesiastical preferment. It is no part of the gospel, has never been practiced in the true Church in any age, but has been found in the false churches of Christendom, from the earliest days of the era of apostasy to the present. The name is derived from Simon the sorcerer (commonly called by the scholars Simon Magus, meaning Simon the magician), because he — having seen miracles performed under the hands of the ancient apostles — sought to buy from Peter the power to confer the gift of the Holy Ghost." (*Mormon Doctrine*, 2nd ed., p. 734.)

22. The thought of thine heart] "Our thoughts will reward or condemn us before the judgment bar. (Alma 12:12-14.) The righteous and the wicked are divided by their thoughts. . . . Righteous thoughts lead to salvation, wicked thoughts to damnation." (*Mormon Doctrine*, 2nd ed., p. 792.)

23. "All men that are in a state of nature, or I would say, in a carnal state, are in the gall of bitterness and in the bonds of iniquity; they are without God in the world, and they have gone contrary to the nature of God; therefore, they are in a state contrary to the nature of happiness." (Alma 41:11.)

PHILIP PREACHES CHRIST, BAPTIZES EUNUCH

ACTS 8:26-40.

26 And the angel of the Lord spake unto Philip, saying, Arise, and go toward the south unto the way that goeth down from Jerusalem unto Gaza, which is desert.

27 And he arose and went: and, behold, a man of Ethiopia, an eunuch of great authority under Candace queen of the Ethiopians, who had the charge of all her treasure, and had come to Jerusalem for to worship,

28 Was returning, and sitting in his chariot read Esaias the prophet.

29 Then the Spirit said unto Philip, Go near, and join thyself to this chariot.

30 And Philip ran thither to *him*, and heard him read the prophet Esaias, and said, Understandest thou what thou readest?

31 And he said, How can I, except some man should guide me? And he desired Philip that he would come up and sit with him.

32 The place of the scripture which he read was this, He was led as a sheep to the slaughter; and like a lamb dumb before his shearer, so opened he not his mouth:

33 In his humiliation his judgment was taken away: and who shall declare his generation? for his life is taken from the earth.

34 And the eunuch answered Philip, and said, I pray thee, of whom speaketh the prophet this? of himself, or of some other man?

35 Then Philip opened his mouth, and began at the same scripture, and preached unto him Jesus.

36 And as they went on *their* way, they came unto a certain water: and the eunuch said, See, *here is* water; what doth hinder me to be baptized?

37 And Philip said, If thou believest with all thine heart, thou mayest. And he answered and said, I believe that Jesus Christ is the Son of God.

38 And he commanded the chariot to stand still: and they

went down both into the water, both Philip and the eunuch; and he baptized him.

39 And when they were come up out of the water, the Spirit of the Lord caught away Philip, that the eunuch saw him no more: and he went on his way rejoicing.

40 But Philip was found at Azotus: and passing through he preached in all the cities, till he came to Caesarea.

26. As occasions warrant (in the true Church) angels, who are themselves missionaries, minister to their mortal missionary counterparts.

27. A man of Ethiopia, an eunuch of great authority] Perhaps this mighty man from the court of Candace came in at least partial fulfilment of David's prophecy: "Princes shall come out of Egypt; Ethiopia shall soon stretch out her hand unto God." (Ps. 68:31.) Eunuchs, despite their handicaps, have the Lord's specific promise that they shall inherit the fulness of his kingdom if they are true and faithful to their gospel covenants. (Isa. 66:1-8.)

29. So frequently (in the true Church) that it becomes almost commonplace, the Holy Ghost speaks to the Lord's ministers giving needed counsel, direction, and encouragement.

30-38. Teach, testify, and baptize — such is the proselyting program of true ministers. It is not enough for investigators to read the record of God's dealings with ancient people who communed with Deity. They must be taught by living persons who interpret the scripture by the power of the Spirit, who seal their teachings with personal testimony, and who then perform a baptism which God himself recognizes. The ability to teach the gospel with persuasive power and converting zeal is itself one of the gifts of the Spirit.

32-33. The Eunuch was reading the 53rd chapter of Isaiah, a part of which is here quoted. This entire chapter is quoted and then explained, in part at least, by Abinadi as recorded in Mosiah chapters 14 and 15.

35. Preached unto him Jesus] Taught him the gospel; explained to him the plan of salvation, probably in some considerable detail.

38. They went down both into the water] Baptism by immersion is indicated, the only then known or practiced mode.

39. The Spirit of the Lord caught away Philip] Nephi the son of Lehi and Nephi the son of Helaman both had this same experience. (1 Ne. 11:1; Hela. 10:16-17.) Apparently some similar experiences were known in Old Testament times. (1 Kings 18:12; 2 Kings 2:16.)

JESUS APPEARS TO SAUL

ACTS 9:1-9.

1 And Saul, yet breathing out threatenings and slaughter against the disciples of the Lord, went unto the high priest,

2 And desired of him letters to Damascus to the synagogues, that if he found any of this way, whether they were men or women, he might bring them bound unto Jerusalem.

3 And as he journeyed, he came near Damascus: and suddenly there shined round about him a light from heaven:

4 And he fell to the earth, and heard a voice saying unto him, Saul, Saul, why persecutest thou me?

5 And he said, Who art thou, Lord? And the Lord said, I am Jesus whom thou persecutest: *it is* hard for thee to kick against the pricks.

6 And he trembling and astonished said, Lord, what wilt thou have me to do? And the Lord *said* unto him, Arise, and go into the city, and it shall be told thee what thou must do.

7 And the men which journeyed with him stood speechless, hearing a voice, but seeing no man.

8 And Saul arose from the earth; and when his eyes were opened, he saw no man: but they led him by the hand, and brought *him* into Damascus.

9 And he was three days without sight, and neither did eat nor drink.

I.V. ACTS 9:7.

7 And **they who were journeying** with him **saw indeed the light, and were afraid; but they heard not the voice of him who spake to him.**

Why did Jesus appear to Saul? Clearly the persecuted Nazarene came to call Saul to service in the Church under such circumstances as to rank him (in due course) with the other apostles who had seen the risen Lord.

But why Saul, why this man who hated the Lord and sought to slay his saints? There can be only one answer — pre-existence; Saul had gained the talents and risen to the spiritual stature in the pre-mortal life which qualified him to stand as an apostolic minister of Him who now chastened him on the Damascus road.

Paul's call from rebellion to righteousness is comparable in many ways to that of the Nephite, Alma the younger. This American Paul, aided by the four sons of Mosiah, was seeking to destroy the Church of God when an angel with the voice of thunder, and as the earth shook, called him to turn and pursue that course which would lead thousands of earth's pilgrims to a celestial haven. (Mosiah 27.)

1. Threatenings and slaughter] There is neither excuse nor mitigation for religious persecution. Life taken because of misdirected religious zeal is still murder. Joseph Smith was both martyred and murdered. Saul's course of seeking to slay the saints was depraved and devil-devised, which he frankly confessed in his later ministry. (Acts 22:4; 26:10-11.)

The high priest] "The Romans allowed the Sanhedrin to exercise civil and criminal jurisdiction (except in capital cases) over the whole Jewish community, even outside Palestine." (*Dummelow*, p. 830.)

2. Letters . . . to the synagogues] Apparently the Jewish converts to Christianity still assembled in the synagogues and were certainly known to and could be identified by the local rabbis. (Acts 26:11.)

4. Why persecutest thou me?] To persecute the saints is to fight against God. Whether a man's acts be good or ill, the same law applies: "Inasmuch as ye have done it unto one of the least of these my brethren, ye have done it unto me." (Matt. 25:40.)

5. Kick against the pricks] "The metaphor of an ox, only driving the goad deeper by kicking against it, is a classic one, and here forcibly expresses, not only the vanity of all his measures for crushing the gospel, but the deeper wound which every such effort inflicted upon himself." (*Jamieson*, p. 183.)

6. Jesus had come from the courts of glory to chasten and reprove Saul. Why, then, did not the Lord tell his future minister how to turn from the error of his ways? Why appear to him without delivering the whole message? Simply because the Lord had a servant named Ananias whose commission and work it was to teach and baptize Paul. The presiding officer of heaven and earth would not overstep the bounds of his own laws. He had delegated power to his local officer to handle matters of this sort and to him even the future apostle to the Gentiles must apply for counsel and direction. See *Commentary I*, pp. 303-305.

9. Alma remained in a trance for two days and two nights, during which time he received a marvelous spiritual manifestation and regeneration, was born again, and heard the voice of the Lord. (Mosiah 27:22-31.) Saul, similarly, during his three sightless days commenced the character transformation which in due course would change the history of Christianity. What anguish of soul he must have felt, what fires of conscience, what godly sorrow for sin, as he humbled himself preparatory to submitting to the direction of Ananias.

I.V. 7. Changes in this verse make it conform with Paul's own account. (Acts 22:9.)

SAUL RECEIVES SIGHT, IS BAPTIZED

ACTS 9:10-19a.

10 And there was a certain disciple at Damascus, named Ananias; and to him said the Lord in a vision, Ananias. And he said, Behold, I *am here*, Lord.

11 And the Lord *said* unto him, Arise, and go into the street which is called Straight, and enquire in the house of Judas for *one* called Saul, of Tarsus: for, behold, he prayeth,

12 And hath seen in a vision a man named Ananias coming in, and putting *his* hand on him, that he might receive his sight.

13 Then Ananias answered, Lord, I have heard by many of this man, how much evil he hath done to thy saints at Jerusalem:

14 And here he hath authority from the chief priests to bind all that call on thy name.

15 But the Lord said unto him, Go thy way: for he is a chosen vessel unto me, to bear my name before the Gentiles, and kings, and the children of Israel:

16 For I will show him how great things he must suffer for my name's sake.

17 And Ananias went his way, and entered into the house; and putting his hands on him said, Brother Saul, the Lord, *even* Jesus, that appeared unto thee in the way as thou camest, hath sent me, that thou mightest receive thy sight, and be filled with the Holy Ghost.

18 And immediately there fell from his eyes as it had been scales: and he received sight forthwith, and arose, and was baptized.

19a And when he had received meat, he was strengthened.

There is divine direction where choice souls are concerned. Often they are led to the truth by miraculous means. Dreams, visions, impressions from the Spirit, and various seeming happenstances take place which help spiritually gifted persons to find the gospel.

10-16. What a shock it must have been to the primitive saints, first, to find Saul within the gospel fold, and, later, to be called to sustain him as a special witness of the Lord's name in all the earth. And yet, when the Lord's will is made manifest, his true saints always bow in humble submission.

12. Saul apparently received great spiritual manifestations during his three days of fasting, blindness, and prayer. At least we here learn he had another vision before his coming baptism.

15. A chosen vessel] Saul was foreordained; nothing he had done on earth qualified him for what was ahead; but his native spiritual endowment, nurtured and earned in pre-existence, prepared him for the coming ministry.

17. Be filled with the Holy Ghost] To occur after his baptism.

18. He received sight] A miracle, one of the signs promised the faithful. **Baptized]** Saul has seen the resurrected Son of God, received visions, been the recipient of miracles wrought on his behalf, and yet none of these sufficed to prepare him for church membership or ministerial service. Baptism is the gate for all — Christ, Paul, every accountable person.

91

SAUL, LATER PAUL, BEGINS HIS MINISTRY

ACTS 9:19b-31.

19b Then was Saul certain days with the disciples which were at Damascus.

20 And straightway he preached Christ in the synagogues, that he is the Son of God.

21 But all that heard *him* were amazed, and said; Is not this he that destroyed them which called on this name in Jerusalem, and came hither for that intent, that he might bring them bound unto the chief priests?

22 But Saul increased the more in strength, and confounded the Jews which dwelt at Damascus, proving that this is very Christ.

23 And after that many days were fulfilled, the Jews took counsel to kill him:

24 But their laying await was known of Saul. And they watched the gates day and night to kill him.

25 Then the disciples took him by night, and let *him* down by the wall in a basket.

26 And when Saul was come to Jerusalem, he assayed to join himself to the disciples: but they were all afraid of him, and believed not that he was a disciple.

27 But Barnabas took him, and brought *him* to the apostles, and declared unto them how he had seen the Lord in the way, and that he had spoken to him, and how he had preached boldly at Damascus in the name of Jesus.

28 And he was with them coming in and going out at Jerusalem.

29 And he spake boldly in the name of the Lord Jesus, and disputed against the Grecians: but they went about to slay him.

30 *Which* when the brethren knew, they brought him down to Caesarea, and sent him forth to Tarsus.

31 Then had the churches rest throughout all Judea and Galilee and Samaria, and were edified; and walking in the fear of the Lord, and in the comfort of the Holy Ghost, were multiplied.

What miracles God, by his Spirit, works in the life of a convert! Indeed, what greater miracle is there than for a sin-laden soul to become clean, for an enemy of God to become his friend, for Satan's ally to enlist in the cause of righteousness?

And so Saul, who once wrecked havoc with the Church, is now to become Paul, the son of Him whose cross he has chosen to bear. Hatred of Christ has turned to love. Rebellion is replaced with righteousness. Already the man from Tarsus is one with the saints and has commenced his ministry as a missionary, scriptorian, theologian, a preacher of righteousness, a student of the law. Soon he will become the apostle to the Gentiles, a special witness of Christ his adopted Lord, and an author of world renown. There are yet to come visions, revelations, and heavenly manifestations equalling those of Peter and the chiefest apostles. Finally that God who cannot lie is to make sure the calling and election of this same Paul, thus guaranteeing him a place of exaltation in the highest heaven of the celestial world. Paul is a prototype of what man can do to serve God in this life and to save and exalt himself in the realms of glory.

Paul was a small man physically, a giant spiritually. In outward appearance he had little to recommend him; his features and physique probably repelled rather than attracted others. But because of his inward grace and goodness, and as a result of his overpowering zeal for Christ, he radiated an influence that led thousands to forsake all in the Master's Cause. From the Prophet Joseph Smith we have received the following revealed knowledge about him: "He is about five feet high; very dark hair; dark complexion; dark skin; large Roman nose; sharp face; small black eyes, penetrating as eternity; round shoulders; a whining voice, except when elevated, and then it almost resembled the roaring of a lion. He was a good orator, active and diligent, always employing himself in doing good to his fellow man." (*Teachings*, p. 180.)

20. Straightway he preached Christ] Paul was already a theologian in the intellectual sense; he had searched the scriptures and studied the Messianic prophecies. Now, enlightened by the Spirit, he knew their true meaning, and so he set forth immediately to follow the course which was to be his as long as breath remained in his body — a course of teaching and testifying that salvation was in the risen Christ.

23. Jews took counsel to kill him] How the tables have turned! Was it only yesterday when Saul was consenting to the death of Stephen? Now his own life is in jeopardy as he feels the persecutors fury. Truly murder is Mahan's most destructive weapon against the truth.

PETER RAISETH DORCAS FROM DEATH

ACTS 9:32-43.

32 And it came to pass, as Peter passed throughout all *quarters*, he came down also to the saints which dwelt at Lydda.

33 And there he found a certain man named Æneas, which had kept his bed eight years, and was sick of the palsy.

34 And Peter said unto him, Æneas, Jesus Christ maketh thee whole: arise, and make thy bed. And he arose immediately.

35 And all that dwelt at Lydda and Saron saw him, and turned to the Lord.

36 Now there was at Joppa a certain disciple named Tabitha, which by interpretation is called Dorcas: this woman was full of good works and alms-deeds which she did.

37 And it came to pass in those days, that she was sick, and died: whom when they had washed, they laid *her* in an upper chamber.

38 And forasmuch as Lydda was nigh to Joppa, and the disciples had heard that Peter was there, they sent unto him two men, desiring *him* that he would not delay to come to them.

39 Then Peter arose and went with them. When he was come, they brought him into the upper chamber: and all the widows stood by him weeping, and showing the coats and garments which Dorcas made, while she was with them.

40 But Peter put them all forth, and kneeled down, and prayed; and turning *him* to the body said, Tabitha, arise. And she opened her eyes: and when she saw Peter, she sat up.

41 And he gave her *his* hand, and lifted her up, and when he had called the saints and widows, presented her alive.

42 And it was known throughout all Joppa; and many believed in the Lord.

43 And it came to pass, that he tarried many days in Joppa with one Simon a tanner.

Peter walked where Jesus walked; the servant wore the shoes of the Master.

In Capernaum, probably in the home of Peter, "one sick of the palsy" had been lowered through the roof, and Peter had heard the Master command: "Arise, and take up thy bed, and walk." (*Commentary I*, pp. 175-180.) Now that same apostle, at the bedside of palsied Aeneas, and in his Master's name, said simply: "Arise, and make thy bed."

In the home of Jairus, Peter had seen the Lord put forth the weeping multitude and heard him say to the deceased damsel: "Maid, arise." (*Commentary I*, pp. 314-317.) Now, serving in the Master's stead, Peter put forth the weeping mourners, knelt in prayer, and then with Christ-like simplicity commanded: "Tabitha, arise."

33. Palsy] A form of paralysis.

36. Dorcas] How many faithful and but little known women there have been in the congregations of the saints in all ages:

The wise hearted women in Israel, who prepared furnishings for the tabernacle (Ex. 35:25-26);

The widow of Zarephath, who served Elijah and whose son he raised from the dead (1 Kings 17; Luke 4:25-26);

Mary and Martha of Bethany with whom Jesus associated (*Commentary I*, pp. 697-701), and whose brother Lazarus he raised from the dead (John 11:1-46);

Mary of Magdala, the first mortal to see the resurrected Lord (*Commentary I*, pp. 842-843);

Mary, the mother of James, Salome, Joanna, and the other women with them, to whom also the risen Lord appeared (*Commentary I*, pp. 844-846);

Mary the mother of Jesus, and the other women, who continued with the saints in prayer and supplication after our Lord's ascension (Acts 1:13-14);

Lois, the grandmother, and Eunice, the mother, of Timothy (2 Tim. 1:5);

Those unnamed women who labored with Paul, but "whose names are in the book of life" (Philip. 4:3);

And many others, including Dorcas, oftimes called the Relief Society Sister of the New Testament, because her life, through good deeds, bore witness that "charity never faileth."

41. Presented her alive] See *Commentary I*, p. 256.

AN ANGEL MINISTERETH TO CORNELIUS

ACTS 10:1-8.

1 There was a certain man in Caesarea called Cornelius, a centurion of the band called the Italian *band*,

2 *A* devout *man*, and one that feared God with all his house, which gave much alms to the people, and prayed to God alway.

3 He saw in a vision evidently about the ninth hour of the day an angel of God coming in to him, and saying unto him, Cornelius.

4 And when he looked on him, he was afraid, and said, What is it, Lord? And he said unto him, Thy prayers and thine alms are come up for a memorial before God.

5 And now send men to Joppa, and call for *one* Simon, whose surname is Peter:

6 He lodgeth with one Simon a tanner, whose house is by the sea side: he shall tell thee what thou oughtest to do.

7 And when the angel which spake unto Cornelius was departed, he called two of his household servants, and a devout soldier of them that waited on him continually:

8 And when he had declared all *these* things unto them, he sent them to Joppa.

"God's messengers, those individuals whom he sends (often from his personal presence in the eternal worlds), to deliver his messages (Luke 1:11-38); to minister to his children (Acts 10:1-8, 30-32); to teach them the doctrines of salvation (Mosiah 3); to call them to repentance (Moro. 7:31); to give them priesthood and keys (D. & C. 13; 128:20-21); to save them in perilous circumstances (1 Ne. 3:29-31; Dan. 6:22); to guide them in the performance of his work (Gen. 24:7); to gather his elect in the last days (Matt. 24:31); to perform all needful things relative to his work (Moro. 7:29-33) — such messengers are called *angels*." (*Mormon Doctrine*, 2nd ed., p. 35.)

" 'Angels speak by the power of the Holy Ghost; wherefore, they speak the words of Christ.' (2 Ne. 32:3.) They are ministers of Christ. 'They are subject unto him, to minister according to the word of his command, showing themselves unto them of strong faith and a firm mind in every form of godliness. And the office of their ministry is to call men unto repentance, and to fulfil and to do the work of the covenants of the Father, which he hath made unto the children of men, to prepare the way among the children of men, by declaring the word of Christ unto the chosen vessels of the Lord, that they may bear testimony of him.' (Moro. 7:30-31.)

"By the ministering of angels to men in modern times the Lord's great work of restoration is being accomplished. By this means the Book of Mormon came forth (D. & C. 20:8-12); by it the gospel of salvation was restored to earth. (Rev. 14:6-7; D. & C. 20:35; 133:36-40.) It was under the hands of angelic ministrants that the Aaronic and Melchizedek powers were conferred again upon men (D. & C. 13; 20:12-13); because they heard the voice of angels men again were commissioned to use the keys of the kingdom (D. & C. 110:11-16; 128:20-21); and by the ministering of angels the world is called to repentance. (D. & C. 43:25.)

"Indeed, from Adam to the present moment, whenever men have had sufficient faith, angels have ministered unto them. So invarying is this principle that it stands forth as the conclusive test of the divinity of any organization on earth. If angels minister to a people, they are the Lord's people, and his kingdom is with them. If angels do not minister unto them, they are not the Lord's people, and his kingdom is not with them. (Moro. 7:27-38.)" (*Mormon Doctrine*, 2nd ed., p. 503.)

1. Cornelius, a centurion] "A Roman legionary officer commanding a century (i.e. from 50 to 100 men, the hundredth part of a legion), and occupying the social position of a modern sergeant or non-commissioned officer." (*Dummelow*, p. 653.)

2-6. Here stands a man who is prayerful, pious, devout, and godfearing; whose charitable deeds are had in remembrance before the Eternal Throne; whose faith and godly conduct enable him to see within the veil and to converse with heavenly beings — and yet this man is not a candidate for salvation; he is not so much as on the strait and narrow path leading to eternal life!

How then can any man hope for salvation? The angel answers: 'Send for Peter. He will teach you the gospel; he will baptize you in water and bring you into the fold of Christ where you can become a new creature by the power of the Holy Ghost, thus putting off the natural man and becoming a saint through the atonement of Christ the Lord.' What a message thunders forth to the pious and good among all churches from this heaven-directed experience of Cornelius!

PETER, THE SEER, SEETH A VISION

ACTS 10:9-20.

9 On the morrow, as they went on their journey, and drew nigh unto the city, Peter went up upon the housetop to pray about the sixth hour:

10 And he became very hungry, and would have eaten: but while they made ready, he fell into a trance,

11 And saw heaven opened, and a certain vessel descending unto him, as it had been a great sheet knit at the four corners, and let down to the earth:

12 Wherein were all manner of fourfooted beasts of the earth, and wild beasts, and creeping things, and fowls of the air.

13 And there came a voice to him, Rise, Peter; kill and eat.

14 But Peter said, Not so, Lord; for I have never eaten any thing that is common or unclean.

15 And the voice *spake* unto him again the second time, What God hath cleansed, *that* call not thou common.

16 This was done thrice: and the vessel was received up again into heaven.

17 Now while Peter doubted in himself what this vision which he had seen should mean, behold, the men which were sent from Cornelius had made enquiry for Simon's house, and stood before the gate,

18 And called, a n d asked whether Simon, which was surnamed Peter, were lodged there.

19 While Peter thought on the vision, the Spirit said unto him, Behold, three men seek thee.

20 Arise therefore, and get thee down, and go with them, doubting nothing: for I have sent them.

10. A trance] See 2 Cor. 12:1-6. "Sometimes prophets go into trances in connection with the receipt of visions. That is, they are so completely overshadowed by the Spirit that to all outward appearances normal bodily functions are suspended. Such was the case with Balaam when he saw the coming of Christ and the triumph of Israel (Num. 24.) Peter 'fell into a trance' when he received the vision commanding him to take the gospel to the Gentiles. (Acts 10:9-48.) Paul 'was in a trance' when the Lord came to him with the command to leave Jerusalem and carry the message of salvation to the Gentiles. (Acts 22:17-21.)

"A similar experience happened to the Prophet Joseph Smith in connection with the First Vision; he was not in control of all his bodily powers when the Father and the Son appeared to him. 'When I came to myself again, I found myself lying on my back, looking up into heaven,' he said. 'When the light had departed, I had no strength; but soon recovering in some degree, I went home.' (Jos. Smith 2:20.)" (*Mormon Doctrine*, 2nd ed., pp. 802-803.)

12. For dietary, health, and religious reasons, Israel had been commanded, as part of the Levitical law, not to eat many types of flesh. (Lev. 11.)

17. What this vision . . . should mean] Peter as yet knew not the meaning of his vision. Even to his chief prophets, the Lord reveals his mind and purposes a step at a time. Visions dealing with current and historical events, and with the destinies and lives of individuals, often become clear and comprehensible by degrees.

19. The Spirit said] By the power of the Holy Ghost, through the still small voice, the voice of revelation, Peter received the mind of the Lord. (D. & C. 8:1-3.)

GOD SENDETH THE GOSPEL TO THE GENTILES

ACTS 10:21-35.

21 Then Peter went down to the men which were sent unto him from Cornelius; and said, Behold, I am he whom ye seek: what *is* the cause wherefore ye are come?

22 And they said, Cornelius the centurion, a just man, and one that feareth God, and of good report among all the nation of the Jews, was warned from God by an holy angel to send for thee into his house, and to hear words of thee.

23 Then called he them in, and lodged *them*. And on the morrow Peter went away with them, and

certain brethren from Joppa accompanied him.

24 And the morrow after they entered into Caesarea. And Cornelius waited for them, and had called together his kinsmen and near friends.

25 And as Peter was coming in, Cornelius met him, and fell down at his feet, and worshipped *him*.

26 But Peter took him up, saying, Stand up; I myself also am a man.

27 And as he talked with him, he went in, and found many that were come together.

28 And he said unto them, Ye know how that it is an unlawful thing for a man that is a Jew to keep company, or come unto one of another nation; but God hath showed me that I should not call any man common or unclean.

29 Therefore came I *unto you* without gainsaying, as soon as I was sent for: I ask therefore for what intent ye have sent for me?

30 And Cornelius said, Four days ago I was fasting until this hour; and at the ninth hour I prayed in my house, and, behold, a man stood before me in bright clothing,

31 And said, Cornelius, thy prayer is heard, and thine alms are had in remembrance in the sight of God.

32 Send therefore to Joppa, and call hither Simon, whose surname is Peter; he is lodged in the house of *one* Simon a tanner by the sea side: who, when he cometh, shall speak unto thee.

33 Immediately therefore I sent to thee; and thou hast well done that thou art come. Now therefore are we all here present before God, to hear all things that are commanded thee of God.

34 Then Peter opened *his* mouth, and said, Of a truth I perceive that God is no respecter of persons:

35 But in every nation he that feareth him, and worketh righteousness, is accepted with him.

Deity is now going to put into full force and operation his decree that the gospel is for all men everywhere. For nearly a millennium and a half his law had gone to Israel only. Jesus himself, with slight and exceptional variations, had neither taught nor healed the Gentiles. "I am not sent but unto the lost sheep of the house of Israel," he said. (Matt. 15:24.) During his mortal ministry he restricted his apostles with this command: "These twelve Jesus sent forth, and commanded them, saying, Go not into the way of the Gentiles, and into any city of the Samaritans enter ye not: But go rather to the lost sheep of the house of Israel." (Matt. 10:5-6.) See Acts 13:42-49.

After his resurrection, however, Jesus issued a new decree and broadened the field of gospel preaching to include all men. "Go ye into all the world, and preach the gospel to every creature," he said. (Mark 16:15.) Thus the decree to go to the Gentiles was already in force before Peter received his vision, but the full and true meaning had not yet burst upon the Lord's apostolic ministers. With this heaven-directed experience, Peter finally swings the gospel door open to the Gentile nations, although in practice, as Paul was soon to learn, there would yet be difficult doctrinal, administrative, and procedural problems to be solved. (Acts 15:1-35.)

24. Called together his kinsmen and near friends] A typical, almost invarying course; those who receive the light and truth from a divine source immediately desire to share it with those closest to them.

25-26. Similarly John sought to worship the messenger who opened the visions of eternity to him. (Rev. 19:10.) Investigators and new converts often have great respect and love for the missionaries who bring them the gospel.

28. Peter now knows the meaning of his vision. (Acts 10:9-16.)

30. A man] An angel. "These messengers, agents, angels of the Almighty, are chosen from among his offspring and are themselves pressing forward along the course of progression and salvation, all in their respective spheres." (*Mormon Doctrine*, 2nd ed., p. 35.)

34. God is no respecter of persons] It is not Israel only, to the exclusion of the Gentile nations; it is not the Latter-day Saints only, leaving the sectarians without hope; it is not one people or race or nation, selected out of all others, upon whom the blessings of God are showered. All souls in all ages are precious in the sight of a loving Father. Blessings received flow from obedience. See Jas. 2:1-9. (Third Article of Faith.)

GOSPEL TAUGHT BY WITNESSES

ACTS 10:36-43.

36 The word which *God* sent unto the children of Israel, preaching peace by Jesus Christ: (he is Lord of all:)

37 That word, *I say*, ye know, which was published throughout all Judea, and began from Galilee, after the baptism which John preached;

38 How God anointed Jesus of Nazareth with the Holy Ghost and with power: who went about doing good, and healing all that were oppressed of the devil; for God was with him.

39 And we are witnesses of all things which he did both in the land of the Jews, and in Jerusalem; whom they slew and hanged on a tree:

40 Him God raised up the third day, and shewed him openly;

41 Not to all the people, but unto witnesses chosen before of God, *even* to us, who did eat and drink with him after he rose from the dead.

42 And he commanded us to preach unto the people, and to testify that it is he which was ordained of God *to be* the Judge of quick and dead.

43 To him gave all the prophets witness, that through his name whosoever believeth in him shall receive remission of sins.

Peter does not argue; he does not contend. There is no debate; in this instance he does not even quote the ancient scriptures to prove his points. He simply announces the divine Sonship and ministry of Jesus and bears testimony of the truth of his message.

This is the way true ministers always operate. Being the Lord's agents and having the guidance of the Holy Spirit, they simply announce their message, or teach the doctrines they are sent to proclaim; then they seal their announcements and teachings with pure testimony. They are sent out to "testify and warn the people." (D. & C. 88:81.) Alma, for instance, recounted what the ancient prophets had taught on a particular subject, told what he knew about it, and then said: "I am commanded to stand and testify unto this people the things which have been spoken by our fathers concerning the things which are to come. And this is not all. Do ye not suppose that I know of these things myself? Behold, I testify unto you that I do know that these things whereof I have spoken are true. And how do ye suppose that I know of their surety? Behold, I say unto you they are made known unto me by the Holy Spirit of God. Behold, I have fasted and prayed many days that I might know these things of myself. And now I do know of myself that they are true; for the Lord God hath made them manifest unto me by his Holy Spirit; and this is the spirit of revelation which is in me." (Alma 5:44-46.)

Since true religion comes from God and deals with the things of the Spirit, there is no way to teach or testify with converting result except by the power and authorization of the Spirit. So important and undeviating is this principle that the Lord says: "And the Spirit shall be given unto you by the prayer of faith; and if ye receive not the Spirit ye shall not teach." (D. & C. 42:14.)

36. 'God sent Jesus Christ — he is Lord of all! — to Israel with the message of salvation.'

39. We are witnesses] See *Commentary I*, pp. 197-200.

41. Witnesses . . . who did eat and drink with him after he rose from the dead] Peter (and the other apostles) did not know and testify that Jesus was Lord of all simply because Isaiah had so foretold (Isa. 53), or through some intellectual process that convinced them mentally that such must be so. Their testimony was plain, clear, and convincing: 'After he rose from the dead, we felt the nail marks in his hands and feet; we thrust our hands into the gaping wound where the spear pierced his side; we saw him eat fish and an honeycomb; we know he rose from the grave, and therefore is Lord of all.' See *Commentary I*, pp. 851-853.

43. What a glorious pronouncement this is! Salvation for all men in all ages is centered in and comes because of belief in Christ. Did Isaiah preach remission of sins by baptism for those who believed in Christ and accepted him as the Son of God? Did Abraham, Moses, and all the prophets proclaim this same plan and system of salvation? Verily, Yes. From Adam to the present moment, every prophet and preacher of righteousness who has dwelt on earth has had as the burden of his message that salvation centered in Christ; that he was to be (or has become) the Son of God; that through his redemption, immortality and eternal life come to mortal man; and that faith, repentance, baptism, receipt of the Holy Ghost, and righteous living are essential to salvation.

There was not one system of salvation for those in the patriarchal age, another for Israel and her tribes, and another for those of the Christian Era. All the prophets testified of Christ, and it was this very knowledge and testimony that placed them in the category of prophets. See *Commentary I*, pp. 251-253; Rev. 19:9b-10.

Speaking in the pre-Christian Era, Abinadi, a Hebrew prophet on the American continent, taught as Peter did, in these words: "There could not any man be saved except it were through the redemption of God. For behold, did not Moses prophesy unto them concerning the coming of the Messiah, and that God should redeem his people? Yea, and even all the prophets who have prophesied ever since the world began — have they not spoken more or less concerning these things? Have they not said that God himself should come down among the children of men, and take upon him the form of man, and go forth in mighty power upon the face of the earth? Yea, and have they not said also that he should bring to pass the resurrection of the dead, and that he, himself, should be oppressed and afflicted?" (Mosiah 13:32-35.)

Then he asks: "Yea, even doth not Isaiah say: Who hath believed our report," and so forth (Mosiah 14), as he proceeds to quote what is the 53rd chapter of the writings of that great Messianic prophet. Truly it is a glorious concept that Christ has been, is, and ever shall be the center of the teachings of all the prophets, and that it is through him, and him only, that remission of sins and consequent salvation come!

GOD GIVETH THE HOLY GHOST TO GENTILES

ACTS 10:44-48.

44 While Peter yet spake these words, the Holy Ghost fell on all them which heard the word.

45 And they of the circumcision which believed were astonished, as many as came with Peter, because that on the Gentiles also

was poured out the gift of the Holy Ghost.

46 For they heard them speak with tongues, and magnify God. Then answered Peter,

47 Can any man forbid water, that these should not be baptized, which have received the Holy Ghost as well as we?

48 And he commanded them to be baptized in the name of the Lord. Then prayed they him to tarry certain days.

God here pours out the Holy Ghost upon Cornelius, his kindred, and friends as a sign to Peter (and through him to all Israel) that the gospel was now to go to the Gentiles. The Holy Ghost is the greatest gift a man can receive in this life, and it comes to those who believe and obey the laws of the gospel. Since the Gentiles are here so visibly anointed with this heavenly endowment, it is evident that the Lord is offering to them the gifts and blessings of that gospel which heretofore has been preached almost exclusively to the house of Israel.

Two basic and fundamental gospel doctrines must be known to understand this spiritual outpouring of divine grace: 1. The nature and kind of being the Holy Ghost is; and 2. What is meant by the gift of the Holy Ghost.

As to the Holy Ghost *himself*, the scriptural teachings are summarized as follows: "The Holy Ghost is the third member of the Godhead. He is a Personage of Spirit, a Spirit Person, a Spirit Man, a Spirit Entity. He can be in only one place at one time, and he does not and cannot transform himself into any other form or image than that of the Man whom he is, though his power and influence can be manifest at one and the same time through all immensity. (D. & C. 130:22-23; *Teachings*, p. 190, 275-276; *Gospel Doctrine*, 5th ed., pp. 59-62.)

"He is the Comforter, Testator, Revelator, Sanctifier, Holy Spirit, Holy Spirit of Promise, Spirit of Truth, Spirit of the Lord, and Messenger of the Father and the Son, and his companionship is the greatest gift that mortal man can enjoy. His mission is to perform all of the functions appertaining to the various name-titles which he bears. Because he is a Spirit Personage, he has power — according to the eternal laws ordained by the Father —

to perform essential and unique functions for men." (*Mormon Doctrine*, 2nd ed., p. 359.) See *Commentary I*, pp. 752-756.

As to the gift of the Holy Ghost *itself*, the scriptural accounts reveal: " 'There is a difference between the Holy Ghost and the gifts of the Holy Ghost,' the Prophet taught. (*Teachings*, p. 199.) As the third member of the Godhead, the Holy Ghost is a Personage of Spirit; the gift of the Holy Ghost, however, is the right, based on faithfulness, to the constant companionship of that member of the Godhead. It is the right to receive revelation, guidance, light, and truth from the Spirit. 'The presentation or "gift" of the Holy Ghost,' President Joseph F. Smith said, 'simply confers upon a man the right to receive at any time, when he is worthy of it and desires it, the power and light of truth of the Holy Ghost, although he may often be left to his own spirit and judgment.' (*Gospel Doctrine*, 5th ed., pp. 60-61.)

"Joseph Smith explained: 'Cornelius received the Holy Ghost before he was baptized, which was the convincing power of God unto him of the truth of the gospel, but he could not receive the gift of the Holy Ghost until after he was baptized. Had he not taken this sign or ordinance upon him, the Holy Ghost which convinced him of the truth of God, would have left him. Until he obeyed these ordinances and received the gift of the Holy Ghost, by the laying on of hands, according to the order of God, he could not have healed the sick or commanded an evil spirit to come out of a man, and it obey him.' (*Teachings*, p. 199.)

"In similar manner, in this day, many nonmembers of the Church, 'by the power of the Holy Ghost' (Moro. 10:4-5), learn that the Book of Mormon is true, or that Joseph Smith is a Prophet of God, but unless they repent and are baptized that flash of testimony leaves them. They never receive the continuing, renewed assurance that comes from the companionship of that Spirit Being whose mission it is to whisper truth to the spirits within men. (*Teachings*, pp. 198-199.)

"Further, the fact that a person has had hands laid on his head and a legal administrator has declared, 'Receive the Holy Ghost, does not guarantee that the gift itself has actually been enjoyed. The gift of the Holy Ghost is the right to have the constant companionship of the Spirit; the actual enjoyment of the gift, the actual receipt of the companionship of the Spirit, is based on personal righteousness; it does not come unless and until the person is worthy to receive it. The Spirit will not dwell in an unclean tabernacle. (1 Cor. 3:16-17; 6:19.) Those who actually enjoy the gift or presentment of the Holy Ghost are the ones who are born again, who have become new creatures of the Holy Ghost. (Mosiah 27:24-26.)

"Even a righteous person is often left to himself so that he does not at all times enjoy the promptings of revelation and light from the Holy Ghost. 'Every elder of the Church who has received the Holy Ghost by the laying on of hands, by one having authority, has power to confer that gift upon another; it does not follow that a man who has received the presentation or gift of the Holy Ghost shall always receive the recognition and witness and presence of the Holy Ghost himself; or he may receive all these, and yet the Holy Ghost not tarry with him, but visit him from time to time (D. & C. 130:23); and neither does it follow that a man must have the Holy Ghost present with him when he confers the Holy Ghost upon another, but he possesses the gift of the Holy Ghost, and it will depend upon the worthiness of him unto whom the gift is bestowed whether he receives the Holy Ghost or not.' (*Gospel Doctrine*, 5th ed., p. 61.)" (*Mormon Doctrine*, 2nd ed., pp. 312-313.) See *Commentary I*, pp. 856-857.

48. He commanded them to be baptized] Baptism is a commandment of God! It is not something offered to men without further inducement or encouragement. Men are commanded to be baptized, and those who remain unbaptized are breaking the commandment and are in rebellion against God. "The Pharisees and lawyers rejected the counsel of God against themselves, being not baptized." (Luke 7:30.) In Jesus' own language, the mandatory requirement to be baptized was given to the Nephites thus: "Now this is the commandment: Repent, all ye ends of the earth, and come unto me and be baptized in my name, that ye may be sanctified by the reception of the Holy Ghost, that ye may stand spotless before me at the last day." (3 Ne. 27:20.)

GOD GRANTS GIFT OF REPENTANCE TO GENTILES

ACTS 11:1-18.

1 And the apostles and brethren that were in Judea heard that the Gentiles had also received the word of God.

2 And when Peter was come up to Jerusalem, they that were of the circumcision contended with him,

3 Saying, Thou wentest in to men uncircumcised, and didst eat with them.

4 But Peter rehearsed *the matter* from the beginning, and expounded *it* by order unto them, saying,

5 I was in the city of Joppa praying: and in a trance I saw a vision, A certain vessel descend, as it had been a great sheet, let down from heaven by four corners; and it came even to me:

6 Upon the which when I had fastened mine eyes, I considered, and saw four-footed beasts of the earth, and wild beasts, and creeping things, and fowls of the air.

7 And I heard a voice saying unto me, Arise, Peter; slay and eat.

8 But I said, Not so, Lord: for nothing common or unclean hath at any time entered into my mouth.

9 But the voice answered me again from heaven, What God hath cleansed, *that* call not thou common.

10 And this was done three times: and all were drawn up again into heaven.

11 And, behold, immediately there were three men already come unto the house where I was, sent from Caesarea unto me.

12 And the spirit bade me go with them, nothing doubting. Moreover these six brethren accompanied me, and we entered into the man's house:

13 And he showed us how he had seen an angel in his house, which stood and said unto him, Send me to Joppa, and call for Simon, whose surname is Peter;

14 Who shall tell thee words, whereby thou and all thy house shall be saved.

15 And as I began to speak, the Holy Ghost fell on them, as on us at the beginning.

16 Then remembered I the word of the Lord, how that he said, John indeed baptized with water; but ye shall be baptized with the Holy Ghost.

17 Forasmuch then as God gave them the like gift as *he did* unto us, who believed on the Lord Jesus Christ; what was I, that I could withstand God?

18 When they heard these things, they held their peace, and glorified God, saying, Then hath God also to the Gentiles granted repentance unto life.

Peter is now called upon to recount and report upon the spiritual experiences which led him to take the gospel to the Gentiles. In response, his apostolic associates and the church members in Jerusalem rejoice because God has now "granted" to the Gentiles also "repentance unto life."

That is — repentance is a gift of God, a part of his gospel plan. It is the way and the means whereby souls are cleansed and saved. It operates because of the atoning sacrifice of Christ and is far more than the forsaking of evil; it includes the acceptance of Christ and the cleansing power of his blood. Any Gentiles in any age had been free to forsake sin and live better lives, but now God was granting them his gift, "repentance unto life," the privilege and power to become clean through the gospel and thus to be heirs of salvation with Israel. See 2 Cor. 2:1-17.

"Because all acountable men are stained by sin (Eccles. 7:20; Rom. 3:10; 1 John 1:8-10), and because no unclean thing can enter into the kingdom of heaven (Alma 11:37; 3 Ne. 27:19; Moses 6:57), a merciful God has ordained the law of repentance whereby the human soul may be cleansed and conditioned for eternal life in his everlasting presence. Repentance is the process whereby a mortal soul — unclean and stained with the guilt of sin — is enabled to cast off the burden of guilt, wash away the filth of iniquity, and become clean every whit, entirely free from the bondage of sin. (D. & C. 58:42-43; 64:3-13; Isa. 1:16-20; Ezek. 18:19-31; 33:7-20.)

"To gain forgiveness through repentance a person must have a conviction of guilt, a godly sorrow for sin, and a contrite spirit. He must desire to be relieved of the burden of sin, have a fixed determination to forsake his evil ways, be willing to confess his sins, and forgive those who have trespassed against him; he must accept the cleansing power of the blood of Christ as such is offered through the waters of baptism and the conferral of the Holy Ghost. (*Articles of Faith*, pp. 109-116.)

"Repentance is essential to salvation; without it no accountable person can be saved in the kingdom of God. (D. & C. 20:29; Moses 6:52-53, 57; 3 Ne. 9:22.) It is a prerequisite to baptism and hence to membership in the kingdom of God on earth. (D. & C. 18:41; 20:71; 33:11; 49:13.) It is a requirement made of every accountable person, that is of those 'having knowledge' (D. & C. 29:49), and parents are obligated to teach repentance to their children to qualify them for baptism when they reach the years of accountability. (D. & C. 68:25-27.)

" 'Every man must repent or suffer.' In the event of repentance, the law of mercy prevails, and the penitent person is saved from suffering. 'I, God, have suffered these things for all, that they might not suffer if they would repent; But if they would not repent they must suffer even as I; Which suffering caused myself, even God, the greatest of all, to tremble because of pain, and to bleed at every pore, and to suffer both body and spirit.' Hence comes the Lord's imperative command to repent. (D. & C. 19:4-20.) Where there is no repentance, the law of justice takes precedence and remission of sins is gained through suffering rather than as a gift of God through the blood of Christ. (Alma 42:22-24.)" (*Mormon Doctrine*, 2nd ed., pp. 630-631.) See *Commentary I*, pp. 475-476.

1. **The word of God**] The gospel.

2. **Circumcision**] See Acts 15:1-35. **Contended with him**] Peter was no autocrat who ruled over the apostles or whose decisions and views were accepted as infallible. They asked for and he gave a temperate and judicious report of his experiences, which they, guided by the same Spirit which had directed him, thereupon accepted with approving endorsement.

14. To be saved men must believe and conform to the teachings of the gospel.

DISCIPLES CALLED CHRISTIANS AT ANTIOCH

ACTS 11:19-26.

19 Now they which were scattered abroad upon the persecution that arose about Stephen travelled as far as Phenice, and Cyprus, and Antioch, preaching the word to none but unto the Jews only.

20 And some of them were men of Cyprus and Cyrene, which, when they were come to Antioch, spake unto the Grecians, preaching the Lord Jesus.

21 And the hand of the Lord was with them: and a great number believed, and turned unto the Lord.

22 Then tidings of these things came unto the ears of the church which was in Jerusalem: and they sent forth Barnabas, that he should go as far as Antioch.

23 Who, when he came, and had seen the grace of God, was glad, and exhorted them all, that with purpose of heart they would cleave unto the Lord.

24 For he was a good man, and full of the Holy Ghost, and of faith: and much people was added unto the Lord.

25 Then departed Barnabas to Tarsus, for to seek Saul:

26 And when he had found him, he brought him unto Antioch. And it came to pass, that a whole year they assembled themselves with the church, and taught much people. And the disciples were called Christians first in Antioch.

19-21. Scattered by persecution the Lord's saints take his gospel to Jews and Gentiles alike in new areas, thus spreading the truth and building up the Church. This personal missionary zeal is one of the greatest evidences of the truth and divinity of the true Christian Church. Every new convert promises in the waters of baptism to stand as a witness of the Lord Jesus and his work "at all times and in all things, and in all places . . . even until death." (Mosiah 18:9.) The divine decree is: "It becometh every man who hath been warned to warn his neighbor." (D. & C. 88:81.) Where the true Church is there the members generally will be imbued with missionary zeal. The common slogan in The Church of Jesus Christ of Latter-day Saints is — Every Member a Missionary. See Acts 16:1-15.

22-24. Obviously among the scattered saints there were priesthood bearers who had power and authority from the apostles to baptize new converts and build up branches of the Church. Barnabas went forth from Jerusalem to the new congregations to hold conferences with them, to strengthen them in the faith, to give needed counsel from the General Authorities at the center of the Church.

25-26. Seemingly, Saul would be chosen for this service because of his leanings to and love for the Gentile converts.

26. Called Christians first in Antioch] Christians is an obvious name for the followers of Christ, for those who believe he is the Son of God and that salvation of all degrees comes because of him and his atoning sacrifice. Since there have been followers of Christ in successive gospel dispensations from Adam to the present, these all would have been known as Christians or some equivalent, synonymous term. By saying the saints were called Christians first in Antioch means that for the first time in the meridian dispensation there was a sufficient church membership so that nonmembers recognized the saints as a separate and distinct organization, one severed and apart from the Jewish synagogue and community.

As far as the rejectors and detractors of Christ were concerned, the term *Christian* was probably first used in derision. Such was clearly the case among the Nephites. The Book of Mormon account, recording events in about the year 73 B.C. — well over a century before the Antioch congregation came into being — says: "Christians . . . For thus were all the true believers of Christ, who belonged to the church of God, called by those who did not belong to the church." (Alma 46:13-16.)

A somewhat analogous situation exists in this dispensation with reference to the term *Mormons*. With the restoration for the final time on earth of the same gospel and the same knowledge about Christ which was possessed and enjoyed by the saints of old, the Lord specified that the name of his Church should be, "The Church of Jesus Christ of Latter-day Saints." (D. & C. 115:4.) The newly designated saints, however, were members of that Church because they knew by revelation from the Spirit that the Book of Mormon is a companion volume to the Bible, a volume of holy scripture containing the mind and will of God. Believers in this book, which is itself a new witness for Christ, and though they themselves were in fact Christians of like kind and type as those of the meridian of time, were soon, derisively at first, called Mormons. It must be understood that this is not the name of the Church, but in the sense that it is used as a synonym for that name, it is not offensive to those to whom it has been applied.

Are Mormons Christians? The answer depends on what is meant by Christians. If Christians are people with the defined view that salvation comes only through the complete gospel of Christ, Mormons are truly Christians in the precise and full meaning of the term.

If Christians are people (and this is the standard definition of the clergy of the day) who believe in the holy trinity as defined and set forth in the Nicene, Athanasian, and Apostles creeds, meaning that God is a three-in-one nothingness, a spirit essence filling immensity, an incorporeal and uncreated being incapable of definition or mortal comprehension — then Mormons, by a clergy-chosen definition, are ruled out of the fold of Christ.

But if by Christians is meant the saints of God in Antioch and elsewhere who believe and live as they did; if by Christians is meant those who accept Christ as the literal Son of God; who believe that miracles and signs follow true believers; who believe in kingdoms of glory, revelation, the gathering of Israel, and Melchizedek and Aaronic priesthoods; who believe there must be apostles and prophets in the Church; and who believe in all respects as did holy men of old — then Mormons are Christians and they have the only pure and perfect Christianity now on earth. Indeed, Mormonism is pure, unadulterated Christianity, restored anew in all its grandeur and glory.

ANCIENT CHURCH GUIDED BY REVELATION

ACTS 11:27-30.

27 And in these days came prophets from Jerusalem unto Antioch.

28 And there stood up one of them named Agabus, and signified by the spirit that there should be great dearth throughout all the

113

world: which came to pass in the days of Claudius Caesar.

29 Then the disciples, every man according to his ability, determined to send relief unto the brethren which dwelt in Judea:

30 Which also they did, and sent it to the elders by the hands of Barnabas and Saul.

Revelation is the rock upon which the true Church is built. Where there is direct revelation from God, there is the true Church; where revelation has ceased, true religion no longer exists. Man cannot create true religion anymore than he can resurrect himself or save his own soul. True religion comes from God and is known only by revelation. (*Mormon Doctrine*, 2nd ed., pp. 643-651.) See *Commentary I*, pp. 290-292; 380-390; 1 Cor. 2:9-16.

True religion provides revelation in both temporal and spiritual fields. The Lord gives direction in the spiritual realm by revealing the plan of salvation, in the temporal by making known what is to be in the particular day and age. All of the prophets receive direction where spiritual things are concerned; each prophet, for his day and situation, receives whatever guidance is needed in temporal matters. Noah, Moses, Elijah, and all the prophets gave revealed guidance in temporal as well as spiritual concerns. Is there any reason to believe that in this atomic age, this age of war and communistic treachery, revelation is any less needed in temporal affairs than it was in the building of an ark, the leading of Israel out of Egypt, or the calling down of fire from heaven upon the priests of Baal?

29. See Acts 4:32-37.

30. Elders] "One of the ordained offices in the Melchizedek Priesthood is that of an *elder*. (D. & C. 20:60; 55:2; 107:7; Acts 14:23; Tit. 1:5.) This office grows out of and is an appendage to the higher priesthood. (D. & C. 84:29; 107:5.) As far as we know, there were no ordained elders in the Church until the day of Moses, just as there was no Aaronic Priesthood until that day.

"There were, of course, ordained elders in ancient Israel (Ex. 24:9-11; Num. 11:16), among the Nephites both in their early and latter history (Alma 4:7, 16; 6:1; Moro. 3:1; 4:1; 6:1; 7), and among

114

the meridian saints. In New Testament usage the term is a translation of the Greek presbyter. (1 Tim. 5:1, 17, 19.) The ordination of elders in modern times began with Joseph Smith and Oliver Cowdery on April 6, 1830. (*Doctrines of Salvation,* vol. 3, pp. 146-147.)

"Elders are ministers of Christ; they are called to administer in spiritual things (D. & C. 107:12), 'To teach, expound, exhort, baptize, and watch over the church; And to confirm the church by the laying on of the hands, and the giving of the Holy Ghost. . . . The elders are to conduct the meetings as they are led by the Holy Ghost, according to the commandments and revelations of God.' (D. & C. 20:42-45; 46:2.) They are to preach the gospel (D. & C. 53:3), teach from the scriptures (D. & C. 42.12), administer to the sick (D. & C. 42:43-52; Jas. 5:14-15), function in the church court system (D. & C. 42:80), and perform any duty that can be done by a holder of the lesser priesthood. (D. & C. 20:38-67.)" (*Mormon Doctrine,* 2nd ed., p. 215.)

AN ANGEL FREES PETER FROM PRISON

ACTS 12:1-19.

1 Now about that time Herod the king stretched forth *his* hands to vex certain of the church.

2 And he killed James the brother of John with the sword.

3 And because he s a w it pleased the Jews, he proceeded further to take Peter also. (Then were the days of unleavened bread.)

4 And when he had apprehended him, he put *him* in prison, and delivered *him* to four quaternions of soldiers to keep him; intending after Easter to bring him forth to the people.

5 Peter therefore was kept in prison: but prayer was made without ceasing of the church unto God for him.

6 And when Herod would have brought him forth, the same night Peter was sleeping between two soldiers, bound with two chains: and the keepers before the door kept the prison.

7 And, behold, the angel of the Lord came upon *him,* and a light shined in the prison: and he smote Peter on the side, and raised him up, saying, Arise up quickly. And his chains fell off from *his* hands.

8 And the angel said unto him, Gird thyself, and bind on thy sandals. And so he did. And he saith unto him, Cast thy garment about thee, and follow me.

9 And he went out, and followed him; and wist not that it was true which was done by the angel; but thought he saw a vision.

10 When they were past the first and the second ward, they came unto the iron gate that leadeth unto the city; which opened to them of his own accord: and they went out, and passed on through one street; and forthwith the angel departed from him.

11 And when Peter was come to himself, he said, Now I know of a surety, that the Lord hath sent his angel, and hath delivered me out of the hand of Herod, and *from* all the expectation of the people of the Jews.

12 And when he had considered *the thing*, he came to the house of Mary the mother of John, whose surname was Mark; where many were gathered together praying.

13 And as Peter knocked at the door of the gate, a damsel came to hearken, named Rhoda.

14 And when she knew Peter's voice, she opened not the gate for gladness, but ran in, and told how Peter stood before the gate.

15 And they said unto her, Thou art mad. But she constantly affirmed that it was even so. Then said they, It is his angel.

16 But Peter continued knocking: and when they had opened *the door*, and saw him, they were astonished.

17 But he, beckoning unto them with the hand to hold their peace, declared unto them how the Lord had brought him out of the prison. And he said, Go show these things unto James, and to the brethren. And he departed, and went into another place.

18 Now as soon as it was day, there was no small stir among the soldiers, what was become of Peter.

19 And when Herod had sought for him, and found him not, he examined the keepers, and commanded that *they* should be put to death. And he went down from Judea to Caesarea, and *there* abode.

Peter is arrested by Herod and sentenced to be slain; he is imprisoned in a cell with guards at the locked doors; he lies chained to two soldiers; a great iron gate with more guards closes in the prison itself; a total of 16 soldiers have the lone apostle in their charge. The Church prays for his deliverance, while Peter sleeps (as his Master had done when the storm threatened their ship on the Sea of Galilee); and lo, God sendeth an angel and Peter is freed. When no recourse remains but through divine intervention, the miraculous deliverance is accomplished. God does for man what he cannot do for himself. See Acts 5:17-26.

2. Martyrdom] See Rev. 6:9-11.

4. Four quarternions of soldiers] Four parties of four each, to stand guard in alternate shifts. **After Easter]** After the Passover; there was as yet no such thing as an Easter festival.

10. The second ward] The second guard of soldiers.

15. It is his angel] 'It is his spirit,' meaning he has already been executed.

17. James] Either James the Lord's brother, now also an apostle (Gal. 1:19), or James the son of Alpheus, one of whom was in Jerusalem at the moment.

THE LORD SLAYS HEROD BY DISEASE

ACTS 12:20-23.

20 And Herod was highly displeased with them of Tyre and Sidon: but they came with one accord to him, and, having made Blastus the king's chamberlain their friend, desired peace; because their country was nourished by the king's *country*.

21 And upon a set day Herod, arrayed in royal apparel, sat upon his throne, and made an oration unto them.

22 And the people gave a shout, *saying, It is* the voice of a god, and not of a man.

23 And immediately the angel of the Lord smote him, because he gave not God the glory: and he was eaten of worms, and gave up the ghost.

Herod Agrippa I, king in Jerusalem and Judea, died by the Lord's hand as surely as though a destroying angel had slain him with the sword of vengeance. Though such expressions as "destroying angel" and "sword of vengeance" may be figurative, they are intended to convey the reality that the Lord's hand is involved

117

in what takes place and that he is using his powers to bring to pass his ends. Deity, for instance, slew the firstborn in all the houses of Egypt (Ex. 12:23, 29), and this is figuratively spoken of as having been done by "the destroying angel." (D. & C. 89:21.)

Though in this instance Herod may have been smitten by an angel in the literal sense, it is more probable to suppose that the angelic smitting is a figure of speech meaning that the Lord caused disease to destroy, in a dramatic and awesome way, the mortal body of one who had already slain James and who had chosen to make God his enemy. In any event the Lord does use diseases and other temporal disturbances and afflictions to carry out his purposes — the temporal destructions that occur being symbolical of the eternal spiritual disease and death which the wicked also inherit.

"Disease comes both because of failure to obey the laws of health and because of failure to keep the other commandments of God. Righteous persons frequently become ill and suffer bodily afflictions simply because they have been exposed to disease, and the contaminating germs have power over their bodies. Sometimes by faith the righteous escape plagues that are sweeping the land; and often, having become sick, the gift of healing restores the obedient to full physical well-being.

"But when the Lord's people rebel, he sends diseases upon them. To disobedient Israel came this curse: 'The Lord will smite thee with the botch of Egypt, and with the emerods, and with the scab, and with the itch, whereof thou canst not be healed. The Lord shall smite thee with madness, and blindness, and astonishment of heart. . . . The Lord will make thy plagues wonderful, and the plagues of thy seed, even great plagues, and of long continuance, and sore sicknesses, and of long continuance. Moreover he will bring upon thee all the diseases of Egypt, which thou wast afraid of; and they shall cleave unto thee. Also every sickness, and every plague, which is not written in the book of this law, them will the Lord bring upon thee, until thou be destroyed.' (Deut. 28:27-28, 59-61; Mosiah 17:16; Alma 15:3-5.) On the other hand, the promise was that by obedience all this would be avoided. (Ex. 15:26; Deut. 7:15, 28.)" (*Mormon Doctrine*, 2nd ed., p. 199.)

SAUL AND BARNABAS CALLED TO THE MINISTRY

ACTS 12:24-25; 13:1-5.

24 But the word of God grew and multiplied.

25 And Barnabas and Saul returned from Jerusalem, when they had fulfilled *their* ministry, and took with them John, whose surname was Mark.

1 Now there were in the church that was at Antioch certain prophets and teachers; as Barnabas, and Simeon that was called Niger, and Lucius of Cyrene, and Manaen, which had been brought up with Herod the tetrarch, and Saul.

2 As they ministered to the Lord, and fasted, the Holy Ghost said, Separate me Barnabas and Saul for the work whereunto I have called them.

3 And when they had fasted and prayed, and laid *their* hands on them, they sent *them* away.

4 So they, being sent forth by the Holy Ghost, departed unto Seleucia; and from thence they sailed to Cyprus.

5 And when they were at Salamis, they preached the word of God in the synagogues of the Jews: and they had also John to *their* minister.

13:1. Prophets and teachers] Not one prophet, but many; not one teacher, but many — with those named being examples. There are always prophets and teachers — a great host of them — in the true Church. Indeed, where the Lord's prophets and teachers are found, there is the Lord's Church; and where such are not found, there the true Church is not. See *Commentary I*, pp. 251-253; Rev. 19:9-10.

2. The Holy Ghost said] The Lord Jesus Christ said; but the instruction came by the power of the Holy Ghost, that is, the Lord spoke to them by the voice of the Spirit. The Holy Ghost is God's minister to give revelation, to convey his mind and will to men. "I will tell you in your mind and in your heart," the Lord says, "by the Holy Ghost, which shall come upon you and which shall dwell in your heart. Now, behold, this is the spirit of revelation." (D. & C. 8:2-3.) And the receipt of continuous revelation is the proof positive of the identity of the true Church. Where there is revelation from the Holy Ghost — revelation in the full, complete, and literal sense, revelation dealing with all things both temporal and spiritual — there is the true Church; but where such is not found, there the true Church is not.

The work whereunto I have called them] What work? Apparently they were being set apart as missionaries, for they immediately went forth to preach the gospel and administer its ordinances according to the pattern set by Jesus. But who is to say whether more than this was involved? Obviously they both already held the Melchizedek Priesthood and were elders. Were they now being ordained seventies? Such is an apostolic and a missionary office. From this time on Luke refers to them as apostles. Could this have been their ordination as such, or their setting apart as members of the Council of the Twelve? If so, and such is a distinct possibility, one or more of the other apostles would have been present to confer upon them the keys of the kingdom. But whatever office or position was involved, Saul and Barnabas were now going forth as legal administrators, on the Lord's errand, called by revelation, and authorized to serve and minister by the laying on of the hands of the Lord's anointed — all of which sets the pattern for ministerial service for all true ministers in all ages.

3. Fasted and prayed] See *Commentary I*, pp. 237-238.

Laid their hands on them] Saul and Barnabas were called by prophecy and were either ordained or set apart or both by the laying on of hands, all in accord with the Lord's law "that a man must be called of God, by prophecy, and by the laying on of hands, by those who are in authority to preach the Gospel and administer in the ordinances thereof." (Fifth Article of Faith.)

There are two types of ministerial calls in the Church — those to ordained offices, and those to administrative or set apart positions. Both kinds of calls are made by prophecy, that is by the spirit of inspiration, but one type is of a permanent nature and the other is temporary. Brethren are ordained to offices in the priesthood, which offices they hold ever thereafter, in time and in eternity. Hence the common saying, "Once a bishop, always a bishop." But brethren are set apart to serve as missionaries, on high councils, in positions of presidency, as bishops of designated wards. The setting apart empowers the priesthood holder to serve in the administrative or ecclesiastical position for the period of the assignment.

Priesthood is the power and authority of God delegated to man on earth to act in all things for the salvation of men. Where men are actually endowed with power from on high, with the priesthood of the Almighty, there is the true Church, and where the priesthood is not, there the true Church is not. See Heb. 7:1-3.

SAUL, NOW PAUL, CURSES A SORCERER

ACTS 13:6-12.

6 And when they had gone through the isle unto Paphos, they found a certain sorcerer, a false prophet, a Jew, whose name *was* Bar-jesus:

7 Which was with the deputy of the country, Sergius Paulus, a prudent man; who called for Barnabas and Saul, and desired to hear the word of God.

8 But Elymas the sorcerer (for so is his name by interpretation) withstood them, seeking to turn away the deputy from the faith.

9 Then Saul, (who also *is called* Paul,) filled with the Holy Ghost, set his eyes on him,

10 And said, O full of all subtilty and all mischief, *thou* child of the devil, *thou* enemy of all righteousness, wilt thou not cease to pervert the right ways of the Lord?

11 And now, behold, the hand of the Lord *is* upon thee, and thou shalt be blind, not seeing the sun for a season. And immediately there fell on him a mist and a darkness; and he went about seeking some to lead him by the hand.

12 Then the deputy, when he saw what was done, believed, being astonished at the doctrine of the Lord.

6. **Sorcerer**] See Acts 8:5-13. **A false prophet**] What is a false prophet? In this instance Elymas the sorcerer is so designated. In modern times, however, since it is not common among the religions of the world generally to point to certain persons as prophets, it also is not the common practice to point to the false imitators of the truth and designate them as false prophets. Nevertheless since a true prophet by definition is a minister or religious

teacher who receives revelation from God, it follows that a false prophet is a person who pretends to be a minister of Christ and a teacher of his truths who does not in fact receive revelation. Thus Joseph Smith said: "When a man goes about prophesying, and commands men to obey his teachings, he must either be a true or false prophet. False prophets always arise to oppose the true prophets, and they will prophesy so very near the truth that they will deceive almost the very chosen ones." (*Teachings*, p. 365.) Also: "If I profess to be a witness or teacher, and have not the spirit of prophecy, which is the testimony of Jesus, I must be a false witness; but if I be a true teacher and witness, I must possess the spirit of prophecy, and that constitutes a prophet; and any man who says he is a teacher or preacher of righteousness, and denies the spirit of prophecy, is a liar, and the truth is not in him; and by this key false teachers and impostors may be detected." (*Teachings*, p. 269.)

8-11. A somewhat similar experience occurred in the ministry of Alma when he cursed the Anti-Christ Korihor. (Alma 30.) "Cursings are the opposite of blessings, and the greater the opportunity given a people to earn blessings, the more severe will be the cursings heaped upon them, if they do not measure up and gain the proffered rewards. Failure to pay tithing, for instance, brings condemnation upon the covenant people, whereas the people of the world — not being specifically obligated to keep this law — do not suffer the same penalties for nontithepaying. (Mal. 3:7-12.) 'Hearken and hear, O ye my people, saith the Lord and your God, ye whom I delight to bless with the greatest of all blessings, ye that hear me; and ye that hear me not will I curse, that have professed my name, with the heaviest of all cursings.' (D. & C. 41:1.)

"Those who persecute the saints shall be cursed with the damnation of hell. (D. & C. 121:11-25.) To those on his left hand the Lord shall say: 'Depart from me, ye cursed, into everlasting fire, prepared for the devil and his angels.' (D. & C. 29:28, 41; Matt. 25:40.)

"Cursings as well as blessings may be administered by the power and authority of the priesthood (D. & C. 124:93), but the Lord's earthly agents are sent forth primarily to bless and not to curse, and no curse should ever be decreed except by direct revelation from the Lord commanding such to be done. The true spirit of the gospel is exemplified in the counsel, 'Love your enemies, bless them that curse you, do good to them that hate you, and pray for them which despitefully use you, and persecute you.' (Matt. 5:44.) 'Bless, and curse not.' (Rom. 12:14.)

"President Joseph F. Smith explained, when speaking of the priesthood: 'It is the same power and priesthood that was committed to the disciples of Christ while he was upon the earth, that whatsoever they should bind on earth should be bound in heaven, and that whatsoever they should loose on earth should be loosed in heaven, and whosoever they blessed should be blessed, and if they cursed, in the spirit of righteousness and meekness before God, God would confirm that curse; but men are not called upon to curse mankind; that is not our mission; it is our mission to preach righteousness to them. It is our business to love and to bless them, and to redeem them from the fall and from the wickedness of the world. This is our mission and our special calling. God will curse and will exercise his judgment in those matters. "Vengeance is mine," saith the Lord, and "I will repay." (Rom. 12:19.) We are perfectly willing to leave vengeance in the hands of God and let him judge between us and our enemies, and let him reward them according to his own wisdom and mercy.' (*Gospel Doctrine*, 5th ed., p. 140.)" (*Mormon Doctrine*, 2nd ed., pp. 175-176.)

10. Harsh words these! But why not? Elymas sought to keep the Roman pro-consul, for such was his rank and status, from receiving the gospel and becoming an heir of salvation. Hence he was engaged in Satan's work. What a crime it is in the sight of Heaven to teach false doctrines and thereby keep men from salvation!

SAVIOR CAME AS SEED OF DAVID

ACTS 13:13-25.

13 Now when Paul and his company loosed from Paphos, they came to Perga in Pamphylia: and John departing from them returned to Jerusalem.

14 But when they departed from Perga, they came to Antioch

123

in Pisidia, and went into the synagogue on the sabbath day, and sat down.

15 And after the reading of the law and the prophets the rulers of the synagogue sent unto them, saying, Ye men *and* brethren, if ye have any word of exhortation for the people, say on.

16 Then Paul stood up, and beckoning with *his* hand said, Men of Israel, and ye that fear God, give audience.

17 The God of this people of Israel chose our fathers, and exalted the people when they dwelt as strangers in the land of Egypt, and with an high arm brought he them out of it.

18 And about the time of forty years suffered he their manners in the wilderness.

19 And when he had destroyed seven nations in the land of Chanaan, he divided their land to them by lot.

20 And after that he gave *unto them* judges about the space of

four hundred and fifty years, until Samuel the prophet.

21 And afterward they desired a king: and God gave unto them Saul the son of Cis, a man of the tribe of Benjamin, by the space of forty years.

22 And when he had removed him, he raised up unto them David to be their king; to whom also he gave testimony, and said, I have found David the *son* of Jesse, a man after mine own heart, which shall fulfil all my will.

23 Of this man's seed hath God according to *his* promise raised unto Israel a Saviour, Jesus:

24 When John had first preached before his coming the baptism of repentance to all the people of Israel.

25 And as John fulfilled his course, he said, Whom think ye that I am? I am not *he*. But, behold, there cometh one after me, whose shoes of *his* feet I am not worthy to loose.

13. Later Paul is to refuse to accept John Mark as a missionary companion because of this failure of Mark, for an unspecified reason, to press forward as Paul deemed proper. (Acts 15:36-41.)

14-22. Apparently no introduction to the doctrine of the divine Sonship of our Lord had as great an appeal to the Jews as this historical approach. Peter and Stephen had laid similar foundations for their testimonies. (Acts 2; 3; 4; 7.)

23. Of this man's seed] Christ is the Son of David; he was born in mortality as the literal seed and descendant of Israel's great king. Both Mary (his actual mother) and Joseph (his reputed father) were descendants of David. From Mary our Lord inherited the blood of David; from Joseph came the right of kingship, meaning that if there had been a temporal ruler sitting upon the throne of David, such would have been Joseph and later Jesus. (James E. Talmage, *Jesus the Christ*, pp. 83-87, 89-90.) See *Commentary I*, pp. 92-95.)

A Saviour] But Jesus was more than the Son of David; as the Son of God he was the Savior of the world. He came "to save that which was lost" (Matt. 18:11), not to save people in their sins but from their sins. (Acts 13:38.) He came to bring salvation to all "who believe on his name." (Alma 11:37-45.)

PAUL OFFERS GOSPEL TO ISRAEL

ACTS 13:26-41.

26 Men *and* brethren, children of the stock of Abraham, and whosoever among you feareth God, to you is the word of this salvation sent.

27 For they that dwell at Jerusalem, and their rulers, because they knew him not, nor yet the voices of the prophets which are read every sabbath day, they have fulfilled *them* in condemning *him*.

28 And though they found no cause of death *in him*, yet desired they Pilate that he should be slain.

29 And when they had fulfilled all that was written of him, they took *him* down from the tree, and laid *him* in a sepulchre.

30 But God raised him from the dead:

31 And he was seen many days of them which came up with him from Galilee to Jerusalem, who are his witnesses unto the people.

32 And we declare unto you glad tidings, how that the promise which was made unto the fathers,

33 God hath fulfilled the same unto us their children, in that he hath raised up Jesus again; as it is also written in the second psalm, Thou art my Son, this day have I begotten thee.

34 And as concerning that he raised him up from the dead, *now* no more to return to corruption, he said on this wise, I will give you the sure mercies of David.

35 Wherefore he saith also in another *psalm*, Thou shalt not suffer thine Holy One to see corruption.

36 For David, after he had served his own generation by the will of God, fell on sleep, and was laid unto his fathers, and saw corruption:

37 But he, whom God raised again, saw no corruption.

38 Be it known unto you therefore, men *and* brethren, that through this man is preached unto you the forgiveness of sins:

39 And by him all that believe are justified from all things, from which ye could not be justified by the law of Moses.

40 Beware therefore, lest that come upon you, which is spoken of in the prophets;

41 Behold, ye despisers, and wonder, and perish: for I work a work in your days, a work which ye shall in no wise believe, though a man declare it unto you.

26. Paul addresses himself to the Jews and to Jewish converts. It is to them he offers the gospel first, not the Gentiles.

27. How history repeats itself! Every Sabbath the Jews read "the voices of the prophets" which testified of Jesus and his ministry, without understanding or actually believing what they supposed they knew and understood. In modern times the divines and theologians of Christendom study the Biblical prophecies of the apostasy and the final restoration of the gospel, without the insight to see their fulfilment in Joseph Smith and his associates.

30-41. Paul testifies that Jesus is the Christ. True he quotes selected Messianic prophecies to show his witness is in harmony with what other prophets have foretold. But the burden of his message is one of announcement, of bearing record that Jesus was raised from the dead; that he was seen of witnesses who now declare the glad tidings of salvation to others; that the Messianic prophecies are fulfilled in him; that forgiveness of sins is available through his blood; that men are justified through Christ and not Moses; and that those who reject him shall perish. It is testimony, not argument and scholarship, which the Lord uses to send his gospel to the world.

33-41. It is the resurrection of Christ which proves the truth and divinity of the Christian faith. Jesus is shown to be the

Son of God because he rose from the dead. The Messianic prophecies are known to apply to him because he broke the bands of death. As recorded by David, Elohim says to Jehovah: "Thou art my Son; this day have I begotten thee." (Ps. 2:7.) This, Paul shows, is fulfilled in Christ because "God raised him from the dead." And so it is with all the Messianic prophecies; their fulfilment is known because Christ gained the victory over death.

34. The sure mercies of David] David was promised a resurrection, "for thou wilt not leave my soul in hell," he wrote, "neither wilt thou suffer thine Holy One to see corruption." (Ps. 16:10.) This merciful promise of redemption, this manifestation of the loving kindness of the Lord (Ps. 89:48-49), is described by Isaiah as "an everlasting covenant . . . even the sure mercies of David." (Isa. 55:3.)

33-35. Paul shows that Christ's resurrection also was foretold in that he, not David, was the one whose soul should not see corruption.

38. There is no forgiveness of sins except in and through and because of Christ. Except for his atoning sacrifice all men would remain everlastingly bound by the chains of sin.

39. Justified] See Rom. 3:21-31.

41. Here Paul exercises the prophetic prerogative of giving an interpreting, substance quotation from the ancient scriptures and of applying it out of context for his own purpose. What Habakkuk actually said, and that with original reference to the Chaldean armies, was: "Behold ye among the heathen, and regard, and wonder marvellously: for I will work a work in your days, which ye will not believe, though it be told you." (Hab. 1:5.)

PAUL TAKES GOSPEL TO GENTILES

ACTS 13:42-49.

42 And when the Jews were gone out of the synagogue, the Gentiles besought that these words might be preached to them the next sabbath.

43 Now when the congregation was broken up, many of the

Jews and religious proselytes followed Paul and Barnabas: who, speaking to them, persuaded them to continue in the grace of God.

44 And the next sabbath day came almost the whole city together to hear the word of God.

45 But when the Jews saw the multitudes, they were filled with envy, and spake against those things which were spoken by Paul, contradicting and blaspheming.

46 Then Paul and Barnabas waxed bold, and said, It was necessary that the word of God should first have been spoken to you: but seeing ye put it from you, and judge yourselves unworthy of everlasting life, lo, we turn to the Gentiles.

47 For so hath the Lord commanded us, *saying,* I have set thee to be a light of the Gentiles, that thou shouldest be for salvation unto the ends of the earth.

48 And when the Gentiles heard this, they were glad, and glorified the word of the Lord: and as many as were ordained to eternal life believed.

49 And the word of the Lord was published throughout all the region.

I.V. ACTS 13:48.

48 And when the Gentiles heard this, they were glad, and glorified the word of the Lord; **and as many as believed were ordained unto eternal life.**

42. The Gentiles] See Acts 10:21-35.

43. Many Jews were converted and accepted the gospel.

45. Contradicting and blaspheming] These are two sins of which those who actively oppose the truth are always guilty. In the very nature of things, active opposition to the gospel cause consists of contradicting the truth and of blaspheming sacred things, whether the opposition is against Paul and Barnabas or Joseph Smith and Brigham Young. "Blasphemy consists in either or both of the following: 1. Speaking irreverently, evilly, abusively, or scurrilously against God or sacred things; or 2. Speaking profanely or falsely about Deity.

"Among a great host of impious and sacrilegious speaking that constitute blasphemy are such things as: Taking the name of God in vain; evil-speaking about the Lord's anointed; belittling sacred temple ordinances, or patriarchal blessings, or sacramental administrations; claiming unwarranted divine authority; and promulgating with profane piety a false system of salvation." (*Mormon Doctrine*, 2nd ed., p. 90.)

46. The divine plan called for offering the gospel to the Jews before it was taken to the Gentiles. True the saving truths are for "all mankind" (Third Article of Faith), but not to all men at once; there is a scheduled range of priorities; one nation is offered gospel light at one time and another on a different occasion; many people have no contact with true ministers in this life and will get their opportunities in the spirit world.

In the dispensation of the fulness of times the priorities where Jews and Gentiles are concerned have been reversed. In this age the gospel goes first to the Gentiles and at a later time will go to the Jews. Nephi summarized the priority system as it was arranged for both dispensations in these words: "There is one God and one Shepherd over all the earth. And the time cometh that he shall manifest himself unto all nations, both unto the Jews and also unto the Gentiles; and after he has manifested himself unto the Jews and also unto the Gentiles, then he shall manifest himself unto the Gentiles and also unto the Jews, and the last shall be first, and the first shall be last." (1 Ne. 13:41-42.) See Acts 1:1-8.

Judge yourselves] In a very real sense men judge themselves. "They are their own judges," Alma said, "whether to do good or do evil." (Alma 41:7.) By rejecting the gospel, thus judging themselves "unworthy of everlasting life," they have fixed the state of their eternal inheritance. None who have opportunity to accept the gospel in this life, for instance, and who do not do so, can ever rise higher in the kingdoms of glory than the terrestrial world. (D. & C. 76:71-80.)

47. Now Paul calls on Isaiah to show the gospel was destined for Gentile ears. He chooses a passage which speaks both of Christ and his servants taking salvation to those not of Israelitish lineage. (Isa. 49.) As Simeon had prophesied, Christ was "a light to lighten the Gentiles" (Luke 2:32), and the hour had now come to take the gospel to them in power.

48. Ordained to eternal life] See Rom. 8:28-34a.

PERSECUTION ATTENDS SPREAD OF GOSPEL

ACTS 13:50-52; 14:1-7.

50 But the Jews stirred up the devout and honourable women, and the chief men of the city, and raised persecution against Paul and Barnabas, and expelled them out of their coasts.

51 But they shook off the dust of their feet against them, and came unto Iconium.

52 And the disciples were filled with joy, and with the Holy Ghost.

1 And it came to pass in Iconium, that they went both together into the synagogue of the Jews, and so spake, that a great multitude both of the Jews and also of the Greeks believed.

2 But the unbelieving Jews stirred up the Gentiles, and made their minds evil affected against the brethren.

3 Long time therefore abode they speaking boldly in the Lord, which gave testimony unto the word of his grace, and granted signs and wonders to be done by their hands.

4 But the multitude of the city was divided: and part held with the Jews, and part with the apostles.

5 And when there was an assault made both of the Gentiles, and also of the Jews with their rulers, to use *them* despitefully, and to stone them,

6 They were ware of *it*, and fled unto Lystra and Derbe, cities of Lycaonia, and unto the region that lieth round about:

7 And there they preached the gospel.

13:50. Devout and honourable women] How important and influential is the place of women, whether for or against the truth as the case may be. These women, probably wives of the chief men of the city (and therefore considered to be honorable), though devout, though sincere, though conscientiously believing their course was right, were persecuting Christ, as Paul himself had done aforetime. See Acts 5:33-41.

51. Shook off the dust of their feet] See *Commentary I*, pp. 326-327.

14:2. Why is it that unbelievers stir themselves and others up to persecute the saints? Why should one person feel so strongly about what others believe as to seek to imprison and slay them?

From a purely rational standpoint there is no sensible explanation. But religion involves feelings and emotions; prejudices become deep seated; passions consume the whole being; and Satan takes control of his persecuting agent. When emotions, passions, and man's innate religious feelings become so distorted and perverted as to place the human soul under Satan's control, these feelings then find expression in persecution.

4. The apostles] Luke, for the first time, so designates Paul and Barnabas. All of the brethren in the Church who knew by personal revelation that Jesus was the Christ, meaning all who had testimonies given by the Holy Ghost of his divine Sonship, were witnesses of the Lord. Such were Stephen, Philip, Prochorus, Nicanor, Timon, Parmenas, Nicolas, Ananias, John Mark, Simeon, Lucius, Manaen, Judas Barsabas, Silas, Timotheus, Apollos, Sopater, Aristarchus, Secundus, Gaius, Tychicus, Trophimus, Agabus, Mnason — all of whom are mentioned in Acts and are variously referred to as prophets, teachers, and disciples, but none of whom are called apostles. Only Barnabas, Paul, Matthias, James the Lord's brother, and the original Twelve are singled out to carry the apostolic appelation. The clear inference thus is that the name is being reserved for those who were ordained to the office of apostle in the Melchizedek Priesthood and therefore that Paul and Barnabas were members of the Council of the Twelve, having filled vacancies in the normal course of events. President Joseph Fielding Smith has written: "Paul was an ordained apostle, and without question he took the place of one of the other brethren in that Council." (Joseph Fielding Smith, *Doctrines of Salvation*, vol. 3, p. 153.)

PAUL AND BARNABAS HAILED AS GODS

ACTS 14:8-18.

8 And there sat a certain man at Lystra, impotent in his feet, being a cripple from his mother's womb, who never had walked:

9 The same heard Paul speak: who stedfastly beholding him, and perceiving that he had faith to be healed,

10 Said with a loud voice, Stand upright on thy feet. And he leaped and walked.

11 And when the people saw what Paul had done, they lifted

up their voices, saying in the speech of Lycaonia, The gods are come down to us in the likeness of men.

12 And they called Barnabas, Jupiter; and Paul, Mercurius, because he was the chief speaker.

13 Then the priest of Jupiter, which was before their city, brought oxen and garlands unto the gates, and would have done sacrifice with the people.

14 *Which* when the apostles, Barnabas and Paul, heard *of*, they rent their clothes, and ran in among the people, crying out,

15 And saying, Sirs, why do ye these things? We also are men of like passions with you, and preach unto you that ye should turn from these vanities unto the living God, which made heaven, and earth, and the sea, and all things that are therein:

16 Who in times past suffered all nations to walk in their own ways.

17 Nevertheless he left not himself without witness, in that he did good, and gave us rain from heaven, and fruitful seasons, filling our hearts with food and gladness.

18 And with these sayings scarce restrained they the people, that they had not done sacrifice unto them.

8-10. Healings] See Acts 3:1-16.

11-12. These pagan people believed that their gods visited the earth in human form, an obvious outgrowth of the true accounts of heavenly messengers (including Deity himself) visiting righteous men in ages past.

13. To Adam the Lord revealed the law of sacrifice (Moses 5:5-8); this continued among the saints as part of the true gospel in every dispensation until the atoning sacrifice of Christ was completed. The presence of this practice among people who did not possess true religion simply means that some fragments of the truth had been preserved and were being imitated. (*Mormon Doctrine*, 2nd ed., pp. 664-667.)

14. The apostles, Barnabas and Paul] See Acts 14:1-7.

PAUL STONED, REVIVED, PREACHES

ACTS 14:19-28.

19 And there came thither *certain* Jews from Antioch and Iconium, who persuaded the people, and, having stoned Paul, drew *him* out of the city, supposing he had been dead.

20 Howbeit, as the disciples stood round about him, he rose up, and came into the city: and the

next day he departed with Barnabas to Derbe.

21 And when they had preached the gospel to that city, and had taught many, they returned again to Lystra, and *to* Iconium, and Antioch,

22 Confirming the souls of the disciples, *and* exhorting them to continue in the faith, and that we must through much tribulation enter into the kingdom of God.

23 And when they had ordained them elders in every church, and had prayed with fasting, they commended them to the Lord, on whom they believed.

24 And after they had passed throughout Pisidia, they came to Pamphylia.

25 And when they had preached the word in Perga, they went down into Attalia:

26 And thence sailed to Antioch, from whence they had been recommended to the grace of God for the work which they fulfilled.

27 And when they were come, and had gathered the church together, they rehearsed all that God had done with them, and how he had opened the door of faith unto the Gentiles.

28 And there they abode long time with the disciples.

19. Satan sometimes seems to inspire almost as much zeal in his followers as the Lord does in his disciples. Here zealous, Jewish bigots travel from Antioch and Iconium to Lycaonia to continue their warfare against God, even as Paul himself once traveled from Jerusalem toward Damascus with the same end in view. And how fickle and unstable are those whose understanding of the truth centers almost solely upon a miracle — one moment they are hailing Paul as a god, the next seeking his life. See Acts 5:33-42.

20. Without question Paul's recovery was miraculous. The natural presumption is that Barnabas raised him from death or near death. But however the miracle occurred — stoned, bruised, and deemed dead — Paul would not have been ready to travel the next day without divine intervention.

22. Confirming the souls of the disciples] Renewing their faith; testifying anew to them of the divinity of the work; teaching them more of the gospel; assuring them repeatedly of the truth of the gospel; feeding their souls with spiritual food — all of which is a continuing requisite in the Church.

Exhorting them to continue in the faith] Salvation is not won by confessing the Lord Jesus with one's lips, but by enduring to the end, by keeping the commandments after baptism.

Tribulation] "As part of their mortal probation the saints are called upon to pass through tribulations, that is to undergo severe afflictions, distress, and deep sorrow. (D. & C. 78:14; 109:5; 112:13; 122:5.) 'In the world ye shall have tribulation,' our Lord said. (John 16:33.)

" 'Tribulation worketh patience' (Rom. 5:3; 12:12; D. & C. 54:10), and it is only 'through much tribulation' that men may 'enter into the kingdom of God.' (Acts 14:22.) 'He that is faithful in tribulation, the reward of the same is greater in the kingdom of heaven. Ye cannot behold with your natural eyes, for the present time, the design of your God concerning those things which shall come hereafter, and the glory which shall follow after much tribulation. For after much tribulation come the blessings.' (D. & C. 58:2-4; 103:12.) Exalted beings are described in these words: 'These are they which came out of great tribulation, and have washed their robes, and made them white in the blood of the Lamb.' (Rev. 7:14.) The saints glory in tribulation. (Rom. 5:3; D. & C. 127:2.)" (*Mormon Doctrine*, 2nd ed., p. 809.)

23. Ordained . . . elders in every church] See Acts 11:27-30.

Prayed with fasting] See *Commentary I*, pp. 237-238.

27. Gathered the church together] Held a conference; assembled the saints from the various branches so they could all worship together and rejoice in the spread of the gospel among the Gentiles.

CHURCH DECIDES QUESTION OF CIRCUMCISION

ACTS 15:1-35.

1 And certain men which came down from Judea taught the brethren, *and said*, Except ye be circumcised after the manner of Moses, ye cannot be saved.

2 When therefore Paul and Barnabas had no small dissension and disputation with them, they determined that Paul and Barnabas, and certain other of them, should go up to Jerusalem unto

the apostles and elders about this question.

3 And being brought on their way by the church, they passed through Phenice and Samaria, declaring the conversion of the Gentiles; and they caused great joy unto all the brethren.

4 And when they were come to Jerusalem, they were received of the church, and *of* the apostles and elders, and they declared all things that God had done with them.

5 But there rose up certain of the sect of the Pharisees which believed, saying, That it was needful to circumcise them, and to command *them* to keep the law of Moses.

6 And the apostles and elders came together for to consider of this matter.

7 And when there had been much disputing, Peter rose up, and said unto them, Men *and* brethren, ye know how that a good while ago God made choice among us, that the Gentiles by my mouth should hear the word of the gospel, and believe.

8 And God, which knoweth the hearts, bare them witness, giving them the Holy Ghost, even as *he* did unto us;

9 And put no difference betwen us and them, purifying their hearts by faith.

10 Now therefore why tempt ye God, to put a yoke upon the neck of the disciples, which neither our fathers nor we were able to bear?

11 But we believe that through the grace of the Lord Jesus Christ we shall be saved, even as they.

12 Then all the multitude kept silence, and gave audience to Barnabas and Paul, declaring what miracles and wonders God had wrought among the Gentiles by them.

13 And after they had held their peace, James answered, saying, Men *and* brethren, hearken unto me:

14 Simeon hath declared how God at the first did visit the Gentiles, to take out of them a people for his name.

15 And to this agree the words of the prophets; as it is written,

16 After this I will return, and will build again the tabernacle of David, which is fallen down; and I will build again the ruins thereof, and I will set it up:

17 That the residue of men might seek after the Lord, and all the Gentiles, upon whom my name is called, saith the Lord, who doeth all these things.

18 Known unto God are all his works from the beginning of the world.

19 Wherefore my sentence is, that we trouble not them, which

from among the Gentiles are turned to God:

20 But that we write unto them, that they abstain from pollutions of idols, and *from* fornication, and *from* things strangled, and *from* blood.

21 For Moses of old time hath in every city them that preach him, being read in the synagogues every sabbath day.

22 Then pleased it the apostles and elders, with the whole church, to send chosen men of their own company to Antioch with Paul and Barnabas; *namely,* Judas surnamed Barsabas, and Silas, chief men among the brethren:

23 And they wrote *letters* by them after this manner; The apostles and elders and brethren *send* greeting unto the brethren which are of the Gentiles in Antioch and Syria and Cilicia:

24 Forasmuch as we have heard, that certain which went out from us have troubled you with words, subverting your souls, saying, Ye *must* be circumcised, and keep the law: to whom we gave no *such* commandment:

25 It seemed good to us, being assembled with one accord, to send chosen men unto you with our beloved Barnabas and Paul,

26 Men that have hazarded their lives for the name of our Lord Jesus Christ.

27 We have sent therefore Judas and Silas, who shall also tell *you* the same things by mouth.

28 For it seemed good to the Holy Ghost, and to us, to lay upon you no greater burden than these necessary things;

29 That ye abstain from meats offered to idols, and from blood, and from things strangled, and from fornication: from which if ye keep yourselves, ye shall do well. Fare ye well.

30 So when they were dismissed, they came to Antioch: and when they had gathered the multitude together, they delivered the epistle:

31 *Which* when they had read, they rejoiced for the consolation.

32 And Judas and Silas, being prophets also themselves, exhorted the brethren with many words, and confirmed *them.*

33 And after they had tarried *there* a space, they were let go in peace from the brethren unto the apostles.

34 Notwithstanding it pleased Silas to abide there still.

35 Paul also and Barnabas continued in Antioch, teaching and preaching the word of the Lord, with many others also.

"In token and remembrance of the everlasting covenant made by God with Abraham, Deity instituted the law of circumcision. As revealed to Joseph Smith, the circumstances and conditions calling forth the revelation of this law of circumcision were these: 'My people have gone astray from my precepts, and have not kept mine ordinances, which I gave unto their fathers,' the Lord said to Abraham, 'And they have not observed mine anointing, and the burial, or baptism wherewith I commanded them; But they have turned from the commandment, and taken unto themselves the washing of children, and the blood of sprinkling; And have said that the blood of the righteous Abel was shed for sins; and have not known wherein they are accountable before me.

" 'But as for thee, behold, I will make my covenant with thee, and thou shalt be a father of many nations. And this covenant I make, that thy children may be known among all nations. Neither shall thy name any more be called Abram, but thy name shall be called Abraham; for, a father of many nations have I made thee. And I will make thee exceedingly fruitful, and I will make nations of thee, and kings shall come of thee, and of thy seed. And I will establish a covenant of circumcision with thee, and it shall be my covenant between me and thee, and thy seed after thee, in their generations; that thou mayest know for ever that children are not accountable before me until they are eight years old. And thou shalt observe to keep all my covenants wherein I covenanted with thy fathers; and thou shalt keep the commandments which I have given thee with mine own mouth, and I will be a God unto thee and thy seed after thee. And I will give unto thee and thy seed after thee, a land wherein thou art a stranger; all the land of Canaan, for an everlasting possession; and I will be their God.

" 'And God said unto Abraham, Therefore thou shalt keep my covenant, thou and thy seed after thee, in their generations. And this shall be my covenant which ye shall keep between me and thee and thy seed after thee; every man child among you shall be circumcised. And ye shall circumcise the flesh of your foreskin; and it shall be a token of the covenant betwixt me and you. And he that is eight days old shall be circumcised among you, every man child in your generations; He that is born in the house, or bought with money of any stranger, which is not of thy seed. He that is born in thy house, and he that is bought with thy money, must needs be circumcised, and my covenant shall be in your flesh for an everlasting covenant. And the uncircumcised man child, whose flesh of his foreskin is not circumcised, that soul shall be cut off from his people, he hath broken my covenant.' (*Inspired Version*, Gen. 17:4-20.)

"One of the provisions of this law of circumcision was that it should be practiced by the chosen seed, to identify and distinguish them, until the day of the mortal ministry of Christ. From Abraham to the meridian of time, the gospel and such of the laws of salvation as were revealed in any period were reserved almost exclusively for the seed of Abraham in whose flesh the token of circumcision was found.

"But beginning in the meridian of time the Lord's eternal plans called for sending the gospel to all the world; the Gentile nations were to be invited to come to Christ and be heirs of salvation. The laws of salvation were to be offered to those in whose flesh the token of the everlasting covenant was not found. Christ himself limited his ministry to the house of Israel; 'I am not sent but unto the lost sheep of the house of Israel,' he said. (Matt. 15:24.) But he sent his apostolic ministers to preach to all men (Mark 16:15), it being pointedly revealed to Peter that the gospel was for Gentiles as well as Jews. (Acts 10.) Accordingly, the need for the special token in the flesh no longer existed, and so circumcision as a gospel ordinance was done away in Christ.

"Mormon received this revelation: 'Little children are whole, for they are not capable of committing sin; wherefore the curse of Adam is taken from them in me, that it hath no power over them; and the law of circumcision is done away in me.' (Moro. 8:8.) The disciples in the Old World received a similar revelation and with the approval of the Holy Ghost discontinued the practice of circumcision, rejecting the doctrine of those who claimed that circumcision was still essential to salvation. (Acts 15.) Paul, the apostle to the Gentiles, of necessity had to write and teach much about circumcision so that his converts would understand that it was done away in Christ. (Rom. 2; 3; 4; 1 Cor. 7:19; Gal. 5:6; 6:15; Col. 2:11; 3:11.)

"By the time of Paul the apostate Jews, as with the people of Abraham's day, had lost the knowledge 'that children are not accountable . . . until they are eight years old.' (*Inspired Version*, Gen. 17:11.) Rather they had a tradition that little children were unholy and that circumcision was essential to their cleansing. Those thus circumcised were then 'brought up in subjection to the law of Moses,' and giving 'heed to the traditions of their fathers,' they 'believed not the gospel of Christ, wherein they became unholy.' (D. & C. 74.) It was while struggling to solve this difficult problem that Paul gave some of his counsel on marriage, which counsel can only be understood in the light of the then existing circumcision difficulties. (1 Cor. 7.)" (*Mormon Doctrine*, 2nd ed., pp. 142-144.) See *Commentary I*, pp. 88-90.

1. Certain men . . . from Judea] They came from the headquarters of the Church, probably had been sent by the apostles (v. 24), and were good and acceptable brethren; but on the issue of circumcision they erred, teaching false doctrine and not being led by the Spirit. Since the Lord often leaves his servants to struggle with and work out solutions for difficult problems, before they finally receive his mind and voice by revelation, similar situations arise in the Church today. For instance, brethren who go forth today to preach and to confirm the churches sometimes take it upon themselves to advocate political, educational, and social philosophies which seem right to them — on occasions even claiming such are essential to salvation — which in fact are not the voice of God to his people.

Circumcised after the manner of Moses] This is not circumcision as an operation for reasons of health or personal hygiene, but circumcision as a saving ordinance, as a part of the plan of salvation.

2. Unity in doctrine and practice is an absolute essential within the true Church. One branch of the Church cannot cleave to one standard and another to a different one. Either circumcision is essential to salvation or it is not, and different groups within the Church do not have power to make their own choice in the matter. And so it is with baptism, miracles, church organization, and all of the doctrines of the kingdom — there can be only one true standard. If there are differences among Christian churches today, it is time the apologists of the conflicting views went up to Jerusalem, as it were, to the apostles and elders to find the truth.

5. Circumcision was the token, cut into the very flesh of the Hebrews, which bore record that they were the seed of Abraham and were under covenant to keep the law of Moses. It was a symbol of the acceptance or rejection of a whole system of worship. When Paul and the others debate whether circumcision is essential to salvation, what they are really considering is whether the law of Moses is still in force or has been fulfilled in Christ. To catch the vision of the issue confronting the restored and newly established Christian Church, it is necessary to understand what was involved in the law of Moses and the relationship of that law to the gospel of Christ.

"To Moses the Lord first gave the higher priesthood and revealed the fulness of the gospel. But Israel rebelled and manifest such gross unworthiness that their God took from them the power whereby they could have become a kingdom of priests and of kings and gave them instead a lesser law, a law of carnal commandments, a preparatory gospel, a schoolmaster to bring them to Christ and the fulness of his gospel. He gave them instead the law of Moses. (D. & C. 84: 17-28; Gal. 3; Heb. 4: 2; *Inspired Version,* Ex. 34:1-2.)

"Moses received by revelation many great gospel truths, as for instance the Ten Commandments recorded in the 20th chapter of Exodus. These gospel truths, being eternal in their nature, are part of the fulness of the everlasting gospel; they have always been in force in all dispensations. They are part of 'the law of Christ.' (D. & C. 88:21.) But the particular things spoken of in the scriptures as the law of Moses were the ordinances and performances that were 'added because of transgressions.' (Gal. 3:19.) They were the 'divers washings, and carnal ordinances, imposed on them until the time of reformation.' (Heb. 9:10.) They were 'the law of commandments contained in ordinances.' (Eph. 2:15.) In great detail they are recorded in Exodus, Leviticus, Numbers, and Deuteronomy, and were preserved on the brass plates which the Nephites took with them. (1 Ne. 4:15-16.)

"Abinadi said that the law of Moses was given to point the attention of the people forward to Christ and that all things in it 'were types of things to come.' Israel was given, he said, 'a very strict law; for they were a stiffnecked people, quick to do iniquity, and slow to remember the Lord their God; Therefore there was a law given them, yea, a law of performances and of ordinances, a law which they were to observe strictly from day to day, to keep them in remembrance of God and their duty towards him.' (Mosiah 13:27-32.) Paul said 'the law was our schoolmaster to bring us unto Christ.' (Gal. 3:24.) It was 'the law of carnal commandments' (D. & C. 84:27; Heb. 7:16) because it was given to teach those belonging to the chosen race to bridle their passions, to overcome the lusts of the flesh, to triumph over carnal things, and to advance to the place where the Spirit of the Lord could have full flow in their hearts.

"Salvation is in Christ and not in the law of Moses. 'Salvation doth not come by the law alone,' Abinadi explained, 'and were it not for the atonement, which God himself shall make for the sins and iniquities of his people, . . . they must unavoidably perish, notwithstanding the law of Moses.' (Mosiah 13:27-28.) Rather, as Nephi taught, the law was given to prove to the people 'the truth of the coming of Christ; for, for this end hath the law of Moses been given; and all things which have been given of God from the beginning of the world, unto man, are the typifying of him.' (2 Ne. 11:4.) Paul also found it necessary to teach with great force that men are saved by the grace of God, 'Not of works,' that is, the works of the law of Moses. (Eph. 2.)

"At any time in ancient Israel when the Melchizedek Priesthood was operative and when the people were enjoying its blessings — even though they continued to keep the formalities of the law of Moses — the law itself became dead to them. The Nephites, for instance, prior to the ministry of our Lord among them, had only the Melchizedek Priesthood, and during that entire 600 year period they kept the law of Moses. (2 Ne. 5:10; Jar. 5; Mosiah 2:3.) They, of course, had the fulness of the gospel, and thus Nephi recorded: 'It is by grace that we are saved, after all we can do. And, notwithstanding we believe in Christ, we keep the law of Moses, and look forward with steadfastness unto Christ, until the law shall be fulfilled. For, for this end was the law given; wherefore the law hath become dead unto us, and we are made alive in Christ because of our faith; yet we keep the law because of the commandments.' (2 Ne. 25:23-25.)

"In Christ the law of Moses, that is, the law of carnal commandments, was fulfilled. The great and eternal gospel truths revealed through Moses remained in force, but the lesser law that had pointed the attention of the people forward to the coming of the Lord became a dead letter. 'Think not that I am come to destroy the law or the prophets,' our Lord proclaimed. 'I am not come to destroy but to fulfil; For verily I say unto you, one jot nor one tittle hath not passed away from the law, but in me it hath all been fulfilled.' (3 Ne. 12:17-18.)

" 'Behold, I say unto you that the law is fulfilled that was given unto Moses. Behold, I am he that gave the law, and I am he who covenanted with my people Israel; therefore, the law in me is fulfilled, for I have come to fulfil the law; therefore it hath an end. Behold, I do not destroy the prophets, for as many as have not been fulfilled in me, verily I say unto you, shall all be fulfilled. And because I said unto you that old things have passed away, I do not destroy that which hath been spoken concerning things which are to come. For behold, the covenant which I have made with my people is not all fulfilled; but the law which was given unto Moses hath an end in me. Behold, I am the law, and the light. Look unto me, and endure to the end, and ye shall live; for unto him that endureth to the end will I give eternal life.' (3 Ne. 15:4-9.)" (*Mormon Doctrine*, 2nd ed., pp. 434-436.) See Rom. 2:17-29; 3:1-20; Gal. 2:11-21.

6-11. With insight and inspiration Peter strikes at the heart of the controversy over circumcision. It is not circumcision as such, but rather: Can the gospel be offered to uncircumcised Gentiles or is it limited to circumcised Israel? Are people who do not keep the law of Moses eligible to inherit the blessings of salvation which Christ came to bring? Who can be saved through the gospel — those (according to the view of believing Pharisees) in whose flesh is found the token of the covenant God made with Abraham, or people (in the view of Paul and Barnabas) among all nations and kindreds? Is salvation in Moses or in Christ? And since these are the issues, there really is nothing to decide. God has already spoken on the matter. Peter himself has received the revelation. The gospel is for all men and therefore circumcision — with all that it symbolizes — is not essential to salvation.

7. By my mouth] Peter is the president of the Church; he receives and announces the mind and will of Deity on all matters.

13. James] "James the Lord's brother," now one of the Twelve. (Gal. 1:19.) "James the brother of John," has already been slain by Herod Agrippa. (Acts 12:2.)

14. Simeon] Ancient Hebrew form of Simon (Peter).

16-17. James here quotes, not literally but in substance, Amos 9:11-12 — a part of a more extensive prophecy which first announces the scattering of Israel; says the gospel will then go to "the heathen," meaning the Gentiles; and that at a still later day Israel will be gathered again to the land of her inheritance. (Amos 9:9-15.)

19. My sentence is] My proposal or recommendation is. Uninspired commentators and others who are unaware of the true system of apostolic succession falsely assume that James was making a decision in the case and therefore was head of the Church in Jerusalem, having some pre-eminence over Peter. Some Protestants have argued that Peter could not have fathered a church in Rome because James and not Peter is in fact here shown to be the chief officer of the Christian kingdom. Interesting as this may be, the fact is Peter was the presiding officer in the Church and had in fact rendered and announced judgment on the issue of circumcision. (Verses 7-11.) James is simply proposing the detailed instructions to put in force the decision already announced by Peter.

20. Abstain from pollutions of idols] 29. Abstain from meats offered to idols] "Things polluted by having been offered in sacrifice to idols. The heathen were accustomed to give away or sell portions of such animals. From such food James would enjoin the Gentile converts to abstain, lest it should seem to the Jews that they were not entirely weaned from idolatry." (*Jamieson*, p. 194.)

From fornication] "The characteristic sin of heathendom, unblushingly practiced by all ranks and classes, and the indulgence of which on the part of the Gentile converts would to the Jews, whose Scripture branded it as an abomination of the heathen, proclaim them to be yet joined to their old idols." (*Jamieson*, pp. 194-195.)

From things strangled, and from blood] These prohibitions were part of the law of Moses. (Lev. 3:17; 7:26; 17:10-14.) There is no apparent reason why they should have been imposed on Gentile converts (or, for that matter, why Jewish converts should continue to conform to them), since the provisions of that law were fulfilled. Some ancient manuscripts omit them, and it seems reasonable to suppose they were not part of the original decree.

21. If this verse means "that Jewish Christians are still to attend the synagogue services and to keep the law" (*Dummelow*, p. 839), then there is some error or omission in the record as we have it. The law was fulfilled and there was no more reason for a Jew to keep it than there was for a Gentile. Salvation was in Christ and his gospel and came to all on the same terms and conditions.

28. The Church was governed by revelation. The Lord's will was manifest by the power of the Spirit, and all members of the kingdom were bound by the revealed word. In this instance the decision apparently was both reached and ratified by following the revealed procedure used by the Prophet in translating the Book of Mormon. That is, the Lord's agent struggled and labored with the problem, searched the scriptures, sought for possible conclusions, and did the best they could to solve the problem on the basis of the sound principles which they knew. Having arrived at what they considered to be an appropriate solution — that is, adopting James' statements which were based on Peter's announcement of principle — they then asked the Lord if their conclusions were true and in accord with his mind. The answer, coming by the power of the Spirit, certified to the verity of their conclusion, and thus, in effect, this was receiving revelation by a course of spiritual confirmation. (D. & C. 8 and 9.)

PAUL CHOOSES SILAS AS HIS COMPANION

ACTS 15:36-41.

36 And some days after Paul said unto Barnabas, Let us go again and visit our brethren in every city where we have preached the word of the Lord, *and see* how they do.

37 And Barnabas determined to take with them John, whose surname was Mark.

38 But Paul thought not good to take him with them, who departed from them from Pamphylia,

and went not with them to the work.

39 And the contention was so sharp between them, that they departed asunder one from the other: and so Barnabas took Mark, and sailed unto Cyprus;

40 And Paul chose Silas, and departed, being recommended by the brethren unto the grace of God.

41 And he went through Syria and Cilicia, confirming the churches.

Even apostles and prophets, being mortal and subject to like passions as other men, have prejudices which sometimes are reflected in ministerial assignments and decisions. But the marvel is not the isolated disagreements on details, but the near universal unity on basic principles; not the occasional personality conflicts, but the common acceptance, for the good of the work, of the faults of others. It is not the conflict between Paul and Barnabas which concerns us, but the fact that they (being even as we are) rose thereafter to spiritual heights where they saw visions, received revelations, and made their callings and elections sure — the fact of their disagreement thus bearing witness that we in our weaknesses can also press forward to that unity and perfection which shall assure us of salvation.

Jarrings and contentions] See 2 Tim. 2:14-26. **Unity]** See 1 Cor. 1:1-16.

SPIRIT DIRECTS PREACHING OF GOSPEL

ACTS 16:1-15.

1 Then came he to Derbe and Lystra: and, behold, a certain disciple was there, named Timotheus, the son of a certain woman, which was a Jewess, and believed; but his father *was* a Greek.

2 Which was well reported of by the brethren that were at Lystra and Iconium.

3 Him would Paul have to go forth with him; and took and circumcised him because of the Jews which were in those quarters: for they knew all that his father was a Greek.

4 And as they went through the cities, they delivered them the decrees for to keep, that were ordained of the apostles and elders which were at Jerusalem.

5 And so were the churches established in the faith, and increased in number daily.

6 Now when they had gone throughout Phrygia and the region of Galatia, and were forbidden of the Holy Ghost to preach the word in Asia,

7 After they were come to Mysia, they assayed to go into Bithynia: but the Spirit suffered them not.

8 And they passing by Mysia came down to Troas.

9 And a vision appeared to Paul in the night; There stood a man of Macedonia, and prayed him, saying, Come over into Macedonia, and help us.

10 And after he had seen the vision, immediately we endeavoured to go into Macedonia, assuredly gathering that the Lord had called us for to preach the gospel unto them.

11 Therefore loosing from Troas, we came with a straight course to Samothracia, and the next *day* to Neapolis;

12 And from thence to Philippi, which is the chief city of that part of Macedonia, *and* a colony: and we were in that city abiding certain days.

13 And on the sabbath we went out of the city by a river side, where prayer was wont to be made; and we sat down, and spake unto the women which resorted *thither.*

14 And a certain woman named Lydia, a seller of purple, of the city of Thyatira, which worshipped God, heard *us:* whose heart the Lord opened, that she attended unto the things which were spoken of Paul.

15 And when she was baptized, and her household, she besought *us,* saying, If ye have judged me to be faithful to the Lord, come into my house, and abide *there.* And she constrained us.

I.V. ACTS 16:13.

13 And on the Sabbath we went out of the city by a river side, where the people resorted for prayer to be made; and we sat down, and spake unto the women which resorted thither.

There is only one way to build up and strengthen the Church; only one way to preach the gospel in the nations of the earth; only one way for the ministers of salvation to know where to go and what to say — and that one way is to receive revelation from the Lord. Without revelation the affairs of the Church cannot be conducted and the missionary work carried forward. Revelation is the rock upon which God's true kingdom is established. See *Commentary I*, pp. 290-292; 380-390; Acts 11:27-30; 1 Cor. 2:9-16.

1-3. In circumcising Timothy, Paul apparently was humoring the Jews. As far as the gospel law was concerned, the act was wrong and should not have been performed. Circumcision (as no one knew better than Paul!) was a thing of the past. But seemingly the social pressures were such that if the ordinances had not been performed in this case, it would have alienated the Jewish community and stopped them from investigating the gospel. Hence Paul performed an unnecessary and in fact an improper act to attract the Jews toward that religion which would teach them in due course that the law of circumcision was fulfilled in Christ. See Acts 15:1-35.

6-15. Here the Lord commands his missionaries not to preach the gospel in Asia or Bithynia, but instead to go to Macedonia. Why? It is simply a matter of sending missionaries where there are more receptive people. Of course those in Asia and elsewhere were entitled to hear the truth; all men are; but every man in his day and time and season. The Lord establishes his own system of priorities and since the laborers are few and cannot be everywhere, they are sent, by revelation, to those peoples who in God's wisdom deserve to hear the truth first. See *Commentary I*, pp. 240-244; 265-266; 323-328.

Every member a missionary] See Acts 11:19-26.

PAUL CASTS EVIL SPIRIT OUT OF SOOTHSAYER

ACTS 16:16-21.

16 And it came to pass, as we went to prayer, a certain damsel possessed with a spirit of divination met us, which brought her masters much gain by soothsaying:

17 The same followed Paul and us, and cried, saying, These men are the servants of the most high God, which show unto us the way of salvation.

18 And this did she many days. But Paul, being grieved, turned and said to the spirit, I command thee in the name of Jesus Christ to come out of her. And he came out the same hour.

19 And when her masters saw that the hope of their gains was gone, they caught Paul and Silas, and drew *them* into the marketplace unto the rulers,

20 And brought them to the magistrates, saying, These men, being Jews, do exceedingly trouble our city,

21 And teach customs, which are not lawful for us to receive, neither to observe, being Romans.

16. As we went to prayer] To a prayer meeting, an appointed meeting of worship where Deity would be entreated to pour out special blessings upon them.

A spirit of divination] "True religion provides for a revelation of future events by prophets sent of God. False religions — whose ministers have no communion with Deity — frequently imitate the true practice by engaging in divination. This practice is an attempt to foretell the future by auguries, omens, presages, or forebodings. Among primitive peoples it frequently meant interpreting dreams or other signs or seeking peculiarities in the entrails of sacrificial victims. A diviner is one who attempts to foretell the future by divination. Soothsayers act by the 'spirit of divination.' (Acts 16:16-18.) The Lord's people are commanded not to engage in divination of any sort. (Deut. 18:9-14.)" (*Mormon Doctrine*, 2nd ed., pp. 202-203.) See Acts 8:5-13.

Soothsaying] "A soothsayer is one of Satan's substitutes for a seer or a prophet. His mission is to foretell the future by the power of the evil one. Such false prophets were common anciently in the Eastern nations (Isa. 2:6; Dan. 2:27; 5:11; 2 Ne. 12:6), but they were not permitted in Israel (Josh. 13:22), and the penalty for practicing soothsaying was death. (Lev. 20:6, 27.) When the final latter-day triumph of Israel is achieved the Lord has promised to cut off witchcrafts and soothsayers out of the land. (3 Ne. 21:16; Mic. 5:12.)" (*Mormon Doctrine*, 2nd ed., p. 746.)

17-18. The testimony of the devil-led damsel was true. Paul and Silas were prophets; they had the words and power of salvation. But true testimony from Satan's servants does not lead to salvation. In effect the damsel was saying: 'Go ahead and believe in Paul and Silas and this Jesus whom they preach. I agree they and their Master are of God; and since we are now united on that point, you can also continue to follow me and enjoy the fruits of my divination.' And how many other practitioners of false religions there are who give lip service to Jesus and his doctrines so that people will the more readily follow them and their special brand of "saving" grace. It was for the very reason here involved that Jesus himself forbade the devils whom he cast out to testify that he was the Son of God. (Luke 4:41.)

In the name of Jesus Christ . . . come out of her] "In my name shall they cast out devils" (Mark 16:17) — that is, they "shall" if they "believe" the very gospel revealed and taught by Christ. Thus, the power to cast out devils is one of the signs of the true Church.

19. When the devil departed from the damsel she no longer could divine the future, a change immediately evident to her masters whose source of income thereby ended.

21. Not lawful for us to receive] How common it has been in all ages and among almost all peoples to pass laws making it unlawful to believe true religion. Such laws underlay the whole history of western Europe during the dark ages, and even to this day, in some parts of the world, it is a criminal offense to preach any doctrine not sanctioned by man's law.

BELIEVE ON THE LORD AND BE SAVED

ACTS 16:22-40.

22 And the multitude rose up together against them: and the magistrates rent off their clothes, and commanded to beat *them.*

23 And when they had laid many stripes upon them, they cast *them* into prison, charging the jailor to keep them safely:

24 Who, having received such a charge, thrust them into the inner prison, and made their feet fast in the stocks.

25 And at midnight Paul and Silas prayed, and sang praises unto God: and the prisoners heard them.

26 And suddenly there was a great earthquake, so that the foundations of the prison were shaken: and immediately all the doors were opened, and every one's bands were loosed.

27 And the keeper of the prison awaking out of his sleep, and seeing the prison doors open, he drew out his sword, and would have killed himself, supposing that the prisoners had been fled.

28 But Paul cried with a loud voice, saying, Do thyself no harm: for we are all here.

29 Then he called for a light, and sprang in, and came trembling, and fell down before Paul and Silas,

30 And brought them out, and said, Sirs, what must I do to be saved?

31 And they said, Believe on the Lord Jesus Christ, and thou shalt be saved, and thy house.

32 And they spake unto him the word of the Lord, and to all that were in his house.

33 And he took them the same hour of the night, and washed *their* stripes; and was baptized, he and all his, straightway

34 And when he had brought them into his house, he set meat before them, and rejoiced, believing in God with all his house.

35 And when it was day, the magistrates sent the serjeants, saying, Let those men go.

36 And the keeper of the prison told this saying to Paul, The magistrates have sent to let you go: now therefore depart, and go in peace.

37 But Paul said unto them, They have beaten us openly uncondemned, being Romans, and have cast *us* into prison; and now do they thrust us out privily? nay verily; but let them come themselves and fetch us out.

BELIEVE ON THE LORD AND BE SAVED

38 And the serjeants told these words unto the magistrates: and they feared, when they heard that they were Romans.

39 And they came and besought them, and brought *them*

out, and desired *them* to depart out of the city.

40 And they went out of the prison, and entered into *the house of* Lydia: and when they had seen the brethren, t h e y comforted them, and departed.

22-24. Two Romans, citizens of the mightiest empire on earth — entitled thereby to an impartial trial; to an appeal to the emperor; to freedom from degrading punishments, including bonds, scourging, and crucifixion — are here condemned without a trial, scourged without mercy, imprisoned in bonds in a damp and pestilential cell, all for the testimony of Jesus and the hope of a better resurrection.

25. Prayer and praise in their persecutor's prison — how fitting for two missionaries who are overcoming this world and centering their hearts on a better one to come!

26. Prisons lose their power when God so purposes. Daniel remains unharmed in a den of lions. (Dan. 6.) Alma and Amulek walk free as the falling prison walls slay their persecutors. (Alma 14.) Nephi and Lehi are encircled by fire from heaven and the earth shakes as they go free. (Hela. 5.) Peter follows an angelic guide as he goes out of Herod's prison. (Acts 12:1-19.) And now Paul and Silas, and all who are imprisoned with them, have their bands loosed in a miraculous manner.

27-29. Apparently the prison held those guilty of capital offenses whose escape, by Roman custom, would have meant the forfeiture of the jailer's life. Paul knowing or sensing the contemplated suicide calls out and saves the temporal life of the man to whom almost immediately he will offer also spiritual life.

30-34. Is belief alone enough to bring salvation to the contrite soul? Assuredly yes, if by belief is meant the ringing declaration of him who, baptizing our Lord, then testified: "He that believeth on the Son hath everlasting life" (John 3:36); or if by belief is meant the pronouncement of Jesus: "He that believeth on me, the works that I do shall he do also; and greater works than these shall he do" (John 14:12); or if by belief is meant that pure, perfect faith in Christ which presupposes and in fact cannot exist without the works of righteousness. (*Mormon Doctrine*, 2nd ed., pp. 78-80; See Heb. 11:1-3.) But belief alone is scarcely the beginning of that course leading to a celestial inheritnace if it is isolated as a thing apart, if it is supposed that it does not embrace within its folds both baptism and a subsequent course of enduring to the end. (2 Ne. 31:15-21.) And in the very case at hand, Paul and Silas teach the gospel to the whole group, baptize them, and without question give them the gift of the Holy Ghost, thus starting them out in the direction of salvation.

PAUL AND SILAS PREACH AMID PERSECUTION

ACTS 17:1-14.

1 Now when they had passed through Amphipolis, and Apollonia, they came to Thessalonica, where was a synagogue of the Jews:

2 And Paul, as his manner was, went in unto them, and three sabbath days reasoned with them out of the scriptures,

3 Opening and alleging, that Christ must needs have suffered, and risen again from the dead; and that this Jesus, whom I preach unto you, is Christ.

4 And some of them believed, and consorted with Paul and Silas; and of the devout Greeks a great multitude, and of the chief women not a few.

5 But the Jews which believed not, moved with envy, took unto them certain lewd fellows of the baser sort, and gathered a company, and set all the city on an uproar, and assaulted the house of Jason, and sought to bring them out to the people.

6 And when they found them not, they drew Jason and certain brethren unto the rulers of the city, crying, These that have turned the world upside down are come hither also;

7 Whom Jason hath received: and these all do contrary to the decrees of Caesar, saying that there is another king, *one* Jesus.

8 And they troubled the people and the rulers of the city, when they heard these things.

9 And when they had taken security of Jason, and of the other, they let them go.

10 And the brethren immediately sent away Paul and Silas by night unto Berea: who coming *thither* went into the synagogue of the Jews.

11 These were more noble than those in Thessalonica, in that they received the word with all readiness of mind, and searched the scriptures daily, whether those things were so.

12 Therefore many of them believed; also of honourable women which were Greeks, and of men, not a few.

13 But when the Jews of Thessalonica had knowledge that the word of God was preached of Paul at Berea, they came thither also, and stirred up the people.

14 And then immediately the brethren sent away Paul to go as it were to the sea: but Silas and Timotheus abode there still.

2-4. Paul's manner of preaching to nonmembers was this: 1. Reason with them out of the scriptures, showing the promises that Christ should come bringing salvation; and 2. Testify that Jesus whom he, Paul, preached was the promised Messiah. Today the elders of Israel follow the same pattern in their missionary work. They reason with people showing the scriptural promises of a latter-day restoration, as well as the logic and sense of the newly revealed doctrines. Then they climax their teachings by testifying that Joseph Smith was the mighty prophet of the restoration, and that his teachings (such as the Book of Mormon) are the mind and will and voice of God to men now living.

5. Certain lewd fellows of the baser sort] Persecution is the weapon of wicked and debased people, people whose consciences are not troubled by acts of arson, rapine, sex defilement, and murder. And, as here, it is commonly stirred up and promoted by religious zealots whose false beliefs cry out for the support of force. Righteous people do not persecute their fellow beings, for persecution itself is a sin. In this dispensation, the persecutions in Missouri, Illinois, Utah, and elsewhere were and are committed by people with criminal proclivities and at the instigation and encouragement of professors of religion.

11. Honest and upright people search the scriptures, investigate the gospel, and learn for themselves of the truth of the message which God's witnesses carry to the world.

"WE ARE THE OFFSPRING OF GOD"

ACTS 17:15-34.

15 And they that conducted Paul brought him unto Athens: and receiving a commandment unto Silas and Timotheus for to come to him with all speed, they departed.

16 Now while Paul waited for them at Athens, his spirit was stirred in him, when he saw the city wholly given to idolatry.

17 Therefore disputed he in the synagogue with the Jews, and with the devout persons, and in the market daily with them that met with him.

18 Then certain philosophers of the Epicureans, and of the Stoics, encountered him. And some said, What will this babbler say? other some, He seemeth to be a setter forth of strange gods: because he preached unto them Jesus, and the resurrection.

19 And they took him, and brought him unto Areopagus, saying, May we know what this new doctrine, whereof thou speakest, is?

20 For thou bringest certain strange things to our ears: we would know therefore what these things mean.

21 (For all the Athenians and strangers which were there spent their time in nothing else, but either to tell, or to hear some new thing.)

22 Then Paul stood in the midst of Mars' hill, and said, Ye men of Athens, I perceive that in all things ye are too superstitious.

23 For as I passed by, and beheld your devotions, I found an altar with this inscription, TO THE UNKNOWN GOD. Whom therefore ye ignorantly worship, him declare I unto you.

24 God that made the world and all things therein, seeing that he is Lord of heaven and earth, dwelleth not in temples made with hands;

25 Neither is worshipped with men's hands, as though he needed any thing, seeing he giveth to all life, and breath, and all things;

26 And hath made of one blood all nations of men for to dwell on all the face of the earth, and hath determined the times before appointed, and the bounds of their habitation;

27 That they should seek the Lord, if haply they might feel after him, and find him, though he be not far from every one of us:

28 For in him we live, and move, and have our being; as certain also of your own poets have said, For we are also his offspring.

29 Forasmuch then as we are the offspring of God, we ought not

to think that the Godhead is like unto gold, or silver, or stone, graven by art and man's device.

30 And the times of this ignorance God winked at; but now commandeth all men every where to repent:

31 Because he hath appointed a day, in the which he will judge the world in righteousness by *that* man whom he hath ordained; *whereof* he hath given assurance unto all *men*, in that he hath raised him from the dead.

32 And when they heard of the resurrection of the dead, some mocked: and others said, We will hear thee again of this *matter*.

33 So Paul departed from among them.

34 Howbeit certain men clave unto him, and believed: among the which *was* Dionysius, the Areopagite, and a woman named Damaris, and others with them.

I.V. ACTS 17:27.

27 That they should seek the Lord, **if they are willing to find him, for he is** not far from every one of us;

16. **Idolatry**] Athens was the world center of idol worship. Temples, statues, and altars were everywhere. "Petronius, a contemporary writer at Nero's court, says satirically that it was easier to find a god at Athens than a man." (*Jamieson*, p. 201.) "Philostratus says, 'It is more prudent to speak well of all gods, especially at Athens, where altars are erected even to unknown gods.' At Athens during a plague Epimenides let loose at the Aeropagus black and white sheep, and commanded the Athenians to sacrifice 'to the proper god,' wherever the sheep lay down. Often 'the proper god' could not be clearly ascertained, and so an altar was raised to an unknown god." (*Dummelow*, p. 842.)

18. **Philosophers**] " 'Philosophy is the account which the human mind gives to itself of the constitution of the world,' says Emerson, the modern philosopher. (Cited Orson F. Whitney, *Saturday Night Thoughts*, p. 265.) 'We shall define philosophy as total perspective, as mind overspreading life and forging chaos into unity,' another modern philosopher, Will Durant, says. It includes 'all questions that vitally affect the worth and significance of human life,' including 'the realm of ethics, and . . . the nature of the good life.' (Will Durant, *Mansions of Philosophy*, p. ix.) 'Only philoso-

phy can give us wisdom,' he also opines. 'Philosophy accepts the hard and hazardous task of dealing with problems . . . like good and evil, beauty and ugliness, order and freedom, life and death.' (Will Durant, *Story of Philosophy*, pp. 2-3.)

"Every basic text on philosophy, such as Mr. Durant's *Mansions of Philosophy*, will contain, among other things, discussions relative to: God and immortality; morals, morality, and immorality; matter, life, and mind; existence, ethics, and truth; reason, instinct, and materialism; life and death; love, marriage, and social relations; the quest of happiness; the elements of character; freedom, the function of religion, and Christianity.

"It should be evident to everyone who has even a casual knowledge of God, the gospel, and the laws of salvation, that philosophy is in effect a religion which, ruling out revelation, attempts to decide eternal realities by reason alone. In large part it is an attempt to explain, Where we came from, Why we are here, and Where we are going, without reference to the revelations of the Almighty.

"Philosophy is a system of general beliefs and views about God, existence, right and wrong, agency, immortality, and so forth — all of which views rule out the true and living God and the revelations that come through his prophets. Philosophers, it is true, may profess to believe in God, but their beliefs will be of the apostate variety; they will worship laws, forces, or the ethereal spirit essence described in the creeds of sectarianism." (*Mormon Doctrine*, 2nd ed., pp. 572-573.)

18. Epicureans] "A well known school of atheistic materialists, who taught that pleasure was the chief end of human existence; a principle which the more rational interpreted in a refined sense, while the sensual explained it in its coarser meaning." **Stoicks]** "A celebrated school of severe and lofty pantheists, whose principle was that the universe was under the law of an iron necessity, the spirit of which was what is called Deity: and that a passionless conformity of the human will to this law, unmoved by all external circumstances and changes, is the perfection of virtue." (*Jamieson*, p. 202.)

This babbler] 'This shallow talker, this unlearned prater, this pretended religious teacher (this Mormon elder) who comes to teach us — wise philosophers that we are — with his foolish and idle words.'

Strange gods] Christ is indeed a strange god to a philosopher, for our Lord's divine Sonship, and the consequent power of immortality vested in him, can be known and understood only by revelation (1 Cor. 12:3), and philosophers substitute reason for revelation in seeking answers to the eternal verities.

19. Areopagus] The Hill of Ares (Mars Hill), an eminence where the Court of the Areopagus met to pass judgment on criminals and to decide questions of religion. Paul may have been appearing before the court or speaking to an informal gathering at the open air site where the court sat.

22-31. Speaking with prophetic power Paul proclaims the nature and kind of being that God is. His hearers have no knowledge of the ancient revelations nor of the ministry of God's Son among mortals. And so, the Apostle simply announces who Deity is and what he has done for man, and then reasons with his hearers to show that his pronouncements make sense to the philosophic mind.

He announces that God is the Creator of all things and reasons that as a consequence Deity does not dwell in small buildings made by men.

He announces that Deity has given life and existence to all things and reasons that these created things cannot then add glory to their Creator by their own weak powers.

He announces that God has made all men as members of the same family, sending designated parts of the family to earth from time to time, and reasons that men should therefore seek their Maker.

He announces that God is omnipresent and reasons that he is therefore readily available to all men everywhere.

And then as the supreme and glorious climax of his Spirit-sponsored sermon, he announces that God is our Father, that we are his offspring, and reasons that Deity therefore cannot be an idol; in effect he is saying that since God and man are of the same race, Deity must therefore be an exalted Man.

He concedes that false worship was tolerated in the days of darkness and ignorance, but explains that when light comes into the world men are commanded to repent and accept the truth.

And finally, he announces that Jesus shall judge all men, and reasons that such coming judgment is proven by the fact that he rose from the dead.

22. Superstitious] Superstition is a form of false worship which substitutes belief in omens, charms, and the like for the true signs and wonders of revealed religion. It is based on fear and credulity and is found almost everywhere among pagan people and to some extent in some of the sects of modern Christendom. (*Mormon Doctrine*, 2nd ed., p. 772.)

23. THE UNKNOWN GOD] "Finding on Mars hill 'an altar with this inscription, TO THE UNKNOWN GOD,' Paul took occasion to reveal to the Athenians the true nature of the living God, as though he were merely giving them a correct understanding of what they already believed. (Acts 17:22-31.) Similarly today, the Elders of Israel go forth among so-called Christian peoples who are worshiping an Unknown God (who chances to have the same names as the true and living God), and the elders proceed to reveal the true nature of God, as though they are explaining what the people already believe.

"In reality, the God of the saints is a Known God who has revealed himself to modern men; the Deity of the sectarian Christians is an Unknown God, who does not appear to men, though in some vague way he is supposed to have done so anciently. The saints say that it is life eternal to know the only true God and Jesus Christ whom he hath sent (John 17:3); apostate Christendom says — officially and formally in the accepted and approved creeds — that God is immaterial, uncreated, and incomprehensible.

"The only similarity between the Known and the Unknown Gods is that they both bear the same names, and the profession is made that they both have the same characteristics and attributes. For that matter the Athenians probably ascribed to their Unknown God many of the same characteristics and attributes that the sectarians ascribe to the mysterious all-pervading essence which they suppose is their God. Acceptance of the gospel, in large measure, consists in coming to the true knowledge of God, in replacing apostate views about an Unknown God with the light of heaven so that the convert begins to know God and the Son who was sent of God." (*Mormon Doctrine*, 2nd ed., pp. 815-816.)

24. God that made the world] The Father, not the Son. Though Christ is the Creator of all things, he acted under the direction and used the power of the Father. (Moses 1:33.) See Col. 1:13-19. "By definition, God (generally meaning the Father) is the one supreme and absolute Being; the ultimate source of the universe; the all-powerful, all-knowing, all-good Creator, Ruler, and Preserver of all things. Of him, when considering the object upon which faith rests, the Prophet observes 'that God is the only supreme governor and independent Being in whom all fulness and perfection dwell; who is omnipotent, omnipresent, and omniscient; without beginning of days or end of life; and that in him every good gift and every good principle dwell; and that he is the Father of lights; in him the principle of faith dwells independently, and he is the object in whom the faith of all other rational and accountable beings centers for life and salvation.' (*Lectures on Faith*, p. 9.)" (*Mormon Doctrine*, 2nd ed., pp. 317-318.)

Temples made with hands] See Acts 7:48-50.

26. One blood] All men are brothers; Adam is their common father; there are no men on earth who are not lineal descendants of "the first man of all men." (Moses 1:34.) "Adam and Eve . . . have brought forth children; yea, even the family of all the earth." (2 Ne. 2:19-20.)

The times before appointed, and the bounds of their habitation] God sends his spirit children to earth on a regular, organized schedule. There is nothing haphazard or accidental about the peopling of the earth or the assignment of various land areas to the races of men. "The race and nation in which men are born in this world is a direct result of their pre-existent life. All the spirit hosts of heaven deemed worthy to receive mortal bodies were foreordained to pass through this earthly probation in the particular race and nation suited to their needs, circumstances, and talents. 'When the Most High divided to the nations their inheritance, when he separated the sons of Adam,' Moses said with reference to pre-existence, 'he set the bounds of the people according to the number of the children of Israel.' (Deut. 32:8.) Not only Israel, but all groups were thus foreknown and their total memberships designated in the pre-mortal life." (*Mormon Doctrine*, 2nd ed., p. 616.)

28. In him we live, and move, and have our being] In his presence; or, in that "light which proceedeth forth from the presence of God to fill the immensity of space." (D. & C. 88:12.) God, a person, is omnipresent because of this light, this power or influence, this spirit which is everywhere present. See Jas. 1:17-21.

29. We are the offspring of God] He is our Eternal Father; we have also an Eternal Mother. There is no such thing as a father without a mother, nor can there be children without parents. We were born as the spirit children of Celestial Parents long before the foundations of this world were laid. (*Mormon Doctrine*, 2nd ed., pp. 516-517.) See Heb. 12:9-10.

The Godhead] "Three glorified, exalted, and perfected personages comprise the Godhead or supreme presidency of the universe. (*Doctrines of Salvation*, vol. 1, pp. 1-55.) They are: God the Father; God the Son; and God the Holy Ghost. . . . Perhaps no better statement defining the Godhead and showing the relationship of its members to each other has been written in this dispensation than that given by the Prophet Joseph Smith in the *Lectures on Faith*. 'There are two personages who constitute the great, matchless, governing, and supreme, power over all things, by whom all things were created and made, that are created and made, whether visible or invisible, whether in heaven, on earth, or in the earth, under the earth, or throughout the immensity of space. They are the Father and the Son — the Father being a personage of spirit [meaning that he has a spiritual body which by revealed definition is a resurrected body of flesh and bones (1 Cor. 15:44-45; D. & C. 88:27)], glory, and power, possessing all perfection and fulness; the Son, who was in the bosom of the Father, a personage of tabernacle, made or fashioned like unto man, or being in the form and likeness of man, or rather man was formed after his likeness and in his image; he is also the express image and likeness of the personage of the Father, possessing all the fulness of the Father, or the same fulness with the Father; being begotten of him, and ordained from before the foundation of the world to be a propitiation for the sins of all those who should believe on his name, and is called the Son because of the flesh, and descended in suffering below that which man can suffer; or, in other words, suffered greater sufferings, and was exposed to more powerful contradictions than any man can be.

'But, notwithstanding all this, he kept the law of God, and remained without sin, showing thereby that it is in the power of man to keep the law and remain also without sin; and also, that by him a righteous judgment might come upon all flesh, and that all who walk not in the law of God may justly be condemned by the law, and have no excuse for their sins.

'And he being the Only Begotten of the Father, full of grace and truth, and having overcome, received a fulness of the glory of the Father, possessing the same mind with the Father, which mind is the Holy Spirit, that bears record of the Father and the Son, and these three are one; or, in other words, these three constitute the great, matchless, governing and supreme, power over all things; by whom all things were created and made that were created and made, and these three constitute the Godhead, and are one; the Father and the Son possessing the same mind, the same wisdom, glory, power, and fulness — filling all in all; the Son being filled with the fulness of the mind, glory, and power; or, in other words, the spirit, glory, and power, of the Father, possessing all knowledge and glory, and the same kingdom, sitting at the right hand of power, in the express image and likeness of the Father, mediator for man, being filled with the fulness of the mind of the Father; or, in other words, the Spirit of the Father, which Spirit is shed forth upon all who believe on his name and keep his commandments.

'And all those who keep his commandments shall grow up from grace to grace, and become heirs of the heavenly kingdom, and joint-heirs with Jesus Christ; possessing the same mind, being transformed into the same image or likeness, even the express image of him who fills all in all; being filled with the fulness of his glory, and become one in him, even as the Father, Son and Holy Spirit are one.' (*Lectures on Faith,* pp. 50-51.)" (*Mormon Doctrine,* 2nd ed., pp. 319-321.)

30. Those who in ignorance of the truth worship idols — or false gods of any kind — are not condemned until the truth is available to them. Then they are commanded to repent of their false worship and conform to the truth.

31. The resurrection of Jesus proves his divine Sonship, including the fact that he shall judge the world.

32. Resurrection] See 1 Cor. 15:1-11.

PAUL PREACHES TO JEW AND GENTILE ALIKE

ACTS 18:1-11.

1 After these things Paul departed from Athens, and came to Corinth;

2 And found a certain Jew named Aquila, born in Pontus, lately come from Italy, with his wife Priscilla; (because that Claudius had commanded all Jews to depart from Rome:) and came unto them.

3 And because he was of the same craft, he abode with them, and wrought: for by their occupation they were tentmakers.

4 And he reasoned in the synagogue every sabbath, and persuaded the Jews and the Greeks.

5 And when Silas and Timotheus were come from Macedonia, Paul was pressed in the spirit, and testified to the Jews *that* Jesus *was* Christ.

6 And when they opposed themselves, and blasphemed, he shook *his* raiment, and said unto them, Your blood *be* upon your own heads; I *am* clean: from henceforth I will go unto the Gentiles.

7 And he departed thence, and entered into a certain *man's* house, named Justus, *one* that worshipped God, whose house joined hard to the synagogue.

8 And Crispus, the chief ruler of the synagogue, believed on the Lord with all his house; and many of the Corinthians hearing believed, and were baptized.

9 Then spake the Lord to Paul in the night by a vision, Be not afraid, but speak, and hold not thy peace:

10 For I am with thee, and no man shall set on thee to hurt thee: for I have much people in this city.

11 And he continued *there* a year and six months, teaching the word of God among them.

3. Tentmakers] Jesus was a carpenter, Peter a fisherman, Matthew a tax collector; Brigham Young was a carpenter, painter, and glazier, Heber J. Grant a businessman, David O. McKay a teacher; Paul and Aquila were tentmakers; none of them were trained in the rabbinical schools or theological seminaries of their days. Thus: 1. Work is honorable, indeed is an essential part of one's mortal probation; and 2. Worldly scholarship as found in the schools of the day is not an essential prerequisite to ministerial service.

4. He reasoned] 5. And testified] Perfect missionary that he wás, Paul presented the doctrines of salvation as reasonably and logically as his keen intellectual capacity permitted. But souls are not converted by intellectual power alone, and so Paul acted as a witness and bore that testimony which God by the power of his Spirit had placed in the heart of this ancient apostle.

5. Pressed in the spirit] The Holy Spirit spoke to Paul's spirit with such force and certainty, commanding him to preach the word, that he felt a compulsion, a pressing urgency, to testify of Christ and the plan of salvation.

6. Shook his raiment] See Acts 20:13-27. Paul is here following the Israelitish custom of dramatizing his personal freedom from responsibility where the sins of his hearers are concerned. The Nephite prophet Jacob did the same thing as part of his preaching on the American Continent. (2 Ne. 9:44; Jac. 1:19; 2:2.)

I will go unto the Gentiles] See Acts 10:21-35; 13:42-49.

9-10. Church guided by revelation] See Acts 11:27-30.

PAUL TEACHES, MINISTERS, TRAVELS

ACTS 18:12-23.

12 And when Gallio was the deputy of Achaia, the Jews made insurrection with o n e accord against Paul, and brought him to the judgment seat,

13 Saying, This *fellow* persuadeth men to worship God contrary to the law.

14 And when Paul was now about to open *his* mouth, Gallio said unto the Jews, If it were a matter of wrong or wicked lewdness, O *ye* Jews, reason would that I should bear with you:

15 But if it be a question of words and names, and *of* your law, look ye *to it;* for I will be no judge of such *matters.*

16 And he drave them from the judgment seat.

17 Then all the Greeks took Sosthenes, the chief ruler of the synagogue, and beat *him* before the judgment seat. And Gallio cared for none of those things.

18 And Paul *after this* tarried *there* yet a good while, and then took his leave of the brethren, and sailed thence into Syria, and with him Priscilla and Aquila; having shorn *his* head in Cenchrea: for he had a vow.

19 And he came to Ephesus, and left them there: but he himself entered into the synagogue, and reasoned with the Jews.

20 When they desired *him* to tarry longer time with them, he consented not;

21 But bade them farewell, saying, I must by all means keep this feast that cometh in Jerusalem: but I will return again unto you, if God will. And he sailed from Ephesus.

22 And when he had landed at Caesarea, and gone up, and saluted the church, he went down to Antioch.

23 And after he had spent some time *there*, he departed, and went over *all* the country of Galatia and Phrygia in order, strengthening all the disciples.

13. Worship God contrary to the law] See Acts 4:13-22; 16:21. When the laws of the land either prescribe or proscribe modes and systems of worship, such is not of God. (D. & C. 134:4.) The Lord's plan of agency says: 'Choose ye this day whom ye will serve, for in no other way can you work out your salvation.' Lucifer's program of compulsion replies 'You have no choice but to worship as I decree, and I shall entice men to pass laws forbidding true and compelling false worship.'

14-17. Gallio refused to use the religious laws of the Jews as an excuse for imposing criminal penalties on the saints; he properly limited his jurisdiction to the laws of the land. Well might Pilate and Festus and Agrippa have had like wisdom when matters affecting the destiny of God's earthly kingdom came before them for judgment. Yet Gallio, with callous disregard of the rights of his subjects, permitted the Greeks to beat Sosthenes before the judgment seat itself.

18. Paul . . . had a vow] "As an incentive to greater personal righteousness, it is a wholesome and proper thing for the saints to make frequent vows to the Lord. These are solemn promises to perform some duty, refrain from some sin, keep some commandment, or press forward in greater service in the kingdom. Thus Jacob vowed to accept Jehovah as his God and to pay an honest tithing (Gen. 28:20-22), and Hannah vowed to give Samuel to the Lord for his service. (1 Sam. 1:9-18.)

"The saints should offer their vows both on the Lord's day and on all days (D. & C. 59:8-12); and once offered, they are to be kept. (D. & C. 108:3; Num. 30:2; Eccles. 5:4-5.) When vows are made in righteousness, they are sealed by the Holy Spirit of promise, and the Lord's blessings attend their performance. (D.&C. 132:7.)" (*Mormon Doctrine*, 2nd ed., p. 825.)

What Paul's vow was is not clear. From the fact that he shaved his head it is assumed he may have been following the Jewish custom where Nazarites are concerned. (Num. 6.) If so he was performing an unnecessary and improper rite, for the apparent purpose of humoring either the Jewish segment of the Church or prospective Jewish converts or both. Compare Acts 21:17-26.

21. If God will] See Jas. 4:13-17.

TRUE BAPTISM INCLUDES WATER AND THE SPIRIT

ACTS 18:24-28; 19:1-7.

24 And a certain Jew named Apollos, born at Alexandria, an eloquent man, *and* mighty in the scriptures, came to Ephesus.

25 This man was instructed in the way of the Lord; and being fervent in the spirit, he spake and taught diligently the things of the Lord, knowing only the baptism of John.

26 And he began to speak boldly in the synagogue: whom when Aquila and Priscilla had heard, they took him unto *them*, and expounded unto him the way of God more perfectly.

27 And when he was disposed to pass into Achaia, the brethren wrote, exhorting the disciples to receive him: who, when he was come, helped them much which had believed through grace:

28 For he mightily convinced the Jews, *and that* publicly, showing by the scriptures that Jesus was Christ.

1 And it came to pass, that, while Apollos was at Corinth, Paul having passed through the upper coasts came to Ephesus: and finding certain disciples,

2 He said unto them, Have ye received the Holy Ghost since ye believed? And they said unto him, We have not so much as heard whether there be any Holy Ghost.

3 And he said unto them, Unto what then were ye baptized? And they said, Unto John's baptism.

4 Then said Paul, John verily baptized with the baptism of repentance, saying unto the people, that they should believe on him which should come after him, that is, on Christ Jesus.

5 When they heard *this*, they were baptized in the name of the Lord Jesus.

6 And when Paul had laid *his* hands upon them, the Holy Ghost came on them; and they spake with tongues, and prophesied.

7 And all the men were about twelve.

To admit a person into God's Church on earth and thereafter into God's kingdom in heaven, he must be "born of water and of the Spirit." (John 3:5.) Immersion in water under the hands of a legal administrator opens the door to the kingdom of God both on earth and in heaven because it makes available that most transcendent of all gifts — the gift of the Holy Ghost. Unless and until a person is baptized by the Spirit, his soul is not cleansed, evil and iniquity are not burned out of him as by fire, and he cannot go where God and Christ are.

Joseph Smith taught: "Baptism is a holy ordinance preparatory to the reception of the Holy Ghost; it is the channel and key by which the Holy Ghost will be administered." (*Teachings*,

p. 148.) Also: "You might as well baptize a bag of sand as a man, if not done in view of the remission of sins and getting of the Holy Ghost. Baptism by water is but half a baptism, and is good for nothing without the other half — that is, the baptism of the Holy Ghost." (*Teachings*, pp. 314, 360.) **Mode of baptism]** See Rom. 6:1-11.

18:24-26. Apparently Apollos was a persuasive, dynamic disciple of John, who had not yet forsaken the forerunner and come to the full faith. He was a fervent, devout theologian who searched and expounded the scriptures and sought to save souls. But until taught by Aquila and Priscilla, he had not accepted the fulness of the gospel. How like him are some of the devout Christian preachers of this day. They have a measure of the truth, have searched the ancient scriptures, and they seek to save souls, not knowing that to do so they must first receive the gospel fulness as preached by the Mormon Aquilas and Priscillas.

24. Scriptures] See 2 Tim. 3:14-17.

27. Believed through grace] It is through the grace of God — his love, mercy, and condescension — that the gospel is available for men to believe; and it is by grace that men are able to comprehend the things of the Spirit and thereby receive the saving truths of the gospel.

19:1-7. John had not baptized these disciples. Had he done so he would have sent them to Christ and the apostles to be baptized "with the Holy Ghost, and with fire." (Matt. 3:11.) But, as the Prophet expressed it, "some sectarian Jew had been baptizing like John" (*Teachings*, p. 263), that is, some self-appointed minister had come along, as modern divines do, and assumed the prerogative to imitate the legal administrations of the past. Hence these receptive believers were baptized over again by a legal administrator other than Paul (1 Cor. 1:12-16), who, however, then conferred upon them the gift of the Holy Ghost.

6. Tongues and prophecy compared] See 1 Cor. 14:6-28.

ALL ASIA HEARD THE GOSPEL

ACTS 19:8-10.

8 And he went into the synagogue, and spake boldly for the space of three months, disputing and persuading the things concerning the kingdom of God.

9 But when divers were hardened, and believed not, but spake evil of that way before the multitude, he departed from them, and separated the disciples, disputing daily in the school of one Tyrannus.

10 And this continued by the space of two years; so that all they which dwelt in Asia heard the word of the Lord Jesus, both Jews and Greeks.

Paul the missionary, with zeal and devotion, continued to preach and teach, in the synagogues, in the schools of philosophy, everywhere he could gain a congregation. He did then what latter-day elders are commanded to do now: "Confound your enemies; call upon them to meet you both in public and in private; and inasmuch as ye are faithful their shame shall be made manifest." (D. & C. 71:7.) "Contend thou, therefore, morning by morning; and day after day let thy warning voice go forth; and when the night cometh let not the inhabitants of the earth slumber, because of thy speech." (D. & C. 112:5.)

And so, all Asia heard the word — not in the sense that each soul was taught the plan of salvation, but in that all had the opportunity to seek and find the truth if they desired it. That seven major units of the Church were established in Asia is known from the revelation received by John on Patmos. (Rev. 1:11.) Paul's ministry undoubtedly played an important part in the establishment of these churches.

GOD WROUGHT SPECIAL MIRACLES BY PAUL

ACTS 19:11-12.

11 And God wrought special miracles by the hands of Paul:

12 So that from his body were brought unto the sick handkerchiefs or aprons, and the diseases departed from them, and the evil spirits went out of them.

168

Healings come by the power of faith; there is no healing virtue or power in any item of clothing or other object, whether owned by Paul or Jesus or anyone. But rites and objects may be used to help increase faith. "When a man works by faith," the Prophet said, "he works by mental exertion instead of physical force." (*Lectures on Faith*, p. 61.) See *Commentary I*, pp. 157-159. In this connection there are occasions when ordinances or performances or objects may be used to help center the mental faculties of a person on those things which will cause faith to increase.

Thus Jesus used spittle and clay to anoint the eyes of a blind man, not that there was any healing power in the mud paste spread on the sightless eyes, but the physical act aided the mental labor out of which faith grew. (*Commentary I*, pp. 379-380.) The same principle is seen in the healing of the woman who touched Jesus' garments (*Commentary I*, pp. 317-319), in the dead being raised by touching the bones of Elisha (2 Kings 13:20-21), and in the very ordinance of admistering to the sick through the formalities of anointing with oil and laying on of hands.

Similar miracles to those wrought through Paul have occurred in this dispensation. On that memorable July 22, 1839, at Montrose, Iowa, for instance, when the Prophet healed the sick in great numbers, he took a silk handkerchief from his pocket, gave it to Wilford Woodruff, and told him to go and use it in the healing of two children of a nonmember of the Church. Elder Woodruff, as instructed, used the handkerchief in wiping the faces of the sick children and they were healed. (Joseph Fielding Smith, *Essentials in Church History*, pp. 270-271.)

EXORCISTS CANNOT CAST OUT DEVILS

ACTS 19:13-20.

13 Then certain of the vagabond Jews, exorcists, took upon them to call over them which had evil spirits the name of the Lord Jesus, saying, We adjure you by Jesus whom Paul preacheth.

14 And there were seven sons of *one* Sceva, a Jew, *and* chief of the priests, which did so.

169

15 And the evil spirit answered and said, Jesus I know, and Paul I know; but who are ye?

16 And the man in whom the evil spirit was leaped on them, and overcame them, and prevailed against them, so that they fled out of that house naked and wounded.

17 And this was known to all the Jews and Greeks also dwelling at Ephesus; and fear fell on them all, and the name of the Lord Jesus was magnified.

18 And many that believed came, and confessed, and showed their deeds.

19 Many of them also which used curious arts brought their books together, and burned them before all *men:* and they counted the price of them, and found *it fifty* thousand *pieces* of silver.

20 So mightly grew the word of God and prevailed.

Satan has a substitute for every doctrine and ordinance of the gospel. "In imitation of the true order whereby devils are cast out of people, false ministers (having no actual priesthood power) attempt to cast them out by exorcism. This ungodly practice was probably more common anciently than it is now, because few people today believe either in miracles or in the casting out of literal devils. But over the years it has not been uncommon for so-called priests to attempt to expel evil spirits from persons or drive them away from particular locations by incantations, conjuration, or adjuration. Commonly some holy name is used in these false rituals." (*Mormon Doctrine*, 2nd ed., p. 259.)

13-16. How literal a thing it is to be possessed by evil spirits. Devils are spirit men and women; by conformity to laws but slightly understood by us, they have power to enter and control the bodies of mortals. Then by the power of the priesthood, but not through incantations or exorcism, they may be cast out of their illegally inhabited tenements. See *Commentary I*, pp. 166-169; 266-269; 307-314.)

19. Curious arts] Witchcrafts, sorcery, spiritualism, exorcism, and the like. See Acts 8:5-13; 16:16-21.

Book burning] We are troubled to read of Bible burning affrays and of the destruction of libraries to stop the spread of Christianity or of learning in general. But book burning is not always bad. It depends upon the books. Pornographic writings and pictures should be destroyed. The oaths and evils of Cain and Gadianton should not be recorded for men to read. (Alma 37:25-31; Hela. 6:17-27.)

PRIESTCRAFT FIGHTS TRUE RELIGION

ACTS 19:21-41.

21 After these things were ended, Paul purposed in the spirit, when he had passed through Macedonia and Achaia, to go to Jerusalem, saying, After I have been there, I must also see Rome.

22 So he sent into Macedonia two of them that ministered unto him, Timotheus and Erastus; but he himself stayed in Asia for a season.

23 And the same time there arose no small stir about that way.

24 For a certain *man named* Demetrius, a silversmith, which made silver shrines for Diana, brought no small gain unto the craftsmen;

25 Whom he called together with the workmen of like occupation, and said, Sirs, ye know that by this craft we have our wealth.

26 Moreover ye see and hear, that not alone at Ephesus, but almost throughout all Asia, this Paul hath persuaded and turned away much people, saying that they be no gods, which are made with hands:

27 So that not only this our craft is in danger to be set at nought; but also that the temple of the great goddess Diana should be despised, and her magnificence should be destroyed, whom all Asia and the world worshippeth.

28 And when they heard *these sayings*, they were full of wrath, and cried out, saying, Great *is* Diana of the Ephesians.

29 And the whole city was filled with confusion: and having caught Gaius and Aristarchus, men of Macedonia, Paul's companions in travel, they rushed with one accord into the theatre.

30 And when Paul would have entered in unto the · people, the disciples suffered him not.

31 And certain of the chief of Asia, which were his friends, sent unto him, desiring *him* that he would not adventure himself into the theatre.

32 Some therefore cried one thing, and some another: for the assembly was confused; and the more part knew not wherefore they were come together.

33 And they drew Alexander out of the multitude, the Jews put-

ting him forward. And Alexander beckoned with the hand, and would have made his defence unto the people.

34 But when they knew that he was a Jew, all with one voice about the space of two hours cried out, Great *is* Diana of the Ephesians.

35 And when the townclerk had appeased the people, he said, Ye men of Ephesus, what man is there that knoweth not how that the city of the Ephesians is a worshipper of the great goddess Diana, and of the *image* which fell down from Jupiter?

36 Seeing t h e n that these things cannot be spoken against, ye ought to be quiet, and to do nothing rashly.

37 For ye have brought hither these men, which are neither robbers of churches, nor yet blasphemers of your goddess.

38 Wherefore if Demetrius, and the craftsmen which are with him, have a matter against any man, the law is open, and there are deputies: let them implead one another.

39 But if ye enquire any thing concerning other matters, it shall be determined in a lawful assembly.

40 For we are in danger to be called in question for this day's uproar, there being no cause whereby we may give an account of this concourse.

41 And when he had thus spoken, he dismissed the assembly.

Paul preached and ministered in the power and authority of the priesthood. The pagan priests of Ephesus taught and made their livelihood through priestcraft. Priesthood and priestcraft are two opposites; one is of God, the other of the devil; one is spiritual and godly, the other is carnal and evil.

Priesthood is the power and authority of God delegated to man on earth to act in all things for the salvation of men. Priestcraft is Satan's substitute for this true power and authority. The Lord's Church is administered by priesthood; Satan's church organizations, all of them, are governed through a system of priestcraft. Nephi said, "Priestcrafts are that men preach and set themselves up for a light unto the world, that they may get gain and praise of the world; but they seek not the welfare of Zion." (2 Ne. 26:29.)

24. Made silver shrines for Diana] These were various small models of such things as the Ephesian Temple, or the goddess Diana, which worshipers purchased for their religious significance.

27. Our craft is in danger] So often religious zeal becomes the hypocritical cloak of self-interest.

29. The theatre] There was room therein for more than 24,000 people.

The temple of the great goddess Diana] "It was reckoned one of the wonders of the world. It was built about 550 B.C., of pure white marble, and though burned by a fanatic on the night of the birth of Alexander the Great, B.C. 356, was rebuilt with more splendour than before. It was 425 feet long, by 220 broad, and the columns, 127 in number, were sixty feet in height, each of them the gift of a king, and thirty-six of them enriched with ornament and colour. It was what the Bank of England is in the modern world, the larger portion of the wealth of Western Asia being stored up in it. It was constantly receiving new decorations and additional buildings, statues, and pictures by the most cele-brated artists, and kindled unparalleled admiration, enthusiasm, and superstition. Its very site is now a matter of uncertainty. The little wooden image of Diana was as primitive and rude as its shrine was sumptuous; not like the Greek Diana, in the form of an imposing huntress, but quite Asiatic, in the form of a many-breasted female (emblematic of the manifold ministrations of Nature to man), terminating in a shapeless block. Like some other far-famed idols, it was believed to have fallen from heaven (v. 35), and models of it were not only sold in immense numbers to private persons, but set up for worship in other cities." (*Jamieson*, pp. 206-207.)

Diana . . . whom all . . . the world worshippeth] What does it matter how many adherents a false religion claims? Suppose all men worshiped Diana forever, would any of them gain salvation as a result? Nephi saw that in the last days the Church of the Devil would have "dominion over all the earth, among all nations, kin-dreds, tongues, and people," and that the membership of the Church of the Lamb of God would be slight by comparison. (1 Ne. 14:11-12.)

29-31. Wise counsel from the saints and his gentile friends kept Paul from personal participation in the devil-led demonstration, thereby probably saving his life.

32. How often "the more part" of a mob scarcely know the reason, the cause, the excuse, that unites them as persecutors and defamers of others.

33-34. Lest the rage of the mob be turned on them, the Jews (who themselves were opposed to idol worship) apparently sought to disassociate themselves from Paul and the saints. But even their defense was shouted down with the fanatical chant, "Great is Diana of the Ephesians."

35-41. In the providences of God there is often a townclerk, a Gamaliel (Acts 5:33-40), or an Alexander W. Doniphan (Joseph Fielding Smith, *Essentials in Church History*, p. 241), to come to the aid of the saints.

PAUL RAISETH EUTYCHUS FROM DEATH

ACTS 20:1-12.

1 And after the uproar was ceased, Paul called unto *him* the disciples, and embraced *them*, and departed for to go into Macedonia.

2 And when he had gone over those parts, and had given them much exhortation, he came into Greece.

3 And *there* a b o d e three months. And when the Jews laid wait for him, as he was about to sail into Syria, he purposed to return through Macedonia.

4 And there accompanied him into Asia Sopater of Berea; and of the Thessalonians, Aristarchus and Secundus; and Gaius of Derbe, and Timotheus; and of Asia, Tychicus and Trophimus.

5 These going before tarried for us at Troas.

6 And we sailed away from Philippi after the days of unleavened bread, and came unto them to Troas in five days; where we abode seven days.

7 And upon the first *day* of the week, when the disciples came together to break bread, Paul preached unto them, ready to depart on the morrow; and continued his speech until midnight.

8 And there were many lights in the upper chamber, where they were gathered together.

9 And there sat in a window a certain young man named Eutychus, being fallen into a deep sleep: and as Paul was long preaching, he sunk down with sleep, and fell down from the third loft, and was taken up dead.

10 And Paul went down, and fell on him, and embracing *him* said, Trouble not yourselves: for his life is in him.

11 When he therefore was come up again, and had broken bread, and eaten, and talked a long while, even till break of day, so he departed.

12 And t h e y brought the young man alive, and were not a little comforted.

Paul joins Jesus, Peter, Elijah, Elisha, Nephi the disciple, Wilford Woodruff, Lorenzo Snow, and other unnamed and unknown prophets, who with like faith raised the dead. But what is death to the Lord? Is anything too hard for him? Why should not the creator and controller of all things speak, either by his own voice or the voice of his servants, and revive the dead for a further sojourn in the flesh? See Acts 9:32-43.

7. The first day of the week] Already the apostolic instituted practice of worshiping and partaking of the sacrament on the Lord's day, the first day of the week, had been inaugurated. See Rev. 1:9-11.

9. Paul was long preaching] Sermons can and sometimes should be long. The modern penchant for capsule presentations often deprives men from coming to a full knowledge of the doctrines of salvation. Who among us would object to listening to Paul or Peter or Joseph Smith for as many consecutive hours as human strength allowed?

10. Paul apparently followed somewhat the same course pursued by Elijah when that ancient worthy raised from death the son of the widow of Zarephath (1 Kings 17:8-23), and of Elisha when he raised the son of the Shunammite. (2 Kings 4:18-37.)

PAUL FREE FROM BLOOD OF ALL MEN

ACTS 20:13-27.

13 And we went before to ship, and sailed unto Assos, there intending to take in Paul: for so had he appointed, minding himself to go afoot.

14 And when he met with us at Assos, we took him in, and came to Mitylene.

15 And we sailed thence, and came the next *day* over against Chios; and the next *day* we arrived at Samos, and tarried at Trogyllium; and the next *day* we came to Miletus.

16 For Paul had determined to sail by Ephesus, because he would not spend the time in Asia: for he hasted, if it were possible for him, to be at Jerusalem the day of Pentecost.

17 And from Miletus he sent to Ephesus, and called the elders of the church.

18 And when they were come to him, he said unto them, Ye know, from the first day that I came into Asia, after what manner I have been with you at all seasons,

19 Serving the Lord with all humility of mind, and with many tears, and temptations, which befell me by the lying in wait of the Jews:

20 *And* how I kept back nothing that was profitable *unto you*, but have showed you, and have taught you publicly, and from house to house,

21 Testifying both to the Jews, and also to the Greeks, repentance toward God, and faith toward our Lord Jesus Christ.

22 And now, behold, I go bound in the spirit unto Jerusalem, not knowing the things that shall befall me there:

23 Save that the Holy Ghost witnesseth in every city, saying that bonds and afflictions abide me.

24 But none of these things move me, neither count I my life dear unto myself, so that I might finish my course with joy, and the ministry, which I have received of the Lord Jesus, to testify the gospel of the grace of God.

25 And now, behold, I know that ye all, among whom I have gone preaching the kingdom of God, shall see my face no more.

26 Wherefore I take you to record this day, that I *am* pure from the blood of all *men*.

27 For I have not shunned to declare unto you all the counsel of God.

I.V. ACTS 20:21.

21 Testifying both to the Jews, and also to the Greeks, repentance toward God, and faith **on the name of** our Lord Jesus Christ.

176

God's servants must, at the peril of their own salvation, deliver the message entrusted to them. (D. & C. 4:2.) If they raise the warning voice as directed by the Lord (D. & C. 88:81), they are free from the blood and sins of those to whom they are sent. If they fail to warn the wicked, the Lord holds them accountable for the sins of the unrepentant. (Ezek. 3:17-21; 33:7-9.) Paul here announces that he has been true to the trust imposed upon him and is thus free from personal responsibility for the sins of those to whom he was sent to minister.

17. The elders of the church] See Acts 11:27-30.

21. Faith both precedes and follows repentance. Because of faith men desire to become clean through repentance, and having thus been cleansed, they gain increased desires to become like God by perfecting their faith.

23-24. By revelation Paul knew of the persecutions and afflictions ahead. But what did these matter in the eternal perspective? Had not even Jesus, the Lord, "for the joy that was set before him endured the cross?" (Heb. 12:2.)

24. The gospel of the grace of God] The good news that because of his love, mercy, and condescension God had made salvation available through Jesus Christ. See Rom. 4:1-25.

25. Preaching the kingdom of God] Preaching that salvation is in Christ; that those who repent and enter his earthly kingdom, and who then keep his commandments, shall gain an inheritance in his heavenly kingdom.

PAUL PREDICTS APOSTASY AND CULTISM

ACTS 20:28-32.

28 Take heed therefore unto yourselves, and to all the flock, over the which the Holy Ghost hath made you overseers, to feed the church of God, which he hath purchased with his own blood.

29 For I know this, that after my departing shall grievous wolves enter in among you, not sparing the flock.

30 Also of your own selves shall men arise, speaking perverse things, to draw away disciples after them.

177

31 Therefore watch, and remember, that by the space of three years I ceased not to warn every one night and day with tears.

32 And now, brethren, I commend you to God, and to the word of his grace, which is able to build you up, and to give you an inheritance among all them which are sanctified.

28. The Holy Ghost hath made you overseers] God calls his own ministers. All calls to the ministry should come by revelation. Unless and until God speaks, no man can represent the Lord in the ministry. (John 15:16; Fifth Article of Faith.)

Feed the church of God] Teach the doctrines of salvation; supply spiritual food; bear testimony of our Lord's divine Sonship — anything short of such a course is unworthy of a true minister who has been called by revelation. Only when the Church is fed the bread of life are its members kept in paths of righteousness. It is the spiritually illiterate who become cultists and who forsake the faith.

Purchased with his own blood] See Heb. 10:1-18.

29-30. Which is worse, persecution from without, which drives men from the truth, or heresy from within, which perverts and twists the truth until all saving power is drained from it?

Theretofore persecution had been Satan's tool to prevent the spread of the gospel, now he was beginning to use a new weapon — dissension from within, perversion of the truth, the formation of conflicting cults and sects within the so-called Christian fold. How well this second approach succeeded is everywhere apparent.

32. Them which are sanctiifed] See 1 Thess. 4:1-8.

"IT IS MORE BLESSED TO GIVE THAN TO RECEIVE"

ACTS 20:33-38.

33 I have coveted no man's silver, or gold, or apparel.

34 Yea, ye yourselves know, that these hands have ministered unto my necessities, and to them that were with me.

35 I have showed you all things, how that so labouring ye ought to support the weak, and to remember the words of the Lord

178

Jesus, how he said, It is more blessed to give than to receive.

36 And when he had thus spoken, he kneeled down, and prayed with them all.

37 And they all wept sore, and fell on Paul's neck, and kissed him,

38 Sorrowing most of all for the words which he spake, that they should see his face no more. And they accompanied him unto the ship.

33-35. Though the laborer is worthy of his hire, true ministers are never a burden on those they serve. See 1 Cor. 9:13-18. King Benjamin, the great Nephite prophet-teacher, followed the same course here stated by Paul. "I . . . have not sought gold nor silver nor any manner of riches of you," the Nephite leader told his people, "And even I, myself, have labored with mine own hands that I might serve you, and that ye should not be laden with taxes, and that there should nothing come upon you which was grievous to be borne." (Mosiah 2:12-14.)

35. It is more blessed to give than to receive] Thanks be to Paul (and Luke his scribe) for preserving for us this golden gem from the lips of the Master Teacher. How wondrous it will be, in some future millennial day, to have the full revealed account of all that Jesus said and taught during his mortal ministry.

SPIRIT OF PROPHECY MANIFEST IN THE CHURCH

ACTS 21:1-16.

1 And it came to pass, that after we were gotten from them, and had launched, we came with a straight course unto Coos, and the *day* following unto Rhodes, and from thence unto Patara:

2 And finding a ship sailing over unto Phenicia, we went aboard, and set forth.

3 Now when we had discovered Cyprus, we left it on the left hand, and sailed into Syria, and landed at Tyre: for there the ship was to unlade her burden.

4 And finding disciples, we tarried there seven days: who said to Paul through the Spirit, that he should not go up to Jerusalem.

5 And when we had accomplished those days, we departed

179

and went our way; and they all brought us on our way, with wives and children, till *we were* out of the city: and we kneeled down on the shore, and prayed.

6 And when we had taken our leave one of another, we took ship; and they returned home again.

7 And when we had finished *our* course from Tyre, we came to Ptolemais, and saluted the brethren, and abode with them one day.

8 And the next *day* we that were of Paul's company departed, and came unto Caesarea: and we entered into the house of Philip the evangelist, which was *one* of the seven; and abode with him.

9 And the same man had four daughters, virgins, which did prophesy.

10 And as we tarried *there* many days, there came down from Judea a certain prophet, named Agabus.

11 And when he was come unto us, he took Paul's girdle and bound his own hands and feet, and said, Thus saith the Holy Ghost, So shall the Jews at Jerusalem bind the man that owneth this girdle, and shall deliver *him* into the hands of the Gentiles.

12 And when we heard these things, both we, and they of that place, besought him not to go up to Jerusalem.

13 Then Paul answered, What mean ye to weep and to break mine heart? for I am ready not to be bound only, but also to die at Jerusalem for the name of the Lord Jesus.

14 And when he would not be persuaded, we ceased, saying, The will of the Lord be done.

15 And after those days we took up our carriages, and went up to Jerusalem.

16 There went with us also *certain* of the disciples of Caesarea, and brought with them one Mnason of Cyprus, an old disciple, with whom we should lodge.

Revelation is the rock foundation upon which Christ built his Church. See *Commentary I*, pp. 380-390. The spirit of prophecy is always found in the earthly kingdom of God. See Rev. 19:9b-10. Where these are, there is the Church and kingdom of God on earth; where these are not, there the Church and kingdom is not. Whenever the Church ceases to receive revelation, and whenever the spirit of prophecy is not found among its members, it ceases to be the Lord's Church. Revelation and the spirit of prophecy are not confined to the President of the Church, to the General Authorities, or to church officers. Others, as well as Paul, here receive knowledge from the Spirit that he should not go up to Jerusalem and also of the fate there awaiting him if he did.

4-15. Should Paul have gone to Jerusalem? Did the journey accord with the will and purposes of the Lord?

Whatever the answers to these questions may be, it is clear that Paul was forewarned of the persecutions and trials that would attend such a journey. He had received whisperings from the Spirit saying that bonds and afflictions awaited him in Jerusalem. (Acts 20:22-24.) Now he is told flatly, not merely by the voice of sympathetic brethren who fear for his safety, but by the voice of revelation given by the Holy Ghost, that he should not go up, although the meaning of the warning may have been that he should not go unless he was prepared to face the promised trials. Also, Agabus, apparently learning of Paul's determination to face persecution and even death in Jerusalem, comes and tells him in the Lord's name that in Jerusalem he will be bound by the Jews and delivered to the Gentiles.

However, out of his journey to Jerusalem came the arrest which enabled him, while in Roman custody, to testify before the Jews of Jerusalem, before Festus and then Agrippa, on the island of Melita, and in Rome itself. To take the witness of Christ to kings and rulers, it oftentimes seems to require the arrest and trial of the Lord's servants. Surely Paul's trip to Jerusalem tested his metal and ennobled his soul, and because of it, he gained opportunities to stand in defense of truth and righteousness which otherwise would have been denied him.

8. Philip the evangelist] Originally a holder of the Aaronic Priesthood (Acts 6:1-6), later a missionary of great renown (Acts 8:5-40), it appears, assuming the accuracy of the account, that Philip now has been ordained a patriarch. See Eph. 4:7-16.

9. Four daughters . . . did prophesy] Though men are appointed to hold rule in the home and in the Church, women are not one whit behind them in spiritual endowments. They prophesy, receive visions, entertain angels (Alma 32:23), enjoy the gifts of the Spirit, and qualify with their husbands for full exaltation in the highest heaven.

11. Prophets often dramatize their inspired predictions. By binding his own hands and feet with Paul's girdle, Agabus delivered his message with far greater impact than he could have done with words alone.

Thus saith the Holy Ghost] 'Thus saith the Lord, by the power of the Holy Ghost.' The Holy Ghost is God's minister and spokesman, saying and speaking those things, in the Lord's name, which Deity would have said had he been present personally; or, occasionally, as here, speaking in the first person as though he were the Lord. The most expressive instance of this latter type of speaking, this speaking by divine investiture of authority, as it were, is seen in the experience of Adam when "the Holy Ghost fell upon" him, "saying: I am the Only Begotten of the Father." (Moses 5:9.)

14. The will of the Lord be done] A statement of resignation, of submission, of agreement to a course which none could dissuade Paul from pursuing.

CONVERSION IS A GRADUAL PROCESS

ACTS 21:17-26.

17 And when we were come to Jerusalem, the brethren received us gladly.

18 And the *day* following Paul went in with us unto James; and all the elders were present.

19 And when he had saluted them, he declared particularly what things God had wrought among the Gentiles by his ministry.

20 And when they heard *it*, they glorified the Lord, and said unto him, Thou seest, brother, how many thousands of Jews there are which believe; and they are all zealous of the law:

21 And they are informed of thee, that thou teachest all the Jews which are among the Gentiles to forsake Moses, saying that they ought not to circumcise *their* children, neither to walk after the customs.

22 What is it therefore? the multitude must needs come together: for they will hear that thou art come.

23 Do therefore this that we say to thee: We have four men which have a vow on them;

24 Them take, and purify thyself with them, and be at charges with them, that they may shave *their* heads: and all may know that those things, whereof they were informed concerning thee, are nothing; but *that* thou thyself also walkest orderly, and keepest the law.

25 As touching the Gentiles which believe, we have written *and* concluded that they observe no such thing, save only that they keep themselves from *things* offered to idols, and from blood, and from strangled, and from fornication.

26 Then Paul took the men, and the next day purifying himself with them entered into the temple, to signify the accomplishment of the days of purification, until that an offering should be offered for every one of them.

I.V. ACTS 21:25.

25 As touching the Gentiles which believe, we have written and concluded that they observe no such thing, save only that they keep themselves from things offered to idols, and from blood, and from **things** strangled, and from fornication.

This is an extremely difficult passage to explain in such a way as to do credit to Paul, or to James the Lord's brother, or to the leading brethren in the Church, or to the Jewish segment of the Church established in Jerusalem.

A quarter of a century has passed since the death of the Lord; the law of Moses is fulfilled; circumcision is no longer an approved part of true worship; the peculiar customs and practices of the Jews are false and damning; the Nazarite system of vows and sacrifices is destructive of that faith which, centered in Christ, leads to life and salvation.

And yet to humor Jewish-Christians — particularly converted church members who still practice false rites and cling to false ordinances; who are giving lip service to Christ while following the Mosaic performances which Christ abolished; who are Christian in name, but largely Jewish in act; who have had the laying on of hands for the gift of the Holy Ghost, but have never attained the spiritual maturity to gain the full companionship of that member of the Godhead — to humor these weak members of the Church,

Paul is asked, officially, as a matter of church discipline to pretend that he is a Jew who keeps the Law of Moses.

Why? What justification can there possibly be for these early saints to reject the spirit and practice of true religion and pretend to conform to the dead letter of a dead law, to a law which can lead nowhere except to spiritual death? The explanation lies in the semi-converted status of the Jewish saints of Jerusalem. As with all men, the Lord was giving gospel truths to them line upon line, precept upon precept. It was better to have them in the Church, seeking the Spirit, striving to keep the commandments, and trying to work out their salvation, than to leave them without the fold until they gained a full knowledge of all things. Even Peter was not converted to the full until long after he was ordained an apostle.

And so it is today — conversion is a gradual process. There are many sectarian concepts and practices which individuals who are in the Church must abandon before the gospel system becomes perfect. If there is a lesson for us in these events, it is that staunch and stable members of the Church should be tolerant and charitable toward persons newly coming out of the darkness of the world into the light of the gospel.

18. James] The Lord's brother, now one of the apostles. (Gal. 1:19.)

19-20. Paul's ministry among the Gentiles, as reported by him in detail, had the full approval of the leading brethren of the Church.

23-26. See Acts 18:12-23. **25.** See Acts 15:1-35.

PAUL PERSECUTED, ARRESTED, BOUND

ACTS 21:27-39.

27 And when the seven days were almost ended, the Jews which were of Asia, when they saw him in the temple, stirred up all the people, and laid hands on him,

28 Crying out, Men of Israel, help: This is the man, that teacheth all *men* every where against the people, and the law, and this place: and further brought Greeks also into the temple, and hath polluted this holy place.

29 (For they had seen before with him in the city Trophimus an Ephesian, whom they supposed that Paul had brought into the temple.)

30 And all the city was moved, and the people ran together: and they took Paul, and drew him out of the temple: and forthwith the doors were shut.

31 And as they went about to kill him, tidings came unto the chief captain of the band, that all Jerusalem was in an uproar.

32 Who immediately took soldiers and centurions, and ran down unto them: and when they saw the chief captain and the soldiers, they left beating of Paul.

33 Then the chief captain came near, and took him, and commanded *him* to be bound with two chains; and demanded who he was, and what he had done.

34 And some cried one thing, some another, among the multi-tude: and when he could not know the certainty for the tumult, he commanded him to be carried into the castle.

35 And when he came upon the stairs, so it was, that he was borne of the soldiers for the violence of the people.

36 For the multitude of the people followed after, crying, Away with him.

37 And as Paul was to be led into the castle, he said unto the chief captain, May I speak unto thee? Who said, Canst thou speak Greek?

38 Art not thou that Egyptian, which before these days madest an uproar, and leddest out into the wilderness four thousand men that were murderers?

39 But Paul said, I am a man *which am* a Jew of Tarsus, *a city* in Cilicia, a citizen of no mean city: and, I beseech thee, suffer me to speak unto the people.

Is not this scene reminiscent of the babble and confusion, the mobocracy, the spirit of hate and murder which attended the last days of our Lord's mortal life? But why should such things be? Why should one group of religionists persecute another? Suppose some people do have different religious beliefs than others, what of it? Why should men be persecuted for what they believe?

The fact that there is religious persecution is one of the great evidences of the existence and influence of Satan. There is no reason to persecute people for their beliefs unless it makes a difference what they believe. Satan, knowing full well that men are saved by believing one set of principles and damned for accepting another, has a personal interest in all religious persecution. By keeping the spirit of persecution alive in the hearts of men, he can hinder and damage the spirit which leads men to piety and worship. And he can then wield the sword of persecution with full strength when he encounters the true religion revealed from heaven. See Acts 5:33-42; 17:1-14.

27-30. Paul is here accused, falsely, of taking a Gentile from the outer court of the Gentiles, into the inner court of Israel. Aliens, meaning unbelievers in the religion of the Jews, who thus overstepped their bounds were worthy of death according to Jewish law, a law which the Jews were then powerless to enforce.

PAUL RECOUNTS STORY OF HIS CONVERSION

ACTS 21:40; 22:1-16.

40 And when he had given him license, Paul stood on the stairs, and beckoned with the hand unto the people. And when there was made a great silence, he spake unto *them* in the Hebrew tongue, saying,

1 Men, brethren, and fathers, hear ye my defence *which I make* now unto you.

2 (And when they heard that he spake in the Hebrew tongue to them, they kept the more silence: and he saith,)

3 I am verily a man *which am* a Jew, born in Tarsus, *a city* in Cilicia, yet brought up in this city at the feet of Gamaliel, *and* taught according to the perfect manner of the law of the fathers, and was zealous toward God, as ye all are this day.

4 And I persecuted this way unto the death, binding and delivering into prisons both men and women.

5 As also the high priest doth bear me witness, and all the estate of the elders: from whom also I received letters unto the brethren, and went to Damascus, to bring them which were there bound unto Jerusalem, for to be punished.

6 And it came to pass, that, as I made my journey, and was come nigh unto Damascus about noon, suddenly there shone from heaven a great light round about me.

7 And I fell unto the ground, and heard a voice saying unto me, Saul, Saul, why persecutest thou me?

8 And I answered, Who art thou, Lord? And he said unto me, I am Jesus of Nazareth, whom thou persecutest.

9 And they that were with me saw indeed the light, and were afraid; but they heard not the voice of him that spake to me.

10 And I said, What shall I do, Lord? And the Lord said unto me, Arise, and go into Damascus; and there it shall be told thee of all things which are appointed for thee to do.

11 And when I could not see for the glory of that light, being led by the hand of them that were with me, I came into Damascus.

12 And one Ananias, a devout man according to the law, having a good report of all the Jews which dwelt *there*,

13 Came unto me, and stood, and said unto me, Brother Saul, receive thy sight. And the same hour I looked up upon him.

14 And he said, The God of our fathers hath chosen thee, that thou shouldest know his will, and see that Just One, and shouldest hear the voice of his mouth.

15 For thou shalt be his witness unto all men of what thou hast seen and heard.

16 And now why tarriest thou? arise, and be baptized, and wash away thy sins, calling on the name of the Lord.

How many times had Paul borne this testimony? The story itself is first recounted in Acts 9, but here we have it in Paul's own words, words that burn like fire into the hearts of those with sufficient spiritual endowment to believe the truth. There is no debate where testimony is concerned; a testimony is either true or false; there is no other issue to decide. Jesus said, "I am the Son of God" (John 10:36), Joseph Smith, "I saw two Personages, whose brightness and glory defy all description, standing above me in the air" (Jos. Smith 2:17), and Paul, 'I saw a light and heard a voice.' And in this manner is the witness of the truth proclaimed to the world. Those who hear, or to whom a knowledge of the testimony comes, accept or reject it at the peril of their own salvation. See Acts 9:1-9; 9:10-19a.

PAUL IN A TRANCE SEETH JESUS

ACTS 22:17-21.

17 And it came to pass, that, when I was come again to Jerusalem, even while I prayed in the temple, I was in a trance;

18 And saw him saying unto me, Make haste, and get thee quickly out of Jerusalem: for they

will not receive thy testimony concerning me.

19 And I said, Lord, they know that I imprisoned and beat in every synagogue them that believed on thee:

20 And when the blood of thy martyr Stephen was shed, I also was standing by, and consenting unto his death, and kept the raiment of them that slew him.

21 And he said unto me, Depart: for I will send thee far hence unto the Gentiles.

17. A trance] See Acts 10:9-20.

18-21. For the first time we here learn that the Lord Jesus appeared again to Paul when the Apostle first visited Jerusalem to report his labors and participate in the council which determined the issue of circumcision. See Acts 15:1-35. It was in this appearance that the converted Paul received the direct and personal commission to go to the Gentiles. See Acts 13:42-49.

19-20. See Acts 8:1b-4.

PAUL SMITTEN AT ANANIAS' ORDER

ACTS 22:22-30; 23:1-5.

22 And they gave him audience unto this word, and *then* lifted up their voices, and said, Away with such a *fellow* from the earth: for it is not fit that he should live.

23 And as they cried out, and cast off *their* clothes, and threw dust into the air,

24 The chief captain commanded him to be brought into the castle, and bade that he should be examined by scourging; that he might know wherefore they cried so against him.

25 And as they bound him with thongs, Paul said unto the centurion that stood by, Is it lawful for you to scourge a man that is a Roman, and uncondemned?

26 When the centurion heard *that*, he went and told the chief captain, saying, Take heed what thou doest: for this man is a Roman.

27 Then the chief captain came, and said unto him, Tell me, art thou a Roman? He said, Yea.

28 And the chief captain answered, With a great sum obtained I this freedom. And Paul said, But I was *free* born.

29 Then straightway they departed from him which should have examined him: and the chief captain also was afraid, after he knew that he was a Roman, and because he had bound him.

30 On the morrow, because he would have known the certainty wherefore he was accused of the Jews, he loosed him from *his* bands, and commanded the chief priests and all their council to appear, and brought Paul down, and set him before them.

1 And Paul, earnestly beholding the council, said, Men *and* brethren, I have lived in all good conscience before God until this day.

2 And the high priest Ananias commanded them that stood by him to smite him on the mouth.

3 Then said Paul unto him, God shall smite thee, *thou* whited wall: for sittest thou to judge me

after the law, and commandest me to be smitten contrary to the law?

4 And they that stood by said, Revilest thou God's high priest?

5 Then said Paul, I wist not, brethren, that he was the high priest: for it is written, Thou shalt not speak evil of the ruler of thy people.

I.V. ACTS 22:29-30.

29 Then straightway they departed from him which should have examined him, and the chief captain also was afraid; **and he loosed him from his bands,** after he knew that he was a Roman, and because he had bound him.

30 On the morrow, because he would have known the certainty wherefore he was accused of the Jews, he commanded the chief priests and all their council to appear, and brought Paul down, and set him before them.

Several striking similarities — with one vivid contrast, in particular — are seen between the arrest and demeaning of Jesus and of Paul. Both were persecuted by violent and unreasoning mobs of religious fanatics; both heard the same murderous cry raised against them, "Away with him" (John 19:15); both arrests were made by Roman power; in both cases an examination by the cruelty of scourging was decreed, though only Jesus was in fact scourged. In both cases the whole Jewish nation, as represented by the Sanhedrin itself, was raising its voice against the Lord's anointed, and in each instance the high priest himself became the chief inquisitor. And each of the high priests acted contrary to the law by which he was governed, Caiaphas, in the case of

189

Jesus, demanding an illegal confession, among other things, and Ananias, in the case of Paul, commanding him to be smitten for presuming to raise his voice in his own defense.

But Jesus, both before Annas and Caiaphas, in full control of himself and the situation, stood silently or spoke discreetly as the occasion warranted, bearing with a divine dignity beyond compare the insults and infamy heaped upon him. Paul, on the other hand (shall we not say in righteous anger?) called down the curse of the Almighty on Ananias for the act of violence which he ordered.

It is a common habit of writers and commentators to compare Paul unfavorably with Jesus, even though Paul's immediate and appropriately worded apology does itself show forth a divine dignity worthy of a Greater even than he. Let us grant that none can compare with the Master, but even then, why speak ill of Paul for proclaiming, almost by instinct, the very curse that Ananias deserved, a curse which did in fact in later years come upon him when he was slain by an assassin during the Jewish war? For that matter, the high priests before whom Jesus stood, though our Lord did not utter the decrees vocally, were also in fact spiritually smitten and destroyed by the Almighty for their accursed roles in the trials and death of our Lord. See *Commentary I*, pp. 777-817.

23:3. Thou whited wall] Thou hypocrite (Matt. 23:27-28), the allusion being to the practice of washing dirty walls with lime to hide the filth.

5. Some local and unnamed circumstance had kept from Paul the fact that Ananias was the high priest. The apostle's apology, however, for the stated reason that the high priest was the ruler of the people was in reality unnecessary. The fact was that the kingdom, with all its rule and dominion, had been wrested from the Jews by their Roman overlords. The high priest was without civic power, and Paul, as a Christian, was no longer subject to any religious direction from either the high priest or the Sanhedrin. It was as though a Mormon elder, converted from Catholicism, was voluntarily submitting to an investigation before a Papal court. Paul was thus being overly gracious to his captors.

THE LORD AGAIN APPEARETH TO PAUL

ACTS 23:6-11.

6 But when Paul perceived that the one part were Sadducees, and the other Pharisees, he cried out in the council, Men *and* brethren, I am a Pharisee, the son of a Pharisee: of the hope and resurrection of the dead I am called in question.

7 And when he had so said, there arose a dissension between the Pharisees and the Sadducees: and the multitude was divided.

8 For the Sadducees say that there is no resurrection, neither angel, nor spirit: but the Pharisees confess both.

9 And there arose a great cry: and the scribes *that were* of the Pharisees' part arose, and strove, saying, We find no evil in this man: but if a spirit or an angel hath spoken to him, let us not fight against God.

10 And when there arose a great dissension, the chief captain, fearing lest Paul should have been pulled in pieces of them, commanded the soldiers to go down, and to take him by force from among them, and to bring *him* into the castle.

11 And the night following the Lord stood by him, and said, Be of good cheer, Paul: for as thou hast testified of me in Jerusalem, so must thou bear witness also at Rome.

In his persecuted and straitened state, Paul needed comfort and assurance from on high. How shall such be given him? The Lord could have sent an angel; he could have spoken by the power of the Holy Spirit to the spirit within Paul; or he could have opened the heavens and let him see again the wonders of eternity. But this time — thanks to his valiant service, his unwearying devotion, his willingness to suffer even unto death in the Cause of Christ — this time Paul was blessed with the personal ministrations of the Lord of heaven himself. Jesus stood at his side. Without question much was said and much transpired, of which there has been preserved to us only the promise that the Lord's special apostle would yet bear witness of the Master in Rome. See Heb. 12:11-17.

6-8. The Jews as a whole were like modern Christians as a whole. All of them did not by any means believe the same things.

191

There were sects among them. Doctrinally a Sadducee was as far removed from a Pharisee as is a Unitarian from an old time Baptist. The division of religiously inclined people into contending sects and groups is one of Satan's most universally used tools.

FORTY JEWS PLOT PAUL'S DEATH

ACTS 23:12-31.

12 And when it was day, certain of the Jews banded together, and bound themselves under a curse, saying that they would neither eat nor drink till they had killed Paul.

13 And they were more than forty which had made this conspiracy.

14 And they came to the chief priests and elders, and said, We have bound ourselves under a great curse, that we will eat nothing until we have slain Paul.

15 Now therefore ye with the council signify to the chief captain that he bring him down unto you to morrow, as though ye would enquire something more perfectly concerning him: and we, or ever he come near, are ready to kill him.

16 And when Paul's sister's son heard of their lying in wait, he went and entered into the castle, and told Paul.

17 Then Paul called one of the centurions unto *him*, and said, Bring this young man unto the chief captain: for he hath a certain thing to tell him.

18 So he took him, and brought *him* to the chief captain, and said, Paul the prisoner called me unto *him*, and prayed me to bring this young man unto thee, who hath something to say unto thee.

19 Then the chief captain took him by the hand, and went *with him* aside privately, and asked *him*, What is that thou hast to tell me?

20 And he said, The Jews have agreed to desire thee that thou wouldst bring down Paul to morrow into the council, as though they would enquire somewhat of him more perfectly.

21 But do not thou yield unto them: for there lie in wait for him of them more than forty men, which have bound themselves with an oath, that they will neither eat nor drink till they have killed him: and now are they ready, looking for a promise from thee.

22 So the chief captain *then* let the young man depart, and charged *him*, *See thou* tell no man

that thou hast showed these things to me.

23 And he called unto *him* two centurions, saying, Make ready two hundred soldiers to go to Caesarea, and horsemen threescore and ten, and spearmen two hundred, at the third hour of the night;

24 And provide *them* beasts, that they may set Paul on, and bring *him safe* unto Felix the governor.

25 And he wrote a letter after this manner:

26 Claudius Lysias unto the most excellent governor Felix *sendeth* greeting.

27 This man was taken of the Jews, and should have been killed of them: then came I with an army, and rescued him, having understood that he was a Roman.

28 And when I would have known the cause wherefore they accused him, I brought him forth into their council:

29 Whom I perceived to be accused of questions of their law, but to have nothing laid to his charge worthy of death or of bonds.

30 And when it was told me how that the Jews laid wait for the man, I sent straightway to thee, and gave commandment to his accusers also to say before thee what *they had* against him. Farewell.

31 Then the soldiers, as it was commanded them, took Paul, and brought *him* by night to Antipatris.

I.V. ACTS 23:27.

27 This man was taken of the Jews, and **would** have been killed of them; then came I with an army, and rescued him, having understood that he was a Roman.

Shades of Cain and Gadianton! (Alma 37:25-31; Hela. 6:15-30; 4 Ne. 42; Ether 8; 10:33.) God permitted his ancient saints to swear with an oath that they would perform some righteous act at the peril of their lives. See *Commentary I*, pp. 225-227. Satan on the other hand directed those who had fully given themselves into his hands and service to covenant by solemn adjuration to spread evil and iniquity on earth even at the peril of their lives.

12. Bound themselves under a curse] A perfect description of a devil-directed oath. In effect these ancient gangsters pledged, in God's name, that their lives or Paul's would be forfeit — thereby bringing the eternal curse of God upon them.

29. Nothing . . . worthy of death or of bonds] As with Jesus, so with Paul. (Luke 23:4.)

PAUL ACCUSED BEFORE FELIX

ACTS 23:32-35; 24:1-27.

32 On the morrow they left the horsemen to go with him, and returned to the castle:

33 Who, when they came to Caesarea, and delivered the epistle to the governor, presented Paul also before him.

34 And when the governor had read *the letter*, he asked of what province he was. And when he understood that *he was* of Cilicia;

35 I will hear thee, said he, when thine accusers are also come. And he commanded him to be kept in Herod's judgment hall.

1 And after five days Ananias the high priest descended with the elders, and *with* a certain orator *named* Tertullus, who informed the governor against Paul.

2 And when he was called forth, Tertullus began to accuse *him*, saying, Seeing that by thee we enjoy great quietness, and that very worthy deeds are done unto this nation by thy providence,

3 We accept *it* always, and in all places, most noble Felix, with all thankfulness.

4 Notwithstanding, that I be not further tedious unto thee, I

pray thee that thou wouldest hear us of thy clemency a few words.

5 For we have found this man a pestilent *fellow*, and a mover of sedition among all the Jews throughout the world, and a ringleader of the sect of the Nazarenes:

6 Who also hath gone about to profane the temple: whom we took, and would have judged according to our law.

7 But the chief captain Lysias came *upon us*, and with great violence took *him* away out of our hands,

8 Commanding his accusers to come unto thee: by examining of whom thyself mayest take knowledge of all these things, whereof we accuse them.

9 And the Jews also assented, saying that these things were so.

10 Then Paul, after that the governor had beckoned unto him to speak, answered, Forasmuch as I know that thou hast been of many years a judge unto this nation, I do the more cheerfully answer for myself:

11 Because that thou mayest understand, that there are yet

but twelve days since I went up to Jerusalem for to worship.

12 And they neither found me in the temple disputing with any man, neither raising up the people, neither in the synagogues, nor in the city:

13 Neither can they prove the things whereof they now accuse me.

14 But this I confess unto thee, that after the way which they call heresy, so worship I the God of my fathers, believing all things which are written in the law and in the prophets:

15 And have hope toward God, which they themselves also allow, that there shall be a resurrection of the dead, both of the just and unjust.

16 And herein do I exercise myself, to have always a conscience void of offence toward God, and *toward* men.

17 Now after many years I came to bring alms to my nation, and offerings.

18 Whereupon certain Jews from Asia found me purified in the temple, neither with multitude, nor with tumult.

19 Who ought to have been here before thee, and object, if they had ought against me.

20 Or else let these same *here* say, if they have found any evil doing in me, while I stood before the council,

21 Except it be for this one voice, that I cried standing among them, Touching the resurrection of the dead I am called in question by you this day.

22 And when Felix heard these things, having more perfect knowledge of *that* way, he deferred them, and said, When Lysias the chief captain shall come down, I will know the uttermost of your matter.

23 And he commanded a centurion to keep Paul, and to let *him* have liberty, and that he should forbid none of his acquaintance to minister or come unto him.

24 And after certain days, when Felix came with his wife Drusilla, which was a Jewess, he sent for Paul, and heard him concerning the faith in Christ.

25 And as he reasoned of righteousness, temperance, a n d judgment to come, Felix trembled, and answered, Go thy way for this time; when I have a convenient season, I will call for thee.

26 He hoped also that money should have been given him of Paul, that he might loose him: wherefore he sent for him the oftener, and communed with him.

27 But after two years Porcius Festus came into Felix' room: and Felix, willing to show the Jews a pleasure, left Paul bound.

Justice as we know it was little regarded in Paul's day. Without a formal trial, to appease the Jews, and in hope of receiving money for his release, the Roman governor of Judea, Antonius Felix, kept Paul a prisoner for two wearisome years. True the Apostle was thereby protected from the murderous hatred of the Jews and the persecuting zeal of the Sanhedrin; true he was granted sufficient liberty to write and do some teaching; but nonetheless as a prisoner in the Cause of Christ, he was denied the full missionary privileges of the past quarter century.

We must assume that the Church did not grow as rapidly and that its members were not perfected as speedily as would have been the case had the great persuasive powers and energies of this mighty proselyter been used to the full during this period. No doubt this experience taught Paul that even he was not indispensable, and perchance his soul was further sanctified by suffering, but with it all the Lord's apostle was in fact a prisoner, held wickedly and unjustly by the forces of evil, all to the detriment of the work.

24:3. Felix] Procurator of Judea from about 52 to 58 A.D. Noted for his folly, cruelty, and lust, he was then living in an adulterous relationship with Drusilla, whom he had persuaded to desert her husband to be his "wife."

16. A conscience void of offense toward God, and toward men] Interestingly, this is almost the verbatim language used by Joseph Smith when he was being taken to Carthage two or three days previous to his assassination. (D. & C. 135:4.)

PAUL APPEALS TO CAESAR

ACTS 25:1-22.

1 Now when Festus was come into the province, after three days he ascended from Caesarea to Jerusalem.

2 Then the high priest and the chief of the Jews informed him against Paul, and besought him,

3 And desired favour against him, that he would send for him to Jerusalem, laying wait in the way to kill him.

4 But Festus answered, that Paul should be kept at Caesarea, and that he himself would depart shortly *thither*.

196

5 Let them therefore, said he, which among you are able, go down with *me*, and accuse this man, if there be any wickedness in him.

6 And when he had tarried among them more than ten days, he went down unto Caesarea; and the next day sitting on the judgment seat commanded Paul to be brought.

7 And when he was come, the Jews which came down from Jerusalem stood round about, and laid many and grievous complaints against Paul, which they could not prove.

8 While he answered for himself, Neither against the law of the Jews, neither against the temple, nor yet against Caesar, have I offended any thing at all.

9 But Festus, willing to do the Jews a pleasure, answered Paul, and said, Wilt thou go up to Jerusalem, and there be judged of these things before me?

10 Then said Paul, I stand at Caesar's judgment seat, where I ought to be judged: to the Jews have I done no wrong, as thou very well knowest.

11 For if I be an offender, or have committed any thing worthy of death, I refuse not to die: but if there be none of these things whereof these accuse me, no man may deliver me unto them. I appeal unto Caesar.

12 Then Festus, when he had conferred with the council, answered, Hast thou appealed unto Caesar? unto Caesar shalt thou go.

13 And after certain days king Agrippa and Bernice came unto Caesarea to salute Festus.

14 And when they had been there many days, Festus declared Paul's cause unto the king, saying, There is a certain man left in bonds by Felix:

15 About whom, when I was at Jerusalem, the chief priests and elders of the Jews informed *me*, desiring to *have* judgment against him.

16 To whom I answered, It is not the manner of the Romans to deliver any man to die, before that he which is accused have the accusers face to face, and have licence to answer for himself concerning the crime laid against him.

17 Therefore, when they were come hither, without any delay on the morrow I sat on the judgment seat, and commanded the man to be brought forth.

18 Against whom when the accusers stood up, they brought none accusation of such things as I supposed:

19 But had certain questions against him of their own superstition, and of one Jesus, which was dead, whom Paul affirmed to be alive.

20 And because I doubted of such manner of questions, I asked *him* whether he would go to Jerusalem, and there be judged of these matters.

21 But when Paul had appealed to be reserved unto the hearing of Augustus, I commanded him to be kept till I might send him to Caesar.

22 Then Agrippa said unto Festus, I would also hear the man myself. To morrow, said he, thou shalt hear him.

Falsely imprisoned, with no specific or substantial charge against him, Paul declines to go willingly back to Jerusalem, back to stand in jeopardy before the fanatical mob which had caused the crucifixion of his Lord. Instead, Roman citizen that he was, he appeals unto Caesar. And Caesar's Procurator decrees that unto Caesar shall Christ's apostle bow.

But why? Why all this imprisonment? Why these repeated mock-like-trials before one ruler after another — all to no avail as far as freeing the innocent Paul is concerned. Why does not the Lord send an angel to deliver his apostle, as he did when Peter was imprisoned by Herod? (Acts 12:1-19.)

Clearly it is the design of Deity to use Paul's imprisonment as the means of taking the testimony of Jesus to the great and the mighty of the world. The gospel is for the poor and for the privileged. It is to be "proclaimed by the weak and the simple unto the ends of the world, and before kings and rulers." (D. & C. 1:23.) What matters it that Augustus sits amid Roman might and splendor, with the power of life and death over millions of people, yet his hope, if any, of peace here and eternal life hereafter, is in the hands of the prisoner of Christ who, though in bonds, has eternal power from on high. How better could the witness of the truth be borne to Felix, Festus, Agrippa, and Augustus, with all their court retinues forced to give ear? Compare Acts 11:19-26.

1. Festus] Porcius Festus succeeded Felix as Procurator of Judea in about 58 A.D.

2-3. How intense is the hatred and bitterness of the Jews! Two years after Paul's arrest in Jerusalem, they are still plotting to kill him. Had his message been false or his success slight, Satan would long since have found other enterprises for these Jews whose self-adopted mission was to fight against God.

9. Festus, seeking to placate the Jews, is here suggesting that Paul go to Jerusalem and be tried before the Sanhedrin with the Roman Procurator present (to assure fair play!). The predestined result of such a procedure — as Paul and Festus and the Jews well knew — would have been the conviction and death of Paul.

13-22. That Paul's bonds were the result of religious bigotry and superstitution and were without legal warrant is shown clearly by Festus' recitation to King Agrippa.

PAUL TESTIFIETH BEFORE AGRIPPA

ACTS 25:23-27; 26:1-32.

23 And on the morrow, when Agrippa was come, and Bernice, with great pomp, and was entered into the place of hearing, with the chief captains, and principal men of the city, at Festus' commandment Paul was brought forth.

24 And Festus said, King Agrippa, and all men which are here present with us, ye see this man, about whom all the multitude of the Jews have dealt with me, both at Jerusalem, and *also* here, crying that he ought not to live any longer.

25 But when I found that he had committed nothing worthy of death, and that he himself hath appealed to Augustus, I have determined to send him.

26 Of whom I have no certain thing to write unto my lord. Wherefore I have brought him forth before you, and specially before thee, O king Agrippa, that, after examination had, I might have somewhat to write.

27 For it seemeth to me unreasonable to send a prisoner, and not withal to signify the crimes *laid* against him.

1 Then Agrippa said unto Paul, Thou are permitted to speak for thyself. Then Paul stretched forth the hand, and answered for himself:

2 I think myself happy, king Agrippa, because I shall answer for myself this day before thee touching all the things whereof I am excused of the Jews:

3 Especially *because I know* thee to be expert in all customs and questions which are among the Jews: wherefore I beseech thee to hear me patiently.

199

4 My manner of life from my youth, which was at the first among mine own nation at Jerusalem, know all the Jews;

5 Which knew me from the beginning, if they would testify, that after the most straitest sect of our religion I lived a Pharisee.

6 And now I stand and am judged for the hope of the promise made of God unto our fathers:

7 Unto which *promise* our twelve tribes, instantly serving *God* day and night, hope to come. For which hope's sake, king Agrippa, I am accused of the Jews.

8 Why should it be thought a thing incredible with you, that God should raise the dead?

9 I verily thought with myself, that I ought to do many things contrary to the name of Jesus of Nazareth.

10 Which thing I also did in Jerusalem: and many of the saints did I shut up in prison, having received authority from the chief priests; and when they were put to death, I gave my voice against *them.*

11 And I punished them oft in every synagogue, and compelled *them* to blaspheme; and being exceedingly mad against them, I persecuted *them* even unto strange cities.

12 Whereupon as I went to Damascus with authority and commission from the chief priests,

13 At midday, O king, I saw in the way a light from heaven, above the brightness of the sun, shining round about me and them which journeyed with me.

14 And when we were all fallen to the earth, I heard a voice speaking unto me, and saying in the Hebrew tongue, Saul, Saul, why persecutest thou me? *it is* hard for thee to kick against the pricks.

15 And I said, Who art thou, Lord? And he said, I am *Jesus* whom thou persecutest.

16 But rise, and stand upon thy feet: for I have appeared unto thee for this purpose, to make thee a minister and a witness both of these things which thou hast seen, and of those things in the which I will appear unto thee;

17 Delivering thee from the people, and *from* the Gentiles, unto whom now I send thee,

18 To open their eyes, *and* to turn *them* from darkness to light, and *from* the power of Satan unto God, that they may receive forgiveness of sins, and inheritance among them which are sanctified by faith that is in me.

19 Whereupon, O king Agrippa, I was not disobedient unto the heavenly vision:

20 But showed first unto them of Damascus, and at Jerusalem, and throughout all the coasts of

Judea, and *then* to the Gentiles, that they should repent and turn to God, and do works meet for repentance.

21 For these causes the Jews caught me in the temple, and went about to kill *me.*

22 Having therefore obtained help of God, I continue unto this day, witnessing both to small and great, saying none other things than those which the prophets and Moses did say should come:

23 That Christ should suffer, *and* that he should be the first that should rise from the dead, and should show light unto the people, and to the Gentiles.

24 And as he thus spake for himself, Festus said with a loud voice, Paul, thou art beside thyself; much learning doth make thee mad.

25 But he said, I am not mad, most noble Festus; but speak forth the words of truth and soberness.

26 For the king knoweth of these things, before whom also I speak freely: for I am persuaded that none of these things are hidden from him; for this thing was not done in a corner.

27 K i n g Agrippa, believest thou the prophets? I know that thou believest.

28 Then Agrippa said unto Paul, Almost thou persuadest me to be a Christian.

29 And Paul said, I would to God, that not only thou, but also all that hear me this day, were both almost, and altogether such as I am, except these bonds.

30 And when he had thus spoken, the king rose up, and the governor, and Bernice, and they that sat with them:

31 And when they were gone aside, they talked between themselves, saying, This man doeth nothing worthy of death or of bonds.

32 Then said Agrippa unto Festus, This man might have been set at liberty, if he had not appealed unto Caesar.

25:24. King Agrippa] Herod Agrippa II, the last of the Herodian dynasty, an expert in Jewish affairs and also a vicious and dissolute man.

25. Nothing worthy of death] Then why not release him, as a just and impartial ruler would have done? But no, it is Satan himself who governs the persecution of the saints. And Lucifer will not relent in his evil course until he is bound by a power which even he cannot resist.

27. After two years of imprisonment, the legal charges against Paul had not so much as been determined.

26:6-7. Hope of Israel] See Acts 7:1-36, especially verse 5.

8. It is just as easy to believe in a resurrection as in a creation, to believe that man will live again as to believe that he now lives; resurrection is no more of a riddle than is existence itself; mortal men, by their own power of reason, cannot explain how either of them come to be.

9-11. Paul's sincerity] See Acts 8:1b-4. **10. Saints]** See Philip. 1:1-26.

12-18. See Acts 9:1-9 and Acts 21:4; 22:1-16.

13-15. Speaking of the "bitter persecution and reviling" heaped upon him, Joseph Smith says: "I have thought since, that I felt much like Paul, when he made his defense before King Agrippa, and related the account of the vision he had when he saw a light, and heard a voice; but still there were but few who believed him; some said he was dishonest, others said he was mad; and he was ridiculed and reviled. But all this did not destroy the reality of his vision. He had seen a vision, he knew he had, and all the persecution under heaven could not make it otherwise; and though they should persecute him unto death, yet he knew, and would know to his latest breath, that he had both seen a light and heard a voice speaking unto him, and all the world could not make him think or believe otherwise. So it was with me. I had actually seen a light, and in the midst of that light I saw two Personages, and they did in reality speak to me; and though I was hated and persecuted for saying that I had seen a vision, yet it was true; and while they were persecuting me, reviling me, and speaking all manner of evil against me falsely for so saying, I was led to say in my heart: Why persecute me for telling the truth? I have actually seen a vision; and who am I that I can withstand God, or why does the world think to make me deny what I have actually seen?" (Jos. Smith 2:23-25.)

15-18. How providential it is that Luke here recounts, for the third time in his record of the Acts of the Apostles, the account of Paul's first vision. For now, from Paul's own lips, we learn the very words spoken by the Lord Jesus in calling the Apostle to stand as a witness of eternal truth to all men and to the Gentiles in particular. And the divine commission summarizes perfectly the procedures involved and the blessings resulting from the proclamation of the gospel of peace to the world.

16. A minister and a witness] One without the other does not suffice. No man can be a true minister without also being a personal witness of the divinity of the Lord; and every witness carries the commission to minister to his fellowmen. See Acts 10:36-43.

17. From the day of his first contact with spiritual reality, Paul knew he was destined to be a minister to the Gentiles. See Acts 10:21-35; 13:42-49.

18. A perfect summary of what happens when a person is converted to the truth.

20. Repent . . . and do works meet for repentance] Good works always attend repentance; obedience to God's laws is part of turning from sin to righteousness. Those who truly repent, first turn from evil, then affirmatively work the works of righteousness.

22. Witnessing] See Acts 10: 36-43. **24.** To the spiritually illiterate, accounts of visions and miracles are as the rantings of diseased minds.

PAUL USES GIFT OF SEERSHIP

ACTS 27:1-44.

1 And when it was determined that we should sail into Italy, they delivered Paul and certain other prisoners unto *one* named Julius, a centurion of Augustus' band.

2 And entering into a ship of Adramyttium, we launched, meaning to sail by the coasts of Asia; *one* Aristarchus, a Macedonian of Thessalonica, being with us.

3 And the next *day* we touched at Sidon. And Julius courteously

entreated Paul, and gave *him* liberty to go unto his friends to refresh himself.

4 And when we had launched from thence, we sailed under Cyprus, because the winds were contrary.

5 And when we had sailed over the sea of Cilicia and Pamphylia, we came to Myra, *a city* of Lycia.

6 And there the centurion found a ship of Alexandria sailing into Italy; and he put us therein.

7 And when we had sailed slowly many days, and scarce were come over against Cnidus, the wind not suffering us, we sailed under Crete, over against Salmone;

8 And, hardly passing it, came unto a place which is called The fair havens; nigh whereunto was the city *of* Lasea.

9 Now when much time was spent, and when sailing was now dangerous, because the fast was now already past, Paul admonished *them,*

10 And said unto them, Sirs, I perceive that this voyage will be with hurt and much damage, not only of the lading and ship, but also of our lives.

11 Nevertheless the centurion believed the master and the owner of the ship, more than those things which were spoken by Paul.

12 And because the haven was not commodious to winter in, the more part advised to depart thence also, if by any means they might attain to Phenice, *and there* to winter; *which is* an haven of Crete, and lieth toward the south west and north west.

13 And when the south wind blew softly, supposing that they had obtained *their* purpose, loosing *thence,* they sailed close by Crete.

14 But not long after there arose against it a tempestuous wind, called Euroclydon.

15 And when the ship was caught, and could not bear up into the wind, we let *her* drive.

16 And running under a certain island which is called Clauda, we had much work to come by the boat:

17 Which when they had taken up, they used helps, undergirding the ship; and, fearing lest they should fall into the quicksands, strake sail, and so were driven.

18 And we being exceedingly tossed with a tempest, the next *day* they lightened the ship;

19 And the third *day* we cast out with our own hands the tackling of the ship.

20 And when neither sun nor stars in many days appeared, and no small tempest lay on *us,* all

hope that we should be saved was then taken away.

21 But after long abstinence Paul stood forth in the midst of them, and said, Sirs, ye should have hearkened unto me, and not have loosed from Crete, and to have gained this harm and loss.

22 And now I exhort you to be of good cheer: for there shall be no loss of *any man's* life among you, but of the ship.

23 For there stood by me this night the angel of God, whose I am, and whom I serve,

24 Saying, Fear not, Paul; thou must be brought before Caesar: and, lo, God hath given thee all them that sail with thee.

25 Wherefore, sirs, be of good cheer: for I believe God, that it shall be even as it was told me.

26 Howbeit we must be cast upon a certain island.

27 But when the fourteenth night was come, as we were driven up and down in Adria, about midnight the shipmen deemed that they drew near to some country;

28 And sounded, and found *it* twenty fathoms: and when they had gone a little further they sounded again, and found *it* fifteen fathoms.

29 Then fearing lest we should have fallen upon rocks, they cast four anchors out of the stern, and wished for the day.

30 And as the shipmen were about to flee out of the ship, when they had let down the boat into the sea, under colour as though they would have cast anchors out of the foreship,

31 Paul said to the centurion and the soldiers, Except these abide in the ship, ye cannot be saved.

32 Then the soldiers cut off the ropes of the boat, and let her fall off.

33 And while the day was coming on, Paul besought *them* all to take meat, saying, This day is the fourteenth day that ye have tarried and continued fasting, having taken nothing.

34 Wherefore I pray you to take *some* meat: for this is for your health: for there shall not an hair fall from the head of any of you.

35 And when he had thus spoken, he took bread, and gave thanks to God in presence of them all: and when he had broken *it*, he began to eat.

36 Then were they all of good cheer, and they also took *some* meat.

37 And we were in all in the ship two hundred threescore and sixteen souls.

38 And when they had eaten enough, they lightened the ship, and cast out the wheat into the sea.

39 And when it was day, they knew not the land: but they discovered a certain creek with a shore, into the which they were minded, if it were possible, to thrust in the ship.

40 And when they had taken up the anchors, they committed *themselves* unto the sea, and loosed the rudder bands, and hoised up the mainsail to the wind, and made toward shore.

41 And falling into a place where two seas met, they ran the ship aground; and the forepart stuck fast, and remained unmove-able, but the hinder part was broken with the violence of the waves.

42 And the soldiers' counsel was to kill the prisoners, lest any of them should swim out, and escape.

43 But the centurion, willing to save Paul, kept them from *their* purpose; and commanded that they which could swim should cast *themselves* first *into the sea*, and get to land:

44 And the rest some on boards, and some on broken *pieces* of the ship. And so it came to pass, that they escaped all safe to land.

Two things stand out in these recitations covering Paul's perilous sea voyage: 1. The multitude of details which of themselves bear witness to the veracity of the account; and 2. The spiritual fortitude and power exhibited by Paul, including his exercise of the gift of seership. By fasting and faith Paul prevailed upon the Lord, who sent his angel to deliver the message, to give divine assurance of preservation for all aboard the ill fated vessel. Then he announced in advance exactly what was to happen, exhibiting thereby his powers of seership. See *Commentary I*, pp. 132-134.

33. Fasting] See Acts 12:24-25; 13:1-5.

PAUL HEALS SICK IN MELITA

ACTS 28:1-15.

1 And when they were escaped, then they knew that the island was called Melita.

2 And the barbarous people showed us no little kindness: for they kindled a fire, and received us every one, because of the present rain, and because of the cold.

3 And when Paul had gathered a bundle of sticks, and laid *them* on the fire, there came a viper

out of the heat, and fastened on his hand.

4 And when the barbarians saw the *venomous* beast hang on his hand, they said among themselves, No doubt this man is a murderer, whom, though he hath escaped the sea, yet vengeance suffereth not to live.

5 And he shook off the beast into the fire, and felt no harm.

6 Howbeit they looked when he should have swollen, or fallen down dead suddenly: but after they had looked a great while, and saw no harm come to him, they changed their minds, and said that he was a god.

7 In the same quarters were possessions of the chief man of the island, whose name was Publius; who received us, and lodged us three days courteously.

8 And it came to pass, that the father of Publius lay sick of a fever and of a bloody flux: to whom Paul entered in, and prayed, and laid his hands on him, and healed him.

9 So when this was done, others also, which had diseases in the island, came, and were healed:

10 Who also honoured us with many honours; and when we departed, they laded *us* with such things as were necessary.

11 And after three months we departed in a ship of Alexandria, which had wintered in the isle, whose sign was Castor and Pollux.

12 And landing at Syracuse, we tarried *there* three days.

13 And from thence we fetched a compass, and came to Rhegium: and after one day the south wind blew, and we came the next day to Puteoli:

14 Where we found brethren, and were desired to tarry with them seven days: and so we went toward Rome.

15 And from thence, when the brethren heard of us, they came to meet us as far as Appii forum, and The three taverns: whom when Paul saw, he thanked God, and took courage.

3-5. God preserveth his own, for, as it is written, "They shall take up serpents," and "it shall not hurt them." (Mark 16:18.)

8-9. These healings came by Paul's faith, for the heathen inhabitants of Melita as yet had not so much as heard of those truths and laws out of which faith grows. But who can doubt that Paul, during the three months of his enforced sojourn there, taught them that measure of truth which their circumstances qualified them to receive. In any event the healings stand as a witness of the wondrous goodness and grace of God, poured out liberally upon a spiritually untutored people, because of their kindness toward one of his missionaries and ministers. See Acts 3:1-16.

8. Laid his hands on them] Paul follows the prescribed pattern, ("They shall lay hands on the sick"), and the promised result ("They shall recover"), is immediately forthcoming. (Mark 16:18.) And thus again and anew does Holy Writ testify that where God's true ministers are, there the sick will be healed by the laying on of hands, and that where this gift of the Spirit is not found, there the Church and kingdom of God is not.

PAUL PREACHES IN ROME

ACTS 28:16-31.

16 And when we came to Rome, the centurion delivered the prisoners to the captain of the guard: but Paul was suffered to dwell by himself with a soldier that kept him.

17 And it came to pass, that after three days Paul called the chief of the Jews together: and when they were come together, he said unto them, Men *and* brethren, though I have committed nothing against the people, or customs of our fathers, yet was I delivered prisoner from Jerusalem into the hands of the Romans.

18 Who, when they had examined me, would have let *me* go, because there was no cause of death in me.

19 But when the Jews spake against *it*, I was constrained to appeal unto Caesar; not that I had ought to accuse my nation of.

20 For this cause therefore have I called for you, to see *you*, and to speak with *you*: because that for the hope of Israel I am bound with this chain.

21 And they said unto him, We neither received letters out of Judea concerning thee, neither any of the brethren that came showed or spake any harm of thee.

22 But we desire to hear of thee what thou thinkest: for as concerning this sect, we know that every where it is spoken against.

23 And when they had appointed him a day, there came many to him into *his* lodging; to whom he expounded and testified the kingdom of God, persuading them concerning Jesus, both out of the law of Moses, and *out* of

the prophets, from morning till evening.

24 And some believed the things which were spoken, and some believed not.

25 And when they agreed not among themselves, they departed, after that Paul had spoken one word, Well spake the Holy Ghost by Esaias the prophet unto our fathers,

26 Saying, Go unto this people, and say, Hearing ye shall hear, and shall not understand; and seeing ye shall see, and not perceive:

27 For the heart of this people is waxed gross, and their ears are dull of hearing, and their eyes have they closed; lest they should see with *their* eyes, and hear with *their* ears, and understand with *their* heart, and should be converted, and I should heal them.

28 Be it known therefore unto you, that the salvation of God is sent unto the Gentiles, and *that* they will hear it.

29 And when he had said these words, the Jews departed, and had great reasoning among themselves.

30 And Paul dwelt two whole years in his own hired house, and received all that came in unto him.

31 Preaching the kingdom of God, and teaching those things which concern the Lord Jesus Christ, with all confidence, no man forbidding him.

Now, after so long a time, imprisoned and yet free to dwell in his own hired house, Paul gains the desire of his heart — to preach in Rome! And so, for two years, he preaches the kingdom of God and testifies of Him whose kingdom it is.

20. Hope of Israel] See Acts 7:1-36, especially verse 5.

22. Satan follows a set plan; always his pattern is the same. Paul's Christianity and Joseph Smith's Mormonism — the two being the same identical system of salvation — are everywhere spoken against. And this very fact is one of the great evidences of their truth and divinity. There is no occasion for all false churches to unite against any "sect," as they are pleased to designate the true religion, unless the object of their distaste is in fact the religion of heaven, unless it is that "sect" which bringeth salvation to men. (Jos. Smith 2:20-23.)

23. He expounded and testified] Again as always Paul uses the one approved approach — teach the doctrine, then testify by the power of the Spirit that it is true.

24. Preaching the gospel always creates division among the people — some believe, some disbelieve — and to a degree this is true even within the Church. When a sound doctrinal sermon is preached by the power of the Spirit, spiritually receptive hearers echo the testimony of the speaker with a heartfelt Amen, while those with less heaven-instilled insight quibble, qualify, and reject the saving statements.

25. Isaiah (and all the prophets!) spoke by the power of the Holy Ghost.

26-27. Jesus used this same prophecy of Isaiah to describe the disbelief of that part of the house of Israel among whom he ministered. See *Commentary I*, pp. 281-285.

28. Though Paul was the Apostle to the Gentiles, in each city he went first to the Jews and thereafter to the Gentiles.

The Epistle of Paul
the Apostle to the Romans

Paul's epistle to the Romans is a paradoxical document. On the one hand it is one of the clearest and most profound doctrinal books in the Bible. On the other hand, it is the source of more doctrinal misunderstanding, misinterpretation, and mischief than any other Biblical book, not even excepting the Book of Revelation.

Four things are apparent with reference to this inspired writing of the Apostle:

1. It was written to and for and about the saints and can be understood by them and by them only.

2. It was not written to the world in general, or to any branch of sectarianism in particular, and it is not and cannot be understood by them.

3. It is the source of more sectarian confusion, more false concepts on basic points of doctrine, and results in more wresting of the scriptures, than any other inspired writing now available to men.

4. In it is found the rationale used by Luther in his break with Catholicism.

Romans is indeed a book for God's saints. It was written to those who have the gift of the Holy Ghost, who are spiritually inclined, and who already have a basic understanding of the purposes of the Lord and of his eternal plan of salvation. To such it is a highly edifying and instructive document, one that portrays gospel doctrines in such a way as to expand the mind and to enlighten the understanding. From it those with spiritual insight will gain gospel views which will add peace to their lot here and open the door to higher spiritual attainment hereafter.

Romans defines the gospel and summarizes the laws by obedience to which full salvation comes. It speaks plainly of Adam's fall, which brought death, and Christ's atoning sacrifice, which brought life. It tells how the law of justification works, how men are justified by faith and works, through the blood of Christ. In it are some of the most explicit Biblical teachings on the election of grace, the status of the chosen race, on why salvation cannot come by the law of Moses alone, on why circumcision was done away in Christ, and on how and why salvation was taken to the Gentiles. And it is a chief source of the glorious doctrine of joint-heirship with Christ, that marvelous principle under which men, through celestial marriage and the continuation of the family unit in eternity, can gain exaltation in the highest celestial heaven.

But these and other doctrines, as here presented, are hidden from the world. They are not set forth by Paul from a missionary standpoint, nor are they written with a view of doctrinal exposition. The epistle to the Romans is a letter, not a treatise on gospel subjects. It is not written to the world, but to the saints, to people who already know and understand the doctrines of salvation. Paul's comments on gospel subjects presuppose an extensive prior knowledge on the part of his readers. He does not here expound doctrines as such; he simply comments about them, leaving unsaid the volumes of gospel understanding already possessed by the saints. Romans, hence is not a source of gospel knowledge for the spiritually untutored; it is not the initial place to turn to learn of Christ and his laws. In the hands of the sectarian world, Romans is a book on calculus in the hands of students who are still struggling to learn the basics of common arithmetic.

Providentially, for this age, the Lord has given to his saints and to the world the Book of Mormon. This volume of holy writ sets forth in a pure, plain, and perfect way the true doctrines of Christ, so that those who have an understanding of its teachings are able to reconcile the difficulties and solve the problems of the epistle to the Romans.

In its very nature Romans is an epistle capable of differing interpretations. Those without prior and full knowledge of the doctrines involved find it exceedingly difficult to place Paul's comments about these doctrines into their true perspective. For instance, it is on a misunderstanding of the Apostle's statement about justification by faith alone that the whole sectarian world is led to believe that men are not required to work out their own salvation; and it was this very passage that enabled Martin Luther to justify in his own mind his break with Catholicism, an eventuality of vital importance to the furtherance of the Lord's work on earth.

Truly Romans is a book for the saints of God. They can and should understand it. From it will flow to them a wealth of gospel knowledge, and because of it, as Paul said to the Romans themselves, their salvation will be nearer than when they believed.

THE GOSPEL IS THE POWER OF GOD UNTO SALVATION

ROMANS 1:1-17.

1 Paul, a servant of Jesus Christ, called *to be* an apostle, separated unto the gospel of God,

2 (Which he had promised afore by his prophets in the holy scriptures,)

3 Concerning his Son Jesus Christ our Lord, which was made of the seed of David, according to the flesh;

4 And declared *to be* the Son of God with power, according to the spirit of holiness, by the resurrection from the dead:

5 By whom we have received grace and apostleship, for obedience to the faith among all nations, for his name:

6 Among whom are ye also the called of Jesus Christ:

7 To all that be in Rome, beloved of God, called *to be* saints: Grace to you and peace from God our Father, and the Lord Jesus Christ.

8 First, I thank my God through Jesus Christ for you all, that your faith is spoken of throughout the whole world.

9 For God is my witness, whom I serve with my spirit in the gospel of his Son, that without ceasing I make mention of you always in my prayers;

10 Making request, if by any means now at length I might have a prosperous journey by the will of God to come unto you.

213

11 For I long to see you, that I may impart unto you some spiritual gift, to the end ye may be established;

12 That is, that I may be comforted together with you by the mutual faith both of you and me.

13 Now I would not have you ignorant, brethren, that oftentimes I purposed to come unto you, (but was let hitherto,) that I might have some fruit among you also, even as among other Gentiles.

14 I am debtor both to the Greeks, and to the Barbarians; both to the wise, and to the unwise.

15 So, as much as in me is, I am ready to preach the gospel to you that are at Rome also.

16 For I am not ashamed of the gospel of Christ: for it is the power of God unto salvation to every one that believeth; to the Jew first, and also to the Greek.

17 For therein is the righteousness of God revealed from faith to faith: as it is written, The just shall live by faith.

I.V. ROMANS 1:1, 4-11, 17.

1 Paul, **an apostle, a servant of God, called of Jesus Christ, and separated to preach the gospel,**

4 And declared the Son of God with power, **by the Spirit according to the truth through** the resurrection from the dead;

5 By whom we have received grace and apostleship, **through obedience, and faith in his name, to preach the gospel among all nations;**

6 Among whom **ye also are called** of Jesus Christ;

7 **Wherefore I write to all who are** in Rome, beloved of God, **called saints;** Grace to you, and peace, from God our Father, and the Lord Jesus Christ.

8 First, I thank my God through Jesus Christ, **that you all are steadfast, and** your faith is spoken of throughout the whole world.

9 For God is my witness, **whom I serve, that without ceasing** I make mention of you always in my prayers, **that you may be kept through the Spirit, in the gospel of his Son,**

10 Making request **of you, to remember me in your prayers, I now write unto you, that you will ask him in faith, that if by any means, at length, I may serve you with my labors, and may** have a prosperous journey by the will of God, to come unto you.

11 For I long to see you, that I may impart unto you some spiritual gift, **that it may be established in you to the end;**

17 For therein is the righteousness of God revealed **through faith on his name;** as it is written, The just shall live by faith.

1. Paul] See Acts 9:19b-31; 13:50-52; 14:1-7; 1 Cor. 4:1-21. **Gospel of God . . . 3. Concerning his Son]** God the Eternal Father is the Author of the plan of salvation; he is the creator and source of the gospel; it is his; he established it and brought it into being. There were not two plans offered in the councils of eternity, only one — the Father's. Having presented his plan, having announced the need for a Redeemer who would be born into the world as his Son to put the provisions of his plan into full operation, the Father then asked: "Whom shall I send?" Two of his spirit sons volunteered; Christ was chosen and foreordained to be the Savior. The plan of salvation then became his by adoption, with the gospel thereafter being called the gospel of Jesus Christ. (Moses 4:1-4; Abra. 3:26-28; Heb. 5:8-9.) Joseph Smith said: "God himself, finding he was in the midst of spirits and glory, because he was more intelligent, saw proper to institute laws whereby the rest could have a privilege to advance like himself." (*Teachings*, p. 354.) These laws, instituted by the Father, constitute the gospel of God, which gospel is the plan by which all of his spirit children, Christ included, may gain eternal life. How apt it is, thus, for Paul to speak of it as the gospel of God concerning his Son.

2. Christ came, among other reasons, to restore the gospel, the gospel that was now his; and his work and ministry, and the mighty gospel restoration wrought by him, had been abundantly promised afore by the prophets.

3. Seed of David] See Acts 13:13-15. **4. Son of God]** Christ had power to die because he was the Seed of David and power to come forth in the resurrection because he was the Son of God. From Mary, his mother, he inherited the power to die, and from God, his Father, he inherited the power of immortality, the power to live. And the fact that he rose from the dead, that he was in fact resurrected, proves the fact of his divine Sonship!

I.V. 5. Grace and apostleship] Grace, which is an outpouring of the mercy, love, and condescension of God, and apostleship, meaning personal revelation of the divine Sonship of our Lord, these are received — not without works, not without righteousness, not without merit — but by obedience and faith!

215

6-8. To whom was the Epistle to the Romans written? To the Gentiles in Rome? To the world in general? To sectarian Christians today? Not by any means. If there is any truth the world can gain from this Epistle, such is all to the good. But Paul wrote it to the saints, to members of the Church, to those who already had the gift of the Holy Ghost, to those who had been born again, to those who held the priesthood and enjoyed the gifts of the Spirit. Hence he was writing to people who already knew the doctrines of salvation, and his teachings can only be understood by people who have the same background, the same knowledge, and the same experience as the original recipients of the message. Romans is a sealed book to the sectarian world; it is an open volume of inspiring gospel truth to the saints of God.

7. Saints] See Philip. 1:1-26. **I.V. 9-11.** Changes made in these verses in the *Inspired Version*, though not of transcendent doctrinal importance, do bear convincing witness of the inspiration resting upon the Prophet when he, by the power of the Spirit, corrected the King James Version.

16. The gospel of Christ] "The gospel of Jesus Christ is the plan of salvation. It embraces all the laws, principles, doctrines, rites, ordinances, acts, powers, authorities, and keys necessary to save and exalt men in the highest heaven hereafter. It is the covenant of salvation which the Lord makes with men on earth. Literally, gospel means good tidings from God or God-story. Thus it is the glad tidings or good news concerning Christ, his atonement, the establishment of his earthly kingdom, and a possible future inheritance in his celestial presence." (*Mormon Doctrine*, 2nd ed., p. 331.) **Word and power of gospel]** See 1 Thess. 1:1-10. **Salvation]** See 1 Peter. 1:1-16.

17. From faith to faith] From age of faith to age of faith, that is, from dispensation to dispensation. **Gospel dispensations]** See Eph. 1:9-12.

GOD IS KNOWN BY KNOWING MAN

ROMANS 1:18-25.

18 For the wrath of God is revealed from heaven against all ungodliness and unrighteousness of men, who hold the truth in unrighteousness;

19 Because that which may be known of God is manifest in them; for God hath showed *it* unto them.

20 For the invisible things of him from the creation of the world are clearly seen, being understood by the things that are made, *even* his eternal power and Godhead; so that they are without excuse:

21 Because that, when they knew God, they glorified *him* not as God, neither were thankful; but became vain in their imaginations, and their foolish heart was darkened.

22 Professing themselves to be wise, they became fools,

23 And changed the glory of the uncorruptible God into an image made like to corruptible man, and to birds, and fourfooted beasts, and creeping things.

24 Wherefore God also gave them up to uncleanness through the lusts of their own hearts, to dishonour their own bodies between themselves:

25 Who changed the truth of God into a lie, and worshipped and served the creature more than the Creator, who is blessed for ever. Amen.

I.V. ROMANS 1:18-21.

18 For the wrath of God is revealed from heaven against all ungodliness and unrighteousness of men; **who love not the truth, but remain in unrighteousness,**

19 **After** that which may be known of God is manifest **to** them.

20 For God hath **revealed unto them** the invisible things of him, from the creation of the world, **which** are clearly seen; **things which are not seen** being understood by the things that are made, **through** his eternal power and Godhead; so that they are without excuse;

21 Because that, when they knew God, they glorified him not as God, neither were they thankful, but became vain in their imaginations, and their foolish **hearts were** darkened.

Paul's reasoning here is this: God is revealed in man; that is, man as God's noblest creation, fashioned in fact in his image, is the most perfect earthly manifestation of God.

Thus to know God man has but to know himself. By introspective search in his own soul, man comes to a degree of understanding of God, including Deity's character, perfections, and attributes. As Joseph Smith said, "If men do not comprehend the character of God, they do not comprehend themselves." (*Teachings*, p. 343.)

There is thus, Paul continues, no justification or excuse for man in his wisdom to worship false gods or to turn to idols, for when man lowers his standard of worship to that which is false and corruptible, his ethical standards fall also, and he is left to every evil lust.

19. That which may be known of God, to a degree at least, is manifest in man. That is, man has a body, is endowed with reason and intellect, possesses certain characteristics, enjoys certain attributes, exercises certain powers — and so it is in greater measure with Deity. God is like man because man is like God. See Acts 17:15-34.

20. God and his doings are invisible; man and his works are seen and known; nevertheless God and his works are clearly seen and understood because they are but the perfection and enlargement of the works of man. Man lives and moves and has a being; so does God. Man thinks and reasons; so does God. Man has character, perfections, and attributes; so does God. Man obeys eternal laws and organizes the elements to create a new product; Deity speaks and worlds come rolling into existence.

21-23. Man once knew God by revelation; but this knowledge was lost because of disobedience. Then man, by foolish reason, created his own gods; some of these false gods were the sculptured likenesses of men, as those set up by the Greeks on Mars Hill; others were the images of birds and animals, as found among the Egyptians and Orientals.

25. Worship of any god other than the true God is in fact service to the creature rather than the Creator, for all things are by and from and of Deity. Anciently this meant worship of idols, or mountains, or the sun, moon, and stars. But in modern times this false worship has reached its highest form in two types of devotion: 1. The sectarian concept of God; and 2. The scientific concept of God.

God is an exalted Man from whose presence there proceeds a light and power which fills the immensity of space and which is called the Light of Christ or the Spirit of the Lord. In their worship of a spirit essence that fills immensity, the sectarians are in effect worshiping and serving the creature rather than the Creator.

Similarly when the scientists of the world speak, often in glowing and affirmative terms, of the existence of God, what they mean is that there is law and order in the universe; they mean, in effect, that gravity is God. And it just so happens that there is no more salvation in worshiping the law of gravity, or any of the other laws of the universe, than there is in worshiping a golden calf.

SIN ABOUNDS WHEN TRUTH ABOUT GOD IS LOST

ROMANS 1:26-32.

26 For this cause God gave them up unto vile affections: for even their women did change the natural use into that which is against nature:

27 And likewise also the men, leaving the natural use of the woman, burned in their lust one toward another; men with men working that which is unseemly, and receiving in themselves that recompence of their error which was meet.

28 And even as they did not like to retain God in *their* knowledge, God gave them over to a reprobate mind, to do those things which are not convenient;

29 Being filled with all unrighteousness, fornication, wickedness, covetousness, maliciousness; full of envy, murder, debate, deceit, malignity; whisperers,

30 Backbiters, haters of God, despiteful, proud, boasters, inventors of evil things, disobedient to parents,

31 Without understanding, covenantbreakers, without natural affection, implacable, unmerciful:

32 Who knowing the judgment of God, that they which commit such things are worthy of death, not only do the same, but have pleasure in them that do them.

I.V. ROMANS 1:28, 32.

28 And even as they did not like to retain God in their knowledge, God gave them over to a reprobate mind, **according to some**

219

to do those things which are not convenient:

32 **And some** knowing the judgment of God, that they which com-mit such things are **inexcusable,** not only do the same, but have pleasure in them that do them.

Knowledge of God and his laws is the greatest incentive to personal righteousness known to man. To know that God is a glorified and perfected Person, an exalted Man, a holy Being in whose image man is made; to know that man by obedience to gospel laws can attain a like exaltation; to know that this glorious reward is reserved for those who overcome the world and put first in their lives the things of God's kingdom; to know that this means that man must earn and develop for himself the attributes of godliness — all such knowledge impels man to live a godly life. After announcing that when Christ returns the faithful saints "shall be like him," meaning be glorified and exalted as he is, John adds: "And every man that hath this hope in him purifieth himself, even as he [Christ] is pure." (1 John 3:1-3.) It is no wonder, then, that man is saved no faster than he gains knowledge of God and the laws of salvation.

Conversely, the absence of the knowledge of God and his laws opens the door to a flood of evils. Those who worship false gods are denied the incentives to righteousness that come from conformity to true principles. Ethics grow out of religion, and when men depart from God and his laws, they fall into the practice of all the evils Paul here condemns.

26. For this cause] Because men "changed the truth of God into a lie," because they rejected God and his laws, they were left to wallow in evil, lust, and perversion.

26-32. In verses 26 to 28, homosexual acts of perversion and degeneracy are described. Then verses 29 to 31 say that those so debased are also filled with many heinous sins. And finally verse 32 records "that they which commit such things are worthy of death," apparently meaning that the law of the gospel prescribes the death penalty for homosexual perversions. God himself executed such a penalty on a whole people in the destruction of

Sodom and Gomorrah. (Gen. 18 and 19.) Interestingly, the Prophet's modification of verse 32 limits the application of the death penalty for such offenses to certain persons, which means those who in so sinning are rebelling against high gospel standards which they themselves have covenanted to keep.

ALL MEN JUDGED BY GOSPEL STANDARDS

ROMANS 2:1-16.

1 Therefore thou art inexcusable, O man, whosoever thou art that judgest: for wherein thou judgest another, thou condemnest thyself; for thou that judgest doest the same things.

2 But we are sure that the judgment of God is according to truth against them which commit such things.

3 And thinkest thou this, O man, that judgest them which do such things, and doest the same, that thou shalt escape the judgment of God?

4 Or despisest thou the riches of his goodness and forbearance and longsuffering; not knowing that the goodness of God leadeth thee to repentance?

5 But after thy hardness and impenitent heart treasurest up unto thyself wrath against the day of wrath and revelation of the righteous judgment of God;

6 Who will render to every man according to his deeds:

7 To them who by patient continuance in well doing seek for glory and honour and immortality, eternal life:

8 But unto them that are contentious, and do not obey the truth, but obey unrighteousness, indignation and wrath,

9 Tribulation and anguish, upon every soul of man that doeth evil, of the Jew first, and also of the Gentile;

10 But glory, honour, and peace, to every man that worketh good, to the Jew first, and also to the Gentile:

11 For there is no respect of persons with God.

12 For as many as have sinned without law shall also perish without law: and as many as have sinned in the law shall be judged by the law;

13 (For not the hearers of the law *are* just before God, but the doers of the law shall be justified.

14 For when the Gentiles, which have not the law, do by nature the things contained in the law, these, having not the law, are a law unto themselves:

221

15 Which show the work of the law written in their hearts, their conscience also bearing witness, and *their* thoughts the mean while accusing or else excusing one another;)

16 In the day when God shall judge the secrets of men by Jesus Christ according to my gospel.

I.V. ROMANS 2:1, 16.

1 Therefore thou art inexcusable, O man, whosoever thou art that judgest **thus;** for wherein thou judgest another, thou condemnest thyself; for thou that judgest doest the same things.

16 In the day when God shall judge the secrets of men by Jesus Christ according to **the** gospel.

Some few of earth's inhabitants have the gospel; the great masses of men are not so blessed; but Paul here announces that all men — all living souls, whether they have knowledge of gospel law or not — shall be judged by the law of the gospel. Specifically, he says, those who sin, having not the law, shall perish, meaning they will be condemned for disobedience to a law they never had.

This principle, Paul reasons, is implicit in the whole system of judgment according to works. It is in fact but an extension of the gospel verity that those who work righteousness shall be saved and those who do evil shall be damned. The fact is they are damned through sin whether they had the gospel law or not. And for that matter, since judgment is the Lord's and he will repay, how could anyone ever be judged by any law except his law which is gospel law?

To show the justice of such a course the Apostle, having previously named the sins of sexual perversion, murder, fornication, and wickedness of every sort, now says that the Gentiles who have not the law given them by revelation, nonetheless have the law written in their hearts so that their minds and consciences bear record that they should not violate the laws of God. This is another and quite an expressive way of saying that "the Spirit of Christ is given to every man, that he may know good from evil." (Moro. 7:16; D. & C. 84:46.) Hence every man, in and out of the Church, whether he has the gospel law or not, is accountable for his deeds and will be judged by gospel standards.

Jacob taught this same truth to the Nephites, including in his explanation the gospel verity that where there is no law there is no punishment nor condemnation, and that those without the law are delivered from death, hell, the devil, and endless torment because of the atonement. It should be noted that Jacob in so saying had already aligned his teachings with Paul's by showing that the disobedient shall be damned because of gospel law and thus that the hope he is holding out to them is simply that they will not be sons of perdition. (2 Ne. 9:23-27.) Those who die without law inherit a terrestrial kingdom. (D. & C. 76:71-72.) The wicked and rebellious go to the telestial kingdom. (D. & C. 76:98-105.)

1-3. God's eternal decree is that he himself will judge all men on the same basis used by men in judging their fellowmen. Hence the counsel, "Judge [condemn] not, that ye be not judged [condemned]. For with what judgment ye judge, ye shall be judged: and with what measure ye mete, it shall be measured to you again." (Matt. 7:1-2.) Hence also the revealed announcement that "the wrath of God shall be poured out upon the wicked without measure," and that such shall occur when "the Lord shall come to recompense unto every man according to his work, and measure to every man according to the measure which he has measured to his fellow man." (D. & C. 1:9-10.) **Judgment by works]** See Rev. 20:11-15.

4. The goodness of God leads men to repentance, meaning that "the Spirit giveth light to every man that cometh into the world; and the Spirit enlighteneth every man through the world, that hearkeneth to the voice of the Spirit. And every one that hearkeneth to the voice of the Spirit cometh unto God," and accordingly repents and is baptized so as to be an heir to God's kingdom. (D. & C. 84:46-48.)

5. The day of wrath] The Second Coming, "the day of vengeance." (D. & C. 133:51.)

6-12. Who but Paul — logician, theologian, literary craftsman that he is — could compare so expertly the rewards of righteousness and the punishments of disobedience! And who could show with more telling impact how impartially God's decrees apply to Jew and Gentile alike!

14. Do by nature] By instinct. The natural desire to do good is planted in the hearts of all men because of the Light of Christ.

16. Jesus Christ is Lord and Judge of all: "For the Father judgeth no man, but hath committed all judgment unto the Son." (John 5:22.)

MAN IS NOT JUSTIFIED BY THE LAW OF MOSES

ROMANS 2:17-29; 3:1-20.

17 Behold, thou art called a Jew, and restest in the law, and makest thy boast of God,

18 And knowest *his* will and approvest the things that are more excellent, being instructed out of the law;

19 And art confident that thou thyself art a guide of the blind, a light of them which are in darkness,

20 An instructor of the foolish, a teacher of babes, which hast the form of knowledge and of the truth in the law.

21 Thou therefore which teachest another, teachest thou not thyself? thou that preachest a man should not steal, dost thou steal?

22 Thou that sayest a man should not commit adultery, dost thou commit adultery? thou that abhorrest idols, dost thou commit sacrilege?

23 Thou that makest thy boast of the law, through breaking the law dishonourest thou God?

24 For the name of God is blasphemed among the Gentiles through you, as it is written.

25 For circumcision verily profiteth, if thou keep the law: but if thou be a breaker of the law, thy circumcision is made uncircumcision.

26 Therefore if the uncircumcision keep the righteousness of the law, shall not his uncircumcision be counted for circumcision?

27 And shall not uncircumcision which is by nature, if it fulfil the law, judge thee, who by the letter and circumcision dost transgress the law?

28 For he is not a Jew, which is one outwardly; neither *is that* circumcision, which is outward in the flesh:

29 But he *is* a Jew, which is one inwardly; and circumcision *is*

that of the heart, in the spirit, *and* not in the letter; whose praise *is* not of men, but of God.

1 What advantage then hath the Jew? or what profit *is there* of circumcision?

2 Much every way: chiefly, because that unto them were committed the oracles of God.

3 For what if some did not believe? shall their unbelief make the faith of God without effect?

4 God forbid: yea, let God be true, but every man a liar; as it is written, That thou mightest be justified in thy sayings, and mightest overcome when thou art judged.

5 But if our unrighteousness commend the righteousness of God, what shall we say? *Is* God unrighteous w h o taketh vengeance? (I speak as a man)

6 God forbid: for then how shall God judge the world?

7 For if the truth of God hath more abounded through my lie unto his glory; why yet am I also judged as a sinner?

8 And not *rather*, (as we be slanderously reported, and as some affirm that we say,) Let us do evil, that good may come? whose damnation is just.

9 What then? are we better *than they?* No, in no wise: for we have before proved both Jews and Gentiles, that they are all under sin;

10 As it is written, There is none righteous, no, not one:

11 There is none that understandeth, there is none that seeketh after God.

12 They are all gone out of the way, they are together become unprofitable; there is none that doeth good, no, not one.

13 Their throat *is* an open sepulchre; with their tongues they have used deceit; the poison of asps *is* under their lips:

14 Whose mouth *is* full of cursing and bitterness:

15 Their feet *are* swift to shed blood:

16 Destruction and misery *are* in their ways:

17 And the way of peace have they not known:

18 There is no fear of God before their eyes.

19 Now we know that what things soever the law saith, it saith to them who are under the law: that every mouth may be stopped, and all the world may become guilty before God.

20 Therefore by the deeds of the law there shall no flesh be justified in his sight: for by the law *is* the knowledge of sin.

I.V. ROMANS 3:1-2, 5, 7-9, 20.

1 What advantage then hath the Jew **over the Gentile?** or what profit of circumcision, **who is not a Jew from the heart?**

2 **But he who is a Jew from the heart, I say hath** much every way; chiefly because that unto them were committed the oracles of God.

5 But if **we remain in** our unrighteousness **and** commend the righteousness of God, **how dare we say, God is unrighteous** who taketh vengeance? (I speak as a man **who fears God,**)

7 For if the truth of God hath more abounded through my lie,

(as it is called of the Jews,) unto his glory; why yet am I also judged as a sinner? **and not received? Because we are** slanderously reported;

8 **And** some affirm that we say, **(whose damnation is just,)** Let us do evil that good may come. **But this is false.**

9 **If not so; what then** are we better than they? No, in no wise; for we have **proved before, that Jews and Gentiles** are all under sin.

20 **For by the law is the knowledge of sin; therefore by the deeds of the law shall no flesh be justified in his sight.**

As a prelude to his great proclamation that men are justified by faith in Christ, without reference to the performances of the Mosaic law, Paul here discusses the status of the Jews, through whom the Mosaic requirements were revealed.

Yes, the Jews of old were favored above all people because they alone had the laws of salvation and knew the mind of God. Yes, the Jews had the law of Moses and were therefore under greater obligation to conform to righteous principles than were other men. Yes, the law of circumcision profited men anciently because it bore record of their covenant with and devotion to the God of Israel.

But, No, the Jews of Paul's day were no better off than their Gentile associates because they no longer walked in the paths of their fathers. No, they were no longer lights to the world because they violated the laws which God had given them. No, there was no longer preferential status for them because the gospel is now for all men. No, they were not justified (and thus saved) through conformity to Mosaic principles alone.

And, Yes, as he was now ready to say, both Jew and Gentile must turn to Christ, and worship and serve him with full purpose of heart, to be justified through the cleansing power of his blood. See Acts 15:1-35; Rom. 3:21-31.

2:17-20. The Jews considered themselves to be God's chosen people. Having the law of Moses, they assumed the prerogative to stand as lights to the world and as teachers for all mankind.

21-24. But when violators of the law do the teaching, their professions of religion and morality lead to sacrilege and blasphemy.

25-29. Those to whom Paul is writing know that the law of Moses has been fulfilled, and that circumcision — as a witness of Abrahamic descent, and as a symbol of conformity to Mosaic standards — is no longer a required ordinance for the Lord's people. See Acts 15:1-35. Hence the Apostle explains that there is no reason for circumcision unless the law of Moses is in force; that the righteousness of the Gentiles is as acceptable as though they had the law of Moses; that even under the law, the outward rite of circumcision had no value unless one's heart was right before God and the circumcised person did in fact live the law.

On this same basis we could reason that the outward ordinance of baptism availeth nothing unless there is an inward desire to conform to gospel standards. Thus the true circumcision is that of the heart and the true baptism that of those who are humble and contrite, who repent and covenant to serve God, and who "manifest by their works that they have received of the Spirit of Christ unto the remission of their sins." (D. & C. 20:37.)

I.V. 3:1-2. God is no respecter of persons; Jew and Gentile stand on equal footing before him. But those ancient Israelites who were Jews from the heart, that is who believed the law of God, held a preferential position, because they alone had the revealed plan of salvation. Jesus spoke similarly by saying, "Salvation is of the Jews." (John 4:22.) They were the ones to whom God had spoken.

3. That some of Jewish-Israel of old had rejected the law does not mean the whole nation had been cast off.

4-6; I.V. 5. God is justified in judging and taking vengeance upon those who do not repent and who remain in their unrighteousness.

I.V. 7-9. Paul's reasoning is to this effect: 'The Jews say my teachings are false, and yet they admit good comes from them; but if the fruit is good the tree must be good. The Jews say, slanderously, that I encourage evil to further the work. But those who so claim shall be damned, for my true teaching is that all men are under sin, Jew and Gentile alike, and that to be saved all must come to Christ.'

This same reasoning is common today. People say: 'The fruits of Mormonism are marvelous; their missionary system, their auxiliary organizations, their welfare plan, their building program, and so forth — all these are examples of pure Christianity in action; but their doctrines, their views on theological matters, these are damning.' And the obvious reply is that "a corrupt tree" cannot "bring forth good fruit." "Do men gather grapes of thorns, or figs of thistles?" (Matt. 7:15-20.)

Continuing to follow the pattern of Paul's day, modern enemies of the truth even say: 'Mormons encourage evil to further their cause (plural marriage, for instance, as they falsely suppose).' And the reply today is as it was in Paul's day: 'All such shall be damned, for the true teachings of the restored gospel is that men must accept Christ and obey his laws to be saved.'

9-20. To clinch his argument that no flesh is justified (and therefore saved!) by the deeds of the Mosaic law alone, Paul then quotes six Old Testament passages (Ps. 14:1-3; 5:9; 140:3; 10:7; Isa. 59:7-8; Ps. 36:1) to prove that all men — including those who had the law — are under sin. This reasoning is prelude to his coming announcement that all men, both Jew and Gentile, are justified by faith in Christ.

Justification] See Rom. 3:21-31.

"MAN IS JUSTIFIED BY FAITH"

ROMANS 3:21-31.

21 But now the righteousness of God without the law is manifested, being witnessed by the Law and the Prophets;

22 Even the righteousness of God *which is* by faith of Jesus Christ unto all and upon all them that believe: for there is no difference:

23 For all have sinned, and come short of the glory of God;

24 Being justified freely by his grace through the redemption that is in Christ Jesus:

25 Whom God hath set forth *to be* a propitiation through faith in his blood, to declare his righteousness for the remission of sins that are past, through the forbearance of God;

26 To declare, *I say,* at this time his righteousness: that he might be just, and the justifier of him which believeth in Jesus.

27 Where *is* boasting then? It is excluded. By what law? of works? Nay: but by the law of faith.

28 Therefore we conclude that a man is justified by faith without the deeds of the law.

29 *Is he* the God of the Jews only? *is he* not also of the Gentiles? Yes, of the Gentiles also:

30 Seeing *it is* one God, which shall justify the circumcision by faith, and uncircumcision through faith.

31 Do we then make void the law through faith? God forbid: yea, we establish the law.

I.V. ROMANS 3:24, 28, 30.

24 **Therefore** being justified freely by his grace through the redemption that is **only** in Christ Jesus;

28 Therefore we conclude that a man is justified by faith **alone** without the deeds of the law.

30 **Seeing that God will** justify the circumcision by faith, and uncircumcision through faith.

Many Protestants attach greater importance to Paul's statements about being justified by faith alone than they do to almost any other single thing in the Bible. They so interpret these pronouncements as to "justify" themselves in breaking from the Catholic fold; and they erroneously conclude that men are saved by grace alone without doing the works of righteousness.

What is lacking in the sectarian world is a true knowledge of the law of justification. Simply stated that law is this: " 'All covenants, contracts, bonds, obligations, oaths, vows, performances, connections, associations, or expectations' (D. & C. 132:7), in which men must abide to be saved and exalted, must be entered into and performed in righteousness so that the Holy Spirit can justify the candidate for salvation in what has been done. (1 Ne. 16:2; Jac. 2:13-14; Alma 41:15; D. & C. 98; 132:1, 62.) An act that is justified by the Spirit is one that is sealed by the Holy Spirit of Promise, or in other words, ratified and approved by the Holy Ghost. This law of justification is the provision the Lord has placed in the gospel to assure that no unrighteous performance will be binding on earth and in heaven, and that no person will add to his position or glory in the hereafter by gaining an unearned blessing.

"As with all other doctrines of salvation, justification is available because of the atoning sacrifice of Christ, but it becomes operative in the life of an individual only on conditions of personal righteousness. As Paul taught, men are not justified by the works of the Mosaic law alone any more than men are saved by those works alone. The grace of God, manifest through the infinite and eternal atonement wrought by his Son, makes justification a living reality for those who seek righteousness. (Isa. 53:11; Mosiah 14:11.)" (*Mormon Doctrine*, 2nd ed., p. 408.)

21-28. Paul reasons and announces: All men have sinned; none, accordingly, are eligible to receive the glory of God, or in other words, to be saved. How, then, can sinners be saved? What will free them from their burden of sin and leave them clean and spotless? Or, as he expresses it, how can they be justified, meaning how can they be accounted and adjudged to be righteous?

He has already shown there was no power in the law of Moses to do this, for those who had the law, as his quotations proved, were still in their sins. But, he proclaims, by the grace of God redemption from sin is available through Christ. Through his blood all men, Jew and Gentile alike, can gain a remission of their sins.

"MAN IS JUSTIFIED BY FAITH"

What price must men pay for this precious gift? Not conformity to Mosaic standards, not compliance with the ordinances and performances of a dead law, but the price of faith, faith in the Lord Jesus Christ, faith that includes within itself enduring works of righteousness, which faith cannot so much as exist unless and until men conform their lives to gospel standards.

Does salvation come, then, by works? No, not by the works of the law of Moses, and for that matter, not even by the more perfect works of the gospel itself. Salvation comes through Christ's atonement, through the ransom he paid, the propitiation he made; without this no good works on the part of men could redeem them from temporal death, which redemption is resurrection, or redeem them from spiritual death, which redemption is eternal life.

Apparently there were some Roman converts from Judaism who believed the false concept that salvation came through the law of Moses alone, and hence the need for Paul to take the approach and make the explanations here given. That there had been, two hundred years before on the American continent, those who had this false view of the law of Moses, we do know from the Book of Mormon account. To them, Abinadi, discussing these matters said:

"And now ye have said that salvation cometh by the law of Moses. I say unto you that it is expedient that ye should keep the law of Moses as yet; but I say unto you, that the time shall come when it shall no more be expedient to keep the law of Moses. And moreover, I say unto you, that salvation doth not come by the law alone; and were it not for the atonement, which God himself shall make for the sins and iniquities of his people, that they must unavoidably perish, notwithstanding the law of Moses." (Mosiah 13:27-28.)

21. The prophets and teachers in the days of the law of Moses taught that salvation would be offered to the Gentiles who did not have the law.

22. This salvation would come to all through faith in Christ.

24. **His grace]** See Eph. 2:1-10. **Redemption]** See Rev. 5:1-14.

25. Propitiation] See 1 John 1:8-10; 2:1-2. **His blood]** See Heb. 10:1-18.

26. Paul here says that God is just, in that he punishes the sinner, and at the same time that he is a justifier of those who believe in Christ, in that such receive mercy and are not punished. This same principle is taught by Alma in these words: "According to justice, the plan of redemption could not be brought about, only on conditions of repentance of men in this probationary state, yea, this preparatory state; for except it were for these conditions, mercy could not take effect except it should destroy the work of justice. Now the work of justice could not be destroyed; if so, God would cease to be God. And thus we see that all mankind were fallen, and they were in the grasp of justice; yea, the justice of God, which consigned them forever to be cut off from his presence. And now, the plan of mercy could not be brought about except an atonement should be made; therefore God himself atoneth for the sins of the world, to bring about the plan of mercy, to appease the demands of justice, that God might be a perfect, just God, and a merciful God also." (Alma 42:13-15.)

27. The law of faith] Faith operates by law. To obtain faith men must abide the law upon which its receipt is predicated. To exercise the power that is faith men must obey the laws governing such usage. "Three things are necessary in order that any rational and intelligent being may exercise faith in God unto life and salvation," the Prophet Joseph Smith taught. These he named as: 1. " 'The idea that he actually exists'; 2. 'A correct idea of his character, perfections, and attributes'; and 3. 'An actual knowledge that the course of life which he is pursuing is according to his will.' " (*Mormon Doctrine*, 2nd ed., p. 262.) See Heb. 11:1-3.

Those who exercise faith, always and invaringly work miracles, and possess the gifts and signs promised the faithful. Thus when Paul says a man is justified by faith, he means he is justified only if he is keeping the commandments and so living that he has power to work miracles and display the fruits of faith.

30. The circumcision] Jews. **Uncircumcision]** Gentiles.

31. By turning to Christ, those who had the law of Moses fulfil and do honor to that very law, for Christ himself gave the law, and the law was designed to point Israel's attention forward to the coming of Christ and the higher law which he would bring. (Mosiah 13:29-32.)

MAN IS JUSTIFIED BY FAITH, WORKS, AND GRACE

ROMANS 4:1-25.

1 What shall we say then that Abraham our father, as pertaining to the flesh, hath found?

2 For if Abraham were justified by works, he hath *whereof* to glory; but not before God.

3 For what saith the scripture? Abraham believed God, and it was counted unto him for righteousness.

4 Now to him that worketh is the reward not reckoned of grace, but of debt.

5 But to him that worketh not, but believeth on him that justifieth the ungodly, his faith is counted for righteousness.

6 Even as David also describeth the blessedness of the man, unto whom God imputeth righteousness without works,

7 *Saying*, Blessed *are* they whose iniquities are forgiven, and whose sins are covered.

8 Blessed *is* the man to whom the Lord will not impute sin.

9 *Cometh* this blessedness then upon the circumcision *only*, or upon the uncircumcision also? for we say that faith was reckoned to Abraham for righteousness.

10 How was it then reckoned? when he was in circumcision, or in uncircumcision? Not in circumcision, but in uncircumcision.

11 And he received the sign of circumcision, a seal of the righteousness of the faith which *he had yet* being uncircumcised: that he might be the father of all them that believe, though they be not circumcised; that righteousness might be imputed unto them also:

12 And the father of circumcision to them who are not of the circumcision only, but who also walk in the steps of that faith of our father Abraham, which *he had* being *yet* uncircumcised.

13 For the promise, that he should be the heir of the world, *was* not to Abraham, or to his seed, through the law, but through the righteousness of faith.

14 For if they which are of the law *be* heirs, faith is made void,

and the promise made of none effect:

15 Because the law worketh wrath: for where no law is, *there is* no transgression.

16 Therefore *it is* of faith, that *it might be* by grace; to the end the promise might be sure to all the seed; not to that only which is of the law, but to that also which is of the faith of Abraham; who is the father of us all,

17 (As it is written, I have made thee a father of many nations,) before him whom he believed, *even* God, who quickeneth the dead, and calleth those things which be not as though they were.

18 Who against hope believed in hope, that he might become the father of many nations according to that which was spoken, So shall thy seed be.

19 And being not weak in faith, he considered not his own body now dead, when he was about an hundred years old, neither yet the deadness of Sarah's womb:

20 He staggered not at the promise of God through unbelief; but was strong in faith, giving glory to God;

21 And being fully persuaded that, what he had promised, he was able also to perform.

22 And therefore it was imputed to him for righteousness.

23 Now it was not written for his sake alone, that it was imputed to him;

24 But for us also, to whom it shall be imputed, if we believe on him that raised up Jesus our Lord from the dead;

25 Who was delivered for our offences, and was raised again for our justification.

I.V. ROMANS 4:2, 4-7, 16.

2 For if Abraham were justified by **the law of** works, he hath to glory **in himself;** but not of God.

4 Now to him **who is justified by the law of works, is the reward reckoned, not of grace,** but of debt.

5 But to him that **seeketh not to be justified by the law of works,** but believeth on him **who** justifieth **not** the ungodly, his faith is counted for righteousness.

6 Even as David also describeth the blessedness of the man, unto whom God imputeth righteousness without **the law of works,**

7 Saying, Blessed are they **through faith** whose iniquities are forgiven, and whose sins are covered.

16 Therefore **ye are justified of faith and works, through grace,** to the end the promise might be sure to all the seed; not to **them** only **who** are of the law, but to **them** also **who are** of the faith of Abraham; who is the father of us all,

MAN IS JUSTIFIED BY FAITH, WORKS, AND GRACE

Having taught that man is justified by faith in Christ, because of the atonement, and not by the performances of the law of Moses, Paul now takes Abraham as the illustration of this doctrine — Abraham who was justified before there was a law of Moses, Abraham whose faith and works ranked him with the justified before the rite of circumcision was revealed. The high point of the Apostle's presentation, as clarified by the Inspired Version account, is that man is "justified of faith and works, through grace" (*Inspired Version*, v. 16), or, as Nephi expressed it, "Believe in Christ, and . . . be reconciled to God; for we know that it is by grace that we are saved, after all we can do." (2 Ne. 25:23.)

1. Abraham our Father, as pertaining to the flesh] God was their Father — the literal Father of their spirits, the adopted Father of those who had been born again. But men also have fathers of the flesh. (Heb. 12:9.) Abraham was theirs, thus showing that Paul's present remarks were directed, not to Gentiles, but to Jewish converts to Christianity.

2. If Abraham had power to save and redeem himself, he could justly claim the glory that now belongs to Him through whom salvation comes.

3. Abraham believed God] Abraham had faith in Christ, repented of his sins, was baptized in water, received the gift of the Holy Ghost, held the Melchizedek Priesthood, entered into the new and everlasting covenant of marriage, kept the commandments, received revelations, saw visions, entertained angels, walked with God, and was one of the greatest prophets who ever lived. Truly, he believed God; and building on the foundation of the promised atoning sacrifice, he worked out his salvation with fear and trembling before that holy being; and of course he was justified, meaning his course of conduct was imputed unto him for righteousness.

4. But even righteous Abraham could not atone for his own sins. God's grace, manifest through Christ, must ransom him and all men from the fall of Adam.

5. As with Abraham, so with all men. If they will rely on Christ — knowing that he alone can pay the ransom, and that God will not justify the ungodly — they can turn to God, do the works of Abraham, and have their faith counted unto them for righteousness as was his. "Go ye, therefore, and do the works of Abraham; enter ye into my law and ye shall be saved," saith the Lord. (D. & C. 132:32.)

6-8. Blessed are those whose sins are forgiven. **9.** Is this forgiveness reserved only for those who are circumcised? **10.** No, it came to Abraham before he was circumcised. **11.** And then came circumcision as a token and seal of the faith through which already he had been justified.

11. Father of all them that believe] Such is the promise of God unto Abraham, a promise made without reference to lineage or birth as the literal seed of this man who was the Friend of God. The exact words of the divine promise are: "And I will bless them through thy name; for as many as receive this Gospel shall be called after thy name, and shall be accounted thy seed, and shall rise up and bless thee, as their father." (Abra. 2:10.)

13. God's promises, thus, are to those who have faith, irrespective of ancestry. **14.** If not so, that is, if men were saved because of birth in a particular lineage, the promises would be void, for the promises are that all men who have faith shall be saved and be adopted into the lineage of Abraham.

15. The law worketh wrath] Because Israel had the law of Moses, they were favored and blessed above other nations, and yet the law was in fact an outpouring of the wrath of God upon those whom he had chosen to be his own peculiar people. First Deity had given them the fulness of his everlasting gospel, the same gospel Paul was now preaching; they had been commanded to sanctify themselves that they might behold his face, enter into his rest, and gain "the fulness of his glory." "But they hardened their hearts and could not endure his presence; therefore, the Lord in his wrath, for his anger was kindled against them," took from them the gospel and gave them instead a lesser law, the law of Moses. This substitute law, severe and strict in nature, was "the law of carnal commandments, which the Lord in his wrath caused to continue with the house of Aaron among the children of Israel until John." (D. & C. 84:23-27.) It was, as Abinadi expressed it, "a very strict law, . . . a law of performances and of ordinances, a law which they were to observe strictly from day to day, to keep them in remembrance of God and their duty towards him." (Mosiah 13:29-30.)

Where no law is, there is no transgression] The Gentiles who did not have the law of Moses could not be condemned for not living in harmony with its provisions.

I.V. 16. Ye are justified of faith and works, through grace] A perfect, revealed summary of how men are justified! And, as the balance of the verse shows, this process of working out one's salvation applies equally to the literal seed and the adopted seed of Abraham, "who is the father of us all."

Grace] "God's grace consists in his love, mercy, and condescension toward his children. All things that exist are manifestations of the grace of God. The creation of the earth, life itself, the atonement of Christ, the plan of salvation, kingdoms of immortal glory hereafter, and the supreme gift of eternal life — all these things come by the grace of him whose we are.

"Grace is granted to men proportionately as they conform to the standards of personal righteousness that are part of the gospel plan. Thus the saints are commanded to 'grow in grace' (D. & C. 50:40), until they are sanctified and justified, 'through the grace of our Lord and Savior Jesus Christ.' (D. & C. 20:30-32.) Grace is an attribute of perfection possessed by Deity (D. & C. 66:12; 84:102), and Christ himself 'received grace for grace' until finally he gained the fulness of the Father. The same path to perfection is offered to man. 'If you keep my commandments,' the Lord says, 'you shall receive of his fulness, and be glorified in me as I am in the Father; therefore, I say unto you, you shall receive grace for grace.' (D. & C. 93:6-20.)" (*Mormon Doctrine*, 2nd ed., pp. 338-339.)

Salvation by grace] See Eph. 2:1-10. **Falling from grace]** See Heb. 10:19-39. **Justification]** See Rom. 3:21-31.

17-22. Abraham's mighty faith was tested and proved in two ways: 1. He believed God would give Sarah a son, though he and she were past the normal childbearing age; and 2. He believed God would raise Isaac from the dead, if need be, to fulfil the promise, "In Isaac shall thy seed be called." (Gen. 21:12; Heb. 11:17-18.)

23-24. Abraham is a pattern for us. If we believe in Christ as he did, it shall be imputed unto us for righteousness as it was unto him.

25. The very atoning sacrifice itself was wrought out by the Son of God so that men might be justified, that is, so they could do the things which will give them eternal life in the celestial realm. (D. & C. 20:21-30.)

MAN IS JUSTIFIED THROUGH THE BLOOD OF CHRIST

ROMANS 5:1-11.

1 Therefore being justified by faith, we have peace with God through our Lord Jesus Christ:

2 By whom also we have access by faith into this grace wherein we stand, and rejoice in hope of the glory of God.

3 And not only *so*, but we glory in tribulations also: knowing that tribulation worketh patience;

4 And patience, experience; and experience, hope:

5 And hope maketh not ashamed; because the love of God is shed abroad in our hearts by the Holy Ghost which is given unto us.

6 For when we were yet without strength, in due time Christ died for the ungodly.

7 For scarcely for a righteous man will one die: yet peradventure for a good man some would even dare to die.

8 But God commendeth his love toward us, in that, while we were yet sinners, Christ died for us.

9 Much more then, being now justified by his blood, we shall be saved from wrath through him.

10 For if, when we were enemies, we were reconciled to God by the death of his Son, much more, being reconciled, we shall be saved by his life.

11 And not only *so*, but we also joy in God through our Lord Jesus Christ, by whom we have now received the atonement.

MAN IS JUSTIFIED THROUGH THE BLOOD OF CHRIST

Salvation and all things incident thereto center in, revolve around, and are founded upon the atoning sacrifice of Christ. The blessings of baptism and celestial marriage, the sanctifying power of the Spirit, redemption from temporal and spiritual death, eternal life and exaltation — indeed, all spiritual blessings — are living realities because of the atonement. Without that infinite and eternal sacrifice they would not exist, and the whole plan of salvation would fade away into nothingness and be of no value.

Hence, Paul says, truly and properly, that we are justified by Christ's blood. Strictly speaking men are sanctified by the Spirit, and they are justified by the Spirit; but in a larger sense, they are sanctified by the blood, and they are justified by the blood, because the blood of Christ (meaning his atonement, wherein he shed his blood) is the foundation upon which all things rest. Thus, by way of accurate exposition, we are justified by the Spirit because of the blood of Christ. See Heb. 10:1-18. (Mosiah 3:18; 3 Ne. 27:19-20; Moses 6:59-60.)

1. Justified by faith] See Rom. 3:21-31. **Peace with God]** There are only two possible courses for men to pursue: 1. As a friend of God, to be at peace with him; or 2. As his enemy, to be at war with him. Those who keep his commandments and are justified by faith are his friends and have peace with him; those who walk after the manner of the world are his enemies and are at war with him. (See explanation of verse 10 below.) The only way men can gain peace with God is through Christ and obedience to his laws.

2. Grace] See Rom. 4:1-25. **Rejoice in hope of the glory of God]** Rejoice in hope of eternal life, which is God's life and hence consists of the glory of God.

3. We glory in tribulations] See 2 Cor. 7:1-16. **Patience]** See Jas. 5:7-11.

4. Experience] Such is a necessary part of our mortal probation. Of the trials, tribulations, and persecutions heaped upon Joseph Smith, the Lord said: "All these things shall give thee experience, and shall be for thy good." (D. & C. 122:7.) **Hope]** See Rom. 8:20-25.

5. The love of God] Similar language to that of Paul is found in the record of Nephi's conversation with an angel. The heavenly visitant asked: "Knowest thou the meaning of the tree which thy father saw?" Nephi replied: "Yea, it is the love of God, which sheddeth itself abroad in the hearts of the children of men; wherefore, it is the most desirable above all things." To this the angel responded: "Yea, and the most joyous to the soul." (1 Ne. 11:21-23.)

6-9. Herein is the perfect manifestation of the love of God — that he gave his Only Begotten Son to ransom us from the fall. Thus Christ died for us, for sinners, for the ungodly, for all men, that through his blood all might be saved from the wrath of God that awaits the wicked.

10. We were enemies . . . to God] God has friends and he has enemies; his friends love and serve him; his enemies hate and defy him. True, his enemies may pay lip service to his cause, but they reject him by refusing to conform to the laws he has revealed. His friends seek to strengthen the cause of godliness and truth in the world; his enemies choose to walk after the manner of the world and promote that which is carnal and evil. Hence James said: "Know ye not that the friendship of the world is enmity with God? whosoever therefore will be a friend of the world is the enemy of God." (Jas. 4:4.) And the angel said to King Benjamin: "The natural man is an enemy to God, and has been from the fall of Adam, and will be, forever and ever, unless he yields to the enticings of the Holy Spirit, and putteth off the natural man and becometh a saint through the atonement of Christ the Lord, and becometh as a child, submissive, meek, humble, patient, full of love, willing to submit to all things which the Lord seeth fit to inflict upon him, even as a child doth submit to his father." (Mosiah 3:19.)

Reconciled to God] See 2 Cor. 5:12-21. **Saved by his life]** Salvation comes because Christ rose from the dead; without the seal of resurrection, the atoning sacrifice would have failed.

11. The atonement] See Rom. 5:12-21.

ADAM FELL, CHRIST ATONED, MAN SAVED

ROMANS 5:12-21.

12 Wherefore, as by one man sin entered into the world, and death by sin; and so death passed upon all men, for that all have sinned:

13 (For until the law sin was in the world: but sin is not imputed when there is no law.

14 Nevertheless death reigned from Adam to Moses, even over them that had not sinned after the similitude of Adam's transgression, who is the figure of him that was to come.

15 But not as the offence, so also *is* the free gift. For if through the offence of one many be dead, much more the grace of God, and the gift by grace, *which is* by one man, Jesus Christ, hath abounded unto many.

16 And not as *it was* by one that sinned, *so is* the gift: for the judgment *was* by one to condemnation, but the free gift *is* of many offences unto justification.

17 For if by one man's offence death reigned by one; much more they which receive abundance of grace and of the gift of righteousness shall reign in life by one, Jesus Christ.)

18 Therefore as by the offence of one *judgment came* upon all

men to condemnation; even so by the righteousness of one *the free gift came* upon all men unto justification of life.

19 For as by one man's disobedience many were made sinners, so by the obedience of one shall many be made righteous.

20 Moreover the law entered, that the offence might abound. But where sin abounded, grace did much more abound:

21 That as sin hath reigned unto death, even so might grace reign through righteousness unto eternal life by Jesus Christ our Lord.

I.V. ROMANS 5:13-15.

13 (For, **before** the law, sin was in the world; **yet** sin is not imputed **to those who have** no law.

14 **For I say that through the offence,** death reigned from Adam to Moses, even over them that had not sinned after the similitude of Adam's transgression, who is the figure of him that was to come.

15 **But the offence is not as the free gift, for the gift aboundeth.** For, if through the offence of one, many be dead; much more the grace of God, and the gift by grace, **hath abounded** by one man, Jesus Christ, unto many.

241

"Nothing in the entire plan of salvation compares in any way in importance with that most transcendent of all events, the atoning sacrifice of our Lord. It is the most important single thing that has ever occurred in the entire history of created things; it is the rock foundation upon which the gospel and all other things rest. Indeed, all 'things which pertain to our religion are only appendage to it,' the Prophet said. (*Teachings*, p. 121.)

"The doctrine of the atonement embraces, sustains, supports, and gives life and force to all other gospel doctrines. It is the foundation upon which all truth rests, and all things grow out of it and come because of it. Indeed, the atonement is the gospel. . . .

"Salvation comes because of the atonement. Without it the whole plan of salvation would be frustrated and the whole purpose behind the creating and populating of the earth would come to naught. With it the eternal purposes of the Father will roll forth, the purpose of creation be preserved, the plan of salvation made efficacious, and men will be assured of a hope of the highest exaltation hereafter. (*Doctrines of Salvation*, vol. 1, pp. 121-138.) . . .

"A knowledge of two great truths is essential to an understanding of the doctrine of the atonement: 1. The fall of Adam; and 2. The divine Sonship of our Lord.

"Adam's fall brought spiritual and temporal death into the world. Spiritual death is to be cast out of the presence of the Lord (2 Ne. 9:6) and to die as pertaining to things of righteousness, or in other words things of the Spirit. (Hela. 14:15-18.) Temporal death or natural death is the separation of body and spirit, the body going back to the dust from which it was created and the spirit to a world of waiting spirits to await the day of the resurrection.

"To atone is to ransom, reconcile, expiate, redeem, reclaim, absolve, propitiate, make amends, pay the penalty. Thus the atonement of Christ is designed to ransom men from the effects of the fall of Adam in that both spiritual and temporal death are conquered; their lasting effect is nullified. The spiritual death of the fall is replaced by the spiritual life of the atonement, in that all who believe and obey the gospel law gain spiritual or eternal life — life in the presence of God where those who enjoy it are alive to things of righteousness or things of the Spirit. The temporal death of the fall is replaced by the state of immortality which comes because of the atonement and resurrection of our Lord. The body and spirit which separated, incident to what men call the natural death, are reunited in immortality, in an inseparable connection that never again will permit the mortal body to see corruption. (Alma 11:37-45; 12:16-18.) Immortality comes as a free gift, by the grace of God alone, without works of righteousness. Eternal life is the reward for 'obedience to the laws and ordinances of the Gospel.' (Third Article of Faith.)

" 'Adam fell that men might be; and men are, that they might have joy,' Lehi says. 'And the Messiah cometh in the fulness of time, that he may redeem the children of men from the fall.' (2 Ne. 2:25-26.) 'The atonement,' King Benjamin explains, 'was prepared from the foundation of the world for all mankind, which ever were since the fall of Adam, or who are, or who ever shall be, even unto the end of the world.' (Mosiah 4:7.)" (*Mormon Doctrine*, 2nd ed., pp. 60-66; 268-269.) See *Commentary I*, pp. 143-145; 853-856.

12-21. Paul's difficult and complex teachings on the fall and atonement, and on the blessings that flow therefrom, are presented simply and clearly by various Book of Mormon prophets.

As to Adam bringing death — temporal death and spiritual death — into the world —

Lehi taught, "If Adam had not transgressed he would not have fallen, but he would have remained in the garden of Eden." (2 Ne. 2:22.)

Alma amplified this by saying, "The Lord God sent our first parents forth from the garden of Eden, to till the ground, from whence they were taken. . . . But behold, it was appointed unto man to die, . . . and man became lost forever, yea, they became fallen man. And now, ye see by this that our first parents were cut off both temporally and spiritually from the presence of the Lord. . . . Therefore, as the soul could never die, and the fall had brought upon all mankind a spiritual death as well as a temporal, that is, they were cut off from the presence of the Lord, it was expedient that mankind should be reclaimed from his spiritual death." (Alma 42:2-9.)

As to the fall and the atonement —

Lehi summarized the prophetic pronouncements in this field by saying: "Adam fell that men might be; and men are, that they might have joy. And the Messiah cometh in the fulness of time, that he may redeem the children of men from the fall." (2 Ne. 2:25-26.)

Jacob expanded the doctrine by saying: "For as death hath passed upon all men, to fulfil the merciful plan of the great Creator, there must needs be a power of resurrection, and the resurrection must needs come unto man by reason of the fall; and the fall came by reason of transgression; and because man became fallen they were cut off from the presence of the Lord." (2 Ne. 9:6.)

And a thousand years later Moroni was still centering man's attention in Adam and Christ by such declarations as: God "created Adam, and by Adam came the fall of man. And because of the fall of man came Jesus Christ, . . . and because of Jesus Christ came the redemption of man." (Morm. 9:12.)

As to salvation through the atonement —

Of the crowning act of our Lord's life, Jacob said: "It must needs be an infinite atonement — save it should be an infinite atonement this corruption could not put on incorruption. Wherefore, the first judgment which came upon man must needs have remained to an endless duration. And if so, this flesh must have laid down to rot and to crumble to its mother earth, to rise no more." (2 Ne. 9:7.)

Amulek philosophized to the same effect by saying: "It is expedient that an atonement should be made; for according to the great plan of the Eternal God there must be an atonement made, or else all mankind must unavoidably perish; yea, all are hardened; yea, all are fallen and are lost, and must perish except it be through the atonement which it is expedient should be made." (Alma 34:9.)

ADAM FELL, CHRIST ATONED, MAN SAVED

As to redemption from temporal death —

Jacob's teachings on this point were: Christ "cometh into the world that he may save all men if they will hearken unto his voice; for behold, he suffereth the pains of all men, yea, the pains of every living creature, both men, women, and children, who belong to the family of Adam. And he suffereth this that the resurrection might pass upon all men, that all might stand before him at the great and judgment day." (2 Ne. 9:21-22.)

Again, a thousand years later, Moroni echoes the same concept thus: "And because of the redemption of man, which came by Jesus Christ, they are brought back into the presence of the Lord; yea, this is wherein all men are redeemed, because the death of Christ bringeth to pass the resurrection, which bringeth to pass a redemption from an endless sleep, from which sleep all men shall be awakened by the power of God when the trump shall sound; and they shall come forth, both small and great, and all shall stand before his bar, being redeemed and loosed from this eternal band of death, which death is a temporal death." (Morm. 9:13.)

As to redemption from spiritual death —

These are the words of Christ to the Brother of Jared: "Because thou knowest these things ye are redeemed from the fall; therefore ye are brought back into my presence; therefore I show myself unto you. Behold, I am he who was prepared from the foundation of the world to redeem my people. Behold, I am Jesus Christ. I am the Father and the Son. In me shall all mankind have light, and that eternally, even they who shall believe on my name; and they shall become my sons and my daughters." (Ether 3:13-14.)

As to God's grace —

On this great principle Lehi expounded: "Redemption cometh in and through the Holy Messiah; for he is full of grace and truth. . . . How great the importance to make these things known unto the inhabitants of the earth, that they may know that there is no flesh that can dwell in the presence of God, save it be through the merits, and mercy, and grace of the Holy Messiah." (2 Ne. 2:6-8.)

Jacob extolled the wonders of God's grace by exclaiming, "O the wisdom of God, his mercy and grace," as he set forth the blessings which come because of the atonement.

As to the acceptance of the free gift of God's grace —

Lehi draws this conclusion: "And because that they are redeemed from the fall they have become free forever, knowing good from evil; to act for themselves and not to be acted upon, save it be by the punishment of the law at the great and last day, according to the commandments which God hath given. Wherefore, men are free according to the flesh; and all things are given them which are expedient unto man. And they are free to choose liberty and eternal life, through the great mediation of all men, or to choose captivity and death, according to the captivity and power of the devil; for he seeketh that all men might be miserable like unto himself." (2 Ne. 2:26-27.)

As to eternal life coming through both grace and righteousness—

Christ's "sacrifice for sin," Lehi explains, is "to answer the ends of the law, unto all those who have a broken heart and a contrite spirit; and unto none else can the ends of the law be answered. . . . And they that believe in him shall be saved." (2 Ne. 2:7-9.)

But it is Nephi who gave the simplest and most plain exposition on this point. He said: "We know that it is by grace that we are saved, after all we can do." (2 Ne. 25:23.)

As to not imputing sin to those without the law —

Here Jacob makes this plain and clear exposition: "He has given a law; and where there is no law given there is no punishment; and where there is no punishment there is no condemnation; and where there is no condemnation the mercies of the Holy One of Israel have claim upon them, because of the atonement; for they are delivered by the power of him. For the atonement satisfieth the demands of his justice upon all those who have not the law given to them, that they are delivered from that awful monster, death and hell, and the devil, and the lake of fire and brimstone, which is endless torment; and they are restored to that God who gave them breath, which is the Holy One of Israel. But wo unto him that has the law given, yea, that has all the commandments of God, like unto us, and that transgresseth them, and that wasteth the days of his probation, for awful is his state!" (2 Ne. 9:25-27.)

12. Adam brought temporal and spiritual death into the world. The effects of these two deaths then passed upon all mankind. Temporal death is the separation of body and spirit when men pass from this sphere of existence. Spiritual death is to die as pertaining to things of righteousness, and this occurs when men arrive at the years of accountability, unless they are born again through baptism of water and the Spirit. (D. & C. 29:41-42.)

13. Sin did not have its beginning with the law of Moses, but sin, in the sense of violations of that law, was not imputed except to those who had the law.

14. **Death reigned from Adam to Moses]** The argument here is: How could those who lived during this twenty-five-hundred-year period be redeemed temporally (resurrected) or redeemed spiritually (gain eternal life) if salvation was in the law alone rather than in Christ and his atoning sacrifice.

Adam's transgression] Adam alone transgressed the law by which temporal and spiritual death came into the world, and he alone is accountable therefor. "Men will be punished for their own sins, and not for Adam's transgression." (Second Article of Faith.) Hence, Paul explains, other men did not transgress "after the similitude of" Adam.

Figure of him that was to come] Adam was a prototype of Christ. "The first man Adam" brought mortality and spiritual death into the world; "the last Adam," who is Christ, brought immortality and eternal life to men. (1 Cor. 15:45-49.)

15. Even as death passes upon all men because of the fall, so life comes to all through the atonement. And how abundant is God's grace to accomplish such an infinite work!

16. One man, Adam, transgressed and many became sinners; now, by one man, Christ, are many made righteous, through the law of justification.

17. The gift of righteousness] One thing only comes as a free gift to men — the fact of the atoning sacrifice. All other gifts must be earned. That is, God's gifts are bestowed upon those who live the law entitling them to receive whatever is involved. The gift of repentance comes to those who turn to the Lord with broken hearts and contrite spirits; the gift of faith is the heavenly endowment conferred upon those who believe in God and live in harmony with his laws; the gifts of the Spirit, all of them, are reserved for those who qualify themselves to receive them. And so it is with the gift of righteousness; it must be merited; men are adjudged and accounted righteous, that is, they are justified, after they keep the commandments; it is then, and then only, that they receive the needed outpouring of God's grace through which they receive the gift of righteousness.

Reign in life] Inherit eternal life.

18-19. Adam's fall brought death, both temporal and spiritual; Christ's atoning sacrifice brought life, both temporal and spiritual, or in other words, the atonement brought both immortality and eternal life. (D. & C. 29:40-45.)

20-21. Subsequent to Adam's day came the law of Moses, under which law death and sin continued to reign, but now Christ has triumphed over all and has ransomed men from sin and death, from death in that all are raised in immortality, and from sin in that those who forsake evil are raised also unto eternal life. And both of these — both immortality and eternal life — come by the infinite grace of God.

A NEW LIFE BEGINS WITH BAPTISM

ROMANS 6:1-11.

1 What shall we say then? Shall we continue in sin, that grace may abound?

2 God forbid. How shall we, that are dead to sin, live any longer therein?

3 Know ye not, that so many of us as were baptized into Jesus

Christ were baptized into his death?

4 Therefore we are buried with him by baptism into death: that like as Christ was raised up from the dead by the glory of the Father, even so we also should walk in newness of life.

5 For if we have been planted together in the likeness of his death, we shall be also *in the likeness* of *his* resurrection:

6 Knowing this, that our old man is crucified with *him*, that the body of sin might be destroyed, that henceforth we should not serve sin.

7 For he that is dead is freed from sin.

8 Now if we be dead with Christ, we believe that we shall also live with him:

9 Knowing that Christ being raised from the dead dieth no more; death hath no more dominion over him.

10 For in that he died, he died unto sin once: but in that he liveth, he liveth unto God.

11 Likewise reckon ye also yourselves to be dead indeed unto sin, but alive unto God through Jesus Christ our Lord.

I.V. ROMANS 6:7.

7 For he that is dead **to sin** is freed from sin.

Baptized members of God's earthly kingdom walk in a newness of life; they are born again; they become new creatures of the Holy Ghost; they die as pertaining to sin and live in the realm of righteousness; they put off the natural man and become saints through the atonement; they crucify the man of sin, bury their sins in the watery grave of baptism, and come forth resurrected, as it were, to righteousness. **Baptism of water and Spirit]** See Acts 18:24-28; 19:1-7.

2. Dead to sin] True saints are dead to sin; it no longer lives in their lives; they have overcome the world.

3-5. Even the symbolism found in baptism bears record of the death of sin and the birth of righteousness in the life of the true convert. Baptism is performed in similitude of the death, burial, and resurrection of Christ, thus signifying that the baptized convert dies as pertaining to the things of the world, buries his sins in the watery grave of baptism, and comes himself forth, as though resurrected, to live a new life, a life of righteousness, the life of a saint of God.

These similitudes and likenesses used by Paul assume and presuppose that baptism is performed by immersion in water, a thing which was well known and understood by the Romans to whom the Apostle was writing. There is, however, no New Testament statement specifying the mode of baptism in express words. The Book of Mormon account is more specific and particular. It records the words used in the baptismal ordinance and then directs, "And then shall ye immerse them in the water, and come forth again out of the water. And after this manner shall ye baptize." (3 Ne. 11:22-27.)

4. Newness of life] Born again. *Commentary I*, pp. 140-142; 1 John 5:1-5. **6. Our old man is crucified**] "If any man be in Christ, he is a new creature." (2 Cor. 5:17.) In other words, he is a convert; once he was of the world, now he is a saint; he has changed, undergone a conversion from one state to another. The natural man has been put off and the follower of Christ has become a new creature of the Holy Ghost. (Mosiah 3:19; 27:24-26.)

7-11. Even as Christ died and is now resurrected, so every convert to Christ dies as to sin and becomes alive as to righteousness.

SIN BEGETS DEATH: CHRIST BRINGS LIFE

ROMANS 6:12-23.

12 Let not sin therefore reign in your mortal body, that ye should obey it in the lusts thereof.

13 Neither yield ye your members *as* instruments of unrighteousness unto sin: but yield yourselves unto God, as those that are alive from the dead, and your members *as* instruments of righteousness unto God.

14 For sin shall not have dominion over you: for ye are not under the law, but under grace.

15 What then? shall we sin, because we are not under the law, but under grace? God forbid.

16 Know ye not, that to whom ye yield yourselves servants to obey, his servants ye are to whom ye obey; whether of sin unto death, or of obedience unto righteousness?

17 But God be thanked, that ye were the servants of sin, but ye have obeyed from the heart that form of doctrine which was delivered you.

18 Being then made free from sin, ye became the servants of righteousness.

19 I speak after the manner of men because of the infirmity of your flesh: for as ye have yielded your members servants to uncleanness and to iniquity unto iniquity; even so now yield your members servants to righteousness unto holiness.

20 For when ye were the servants of sin, ye were free from righteousness.

21 What fruit had ye then in those things whereof ye are now ashamed? for the end of those things *is* death.

22 But now being made free from sin, and become servants to God, ye have your fruit unto holiness, and the end everlasting life.

23 For the wages of sin *is* death; but the gift of God *is* eternal life through Jesus Christ our Lord.

I.V. ROMANS 6:14, 17, 19.

14 For **in so doing** sin shall not have dominion over you; for ye are not under the law, but under grace.

17 But God be thanked, that ye **are not** the servants of sin, **for** ye have obeyed from the heart that form of doctrine which was delivered you.

19 I speak after the manner of men because of the infirmity of your flesh; for as ye have **in times past** yielded your members servants to uncleanness and to iniquity unto iniquity; even so now yield your members servants to righteousness unto holiness.

Paul is the greatest advocate of personal righteousness, of full obedience to the whole law of the whole gospel, of keeping the commandments, of working out one's "own salvation with fear and trembling" before God (Philip. 2:12) — a concept seemingly concealed from the whole sectarian world. Accordingly, we here find him giving a powerful exhortation to abstain from sin and obey the laws which lead to eternal life.

12. Sin not.

13. Yield yourself to God; keep the commandments.

14-15. Your sins are forgiven because of the grace of God.

16. His servants ye are to whom ye obey] Jesus said: "Who-

251

soever committeth sin is the servant of sin." (John 8:34.) All men serve either God or the devil; there is no neutral ground; the obedient are the servants of God, or the servants of righteousness; the disobedient are the servants of the devil, or the servants of sin. Alma expressed it this way: "If ye are not the sheep of the good shepherd, of what fold are ye? Behold, I say unto you, that the devil is your shepherd, and ye are of his fold. . . . Therefore, if a man bringeth forth good works he hearkeneth unto the voice of the good shepherd, and he doth follow him; but whosoever bringeth forth evil works, the same becometh a child of the devil, for he hearkeneth unto his voice, and doth follow him. And whosoever doeth this must receive his wages of him; therefore, for his wages he receiveth death, as to things pertaining unto righteousness, being dead unto all good works." (Alma 5:39-42.) Mormon said: "A man being a servant of the devil cannot follow Christ; and if he follow Christ he cannot be a servant of the devil." (Moro. 7:11.)

17-20. Those who do not live the gospel are servants of sin; when they accept the gospel and yield themselves to the cause of righteousness, their sins are forgiven through baptism, and they become the servants of righteousness.

21. The fruit of sin is spiritual death.

22. The fruit of righteousness is everlasting life.

23. "Every man receiveth wages of him whom he listeth to obey." (Alma 3:27.) Satan pays his servants with death, spiritual death, death as pertaining to the things of righteousness; Christ rewards those who serve him with life, spiritual life, eternal life, life in the presence of God, enjoying and possessing all that Deity himself has.

LAW OF MOSES IS FULFILLED IN CHRIST

ROMANS 7:1-6.

1 Know ye not, brethren, (for I speak to them that know the law,) how that the law hath do-minion over a man as long as he liveth?

2 For the woman which hath an husband is bound by the law

to *her* husband so long as he liveth; but if the husband be dead, she is loosed from the law of *her* husband.

3 So then if, while *her* husband liveth, she be married to another man, she shall be called an adulteress: but if her husband be dead, she is free from that law; so that she is no adulteress, though she be married to another man.

4 Wherefore, my brethren, ye also are become dead to the law by the body of Christ; that ye should be married to another, *even* to him who is raised from the dead, that we should bring forth fruit unto God.

5 For when we were in the flesh, the motions of sins, which were by the law, did work in our members to bring forth fruit unto death.

6 But now we are delivered from the law, that being dead wherein we were held; that we should serve in newness of spirit, and not *in* the oldness of the letter.

I.V. ROMANS 7:1-2, 5-6.

1 Know ye not, brethren, (for I speak to them that know the law,) how that the law hath dominion over a man **only** as long as he liveth?

2 For the woman which hath **a** husband is bound by the law to her husband **only as** long as he liveth; **for** if the husband be dead, she is loosed from the law of her husband.

5 For when we were in the flesh, the motions of sins, which were **not according to** the law, did work in our members to bring forth fruit unto death.

6 But now we are delivered from the law **wherein we were held, being dead to the law,** that we should serve in newness of spirit, and not in the oldness of the letter.

Paul was an absolute genius at devising illustrations to drive home his gospel teachings. Here he compares Israel's allegiance to the law of Moses with that of a wife to her husband. As long as her husband lives, a wife is bound to him, must obey his laws, and if she be with another, she is an adulteress. But when the husband dies, he can no longer direct her actions, and she is free to marry another; she can no longer be subject to him that is dead.

So with Israel and the law. As long as the law lived, and was therefore in force, Israel was married to it and required to obey its provisions. If she went after other gods, or followed other religions, it was as adultery. But now the law is fulfilled; it no longer lives; it has become dead in Christ; and Israel is married to another, even to Christ, whose gospel law must now be obeyed.

As a matter of fact, whenever the Melchizedek Priesthood — which "administereth the gospel" (D. & C. 84:19) — was found in ancient Israel, the law of Moses was dead, and the people were alive in Christ. Hence, we find Nephi saying, some six hundred years before Christ, "Notwithstanding we believe in Christ, we keep the law of Moses, and look forward with steadfastness unto Christ, until the law shall be fulfilled. For, for this end was the law given; wherefore the law hath become dead unto us, and we are made alive in Christ because of our faith; yet we keep the law because of the commandments." (2 Ne. 25:24-25.)

Law of Moses] See Acts 15:1-35; *Commentary I*, pp. 218-223; 505-507.

LAW OF CHRIST REPLACES LAW OF MOSES

ROMANS 7:7-25.

7 What shall we say then? *Is* the law sin? God forbid. Nay, I had not known sin, but by the law: for I had not known lust, except the law had said, Thou shalt not covet.

8 But sin, taking occasion by the commandment, wrought in me all manner of concupiscence. For without the law sin *was* dead.

9 For I was alive without the law once: but when the commandment came, sin revived, and I died.

10 And t h e commandment, which *was* *ordained* to life, I found *to be* unto death.

11 For sin, taking occasion by the commandment, deceived me, and by it slew *me*.

12 Wherefore the law *is* holy, and the commandment holy, and just, and good.

13 Was then that which is good made death unto me? God forbid. But sin, that it might appear sin, working death in me by that which is good; that sin by the commandment might become exceeding sinful.

14 For we know that the law is spiritual: but I am carnal, sold under sin.

15 For that which I do I allow not: for what I would, that do I not; but what I hate, that do I.

16 If then I do that which I would not, I consent unto the law that *it is* good.

17 Now then it is no more I that do it, but sin that dwelleth in me.

18 For I know that in me (that is, in my flesh,) dwelleth no good thing: for to will is present with me; but *how* to perform that which is good I find not.

19 For the good that I would I do not: but the evil which I would not, that I do.

20 Now if I do that I would not, it is no more I that do it, but sin that dwelleth in me.

21 I find then a law, that, when I would do good, evil is present with me.

22 For I delight in the law of God after the inward man:

23 But I see another law in my members, warring against the law of my mind, and bringing me into captivity to the law of sin which is in my members.

24 O wretched man that I am! who shall deliver me from the body of this death?

25 I thank God through Jesus Christ our Lord. So then with the mind I myself serve the law of God; but with the flesh the law of sin.

I.V. ROMANS 7:9-27.

9 For **once I** was alive without **transgression of** the law, but when the commandment **of Christ** came, sin revived, and I died.

10 **And when I believed not the commandment of Christ which came,** which was ordained to life, I found **it condemned me** unto death.

11 For sin, taking occasion, **denied** the commandment, **and** deceived me; and by it **I was slain.**

12 **Nevertheless, I found the law to be holy,** and the commandment **to be** holy, and just, and good.

13 Was then that which is good made death unto me? God forbid. But sin, that it might appear sin **by that which is good working death in me;** that sin, by the commandment, might become exceeding sinful.

14 For we know that the **commandment** is spiritual; but **when I was under the law, I was yet** carnal, sold under sin.

15 **But now I am spiritual; for that which I am commanded to do, I do; and that which I am commanded not to allow, I allow not.**

16 **For what I know is not right, I would not do; for that which is sin, I hate.**

17 **If then I do not that which I would not allow,** I consent unto the law, that it is good; **and I am not condemned.**

18 Now then, it is no more I that **do sin; but I seek to subdue that** sin **which** dwelleth in me.

19 For I know that in me, that is, in my flesh, dwelleth no good thing; for to will is present with me, but to perform that which is good I find not, **only in Christ.**

20 For the good that I would **have done when under the law, I find not to be good; therefore, I do it not.**

21 But the evil which I would not **do under the law, I find to be good;** that, I do.

22 Now if I do that, **through the assistance of Christ, I would** not **do under the law, I am not under the law; and it is no more** that I seek to do wrong, but to subdue sin that dwelleth in me.

23 I find then **that under the law,** that when I would do good evil **was** present with me; for I delight in the law of God after the inward man.

24 **And now** I see another law, **even the commandment of Christ, and it is imprinted in my mind.**

25 **But my members are warring against the law of my mind,** and bringing me into captivity to the law of sin which is in my members.

26 **And if I subdue not the sin which is in me, but with the flesh** serve the law of sin; O wretched man that I am! who shall deliver me from the body of this death?

27 I thank God through Jesus Christ our Lord, **then, that** so with the mind I myself serve the law of God.

Paul's presentation here is obscure and difficult. From the King James record alone, it is almost impossible to comprehend it. The *Inspired Version* clarifies and improves the account immeasurably. But even the numerous changes and additions made by the Prophet do not leave us with an incisive and plain summary of what the Apostle had in mind.

Something, however, should be said in mitigation of the obscurity and ambiguity of the argument Paul makes. The fact is that the philosophical problems facing his Roman readers were wholly different from those with which we wrestle today. We do not have the Mosaic background, and are not concerned with how the law of Moses died in Christ; we are not confronted with the problem of rationalizing away those performances which had been drilled into Israel for fifteen hundred years; we are not faced with the problem of showing that the gospel grew out of the Mosaic order. Today our problem, in a comparable situation, is one of showing there was a falling away from the doctrines and powers of primitive Christianity, and that growing out of this apostasy there has been a glorious restoration.

Nonetheless, Paul's argument, given of old, does have worth and merit for us; it enables us to get an over-all view of God's dealings with men; it helps us understand better what we do have in the revealed religion which has come to us. In effect Paul is saying that the law of Moses was good in its day, that God gave it for a purpose, but that now it is dead, and in place thereof God has given a higher law to which all men must now turn for salvation.

Law of Moses] See Acts 15:1-35; *Commentary I*, pp. 218-223; 505-507.

7-8. The law of Moses was good in its day, and time, and season; by it Paul learned the course in which he should walk; when he failed to keep the law, he committed sin, sin for which he would not have been accountable except for the law. (D. & C. 82:3-4.)

I.V. 9. Once Paul was alive spiritually, in the sense that he obeyed the law of Moses, which was the spiritual light God had given his people, but when Christ came and fulfilled and replaced the law, then Paul died spiritually, because the law itself was dead, and therefore no longer had any saving grace.

I.V. 10. By not accepting the gospel when it came, so as to be born again and become alive spiritually, Paul was condemned to spiritual death.

I.V. 11. Because of sin he denied the gospel and was slain spiritually, that is, he remained spiritually dead.

I.V. 12. The law of Moses was holy as long as it was in force, and the gospel, which replaced it, is now holy, just, and good.

I.V. 13-16. When Paul was subject to the law of Moses, he was yet carnal, that is, he was yet in his sins; but now, because of the gospel, being born again, he has become spiritual, and the proof of his spirituality is that he keeps the commandments.

I.V. 17. Now, Paul philosophizes, since he obeys the higher gospel law, he cannot be condemned for failure to keep the lesser Mosaic standard. It is as though a Mormon Elder said to a sectarian Christian: "Keep all the good you have in your church and add to it the further light and knowledge we have received in this day," and then asked such person, "How can you be condemned for living all the good principles you already have, simply because you accept the added truths that have come by revelation in this day?"

I.V. 18-27. And so, Paul seeks to overcome sin, to subdue and control the lusts of the flesh; this is possible only through the grace and power of Christ; the natural man needs assistance from Christ to rise above the carnal state, assistance that comes because of the atonement and was not available through the law of Moses alone. But even after the gospel law is imprinted in his mind, carnal desires persist; and if they are not subdued, he is not justified. But praise God, righteousness and salvation are available through Christ, and the faithful shall come off triumphant.

LAW OF CHRIST BRINGS LIFE AND PEACE

ROMANS 8:1-13.

1 *There is* therefore now no condemnation to them which are in Christ Jesus, who walk not after the flesh, but after the Spirit.

2 For the law of the Spirit of life in Christ Jesus hath made me free from the law of sin and death.

3 For what the law could not do, in that it was weak through the flesh, God sending his own Son in the likeness of sinful flesh, and for sin, condemned sin in the flesh:

4 That the righteousness of the law might be fulfilled in us, who walk not after the flesh, but after the Spirit.

5 For they that are after the flesh do mind the things of the flesh; but they that are after the Spirit the things of the Spirit.

6 For to be carnally minded *is* death; but to be spiritually minded *is* life and peace.

7 Because the carnal mind *is* enmity against God: for it is not subject to the law of God, neither indeed can be.

8 So then they that are in the flesh cannot please God.

9 But ye are not in the flesh, but in the Spirit, if so be that the Spirit of God dwell in you. Now if any man have not the Spirit of Christ, he is none of his.

10 And if Christ *be* in you, the body *is* dead because of sin; but the Spirit *is* life because of righteousness.

11 But if the Spirit of him that raised up Jesus from the dead dwell in you, he that raised up Christ from the dead shall also quicken your mortal bodies by his Spirit that dwelleth in you.

12 Therefore, brethren, we are debtors, not to the flesh, to live after the flesh.

13 For if ye live after the flesh, ye shall die: but if ye through the Spirit do mortify the deeds of the body, ye shall live.

I.V. ROMANS 8:8-11, 13.

8 So then they that are **after** the flesh cannot please God.

9 But ye are not **after** the flesh, but **after** the Spirit, if so be that the Spirit of God dwell in you. Now if any man have not the Spirit of Christ, he is none of his.

10 And if Christ be in you, **though the body shall die** because of sin, **yet** the Spirit is life, because of righteousness.

11 **And** if the Spirit of him that raised up Jesus from the dead, dwell in you, he that raised up Christ from the dead shall also quicken your mortal bodies by his Spirit that dwelleth in you.

13 For if ye live after the flesh, **unto sin,** ye shall die; but if ye through the Spirit do mortify the deeds of the body, ye shall live **unto Christ.**

Life and peace come, not through the law of Moses, but through Christ and his saving grace. The Mosaic performances deal with carnal things, the things of the flesh, the things of death. There is no power in them to atone, to ransom, to save, to bring joy and peace here and eternal life hereafter.

But Christ deals with spiritual things, the things of the Spirit, the things that bring life. Because of him, "he who doeth the works of righteousness shall receive his reward, even peace in this world, and eternal life in the world to come." (D. & C. 59:23.)

1. Failure to keep the law of Moses does not condemn church members who keep the commandments of the Lord.

2. The law of the gospel frees men from keeping the law of Moses.

3. The law of Moses could not save men from sin, but the atonement of Christ does.

4. The law of Moses is fulfilled.

5. Those who had the law were concerned with carnal things; those who have the gospel, with spiritual.

6. "To be carnally-minded is death, and to be spiritually-minded is life eternal." (2 Ne. 9:39.)

7. **The carnal mind is enmity against God]** "The natural man is an enemy to God, and has been from the fall of Adam, and will be, forever and ever, unless he yields to the enticings of the Holy Spirit, and putteth off the natural man and becometh a saint through the atonement of Christ the Lord." (Mosiah 3:19.) **Carnality]** See 1 Cor. 3:1-8a.

9. Those who have the Spirit of God are not carnal; unless they have this Spirit they are not Christ's.

10. **If Christ be in you]** Christ dwells in those who have his mind, who believe and think and act as he does. (1 Cor. 2:16.) Thus the Resurrected Lord petitioned his Father with reference to his Nephite disciples, "I pray . . . that I may be in them as thou, Father, art in me, that we may be one, that I may be glorified in them." (3 Ne. 19:29.)

11. If the Spirit of God dwells in you, your body is quickened, you are "changed from" your "carnal and fallen state, to a state of righteousness, being redeemed of God, becoming his sons and daughters." (Mosiah 27:25.)

12-13. Therefore, we are not indebted to the law of Moses for salvation, but to Christ through whose Spirit and power we can overcome the flesh and live in the Spirit.

SONS OF GOD ARE JOINT-HEIRS WITH CHRIST

ROMANS 8:14-19.

14 For as many as are led by the Spirit of God, they are the sons of God.

15 For ye have not received the spirit of bondage again to fear; but ye have received the Spirit of adoption, whereby we cry, Abba, Father.

16 The Spirit itself beareth witness with our spirit, that we are the children of God:

17 And if children, then heirs; heirs of God, and joint-heirs with Christ; if so be that we suffer with him, that we may be also glorified together.

18 For I reckon that the sufferings of this present time *are* not worthy *to be compared* with the glory which shall be revealed in us.

19 For the earnest expectation of the creature waiteth for the manifestation of the sons of God.

I.V. ROMANS 8:18.

18 For I reckon that the sufferings of this present time are not worthy to be **named** with the glory which shall be revealed in us.

14. Sons of God] See Gal. 4:1-7.

15. 'You are no longer servants; you are not in bondage; for you have been adopted as sons into the family of God the Father.' **Abba, Father]** *Abba* is the Aramaic term for Father; and the adopted sons in the family of the Eternal Father are privileged to address him who is the Ruler of the universe in this intimate way.

16. Those who are sons of God know it by the whisperings of the Spirit.

17. Joint-heirs with Christ] "As the literal Son of God — the Firstborn in the spirit, the Only Begotten in the flesh — Christ is the natural heir of his Father. It thus became his right to inherit, receive, and possess all that his Father had. (John 16:15.) And his Father is possessor of all things: the universe; all power, wisdom, and goodness; the fulness of truth and knowledge; and an infinity of all good attributes. By heirship and by obedience, going from grace to grace, the Son attained these same things. (D. & C. 93:5-17.)

"By obedience to the fulness of gospel law, righteous men are adopted into the family of God so that they also become heirs, joint-heirs with Christ (Rom. 8:14-18; Gal. 3:26-29; 4:1-7), inheritors of all that the Father hath. (D. & C. 84:33-41.) In his famous King Follett Sermon, speaking of those who 'shall be heirs of God and joint-heirs with Jesus Christ,' the Prophet asked what their glory should be. Answering his own query, he described joint-heirship as inheriting 'the same power, the same glory and the same exaltation, until you arrive at the station of a God, and ascend the throne of eternal power, the same as those who have gone before.' (*Teachings*, p. 347.)

"A joint-heir is one who inherits equally with all other heirs including the Chief Heir who is the Son. Each joint-heir has an equal and an undivided portion of the whole of everything. If one knows all things, so do all others. If one has all power, so do all those who inherit jointly with him. If the universe belongs to one, so it does equally to the total of all upon whom the joint inheritances are bestowed.

"Joint-heirs are possessors of all things. (D. & C. 50:26-28.) All things are theirs for they have exaltation. (D. & C. 76:50-60.) They are made 'equal' with their Lord. (D. & C. 88:107.) They gain all power both in heaven and on earth and receive the fulness of the Father, and all the knowledge and truth are theirs. (D. & C. 93:15-30.) They are gods. (D. & C. 132:20.) Celestial marriage is the gate to this high state of exaltation. (*Doctrines of Salvation*, vol. 2, pp. 24, 35-39; D. & C. 131:1-4; 132.)" (*Mormon Doctrine*, 2nd ed., pp. 394-395.)

"WE ARE SAVED BY HOPE"

ROMANS 8:20-25.

20 For the creature was made subject to vanity, not willingly, but by reason of him who hath subjected *the same* in hope,

21 Because the creature itself also shall be delivered from the bondage of corruption into the glorious liberty of the children of God.

22 For we know that the whole creation groaneth and travaileth in pain together until now.

23 And not only *they*, but ourselves also, which have the first-

fruits of the Spirit, even we our-selves groan within ourselves, wait-ing for the adoption, *to wit*, the redemption of our body.

24 For we are saved by hope: but hope that is seen is not hope: for what a man seeth, why doth he yet hope for?

25 But if we hope for that we see not, *then* do we with patience wait for *it*.

I.V. ROMANS 8:20.

20 For the creature was made subject to **tribulation** not willing-ly, but by reason of him who hath subjected it in hope;

20. Man is subject to the trials of mortality; if faithful, he receives the hope of eternal life.

20. The creature] 22. The whole creation] Man is the crea-ture; all created beings are the whole of creation. Paul is speak-ing of the need for men, as part of their adoption into the family of God, to become, as Alma expressed it, "new creatures," that is to "be born again; yea, born of God, changed from their carnal and fallen state, to a state of righteousness." (Mosiah 27:25.)

21. Bondage of corruption] Bondage of sin, in which men are bound by the chains of hell. **Liberty of the children of God]** "The truth shall make you free." (John 8:32.)

22. All men are as in the pain of travail, awaiting the new birth of the Spirit.

23. And even the saints who already have the Spirit birth, yet struggle as in travail, awaiting the final redemption of the soul.

24. For we are saved by hope] "As used in the revelations, hope is the desire of faithful people to gain eternal salvation in the kingdom of God hereafter. It is not a flimsy, ethereal desire, one without assurance that the desired consummation will be received, but a desire coupled with full expectation of receiving the coveted reward. Paul, for instance, was not hesitant in affirm-ing that he lived, 'In hope of eternal life, which God, that cannot lie, promised before the world began' (Tit. 1:2), and Peter assured all the elect that 'by the resurrection of Jesus Christ from the dead,' their 'lively hope' of 'an inheritance incorruptible, and undefiled, and that fadeth not away, reserved in heaven' for the saints, had been renewed or 'begotten' again. (1 Pet. 1:1-5.)

"Hope is always centered in Christ (Ps. 31:24; 42:5, 11; 43:5; 146:5); it always pertains to salvation in the kingdom of God (Lam. 3:26; Acts 24:15; Rom. 8:24-25; Heb. 11:1; Col. 1:5, 23); and without hope there can be no salvation. Speaking to the Lord, Moroni said: 'Thou hast prepared a house for man, yea, even among the mansions of thy Father, in which man might have a more excellent hope; wherefore man must hope, or he cannot receive an inheritance in the place which thou hast prepared.' (Ether 12:32.)

"There is only one true hope (Eph. 4:4), 'that blessed hope' (Tit. 2:13), and the saints are commanded to acquire it. (D. & C. 6:19; Alma 7:24.) It is one of the essential qualifications for those who labor in the ministry (D. & C. 4:5); none can assist in the Lord's work without it (D. & C. 12:8; 18:19); those who have it are not ashamed of the testimony they bear (Rom. 5:5); rather, they are commanded to 'be ready always to give an answer to every man' for the hope that is in them. (1 Pet. 3:15.)

"Hope is born of righteousness. 'The hope of the righteous shall be gladness: but the expectation of the wicked shall perish.' (Prov. 10:28; 14:32.) The hope of the wicked 'shall be as the giving up of the ghost.' (Job 11:20.) Hope is found through the gospel; the scriptures themselves have been recorded that men 'might have hope' (Rom. 15:4); and angels minister unto man to confirm that hope. (D. & C. 128:21.) And those who gain the full hope of eternal life purify themselves even as Christ is pure. (1 John 3:1-3.)

"Faith and hope are inseparable. Hope enables men to have faith in the first instance and then because of faith that hope increases until salvation is gained. 'How is it that ye can attain unto faith, save ye shall have hope?' Mormon asks. 'And what is it that ye shall hope for? Behold I say unto you that ye shall have hope through the atonement of Christ and the power of his resurrection, to be raised unto life eternal, and this because of your faith in him according to the promise. Wherefore, if a man have faith he must needs have hope; for without faith there cannot be any hope. And again, behold I say unto you that he cannot have faith and hope, save he shall be meek, and lowly of heart. If so, his faith and hope is vain, for none is acceptable before God, save the meek and lowly in heart.' (Moro. 7:40-44.)

"Moroni quoted the words of Ether who said: 'By faith all things are fulfilled — Wherefore, whoso believeth in God might with surety hope for a better world, yea, even a place at the right hand of God, which hope cometh of faith, maketh an anchor to the souls of men, which would make them sure and steadfast, always abounding in good works, being led to glorify God.' Then Moroni explained that 'faith is things which are hoped for and not seen,' and said that Christ had revealed himself to men, 'that they might hope for those things which they have not seen. Wherefore, ye may also have hope, and be partakers of the gift, if ye will but have faith.' (Ether 12:3-9.) Hope thus is one of the gifts of the Spirit. 'Now the God of hope fill you with all joy and peace in believing,' Paul prayed for the Roman Saints, 'that ye may abound in hope, through the power of the Holy Ghost.' (Rom. 15:13.)" (*Mormon Doctrine*, 2nd ed., pp. 365-366.)

HOW THE SPIRIT MAKETH INTERCESSION FOR MAN

ROMANS 8:26-27.

26 Likewise the Spirit also helpeth our infirmities: for we know not what we should pray for as we ought: but the Spirit itself maketh intercession for us with groanings which cannot be uttered.

27 And he that searcheth the hearts knoweth what *is* the mind of the Spirit, because he maketh intercession for the saints according to *the will of* God.

Christ our Lord is the Intercessor! He it is who advocateth our cause in the courts above and who, as Paul is about to say "maketh intercession for the saints" (verse 27), and "maketh intercession for us." (Verse 34b.) Why, then, does he first say that "the Spirit itself maketh intercession for us with groanings which cannot be uttered," which statement the Prophet Joseph Smith says should better be expressed: "The Spirit maketh intercession for us with striving which cannot be expressed"? (*Teachings*, p. 278.)

The Holy Ghost is a Revelator who gives direction to the faithful, causing them to know and speak the mind and will of the Lord. Perfect prayers are always inspired by the Spirit, and they are always answered, because the Spirit knows beforehand "what ye should pray for." Thus the revelation says: "If ye are purified and cleansed from all sin, ye shall ask whatsoever you will in the name of Jesus and it shall be done. But know this, it shall be given you what you shall ask." (D. & C. 50:29-30.) That is, the uttered prayer will come by revelation from the Spirit. Prayers during the millennium will meet this high standard of excellence, for "in that day whatsoever any man shall ask, it shall be given unto him." (D. & C. 101:27.)

Thus the Spirit maketh intercession for us, in the sense that his words and pleas are planted in the hearts of others who utter them for and on our behalf. The Son of God, for instance, whose mission is one of intercession, "speaketh the words of God: for God giveth not the Spirit by measure unto him." (John 3:34.) That is, all his words and acts are in complete harmony with the Holy Spirit. Thus the Prophet taught: "And he being the Only Begotten of the Father, full of grace and truth, and having overcome, received a fulness of the glory of the Father, possessing the same mind with the Father, which mind is the Holy Spirit, that bears record of the Father and the Son, and these three are one." (*Lectures on Faith*, pp. 50-51.)

And so when our great Intercessor mediates our cause and pleads for us, his brethren, he is pleading for the same things that are in the mind of the Holy Spirit, and in this sense it may be said that the Spirit itself is making intercession. And similarly, when we, as moved upon by the Spirit, pray for each other, it might be said that the Spirit, through us, is interceding for the welfare of our brethren. In the field of intercession, the Spirit operates through other persons.

27. He maketh intercession] Christ does it, because he it is that "knoweth what is the mind of the Spirit."

GOD'S ELECT FOREORDAINED TO ETERNAL LIFE

ROMANS 8:28-34a.

28 And we know that all things work together for good to them that love God, to them who are the called according to *his* purpose.

29 For whom he did foreknow, he also did predestinate *to be* conformed to the image of his Son, that he might be the firstborn among many brethren.

30 Moreover whom he did predestinate, them he also called: and whom he called, them he also justified: and whom he justified, them he also glorified.

31 What shall we then say to these things? If God *be* for us, who *can be* against us?

32 He that spared not his own Son, but delivered him up for us all, how shall he not with him also freely give us all things?

33 Who shall lay any thing to the charge of God's elect? *It is* God that justifieth.

34a Who *is* he that condemneth?

I.V. ROMANS 8:29-31.

29 For him whom he did foreknow, he also did predestinate to be conformed **to his own image,** that he might be the firstborn among many brethren.

30 Moreover, **him** whom he did predestinate, **him** he also called; and **him** whom he called, **him** he also **sanctified;** and **him** whom he **sanctified, him** he also glorified.

31 What shall we then say to these things? If God be for us, who can **prevail** against us?

Paul here begins to comment about foreordination or predestination. Later he will build on this concept in setting forth the doctrine of election (Rom. 9:1-31), and in explaining the foreordination of the house of Israel. (Rom. 10:19-21; 11:1-10.) In each of these presentations, as is the case with most of the doctrinal discussions in his epistles, Paul simply comments about matters already known to and understood by his readers. He does not define or explain the doctrines in any detail. Unfortunately his comments have given rise to major misconceptions in the minds of sectarians who do not have the doctrinal and spiritual background to know what the Apostle means in the brief allusions he makes to the great gospel truths involved. Since the true doc-

267

trines of the gospel have been revealed anew in this day, the Latter-day Saints find themselves in a position comparable to that of the Roman Saints; they can understand Paul's teachings because they already know the doctrinal concepts to which he is alluding.

"To carry forward his own purposes among men and nations, the Lord foreordained chosen spirit children in pre-existence and assigned them to come to earth at particular times and places so that they might aid in furthering the divine will. These pre-existence appointments, made 'according to the foreknowledge of God the Father' (1 Pet. 1:2), simply designated certain individuals to perform missions which the Lord in his wisdom knew they had the talents and capacities to do.

"The mightiest and greatest spirits were foreordained to stand as prophets and spiritual leaders, giving to the people such portion of the Lord's word as was designed for the day and age involved. Other spirits, such as those who laid the foundations of the American nation, were appointed beforehand to perform great works in political and governmental fields. In all this there is not the slightest hint of compulsion; persons foreordained to fill special missions in mortality are as abundantly endowed with free agency as are any other persons. By their foreordination the Lord merely gives them the opportunity to serve him and his purposes if they will choose to measure up to the standard he knows they are capable of attaining." (*Mormon Doctrine*, 2nd ed., pp. 290-292.)

"Predestination is a sectarian substitute for the true doctrine of foreordination. Just as Lucifer 'sought to destroy the agency of man' in pre-existence (Moses 4:3), so through his ministers here he has taught a doctrine, based on scriptural distortions, of salvation and damnation without choice on the part of the individual. Predestination is the false doctrine that from all eternity God has ordered whatever comes to pass, having especial and particular reference to the salvation or damnation of souls. Some souls, according to this false concept, are irrevocably chosen for salvation, others for damnation; and there is said to be nothing any individual can do to escape his predestined inheritance in heaven or in hell as the case may be. . . .

"It is true that the words predestinate and predestinated are found in the King James translation of some of Paul's writings (Rom. 8:29-30; Eph. 1:5, 11), but Biblical revisions use the words foreordain and foreordained, which more accurately convey Paul's views. However, even as the King James Version renders the passages, there is no intimation of any compulsion or denial of free agency, for one of the dictionary definitions of foreordination is predestination, meaning the prior appointment (in pre-existence) of particular persons to perform designated labors or gain particular rewards." (*Mormon Doctrine*, 2nd ed., pp. 588-589.)

28. "Search diligently, pray always, and be believing, and all things shall work together for your good, if ye walk uprightly and remember the covenant wherewith ye have covenanted one with another." (D. & C. 90:24.) **The called]** See Rom. 9:1-31.

29. The noble and great in pre-existence (Abra. 3:22-23) were foreordained to gain eternal life, to become like Christ, to be his brethren in exaltation.

30. Those so foreordained are called and elected to receive the blessings of the gospel in this life; they are justified and sanctified by obedience to its laws; and they are finally glorified with Christ in exaltation.

31. Since God is on the side of his saints, what does it matter who opposes them?

32. Though God spared not his Son, and may not spare his saints, yet shall he not in due season give his saints all things, even as he gave them to his Son?

33-34a. Who then dares to condemn or lay a charge against the saints? If they do, let it be known that God shall be the final judge!

CHRIST MAKETH INTERCESSION FOR MAN

ROMANS 8:34b-39.

34b *It is* Christ that died, yea rather, that is risen again, who is even at the right hand of God, who also maketh intercession for us.

35 Who shall separate us from the love of Christ? *shall* tribula-

tion, or distress, or persecution, or famine, or nakedness, or peril, or sword?

36 As it is written, For thy sake we are killed all the day long; we are accounted as sheep for the slaughter.

37 Nay, in all these things we are more than conquerors through him that loved us.

38 For I am persuaded, that neither death, nor life, nor angels, nor principalities, nor powers, nor things present, nor things to come.

39 Nor height, nor depth, nor any other creature, shall be able to separate us from the love of God, which is in Christ Jesus our Lord.

34b. It is Christ that died, yea rather, that is risen again] The thoughts and hopes of the Lord's saints center — not in a dead, but in a living Christ; not in the agony of his death, but in the triumph and glory of his resurrection; not in the symbol of the cross, but in the upper room where he was seen and felt and where he ate before his worshiping disciples.

Who is even at the right hand of God] The Risen Lord — having a body of flesh and bones as tangible as man's, a body that can be felt and handled, a body that digests food — ascended into heaven and is on the right hand of that holy being who, as his Father, of necessity has the same kind of a body as does the glorified Son. Fathers beget children in their own image and likeness.

Who also maketh intercession for us] "To Christ, the Father has given 'power to make intercession for the children of men' (Mosiah 15:8), that is, he has the role of interceding, of mediating, of praying, petitioning and entreating the Father to grant mercy and blessings to men. (Rom. 8:34; Heb. 7:25.) Lehi said: 'He shall make intercession for all the children of men; and they that believe in him shall be saved. And because of the intercession for all, all men come unto God; wherefore, they stand in the presence of him, to be judged of him according to the truth and holiness which is in him.' (2 Ne. 2:9-10.)

"One of the great Messianic prophecies foretold that Christ would make 'intercession for the transgressors.' (Isa. 53:12; Mosiah 14:12.) His great Intercessory Prayer, excerpts of which are found in the 7th chapter of John, with some of the same petitions later being repeated on behalf of the Nephites (3 Ne. 19), is one of the chief illustrations of his pleadings on behalf of his brethren." (*Mormon Doctrine*, 2nd ed., pp. 387-388.)

35. The love of Christ] "Jesus Christ . . . Who so loved the world that he gave his own life, that as many as would believe might become the sons of God." (D. & C. 34:1-3.) **Persecution]** See *Commentary I*, pp. 328-332; Acts 5:33-42; 14:19-28; 17:1-14; 21:27-39.

36. We are killed] It was ever thus. In every dispensation Satan seeks to slay the saints. But in Paul's day the threat of persecution and death was greater than before or since. He lived, as it were, in the dispensation of persecution and death.

37. More than conquerors] Those who are persecuted for righteousness' sake are more than conquerors, even though they are called upon to lay down their lives in the Cause of Christ. Not only do they overcome or conquer the world, but they go on to eternal glory in the world to come. "And whoso layeth down his life in my cause, for my name's sake, shall find it again, even life eternal." (D. & C. 98:13.)

HOW THE LAW OF ELECTION OPERATES

ROMANS 9:1-33.

1 I say the truth in Christ, I lie not, my conscience also bearing me witness in the Holy Ghost,

2 That I have great heaviness and continual sorrow in my heart.

3 For I could wish that myself were accursed from Christ for my brethren, my kinsmen according to the flesh:

4 Who are Israelites; to whom *pertaineth* the adoption, and the glory, and the covenants, and the giving of the law, and the service *of God*, and the promises;

5 Whose *are* the fathers, and of whom as concerning the flesh Christ *came*, who is over all, God blessed for ever. Amen.

6 Not as though the word of God hath taken none effect. For they *are* not all Israel, which are of Israel:

7 Neither, because they are the seed of Abraham, *are they* all chil-

271

dren; but, In Isaac shall thy seed be called.

8 That is, They which are the children of the flesh, these *are* not the children of God: but the children of the promise are counted for the seed.

9 For this *is* the word of promise, At this time will I come, and Sarah shall have a son.

10 And not only *this;* but when Rebecca also had conceived by one, *even* by our father Isaac;

11 (For *the children* being not yet born, neither having done any good or evil, that the purpose of God according to election might stand, not of works, but of him that calleth;)

12 It was said unto her, The elder shall serve the younger.

13 As it is written, Jacob have I loved, but Esau have I hated.

14 What shall we say then? *Is there* unrighteousness with God? God forbid.

15 For he saith to Moses, I will have mercy on whom I will have mercy, and I will have compassion on whom I will have compassion.

16 So then *it is* not of him that willeth, nor of him that runneth, but of God that showeth mercy.

17 For the scripture saith unto Pharaoh, Even for this same pur-

pose have I raised thee up, that I might show my power in thee, and that my name might be declared throughout all the earth.

18 Therefore hath he mercy on whom he will *have* mercy, and whom he will he hardeneth.

19 Thou wilt say then unto me, Why doth he yet find fault? For who hath resisted his will?

20 Nay but, O man, who art thou that repliest against God? Shall the thing formed say to him that formed *it,* Why hast thou made me thus?

21 Hath not the potter power over the clay, of the same lump to make one vessel unto honour, and another unto dishonour,

22 *What* if God, willing to shew *his* wrath, and to make his power known, endured with much longsuffering the vessels of wrath fitted to destruction:

23 And that he might make known the riches of his glory on the vessels of mercy, which he had afore prepared unto glory,

24 Even us, whom he hath called, not of the Jews only, but also of the Gentiles?

25 As he saith also in Osee, I will call them my people, which were not my people; and her beloved, which was not beloved.

26 And it shall come to pass, *that* in the place where it was said unto them, Ye *are* not my

people; there shall they be called the children of the living God.

27 Esaias also crieth concerning Israel. Though the number of the children of Israel be as the sand of the sea, a remnant shall be saved:

28 For he will finish the work, and cut *it* short in righteousness: because a short work will the Lord make upon the earth.

29 And as Esaias said before, Except the Lord of Sabaoth had left us a seed, we had been as Sodoma, and been made like unto Gomorrha.

30 What shall we say then? That the Gentiles, which followed not after righteousness, have attained to righteousness, even the righteousness which is of faith.

31 But Israel, which followed after the law of righteousness, hath not attained to the law of righteousness.

32 Wherefore? Because *they sought it* not by faith, but as it were by the works of the law. For they stumbled at that stumblingstone;

33 As it is written, Behold, I lay in Sion a stumblingstone and rŏck of offence: and whosoever believeth on him shall not be ashamed.

I.V. ROMANS 9:3-5, 7, 32.

3 (For **once I could have wished** that myself were accursed from Christ,) for my brethren, my kinsmen according to the flesh;

4 Who are Israelites; **of whom are** the adoption, and the glory, and the covenants, and the giving of the law, and the service of God,

5 And the promises **which are made unto** the fathers; and of whom, as concerning the flesh, Christ **was, who is God over all,** blessed for ever. Amen.

7 Neither, because they are **all children** of Abraham, are they **the seed;** but, In Isaac shall thy seed be called.

32 **Wherefore they stumbled at that stumbling-stone, not by faith, but as it were by the works of the law;**

Paul here tells how the election of grace fits into the gospel scheme. His Roman readers knew what he was talking about because they already understood the doctrine of election. Since the sectarian world has little or no comprehension of pre-existence and eternal progression, upon which doctrines the principles of election are based, it is no wonder that these and other teachings of Paul are so completely misconstrued by them.

This doctrine of the election of grace is as follows: "As part of the new song the saints will sing when they 'see eye to eye' and the millennial era has been ushered in will be these words, 'The Lord hath redeemed his people, Israel, According to the election of grace, Which was brought to pass by the faith And covenant of their fathers.' (D. & C. 84:98-102; Rom. 11:1-5.) This election of grace is a very fundamental, logical, and important part of God's dealings with men through the ages. To bring to pass the salvation of the greatest possible number of his spirit children the Lord, in general, sends the most righteous and worthy saints to earth through the lineage of Abraham and Jacob. This course is a manifestation of his grace or in other words his love, mercy, and condescension toward his children.

"This election to a chosen lineage is based on pre-existent worthiness and is thus made 'according to the foreknowledge of God.' (1 Pet. 1:2.) Those so grouped together during their mortal probation have more abundant opportunities to make and keep the covenants of salvation, a right which they earned by pre-existent devotion to the cause of righteousness. As part of this election, Abraham and others of the noble and great spirits were chosen before they were born for the particular missions assigned them in this life. (Abra. 3:22-24; Rom. 9.)

"As with every basic doctrine of the gospel, the Lord's system of election based on pre-existent faithfulness has been changed and perverted by an apostate Christendom. So absurd have been the false conclusions reached in this field that millions of sincere though deceived persons have devoutly believed that in accordance with the divine will men were pre-destined to receive salvation or damnation which no act on their part could change. (*Teachings*, p. 189.)

"Actually, if the full blessings of salvation are to follow, the doctrine of election must operate twice. First, righteous spirits are elected or chosen to come to mortality as heirs of special blessings. Then, they must be called and elected again in this life, an occurrence which takes place when they join the true Church. (D. & C. 53:1.) Finally, in order to reap eternal salvation, they must press forward in obedient devotion to the truth until they make their 'calling and election sure' (2 Pet. 1), that is, are 'sealed up unto eternal life.' (D. & C. 131:5.)" (*Mormon Doctrine*, 2nd ed., pp. 216-217.)

Foreordination] See Rom. 8:28-34a. **Foreordination of Israel**] See Rom. 10:19-21; 11:1-10.

1. **Conscience**] For the generality of mankind, conscience consists in the pleading, striving, and enlightening promptings which come from the Light of Christ. But where the saints of God are concerned, those favored few who have the gift of the Holy Ghost, conscience sometimes includes the whisperings of the Spirit, the still small voice that comes from the Holy Ghost. (*Mormon Doctrine*, 2nd ed., pp. 156-157.)

3. Before his conversion Paul chose to be accursed, meaning that by failing to accept Christ he was choosing to be accursed, and this was so despite the fact he was born in the house of Israel. **My kinsmen according to the flesh**] Paul was of the tribe of Benjamin. (Rom. 11:1.)

4. To Israel God gave these six things:

(1) **The adoption**] Christ is the natural Son of God because God is his Father "after the manner of the flesh." (1 Ne. 11:18.) As such he is God's heir and shall inherit all that his Father hath. Those who are "led by the Spirit of God" (Rom. 8:14) are adopted into the family of God the Father, and thus they become sons of God, joint-heirs with his natural Son, inheriting jointly with him all that the Father hath. See Rom. 8:14-19.

Similarly all those who join the Church have power given them to become the sons and daughters of Jesus Christ by adoption. (D. & C. 39:1-6.) To the Nephite Saints of his day, who had been thus adopted, King Benjamin said: "Because of the covenant which ye have made ye shall be called the children of Christ, his sons, and his daughters; for behold, this day he hath spiritually begotten you; for ye say that your hearts are changed through faith on his name; therefore, ye are born of him and have become his sons and his daughters." (Mosiah 5:7.)

(2) **The glory**] Through sanctification, to "behold the face of God" in this life, and to enter into "the fulness of his glory," which is exaltation, in the life to come. (D. & C. 84:23-24.)

(3) **The covenants**] First to Abraham (Abra. 2:8-11; Gen. 12:1-3; 17:1-14; 23:15-18), then to Isaac (Gen. 26:2-5), and then to Jacob (Gen. 28:1-4, 10-15; 35:9-13) God gave the covenants of salvation, exaltation, and eternal increase through the patriarchal order. (D. & C. 132:29-37.) The blessings of these covenants were passed on to the whole house of Israel, the members of that chosen people thus becoming the children of the covenant. (3 Ne. 20:25-27.) These same blessings are now available to latter-day Israel, and are, in the main, received by them in the temples.

(4) **The giving of the law**] Only Israel had either the law of the gospel or the law of Moses. Paul is here speaking of the Mosaic system, although from time to time some in Israel, as for instance the Nephite portion of that people, did in fact have the law of the gospel in addition to the law of Moses.

(5) **The service of God**] Others served tribal or local false gods; only Israel knew the Living Lord, had his laws, and were priviliged to serve him, thereby becoming heirs of salvation in his everlasting kingdom.

(6) **The promises**] These include the covenants, with particular reference to the fact that the seed of Abraham, of Isaac, and of Jacob would inherit the same blessings possessed by those ancient patriarchs. These promises have also been given to the Latter-day Saints who are gathered Israel.

6-8. The house of Israel was a distinct people in pre-existence; that is, by obedience and devotion, certain of the spirit children of the Father earned the right to be born in the lineage of Abraham, of Isaac, and of Jacob, and of being natural heirs to the blessings of the gospel. But some of them, after such a favored birth, after being numbered with the chosen seed, turn from the course of righteousness and become children of the flesh; that is, they walk after the manner of the world, rejecting the spiritual blessings held in store for Israel. They are disinherited; they shall

276

not continue as children in the family of the prophets when the chosen race continues as a distinct people in the eternal worlds. Thus they are descendants of the prophets in this life but shall not inherit with the sons of God in the life to come.

11-12. God chose Jacob over Esau while the two were yet in Rebecca's womb and before either, as far as the works of this life are concerned, had earned any preferential status. Why? It is a pure matter of pre-existence. Jacob was coming into the world with greater spiritual capacity than Esau; he was foreordained to a special work; he was elected to serve in a chosen capacity.

13. Then through the lineage of Jacob, God sent those valiant spirits, those noble and great ones, who in his infinite wisdom and foreknowledge he knew would be inclined to serve him. Through Esau came those spirits of lesser valiance and devotion. Hence, in the very nature of things, many of Jacob's seed were righteous in this life, and many of Esau's were wicked, causing Malachi to say in the Lord's name, some fifteen hundred years later, that God loved the house of Jacob and hated the house of Esau. (Mal. 1:2-3.)

14-21. Then Paul asks: 'Is God unrighteous because he favors some people over others? The Israelites over the Egyptians, for instance?' Those who so maintain, Paul says, are resisting God and contending against him. The rationale of his argument is: Of course God is just in having a chosen people, for they earned the right to their preferential status by obedience and conformity in pre-existence. This same explanation shows why some people are born into the worlds as natural heirs of the priesthood and others are denied the fulness of its blessings.

22. Vessels of wrath fitted to destruction] The rebellious and disobedient; those, as the seed of Esau, who waste the days of their probation and walk in carnal paths.

23. Vessels of mercy, which he had afore prepared unto glory] Obedient and righteous persons, those, as the seed of Israel, who were foreordained in the pre-mortal life to receive that glory which is eternal life.

24-29. And who was foreordained to gain salvation? The house of Israel, of course, but also many of the Gentiles, an expansion of the doctrine of election which Paul proceeds to prove by the mouths of Hosea and Isaiah. (Hos. 1:10; 2:23; Isa. 1:9; 10:22-23.)

30-33. 'What then is the conclusion of the whole matter? It is that the Gentiles who once were unrighteous have now become righteous through Christ. It is that the Jews, supposing that the law alone is enough, have failed to gain righteousness through Christ. It is that both Jew and Gentile can be saved by faith in Christ.'

HOW FAITH AND SALVATION COME

ROMANS 10:1-18.

1 Brethren, my heart's desire and prayer to God for Israel is, that they might be saved.

2 For I bear them record that they have a zeal of God, but not according to knowledge.

3 For they being ignorant of God's righteousness, and going about to establish their own righteousness, have not submitted themselves unto the righteousness of God.

4 For Christ *is* the end of the law for righteousness to every one that believeth.

5 For Moses describeth the righteousness which is of the law, That the man which doeth those things shall live by them.

6 But the righteousness which is of faith speaketh on this wise, Say not in thine heart, Who shall

ascend into heaven? (that is, to bring Christ down *from above:*)

7 Or, Who shall descend into the deep? (that is, to bring up Christ again from the dead.)

8 But what saith it? The word is nigh thee, *even* in thy mouth, and in thy heart: that is, the word of faith, which we preach;

9 That if thou shalt confess with thy mouth the Lord Jesus, and shalt believe in thine heart that God hath raised him from the dead, thou shalt be saved.

10 For with the heart man believeth unto righteousness; and with the mouth confession is made unto salvation.

11 For the scripture saith, Whosoever believeth on him shall not be ashamed.

12 For there is no difference between the Jew and the Greek:

for the same Lord over all is rich unto all that call upon him.

13 For whosoever shall call upon the name of the Lord shall be saved.

14 How then shall they call on him in whom they have not believed? and how shall they believe in him of whom they have not heard? and how shall they hear without a preacher?

15 And how shall they preach, except they be sent? as it is written, How beautiful are the feet of them that preach the gospel of peace, and bring glad tidings of good things!

16 But they have not all obeyed the gospel. For Esaias saith, Lord, who hath believed our report?

17 So then faith *cometh* by hearing, and hearing by the word of God.

18 But I say, Have they not heard? Yes verily, their sound went into all the earth, and their words unto the ends of the world.

I.V. ROMANS 10:15-18.

15 And how shall they preach, except they be sent? as it is written, How beautiful are the feet of them that preach the gospel of peace, and bring glad tidings of good things!

16 So then faith cometh by hearing, and hearing by the word of God.

17 But I say, Have they not heard? Yes verily, their sound went into all the earth, and their words unto the ends of the world.

18 But they have not all obeyed the gospel. For Esaias saith, Lord, who hath believed our report?

1. True ministers of Christ seek to save souls. Nephi expressed it thus: "For the fulness of mine intent is that I may persuade men to come unto the God of Abraham, and the God of Isaac, and the God of Jacob, and be saved." (1 Ne. 6:4.)

2. **A zeal of God, but not according to knowledge]** Of whom speaketh the Apostle? Of the Jews only? Or of the sectarians? Of the Catholics? Of the non-Christians? Of all those who zealously, devoutly, and courageously follow a course of worship which is not the Lord's one and only plan of salvation? Yea, of them all. For salvation comes by obedience to the laws upon which its receipt is predicated and in no other way.

3. Jewish Israel as a whole was ignorant of the saving truths of the gospel, choosing instead to establish and defend the law of Moses which was now fulfilled. Or: Modern Christians as a whole are ignorant of God's true purposes as manifest through Joseph Smith and the restoration, choosing instead to establish and defend those remnants of ancient Christianity which they still possess.

4-5. God gave his law to Israel and commanded them to walk in his statutes and judgments, with the promise that by so doing they would be saved. (Lev. 18:1-5.) Now that law has an end in Christ, and salvation is available only for those who believe in him.

6-8. In these verses Paul draws a parallel between his teachings and those of Moses. In summarizing for Israel the statutes and judgments of God, Moses told the people that he had set before them life and death, blessing and cursing, and that if they would keep the commandments they would be saved, otherwise damnation was their lot. As part of his exhortation, to drive home the fact that they had been taught the law to the full, Moses said: "For this commandment which I command thee this day, it is not hidden from thee, neither is it far off. It is not in heaven, that thou shouldest say, Who shall go up for us to heaven, and bring it unto us, that we may hear it, and do it? Neither is it beyond the sea, that thou shouldest say, Who shall go over the sea for us, and bring it unto us, that we may hear it, and do it? But the word is very nigh unto thee, in thy mouth, and in thy heart, that thou mayest do it." (Deut. 30:11-14.)

Now Paul, knowing his hearers have had as much opportunity to learn the new law as Israel had to know the old one, and to drive home the fact that they must now turn to Christ, paraphrases the statements made by Moses. Those in his day, he says, do not need to ascend to heaven to learn of Christ and salvation. Neither do they need to seek Christ over the sea, or in any distant and hidden place. As it was in ancient Israel, the truths of salvation are very near, so near that they are already in their minds and hearts.

9. Based on Moses' language that "the word is very nigh unto thee, in thy mouth, and in thy heart" (Deut. 30:14), Paul here makes one of the most glorious proclamations of revealed religion. The word of salvation, the word already in their mouths, is to confess the divine Sonship of Christ; that which they must believe with all their souls is that God has raised him from the dead, thereby showing that he is the Son of God and that salvation is in him.

And Paul's proclamation accords with all the words of all the prophets of all the ages. "He that believeth on the Son hath everlasting life." (John 3:36.) Thus it is everlastingly. But the belief involved is that belief which moves mountains, which raises the dead, which works miracles, all in accord with the promise, "He that believeth on me, the works that I do shall he do also; and greater works than these shall he do." (John 14:12.)

11. This is Paul's rendition of part of Isaiah 28:16, as shown by his quotation of the whole verse in Romans 9:33, and it is a much improved rendition.

12-13. All men of every nation and lineage who call upon the true God for deliverance shall be saved. Joel so prophesied (Joel 2:32), and Paul reaffirms the doctrine. But to call upon God in the sense meant involves a knowledge of him, the acceptance of the gospel of his Son, and total adherence to its truths — all in harmony with the scripture which saith: "Whatsoever ye shall ask the Father in my name, which is right, believing that ye shall receive, behold it shall be given unto you." (3 Ne. 18:20.)

15. How shall they preach, except they be sent] What a denunciation this is of self-appointed ministers, ministers who become such because of a feeling in their heart that they want to do good, to preach the gospel, to do missionary work among the benighted of the earth! Was it not Paul's Lord who said, "Ye have not chosen me, but I have chosen you, and ordained you." (John 15:16.) Truly, "a man must be called of God, by prophecy, and by the laying on of hands, by those who are in authority, to preach the Gospel and administer in the ordinances thereof." (Fifth Article of Faith.) Those who have desires to do good, and do it, shall be rewarded, but it is not within the province of any man to set himself up as a minister of Christ or a light to the world. No man can give himself the power to baptize, or to confer the Holy Ghost, or to preach, or to seal men up unto eternal life in God's kingdom. True legal administrators are "called of God, as was Aaron." (Heb. 5:4.)

At this point Paul gives a paraphrasing quotation from Isaiah, whose actual words were: "How beautiful upon the mountains are the feet of him that bringeth good tidings, that publisheth peace; that bringeth good tidings of good, that publisheth salvation; that saith unto Zion, Thy God reigneth!" (Isa. 52:7.)

Extolling the work and peaching of "all the holy prophets," Abinadi said: "And these are they who have published peace, who have brought good tidings of good, who have published salvation; and said unto Zion: Thy God reigneth! And O how beautiful upon the mountains were their feet! And again, how beautiful upon the mountains are the feet of those that are still publishing peace! And again, how beautiful upon the mountains are the feet of those who shall hereafter publish peace, yea, from this time henceforth and forever! And behold, I say unto you, this is not all. For O how beautiful upon the mountains are the feet of him that bringeth good tidings, that is the founder of peace, yea, even the Lord, who has redeemed his people; yea, him who has granted salvation unto his people; For were it not for the redemption which he hath made for his people, which was prepared from the foundation of the world, I say unto you, were it not for this, all mankind must have perished." (Mosiah 15:14-19.)

17. Joseph Smith said: "Faith comes by hearing the word of God, through the testimony of the servants of God; that testimony is always attended by the spirit of prophecy and revelation." (*Teachings*, p. 148.) In other words faith follows preaching when: 1. The true gospel is taught; 2. Those who teach it are legal administrators who have been sent of God; 3. They teach by the power of the Spirit, so their preaching is attended by the spirit of prophecy and revelation; and 4. Those who hear the message receive the gifts of the Spirit, for the promise is that signs always have and always will accompany belief in the same gospel preached by Jesus and the apostles of old. (Mark 16:15-18.)

ISRAEL CHOSEN ACCORDING TO THE ELECTION OF GRACE

ROMANS 10:19-21; 11:1-10.

19 But I say, Did not Israel know? First Moses saith, I will provoke you to jealousy by *them that are* no people, *and* by a foolish nation I will anger you.

20 But Esaias is very bold, and saith, I was found of them that sought me not; I was made manifest unto them that asked not after me.

21 But to Israel he saith, All day long I have stretched forth my hands unto a disobedient and gainsaying people.

1 I say then, Hath God cast away his people? God forbid. For I also am an Israelite, of the seed of Abraham, *of* the tribe of Benjamin.

2 God hath not cast away his people which he foreknew. Wot ye not what the scripture saith of Elias? how he maketh intercession to God against Israel, saying,

3 Lord, they have killed thy prophets, and digged down thine altars; and I am left alone, and they seek my life.

4 But what saith the answer of God unto him? I have reserved to myself seven thousand men, who have not bowed the knee to *the image of* Baal.

5 Even so then at this present time also there is a remnant according to the election of grace.

6 And if by grace, then *is it* no more of works: otherwise grace is no more grace. But if *it be* of works, then is it no more grace: otherwise work is no more work.

7 What then? Israel hath not obtained that which he seeketh for; but the election hath obtained it, and the rest were blinded

8 (According as it is written, God hath given them the spirit of slumber, eyes that they should not see, and ears that they should not hear;) unto this day.

9 And David saith, Let their table be made a snare, and a trap, and a stumblingblock, and a recompence unto them:

10 Let their eyes be darkened, that they may not see, and bow down their back alway.

I.V. ROMANS 10:19; 11:2, 7.

19 But I say, Did not Israel know? **Now** Moses saith, I will provoke you to jealousy by them that are no people, and by a foolish nation I will anger you.

2 God hath not cast away his people which he foreknew. **Know**

ye not what the Scripture saith of Elias? how he maketh com-plaint to God against Israel, say-ing,

7 What then? Israel hath not obtained that which they seek for; but the election hath obtained it, and the rest were blinded,

Israel is an eternal people. Members of that chosen race first gained their inheritance with the faithful in the pre-mortal life. Israel was a distinct people in pre-existence. Many of the valiant and noble spirits in that first estate were chosen, elected, and foreordained to be born into the family of Jacob, so as to be natural heirs of all of the blessings of the gospel. It was to their pre-existent status that Moses alluded when, in speaking to mortal Israel, he said: "Remember the days of old, consider the years of many generations: ask thy father, and he will shew thee; thy elders, and they will tell thee. When the most High divided to the nations their inheritance, when he separated the sons of Adam, he set the bounds of the people according to the number of the children of Israel. For the Lord's portion is his people; Jacob is the lot of his inheritance." (Deut. 32:7-9.) Those of mor-tal Israel who walk uprightly in this second estate shall have eter-nal inheritance with Israel in the world to come. Foreordination] See Rom. 8:28-34a. Election] See Rom. 9:1-33.

10:19-21; 11:1-4] Did not ancient Israel know and keep the statutes and judgments of God? Some did; others did not. Thus the Lord, by the mouth of Moses, said such things as: "They are a very froward generation, children in whom is no faith," and hence the blessings shall go to other nations, who shall conse-quently provoke Israel to anger and jealousy. (Deut. 32:20-21.) Isaiah speaks of the same thing, Paul explains, saying even more plainly than did Moses that because Israel was "a rebellious people, which walketh in a way that was not good," that the Lord would then be found and accepted by other people (the Gentiles) who had not previously known him. (Isa. 65:1-2.) However, not all Israel was apostate, for when Elijah complained that he alone had remained true to the Lord, the reply came from Deity that there were yet seven thousand who had not bowed the knee to Baal. (1 Kings 19.)

5. A remnant according to the election of grace] As in the day of Elijah, so in the day of Paul, a few of Israel, a few of those foreordained and elected to receive the blessings of God in this life, a remnant of a once great nation, had remained faithful and true.

6-7. Grace . . . works . . . election] Israel, by God's grace, was elected to receive the blessings and glories of true religion, not by any works done in this life, but by grace alone (as far as this life is concerned) — all because of pre-existence and the law of foreordination. But, unhappily, only a few, those with especial spiritual talents, were in fact receiving the blessings in Paul's day.

8-10. And now, as though the point has not been driven home to the full, Paul calls upon Isaiah and David (paraphrasing their prophecies, as his custom was) to testify that Israel should sleep and slumber spiritually, with that which should have been for their welfare becoming a trap unto them. (Isa. 29:10; Ps. 69:22-23.)

GENTILES GRAFTED INTO ISRAEL

ROMANS 11:11-24.

11 I say then, Have they stumbled that they should fall? God forbid: but *rather* through their fall salvation *is come* unto the Gentiles, for to provoke them to jealousy.

12 Now if the fall of them *be* the riches of the world, and the diminishing of them the riches of the Gentiles; how much more their fulness?

13 For I speak to you Gentiles, inasmuch as I am the apostle of the Gentiles, I magnify mine office:

14 If by any means I may provoke to emulation *them which are* my flesh, and might save some of them.

15 For if the casting away of them *be* the reconciling of the world, what *shall* the receiving *of them be*, but life from the dead?

16 For if the firstfruit *be* holy, the lump *is* also *holy*: and if the root *be* holy, so *are* the branches.

17 And if some of the branches be broken off, and thou, being a wild olive tree, wert graffed in among them, and with them partakest of the root and fatness of the olive tree;

18 Boast n o t against the branches. But if thou boast, thou

bearest not the root, but the root thee.

19 Thou wilt say then, The branches were broken off, that I might be graffed in.

20 Well; because of unbelief they were broken off, and thou standest by faith. Be not high-minded, but fear:

21 For if God spared not the natural branches, *take heed* lest he also spare not thee.

22 Behold therefore the goodenss and severity of God: on them which fell, severity; but toward thee, goodness, if thou continue in *his* goodness: otherwise thou also shalt be cut off.

23 And they also, if they abide not still in unbelief, shall be graffed in: for God is able to graff them in again.

24 For if thou wert cut out of the olive tree which is wild by nature, and wert graffed contrary to nature into a good olive tree: how much more shall these, which be the natural *branches*, be graffed into their own olive tree?

I.V. ROMANS 11:15-19, 23-24.

15 For if the casting away of them is the reconciling of the world, what shall the **restoring** of them be, but life from the dead?

16 For if the first fruit is holy, the lump is also holy; and if the root is holy, so are the branches.

17 And if some of the branches be broken off, and thou, being a wild olive tree, **wast grafted** in among them, and with them partakest of the root and fatness of the olive tree;

18 Boast n o t against the branches, **for** thou bearest not the root, but the root thee.

19 **For if thou boast,** thou wilt say, The branches were broken off, that **we** might be **grafted** in.

23 And they also, if they abide not still in unbelief, shall be **grafted** in; for God is able to **graft** them in again.

24 For if thou **wast** cut out of the olive tree which is wild by nature, and **wast grafted** contrary to nature into a good olive tree; how much more shall these, which be the natural branches, be **grafted** into their own olive tree?

The promises were made to Israel, not to the Gentiles, with the understanding that those Gentiles who did repent and receive the truth would be adopted into the house of Israel. The promises were made to Abraham and to his seed, "that is to say, the literal seed, or the seed of the body," but in the promises this assurance also was given to Abraham: "As many as receive this Gospel shall be called after thy name, and shall be accounted thy seed, and shall rise up and bless thee, as their father." (Abra. 2:8-11.)

Of this adoption into the house of Israel, the Prophet Joseph Smith said: The Holy Ghost "is more powerful in expanding the mind, enlightening the understanding, and storing the intellect with present knowledge, of a man who is of the literal seed of Abraham, than one that is a Gentile, though it may not have half as much visible effect upon the body; for as the Holy Ghost falls upon one of the literal seed of Abraham, it is calm and serene; and his whole soul and body are only exercised by the pure spirit of intelligence; while the effect of the Holy Ghost upon a Gentile, is to purge out the old blood, and make him actually of the seed of Abraham. That man that has none of the blood of Abraham (naturally) must have a new creation by the Holy Ghost. In such a case, there may be more of a powerful effect upon the body, and visible to the eye, than upon an Israelite, while the Israelite at first might be far before the Gentile in pure intelligence." (*Teachings*, pp. 149-150.)

In his presentation to the Romans, Paul — who has been advocating the cause of the Gentiles, showing by reason and revelation that they too are entitled to the gospel — now explains that the gospel blessings come to the Gentiles because they are adopted into the house of Israel; that is, using the common figure that Israel was likened to a tame olive tree, Paul says that the Gentiles, as branches of a wild olive tree, are being grafted into the roots of the tame tree, the roots to whom the promises appertain.

Zenos, one of ancient Israel's prophets, wrote an allegory concerning the tame and wild olive trees. That portion, as preserved in the Book of Mormon, which pertains to Paul's day, includes these pronouncements: "Thus saith the Lord, I will liken thee, O house of Israel, like unto a tame olive-tree, which a man took and nourished in his vineyard; and it grew, and waxed old, and began to decay. . . . And it came to pass that the master of the vineyard saw it, and he said unto his servant: It grieveth me that I should lose this tree; wherefore, go and pluck the branches from a wild olive-tree, and bring them hither unto me; and we will pluck off those main branches which are beginning to wither away, and we will cast them into the fire that they may be burned. . . . Take thou the branches of the wild olive-tree, and graft them in, in the stead thereof; and these which I have plucked off I will cast into the fire and burn them, that they may not cumber the ground of my vineyard. . . . And it came to pass that the Lord of the vineyard looked and beheld the tree in the which the wild olive branches had been grafted; and it had sprung forth and begun to bear fruit. And he beheld that it was good; and the fruit thereof was like unto the natural fruit. And he said unto the servant: Behold, the branches of the wild tree have taken hold of the moisture of the root thereof, that the root thereof hath brought forth much strength; and because of the much strength of the root thereof the wild branches have brought forth tame fruit. Now, if we had not grafted in these branches, the tree thereof would have perished. And now, behold, I shall lay up much fruit, which the tree thereof hath brought forth; and the fruit thereof I shall lay up against the season, unto mine own self." (Jacob 5:3, 7, 9, 17-18.)

11-15. Is Israel cast off forever? No. Though she now has fallen, and salvation has gone instead to the Gentiles, in the last days Israel shall return, as though from the dead. In the meantime Paul, though his mission is to the Gentiles, will strive to get Israel to emulate the Gentiles that he might perchance save some of them.

16. If the firstfruit be holy, the lump is also holy] Paul here refers to the heave offering in which Israel offered a cake of dough made of the firstfruits of the harvest. (Num. 15:17-21.) As this offering of a single cake signified that the whole harvest was hallowed, so the ancient separation of the Jews from among all people, as an offering to God, now hallowed all people for the receipt of the truth.

16-24. To catch the full vision of Paul's comments about the tame and wild olive trees, Paul's readers must have had the equivalent of the knowledge found in Zenos' allegory. And, indeed, that account itself speaks of the latter-day grafting in of the natural branches again. "Let us take of the branches of these which I have planted in the nethermost parts of my vineyard," Zenos records, "and let us graft them into the tree from whence they came; and let us pluck from the tree those branches whose fruit is most bitter, and graft in the natural branches of the tree in the stead thereof." (Jacob 5:52.)

WHAT IS THE FULNESS OF THE GENTILES?

ROMANS 11:25-36.

25 For I would not, brethren, that ye should be ignorant of this mystery, lest ye should be wise in your own conceits; that blindness in part is happened to Israel, until the fulness of the Gentiles be come in.

26 And so all Israel shall be saved: as it is written, There shall come out of Sion the Deliverer, and shall turn away ungodliness from Jacob:

27 For this *is* my covenant unto them, when I shall take away their sins.

28 As concerning the gospel, *they are* enemies for your sakes: but as touching the election, *they are* beloved for the fathers' sakes.

29 For the gifts and calling of God *are* without repentance.

30 For as ye in times past have not believed God, yet have now obtained mercy through their unbelief:

31 Even so have these also now not believed, that through your mercy they also may obtain mercy.

32 For God hath concluded them all in unbelief, that he might have mercy upon all.

33 O the depth of the riches both of the wisdom and knowledge of God! how unsearchable *are* his judgments, and his ways past finding out!

34 For who hath known the mind of the Lord? or who hath been his counsellor?

35 Or who hath first given to him, and it shall be recompensed unto him again?

36 For of him, and through him, and to him, *are* all things: to whom *be* glory for ever. Amen.

I.V. ROMANS 11:26.

26 And **then** all Israel shall be saved; as it is written, There shall come out of Sion the Deliverer, and shall turn away ungodliness from Jacob;

25. The fulness of the Gentiles] Eventually every living soul shall hear the message of salvation. "For verily the voice of the Lord is unto all men, and there is none to escape; and there is no eye that shall not see, neither ear that shall not hear, neither heart that shall not be penetrated." (D. & C. 1:2.) But gospel truths go to those of the various nations of the earth on a priority basis. Whole races and nations of men shall first hear the word in the spirit world; others shall have the testimony of Christ borne to them while here in mortality.

For the nearly two thousand years between Abraham and Christ, the statutes and judgments of God were reserved almost exclusively for the seed of Abraham and for the house of Israel. During the mortal ministry of our Lord, the message was limited to Israel, to the Jews, and it was not then offered to the Gentiles. After Jesus' resurrection, Peter opened the door to the preaching of the gospel of the Gentiles, and Paul became their chief apostolic advocate and teacher. Thus there was a period or time appointed for the Jews to hear the word, and then a period of time for the Gentiles to take precedence. The times of the Gentiles is the period during which the gospel goes to them on a preferential basis, and this will continue until they have had a full opportunity to accept the truth, or in other words until the fulness of the Gentiles. Then the message will go again to the Jews, meaning to the Jews as a nation and as a people.

Jesus said that the Jews would be "scattered among all nations," which is the now existing situation. "But they shall be gathered again," he continued. "But they shall remain until the times of the Gentiles be fulfilled. . . . And when the times of the Gentiles is come in, a light shall break forth among them that sit in darkness, and it shall be the fulness of my gospel; But they receive it not; for they perceive not the light, and they turn their hearts from me because of the precepts of men. And in that generation shall the times of the Gentiles be fulfilled." (D. & C. 45:19, 25, 28-30.)

Gentiles] See Acts 10:21-35. **First shall be last]** See Acts 13:42-49. **Times of the Gentiles]** See *Commentary I*, pp. 654-658.

26-27. Salvation will come again to the Jews as a nation at the Second Coming, the day when the Deliverer comes again, the day when the times of the Gentiles is fulfilled. Then he will take away their sins, and they again shall be his people as in days of old.

28-32. Because the Jews (as a nation) rejected the gospel in Paul's day, it was taken to the Gentiles; because the Gentiles (as a whole) shall reject the gospel in this day, it shall be taken again to the Jews, when the fulness of the Gentiles comes in.

29. The gifts and calling of God are without repentance] God bestows gifts and graces upon men and calls them to his holy work without reference to any achievements or preparations on their part — as far as this life is concerned. Men are elected, called, foreordained, all on the basis of pre-existent preparation. Thus Joseph Smith was called to stand as one of the mightiest prophets of the ages, called as it were without repentance; that is, he had not received the gospel, he had not established himself as a leader of power and influence; he was called, rather, according to the foreknowledge of God because of the talents and capacities earned in the pre-mortal life.

33. "Great is his wisdom, marvelous are his ways, and the extent of his doings none can find out." (D. & C. 76:2.)

36. "By him, and through him, and of him, the worlds are and were created." (D. & C. 76:24.)

"PRESENT YOUR BODIES A LIVING SACRIFICE . . . TO GOD"

ROMANS 12:1-3.

1 I beseech you therefore, brethren, by the mercies of God, that ye present your bodies a living sacrifice, holy, acceptable unto God, *which is* your reasonable service.

2 And be not conformed to this world: but be ye transformed by the renewing of your mind, that ye may prove what *is* that good, and acceptable, and perfect, will of God.

3 For I say, through the grace given unto me, to every man that is among you, not to think *of himself* more highly than he ought to think; but to think soberly, according as God hath dealt to every man the measure of faith.

1. Present your bodies a living sacrifice] Sacrifices are of two kinds: living and dead, or in other words, temporal and spiritual. Under the law of Moses, animals were slain in similitude of the coming sacrifice of the Son of God; such were temporal sacrifices, sacrifices involving death. But under the law of Christ, men are called upon to make living sacrifices, to sacrifice themselves by obedience to the laws and ordinances of the gospel.

Paul is here alluding to the fact that the old sacrifices, those unto death, are abolished, that they have been replaced with a new order, sacrifices unto life. As with almost all doctrines, this is taught in the Book of Mormon with greater plainness and perfection than in the Bible. To the Nephites, after his resurrection, the Lord Jesus said: "Ye shall offer up unto me no more the shedding of blood; yea, your sacrifices and your burnt offerings shall be done away, for I will accept none of your sacrifices and your burnt offerings. And ye shall offer for a sacrifice unto me a broken heart and a contrite spirit. And whoso cometh unto me with a broken heart and a contrite spirit, him will I baptize with fire and with the Holy Ghost." (3 Ne. 9:19-20.) Thus to present one's body as a living sacrifice is to come forth with a broken heart and a contrite spirit through obedience.

2. Be not conformed to this world] Live not after the manner of the world, where lust, evil, and carnality prevail; overcome the world; be a saint in very deed. **World]** See 1 John 2:15-17; *Commentary I*, pp. 749-752.

Be ye transformed] Become a new creature of the Holy Ghost. Crucify the lusts of the flesh. Be born again. **Born again]** See 1 John 5:1-5; *Commentary I*, pp. 140-142.

Renewing of your mind] Thoughts father deeds. Men do what they think. To be virtuous they must heed the command: "Let virtue garnish thy thoughts unceasingly." (D. & C. 121:45.) Thus those who leave the world and turn to Christ must renew their minds by thinking pure and wholesome thoughts; they must forsake the mind that revels in carnal thoughts and cleave to the mind that ponders the things of the Spirit. "To be carnally-minded is death, and to be spiritually-minded is life eternal." (2 Ne. 9:39.)

3. Shun pride. Be humble.

SAINTS TO USE OWN GRACE-GIVEN GIFTS

ROMANS 12:4-8.

4 For as we have many members in one body, and all members have not the same office:

5 So we, *being* many, are one body in Christ, and every one members one of another.

6 Having then gifts differing according to the grace that is given to us, whether prophecy, *let us prophecy* according to the proportion of faith;

7 Or ministry, *let us wait* on *our* ministering: or he that teacheth, on teaching;

8 Or he that exhorteth, on exhortation: he that giveth, *let him do it* with simplicity; he that ruleth, with diligence; he that showeth mercy, with cheerfulness.

Members of the Church should use, and be called to positions which enable them to use, the specific talents and gifts with which they are endowed. Musicians belong in the choir, preachers in the pulpit, teachers in the classroom, and prophets in positions of presidency. Those who can influence the young and rising generation for good should be appointed to do so; those having converting power and zeal should labor as missionaries; and those with financial and business ability should be assigned to build up the kingdom temporally. A bishop may not be a farmer, nor an apostle a financier; but there will be others who can serve in these areas. And one of the talents of superior leaders is their ability to call the right person to serve in the right position at the right time.

LIVE AS BECOMETH SAINTS

ROMANS 12:9-21.

9 *Let* love be without dissimulation. Abhor that which is evil; cleave to that which is good.

10 *Be* kindly affectioned one to another with brotherly love; in honour preferring one another;

11 Not slothful in business; fervent in spirit; serving the Lord;

12 Rejoicing in hope; patient in tribulation; continuing instant in prayer;

13 Distributing to the necessity of saints; given to hospitality.

293

14 Bless them which persecute you: bless, and curse not.

15 Rejoice with them that do rejoice, and weep with them that weep.

16 *Be* of the same mind one toward another. Mind not high things, but condescend to men of low estate. Be not wise in your own conceits.

17 Recompense to no man evil for evil. Provide things honest in the sight of all men.

18 If it be possible, as much as lieth in you, live peaceably with all men.

19 Dearly beloved, avenge not yourselves, but *rather* give place unto wrath: for it is written, Vengeance *is mine;* I will repay, saith the Lord.

20 Therefore if thine enemy hunger, feed him; if he thirst, give him drink: for in so doing thou shalt heap coals of fire on his head.

21 Be not overcome of evil, but overcome evil with good.

Paul is the apostle of good works, of personal righteousness, of keeping the commandments, of pressing forward with a steadfastness in Christ, of earning the right to eternal life by obedience to the laws and ordinances of the gospel. All these good works, however, are meritorious, as he has already told the Romans, only because of the atoning sacrifice of Christ.

And so now Paul builds on the doctrinal foundation he has already laid by naming in terse, epigramatic statements many of the things which saints must do to "work out" their "own salvation with fear and trembling." (Philip. 2:12.) And how perfect his approach is: first, teach the doctrines; then, exhort to righteousness. Ethical standards grow out of religion. A knowledge of the doctrines of salvation is both the reason for and the incentive to the living of goodly lives. Exhortations mean little unless they rest on a doctrinal foundation. The incentive to conform to gospel standards grows out of a knowledge of gospel laws. Encouraging chastity among those who are ignorant of God and his laws has little effect, but teaching it to those who already know through purity and morality they can be saved has a profound effect. As to the relationship between religion and ethics, between the word of God and living upright lives, the Nephite scriptures say: "And now, as the preaching of the word had a great tendency to lead the people to do that which was just — yea, it had had more powerful effect upon the minds of the people than the sword, or anything else, which had happened unto them — therefore Alma thought it was expedient that they should try the virtue of the word of God." (Alma 31:5.)

9-21. This whole passage, as much perhaps as any other, shows the scholarship, the literary craftsmanship, and the pure inspiration that flowed from the pen of Paul. How better could any of these exhortations been phrased? Does not the language compare favorably with that used by the Lord Jesus himself as he ministered among men?

BE SUBJECT UNTO GOD'S MINISTERS

ROMANS 13:1-7.

1 Let every soul be subject unto the higher powers. For there is no power but of God: the powers that be are ordained of God.

2 Whosoever therefore resisteth the power, resisteth the ordinance of God: and they that resist shall receive to themselves damnation.

3 For rulers are not a terror to good works, but to the evil. Wilt thou then not be afraid of the power? do that which is good, and thou shalt have praise of the same:

4 For he is the minister of God to thee for good. But if thou do that which is evil, be afraid; for he beareth not the sword in vain: for he is the minister of God, a revenger to *execute* wrath upon him that doeth evil.

5 Wherefore *ye* must needs be subject, not only for wrath, but also for conscience sake.

6 For for this cause pay ye tribute also: for they are God's ministers, attending continually upon this very thing.

7 Render therefore to all their dues: tribute to whom tribute *is due;* custom to whom custom; fear to whom fear; honour to whom honour.

I.V. ROMANS 13:1-2, 4, 6-7.

1 Let every soul be subject unto the higher powers. For there is no power **in the church** but of God; the powers that be are ordained of God.

2 Whosoever therefore resisteth the power, resisteth the ordinance of God; and they that resist shall receive to themselves **punishment.**

4 For he is the minister of God to thee for good. But if thou do that which is evil be afraid;

295

for he beareth not the **rod** in vain; for he is the minister of God, a revenger to execute wrath upon him that doeth evil.

6 **For,** for this cause pay ye **your consecrations** also **unto them;** for they are God's ministers, attending continually upon this very thing.

7 **But first,** render to all their dues, **according to custom,** tribute to whom tribute, custom to whom custom, **that your consecrations may be done in fear of him to whom fear belongs, and in honor of him to whom honor belongs.**

To gain salvation the saints must be subject to God's ministers. The doctrines and ordinances of the gospel cannot be separated from those appointed to teach Christ's gospel and perform his ordinances. Those who accept the gospel do so by submitting to the will and dictation of Christ. They come to the legal administrators who teach the doctrines of Christ and who perform the ordinances of salvation in his name and by his authority.

God's truths cannot be accepted in an abstract and impersonal way; they must always be taught by someone sent of God. "How shall they preach, except they be sent?" (Rom. 10:15.) And gospel ordinances cannot be performed except by commissioned servants empowered so to act by their Master. It is an eternal, invarying verity that salvation seekers must submit to the direction of those whom God has placed over them in his kingdom; otherwise they cannot be saved. The saints, therefore, must be subject to God's ministers.

Conformity to church discipline sanctifies the soul. "I will prove you in all things, whether you will abide in my covenant, even unto death, that you may be found worthy," the Lord says. (D. & C. 98:14.) The Lord's covenant or gospel is always administered by those whom he has appointed so to act, and as a consequence the saints are bound to take counsel and direction from them. Thus when the President of the Church, the stake president, the bishop, or any duly commissioned church officer counsels those over whom he presides to follow a certain course, the church members involved must do so at the peril of losing their salvation. Paul's pronouncement, as restored to its original state by the Inspired Version, so specifies.

Civil powers] See 1 Pet. 2:13-25.

"LOVE IS THE FULFILLING OF THE LAW"

ROMANS 13:8-10.

8 Owe no man any thing, but to love one another: for he that loveth another hath fulfilled the law.

9 For this, Thou shalt not commit adultery, Thou shalt not kill, Thou shalt not steal, Thou shalt not bear false witness, Thou shalt not covet; and if *there be* any other commandment, it is briefly comprehended in this saying, namely, Thou shalt love thy neighbour as thyself.

10 Love worketh no ill to his neighbour: therefore love *is* the fulfilling of the law.

"Many attributes and feelings are embraced in gospel love: devotion, adoration, reverence, tenderness, mercy, compassion, condescension, grace, service, solicitude, gratitude, kindness. Love's chief manifestation is seen in the grace of God as this is found in the infinite and eternal atonement." (*Mormon Doctrine*, 2nd ed., pp. 459-460.) See *Commentary I*, pp. 229-230; 725-727; 746-749. **Love between husband and wife]** See Eph. 5:22-33.

8. 'Free yourself from all debt, except to love one another.' Men are commanded to love God and their fellow men; failure so to do is disobedience and therefore sin. Men owe a debt of love to Deity and to their fellow beings, and through love they obey or keep or fulfil the law.

9-10. Those who truly love their fellow mortals thereby automatically keep all the commandments, which obedience constitutes total conformity to or fulfilment of the whole law.

RIGHTEOUSNESS LEADS TO SALVATION

ROMANS 13:11-14.

11 And that, knowing the time, that now *it is* high time to awake out of sleep: for now *is* our salvation nearer than when we believed.

12 The night is far spent, the day is at hand: let us therefore cast off the works of darkness, and let us put on the armour of light.

13 Let us walk honestly, as in the day; not in rioting and drunkenness, not in chambering and wantonness, not in strife and envying.

14 But put ye on the Lord Jesus Christ, and make not provision for the flesh, to *fulfill* the lusts *thereof*.

I.V. ROMANS 13:14.

14 But put ye on the Lord Jesus Christ, and make not provision for the flesh, to **gratify** the lusts thereof.

Salvation is available because of the atonement, but it is gained through personal righteousness, as Paul proclaims again and again. **Salvation]** See 1 Pet. 1:1-16. **Work out your salvation]** See Philip. 2:12-16.

11. Now is our salvation nearer than when we believed] 'We are nearer the goal of salvation now than when we first accepted the gospel; we have made progress along the path leading to eternal life; through continued obedience we have acquired more of the attributes of godliness and become more Christlike.'

Since salvation consists in having the character, perfections, and attributes of Deity, and since all things are governed and controlled by law, it is a self-evident truth that some people are nearer to gaining eternal life than are others. Some have just entered the gate of repentance and baptism and have thus just started out in the direction of salvation; others, through long devotion and obedience after baptism, have begun to acquire measurably the attributes of godliness, and hence are nearer the goal than are the newborn babes in Christ.

12-14. Keep the commandments.

ARE MEAT, DRINK, SABBATH DAY, MATTERS OF RELIGION?

ROMANS 14:1-23.

1 Him that is weak in the faith receive ye, *but* not to doubtful disputations.

2 For one believeth that he may eat all things: another, who is weak, eateth herbs.

3 Let not him that eateth despise him that eateth not; and let

not him which eateth not judge him that eateth: for God hath received him.

4 Who art thou that judgest another man's servant? to his own master he standeth or falleth. Yea, he shall be holden up: for God is able to make him stand.

5 One man esteemeth one day above another: another esteemeth every day *alike*. Let every man be fully persuaded in his own mind.

6 He that regardeth the day, regardeth *it* unto the Lord; and he that regardeth not the day, to the Lord he doth not regard *it*. He that eateth, eateth to the Lord, for he giveth God thanks; and he that eateth not, to the Lord he eateth not, and giveth God thanks.

7 For none of us liveth to himself, and no man dieth to himself.

8 For whether we live, we live unto the Lord; and whether we die, we die unto the Lord: whether we live therefore, or die, we are the Lord's.

9 For to this end Christ both died, and rose, and revived, that he might be Lord both of the dead and living.

10 But why dost thou judge thy brother? or why dost thou set at nought thy brother? for we shall all stand before the judgment seat of Christ.

11 For it is written, *As* I live, saith the Lord, every knee shall bow to me, and every tongue shall confess to God.

12 So then every one of us shall give account of himself to God.

13 Let us not therefore judge one another any more: but judge this rather, that no man put a stumblingblock or an occasion to fall in *his* brother's way.

14 I know, and am persuaded by the Lord Jesus, that *there is* nothing unclean of itself: but to him that esteemeth any thing to be unclean, to him *it is* unclean.

15 But if thy brother be grieved with *thy* meat, now walkest thou not charitably. Destroy not him with thy meat, for whom Christ died.

16 Let not then your good be evil spoken of:

17 For the kingdom of God is not meat and drink; but righteousness, and peace, and joy in the Holy Ghost.

18 For he that in these things serveth Christ *is* acceptable to God, and approved of men.

19 Let us therefore follow after the things which make for peace, and things wherewith one may edify another.

20 For meat destroy not the work of God. All things indeed *are* pure; but *it is* evil for that man who eateth with offence.

21 *It is* good neither to eat flesh, nor to drink wine, nor *any thing* whereby thy brother stumbleth, or is offended, or is made weak.

22 Hast thou faith? have *it* to thyself before God. Happy *is* he that condemneth not himself in that thing which he alloweth.

23 And he that doubteth is damned if he eat, because *he eateth* not of faith: for whatsoever *is* not of faith is sin.

I.V. ROMANS 14:11, 15, 23.

11 For **I live, saith the Lord, as it is written. And** every knee shall bow to me, and every tongue shall **swear** to God.

15 But if t h y brother be grieved with thy meat, **thou walkest not charitably if thou eatest. Therefore** destroy not him with thy meat, for whom Christ died.

23 And he that doubteth is **condemned** if he eat, because **it** is not of faith; for whatsoever is not of faith is sin.

Two of the dead performances of the Mosaic law are here raising their ugly heads to plague the Jewish converts in Rome. These are: 1. The ancient dietary restrictions, such as the prohibitions in Leviticus 11 against eating certain animals, fowl, fish, and creeping things, some thirty-two of which happen to be prohibited by name; and 2. The strict commandment that Israel should observe an appointed weekly Sabbath as a sign and witness that they were the Lord's people. This Sabbath was in commemoration of their deliverance from Egyptian bondage, and as a consequence fell on a different day each week. **Sabbath Day]** See Rev. 1:9-11.

But now Christ has come; the law is fulfilled; its performances are no longer binding. On the point of dietary restrictions, Jesus himself has said: "Do ye not perceive, that whatsoever thing from without entereth into the man, it cannot defile him; Because it entereth not into his heart, but into the belly, and goeth out into the draught, purging all meats?" (Mark 7:18-19.) And as to the Sabbath Day, the apostles have now decreed that worship reserved for that day should be transferred to Sunday, the Lord's Day, and should be in commemoration of Christ's coming forth in the resurrection.

However, some of the Jewish converts, apparently not fully envisioning the new order of things, are still trying to live the dead law. Also there seem to be among the Roman Saints those who have other self-imposed and foolish personal rules where eating and drinking are concerned, even as there are Word of Wisdom faddists in the Church today.

Paul's approach to the problem follows the pattern set by the apostles in deciding the question of circumcision. (Acts 15:1-35.) Since eating and drinking, and even some matters connected with Sabbath observance, are not to be compared in importance with the great basic realities of Christianity, such as the divine Sonship of Christ, Paul wisely takes a tolerant view. Bear with the weak, he says. It is not their dietary preferences that will save them, but their faith in Christ. Granted that the faddists and extremists are still worshiping to some extent at the shrine of Moses, yet exhibit Christian charity toward them. Until they grow in faith, a severe and strict approach may drive them from the fold of fellowship and lose them to the Cause. All men are foolish to some extent, and it becometh saints to bear with each other, that all eventually may be strong and sound and stable, anchored securely on the true foundation which Christ laid. And as it was in Paul's day, so should it be in ours.

1. Faith comes by hearing the truth from the lips of a legal administrator who speaks by the power of the Spirit and not by argument or debate. The spirit of contention is of the devil.

2-4. Church members should not condemn and sit in judgment upon each other; judgment is the Lord's.

5-6. It is not *the* day but *a* day that is important in Sabbath observance. Labor on the Sabbath is *malum prohibitum* and not *malum in se;* that is, it is wrong because it is prohibited and not wrong in itself, as is the case, for instance, with murder and stealing.

7-9. In life and in death we are the Lord's; he has bought us with his blood. (1 Cor. 6:20.)

10-12. Jehovah said to Isaiah: "Look unto me, and be ye saved, all the ends of the earth: for I am God, and there is none else. I have sworn by myself, the word is gone out of my mouth in righteousness, and shall not return, That unto me every knee shall bow, every tongue shall swear." (Isa. 45:22-23.) Paul, by the spirit of revelation, quotes from this ancient declaration and applies it pointedly and specifically to Christ — thus making Jehovah and Christ the same being.

13-23. Humor those who are weak in the faith; let them be Word of Wisdom fanatics until they learn better; hold up before them the great spiritual reality that the gospel is not meat and drink, but righteousness, and peace, and joy in the Holy Ghost; labor for their perfections, but do not contend, do not cast them off because they are not yet stable and sound.

23. Whatsoever is not of faith is sin] This law applies to the saints, to those who have the light, who know that salvation is in Christ, to those who are under covenant to keep the commandments. It is not applicable to the world in general, for sin is not imputed where there is no law. Thus the saints are guilty of sin when they fall short of those high standards they are obligated to attain. In the field of the Word of Wisdom, for instance, it is a sin for a Latter-day Saint to use tea, coffee, tobacco, or liquor, but it is not a sin for a nonmember of the Church so to do.

TRUE SAINTS FELLOWSHIP EACH OTHER

ROMANS 15:1-7.

1 We then that are strong ought to bear the infirmities of the weak, and not to please ourselves.

2 Let every one of us please *his* neighbour for *his* good to edification.

3 For even Christ pleased not himself; but, as it is written, The reproaches of them that reproached thee fell on me.

4 For whatsoever things were written aforetime were written for our learning, that we through patience and comfort of the scriptures might have hope.

5 Now the God of patience and consolation grant you to be likeminded one toward another according to Christ Jesus:

6 That ye may with one mind *and* one mouth glorify God, even the Father of our Lord Jesus Christ.

7 Wherefore receive ye one another, as Christ also received us to the glory of God.

I.V. ROMANS 15:5.

5 Now the God of patience and consolation grant you to be likeminded one toward another according **as** Christ Jesus **was;**

Christ, the prototype of all good and perfect things, fellow-shiped us, as his brethren, in our weaknesses and with our infirmities. Now we should fellowship each other, those who are strong in the faith helping the weak, bearing their spiritual shortcomings, until all are like-minded and have become one with each other. **Fellowship with God]** See 1 John 1:1-7.

1-3. Those who are Christ's are called upon, not to please themselves, but to serve each other, even as he served us.

4. Scriptures] See 2 Tim. 3:14-17.

6. One mind and one mouth] See 1 Cor. 1:1-16.

GOSPEL GIFTS POURED OUT UPON GENTILES

ROMANS 15:8-33.

8 Now I say that Jesus Christ was a minister of the circumcision for the truth of God, to confirm the promises *made* unto the fathers:

9 And that the Gentiles might glorify God for *his* mercy; as it is written, For this cause I will confess to thee among the Gentiles, and sing unto thy name.

10 And again he saith, Rejoice, ye Gentiles, with his people.

11 And again, Praise the Lord, all ye Gentiles; and laud him, all ye people.

12 And again, Esaias saith, There shall be a root of Jesse, and he that shall rise to reign over the Gentiles; in him shall the Gentiles trust.

13 Now the God of hope fill you with all joy and peace in believing, that ye may abound in hope, through the power of the Holy Ghost.

14 And I myself also am persuaded of you, my brethren, that ye also are full of goodness, filled with all knowledge, able also to admonish one another.

15 Nevertheless, brethren, I have written the more boldly unto you in some sort, as putting you in mind, because of the grace that is given to me of God,

16 That I should be the minister of Jesus Christ to the Gentiles, ministering the gospel of God, that the offering up of the Gentiles might be acceptable, being sanctified by the Holy Ghost.

17 I have therefore whereof I may glory through Jesus Christ in those things which pertain to God.

18 For I will not dare to speak of any of those things which Christ

hath not wrought by me, to make the Gentiles obedient, by word and deed,

19 Through mighty signs and wonders, by the power of the Spirit of God; so that from Jerusalem, and round about unto Illyricum, I have fully preached the gospel of Christ.

20 Yea, so have I strived to preach the gospel, not where Christ was named, lest I should build upon another man's foundation:

21 But as it is written, To whom he was not spoken of, they shall see: and they that have not heard shall understand.

22 For which cause also I have been much hindered from coming to you.

23 But now having no more place in these parts, and having a great desire these many years to come unto you;

24 Whensoever I take my journey into Spain, I will come to you: for I trust to see you in my journey, and to be brought on my way thitherward by you, if first I be somewhat filled with your *company*.

25 But now I go unto Jerusalem to minister unto the saints.

26 For it hath pleased them of Macedonia and Achaia to make a certain contribution for the poor saints which are at Jerusalem.

27 It hath pleased them verily; and their debtors they are. For if the Gentiles have been made partakers of their spiritual things, their duty is also to minister unto them in carnal things.

28 When therefore I have performed this, and have sealed to them this fruit, I will come by you into Spain.

29 And I am sure that, when I come unto you, I shall come in the fulness of the blessing of the gospel of Christ.

30 Now I beseech you, brethren, for the Lord Jesus Christ's sake, and for the love of the Spirit, that ye strive together with me in *your* prayers to God for me;

31 That I may be delivered from them that do not believe in Judea; and that my service which *I have* for Jerusalem may be accepted of the saints;

32 That I may come unto you with joy by the will of God, and may with you be refreshed.

33 Now the God of peace *be* with you all. Amen.

I.V. ROMANS 15:24.

24 **When** I take my journey into Spain, I will come to you; **for** I trust to see you in my journey, and to be brought on my way thitherward by you, if first I be somewhat filled **through** your **prayers.**

8. Jesus Christ was a minister of the circumcision] How can this be since Christ came to fulfil and replace the ancient order? Since it was he who said: "The law of circumcision is done away in me"? (Moro. 8:8.) Paul's explanation is both wondrous and inspiring. Says he: 'Jehovah who gave the law of circumcision is Christ, and in his mortal ministry he came both to confirm and to fulfil his own law.'

9. As proof of this exposition, Paul says further: 'It was Christ, speaking anciently under his designation as the great Jehovah, who said his gospel would go to the Gentiles.'

9-12. Paul cites Psalm 18:19, Deuteronomy 32:43, Psalm 117:1, and Isaiah 11:1, 10 to show that nations other than Israel, meaning Gentile peoples, were destined to receive the gospel. **Gentiles]** See Acts 10:21-35.

12. Root of Jesse] The Stem of Jesse spoken of by Isaiah is Christ. As to the Root of Jesse: "Behold, thus saith the Lord, it is a descendant of Jesse, as well as of Joseph, unto whom rightly belongs the priesthood, and the keys of the kingdom, for an ensign, and for the gathering of my people in the last days." (D. & C. 113:6.)

13-19, 27. Now as the crowning proof that the gospel has gone and should go to the Gentiles, Paul names some of the gifts and graces which God has poured out upon them. They have received the power of the Holy Ghost and are full of goodness and knowledge; their offerings are sanctified by the Spirit, and they are partakers of spiritual things. Among them, by faith, signs and wonders and mighty miracles have been wrought — the lame walk, the blind see, the dead are raised — none of which could happen without God's sanction and power. **Gentiles as fellowheirs]** See Eph. 2:19-22; 3:1-12.

30. Strive together with me in your prayers to God for me] Prayers — which God hears! — are not perfunctory, ritualistic recitations. They should manifest the strivings and strugglings of the soul. Mormon says men should pray "with real intent of heart," and "with all the energy of heart." (Moro. 7:9, 48.) **Prayer]** See 1 John 3:19-24.

PAUL SALUTES DIVERS SAINTS

ROMANS 16:1-27.

1 I commend unto you Phebe our sister, which is a servant of the church which is at Cenchrea:

2 That ye receive her in the Lord, as becometh saints, and that ye assist her in whatsoever business she hath need of you: for she hath been a succourer of many, and of myself also.

3 Greet Priscilla and Aquila my helpers in Christ Jesus:

4 Who have for my life laid down their own necks: unto whom not only I give thanks, but also all the churches of the Gentiles.

5 Likewise *greet* the church that is in their house. Salute my wellbeloved Epaenetus, who is the firstfruits of Achaia unto Christ.

6 Greet Mary, who bestowed much labour on us.

7 Salute Andronicus and Junia, my kinsmen, and my fellow-prisoners, who are of note among the apostles, who also were in Christ before me.

8 Greet Amplias my beloved in the Lord.

9 Salute Urbane, our helper in Christ, and Stachys my beloved.

10 Salute Appelles approved in Christ. Salute them which are of Aristobulus' *household*.

11 Salute Herodian my kinsman. Greet them that be of the *household* of Narcissus, which are in the Lord.

12 Salute Tryphena and Tryphosa, who labour in the Lord. Salute the beloved Persis, which laboured much in the Lord.

13 Salute Rufus chosen in the Lord, and his mother and mine.

14 Salute Asyncritus, Phlegon, Hermas, Patrobas, Hermes, and the brethren which are with them.

15 Salute Philologus, and Julia, Nereus, and his sister, and Olympas, and all the saints which are with them.

16 Salute one another with an holy kiss. The churches of Christ salute you.

17 Now I beseech you, brethren, mark them which cause divisions and offences contrary to the doctrine which ye have learned; and avoid them.

18 For they that are such serve not our Lord Jesus Christ, but their own belly; and by good words and fair speeches deceive the hearts of the simple.

19 For your obedience is come abroad unto all *men*. I am glad therefore on your behalf: but yet I would have you wise unto that

which is good, and simple concerning evil.

20 And the God of peace shall bruise Satan under your feet shortly. The grace of our Lord Jesus Christ *be* with you. Amen.

21 Timotheus my workfellow, and Lucius, and Jason, and Sosipater, my kinsmen, salute you.

22 I Tertius, who wrote *this* epistle, salute you in the Lord.

23 Gaius mine host, and of the whole church saluteth you. Erastus the chamberlain of the city saluteth you, and Quartus a brother.

24 The grace of our Lord Jesus Christ *be* with you all. Amen.

25 Now to him that is of power to stablish you according to my gospel, and the preaching of Jesus Christ, according to the revelation of the mystery, which was kept secret since the world began,

26 But now is made manifest, and by the scriptures of the proph-ets, according to the commandment of the everlasting God, made known to all nations for the obedience of faith:

27 To God only wise, *be* glory through Jesus Christ for ever. Amen.

I.V. ROMANS 16:10-11, 16, 25.

10 Salute Apelles approved in Christ. Salute them which are of Aristobulus' **church.**

11 Salute Herodion my kinsman. Greet them that be of the **church** of Narcissus, which are in the Lord.

16 Salute one another with **a** holy **salutation.** The churches of Christ salute you.

25 Now to him that is of power to stablish you according to **the** gospel, and the preaching of Jesus Christ, according to the revelation of the mystery, which was kept secret since the world began,

Words of greeting, commendation, and warning are here sent by Paul to his special friends and fellow laborers in Rome, to those who had struggled and suffered with him in spreading the truth, to those who in effect were to him as Elisha who "poured water on the hands of Elijah." (2 Kings 3:11.) Among those named are several women and representatives of various nations. Shall not these favored ones receive like glory and reward in the kingdoms of glory with the Apostle whose fellow witnesses they are?

1. A servant of the church] Are not all so designated who hold positions in the Church and who labor diligently therein?

307

2. One saint succors another, and he a third, and so the goodness of the gospel spreads among all who will receive it.

4. The churches of the Gentiles] Congregations, wards, branches, or stakes established among the Gentiles.

5. The church that is in their house] How often small, struggling branches of the Church meet in the homes of faithful members, pending the time when growth and strength permit the erection of a house of worship.

7. Paul had kinsmen who joined the Church before he did, kinsmen who bore apostolic witness of the divine Sonship and who held positions of note among the brethren.

17. Avoid cultists. See Acts 20:28-32.

19. Simple concerning evil] The saints have no need to learn of sin; so often a knowledge of evil becomes an invitation to sin.

20. Bruise Satan under your feet] Those who overcome the world trample Satan under their feet by rejecting his enticings; conversely, those who reject Christ and his counsels thereby trample him under their feet. (1 Ne. 19:7.)

25-26. According to the commandment of the everlasting God, as revealed to the apostles and as foretold in the scriptures, the gospel is now for all nations.

Subscription] Euthalius, a bishop of the fifth century, is said to have written the subscriptions to the epistles.

The First Epistle of Paul the Apostle to the Corinthians

Ancient Corinth was a city of debauchery, lewdness, and evil. Even by pagan standards the Corinthians were notoriously sensual and immoral. Their very religion itself centered around the worship of Aphrodite (Venus) and included the sacrificing of chastity by virgins. Drunkenness, lasciviousness, and sex sin were proverbial. And as is natural in such a society, the people of the Roman colony of Corinth were given to faction and strife, and to the solving of moral issues through philosophical contention.

In this climate of evil, Paul had raised up a congregation of saints who forsook the world that was Corinth and sought for a better life in the Cause of Christ. But these new and in some cases only semi-converted saints soon reeked with troubles in their own select group. Factions arose in the Church; some sought to solve spiritual problems by reason and philosophical dispute; the gifts of the Spirit and the partaking of the Lord's Supper were twisted and debased; some rejected Paul as an apostle, others denied the resurrection; and immoral and wanton conduct was found among those who had once turned from Satan to Christ.

Paul himself had personal knowledge of the temper and feelings of the people. By the whisperings of the Spirit, he knew what should be said to them to reclaim them to the gospel standard. Hence, he had written them an epistle directing among other things that they refrain from associating with fornicators. (1 Cor. 5:9.) What else this espistle commanded, we can only speculate, but undoubtedly it summarized many basic gospel doctrines and exhorted the Corinthian Saints to serve God and keep his commandments.

Upon receipt of this epistle, the contentious souls in the Corinthian congregation wrote a reply, taking issue with some of the doctrines of the Apostles and asking detailed questions about his

309

teachings. Thereupon, with vigor and true apostolic zeal, Paul wrote a second epistle, canonized and known as First Corinthians, which answered the points raised by his detractors and further amplified the teachings of the original letter.

Unfortunately we do not know what was said in Paul's prior epistle to the Corinthians, nor in their reply to him. All that has come to us is his reply to the reply. We have, thus, only a few comments about certain aspects of the doctrines they were considering. One cannot, for instance, learn the doctrine of eternal marriage by studying First Corinthians, for it is not there recorded. What one does find is an application of the doctrine to a special situation, which application cannot be understood without a prior knowledge of the doctrine itself.

In addition to his personal knowledge and to these other documents unknown to us but available to him, Paul had received detailed oral reports about conditions in Corinth from members of the household of Chloe. (1 Cor. 1:11.) Here again we are without background information which would be most helpful in putting First Corinthians into its proper perspective.

But with it all, the document, as we now have it, is an inspired and inspiring recitation of some of the most glorious aspects of the doctrines of salvation. In it we read profound explanations of spiritual gifts, of the resurrection, and of degrees of glory in the world to come. We learn of baptism for the dead, are reminded that Christ is the God of Israel, and that there are gods many and lords many. We read of charity, unity, moral cleanliness, personal revelation, the sacrament, the spiritual powers of the saints, and much, much more. Truly the Lord's hand has been in the preservation of this storehouse of gospel knowledge, so needed for our edification and guidance.

"IS CHRIST DIVIDED?"

I CORINTHIANS 1:1-16.

1 Paul, called *to be* an apostle of Jesus Christ through the will of God, and Sosthenes *our* brother,

2 Unto the church of God which is at Corinth, to them that are sanctified in Christ Jesus, called *to be* saints, with all that in every place call upon the name

of Jesus Christ our Lord, both theirs and ours:

3 Grace *be* unto you, and peace, from God our Father, and *from* the Lord Jesus Christ.

4 I thank my God always on your behalf, for the grace of God which is given you by Jesus Christ;

5 That in every thing ye are enriched by him, in all utterance, and *in* all knowledge;

6 Even as the testimony of Christ was confirmed in you:

7 So that ye come behind in no gift; waiting for the coming of our Lord Jesus Christ:

8 Who shall also confirm you unto the end, *that ye may be* blameless in the day of our Lord Jesus Christ.

9 God *is* faithful, by whom ye were called unto the fellowship of his Son Jesus Christ our Lord.

10 Now I beseech you, brethren, by the name of our Lord Jesus Christ, that ye all speak the same thing, and *that* there be no divisions among you; but *that* ye be perfectly joined together in the same mind and in the same judgment.

11 For it hath been declared unto me of you, my brethren, by them *which are of the house* of Chloe, that there are contentions among you.

12 Now this I say, that every one of you saith, I am of Paul; and I of Apollos; and I of Cephas; and I of Christ.

13 Is Christ divided? was Paul crucified for you? or were ye baptized in the name of Paul?

14 I thank God that I baptized none of you, but Crispus and Gaius;

15 Lest any should say that I had baptized in mine own name.

16 And I baptized also the household of Stephanas: besides, I know not whether I baptized any other.

I.V. I CORINTHIANS 1:1, 12.

1 Paul, **an apostle, called of Jesus Christ** through the will of God; and Sosthenes our brother,

12 Now this I say, that **many** of you saith, I am of Paul; and I of Apollos; and I of Cephas; and I of Christ.

I.V. 1. Paul an apostle] See Acts 13:50-52; 14:1-7; 1 Cor. 4:1-21. **Called of Jesus Christ**] Neither apostles nor any church officers call themselves. Either they are called of God or they are not, and if they are not their teachings and performances have no saving virtue and are not binding in heaven.

2. The church of God] The Church of Jesus Christ, for he is God, and his is the name the saints take upon themselves in the waters of baptism. (D. & C. 18:21-25.) As with all people and all organizations, the proper name is one of the chief marks of identification. In the case of his Church, the Lord has been very express and specific as to the exact name which should be used. When the Church was first organized in this dispensation, it was known as the *Church of Christ* (D. & C. 20:1), which name was later amplified by revelation to be *The Church of Jesus Christ of Latter-day Saints.* (D. & C. 115:4.)

When the Nephite disciples asked: "Lord, . . . tell us the name whereby we shall call this church," the Resurrected Lord, by way of explanation and commandment replied: "Ye must take upon you the name of Christ, which is my name. For by this name shall ye be called at the last day; And whoso taketh upon him my name, and endureth to the end, the same shall be saved at the last day. Therefore, whatsoever ye shall do, ye shall do it in my name; therefore ye shall call the church in my name; and ye shall call upon the Father in my name that he will bless the church for my sake. And how be it my church save it be called in my name? For if a church be called in Moses' name then it be Moses' church; or if it be called in the name of a man then it be the church of a man; but if it be called in my name then it is my church, if it so be that they are built upon my gospel." (3 Ne. 27:3-8.)

Sanctified in Christ] See 1 Thess. 4:1-8. **Called to be saints]** Called out of the world and into the Church, called by the election of grace, which includes being foreordained to be members of the Church. See Rom. 8:28-34a; 9:1-33.

2-9. Paul is writing to able, conscientious, faithful saints, not to the world. He is giving counsel to those who have the gift of the Holy Ghost and who already know the doctrines of salvation, not to sectarians, and not to mankind in general. Among them, as almost always is the case, are the weak and dissident members, those who need counsel, direction, and encouragement, but with it all they are God's chosen people — a fact which must be crystal clear if we are to comprehend the counsel about to fall from the Apostle's lips.

4. Grace of God] See Rom. 4:1-25. **6. Testimony of Christ]** See Rev. 19:9b-10. **8. Day of our Lord Jesus Christ]** Second Coming. **9. Fellowship of his Son]** See Rom. 15:1-7; 1 John 1:1-7.

10. Unity within the Church and among the saints is the goal of the gospel. There is no place in the Church of God for division, for disagreement on doctrine, for cults and cliques, for liberal views as contrasted with conservative concepts. Among the faithful saints there is only one mind and one judgment and these are the Lord's; those with the full enjoyment of the Spirit learn the Lord's views on all things and conform their minds and hearts to his, becoming one with him. "Be one; and if ye are not one ye are not mine," is his everlasting decree to his saints. (D. & C. 38:27.) See *Commentary I*, pp. 426-427; 765-767.

11. Contentions] See 2 Tim. 2:14-26.

12. Perfect unity is a goal the Church is still seeking. There are today Word of Wisdom faddists who will not use white flour or refined sugar; there are so-called liberals who think the problems of religion can be solved by dialogues and discussions without reference to revelation; there are others who maintain the Church should follow the world's course of social progress; there are those who try and harmonize the evolutionary concepts of the day with the revealed account of the fall and atonement; and there are others who profess to believe that full salvation is reserved for those who practice plural marriage, and so on. In other words, there are some of one philosophy and some of another, some follow the advocates of this cultish view and some of that.

How apt it is that the Lord chose to paraphrase Paul's language concerning divisive groups in the Church, when he spoke of those who shall be thrust down to hell, and who after their sufferings shall come forth to receive a telestial inheritance. "These are they who are of Paul, and of Apollos, and of Cephas. These are they who say they are some of one and some of another — some of Christ and some of John, and some of Moses, and some of Elias, and some of Esaias, and some of Isaiah, and some of

Enoch; But received not the gospel, neither the testimony of Jesus, neither the prophets, neither the everlasting covenant." (D. & C. 76:99-101.)

13. Is Christ divided?] There is and can be only one true Church on earth. (D. & C. 1:30.) To imagine that two organizations teaching different systems of salvation can both be true is a philosophical absurdity that is almost unbelievable. God cannot have a body of flesh and bones and also be a spirit essence without a body. Two conflicting religions can both be false, but only one can be true. Truth is truth; all truth is in harmony with all truth. There are not and cannot be two ways to gain celestial glory. Christ is not divided. The mere existence of the conflicting sects of Christendom is conclusive proof of the great apostasy. The fact that any or all of them, as Paul expressed it, say, "I am of Christ," has almost no bearing whatever on the issue. Even the members of the Church itself who were making this claim, without also receiving the fulness of the law and accepting the whole gospel, were among those severely rebuked by the inspired writer.

PREACH CHRIST AND SAVE SOULS

I CORINTHIANS 1:17-25.

17 For Christ sent me not to baptize, but to preach the gospel: not with wisdom of words, lest the cross of Christ should be made of none effect.

18 For the preaching of the cross is to them that perish foolishness; but unto us which are saved it is the power of God.

19 For it is written, I will destroy the wisdom of the wise, and will bring to nothing the understanding of the prudent.

20 Where is the wise? where is the scribe? where is the disputer of this world? hath not God made foolish the wisdom of this world?

21 For after that in the wisdom of God the world by wisdom knew not God, it pleased God by the foolishness of preaching to save them that believe.

22 For the Jews require a sign, and the Greeks seek after wisdom:

23 But we preach Christ crucified, unto the Jews a stumblingblock, and unto the Greeks foolishness;

24 But unto them which are called, both Jews and Greeks, Christ the power of God, and the wisdom of God.

25 Because the foolishness of God is wiser than men; and the weakness of God is stronger than men.

17. Paul's commission was to declare the doctrines of salvation in plainness and to testify of their truth. Many were baptized and became heirs of salvation, but, as with the Lord's latter-day ministers, he was sent also to raise the warning voice whether men believed or not, so that all would be left without excuse in the day of judgment. (D. & C. 88:81-82.) **Preach the gospel]** See 2 Tim. 4:1-5. **Not with wisdom of words]** Not with oratorical power, not with the witchery of words, but in a plain, simple, and compelling manner. (2 Ne. 25:1-7.)

18-19. Gospel truths seem like foolish nonsense to the spiritually illiterate, but to the saints (who if they continue faithful shall be saved!) they are as the voice of God.

20-21. God is known only by revelation. All the wisdom of all the world combined cannot search him out. He stands revealed or remains forever unknown. Religion is a thing of the Spirit; it is made known by revelation; hence, it is foolishness to the carnal mind. And thus the only ministers who can save people through their preaching are those to whom God is revealed and who preach by the power of the Spirit. Scientific research, of course, sustains and supports many of the truths of revealed religion. For instance, the ordered system which prevails in the universe, of itself bears record of a Supreme Intelligence.

23. We preach Christ crucified] To preach the gospel is to preach the atoning sacrifice of Christ, for the atonement is the gospel. (3 Ne. 27:13-21.) All doctrines and principles rest on and are efficacious because of the shedding of his blood. Thus none actually preach the gospel in purity unless they testify (as a result of personal revelation!) of Christ and declare the doctrines that lead men to be like him.

GOSPEL PREACHED BY THE WEAK AND SIMPLE

I CORINTHIANS 1:26-31.

26 For ye see your calling, brethren, how that not many wise men after the flesh, not many mighty, not m a n y noble, *are called:*

27 But God hath chosen the foolish things of the world to confound the wise; and God hath chosen the weak things of the world to confound the things which are mighty;

28 And base things of the world, and things which are despised, hath God chosen, *yea,* and things which are not, to bring to nought things that are:

29 That no flesh should glory in his presence.

30 But of him are ye in Christ Jesus, who of God is made unto us wisdom, and righteousness, and sanctification, and redemption:

31 That, according as it is written, He that glorieth, let him glory in the Lord.

I.V. I CORINTHIANS 1:26, 28.

26 For ye see your calling, brethren, how that not many wise men after the flesh, not many mighty, not m a n y noble, are **chosen;**

28 And base things of the world, and things which are despised, hath God chosen, yea, and things which are not, to bring to naught things that are **mighty;**

Question: Who is better qualified to preach the gospel, a fifty-year-old college president of world renown who has many scholastic degrees, or a nineteen-year-old high school graduate who has no scholastic stature whatever?

Answer: The one who has a testimony of the gospel and who is so living as to have the companionship and guidance of the Holy Spirit.

Question: How is it that the weak things of the earth confound the mighty and strong?

Answer: True religion is not a matter of intellectuality or of worldly prominence or renown, but of spirituality; and they are not weak but strong in the realm of spiritual things.

Question: How is it that weak and untried persons have spiritual powers and understanding which is often denied the learned and worldly wise?

316

Answer: It is in large measure a matter of pre-existent preparation. Some people developed in the pre-mortal life the talents to recognize truth, to comprehend spiritual things, to receive revelation from the Spirit; others did not. Those so endowed spiritually were foreordained and sent to earth to serve at God's command as his ministers.

Hence, we find Paul extolling the spiritual powers of the weak and the simple and decrying the foolishness of the worldly wise who seek religious preferment and status on the basis of intellectuality and persuasive powers. In our day the Lord has taken the same approach. "I call upon the weak things of the world," he said, "those who are unlearned and despised, to thrash the nations by the power of my Spirit." (D. & C. 35:13.) To Joseph Smith he said: "I have raised you up, that I might show forth my wisdom through the weak things of the earth." (D. & C. 124:1, 17-24.)

30. God's ministers, who have the Holy Spirit, are in Christ; they receive by revelation that wisdom about righteousness, sanctification, and redemption which guides men to salvation.

31. **Glory in the Lord]** See 2 Cor. 10:1-18; 11:1-11.

GOSPEL PREACHED IN POWER BY THE SPIRIT

I CORINTHIANS 2:1-8.

1 And I, brethren, when I came to you, came not with excellency of speech or of wisdom, declaring unto you the testimony of God.

2 For I determined not to know any thing among you, save Jesus Christ, and him crucified.

3 And I was with you in weakness, and in fear, and in much trembling.

4 And my speech and my preaching *was* not with enticing words of man's wisdom, but in demonstration of the Spirit and of power:

5 That your faith should not stand in the wisdom of men, but in the power of God.

6 Howbeit we speak wisdom among them that are perfect: yet not the wisdom of this world, nor of the princes of this world, that come to nought:

317

7 But we speak the wisdom of God in a mystery, *even* the hidden *wisdom*, which God ordained before the world unto our glory:

8 Which none of the princes of this world knew: for had they known *it*, they would not have crucified the Lord of glory.

There was of old, there is now, and to all eternity there shall be only one approved and proper way to preach the gospel — Preach by the power of the Spirit. Anything short of this is not of God and has neither converting nor saving power. All the religious learning, of all the professors of religion, of all the ages is as nothing compared to the Spirit-born testimony of one legal administrator.

Either ministers of religion receive revelation or they do not, and if they do not their words do not carry the final converting seal. Granted they may say things that are true, but truth alone is not enough. Pure religion is a thing of the Spirit and not of the intellect alone, and its truths must be carried into the hearts of hearers by the power of the Spirit, otherwise the human soul is not changed, the old man of sin is not crucified, and the seeker after salvation does not become alive in Christ.

If there is any truth of salvation that Deity has made imperishably clear, it is that first and last, in all ages, now and forever, among the learned and the ignorant for all races and peoples, and for that matter on all the endless worlds of the great Creator, there is one formula and one formula only for conveying saving truth to men — Preach by the power of the Spirit.

In a revelation to Joseph Smith, God commanded his ministers: "If ye receive not the Spirit ye shall not teach." Then he gave them this promise: "As ye shall lift up your voices by the Comforter, ye shall speak and prophesy as seemeth me good; For, behold, the Comforter knoweth all things, and beareth record of the Father and of the Son." (D. & C. 42:14-17.)

Reasoning with his ministers on this subject, the Lord said: "I the Lord ask you this question — unto what were ye ordained?" The answer, in Deity's language: "To preach my gospel by the Spirit, even the Comforter which was sent forth to teach the truth."

Then the Lord asked: "He that is ordained of me and sent forth to preach the word of truth by the Comforter, in the Spirit of truth, doth he preach it by the Spirit of truth or some other way?" And as though his voice thundered from Sinai, the Almighty answered: "If it be by some other way it is not of God."

This revealed reasoning then continues: "And again, he that receiveth the word of truth, doth he receive it by the Spirit of truth or some other way? If it be some other way it is not of God. Therefore, why is it that ye cannot understand and know, that he that receiveth the word by the Spirit of truth receiveth it as it is preached by the Spirit of truth? Wherefore, he that preacheth and he that receiveth, understand one another, and both are edified and rejoice together." (D. & C. 50:13-22.)

From Nephi's inspired writings we learn that one of the signs of the great apostasy is that ministers of religion "shall teach with their learning, and deny the Holy Ghost, which giveth utterance." (2 Ne. 28:4.)

Is it any wonder, then, that Paul, who himself taught and wrote and preached by the power of the Spirit, should divide preachers into two classes: 1. Those who preach with enticing words of man's wisdom; and 2. Those who do so in demonstration of the Spirit and of power.

In this connection, however, it should be pointed out that there is much reasoning and intellectuality in the world which prepares men for that preaching which carries conviction and brings conversion. The Light of Christ is shed forth upon every person born into the world, teaching all men to do good, to love truth, and to come unto the gospel covenant. Those who heed the promptings and follow the pleadings of this Spirit accept and conform to many true principles and are thus ready to accept the fulness of revealed truth when it is taught to them by the power of the Holy Ghost. (D. & C. 88:45-53.)

5-8. Wisdom is of two kinds: 1. The wisdom of men or the wisdom of the world; and 2. The wisdom of God. One is of the intellect alone; the other is in the mind of God and is given to man by revelation. One is "foolishness" and "profiteth" nothing; the other leads to "that happiness which is prepared for the saints." (2 Ne. 9:28, 43.)

SPIRIT REVEALS ALL THINGS TO SAINTS

I CORINTHIANS 2:9-16.

9 But as it is written, Eye hath not seen, nor ear heard, neither have entered into the heart of man, the things which God hath prepared for them that love him.

10 But God hath revealed *them* unto us by his Spirit: for the Spirit searcheth all things, yea, the deep things of God.

11 For what man knoweth the things of a man, save the spirit of man which is in him? even so the things of God knoweth no man, but the Spirit of God.

12 Now we have received, not the spirit of the world, but the spirit which is of God; that we might know the things that are freely given to us of God.

13 Which things also we speak, not in the words which man's wisdom teacheth, but which the Holy Ghost teacheth; comparing spiritual things with spiritual.

14 But the natural man receiveth not the things of the Spirit of God: for they are foolishness unto him: neither can he know *them*, because they are spiritually discerned.

15 But he that is spiritual judgeth all things, yet he himself is judged of no man.

16 For who hath known the mind of the Lord, that he may instruct him? But we have the mind of Christ.

I.V. I CORINTHIANS 2:11.

11 For what man knoweth the things of a man, save the spirit of man which is in him? even so the things of God knoweth no man, **except he has** the Spirit of God.

Personal revelation is the rock foundation upon which true religion rests. All faithful members of the true Church receive revelation. By the laying on of the hands of legal administrators they receive the gift of the Holy Ghost; this gift, by definition and in its nature, is the right to the constant companionship of that member of the Godhead based on faithfulness. And as Joseph Smith said, "No man can receive the Holy Ghost without receiving revelations. The Holy Ghost is a revelator." (*Teachings*, p. 328.) **Church guided by revelation]** See Acts 11:27-30.

9-10. Revelation is for everyone in the Church. "Thus saith the Lord" — to every member of his Church — "I, the Lord, am merciful and gracious unto those who fear me, and delight to honor those who serve me in righteousness and in truth unto the end. Great shall be their reward and eternal shall be their glory. And to them will I reveal all mysteries, yea, all the hidden mysteries of my kingdom from days of old, and for ages to come, will I make known unto them the good pleasure of my will concerning all things pertaining to my kingdom. Yea, even the wonders of eternity shall they know, and things to come will I show them, even the things of many generations. And their wisdom shall be great, and their understanding reach to heaven; and before them the wisdom of the wise shall perish, and the understanding of the prudent shall come to naught. For by my Spirit will I enlighten them, and by my power will I make known unto them the secrets of my will — yea, even those things which eye has not seen, nor ear heard, nor yet entered into the heart of man." (D. & C. 76:5-10; 121:26-28.) Joseph Smith said: "God hath not revealed anything to Joseph, but what he will make known unto the Twelve, and even the least saint may know all things as fast as he is able to bear them." (*Teachings*, p. 149.)

11-12. "We never can comprehend the things of God and of heaven," the Prophet said, except "by revelation." (*Teachings*, p. 292.) That is the sum and substance of the whole matter. Until men receive personal revelation they are without God in the world, they are not on the course leading to salvation, and they cannot go where God and Christ are. Revelation comes from the Holy Ghost. Men may study about religion, about God, and about his laws, but they cannot receive that knowledge of them whom to know is eternal life except by revelation from the Spirit of God. Those who receive revelation are on the path leading to salvation; those who do not receive revelation are not on that path and cannot be saved, unless they repent and get in tune with the Spirit.

13. The Holy Ghost teacheth] The Holy Ghost is a Teacher. (D. & C. 75:10.) "And by the power of the Holy Ghost ye may know the truth of all things." (Moro. 10:5.)

14. The natural man] The worldly man, the man who is carnal, sensual, and devilish by nature, the man who has not put

321

on Christ, who has not been born again by the power of the Spirit. "The natural man is an enemy to God, and has been from the fall of Adam, and will be, forever and ever, unless he yields to the enticings of the Holy Spirit." (Mosiah 3:19.)

16. We have the mind of Christ] Christ acts and speaks by the power of the Spirit. Those saints who walk in the light as he is in the light, who keep his commandments, who actually enjoy the presentment or gift given them following baptism, thereby have his mind. They think what he thinks, know what he knows, say what he would say, and do what he would do in every situation — all by revelation from the Spirit. As joint-heirs with him of the fulness of his Father's kingdom, their destiny is to "be made equal with him." (D. & C. 88:107.)

Joseph Smith taught that the Father and the Son possess "the same mind, the same wisdom, glory, power, and fulness," and that "all those who keep his commandments shall grow up from grace to grace, and become heirs of the heavenly kingdom, and joint-heirs with Jesus Christ; possessing the same mind, being transformed into the same image or likeness, even the express image of him who fills all in all; being filled with the fulness of his glory, and become one in him, even as the Father, Son and Holy Spirit are one." (*Lectures on Faith*, pp. 50-51.)

How God dwells in us] See 1 John 4:7-21.

MILK COMES BEFORE MEAT IN THE CHURCH

I CORINTHIANS 3:1-8a.

1 And I, brethren, could not speak unto you as unto spiritual, but as unto carnal, *even* as unto babes in Christ.

2 I have fed you with milk, and not with meat: for hitherto ye were not able *to bear it*, neither yet now are ye able.

3 For ye are yet carnal: for whereas *there is* among you envying, and strife, and divisions, are ye not carnal, and walk as men?

4 For while one saith, I am of Paul; and another, I *am* of Apollos; are ye not carnal?

5 Who then is Paul, and who *is* Apollos, but ministers by whom

ye believed, even as the Lord gave to every man?

6 I have planted, Apollos watered; but God gave the increase.

7 So then neither is he that planteth any thing, neither he that watereth; but God that giveth the increase.

8a Now he that planteth and he that watereth are one:

I.V. I CORINTHIANS 3:2.

2 I have fed you with milk, and not with meat; for hitherto ye were not able to **receive** it, neither yet now are ye able.

1-4. Carnality] "Since the fall, all men have become carnal, sensual and devilish by nature. (Moses 5:13; 6:49; Alma 42:10; Mosiah 16:1-4; D. & C. 20:20.) In this fallen state they are subject to the lusts, passions, and appetites of the flesh. They are spiritually dead, having been cast out of the presence of the Lord; and thus 'they are without God in the world, and they have gone contrary to the nature of God.' They are in a 'carnal state' (Alma 41:10-11); they are of the world. Carnality connotes worldliness, sensuality, and inclination to gratify the flesh.

"To be saved men must forsake carnality and turn to the things of the Spirit. They 'must be born again; yea, born of God, changed from their carnal and fallen state, to a state of righteousness, being redeemed of God, becoming his sons and daughters.' (Mosiah 27:25.) All accountable persons who have not received the truth and the spiritual re-birth that attends such reception are yet in a carnal state. (Mosiah 4:2; 16:1-4; 26:4; Alma 22:13; 4:10-15.)

"Even members of the Church who have not forsaken the world, and who have not bridled their passions (Alma 38:12), are yet in a carnal state. 'Ye are yet carnal,' Paul said to the Corinthian Saints, 'for whereas there is among you envying, and strife, and divisions, are ye not carnal, and walk as men?' (1 Cor. 3:3; Mosiah 3:19.) 'To be carnally minded is death; but to be spiritually minded is life and peace. Because the carnal mind is enmity against God.' (Rom. 8:6-7; 2 Ne. 9:39.)" (*Mormon Doctrine*, 2nd ed., p. 113.)

2. God's earthly kingdom is a school in which his saints learn the doctrines of salvation. Some members of the Church are being taught elementary courses; others are approaching graduation and can do independent research where the deep and hidden things are concerned. All must learn line upon line and precept upon precept. Alma said: "It is given unto many to know the mysteries of God; nevertheless they are laid under a strict command that they shall not impart only according to the portion of his word which he doth grant unto the children of men, according to the heed and diligence which they give unto him. And therefore, he that will harden his heart, the same receiveth the lesser portion of the word; and he that will not harden his heart, to him is given the greater portion of the word, until it is given unto him to know the mysteries of God until he know them in full." (Alma 12:9-10.)

3. Divisions] See 1 Cor. 1:1-16.

6-8a. One plants, another waters; one sows, another reaps; one makes friends for the Church, another teaches the deep doctrines. What matters it? All are needful; all are ministers; and God giveth the increase. (John 4:36-38.)

"FIRE SHALL TRY EVERY MAN'S WORK"

I CORINTHIANS 3:8b-15.

8b and every man shall receive his own reward according to his own labour.

9 For we are labourers together with God: ye are God's husbandry, *ye are* God's building.

10 According to the grace of God which is given unto me, as a wise masterbuilder, I have laid the foundation, and another buildeth thereon. But let every man take heed how he buildeth thereupon.

11 For other foundation can no man lay than that is laid, which is Jesus Christ.

12 Now if any man build upon this foundation gold, silver, precious stones, wood, hay, stubble;

13 Every man's work shall be made manifest: for the day shall declare it, because it shall be revealed by fire; and the fire shall try every man's work of what sort it is.

14 If any man's work abide which he hath built thereupon, he shall receive a reward.

15 If any man's work shall be burned, he shall suffer loss: but he himself shall be saved; yet so as by fire.

I.V. I CORINTHIANS 3:15.

15 If any man's work shall be burned, he shall suffer loss; but he himself **may** be saved; yet so as by fire.

8b. Laborers in the vineyard are paid for what they personally do.

9. God and his saints are fellow laborers; they are engaged in the same work — the salvation of souls.

10-11. Paul, "as a wise masterbuilder," laid the foundation for the Corinthian Church on Christ and his atoning sacrifice. Similarly, in this day, Joseph Smith said: "The fundamental principles of our religion are the testimony of the apostles and prophets, concerning Jesus Christ, that he died, was buried, and rose again the third day, and ascended into heaven; and all other things which pertain to our religion are only appendages to it." (*Teachings*, p. 121.)

12-15. If the building (and the saints "are God's building"!) conforms to God's blueprint, it will become a stable structure which will withstand the fiery tests; otherwise it will be burned and destroyed. And the same is true of all men, if their works are good, they shall abide the day and not be cast into the fire; otherwise when He who "is like a refiner's fire" (Mal. 3:2), sits in judgment, they "shall be stubble: and the day that cometh shall burn them up." (Mal. 4:1.) **Judgment by works]** See Rev. 20:11-16. **Judgment at Second Coming]** See Rev. 22:6-16.

"If it so be that the church is built upon my gospel," the Lord Jesus proclaimed to the Nephites, "then will the Father show forth his own works in it. But if it be not built upon my gospel, and is built upon the works of men, or upon the works of the devil, verily I say unto you they have joy in their works for a season, and by and by the end cometh, and they are hewn down and cast into the fire, from whence there is no return. For their works do follow them, for it is because of their works that they are hewn done." (3 Ne. 27:10-12.) And as to false churches — churches built upon "gold, silver, precious stone, wood, hay, stubble" — all such shall be burned. "And the great and abominable church, which is the whore of all the earth, shall be cast down by devouring fire." (D. & C. 29:21.)

"YE ARE THE TEMPLE OF GOD"

I CORINTHIANS 3:16-17.

16 Know ye not that ye are the temple of God, and *that* the Spirit of God dwelleth in you?

17 If any man defile the temple of God, him shall God destroy; for the temple of God is holy, which *temple* ye are.

To be clean is to be saved; to be filthy is to be damned. "No unclean thing can inherit the kingdom of heaven." (Alma 11:37; Moses 6:57-61.) The whole plan and system of salvation is designed to enable men to take the worldly souls they now possess and to cleanse and perfect them through baptism of water and of the Spirit. Indeed, the very purpose of baptism is to empower men to "be sanctified by the reception of the Holy Ghost," that they "may stand spotless" before the Lord at the last day. (3 Ne. 27:19-21.)

How apt, then, for Paul, speaking to the saints, to those who have already been cleansed by fire, to remind them that their bodies have thus become temples in which the Spirit of God resides. "Be ye clean that bear the vessels of the Lord" (D. & C. 133:5), he is saying in effect, for your bodies are "the temple of the Holy Ghost which is in you." (1 Cor. 6:19.)

Destruction awaits those who defile their bodies unless they repent. Shortly before the coming of Christ, the Nephites "began to disbelieve in the spirit of prophecy and in the spirit of revelation; and the judgments of God did stare them in the face. . . . The Spirit of the Lord did no more preserve them; yea, it had withdrawn from them because the Spirit of the Lord doth not dwell in unholy temples — Therefore the Lord did cease to preserve them by his miraculous and matchless power, for they had fallen into a state of unbelief and awful wickedness." (Hela. 4:23-25.) Precisely this same thing happened to the Church in the Old World, following the death of the apostles, prophets, and other inspired men who had the spirit of revelation because the Spirit dwelt in them.

Truly, the Spirit will not dwell in an unclean tabernacle!

SAINTS INHERIT ALL THINGS

I CORINTHIANS 3:18-23.

18 Let no man deceive himself. If any man among you seemeth to be wise in this world, let him become a fool, that he may be wise.

19 For the wisdom of this world is foolishness with God. For it is written, He taketh the wise in their own craftiness.

20 And again, The Lord knoweth the thought of the wise, that they are vain.

21 Therefore let no man glory in men. For all things are your's;

22 Whether Paul, or Apollos, or Cephas, or the world, or life, or death, or things present, or things to come; all are your's;

23 And ye are Christ's; and Christ *is* God's.

What is the relative value of intellectuality and spirituality?

In this life, those who are learned, who have intellectual capacity, who gain scholastic degrees, are held up to dignity and renown; their views are sought; their opinions are valued. But from the Lord's eternal perspective, there is almost no language sufficient to depreciate the importance of intellectuality standing alone and to magnify the eternal worth of spirituality.

There is no salvation in intellectuality standing alone. "The wisdom of this world is foolishness with God." But through spirituality the door is open to the saints to progress until they inherit all things — literally, all things — including all the intellectuality known in the world and more. Those who seek the Lord, who find him, who keep his commandments, who grow in the things of the Spirit, shall gain the fulness of the kingdom of the Father. They gain exaltation; they become gods. They inherit all things — literally.

Why then, Paul contends, should the saints glory in intellectuality, in the wisdom of the world? And the Lord, in latter-day revelation, makes the same presentation. Speaking of those who gain exaltation, he says: "All things are theirs, whether life or death, or things present, or things to come, all are theirs and they are Christ's, and Christ is God's. And they shall overcome all things. Wherefore, let no man glory in man, but rather let him glory in God, who shall subdue all enemies under his feet." (D. & C. 76:59-61.)

Exaltation] See 1 John 3:1-3.

APOSTLES SUFFER, MINISTER, KEEP THE FAITH

I CORINTHIANS 4:1-21.

1 Let a man so account of us, as of the ministers of Christ, and stewards of the mysteries of God.

2 Moreover it is required in stewards, that a man be found faithful.

3 But with me it is a very small thing that I should be judged of you, or of man's judgment: yea, I judge not mine own self.

4 For I know nothing by myself; yet am I not hereby justified: but he that judgeth me is the Lord.

5 Therefore judge nothing before the time, until the Lord come, who both will bring to light the hidden things of darkness, and will make manifest the counsels of the hearts: and then shall every man have praise of God.

6 And these things, brethren, I have in a figure transferred to myself and *to* Apollos for your sakes; that ye might learn in us not to think *of men* above that which is written, that no one of you be puffed up for one against another.

7 For who maketh thee to differ *from another?* and what hast thou that thou didst not receive? now if thou didst receive *it*, why dost thou glory, as if thou hadst not received *it?*

8 Now ye are full, now ye are rich, ye have reigned as kings without us: and I would to God ye did reign, that we also might reign with you.

9 For I think that God hath set forth us the apostles last, as it were appointed to death: for we are made a spectacle unto the world, and to angels, and to men.

10 We *are* fools for Christ's sake, but ye *are* wise in Christ; we *are* weak, but ye *are* strong; ye *are* honourable, but we *are* despised.

11 Even unto this present hour we both hunger, and thirst, and are naked, and are buffeted, and have no certain dwellingplace;

12 And labour, working with our own hands: being reviled, we bless; being persecuted, we suffer it:

13 Being defamed, we intreat: we are made as the filth of the world, *and are* the offscouring of all things unto this day.

14 I write not these things to shame you, but as my beloved sons I warn *you.*

15 For though ye have ten thousand instructors in Christ, yet *have ye* not many fathers: for in Christ Jesus I have begotten you through the gospel.

16 Wherefore I beseech you, be ye followers of me.

17 For this cause have I sent unto you Timotheus, who is my beloved son, and faithful in the Lord, who shall bring you into remembrance of my ways which be in Christ, as I teach every where in every church.

18 Now some are puffed up, as though I would not come to you.

19 But I will come to you shortly, if the Lord will, and will know, not the speech of them which are puffed up, but the power.

20 For the kingdom of God *is* not in word, but in power.

21 What will ye? shall I come unto you with a rod, or in love, and *in* the spirit of meekness?

I.V. I CORINTHIANS 4:4-5.

4 For **though** I know nothing **against** myself; yet I am not hereby justified; but he **who** judgeth me is the Lord.

5 Therefore I judge nothing before the time, until the Lord come, who both will bring to light the hidden things of darkness, and will make manifest the counsels of the hearts; and then shall every man have praise of God.

1. Ministers of Christ] Legal administrators holding the priesthood, called and commissioned by Christ to represent him, to stand in his place and stead in teaching the gospel and performing the ordinances of salvation. See Philip. 3:13-21; 1 Thess. 2:1-12.

Stewards of the mysteries of God] True ministers receive revelation and know the mysteries of God. "Salvation cannot come without revelation," the Prophet said. "It is in vain for anyone to minister without it. No man is a minister of Jesus Christ without being a prophet. . . . Men of the present time testify of heaven and hell, and have never seen either; and I will say that no man knows these things without this." (*Teachings*, p. 160.)

2-7. 'As a steward and having received revelation, I have been faithful; nevertheless you have judged me, but that is of no moment. I do not even judge myself, nor would I be justified in so doing, though I am not aware of any fault, for judgment is the Lord's. I pass judgment on none of you, until the Lord comes. Then he shall reveal your hidden acts and make manifest what is in your hearts; then shall those who are saints be rewarded. I speak of myself, and of Apollos, but the principle applies to all of you. You must learn not to think too highly of men, simply because they have gained the wisdom of the world. After all, where did they get the ability to excel? For that matter, what have any of us that did not come from God; and if something comes by inheritance, as a gift, why should be boast about having it?'

7. Who maketh thee to differ from another?] Why does one man have one gift or ability, another something else? One man sings, another preaches; one has athletic prowess, another is an intellectual giant; one solves mathematical problems, another composes music; one is spiritually inclined, another is about as receptive to the voice of revelation as a pine board. Why? It is primarily a matter of pre-existence. All men trained themselves for an infinite period in the schools of eternity before birth into mortality. Men came here with the talents and capacities developed there. Why then, Paul asks, should any man boast because of some God-given gift?

8. Ye are rich, ye have reigned as kings] How often the wealth of the world turns the hearts of the saints from spiritual to worldly things! See 1 Tim. 6:7-10; Jas. 5:1-5. **I would to God ye did reign]** Reign as kings and priests in God's hierarchy. "Seek not for riches but for wisdom, and behold, the mysteries of God shall be unfolded unto you, and then shall you be made rich. Behold, he that hath eternal life is rich." (D. & C. 6:7.)

9. Apostles] "1. An apostle is a special witness of the name of Christ who is sent to teach the principles of salvation to others. He is one who knows of the divinity of the Savior by personal revelation and who is appointed to bear testimony to the world of what the Lord has revealed to him. Every elder in the Church is or should be an apostle; that is, as a minister of the Lord and as a recipient of personal revelation from the Holy Ghost, every elder has the call to bear witness of the truth on all proper occasions. Indeed, every member of the Church should have apostolic insight and revelation, and is under obligation to raise the warning voice. (D. & C. 88:81; Mosiah 18:9.)

"In September, 1832, (nearly two and a half years before there were any ordained apostles in the Church) the Lord said to certain missionaries: 'You are mine apostles, even God's high priests.' (D. & C. 84:63-64.) In fact, Joseph Smith became an apostle in the spring of 1820, as a result of the First Vision, even before priesthood was conferred upon him through the ministration of Peter, James, and John; and after the Church was established, the Lord ordained (meaning decreed) that he continue to serve in this high apostolic station. (D. & C. 20:1-4; 21:1; 27:12; *Doctrines of Salvation*, vol. 3, pp. 144-149.)

"Men are saved by giving heed to the words of the prophets and apostles sent among them and are damned for failure to heed the inspired testimony. (D. & C. 1:14.) And as with nearly all things, the devil offers a spurious substitute to deceive men. These 'are false apostles, deceitful workers, transforming themselves into the apostles of Christ.' (2 Cor. 11:13.) But faithful members of the Church have the assurance that they shall sit in judgment, 'And liars and hypocrites shall be proved by them, and they who are not apostles and prophets shall be known.' (D. & C. 64:37-39; Rev. 2:2.)

"2. In the ordained sense, an apostle is one who is ordained to the office of apostle in the Melchizedek Priesthood. Ordinarily

331

those so ordained are also set apart as members of the Council of the Twelve and are given all of the keys of the kingdom of God on earth. This apostleship carries the responsibility of proclaiming the gospel in all the world and also of administering the affairs of the Church. Christ 'chose twelve, whom also he named apostles' (Luke 6:13), and upon their shoulders the burden of the kingdom rested after he ascended to his Father. (1 Cor. 12:28.) The original Twelve in latter-days were selected by revelation by the Three Witnesses to the Book of Mormon. (D. & C. 18:26-47.)

"The Twelve Disciples among the Nephites ministered in an ordained apostolic capacity. (3 Ne. 18; 19; 27; 28.) In writing about the Book of Mormon, the Prophet said that it 'tells us that our Savior made his appearance upon this continent after his resurrection; that he planted the gospel here in all its fulness, and richness, and power, and blessing; that they had apostles, prophets, pastors, teachers, and evangelists; the same order, the same priesthood, the same ordinances, gifts, powers, and blessings as were enjoyed on the eastern continent.' (*History of the Church,* vol. 4, p. 538.)" (*Mormon Doctrine,* 2nd ed., pp. 46-47.) See *Commentary I,* pp. 209-211.

When ordained apostles are set apart as members of the Council of the Twelve, they are given the keys of the kingdom; that is, they receive the rights and powers of presidency; they are empowered to preside over and to govern and regulate all of the affairs of the kingdom of God on earth which is the Church. See *Commentary I,* pp. 424-426; *Mormon Doctrine,* 2nd ed., pp. 411-413.

1. Us] 6. Us] 8. Us] 9. Us the apostles] Who? Paul and Apollos are named, and all of the apostles are included. Does this, then, mean that Apollos had become one of the Council of the Twelve? Such appears to be the case. Great hosts of the early brethren were apostles in the sense of being special witnesses of the Lord, of having the Spirit certify to their souls the fact of his divine Sonship. But the whole context of Paul's presentation here indicates he is speaking of members of the Twelve as "the ministers of Christ" and not of witnesses in general. He is in fact comparing the suffering and persecution of "the apostles" with other saints who, not having been "appointed to death," have in effect "reigned as kings." See Acts 13:50-52; 14:1-7.

9-13. Appointed to death, etc.] Every dispensation has its own cross to bear. Noah's day alone saw the flood; Abraham's only saw fire from heaven destroy great cities; only in Moses' day were the Lord's people called upon to wander for forty years in the wilderness. And only in time's meridian were persecution and martyrdom singled out as among the chief identifying marks of membership in God's earthly kingdom. The dispensation of the meridian of time was the dispensation of martyrdom, the dispensation of crucifixion, the dispensation when God himself, as well as hosts of those who enlisted in his Cause, were slain by wicked men. In all ages the saints have been persecuted by the world, but in the days of Jesus and Paul the world went wild; persecution was perfected; and the blood of the martyrs under the altar cried unto the Lord for vengeance.

16. Be ye followers of me] Jesus said: "Follow thou me" (2 Ne. 31:10), and, "What manner of men ought ye to be? Verily I say unto you, even as I am." (3 Ne. 27:27.) How glorious it would be if every shepherd, as Paul here does, could say the same to his flock.

20. The kingdom of God is not in word, but in power] O how this truth needs to be thundered into the ears of every living soul. The kingdom of God on earth, the Church of Jesus Christ, the gospel of salvation, are not found in word but in power. It matters not that a people have the word of God, that the Bible is open before them, that they have a record of what God and angels have said, that they know what the doctrines of salvation are. There is no salvation in these things standing alone. Of course men must have the word, of course they must learn the doctrines of salvation. But men do not gain the kingdom of God, the Church, or the gospel until they possess the power. The gospel is the power of God unto salvation. There must be priesthood, the gift of the Holy Ghost, revelation, visions, miracles, glorious manifestations of God's power, or there is no kingdom of God, no Church of Jesus Christ, no saving gospel. Where God's power is manifest, there is the Church and kingdom of God on earth, and where his power is not found, there the Church and kingdom is not.

WHY CHURCH CANNOT FELLOWSHIP SINNERS

I CORINTHIANS 5:1-13.

1 It is reported commonly *that there is* fornication among you, and such fornication as is not so much as named among the Gentiles, that one should have his father's wife.

2 And ye are puffed up, and have not rather mourned, that he that hath done this deed might be taken away from among you.

3 For I verily, as absent in body, but present in spirit, have judged already, as though I were present, *concerning* him that hath so done this deed,

4 In the name of our Lord Jesus Christ, when ye are gathered together, and my spirit, with the power of our Lord Jesus Christ,

5 To deliver such an one unto Satan for the destruction of the flesh, that the spirit may be saved in the day of the Lord Jesus.

6 Your glorying *is* not good. Know ye not that a little leaven leveneth the whole lump?

7 Purge out therefore the old leaven, that ye may be a new lump, as ye are unleavened. For even Christ our passover is sacrificed for us:

8 Therefore let us keep the feast, not with old leaven, neither with the leaven of malice and wickedness; but with the unleavened *bread* of sincerity and truth.

9 I wrote unto you in an epistle not to company with fornicators:

10 Yet not altogether with the fornicators of this world, or with the covetous, or extortioners, or with idolaters; for then must ye needs go out of the world.

11 But now I have written unto you not to keep company, if any man that is called a brother be a fornicator, or covetous, or an idolater, or a railer, or a drunkard, or an extortioner; with such an one no not to eat.

12 For what have I to do to judge them also that are without? do not ye judge them that are within?

13 But them that are without God judgeth. Therefore put away from among yourselves that wicked person.

I.V. I CORINTHIANS 5:3-4, 12.

3 For verily, as absent in body but present in spirit, **I** have judged already **him who hath so done this deed, as though I were present,**

4 In the name of our Lord Jesus Christ, when ye are gathered together, and **have the Spirit,** with the power of our Lord Jesus Christ,

12 For what have I to do to judge them also that are without? do not **they** judge them that are within?

1-8. Apparently a member of the Church in Corinth had married his stepmother, either because she was a widow or had been separated from her prior husband. Such marriages were forbidden by the Mosaic code under penalty of excommunication. (Lev. 18:6-8, 29.) Paul endorses the Mosaic prohibition, describes the intimacies resulting from such unions as fornication, condemns his Corinthian brethren for winking at the offense, and directs the excommunication of the offender. If the sinner were left in the Church, Paul reasons, his influence, as leaven, would spread throughout the whole Church. The Church must, therefore, purge out this old leaven of wickedness and replace it with a new influence or leaven of righteousness.

5. Less than twenty verses farther on in this same epistle, Paul is going to say, in language that cannot be gainsaid, that fornicators cannot inherit the kingdom of God. (1 Cor. 6:9-11.) But in this case he holds out a hope of salvation on certain conditions. Why? This is perhaps the most deep, difficult, and little known doctrine in the Church, one that is wholly unknown in the world. From latter-day revelation we learn that following celestial marriage, a man may make his calling and election sure; that is, he may progress in righteousness until he is sealed up unto eternal life and his exaltation is guaranteed. Such is the state to which Isaiah, Ezekiel, Joseph Smith, Paul himself, and others attained. A person in this state is subject to the law to which Paul here merely alludes, but which is given in more amplified form in the Doctrine and Covenants in these words: "Verily, verily, I say unto you, if a man marry a wife according to my word, [and if their calling and election is made sure], and they are sealed by the Holy Spirit of promise, according to mine appointment, and he or she shall commit any sin or transgression of the new and everlasting covenant whatever, and all manner of blasphemies, and if they commit no murder wherein they shed innocent blood, yet they shall come forth in the first resurrection, and enter into their exaltation; but they shall be destroyed in the flesh, and shall be delivered unto the buffetings of Satan unto the day of redemption, saith the Lord God." (D. & C. 132:26.)

Calling and election sure] See 2 Pet. 1:1-19.

6-8, 12-13. When persons who should be excommunicated remain in the Church, they hold the Church up to ill-repute, hinder the missionary cause, and, by their bad example, influence other church members to walk in unrighteousness. The Lord's plan calls for their severance from the Church. (D. & C. 64:12-14.)

9-13. Paul wrote the Corinthians, in an epistle since lost and unknown, not to company with fornicators. Here he qualifies his previous command. What he intended to forbid was the fellowshiping of such persons in the Church. They should be handled for their membership, unless of course they repent. Now also he extends his instructions to include members of the Church who are covetous, idolaters, railers, drunkards, or extortioners. Manifestly, he explains, to avoid all such who are in the world, would require us to "go out of the world" itself.

TAKE CIVIL CASES TO CHURCH COURTS

I CORINTHIANS 6:1-8.

1 Dare any of you, having a matter against another, go to law before the unjust, and not before the saints?

2 Do ye not know that the saints shall judge the world? and if the world shall be judged by you, are ye unworthy to judge the smallest matters?

3 Know ye not that we shall judge angels? how much more things that pertain to this life?

4 If then ye have judgments of things pertaining to this life, set them to judge who are least esteemed in the church.

5 I speak to your shame. Is it so, that there is not a wise man among you? no, not one that shall be able to judge between his brethren?

6 But brother goeth to law with brother, and that before the unbelievers.

7 Now therefore there is utterly a fault among you, because ye go to law one with another. Why do ye not rather take wrong? why do ye not rather *suffer yourselves to* be defrauded?

8 Nay, ye do wrong, and defraud, and that *your* brethren.

Judges and courts are and always have been part of the kingdom of God on earth. Whenever that kingdom has been set up in it fulness, glory, and power, the church court system has been empowered to handle both civil and ecclesiastical matters. All such cases rested in the hands of the Lord's judges from the day of Adam to the time Saul was chosen to rule in Israel. Since then the perfect law has been modified to fit into world conditions.

In Paul's day there were both church courts and civil courts, as there are today. If the saints go to law with each other, they may choose to do so under either state or church jurisdiction. Paul is here counseling them to handle their own affairs in their own courts, and his counsel is good and might well be followed by church members today. Manifestly where grievances involve non-members of the Church, redress must be sought before civil tribunals. (D. & C. 134:11.)

2. The saints shall judge the world] 3. We shall judge angels] See Rev. 20:4-6.

THE UNRIGHTEOUS SHALL NOT BE SAVED

I CORINTHIANS 6:9-20.

9 Know ye not that the unrighteous shall not inherit the kingdom of God? Be not deceived: neither fornicators, nor idolaters, nor adulterers, nor effeminate, nor abusers of themselves with mankind,

10 Nor thieves, nor covetous, nor drunkards, nor revilers, nor extortioners, shall inherit the kingdom of God.

11 And such were some of you: but ye are washed, but ye are sanctified, but ye are justified in the name of the Lord Jesus, and by the Spirit of our God.

12 All things are lawful unto me, but all things are not expedient: all things are lawful for me, but I will not be brought under the power of any.

13 Meats for the belly, and the belly for meats: but God shall destroy both it and them. Now the body *is* not for fornication, but for the Lord; and the Lord for the body.

14 And God hath both raised up the Lord, and will also raise up us by his own power.

15 Know ye not that your bodies are the members of Christ? shall I then take the members of Christ, and make *them* the members of an harlot? God forbid.

16 What? know ye not that he which is joined to an harlot is

one body? for two, saith he, shall be one flesh.

17 But he that is joined unto the Lord is one spirit.

18 Flee fornication. Every sin that a man doeth is without the body; but he that committeth fornication sinneth against his own body.

19 What? Know ye not that your body is the temple of the Holy Ghost *which is* in you, which ye have of God, and ye are not your own?

20 For ye are bought with a price: therefore glorify God in your body, and in your spirit, which are God's.

I.V. I CORINTHIANS 6:12, 18.

12 All **these** things are **not** lawful unto me, **and** all **these** things are not expedient. All things are **not** lawful for me, **therefore** I will not be brought under the power of any.

18 Flee fornication. Every sin that a man **committeth** is **against the body of Christ, and** he **who** committeth fornication sinneth against his own body.

9-11. To be saved, in the full gospel sense, is to gain the fulness of the celestial kingdom; to be damned is to fall short of full salvation. All sinners shall be damned unless they repent and are baptized. But grievous as are the sins here listed by Paul, yet those Corinthians who were once guilty of them, are now clean, sanctified, justified — all by the power of the Holy Ghost. An even more express and comprehensive listing of sins, which if forsaken, yet allow repentant souls to be saved, is found in the Book of Mormon in these words: "Turn, all ye Gentiles, from your wicked ways; and repent of your evil doings, of your lyings and deceivings, and of your whoredoms, and of your secret abominations, and your idolatries, and of your murders, and your priestcrafts, and your envyings, and your strifes, and from all your wickedness and abominations, and come unto me, and be baptized in my name, that ye may receive a remission of your sins, and be filled with the Holy Ghost, that ye may be numbered with my people who are of the house of Israel." (3 Ne. 30:2.)

Damnation] See *Commentary I,* pp. 434-436. **Eternal damnation]** See Rev. 14:8-11. **Salvation]** See 1 Pet. 1:1-16.

9. The unrighteous] All accountable persons, except those who repent and are baptized, but particularly those guilty of the grosser sins, such as those here listed. "For whoso cometh not unto me," the Lord says, "is under the bondage of sin." (D. & C. 84:51.)

Fornicators] Unmarried persons who have illicit sexual intercourse. "Wo unto them who commit whoredoms, for they shall be thrust down to hell." (2 Ne. 9:36.)

Idolaters] Those who worship idols or who have excessive love or veneration for anything. "Wo unto those that worship idols, for the devil of all devils delighteth in them." (2 Ne. 9:37.)

Adulterers] Married persons who have sexual relations with anyone but their husband or wife. "Thou shalt not commit adultery." (Ex. 20:14.)

Effeminate] Men who have womanlike traits and who engage in sexual perversions.

Abusers of themselves with mankind] Homosexuals. "Thou shalt not lie with mankind, as with womankind: it is abomination." (Lev. 18:22.)

10. Thieves] Those who steal. "Thou shalt not steal." (Ex. 20:15.)

Covetous] Those who have a strong and inordinate desire for possessions or things which belong to another. "Thou shalt not covet thy neighbour's house, thou shalt not covet thy neighbour's wife, nor his manservant, nor his maidservant, nor his ox, nor his ass, nor any thing that is thy neighbour's." (Ex. 20:17.)

Drunkards] Those who are often or habitually intoxicated. The drinking of intoxicating liquors is proscribed by divine edict. (D. & C. 89:5-7.)

Revilers] Persons who heap verbal abuse upon the saints, or who deride, belittle, and mock the truth.

Extortioners] Criminally bent persons who wrest money or property from others by the illegal use of fear.

11. Ye are washed] Ye are baptized. **Ye are sanctified]** Ye are pure and spotless, because sin and iniquity has been burned out of your souls as though by fire. **Ye are justified]** God by his Spirit seals, ratifies, and approves your post-baptismal conduct, because it now conforms to his standards.

13-20. Paul here decries the Corinthian claim that as the hunger of the belly is properly satisfied with food, so sex appetites might properly be fed with fornication. Rather, he acclaims, the bodies of the saints are eternal and will be resurrected; as part of the spiritual body of Christ, they must not be defiled by connections with harlots; they are now Christ's, for he has bought them with his blood and made them temples wherein his Spirit may dwell; since he owns them, he justly decrees they shall be used in righteousness.

19. Your body is the temple of the Holy Ghost] See 1 Cor. 3:16-17.

MARRIAGE IS ORDAINED OF GOD

I CORINTHIANS 7:1-24.

1 Now concerning the things whereof ye wrote unto me: *It is* good for a man not to touch a woman.

2 Nevertheless, *to avoid* fornication, let every man have his own wife, and let every woman have her own husband.

3 Let the husband render unto the wife due benevolence: and likewise also the wife unto the husband.

4 The wife hath not power of her own body, but the husband: and likewise also the husband hath not power of his own body, but the wife.

5 Defraud ye not one the other, except *it be* with consent for a time, that ye may give yourselves to fasting and prayer; and come together again, that Satan tempt you not for your incontinency.

6 But I speak this by permission, *and* not of commandment.

7 For I would that all men were even as I myself. But every man hath his proper gift of God, one after this manner, and another after that.

8 I say therefore to the unmarried and widows, It is good for them if they abide even as I.

9 But if they cannot contain, let them marry: for it is better to marry than to burn.

10 And unto the married I command, *yet* not I, but the Lord,

Let not the wife depart from *her* husband:

11 But and if she depart, let her remain unmarried, or be reconciled to *her* husband: and let not the husband put away *his* wife.

12 But to the rest speak I, not the Lord: If any brother hath a wife that believeth not, and she be pleased to dwell with him, let him not put her away.

13 And the woman which hath an husband that believeth not, and if he be pleased to dwell with her, let her not leave him.

14 For the unbelieving husband is sanctified by the wife, and the unbelieving wife is sanctified by the husband: else were your children unclean; but now are they holy.

15 But if the unbelieving depart, let him depart. A brother or a sister is not under bondage in such *cases:* but God hath called us to peace.

16 For what knowest thou, O wife, whether thou shalt save *thy* husband? or how knowest thou, O man, whether thou shalt save *thy* wife?

17 But as God hath distributed to every man, as the Lord hath called every one, so let him walk. And so ordain I in all churches.

18 Is any man called being circumcised? let him not become un-circumcised. Is any called in uncircumcision? let him not be circumcised.

19 Circumcision is nothing, and uncircumcision is nothing, but the keeping of the commandments of God.

20 Let every man abide in the same calling wherein he was called.

21 Art thou called *being* a servant? care not for it: but if thou mayest be made free, use *it* rather.

22 For he that is called in the Lord, *being* a servant, is the Lord's freeman: likewise also he that is called, *being* free, is Christ's servant.

23 Ye are bought with a price; be not ye the servants of men.

24 Brethren, let every man, wherein he is called, therein abide with God.

I.V. I CORINTHIANS 7:1-2, 5-6, 9.

1 Now concerning the things whereof ye wrote unto me, **saying,** It is good for a man not to touch a woman.

2 Nevertheless, **I say,** to avoid fornication, let every man have his own wife, and let every woman have her own husband.

5 **Depart** ye not one **from** the other, except it be with consent for a time, that ye may give yourselves to fasting and prayer; and come together again, that Satan tempt you not for your incontinency.

6 **And now what I speak is** by permission, and not **by command**ment.

9 But if they cannot **abide,** let them marry; for it is better to marry than **that any should commit sin.**

Marriage is ordained of God. The family unit is the most important organization in time or in eternity. The Church itself is a service agency to aid men in creating and perfecting eternal family units; eternal life and exaltation grow out of the continuation of the family unit in the highest heaven of the celestial world.

The whole plan of salvation revolves around and centers in the family unit. God's work was to create man; Christ's, to redeem him; and man's is to form proper family units, which will give peace and joy to the members in this life and assure them of eternal glory in the life to come. Every healthy and mentally balanced adult on earth, who has a proper opportunity to do so, should marry, and if the Lord's goodness permits, should have children. These truths are found in the teachings of all the prophets of all the ages, Paul included. See *Commentary I,* pp. 544-549; 602-608.

But proper marriage discipline is and must be geared to the circumstances in which people live. Civil marriage only is available to people in the world; celestial marriage is the proper order for the saints. Divorce, except for sex sins, has been the law of God in some dispensations; in others, as in ours, there are other justifiable reasons for dissolving the marriage union. There are occasional instances, as when young men and women go on full-time missions, when marriage should be postponed temporarily. And there are many individual problems which may properly be solved one way for one couple and another for someone else, the solution depending on local circumstances and personal temperaments.

To understand what Paul has here said about marriage, we must put ourselves in the position of the Corinthian Saints, and we must have the prior knowledge which they had. For instance:

MARRIAGE IS ORDAINED OF GOD

1. They knew about the law of eternal marriage and understood full well its relationship to eternal life.

2. They knew Paul had the theoretical knowledge, the practical experience, and the heaven-bequeathed inspiration to guide others who had marital questions and problems.

3. Further, they had asked him to comment on several specific and difficult problems involving members of their congregation. And — unfortunately — we do not know what those problems were. In other words, we have some guarded and carefully phrased answers, with various express exceptions, but we do not know the questions presented nor the situations involved.

4. And finally, Paul did not answer the questions by going back to first principles and talking about the policies and procedures governing the Lord's law of matrimony; instead he assumed such knowledge on the part of his readers (knowledge which, of course, the sectarian world does not have!), and so he simply proceeded to talk about the specific questions, and some of his answers involved exceptions to the general rules of the Church.

Suppose, for instance, a modern apostle — without saying anything about the general laws of marriage — should write answers to such questions as: Is it better to remain single, to forego marriage entirely, or to marry out of the Church? If a husband or wife will not receive the gospel, should divorce follow? Should missionaries marry while on their missions? What about marriage by persons having venereal diseases? And so on. Obviously, in the very nature of things, the most wise and proper comments on these points might not have universal application, and certainly they would not give a good over-all view of the Lord's true marriage discipline. And so it is with Paul's present explanations.

I.V. 1-2. The Corinthians said that in some unusual situation, marriage was improper; Paul replies that the requirement to marry is universal and applies even in such instances.

K.J. 3-5. Conjugal relations have apostolic approval.

6. Having announced that marriage is honorable in all, and the bed undefiled, Paul is now going to give it as his personal opinion that in some cases exceptions may be made.

7. I would that all men were even as I myself] 'I would that all men understood the law of marriage, that all had self-mastery over their appetites, and that all obeyed the laws of God in these respects.'

8-9. Paul here gives a personal opinion that in some cases, about which the Corinthians had asked, unmarried persons and widows should not marry. We do not know to whom the instructions here given apply. In any event, they are an exception to the law, and do not apply, even as a personal opinion, to others than those involved.

10-11. In whatever cases are here involved, the Lord counsels against divorce, and Paul gives a personal opinion that should divorces occur, women should remain unmarried.

12-19. These verses, and particularly verse 14, so troubled the Prophet Joseph Smith, that he inquired of the Lord and received the following explanation: "Now, in the days of the apostles the law of circumcision was had among all the Jews who believed not the gospel of Jesus Christ. And it came to pass that there arose a great contention among the people concerning the law of circumcision, for the unbelieving husband was desirous that his children should be circumcised and become subject to the law of Moses, which law was fulfilled. And it came to pass that the children, being brought up in subjection to the law of Moses, gave heed to the traditions of their fathers and believed not the gospel of Christ, wherein they became unholy. Wherefore, for this cause the apostle wrote unto the church, giving unto them a commandment, not of the Lord, but of himself, that a believer should not be united to an unbeliever; except the law of Moses should be done away among them, That their children might remain without circumcision; and that the tradition might be done away, which saith that little children are unholy; for it was had among the Jews; But little children are holy, being sanctified through the atonement of Jesus Christ; and this is what the scriptures mean." (D. & C. 74:2-7.)

20-24. Both slaves and freemen join the Church, but such does not of itself change their legal status. It is not, however, right that men should be slaves.

344

SHOULD MISSIONARIES BE MARRIED OR SINGLE?

I CORINTHIANS 7:25-40.

25 Now concerning virgins I have no commandment of the Lord: yet I give my judgment, as one that hath obtained mercy of the Lord to be faithful.

26 I suppose therefore that this is good for the present distress, I say, that it is good for a man so to be.

27 Art thou bound unto a wife? seek not to be loosed. Art thou loosed from a wife? seek not a wife.

28 But and if thou marry, thou hast not sinned; and if a virgin marry, she hath not sinned. Nevertheless such shall have trouble in the flesh: but I spare you.

29 But this I say, brethren, the time is short: it remaineth, that both they that have wives be as though they had none;

30 And they that weep, as though they wept not; and they that rejoice, as though they rejoiced not; and they that buy, as though they possessed not;

31 And they that use this world, as not abusing it: for the fashion of this world passeth away.

32 But I would have you without carefulness. He that is unmarried careth for the things that belong to the Lord, how he may please the Lord:

33 But he that is married careth for the things that are of the world, how he may please his wife.

34 There is difference also between a wife and a virgin. The unmarried woman careth for the things of the Lord, that she may be holy both in body and in spirit: but she that is married careth for the things of the world, how she may please her husband.

35 And this I speak for your own profit; not that I may cast a snare upon you, but for that which is comely, and that ye may attend upon the Lord without distraction.

36 But if any man think that he behaveth himself uncomely toward his virgin, if she pass the flower of her age, and need so require, let him do what he will, he sinneth not: let them marry.

37 Nevertheless he that standeth stedfast in his heart, having no necessity, but hath power over his own will, and hath so decreed in his heart that he will keep his virgin, doeth well.

38 So then he that giveth her in marriage doeth well; but he that giveth her not in marriage doeth better.

39 The wife is bound by the law as long as her husband liveth; but if her husband be dead, she is at liberty to be married to whom she will; only in the Lord.

40 But she is happier if she so abide, after my judgment: and I think also that I have the Spirit of God.

I.V. I CORINTHIANS 7:26, 28-33, 36, 38.

26 I suppose therefore that this is good for the present distress, **for a man so to remain that he may do greater good.**

28 But if thou marry, thou hast not sinned; and if a virgin marry, she hath not sinned. Nevertheless, such shall have trouble in the flesh. For I spare you **not.**

29 **But I speak unto you who are called unto the ministry. For** this I say, brethren, the time **that remaineth is but short, that ye shall be sent forth unto the ministry. Even they who have wives, shall be as though they had none; for ye are called and chosen to do the Lord's work.**

30 **And it shall be with them who weep,** as though they wept not; and **them who** rejoice, as though they rejoiced not, and

them who buy, as though they possessed not;

31 **And them who** use this world, as not **using** it; for the fashion of this world passeth away.

32 But I would, **brethren, that ye magnify your calling.** I would have you without carefulness. **For he who** is unmarried, careth for the things that belong to the Lord, how he may please the Lord; **therefore he prevaileth.**

33 But he **who** is married, careth for the things that are, of the world, how he may please his wife; **therefore there is a difference, for he is hindered.**

36 But if any man think that he behaveth himself uncomely toward his virgin **whom he hath** espoused, if she pass the flower of age, and need so require, let him do what he **hath promised,** he sinneth not; let them marry.

38 So then he that giveth **himself** in marriage doeth well; but he that giveth **himself** not in marriage doeth better.

Paul here continues to answer questions on marriage which were posed by his Corinthian fellow saints. It is clear from the Inspired Version corrections and additions that ministerial service of a missionary nature was involved, and the main questions seemed to be: Should engaged persons who are called on missions marry first, or go out on the Lord's errand while single? And if they should serve while single, should certain ones who were already married, receive divorces prior to such service?

In our day when an elder who is engaged to be married is called on a mission, more often than not he fulfils his mission prior to his marriage; occasionally he marries first and leaves his wife for the assigned period of ministerial service. In the earlier days of this dispensation recently married brethren were frequently called to leave their wives and perform missionary service. Obviously the same rule need not and should not apply in every case. A host of personal circumstances and situations are always involved. Ordinarily, and Paul specified this as his opinion, marriage should be deferred.

Marriage] See 1 Cor. 7:1-24.

THERE ARE GODS MANY AND LORDS MANY

I CORINTHIANS 8:1-13.

1 Now as touching things offered unto idols, we know that we all have knowledge. Knowledge puffeth up, but charity edifieth.

2 And if any man think that he knoweth any thing, he knoweth nothing yet as he ought to know.

3 But if any man love God, the same is known of him.

4 As concerning therefore the eating of those things that are offered in sacrifice unto idols, we know that an idol *is* nothing in the world, and that *there is* none other God but one.

5 For though there be that are called gods, whether in heaven or in earth, (as there be gods many, and lords many,)

6 But to us *there is but* one God, the Father, of whom *are* all things, and we in him; and one Lord Jesus Christ, by whom *are* all things, and we by him.

7 Howbeit *there is* not in every man that knowledge: for some with conscience of the idol unto this hour eat *it* as a thing offered unto an idol; and their conscience being weak is defiled.

8 But meat commendeth us not to God: for neither, if we eat, are we the better; neither, if we eat not, are we the worse.

9 But take heed lest by any means this liberty of your's become a stumblingblock to them that are weak.

10 For if any man see thee which hast knowledge sit at meat in the idol's temple, shall not the conscience of him which is weak be emboldened to eat those things which are offered to idols;

11 And through thy knowledge shall the weak brother perish, for whom Christ died?

12 But when ye sin so against the brethren, and wound their weak conscience, ye sin against Christ.

13 Wherefore, if meat make my brother to offend, I will eat no flesh while the world standeth, lest I make my brother to offend.

I.V. I CORINTHIANS 8:4.

4 As concerning therefore the eating of those things **which** are **in the world** offered in sacrifice unto idols, we know that an idol is nothing, and that there is none other God but one.

The Corinthians had asked Paul for counsel about eating meat sacrificed by pagan people to their idols. He replies that in theory it is completely immaterial whether the saints eat such meat or not, because idols are not true gods, and there is actually no religious significance to the pseudo-sacrifices one way or the other. But, he reasons, in practice it may be wise not to eat this meat, since such a course might cause those who are weak in the faith to assume there was virtue and benefit in the sacrifices themselves and therefore to be led astray.

And — praise God for such bursts of inspiration! — in the midst of his relatively unimportant comments about some saints who had been partaking in pagan temples of food sacrificed to idols, Paul summarizes for his Corinthian brethren some of the great truths about the plurality of God. See *Commentary I*, pp. 488-492.

"The Prophet commenting on this passage said: 'Paul had no allusion to the heathen gods. I have it from God, and get over it if you can. I have a witness of the Holy Ghost, and a testimony that Paul had no allusion to the heathen gods in the text.' (*Teachings*, 371.)

"The Prophet also taught — in explaining John's statement, 'And hath made us kings and priests unto God and his Father' (Rev. 1:6) — that there is 'a god above the Father of our Lord Jesus Christ. . . . If Jesus Christ was the Son of God, and John discovered that God the Father of Jesus Christ had a Father, you may suppose that he had a Father also. Where was there ever a son without a father? And where was there ever a father without first being a son? Whenever did a tree or anything spring into existence without a progenitor? And everything comes in this way. Paul says that which is earthly is in the likeness of that which is heavenly. Hence if Jesus had a Father, can we not believe that he had a Father also?' (*Teachings*, pp. 370-373.)

"Indeed, this doctrine of plurality of Gods is so comprehensive and glorious that it reaches out and embraces every exalted personage. Those who attain exaltation are gods. 'Go and read the vision in the Book of Covenants,' the Prophet said. 'There is clearly illustrated glory upon glory — one glory of the sun, another glory of the moon, and a glory of the stars; and as one star differeth from another star in glory, even so do they of the telestial world differ in glory, and every man who reigns in celestial glory is a God to his dominions. . . . They who obtain a glorious resurrection from the dead are exalted far above principalities, powers, thrones, dominions, and angels, and are expressly declared to be heirs of God and joint-heirs with Jesus Christ, all having eternal power.' (*Teachings*, p. 374.)" (*Mormon Doctrine*, 2nd ed., p. 577.)

PAUL REJOICETH IN HIS CHRISTIAN LIBERTY

I CORINTHIANS 9:1-12.

1 Am I not an apostle? am I not free? have I not seen Jesus Christ our Lord? are not ye my work in the Lord?

2 If I be not an apostle unto others, yet doubtless I am to you: for the seal of mine apostleship are ye in the Lord.

3 Mine answer to them that do examine me is this,

4 Have we not power to eat and drink?

5 Have we not power to lead about a sister, a wife, as well as other apostles, and *as* the brethren of the Lord, and Cephas?

6 Or I only and Barnabas, have not we power to forbear working?

7 Who goeth a warfare any time at his own charges? who planteth a vineyard, and eateth not of the fruit thereof? or who feedeth a flock, and eateth not of the milk of the flock?

8 Say I these things as a man? or saith not the law the same also?

9 For it is written in the law of Moses, Thou shalt not muzzle the mouth of the ox that treadeth out the corn. Doth God take care for oxen?

10 Or saith he *it* altogether for our sakes? For our sakes, no doubt, *this* is written: that he

that ploweth should plow in hope; and that he that thresheth in hope should be partaker of his hope.

11 If we have sown unto you spiritual things, *is it* a great thing if we shall reap your carnal things?

12 If others be partakers of *this* power over you, *are* not we rather? Nevertheless we have not used this power; but suffer all things, lest we should hinder the gospel of Christ.

Some, apparently in Corinth, had questioned Paul's claim to the apostleship, such information having come to him either in their letter, which this epistle answers, or in verbal reports made by knowledgeable persons. (1 Cor. 1:11.) In eloquent terms Paul replies that he is an apostle in very deed, for he has seen the Lord; that as such he is entitled to their support, spiritually and temporally; that their very existence as a Corinthian Congregation is proof of his apostleship, meaning that through his instrumentality they had been converted.

But, he says, as an apostle he is still free, free to eat and drink, to work and preach, to plant and harvest, to marry and enjoy family associations, free to do all the things for which he had apparently been criticized.

1. An apostle] See 1 Cor. 4:1-21.

5. 'Do not Barnabas and I have the same right to be married as do Peter, and the other apostles, and the brothers of the Lord?'

6-12. Paul and Barnabas, even as the other apostles, having fed the saints spiritually were entitled, in turn, to be fed temporally.

9-11. If it is proper to let the ox that works in the harvest partake of the corn, surely men who labor to harvest souls are also entitled to have their needs supplied.

GOSPEL PREACHED WITHOUT COST TO ALL

I CORINTHIANS 9:13-18.

13 Do ye not know that they which minister about holy things live *of the things* of the temple?

and they which wait at the altar are partakers with the altar?

14 Even so hath the Lord ordained that they which preach

the gospel should live of the gospel.

15 But I have used none of these things: neither have I written these things, that it should be so done unto me: for *it were* better for me to die, than that any man should make my glorying void.

16 For though I preach the gospel, I have nothing to glory of: for necessity is laid upon me;

yea, woe is unto me, if I preach not the gospel!

17 For if I do this thing willingly, I have a reward: but if against my will, a dispensation *of the gospel* is committed unto me.

18 What is my reward then? *Verily* that, when I preach the gospel, I may make the gospel of Christ without charge, that I abuse not my power in the gospel.

Who pays for the preaching of the gospel? Whence comes the money to pay for the transportation, and for the food, clothing, and shelter of the missionaries? Must people pay to be taught the truth? Or buy their status and place in the kingdom?

Two harmonious principles govern where preaching the gospel and the costs of the kingdom are concerned:

1. "Salvation is free." (2 Ne. 2:4.) It has no price tag; it cannot be purchased with money. None is ever asked to buy saving grace. God's decree is: Every living soul is entitled to hear the truth taught and the testimony of Jesus born by a legal administrator, who has no purpose in preaching except the eternal welfare of his hearers. To all preachers the Lord's directive is: "Freely ye have received, freely give." (Matt. 10:8.)

2. But the ministers of salvation must eat and drink; they must be clothed, marry, raise families, and live as other men do. When all of their time and strength is expended in building up the kingdom, others — happily, those blessed by their ministrations — must supply the just needs and wants of the laborers in the vineyard, for "the laborer is worthy of his hire." (D. & C. 84:79.) "But the laborer in Zion shall labor for Zion; for if they labor for money they shall perish." (2 Ne. 26:31.)

15-16. In Paul's personal ministry, he took pride "that these hands have ministered unto my necessities" (Acts 20:34), that is that he had not been burdensome to the churches.

16. Woe is unto me, if I preach not the gospel] Unless God's ministers labor diligently, they are under condemnation. Those among them who serve God with all their "heart, might, mind and strength," shall "stand blameless" before him "at the last day." (D. & C. 4:2.) Those who are "slothful shall not be counted worthy to stand" in his glorious presence and shall fail to gain the reward they offered to others through their preaching. (D. & C. 107:99-100.)

17. Willing service is required. "He that is compelled in all things, the same is a slothful and not a wise servant; wherefore he receiveth no reward." (D. & C. 58:26.)

WHY PAUL WAS ALL THINGS TO ALL MEN

I CORINTHIANS 9:19-27.

19 For though I be free from all *men*, yet have I made myself servant unto all, that I might gain the more.

20 And unto the Jews I became as a Jew, that I might gain the Jews; to them that are under the law, as under the law, that I might gain them that are under the law;

21 To them that are without law, as without law, (being not without law to God, but under the law to Christ,) that I might gain them that are without law.

22 To the weak became I as weak, that I might gain the weak: I am made all things to all *men*, that I might by all means save some.

23 And this I do for the gospel's sake, that I might be partaker thereof with *you*.

24 Know ye not that they which run in a race run all, but one receiveth the prize? So run, that ye may obtain.

25 And every man that striveth for the mastery is temperate in all things. Now they *do it* to obtain a corruptible crown; but we an incorruptible.

26 I therefore so run, not as uncertainly; so fight I, not as one that beateth the air:

27 But I keep under my body, and bring *it* into subjection: lest that by any means, when I have preached to others, I myself should be a castaway.

I.V. I CORINTHIANS 9:24.

24 Know ye not that they which run in a race **all run,** but **only** one receiveth the prize? So run, that ye may obtain.

Paul here says he made himself all things to all men in an effort to get them to accept the gospel message; that is, he adapted himself to the conditions and circumstances of all classes of people, as a means of getting them to pay attention to his teachings and testimony. And then, lest any suppose this included the acceptance of their false doctrines or practices, or that it in any way involved a compromise between the gospel and false systems of worship, he hastened to add that he and all men must obey the gospel law to be saved.

Our missionary approaches follow the same course today. To gain the interest of the learned, we reason and philosophize; to help the faith-endowed Maori to see the light, we certify of the healing power that is in Christ. There is one approach in finding investigators among the Jews, another among the Buddhists, and still another among the sects of Christendom, but the final teaching is always the same — accept Christ and the legal administrators who he hath sent in this day, and live the laws of the restored gospel.

20. Unto the Jews I became as a Jew] He claimed kinship with them, preached in their synagogues, quoted their prophets, showed how Christ fulfilled the law of Moses, and how the gospel grew naturally out of the foundations laid by their fathers.

To them that are under the law] In certain circumstances he submitted to Jewish laws and traditions; for instance, he circumcised Timothy, who has half a Jew (Acts 16:1-3), and he himself took a Nazarite vow in the temple at Jerusalem, thus holding himself out as both a Jew and a Christian. (Acts 21:20-26.)

21. To them that are without law] Among the pagans at Lystra, he reasoned on the basis of natural religion (Acts 14:8-18); on Mars hill he philosophized and quoted Greek literature (Acts 17:22-31); and he refused to permit Titus, who was a Greek, to be circumcised. (Gal. 2:3-5.)

24-27. Self-discipline is essential to salvation. Even as athletes train for their races by being temperate in the use of food and drink, and then run so as to win the victor's crown, so in the Christian race, shall all those who control their bodies, who subdue the flesh to the Spirit, and who run the race manfully, so shall they all receive an incorruptible crown.

27. Lest . . . I myself should be a castaway] 'Lest I be rejected of God and not gain salvation.' "For although a man may have many revelations, and have power to do many mighty works, yet if he boasts in his own strength, and sets at naught the counsels of God, and follows after the dictates of his own will and carnal desires, he must fall and incur the vengeance of a just God upon him." (D. & C. 3:4.)

CHRIST IS THE GOD OF ISRAEL

I CORINTHIANS 10:1-4.

1 Moreover, brethren, I would not that ye should be ignorant, how that all our fathers were under the cloud, and all passed through the sea;

2 And were all baptized unto Moses in the cloud and in the sea;

3 And did all eat the same spiritual meat;

4 And did all drink the same spiritual drink: for they drank of that spiritual Rock that followed them: and that Rock was Christ.

Who is the God of Israel? Is it the Father or the Son? In the Old Testament account, he is called the Lord Jehovah, the I AM, the God of Abraham, Isaac, and Jacob. Here Paul teaches, truly and clearly, that Christ is the God of Israel, a basic and fundamental gospel truth which remains unknown and hidden to hosts of men in the sectarian world. According to God's revealed word: Elohim is the Father; Jehovah is the Son; and the Holy Ghost is their minister.

Nephi prophesied that the God of Israel, the God of Abraham, Isaac, and Jacob, would yield himself into the hands of sinful men to be crucified (1 Ne. 19:7-17), and when the resurrected Lord ministered among the Nephites he said: "Come forth unto me, that ye may thrust your hands into my side, and also that ye may feel the prints of the nails in my hands and in my feet, that ye may know that I am the God of Israel, and the God of the whole earth, and have been slain for the sins of the world." (3 Ne. 11:14.)

1. Our fathers] Those in ancient Israel were the fathers of the saints in Paul's day, either literally or by adoption. Though the Corinthians, for instance, were Gentiles by birth, they had become Israelites by adoption; in joining the Church they had become the seed of Abraham and had found their inheritance in the house of Jacob. (Abra. 2:10.)

2. Baptized unto Moses] Baptism is an eternal ordinance, which was universally practiced in Israel, whenever that people followed the counsel of her prophets. Indeed, the very law of Moses itself was "the preparatory gospel, . . . the gospel of repentance and of baptism, and the remission of sins." (D. & C. 84:26-27.) All this the Corinthians knew, which makes Paul's analogy even more persuasive, for he is saying that even as Israel, when they passed through the Red Sea, fled from the worldliness of Egypt, so their Christian descendants, through baptism, are to forsake the lusts of the flesh and live godly lives; their fathers, Paul reasons, had been disciples of Moses, as it were, but they are disciples of Moses' Master, who is Christ.

3. Spiritual meat] 4. Spiritual drink] Spiritual Rock] Christ is the bread which came down from heaven, the Bread of Life, the spiritual manna, of which men must eat to gain salvation. (John 6:31-58.) He is the spiritual drink, the living water, the water of life, which if men drink they shall never thirst more. (John 4:6-15.) He is the rock-foundation upon which all must build to gain an inheritance in his Father's kingdom. To eat of the bread and drink of the waters of life is to keep the commandments of God, which includes (as the Corinthians are here being counseled) the forsaking of all that is carnal and evil.

That Rock was Christ] Christ is the Rock (Deut. 32:3-4, 18, 30-31), the Rock of Heaven (Moses 7:53), which signifies his eternal strength and stability, and holds him forth as the sure foundation upon which men must build their eternal homes.

ANCIENT ISRAEL REBELLED AGAINST CHRIST

I CORINTHIANS 10:5-15.

5 But with many of them God was not well pleased: for they were overthrown in the wilderness.

6 Now these things were our examples, to the intent we should not lust after evil things, as they also lusted.

355

7 Neither be ye idolaters, as *were* some of them; as it is written, The people sat down to eat and drink, and rose up to play.

8 Neither let us commit fornication, as some of them committed, and fell in one day three and twenty thousand.

9 Neither let us tempt Christ, as some of them also tempted, and were destroyed of serpents.

10 Neither murmur ye, as some of them also murmured, and were destroyed of the destroyer.

11 Now all these things happened unto them for ensamples: and they are written for our admonition, upon whom the ends of the world are come.

12 Wherefore let him that thinketh he standeth take heed lest he fall.

13 There hath no temptation taken you but such as is common to man: but God *is* faithful, who will not suffer you to be tempted above that ye are able; but will with the temptation also make a way to escape, that ye may be able to bear *it*.

14 Wherefore, my dearly beloved, flee from idolatry.

15 I speak as to wise men; judge ye what I say.

I.V. I CORINTHIANS 10:11.

11 Now, all these things happened unto them for ensamples; and they are written for our admonition **also, and for an admonition for those upon whom the end of the world shall come.**

Paul here says ancient Israel rebelled against the Lord in the following particulars:

1. They rebelled in the wilderness and refused to keep the statutes and judgments of the Lord — for which they were destroyed and denied entrance to the promised land. (Ezek. 20:10-26.)

2. They lusted after the flesh pots of Egypt — for which many were consumed by fire. (Num. 11:1-6.)

3. Some became idolaters, worshiped the idols of Egypt, and even sacrificed their children to Molech — for which they were rejected and scattered. (Ezek. 20:7, 18, 26.)

4. With Aaron's cooperation, they made and worshiped a golden calf; they revelled in pagan displays of nakedness and lewdness before it; and they offered sacrifices to it, acclaiming

the molten calf as their deliverer from Egypt — for which three thousand were slain by the Levites with the sword. (Ex. 32:1-20.)

5. They committed whoredoms with the daughters of Moab, and worshiped and sacrificed to Baal — for which twenty-four thousand (Paul says twenty-three thousand) were slain by plague. (Num. 25:1-9.)

6. Many were bitten by fiery serpents, sent upon them for their wickedness — for which cause "much people of Israel died." (Num. 21:4-9.)

7. Great murmurings rose among them against Moses, Aaron, and the Lord — for which God decreed that the carcases of all who were twenty years of age and upwards, save Caleb and Joshua, should fall in the wilderness, where their children also should wander for forty years. (Num. 14:1-38.)

Having recorded this direful and despairing indictment, the Apostle says plainly that all these rebellions were against the Lord Jesus Christ, who is the God of Israel. See 1 Cor. 10:1-4. Then, says he, these things are not just dead history, they are living examples for us and for all men of all ages, showing that when men rebel against God they are cursed. And finally, he says, that none of them are subject to any temptations which are not common to all men, and that if they will flee from idolatry, be wise, and keep the commandments they shall be saved.

TRUE AND FALSE SACRAMENT CONTRASTED

I CORINTHIANS 10:16-33.

16 The cup of blessing which we bless, is it not the communion of the blood of Christ? The bread which we break, is it not the communion of the body of Christ?

17 For we *being* many are one bread, *and* one body: for we are all partakers of that one bread.

18 Behold Israel after the flesh: are not they which eat of the sacrifices partakers of the altar?

19 What say I then? that the idol is any thing, or that which is offered in sacrifice to idols is any thing?

20 But *I say*, that the things which the Gentiles sacrifice, they

357

sacrifice to devils, and not to God: and I would not that ye should have fellowship with devils.

21 Ye cannot drink the cup of the Lord, and the cup of devils: ye cannot be partakers of the Lord's table, and of the table of devils.

22 Do we provoke the Lord to jealousy? are are stronger than he?

23 All things are lawful for me, but all things are not expedient: all things are lawful for me, but all things edify not.

24 Let no man seek his own, but every man another's *wealth.*

25 Whatsoever is sold in the shambles, *that* eat, asking no question for conscience sake:

26 For the earth *is* the Lord's, and the fulness thereof.

27 If any of them that believe not bid you *to a feast*, and ye be disposed to go; whatsoever is set before you, eat, asking no question for conscience sake.

28 But if any man say unto you, This is offered in sacrifice unto idols, eat not for his sake that showed it, and for conscience sake: for the earth *is* the Lord's, and the fulness thereof:

29 Conscience, I say, not thine own, but of the other: for why is my liberty judged of another *man's* conscience?

30 For if I by grace be a partaker, why am I evil spoken of for that for which I give thanks?

31 Whether therefore ye eat, or drink, or whatsoever ye do, do all to the glory of God.

32 Give none offence, neither to the Jews, nor to the Gentiles, nor to the church of God:

33 Even as I please all *men* in all *things*, not seeking mine own profit, but the *profit* of many, that they may be saved.

I.V. I CORINTHIANS 10:23-24, 27.

23 All things are **not** lawful for me, **for** all things are not expedient; all things are **not** lawful, **for** all things edify not.

24 Let **no** man seek **therefore** his own, but every man another's **good.**

27 If any of them that believe not bid you to a feast, and ye be disposed to **eat;** whatsoever is set before you, eat, asking no questions for conscience' sake.

Paul has been asked: Should the saints eat things sacrificed to idols? Since the sacrifices have no standing before God, what does it matter if members of the Church eat of them?

How powerfully he reasons in reply! First he reminds the Corinthians that they have a true ordinance, the Sacrament of the Lord's Supper, through which they all may become one. Through it they all may receive the guidance and companionship of the Holy Spirit, and by communion with this Spirit they are made one in Christ and thus gain salvation.

Then he speaks of false ordinances which lead not to salvation, but to damnation, not to God, but to Lucifer. Since a sacrifice to an idol is not of God, whence is it? He answers, it is a sacrifice to devils. In effect he is asking, since false ordinances are not of God, whence are they? If, for instance, the saints have a true ordinance of the sacrament, which comes from God, and false churches have false ordinances of the sacrament, whence come these false ordinances? His argument is the same in principle as that used by the Prophet Joseph Smith in contrasting the true sacrifice of Abel and the false sacrifice of Cain. "Cain could have no faith," the Prophet reasoned, because a false ordinance is contrary to the will of God, and it is not possible to "exercise faith contrary to the plan of heaven." (*Teachings*, p. 58.)

16. Cup of blessing] Cup of wine drunk during the Feast of the Passover; used by Jesus to introduce the ordinance of the sacrament, as he and his apostles kept the paschal supper. (*Commentary I*, pp. 716-725.)

Communion] Sacrament. See 1 Cor. 11:20-34.

20. They sacrifice to devils, and not to God] They sacrificed to idols who were false gods, and therefore their rites of worship were being performed to devils. True ordinances please God and bless men; false ordinances please Satan and are devoid of blessings.

Fellowship with devils] Participation in false systems of religion.

21. Cup of the Lord] Sacramental cup. **Cup of devils]** False ordinances, as sacrifices to idols.

PAUL COMPARES STATUS OF MAN AND WOMAN

I CORINTHIANS 11:1-15.

1 Be ye followers of me, even as I also *am* of Christ.

2 Now I praise you, brethren, that ye remember me in all things, and keep the ordinances, as I delivered *them* to you.

3 But I would have you know, that the head of every man is Christ; and the head of the woman *is* the man; and the head of Christ *is* God.

4 Every man praying or prophesying, having *his* head covered, dishonoureth his head.

5 But every woman that prayeth or prophesieth with *her* head uncovered dishonoureth her head: for that is even all one as if she were shaven.

6 For if the woman be not covered, let her also be shorn: but if it be a shame for a woman to be shorn or shaven, let her be covered.

7 For a man indeed ought not to cover *his* head, forasmuch as he is the image and glory of God: but the woman is the glory of the man.

8 For the man is not of the woman; but the woman of the man.

9 Neither was the man created for the woman; but the woman for the man.

10 For this cause ought the woman to have power on *her* head because of the angels.

11 Nevertheless neither is the man without the woman, neither the woman without the man, in the Lord.

12 For as the woman *is* of the man, even so *is* the man also by the woman; but all things of God.

13 Judge in yourselves: is it comely that a woman pray unto God uncovered?

14 Doth not even nature itself teach you, that, if a man have long hair, it is a shame unto him?

15 But if a woman have long hair, it is a glory to her: for *her* hair is given her for a covering.

With apostolic insight, our inspired writer here proclaims certain basic and eternal principles pertaining to men and women and their relationship to each other. In view of these, he then approves or disapproves of certain local customs and traditions — not that the local customs were of themselves either good or bad, but that their practice either added to or diminished from the proper reverence for and adherence to the great basic concepts being set forth.

Paul, thus, names four great gospel principles in this order:

1. As God is the head of Christ, and Christ is the head of man, so man is the head of woman. Such is the Lord's eternal order of government and control. (Verse 3.)

2. As man is the image and glory of God, so woman is the glory of man. Such specifies the relative position of the sexes. (Verse 7.)

3. As the woman, Eve, was created for the man, Adam, and not the reverse, so women are subordinate to men and are subject to their control. Such is the practical rule that does and must exist between the sexes by virtue of the simple fact that there cannot be two equal heads. (Verses 8 and 9.)

4. As eternal life grows out of the continuation of the family unit in eternity, and as a family unit consists of a husband and a wife, so — "in the Lord" — it takes a man and a woman together to gain the glorious state of exaltation. Such is the whole object and end of the gospel, and as such it forms a kind and degree of equality between the sexes, still, however, leaving the man to preside over the woman as God presides over the man. (Verses 11 and 12.)

In connection with these basic gospel principles, Paul comments on local customs and traditions, for instance, that a woman should have her head covered when she prays or prophesies, lest she be as though her head were shaven, which according to local custom would identify her as an adulteress. In the eternal sense it is wholly immaterial whether a woman wears a hat or is bareheaded when she prays. In Paul's day the bare head was irreverent; in our's reverence and respect are shown by removing the hat. In other words, gospel principles are eternal, and it is wise to adhere to the passing customs which signify adherence to that course which adds to rather than detracts from the great and important revealed truths.

1. Christ and his prophets are prototypes. Follow them.

2. **Keep the ordinances]** Keep the commandments.

5. **Every woman that prayeth or prophesieth]** Women are not one whit behind men in spiritual things; perhaps, on the whole, they are ahead of them; in the very nature of things there will be more women than men living in the state of family exaltation hereafter. And women, here and now, are as much entitled to revelation, visions, and gifts of the Spirit as are men.

10. According to custom, wearing a hat was a sign that the woman was in subjection to the man.

ARE THERE HERESIES IN THE TRUE CHURCH?

I CORINTHIANS 11:16-19.

16 But if any man seem to be contentious, we have no such custom, neither the churches of God.

17 Now in this that I declare *unto you* I praise *you* not, that ye come together not for the better, but for the worse.

18 For first of all, when ye come together in the church, I hear that there be divisions among you; and I partly believe it.

19 For there must be also heresies among you, that they which are approved may be made manifest among you.

16-18. Contention] See 2 Tim. 2:14-26. **Unity; Divisions]** See 1 Cor. 1:1-16.

19. Heresies abound in the sectarian world. False doctrines are manifest on every hand. God is not a spirit essence, without body, parts, or passions, that fills immensity and is nowhere in particular present, for instance; nor is it true that revelation ceased with the ancient apostles.

But what of the true Church? Are there heresies within even that divine institution? Paul says such was the case among the Corinthians, and it is apparent that the same thing prevails in the modern kingdom of God on earth. Speaking of our day, Nephi said that "because of pride, and wickedness, and abominations, and whoredoms," all men have "gone astray save it be a few, who are the humble followers of Christ." Then pointing to these true saints, he added: "Nevertheless, they are led, that in many instances they do err because they are taught by the precepts of men." (2 Ne. 28:14.) That is, heresies are found in the Church today, even as in the meridian of time. For instance, what of the views of some on revelation, on the age of the earth, on the theories of organic evolution, on the resurrection of the sons of perdition, on a second chance for salvation, on whether God is progressing in truth and knowledge, and so forth?

The fact is that a major part of the testing process of mortality is to determine how much of the truth the saints will believe while they are walking by faith rather than by sight. And the more truths they accept, the clearer will be their views on spiritual matters, and the more incentive and determination they will have to work out their salvation and gain eternal glory hereafter. Heresies and false teachings are thus used in the testing processes of this mortal probation.

WHY WE PARTAKE OF THE SACRAMENT

I CORINTHIANS 11:20-34.

20 When ye come together therefore into one place, *this* is not to eat the Lord's supper.

21 For in eating every one taketh before *other* his own supper: and one is hungry, and another is drunken.

22 What? have ye not houses to eat and to drink in? or despise ye the church of God, and shame them that have not? What shall I say to you? shall I praise you in this? I praise *you* not.

23 For I have received of the Lord that which also I delivered unto you, That the Lord Jesus the *same* night in which he was betrayed took bread:

24 And when he had given thanks, he brake *it*, and said, Take, eat: this is my body, which is broken for you: this do in remembrance of me.

25 After the same manner also *he took* the cup, when he had supped, saying, This cup is the new testament in my blood: this do ye, as oft as ye drink *it*, in remembrance of me.

26 For as often as ye eat this bread, and drink this cup, ye do show the Lord's death till he come.

27 Wherefore whosoever shall eat this bread, and drink *this* cup of the Lord, unworthily, shall be guilty of the body and blood of the Lord.

28 But let a man examine himself, and so let him eat of *that* bread, and drink of *that* cup.

29 For he that eateth and drinketh unworthily, eateth and drinketh damnation to himself, not discerning the Lord's body.

30 For this cause many *are* weak and sickly among you, and many sleep.

31 For if we would judge ourselves, we should not be judged.

32 But when we are judged, we are chastened of the Lord, that we should not be condemned with the world.

33 Wherefore, my brethren, when ye come together to eat, tarry one for another.

34 And if any man hunger, let him eat at home; that ye come not together unto condemnation. And the rest will I set in order when I come.

I.V. I CORINTHIANS 11:20-21, 29.

20 When ye come together into one place, is it not to eat the Lord's supper?

21 But in eating every one taketh before his own supper; and one is hungry, and another is drunken.

29 For he that eateth and drinketh unworthily, eateth and drinketh condemnation to himself, not discerning the Lord's body.

When Jesus instituted the ordinance of the sacrament, he and his apostles were celebrating the Feast of the Passover; the partaking of the emblems of his broken flesh and spilled blood was a part of and grew out of this paschal meal. With this pattern before them, the early saints apparently adopted the practice of eating together a meal or supper and of then partaking of the sacrament. Abuses involving selfishness and drunkenness seem to have arisen in connection with this feasting. These are here condemned and the saints are counseled to eat at home and then assemble with their fellow church members to renew their covenants in the sacramental ordinance.

23-30. How men eat the flesh and drink the blood of Jesus] See *Commentary I*, pp. 357-360. **Introduction and purpose of the sacrament]** See *Commentary I*, pp. 716-725.

23-25. The ordinance of the sacrament, replacing the ordinance of sacrifice, is the repetitiously performed rite whereby the true saints center their worship in Christ and his atoning sacrifice, and whereby they renew and reaffirm the covenant made in the waters of baptism, thus again attaining a state of full fellowship with the Lord, through the consequent remission of their sins.

26. The sacramental ordinance was destined to continue among the true saints until and after the Second Coming of the Son of Man, when Christ himself will again partake, with all his holy saints, of the emblems of his broken flesh and spilled blood. (D. & C. 27:5-14.)

27-29. Personal worthiness is an essential prerequisite in all gospel ordinances; otherwise the performances are not sealed by the Holy Spirit of Promise, thus gaining efficacy, virtue, and force for this life and for the life to come. (D. & C. 76:53; 132:7.) Thus Moroni counsels: "See that ye partake not of the sacrament of Christ unworthily." (Morm. 9:29.) Similarly, in latter-day revelation we find this decree: "If any have trespassed, let him not partake until he makes reconcilation." (D. & C. 46:4.) And the resurrected Lord, ministering among the Nephites, commands: "Ye shall not suffer any one knowingly to partake of my flesh and blood unworthily, when ye shall minister it; For whoso eateth and drinketh my flesh and blood unworthily eateth and drinketh damnation to his soul; therefore if ye know that a man is unworthy to eat and drink of my flesh and blood ye shall forbid him. Nevertheless, ye shall not cast him out from among you, but ye shall minister unto him and shall pray for him unto the Father, in my name; and if it so be that he repenteth and is baptized in my name, then shall ye receive him, and shall minister unto him of my flesh and blood. But if he repent not he shall not be numbered among my people, that he may not destroy my people, for behold I know my sheep, and they are numbered. Nevertheless, ye shall not cast him out of your synagogues, or your places of worship, for unto such shall ye continue to minister; for ye know not but what they will return and repent, and come unto me with full purpose of heart, and I shall heal them; and ye shall be the means of bringing salvation unto them." (3 Ne. 18:28-32.)

27. Guilty of the body and blood of the Lord] This penalty applies only to those who partake of the sacrament in total and complete unworthiness and rebellion. It is only this class of damned souls upon whose hands, in the full sense of the word, the blood of Christ is found.

30. Both temporal and spiritual sickness and death are here promised those saints who partake unworthily of the sacrament. They are spiritually diseased, and sometimes dead, because of sins committed after baptism, sins which are not remitted anew by obtaining the Holy Spirit poured out upon those who worthily partake of the blessed emblems of Christ's flesh and blood; and, also, "many" among them suffer physical illnesses and temporal death when such, through faith, might be avoided.

HOLY GHOST REVEALS JESUS IS THE CHRIST

I CORINTHIANS 12:1-3.

1 Now concerning spiritual *gifts*, brethren, I would not have you ignorant.

2 Ye know that ye were Gentiles, carried away unto these dumb idols, even as ye were led.

3 Wherefore I give you to understand, that no man speaking by the Spirit of God calleth Jesus accursed: and *that* no man can say that Jesus is the Lord, but by the Holy Ghost.

I.V. I CORINTHIANS 12:1.

1 Now concerning spiritual **things,** brethren, I would not have you ignorant.

1. If the saints are to be saved, they must accept, understand, and experience the gifts of the Spirit. Since religion itself is of the Spirit, and deals with spiritual things, it can be received and known only by the power of the Spirit. Thus where the gifts of the Spirit are manifest, there is true religion; and where the gifts of the Spirit are not manifest, there true religion is not. Hence, in his farewell to the Lamanites, Moroni counseled: "I exhort you, my brethren, that ye deny not the gifts of God, for they are many." (Moro. 10:8.)

Spiritual gifts] See 1 Cor. 12:4-13.

2. Gentiles, which includes all nonmembers of the Church, do not have the gifts of the Spirit; these spiritual outpourings of divine grace are reserved for those who have the gift of the Holy Ghost, who is the very Spirit whose gifts are bestowed upon men.

3. Two principles are here set forth: 1. Any man who has the Spirit praises Christ and testifies of his goodness and mercy; and 2. Christ is and can be known by revelation from the Holy Ghost, and in no other way.

Revelation is the sole and only sure source of knowledge about God and Christ and gospel truths. A knowledge of these things does not and cannot come by reason, research, or rationalization. God stands revealed, or he remains forever unknown. In keeping with this principle, Joseph Smith said that the latter part of verse three should read: "No man can *know* that Jesus is the Lord, but by the Holy Ghost." (*Teachings*, p. 223.)

Paul speaks only of coming to a knowledge of the divine Sonship of our Lord by the Spirit. Moroni, however, in his dissertation on spiritual gifts, amplifies the concept to cover three matters in particular: 1. The Spirit will reveal the truth of the Book of Mormon to those who seek this knowledge in faith; 2. All things may be known by the power of the Holy Ghost; and 3. Christ may be known by this same power. These are his words: "I would exhort you that when ye shall read these things, if it be wisdom in God that ye should read them, that ye would remember how merciful the Lord hath been unto the children of men, from the creation of Adam even down unto the time that ye shall receive these things, and ponder it in your hearts. And when ye shall receive these things, I would exhort you that ye would ask God, the Eternal Father, in the name of Christ, if these things are not true; and if ye shall ask with a sincere heart, with real intent, having faith in Christ, he will manifest the truth of it unto you, by the power of the Holy Ghost. And by the power of the Holy Ghost ye may know the truth of all things. And whatsoever thing is good is just and true; wherefore, nothing that is good denieth the Christ, but acknowledgeth that he is. And ye may know that he is, by the power of the Holy Ghost; wherefore I would exhort you that ye deny not the power of God; for he worketh by power, according to the faith of the children of men, the same today and tomorrow, and forever." (Moro. 10:3-7.)

Jesus taught that "the Comforter, which is the Holy Ghost, whom the Father will send in my name, he shall teach you all things" (John 14:26), and the latter-day revelation on spiritual gifts says this about knowing of Christ's divinity by the power of the Spirit: "To some it is given by the Holy Ghost to know that Jesus Christ is the Son of God, and that he was crucified for the sins of the world. To others it is given to believe on their words, that they also might have eternal life if they continue faithful." (D. & C. 46:13-14.)

GIFTS OF THE SPIRIT IDENTIFY TRUE CHURCH

I CORINTHIANS 12:4-11.

4 Now there are diversities of gifts, but the same Spirit.

5 And there are differences of administrations, but the same Lord.

6 And there are diversities of operations, but it is the same God which worketh all in all.

7 But the manifestation of the Spirit is given to every man to profit withal.

8 For to one is given by the Spirit the word of wisdom: to another the word of knowledge by the same Spirit;

9 To another faith by the same Spirit; to another the gifts of healing by the same Spirit;

10 To another the working of miracles; to another prophecy; to another discerning of spirits; to another *divers* kinds of tongues; to another the interpretation of tongues:

11 But all these worketh that one and the selfsame Spirit, dividing to every man severally as he will.

"By the grace of God — following devotion, faith, and obedience on man's part — certain special spiritual blessings called gifts of the Spirit are bestowed upon men. Their receipt is always predicated upon obedience to law, but because they are freely available to all the obedient, they are called gifts. They are signs and miracles reserved for the faithful and for none else. . . .

"Their purpose is to enlighten, encourage, and edify the faithful so that they will inherit peace in this life and be guided toward eternal life in the world to come. Their presence is proof of the divinity of the Lord's work; where they are not found, there the Church and kingdom of God is not. . . .

"From the writings of Paul (1 Cor. 12; 13; 14), and of Moroni (Moro. 10), and from the revelations received by Joseph Smith (D. & C. 46), we gain a clear knowledge of spiritual gifts and how they operate. Among others, we find the following gifts named either in these three places or elsewhere in the scriptures: the gift of knowing by revelation 'that Jesus Christ is the Son of God, and that he was crucified for the sins of the world' (D. & C. 46:13), and also the gift of believing the testimony of those who have gained this revelation; the gifts of testimony, of knowing that the Book of Mormon is true, and of receiving revelations; the gifts of judgment, knowledge, and wisdom; of teaching, exhortation, and preaching; of teaching the word of wisdom and the word of knowledge; of declaring the gospel and of ministry; the gift of faith, including power both to heal and to be healed; the gifts of healing, working of miracles, and prophesy; the viewing of visions, beholding of angels and ministering spirits, and the discerning of spirits; speaking with tongues, the interpretation of tongues, the interpretation of languages, and the gift of translation; the differences of administration in the Church and the diversities of operation of the Spirit; the gift of seership, 'and a gift which is greater can no man have.' (Mosiah 8:16; Alma 9:21; D. & C. 5:4; 43:3-4; Rom. 12:6-8.) And these are by no means all of the gifts. In the fullest sense, they are infinite in number and endless in their manifestations." (*Mormon Doctrine*, 2nd ed., pp. 314-315.)

4-7. Speaking of the gifts of God, Moroni says: "They are many; and they come from the same God. And there are different ways that these gifts are administered; but it is the same God who worketh all in all; and they are given by the manifestations of the Spirit of God unto men, to profit them." (Moro. 10:8.) Latter-day revelation expresses the same concept this way: "And again, verily I say unto you, I would that ye should always remember, and always retain in your minds what those gifts are, that are given unto the church. For all have not every gift given unto them; for there are many gifts, and to every man is given a gift by the Spirit of God. To some is given one, and to some is given another, that all may be profited thereby. . . . And again, to some it is given by the Holy Ghost to know the differences of administration, as it will be pleasing unto the same Lord, according as the Lord will, suiting his mercies according to the conditions of

369

the children of men. And again, it is given by the Holy Ghost to some to know the diversities of operations, whether they be of God, that the manifestations of the Spirit may be given to every man to profit withal." (D. & C. 46:10-12, 15-16.)

8. "For behold, to one is given by the Spirit of God, that he may teach the word of wisdom; And to another, that he may teach the word of knowledge by the same Spirit." (Moro. 10:9-10.) "And again, verily I say unto you, to some is given, by the Spirit of God, the word of wisdom. To another is given the word of knowledge, that all may be taught to be wise and to have knowledge." (D. & C. 46:17-18.)

The word of wisdom] An endowment of wisdom. See Jas. 1:1-7.

The word of knowledge] An endowment of knowledge, not random knowledge, not knowledge in general or as an abstract principle, but gospel knowledge, a knowledge of God and his laws.

9. "And to another, exceeding great faith; and to another, the gifts of healing by the same Spirit." (Moro. 10:11.) "And again, to some it is given to have faith to be healed; And to others it is given to have faith to heal." (D. & C. 46:19-20.)

Faith] See Heb. 11:1-3. **Gifts of healing]** The power, by faith, to heal men physically and spiritually, even as the Lord Jesus did during his mortal ministry.

10. **The working of miracles]** "And again, to another, that he may work mighty miracles." (Moro. 10:12.) "And again, to some is given the working of miracles." (D. & C. 46:21.) See 1 Cor. 12:28-31.

Prophecy] "And again, to another, that he may prophesy concerning all things." (Moro. 10:13.) "And to others it is given to prophesy." (D. & C. 46:22.) See Rev. 19:9b-10.

Discerning of spirits] "And to others the discerning of spirits." (D. & C. 46:23.) See 1 John 4:1-6.

Tongues . . . interpretation of tongues] "And again, to another, all kinds of tongues; And again, to another, the interpretation of languages and of divers kinds of tongues." (Moro. 10:15-16.) "And again, it is given to some to speak with tongues; And to another is given the interpretation of tongues." (D. & C. 46:24-25.) See Acts 2:1-21; 1 Cor. 14:6-28.

11. "And all these gifts come by the Spirit of Christ; and they come unto every man severally, according as he will. And I would exhort you, my beloved brethren, that ye remember that every good gift cometh of Christ." (Moro. 10:17-18.) "And all these gifts come from God, for the benefit of the children of God. And unto the bishop of the church, and unto such as God shall appoint and ordain to watch over the church and to be elders unto the church, are to have it given unto them to discern all those gifts lest there shall be any among you professing and yet be not of God." (D. & C. 46:26-27.)

Whence come spiritual gifts? Paul says they come from the Spirit, meaning the Holy Ghost. The latter-day revelation on spiritual gifts says they come from God, meaning the Father. Moroni calls them the gifts of God, but says they come from Christ and also that they come by the Spirit of Christ, meaning the light of Christ which proceedeth forth from the presence of God to fill the immensity of space.

And all of these inspired declarations are true; each is in perfect harmony with all of the others. Certainly they are the gifts of the Father, and of the Son, and of the Holy Ghost. They come from the Father in that he is the source and center of creation and of all things; they come from Christ because he represents the Father, acts in his name and power, and is the one to whom all men look for salvation; they come from the Holy Ghost because he is the minister of the Father and the Son, the one appointed to give revelation and to bestow the gifts of the Gods upon men — all of which exemplifies the perfect unity and oneness of the members of the Godhead.

Further, they come by means of the Spirit of Christ, meaning the Light of Christ, because that light is the law by which all things are governed; it is the light in all things, and through all things, and round about all things; it is the agency of God's power; it is the vehicle used by the Holy Ghost to manifest his powers in all places at all times.

EVERY MEMBER HAS HIS OWN GIFT

I CORINTHIANS 12:12-27.

12 For as the body is one, and hath many members, and all the members of that one body, being many, are one body: so also *is* Christ.

13 For by one Spirit are we all baptized into one body, whether *we be* Jews or Gentiles, whether *we be* bond or free; and have been all made to drink into one Spirit.

14 For the body is not one member, but many.

15 If the foot shall say, Because I am not the hand, I am not of the body; is it therefore not of the body?

16 And if the ear shall say, Because I am not the eye, I am not of the body; is it therefore not of the body?

17 If the whole body *were* an eye, where *were* the hearing? If the whole *were* hearing, where *were* the smelling?

18 But now hath God set the members every one of them in the body, as it hath pleased him.

19 And if they were all one member, where *were* the body?

20 But now *are they* many members, yet but one body.

21 And the eye cannot say unto the hand, I have no need of thee: nor again the head to the feet, I have no need of you.

22 Nay, much more those members of the body, which seem to be more feeble, are necessary:

23 And those *members* of the body, which we think to be less honourable, upon these we bestow more abundant honour; and our uncomely *parts* have more abundant comeliness.

24 For our comely *parts* have no need: but God hath tempered the body together, having given more abundant honour to that *part* which lacked:

25 That there should be no schism in the body; but *that* the members should have the same care one for another.

26 And whether one member suffer, all the members suffer with it; or one member be honoured, all the members rejoice with it.

27 Now ye are the body of Christ, and members in particular.

Every converted member of the Church has one or more of the gifts of the Spirit. Following baptism in water, new members of the Church receive the laying on of hands for the gift of the Holy Ghost. This gift is the right to the constant companionship

372

of the Holy Spirit based on faithfulness. Hence, any truly converted person has, as one gift, a witness from the Spirit that the work is true; every person who has a testimony enjoys to one degree or another the companionship of the Spirit; and none can receive the Spirit without partaking of the gifts of the Spirit, for the fact of receiving revelation that the work is true is itself one of the gifts.

But all members are not equally endowed; some possess one gift, some another; a few have a host of gifts; and all of the gifts are found somewhere in the Church. Paul's inspired commentary on this takes the human body as the illustration of the Church; even as one body has many parts or members, so one Church, endowed with one Spirit, has many members with divers gifts.

And the obligation resting upon church members is to "covet earnestly the best gifts" (1 Cor. 12:31), and to use whatever gifts are obtained for the building up of the kingdom and the rolling forth of the Lord's work. Hence the revealed counsel: "Let every man stand in his own office, and labor in his own calling; and let not the head say unto the feet it hath no need of the feet; for without the feet how shall the body be able to stand? Also the body hath need of every member, that all may be edified together, that the system may be kept perfect." (D. & C. 84:109-110.)

Gifts of the Spirit] See 1 Cor. 12:4-11.

APOSTLES, PROPHETS, MIRACLES IDENTIFY TRUE CHURCH

I CORINTHIANS 12:28-31.

28 And God hath set some in the church, first apostles, secondarily prophets, thirdly teachers, after that miracles, then gifts of healings, helps, governments, diversities of tongues.

29 *Are* all apostles? *are* all prophets? *are* all teachers? *are* all workers of miracles?

30 Have all the gifts of healing? do all speak with tongues? do all interpret?

31 But covet earnestly the best gifts: and yet show I unto you a more excellent way.

I.V. I CORINTHIANS 12:31.

31 **I say unto you, Nay; for I have shown unto you a more excellent way, therefore covet earnestly the best gifts.**

28-29. The presence of the gifts of the Spirit identifies the true Church and kingdom of God on earth. Where these are, there is God's Church, and where they are not, there true religion with saving power is not found.

Moroni's statements on this phase of spiritual gifts include this persuasive argument: Christ "is the same yesterday, today, and forever, and that all these gifts of which I have spoken, which are spiritual, never will be done away, even as long as the world shall stand, only according to the unbelief of the children of men. . . . And now I speak unto all the ends of the earth — that if the day cometh that the power and gifts of God shall be done away among you, it shall be because of unbelief. And wo be unto the children of men if this be the case; for there shall be none that doeth good among you, no not one. For if there be one among you that doeth good, he shall work by the power and gifts of God." (Moro. 10:19, 24-25.)

28. God hath set some in the Church] God did it! In his Church there are apostles, prophets, gifts of the Spirit, and so forth. These are essential; there are no substitutes for them; they are either present or the truth of heaven is absent, for it is the eternal decree of the Incarnate Jehovah that all "these signs shall follow them that believe" God's one and only true gospel. (Mark 16:17.) Where all these things are, there is found the power of God unto salvation; where these things are not, whatever parades in the name of religion has no saving power. It is instead "a form of godliness," whose adherents, being without the gifts, of necessity, must and do "deny the power thereof." (Jos. Smith 2:19.)

Apostles] See 1 Cor. 4:1-21. **Prophets]** See Rev. 19:9b-10. **Teachers]** See Eph. 4:7-16; 1 Tim. 1:1-11.

Miracles] Miracles wrought by the power of God are the perfect proof of pure religion. They are always, invariably, everlastingly, unendingly, and without fail, found in the true Church. Their absence is conclusive, absolute, and irrefutable proof of apostasy. It is just as simple as that. In the true Church there are miracles in great numbers; churches without miracles — meaning where the dead are not raised, where the eyes of the blind are not opened, where the ears of the deaf are not unstopped, and where there are not all manner of healings and wonderous things — such churches are not of God and do not have the power to save souls in the celestial kingdom. The seeming and actual miraculous things shown forth by Satan's power are not to be confused with the actual operation of God's power among his earthly children. Those with spiritual insight soon detect the difference, for God's power endures and Satan's fades away.

One of the most powerful and persuasive sermons ever preached on the subject of miracles came from the lips of Moroni. "I speak unto you who deny the revelations of God," he said, "and say that they are done away, that there are no revelations, nor prophecies, nor gifts, nor healing, nor speaking with tongues, and the interpretation of tongues; Behold I say unto you, he that denieth these things knoweth not the gospel of Christ; yea, he has not read the scriptures; if so, he does not understand them. For do we not read that God is the same yesterday, today, and forever, and in him there is no variableness neither shadow of changing? And now if ye have imagined up unto yourselves a god who doth vary, and in whom there is shadow of changing, then have ye imagined up unto yourselves a god who is not a God of miracles. But behold, I will show unto you a God of miracles, even the God of Abraham, and the God of Isaac, and the God of Jacob; and it is that same God who created the heavens and the earth, and all things that in them are." (Morm. 9:7-11.)

Then he lists some of the great events that have and are to occur in the course of God's dealings with men, including the fact that there is to be a resurrection, a final judgment, and a salvation or damnation for all men, and asks: "O all ye that have imagined up unto yourselves a god who can do no miracles, I would ask of you, have all these things passed, of which I have spoken? Has the end come yet? Behold I say unto you, Nay; and God has not ceased to be a God of miracles. Behold, are not the things that God hath wrought marvelous in our eyes? Yea, and who can comprehend the marvelous works of God? Who shall say that it was not a miracle that by his word the heaven and the earth should be; and by the power of his word man was created of the dust of the earth; and by the power of his word have miracles been wrought? And who shall say that Jesus Christ did not many mighty miracles? And there were many mighty miracles wrought by the hands of the apostles. And if there were miracles wrought then, why has God ceased to be a God of miracles and yet be an unchangeable Being? And behold, I say unto you he changeth not; if so he would cease to be God; and he ceaseth not to be God, and is a God of miracles. And the reason why he ceaseth to do miracles among the children of men is because that they dwindle in unbelief, and depart from the right way, and know not the God in whom they should trust.

"Behold, I say unto you that whoso believeth in Christ, doubting nothing, whatsoever he shall ask the Father in the name of Christ it shall be granted him; and this promise is unto all, even unto the ends of the earth. For behold, thus said Jesus Christ, the Son of God, unto his disciples who should tarry, yea, and also to all his disciples, in the hearing of the multitude: Go ye into all the world, and preach the gospel to every creature; And he that believeth and is baptized shall be saved, but he that believeth not shall be damned; And these signs shall follow them that believe — in my name shall they cast out devils; they shall speak with new tongues; they shall take up serpents; and if they drink any deadly thing it shall not hurt them; they shall lay hands on the sick and they shall recover; And whosoever shall believe in my name, doubting nothing, unto him will I confirm all my words, even unto the ends of the earth." (Morm. 9:15-25.)

Gifts of healings] Power to exercise faith sufficient to heal the sick; in part at least this is a matter of causing the sick persons to center their own faith in Christ so that the healing power of faith becomes operative on their behalf. See *Commentary I*, pp. 157-159.

Helps, governments] Church officers and organizations. When our Article of Faith says, "We believe in the same organization that existed in the Primitive Church," it has specific reference to priesthood offices, to "apostles, prophets, pastors, teachers, evangelists," and so forth, to the possession of apostolic power and the keys of the kingdom. These things are the same in all dispensations, and after listing them in our day, the Lord said: "The above offices I have given unto you, and the keys thereof, for helps and for governments, for the work of the ministry and the perfecting of my saints." (D. & C. 124:143.) But in addition to these basic priesthood offices there have always been other helps and governments which are auxiliary to the priesthood. These supplemental church organizations vary from time to time and are geared to the needs of the particular age or hour involved. Indeed, the fact that they change to meet current needs is one of the great evidences of the divinity of the Lord's work; otherwise the saints would have difficulty in solving the problems of whatever day is involved.

Diversities of tongues] See Acts 2:1-21; 1 Cor. 14:6-28.

31. "But ye are commanded in all things to ask of God, who giveth liberally; and that which the Spirit testifies unto you even so I would that ye should do in all holiness of heart, walking uprightly before me, considering the end of your salvation, doing all things with prayer and thanksgiving, that ye may not be seduced by evil spirits, or doctrines of devils, or the commandments of men; for some are of men, and others of devils. Wherefore, beware lest ye are deceived; and that ye may not be deceived seek ye earnestly the best gifts, always remembering for what they are given; For verily I say unto you, they are given for the benefit of those who love me and keep all my commandments, and him that seeketh so to do; that all may be benefited that seek or that ask of me, that ask and not for a sign that they may consume it upon their lusts." (D. & C. 46:7-9.)

"CHARITY IS THE PURE LOVE OF CHRIST"

I CORINTHIANS 13:1-13.

1 Though I speak with the tongues of men and of angels, and have not charity, I am become *as* sounding brass, or a tinkling cymbal.

2 And though I have *the gift of* prophecy, and understand all mysteries, and all knowledge; and though I have all faith, so that I could remove mountains, and have not charity, I am **nothing.**

3 And though I bestow all my goods to feed *the poor*, and though I give my body to be burned, and have not charity, it profiteth me nothing.

4 Charity suffereth long, *and* is kind; charity envieth not; charity vaunteth not itself, is not puffed up,

5 Doth not behave itself unseemly, seeketh not her own, is not easily provoked, thinketh no evil;

6 Rejoiceth not in iniquity, but rejoiceth in the truth;

7 Beareth all things, believeth all things, hopeth all things, endureth all things.

8 Charity never faileth: but whether *there be* prophecies, they shall fail; whether *there be* tongues, they shall cease; whether *there be* knowledge, it shall vanish away.

9 For we know in part, and we prophesy in part.

10 But when that which is perfect is come, then that which is in part shall be done away.

11 When I was a child, I spake as a child, I understood as a child, I thought as a child: but when I became a man, I put away childish things.

12 For now we see through a glass, darkly; but then face to face: now I know in part; but then shall I know even as also I am known.

13 And now abideth faith, hope, charity, these three; but the greatest of these *is* charity.

"Above all the attributes of godliness and perfection, charity is the one most devoutly to be desired. Charity is more than love, far more; it is everlasting love, perfect love, the pure love of Christ which endureth forever. It is love so centered in righteousness that the possessor has no aim or desire except for the eternal welfare of his own soul and for the souls of those around him. (2 Ne. 26:30; Moro. 7:47; 8:25-26.)

" 'Above all things,' the Lord says, 'clothe yourselves with the bond of charity, as with a mantle, which is the bond of perfectness and peace.' (D. & C. 88:125; Col. 3:14.) 'Above all things have fervent charity among yourselves,' Peter said to the saints, 'for charity shall cover the multitude of sins.' (1 Pet. 4:8.) Charity is the crowning virtue, 'the end of the commandment' (1 Tim. 1:5); 'And now abideth faith, hope, charity, these three; but the greatest of these is charity.' (1 Cor. 13:13.)

"CHARITY IS THE PURE LOVE OF CHRIST"

"Charity is an essential qualification for the ministers of Christ (D. & C. 4:5); no one can assist in the Lord's work without it (D. & C. 12:8; 18:19); and the saints of God are commanded to seek and attain it. (D. & C. 121:45; 124:116; 2 Ne. 33:7-9; Alma 7:24; 1 Cor. 16:14; 1 Tim. 4:12; 2 Tim. 2:22; Tit. 2:2; 2 Pet. 1:7.) Charity is a gift of the Spirit which must be gained if one is to have salvation. 'There must be faith,' Moroni writes, 'and if there must be faith there must also be hope; and if there must be hope there must also be charity. And except ye have charity ye can in nowise be saved in the kingdom of God; neither can ye be saved in the kingdom of God if ye have not faith; neither can ye if ye have no hope.' (Moro. 10:20-21.)

"To Moroni the Lord said: 'Faith, hope and charity bringeth unto me — the fountain of all righteousness,' and Moroni replied to the Lord (being, of course, moved upon by the Holy Ghost): 'I remember that thou hast said that thou hast loved the world, even unto the laying down of thy life for the world, that thou mightest take it again to prepare a place for the children of men. And now I know that this love which thou hast had for the children of men is charity; wherefore, except men shall have charity they cannot inherit that place which thou hast prepared in the mansions of thy Father.' (Ether 12:28, 33-34.)

"Both Paul and Mormon wrote of charity in similar language. Either they both had the same words of some earlier prophet before them or the Holy Ghost revealed the same truths to them in almost the same words. Mormon's language included these statements: 'If a man be meek and lowly in heart, and confesses by the power of the Holy Ghost that Jesus is the Christ, he must needs have charity; for if he have not charity he is nothing; wherefore he must needs have charity. And charity suffereth long, and is kind, and envieth not, and is not puffed up, seeketh not her own, is not easily provoked, thinketh no evil, and rejoiceth not in iniquity but rejoiceth in the truth, beareth all things, believeth all things, hopeth all things, endureth all things. Wherefore, my beloved brethren, if ye have not charity, ye are nothing, for charity never faileth. Wherefore, cleave unto charity, which is the greatest of all, for all things must fail — But charity is the pure love of

379

Christ, and it endureth forever; and whoso is found possessed of it at the last day, it shall be well with him. Wherefore, my beloved brethren, pray unto the Father with all the energy of heart, that ye may be filled with this love, which he hath bestowed upon all who are true followers of his Son, Jesus Christ; that ye may become the sons of God; that when he shall appear we shall be like him, for we shall see him as he is; that we may have this hope; that we may be purified even as he is pure.' (Moro. 7:44-48.)" (*Mormon Doctrine*, 2nd ed., pp. 121-122.)

1-3. These verses must be interpreted in the context of Paul's whole presentation on charity and spiritual gifts. They are a form of reasoning and argumentation designed to dramatize the pre-eminent position of charity among the attributes of godliness, and standing alone they are not to be taken literally. It is not possible, for instance, to have faith without first having charity, but by speaking as though faith to move mountains is as nothing compared to charity, the point is driven home that there is nothing so transcendent as having the pure love of Christ in one's soul. In principle, it is as though, in order to emphasize the importance of the family unit, a man should say: "Though I gain exaltation itself, and have not my wife by my side, I shall have nothing" — a thing which is impossible, for exaltation consists in the continuation of the family unit in eternity.

1. Tongues . . . of angels] "Angels speak by the power of the Holy Ghost." (2 Ne. 32:3.)

8-12. Shall the gifts of the Spirit cease? Is there to be a day when the saints shall no longer possess the gifts of prophecy and tongues? Or the gift of knowledge? Yes, in the sense that these shall be swallowed up in something greater, and shall no longer be needed in the perfect day. When the saints know all tongues, none will be able to speak in an unknown tongue. When the saints become as God and know all things — past, present, and future — there will be no need or occasion to prophesy of the future.

13. But some things shall "abide" forever. Among them: Faith, which is the very power of God himself; hope, which is the assurance of eternal life and everlasting progression; and charity, which is the pure love of Christ.

TONGUES AND PROPHECY COMPARED

I CORINTHIANS 14:1-28.

1 Follow after charity, and desire spiritual *gifts*, but rather that ye may prophesy.

2 For he that speaketh in an *unknown* tongue speaketh not unto men, but unto God: for no man understandeth *him;* howbeit in the spirit he speaketh mysteries.

3 But he that prophesieth speaketh unto men *to* edification, and exhortation, and comfort.

4 He that speaketh in an *unknown* tongue edifieth himself; but he that prophesieth edifieth the church.

5 I would that ye all spake with tongues, but rather that ye prophesied: for greater *is* he that prophesieth than he that speaketh with tongues, except he interpret, that the church may receive edifying.

6 Now, brethren, if I come unto you speaking with tongues, what shall I profit you, except I shall speak to you either by revelation, or by knowledge, or by prophesying, or by doctrine?

7 And even things without life giving sound, whether pipe or harp, except they give a distinction in the sounds, how shall it be known what is piped or harped?

8 For if the trumpet give an uncertain sound, who shall prepare himself to the battle?

9 So likewise ye, except ye utter by the tongue words easy to be understood, how shall it be known what is spoken? for ye shall speak into the air.

10 There are, it may be, so many kinds of voices in the world, and none of them *is* without signification.

11 Therefore if I know not the meaning of the voice, I shall be unto him that speaketh a barbarian, and he that speaketh *shall be* a barbarian unto me.

12 Even so ye, forasmuch as ye are zealous of spiritual *gifts*, seek that ye may excel to the edifying of the church.

13 Wherefore let him that speaketh in an *unknown* tongue pray that he may interpret.

14 For if I pray in an *unknown* tongue, my spirit prayeth, but my understanding is unfruitful.

15 What is it then? I will pray with the spirit, and I will pray with the understanding also: I will sing with the spirit, and I will sing with the understanding also.

16 Else when thou shalt bless with the spirit, how shall he that occupieth the room of the unlearned say Amen at thy giving of thanks, seeing he understandeth not what thou sayest?

17 For thou verily givest thanks well, but the other is not edified.

18 I thank my God, I speak with tongues more than ye all:

19 Yet in the church I had rather speak five words with my understanding, that *by my voice* I might teach others also, than ten thousand words in an *unknown* tongue.

20 Brethren, be not children in understanding: howbeit in malice be ye children, but in understanding be men.

21 In the law it is written, With *men of* other tongues and other lips will I speak unto this people; and yet for all that will they not hear me, saith the Lord.

22 Wherefore tongues are for a sign, not to them that believe, but to them that believe not: but prophesying *serveth* not for them that believe not, but for them which believe.

23 If therefore the whole church be come together into one place, and all speak with tongues, and there came in *those that are* unlearned, or unbelievers, will they not say that ye are mad?

24 But if all prophesy, and there come in one that believeth not, or *one* unlearned, he is convinced of all, he is judged of all:

25 And thus are the secrets of his heart made manifest; and so falling down on *his* face he will worship God, and report that God is in you of a truth.

26 How is it then, brethren? when ye come together, every one of you hath a psalm, hath a doctrine, hath a tongue, hath a revelation, hath an interpretation. Let all things be done unto edifying.

27 If any man speak in an *unknown* tongue, *let it be* by two, or at the most *by* three, and *that* by course; and let one interpret.

28 But if there be no interpreter, let him keep silence in the church; and let him speak to himself, and to God.

I.V. I CORINTHIANS 14:2, 4, 13-14, 19, 27.

2 For he that speaketh in **another** tongue speaketh not unto men, but unto God; for no man understandeth him; howbeit in the spirit he speaketh mysteries.

4 He that speaketh in **another** tongue edifieth himself; but he that prophesieth edifieth the church.

13 Wherefore let him that speaketh in **another** tongue pray that he may interpret.

14 For if I pray in **another** tongue, my spirit prayeth, but my understanding is unfruitful.

19 Yet in the church I had rather speak five words with my understanding, that by my voice I might teach others also, than ten thousands w o r d s in **another** tongue.

27 If any man speak in **another** tongue, let it be by two, or at the most by three, and that by course; and let one interpret.

TONGUES AND PROPHECY COMPARED

"Two of the gifts of the Spirit are speaking in tongues and interpretation of tongues. (Moro. 10:15-16; D. & C. 46:24-25; 1 Cor. 12:10, 28, 30; 14.) These gifts have been manifest among the saints in every age (Omni 25; Alma 9:21; 3 Ne. 29:6; Morm. 9:7), and they are desirable and useful in the Lord's work. 'Let the gift of tongues be poured out upon thy people, even cloven tongues as of fire, and the interpretation thereof,' the Prophet prayed at the dedication of the Kirtland Temple. (D. & C. 109:36.)

"Tongues and their interpretation are classed among the signs and miracles which always attend the faithful and which stand as evidences of the divinity of the Lord's work. (Morm. 9:24; Mark 16:17; Acts 10:46; 19:6.) In their more dramatic manifestations they consist in speaking or interpreting, by the power of the Spirit, a tongue which is completely unknown to the speaker or interpreter. Sometimes it is the pure Adamic language which is involved. Frequently these gifts are manifest where the ordinary languages of the day are concerned in that the Lord's missionaries learn to speak and interpret foreign languages with ease, thus furthering the spread of the message of the restoration. When the elders of Israel, often in a matter of weeks, gain fluency in a foreign tongue, they have been blessed with the gift of tongues.

"An ideal and proper use of tongues was shown forth on the day of Pentecost. By using this gift the apostles were enabled to speak in their own tongue and be understood by persons of many different tongues. (Acts 2:1-18.) Indeed, 'the gift of tongues by the power of the Holy Ghost in the Church,' as the Prophet said, 'is for the benefit of the servants of God to preach to unbelievers, as on the day of Pentecost. (Teachings, p. 195.) 'Be not so curious about tongues,' the Prophet also said. 'Do not speak in tongues except there be an interpreter present; the ultimate design of tongues is to speak to foreigners, and if persons are very anxious to display their intelligence, let them speak to such in their own tongues [that is, in the tongues of the foreigners].' (Teachings, pp. 247-248.)

"Caution should always attend the use of the gift of tongues. 'It is not necessary,' for instance, 'for tongues to be taught to the

Church particularly, for any man that has the Holy Ghost, can speak of the things of God in his own tongue as well as to speak in another; for faith comes not by signs, but by hearing the word of God.' (*Teachings*, pp. 148-149.) 'If anything is taught by the gifts of tongues, it is not to be received for doctrine.' (*Teachings*, p. 229.) 'Speak not in the gift of tongues without understanding it, or without interpretation. The devil can speak in tongues; the adversary will come with his work; he can tempt all classes; can speak in English or Dutch. Let no one speak in tongues unless he interpret, except by the consent of the one who is placed to preside; then he may discern or interpret, or another may.' (*Teachings*, p. 162, 212.)

"Tongues and their interpretation are given for special purposes under special circumstances. There are a host of gifts that are far more important and in the use of which there is less chance for deception. The gifts of exhortation, of preaching, of expounding doctrine, of teaching the gospel — though not nearly so dramatic — are far greater and of more value than tongues. 'In the church I had rather speak five words with my understanding, that by my voice I might teach others also,' Paul averred, 'than ten thousand words in an unknown tongue.' (1 Cor. 14:19.)

"As with other spiritual gifts, tongues 'never will be done away,' as long as the earth remains in its present state, 'only according to the unbelief of the children of men.' (Moro. 10:19.) But in the ultimate perfect day the gifts pertaining to tongues 'shall cease.' (1 Cor. 13:8.) Obviously in that final glorious day when the saints know all things (which includes a perfect knowledge of all languages) it will no longer be either necessary or possible to speak in tongues and give interpretation thereto." (*Mormon Doctrine*, 2nd ed., pp. 799-801.)

1. Prophecy is greater than charity, because in order to prophesy a man must first have the pure love of Christ in his soul (which is charity), and then he must attune himself to the Holy Spirit so as to receive the spirit of revelation and of prophecy. Chiefly the gift of prophecy is to know by revelation from the Holy Ghost of the divine Sonship of our Lord. See Rev. 19:9b-10.

5. Tongues and prophecy belong in and are found in the true Church.

16. It is proper practice for the congregation to say Amen at the conclusion of a gospel sermon, thus signifying acceptance of and concurrence in what has been said.

19. Suppose a speaker should say: "God is an exalted Man" — five simple words; would they not, as Paul reasons, be worth more than endless sermons in unknown tongues?

22-23. See Acts 2:1-21.

26. In testimony meetings, members of the congregation, in an orderly manner, are privileged to sing, testify, speak, or exhort, as the Spirit directs.

"YE MAY ALL PROPHESY"

I CORINTHIANS 14:29-40.

29 Let the prophets speak two or three, and let the other judge.

30 If *any thing* be revealed to another that sitteth by, let the first hold his peace.

31 For ye may all prophesy one by one, that all may learn, and all may be comforted.

32 And the spirits of the prophets are subject to the prophets.

33 For God is not *the author* of confusion, but of peace, as in all churches of the saints.

34 Let your women keep silence in the churches: for it is not permitted unto them to speak; but *they are commanded* to be under obedience, as also saith the law.

35 And if they will learn any thing, let them ask their husbands at home: for it is a shame for women to speak in the church.

36 What? came the word of God out from you? or came it unto you only?

37 If any man think himself to be a prophet, or spiritual, let him acknowledge that the things that I write unto you are the commandments of the Lord.

38 But if any man be ignorant, let him be ignorant.

39 Wherefore, brethren, covet to prophesy, and forbid not to speak with tongues.

40 Let all things be done decently and in order.

I.V. I CORINTHIANS 14:34-35.

34 Let your women keep silence in the churches; for it is not permitted unto them to **rule;** but they are commanded to be under obedience, as also saith the law.

35 And if they will learn any thing, let them ask their husbands at home; for it is a shame for women to **rule** in the church.

Paul the prophet, Paul the apostle, Paul the authority on doctrine and spiritual things — drawing on his own experiences and speaking by the power of the Spirit — now puts the capstone on the doctrine of spiritual gifts. He has spoken of these gifts — outlining, defining, exhorting. He has related spiritual gifts to charity and the eternal verities. Now he comes to the Spirit-directed climax: "Let the prophets speak. . . . Ye may all prophesy. . . . Covet to prophesy."

Prophecy stands supreme, the greatest of all the gifts of the Spirit.

Prophecy is revelation; it is testimony; it is Spirit speaking to spirit; it is knowing by revelation that Jesus is the Lord, that salvation is in Christ, that he has redeemed us by his blood.

Prophecy is walking in paths of truth and righteousness; it is living and doing the will of Him whose we are; and in its final and perfect form — known as, "the more sure word of prophecy" —it consists in "a man's knowing that he is sealed up unto eternal life, by revelation and the spirit of prophecy, through the power of the Holy Priesthood." (D. & C. 131:5.)

29. Let the prophets speak] Let those speak who have the testimony of Jesus, who know of spiritual things by revelation, who have tasted the good word of God; let those speak to whom the heavens have been opened, who can testify from personal knowledge, who have gained "words of wisdom . . . even by study and also by faith." (D. & C. 88:118.) Let those speak who can tell what God has revealed to them about his glorious gospel, "for one truth revealed from heaven is worth all the sectarian notions in existence." (*Teachings*, p. 338.)

Let the other judge] And while one prophet speaks, all others present shall give rapt attention to his words, that they, partaking of the same Spirit with which the speaker is endowed, may judge the testimony and doctrine to be good; thus, "he that preacheth and he that receiveth, understand one another, and both are edified and rejoice together." (D. & C. 50:22.)

30. Preaching in the true Church should be by revelation, and revelation is available to all, for all have the gift of the Holy Ghost, which is the right to the constant companionship of the Spirit. Preachers and ministers who are not of God are identified by the fact that they "teach with their learning, and deny the Holy Ghost, which giveth utterance." (2 Ne. 28:4.) "If any man speak," Peter said, "let him speak as the oracles of God." (1 Pet. 4:11.)

31. Ye may all prophesy] Who may prophesy? Who can receive revelation? To whom are visions and heavenly manifestations vouchsafed? Not to members of the Council of the Twelve only, not to bishops and stake presidents alone, not just to the leaders of the Church. Rather, that God who is no respecter of persons and who loves all his children, speaks to every person who will heed his voice. Prophecy is for all: men, women, and children, every member of the true Church; and those who have the testimony of Jesus have the spirit of prophecy, "for the testimony of Jesus is the spirit of prophecy." (Rev. 19:10.) "Would God," said Moses, "that all the Lord's people were prophets, and that the Lord would put his spirit upon them!" (Num. 11:29.)

32. There is nothing disorganized or haphazard about meetings in the Church. Members do not stand and speak at will. (*Teachings*, pp. 208-212.) There are always presiding officers who "conduct all meetings as they are directed and guided by the Holy Spirit." (D. & C. 46:2.)

33. "Behold, mine house is a house of order, saith the Lord God, and not a house of confusion." (D. & C. 132:8.)

34-35. May women speak in Church? Yes, in the sense of teaching, counseling, testifying, exhorting, and the like; no, in the sense of assuming rule over the Church as such, and in attempting to give direction as to how God's affairs on earth shall be regulated: "A woman has no right to found or organize a church — God never sent them to do it." (*Teachings*, p. 212.) Paul is here telling the sisters they are subject to the priesthood, that it is not their province to rule and reign, that the bishop's wife is not the bishop.

37. Paul was counseling by the power of the Spirit, and it follows that any person in tune with the same Spirit shall know the counsel comes from God.

39. Covet to prophesy] What better desire can members of the Church have than this? In effect it means, *Seek the Spirit*, and the companionship of the Spirit is the greatest gift men can receive in this life.

"CHRIST DIED FOR OUR SINS"

I CORINTHIANS 15:1-11.

1 Moreover, brethren, I declare unto you the gospel which I preached unto you, which also ye have received, and wherein ye stand;

2 By which also ye are saved, if ye keep in memory what I preached unto you, unless ye have believed in vain.

3 For I delivered unto you first of all that which I also received, how that Christ died for our sins according to the scriptures;

4 And that he was buried, and that he rose again the third day according to the scriptures:

5 And that he was seen of Cephas, then of the twelve:

6 After that, he was seen of above five hundred brethren at once; of whom the greater part remain unto this present, but some are fallen asleep.

7 After that, he was seen of James; then of all the apostles.

8 And last of all he was seen of me also, as of one born out of due time.

9 For I am the least of the apostles, that am not meet to be called an apostle, because I persecuted the church of God.

10 But by the grace of God I am what I am: and his grace which *was bestowed* upon me was not in vain; but I laboured more abundantly than they all: yet not I, but the grace of God which was with me.

11 Therefore whether *it were* I or they, so we preach, and so ye believed.

For the 58 verses of chapter 15, the Apostle now expounds on the reality, glories, and mysteries of the resurrection, that glorious doctrine that all men shall live again in immortality.

"The resurrection is the creation of an immortal soul; it consists in the uniting or reuniting of body and spirit in immortality. (*Doctrines of Salvation,* vol. 2, pp. 258-301.) A resurrected being is one for whom body and spirit are inseparably connected in a state of incorruption, a state in which there never again can be decay (corruption) or death (separation of body and spirit). (1 Cor. 15; Alma 11:37-46; 12:12-18.) Resurrected beings have bodies of flesh and bones, tangible, corporeal bodies, bodies that occupy space, digest food, and have power, outwardly, to appear as mortal bodies do. (Luke 24.)" (*Mormon Doctrine,* 2nd ed., pp. 637-638.)

1-4. The very gospel of Christ itself is that our Lord was crucified, died, and rose again the third day in glorious immortality. **Gospel]** See Rom: 1:1-17. **Atonement]** See Rom. 5:12-21. **First and Second Resurrections]** See Rev. 20:4-6. **All men resurrected]** See 1 Cor. 15:23-28.

2. Ye are saved, if] Because of the atonement men are saved if, after baptism, they keep the commandments. **Saved by obedience]** See Philip. 2:12-16.

Christ died for our sins] The atonement redeems men "from their spiritual fall" if they repent. (D. & C. 29:44.) "For, behold, the Lord your Redeemer suffered death in the flesh; wherefore he suffered the pain of all men, that all men might repent and come unto him. And he hath risen again from the dead, that he might bring all men unto him, on conditions of repentance." (D. & C. 18:11-12.)

4. He rose again the third day] See *Commentary I,* p. 194-197, 839-850.

5-9. How can Paul, or Peter, or anyone prove that Christ rose from the dead? The fact of resurrection is a spiritual reality, one wholly outside the realm of scientific investigation or proof; it cannot be established by research, or reason, or laboratory experiment. Spiritual truths can be known only by revelation; they are always revealed to the world by witnesses — prophets and righteous men who have seen within the veil, who have heard the voices of beings from another sphere, and who can therefore testify of the things of God. Peter and the others felt the nail marks in the hands of the Risen Lord, thrust their hands into the spear wound in his side, and ate and drank with him after he rose from the dead. (Luke 24; Acts 10:34-43.) Could there be any better evidence than this?

5. He was seen of Cephas] See *Commentary I*, p. 851. **Then of the twelve]** See *Commentary I*, pp. 851-859.

6. He was seen of above five hundred brethren at once] See *Commentary I*, pp. 865-872.

7. He was seen of James] James, the Lord's brother, of which appearance we have no other account. (Gal. 1:19.) **Then of all the apostles]** See *Commentary I*, p. 860; Acts 1:9-14.

8. He was seen of me] See Acts 9:1-9.

"NOW IS CHRIST RISEN FROM THE DEAD"

I CORINTHIANS 15:12-20.

12 Now if Christ be preached that he rose from the dead, how say some among you that there is no resurrection of the dead?

13 But if there be no resurrection of the dead, then is Christ not risen:

14 And if Christ be not risen, then *is* our preaching vain, and your faith *is* also vain.

15 Yea, and we are found false witnesses of God; because we have testified of God that he raised up Christ: whom he raised not up, if so be that the dead rise not.

16 For if the dead rise not, then is not Christ raised:

17 And if Christ be not raised, your faith *is* vain; ye are yet in your sins.

18 Then they also which are fallen asleep in Christ are perished.

19 If in this life only we have hope in Christ, we are of all men most miserable.

20 But now is Christ risen from the dead, *and* become the firstfruits of them that slept.

If Christ was resurrected—a fact which the Apostle has already shown in the only way such a spiritual reality can be proved, that is, by witnesses who saw and talked and felt and ate with the Resurrected Lord — if he was resurrected, then so it is or shall be with all men.

If the resurrection of one man is established, then the resurrection of all men is possible; and if the One known to have come forth from the tomb is also the Son of God — a fact which is itself proved by the resurrection — then his testimony is true that "all that are in the graves shall hear his voice, And shall come forth." (John 5:28-29.)

Indeed, the fact of our Lord's resurrection, and the consequent immortality thereby passed on to all men, lies at the heart and core and center of Christianity. Unless Christ was resurrected, he was not the Son of God; unless he inherited from an Immortal Father the power of immortality, he was as other men, incapable of bursting the bands of death for himself and for all men. The resurrection proves the divine Sonship, and the divine Sonship is established by the fact of resurrection; the two are inseparably connected; both are true, or neither is.

And if Christ is God's Son, then "the gospel of God, . . . Concerning his Son Jesus Christ our Lord" (Rom. 1:1-3), is true, its provisions are in force, and salvation is available to men. But if Christ is not God's Son, there is no atonement, no ransom from temporal and spiritual death, no resurrection, no forgiveness of sin, no eternal life, and, as Paul says, our faith is vain.

Moreover, true religion is not something for this life alone; it does not suffice for men to attain peace here while they let eternity take care of itself; such a limitation would leave the saints as the most miserable of all men. Rather, their hope in Christ is for a better world to come. This life is the time to prepare to meet God; to inherit that eternal life made possible through our Lord's atoning sacrifice is the hope and goal of those whose hearts are set on righteousness.

And that all this and much more may be, "the Holy Messiah," as Jacob taught, "layeth down his life according to the flesh, and taketh it again by the power of the Spirit, that he may bring to pass the resurrection of the dead, being the first that should rise. Wherefore he is the firstfruits unto God." (2 Ne. 2:8-9.)

Resurrection] See 1 Cor. 15:1-11.

CHRIST AND ADAM MAKE RESURRECTION POSSIBLE

I CORINTHIANS 15:21-22.

21 For since by man *came* death, by man *came* also the resurrection of the dead.

22 For as in Adam all die, even so in Christ shall all be made alive.

Christ and Adam are perfectly united in all things, each performing the mission assigned by the Eternal God.

Both are spirit sons of the Father of spirits; both were mighty and great in pre-existence — Christ attaining a state like unto God, and then becoming the Creator of all things; Adam standing next to the Creator in power and dominion, and then leading the armies of heaven when Lucifer and his host rebelled.

Both came into the world as sons of God — Adam, coming before death entered the world; Christ coming as the Only Begotten in the flesh. (Moses 6:22.)

And no two persons ever born on earth had ministries more intimately and essentially connected — Adam coming to bring temporal and spiritual death into the world through his transgression and fall; Christ coming to bring immortality and eternal life through his righteousness and redeeming sacrifice. (2 Ne. 2:6-10, 25-26; 9:6-7; Morm. 9:12-13.)

Adam brought mortality, Christ immortality; Adam brought death, Christ life. Death consists in the separation of body and spirit and is possible only because mortality came into the world through the fall of Adam. Immortal life consists in the reuniting, inseparably, of body and spirit and comes because of the atonement of Christ. Without mortality, there could be no immortality; without Adam there would be no mortality, and without Christ no immortality. The mission of each is tied into one eternal plan, the plan of the Father, the plan which gives immortality to all his children and offers eternal life to them on conditions of obedience to the laws and ordinances of the gospel.

Fall of Adam] See Rom. 5:12-21. **Resurrection]** See 1 Cor. 15:1-11.

IN WHAT ORDER ARE MEN RESURRECTED?

I CORINTHIANS 15:23-28.

23 But every man in his own order: Christ the firstfruits; afterward they that are Christ's at his coming.

24 Then *cometh* the end, when he shall have delivered up the kingdom to God, even the Father; when he shall have put down all rule and all authority and power.

25 For he must reign, till he hath put all enemies under his feet.

26 The last enemy *that* shall be destroyed *is* death.

27 For he hath put all things under his feet. But when he saith all things are put under *him, it is* manifest that he is excepted, which did put all things under him.

28 And when all things shall be subdued unto him, then shall the Son also himself be subject unto him that put all things under him, that God may be all in all.

I.V. I CORINTHIANS 15:24, 26-27.

24 **Afterward** cometh the end, when he shall have delivered up the kingdom to God, even the Father; when he shall have put down all rule, and all authority and power.

26 The last enemy, **death,** shall be destroyed.

27 **For he saith, When it is manifest that he hath put all things under his feet, and that all things are put under,** he is excepted **of the Father who** did put all things under him.

That all men shall come forth in the resurrection is axiomatic. (Alma 40:4.) Jesus promised: "All . . . shall come forth." The issue is not whether men shall be resurrected but when. There are, Jesus continued, two resurrections, "the resurrection of life; and

. . . the resurrection of damnation." (John 5:27-29.) And not only does one of these resurrections precede the other, but there is an order of priority within each period of resurrection. **Resurrection**] See 1 Cor. 15:1-11.

23. Every man in his own order] Order in the resurrection is determined by obedience to gospel law. The most righteous man was first, the most wicked shall be the last; Christ was first, the sons of perdition shall be last.

Christ the firstfruits] Christ's the firstfruits. These are the righteous dead, the faithful saints who come forth in the morning of the first resurrection and enter into celestial rest. At the Second Coming of our Lord, "they who have slept in their graves shall come forth, for their graves shall be opened; and they also shall be caught up to meet him in the midst of the pillar of heaven — They are Christ's, the first fruits, they who shall descend with him first, and they who are on the earth and in their graves, who are first caught up to meet him; and all this by the voice of the sounding of the trump of the angel of God." (D. & C. 88:97-98.)

Christ's at his coming] "And after this another angel shall sound, which is the second trump; and then cometh the redemption of those who are Christ's at his coming; who have received their part in that prison which is prepared for them, that they might receive the gospel, and be judged according to men in the flesh." (D. & C. 88:99.) These are they who lived a terrestrial law. They include: the heathen nations who died without the law of the gospel; others who rejected the gospel in this life, but received it in the spirit world; others who were honorable men by the standards of the world, but who were blinded spiritually; and yet others who were numbered with the saints of God, but who did not endure to the end and were not valiant in defense of truth and righteousness. (D. & C. 76:71-79.) They shall come forth in the latter part of the first resurrection and enter a terrestrial kingdom.

24. Then cometh the end] Afterward cometh the resurrection of damnation. In the fore part of this final resurrection shall come forth those whose inheritance is the telestial world, and in the latter part those who as sons of perdition shall be cast out with Lucifer and his rebel hosts forever. "And again, another trump shall sound, which is the third trump; and then come the spirits of men who are to be judged, and are found under condemnation; And these are the rest of the dead; and they live not again until the thousand years are ended, neither again, until the end of the earth. And another trump shall sound, which is the fourth trump, saying: There are found among those who are to remain until that great and last day, even the end, who shall remain filthy still." (D. & C. 88:100-102.)

WHY THE SAINTS BAPTIZE FOR THE DEAD

I CORINTHIANS 15:29.

29 Else what shall they do which are baptized for the dead, if the dead rise not at all? why are they then baptized for the dead?

'Why do you Corinthian Saints perform baptisms for your dead who died without a knowledge of the gospel, if there is no resurrected state in which they can reap the blessings of this holy ordinance?'

"Based on the eternal principle of vicarious service, the Lord has ordained baptism for the dead as the means whereby all his worthy children of all ages can become heirs of salvation in his kingdom. Baptism is the gate to the celestial kingdom, and except a man be born again of water and of the Spirit he cannot gain an inheritance in that heavenly world. (John 3:3-5.) Obviously, during the frequent periods of apostate darkness when the gospel light does not shine, and also in those geographical areas where legal administrators are not found, hosts of people live and die without ever entering in at the gate of baptism so as to be on the path leading to eternal life. For them a just God has ordained baptism for the dead, a vicarious-proxy labor. (D. & C. 124:28-36; 127; 128; 1 Cor. 15:29.)" (*Mormon Doctrine*, 2nd ed., p. 73.)

Baptism for the dead is thus one of the signs of the true Church. Where a people have the knowledge of this doctrine, together with the power and authority from God to perform the saving ordinances involved, there is the Church and kingdom of God on earth; and where these are not, there the Church and kingdom of God is not.

Salvation for the dead] See 1 Pet. 3:18-22; 4:1-6.

OBEDIENCE BRINGS A BETTER RESURRECTION

I CORINTHIANS 15:30-34.

30 And why stand we in jeopardy every hour?

31 I protest by your rejoicing which I have in Christ Jesus our Lord, I die daily.

32 If after the manner of men I have fought with beasts at Ephesus, what advantageth it me, if the dead rise not? let us eat and drink; for to morrow we die.

33 Be not deceived: evil com-munications corrupt good man-ners.

34 Awake to righteousness, and sin not; for some have not the knowledge of God: I speak *this* to your shame.

I.V. I CORINTHIANS 15:31.

31 I protest **unto you the res-urrection of the dead; and this is my rejoicing** which I have in Christ Jesus our Lord **daily, though I die.**

It is the hope of a better life to come that enables the saints to stand against the perils and enticements of this world. Whenever men gain the Lord's eternal perspective of whence they came, why they are here, and what lies ahead in the eternal realms of living and being, they are able better to govern the deeds done in the flesh. A knowledge of the resurrection thus leads to personal righteousness. **Resurrection]** See 1 Cor. 15:1-11. **Plan of salvation]** See Acts 2:37-40. **Faith enables men to endure sufferings]** See Heb. 11:35b-40.

30-32. 'If there is no resurrection — Why do the saints stand in jeopardy of their lives every hour? Why do they suffer persecution, submit to oppression, and bow before hostility and hate, rather than deny the faith? Why do they let themselves be driven from homes and lands, see their loved ones slain, and suffer death themselves rather than becoming one with the world? Is it not the rejoicing they have daily in the hope of a better resurrection, though they are called upon to die as martyrs of the truth?'

33-34. 'Therefore,' Paul reasons, 'let us keep the commandments and gain the promised blessings, even a better resurrection.'

HOW KINGDOMS OF GLORY ARE ASSIGNED

I CORINTHIANS 15:35-42a.

35 But some *man* will say, How are the dead raised up? and with what body do they come?

36 *Thou* fool, that which thou sowest is not quickened, except it die:

37 And that which thou sowest, thou sowest not that body that shall be, but bare grain, it may chance of wheat, or of some other *grain:*

38 But God giveth it a body as it hath pleased him, and to every seed his own body.

39 All flesh *is* not the same flesh: but *there is* one *kind of* flesh of men, another flesh of beasts, another of fishes, *and* another of birds.

40 *There are* also celestial bodies, and bodies terrestrial: but the glory of the celestial *is* one, and the *glory* of the terrestrial *is* another.

41 *There is* one glory of the sun, and another glory of the moon, and another glory of the stars: for *one* star differeth from *another* star in glory.

42a So also *is* the resurrection of the dead.

I.V. I CORINTHIANS 15:37, 40.

37 And that which thou sowest, thou sowest not that body **which** shall be, but grain, it may **be** of wheat, or some other;

40 Also celestial bodies, and bodies terrestrial, **and bodies telestial;** but the glory of the celestial, one; and the terrestrial, another; **and the telestial, another.**

Resurrection is the father of salvation; salvation grows out of and results from resurrection; only resurrected beings are saved; and the degree of glory gained by immortal beings depends upon the resurrection in which their immortal souls rise from the grave.

Our knowledge of degrees of glory and kinds of salvation is in fact an amplification and explanation of the doctrine of resurrection. "While we were doing the work of translation, which the Lord had appointed unto us," the Prophet writes of himself and Sidney Rigdon, "we came to the twenty-ninth verse of the fifth chapter of John, which was given unto us as follows: Speaking of the resurrection of the dead, concerning those who shall hear the voice of the Son of Man, and shall come forth— They who have done good in the resurrection of the just, and they who have done evil in the resurrection of the unjust — Now this caused us to marvel, for it was given unto us of the Spirit. And while we meditated upon these things, the Lord touched the eyes of our understandings and they were opened, and the glory of the Lord shone round about. And we beheld" the kingdoms of glory in the eternal worlds. (D. & C. 76:15-20.)

35. **How are the dead raised up?**] By the power of God, who created them, as such is made manifest in the atoning sacrifice of his Son. Immortality comes because of Jesus Christ; he is the resurrection and the life, without whom there would be neither immortality nor eternal life. **Resurrection**] See 1 Cor. 15:1-11.

With what body do they come?] The one they are entitled to receive — either a celestial, terrestrial, or telestial body, or a body incapable of abiding the glory found in any of the mansions which are prepared. And the degree of glory gained by each person shall be that which his resurrected and immortal body can abide.

36-38. Even as the seed, sown in the ground, decays that a new plant may live, so our mortal bodies return to the dust that they may rise again in a more glorious state.

39-40. Even as there is a difference between the flesh of men and beasts and fish and birds, so there is a difference between celestial, terrestrial, and telestial bodies.

40. **Celestial bodies**] **Bodies terrestrial**] I.V. 40. **Bodies telestial**] "Now, verily I say unto you, that through the redemption which is made for you is brought to pass the resurrection from the dead. And the spirit and the body are the soul of man. And the resurrection from the dead is the redemption of the soul. And the redemption of the soul is through him that quickeneth all things, in whose bosom it is decreed that the poor and the meek of the earth shall inherit it. Therefore, it must needs be

sanctified from all unrighteousness, that it may be prepared for the celestial glory; For after it hath filled the measure of its creation, it shall be crowned with glory, even with the presence of God the Father; That bodies who are of the celestial kingdom may possess it forever and ever; for, for this intent was it made and created, and for this intent are they sanctified.

"And they who are not sanctified through the law which I have given unto you, even the law of Christ, must inherit another kingdom, even that of a terrestrial kingdom, or that of a telestial kingdom. For he who is not able to abide the law of a celestial kingdom cannot abide a celestial glory. And he who cannot abide the law of a terrestrial kingdom cannot abide a terrestrial glory. And he who cannot abide the law of a telestial kingdom cannot abide a telestial glory; therefore he is not meet for a kingdom of glory. Therefore he must abide a kingdom which is not a kingdom of glory. And again, verily I say unto you, the earth abideth the law of a celestial kingdom, for it filleth the measure of its creation, and transgresseth not the law — Wherefore, it shall be sanctified; yea, notwithstanding it shall die, it shall be quickened again, and shall abide the power by which it is quickened, and the righteous shall inherit it. For notwithstanding they die, they also shall rise again, a spiritual body.

"They who are of a celestial spirit shall receive the same body which was a natural body; even ye shall receive your bodies, and your glory shall be that glory by which your bodies are quickened. Ye who are quickened by a portion of the celestial glory shall then receive of the same, even a fulness.

"And they who are quickened by a portion of the terrestrial glory shall then receive of the same, even a fulness. And also they who are quickened by a portion of the telestial glory shall then receive of the same, even a fulness. And they who remain shall also be quickened; nevertheless, they shall return again to their own place, to enjoy that which they are willing to receive, because they were not willing to enjoy that which they might have received. For what doth it profit a man if a gift is bestowed upon him, and he receive not the gift? Behold, he rejoices not in that which is given unto him, neither rejoices in him who is the giver of the gift." (D. & C. 88:14-33.)

41. Glory of the sun] Celestial glory found only in the celestial kingdom. It is reserved for those "whose bodies are celestial." (D. & C. 76:70.)

Glory of the moon] Terrestrial glory, found only in the terrestrial kingdom. "Those attaining a terrestrial kingdom will be inheritors of terrestrial glory which differs from celestial glory 'as that of the moon differs from the sun in the firmament.' (D. & C. 76:71; 1 Cor. 15:41.) In effect they bask, as does the moon, in reflected glory, for there are restrictions and limitations placed on them. They 'receive of the presence of the Son, but not of the fulness of the Father' (D. & C. 76:77), and to all eternity they remain unmarried and without exaltation. (D. & C. 132:17.)" (*Mormon Doctrine*, 2nd ed., p. 784.)

Glory of the stars] Telestial glory found only in the telestial kingdom. "In the infinite mercy of a beneficent Father it surpasses all mortal understanding, and yet it is in no way comparable to the glory of the terrestrial and celestial worlds. Telestial glory is typified by the stars of the firmament, and 'as one star differs from another star in glory, even so differs one from another in glory in the telestial world' (D. & C. 76:81-112; 1 Cor. 15:41), meaning that all who inherit the telestial kingdom will not receive the same glory." (*Mormon Doctrine*, 2nd ed., p. 778.)

Degrees of glory] See *Commentary I*, pp. 727-730.

"DEATH IS SWALLOWED UP IN VICTORY"

I CORINTHIANS 15:42b-54.

42b It is sown in corruption; it is raised in incorruption:

43 It is sown in dishonour; it is raised in glory: it is sown in weakness; it is raised in power:

44 It is sown a natural body; it is raised a spiritual body. There is a natural body, and there is a spiritual body.

45 And so it is written, The first man Adam was made a living soul; the last Adam *was made* a quickening spirit.

46 Howbeit that *was* not first which is spiritual, but that which is natural; and afterward that which is spiritual.

47 The first man *is* of the earth, earthy: the second man *is* the Lord from heaven.

48 As *is* the earthy, such *are* they also that are earthy: and as *is* the heavenly, such *are* they also that are heavenly.

49 And as we have borne the image of the earthy, we shall also bear the image of the heavenly.

50 Now this I say, brethren, that flesh and blood cannot inherit the kingdom of God; neither doth corruption inherit incorruption.

51 Behold, I show you a mystery; We shall not all sleep, but we shall all be changed,

52 In a moment, in the twinkling of an eye, at the last trump: for the trumpet shall sound, and the dead shall be raised incorruptible, and we shall be changed.

53 For this corruptible must put on incorruption, and this mortal *must* put on immortality.

54 So when this corruptible shall have put on incorruption, and this mortal shall have put on immortality, then shall be brought to pass the saying that is written, Death is swallowed up in victory.

I.V. I CORINTHIANS 15:46, 52.

46 Howbeit, **that which is natural first, and not that which is spiritual; but afterwards,** that which is spiritual;

52 In a moment, in the twinkling of an eye, at the **sound of** the last trump; for the trumpet shall sound, and the dead shall be raised incorruptible, and we shall be changed.

All men shall gain physical perfection in the resurrection; that is, being raised from mortality to immortality, from corruption to incorruption, they shall shuffle off all disease, deformities, bodily disorders, and physical imperfections of every nature, and shall stand thenceforth without physical impairments or deficiencies of any sort. There will be no eyes that do not see, no ears without hearing, no crippled arms or legs, no club feet, no ulcers, no physical pain, no diseases, no corruption, no death. As Alma said: "The soul shall be restored to the body, and the body to the soul; yea, and every limb and joint shall be restored to its body; yea, even a hair of the head shall not be lost; but all things shall be restored to their proper and perfect frame." (Alma 40:23.)

42. Corruption] Mortality. Status of mortal bodies, subject as they are to physical change and decay.

401

Incorruption] Immortality. Status of physical perfection enjoyed by immortal beings, a status without death. As Amulek said: "This mortal body is raised to an immortal body, that is from death, even from the first death unto life, that they can die no more; their spirits uniting with their bodies, never to be divided; thus the whole becoming spiritual and immortal, that they can no more see corruption." (Alma 11:45.)

44. Natural body] Mortal, temporal, or corruptible body, a body of flesh and blood, one in which body and spirit are temporarily connected, one subject to pain, disease, and death.

Spiritual body] Not a spirit body, but an immortal, resurrected, or incorruptible body, a body of flesh and bones, one in which body and spirit are inseparably connected, one not subject to physical pain, disease, or death.

45. A living soul] A mortal soul or person, consisting of a mortal tabernacle temporarily housing an eternal spirit. Thus, "the resurrection from the dead is the redemption of the soul." (D. & C. 88:16.)

A quickening spirit] An immortal soul or person, consisting of a resurrected body housing an eternal spirit everlastingly. It is Christ, as a quickening spirit, who "quickeneth all things," thus bringing to pass "the redemption of the soul." (D. & C. 88:17.)

49. Image of the earthy] Image of Adam or mortality, which is the natural inheritance of all men from Adam.

Image of the heavenly] Image of Christ or immortality, which is the natural inheritance of all men from Christ.

50. Flesh and blood] Mortality, as distinguished from flesh and bones which is descriptive of immortality. The life of the mortal body is in the blood. (Lev. 17:11.)

51-52. "And he that liveth when the Lord shall come, and hath kept the faith, blessed is he; nevertheless, it is appointed to him to die at the age of man. Wherefore, children shall grow up until they become old; old men shall die; but they shall not sleep in the dust, but they shall be changed in the twinkling of an eye." (D. & C. 63:50-51.)

53. "This mortal shall put on immortality, and this corruption shall put on incorruption." (Mosiah 16:10.)

54. Death is swallowed up in victory] To man, nothing is so absolute and final as death; death conquers all; rich and poor, wise and foolish, righteous and wicked, the mighty and the weak — all bow to death, all leave their bodies to rot in the earth. But, praise God!, there is One, even Christ, who, ministering in all the glory of his Father's power, hath gained the victory over the grave, and because of him all men shall live again.

Resurrection] See 1 Cor. 15:1-11. **Sorrow in the resurrection]** See 1 Cor. 15:55-58.

"THE STING OF DEATH IS SIN"

I CORINTHIANS 15:55-58.

55 O death, where *is* thy sting? O grave, where *is* thy victory?

56 The sting of death *is* sin; and the strength of sin *is* the law.

57 But thanks *be* to God, which giveth us the victory through our Lord Jesus Christ.

58 Therefore, my beloved brethren, be ye stedfast, unmoveable, always abounding in the work of the Lord, forasmuch as ye know that your labour is not in vain in the Lord.

Why teach the doctrine of the resurrection? As with all doctrines, a knowledge of it encourages men to live better lives. The mere fact of resurrection, the reality that all shall rise from the dead, this standing alone sheds a flood of light and hope upon all who know of it.

But the detailed doctrine, the doctrine that there are times and kinds of resurrections; that some men shall come forth in the resurrection of life, others in the resurrection of damnation; that some shall be raised with celestial bodies and enter into eternal rest, while others shall remain filthy still; the fact that the righteous shall have righteousness restored to them and the carnal, carnality; that those who overcome the world shall have glory added upon their heads forever, while those who eat with the gluttons, drink with the drunken, and are merry with the unclean, shall rise to a telestial inheritance — all this stands as a great incentive to the saints to keep the commandments. (2 Ne. 9:14-16; Alma 40:24-26; 41:12-15; D. & C. 29:43-45.)

Hence, Paul having taught this doctrine, comes now to the conclusion of the whole matter: The sting of death is sin; therefore, walk as becometh saints.

Resurrection] See 1 Cor. 15:1-11. **Physical perfection in the resurrection]** See 1 Cor. 15:42b-54.

56. The sting of death is sin] "Thou shalt live together in love, insomuch that thou shalt weep for the loss of them that die, and more especially for those that have not hope of a glorious resurrection. And it shall come to pass that those that die in me shall not taste of death, for it shall be sweet unto them; And they that die not in me, wo unto them, for their death is bitter." (D. & C. 42:45-47.)

"STAND FAST IN THE FAITH"

I CORINTHIANS 16:1-24.

1 Now concerning the collection for the saints, as I have given order to the churches of Galatia, even so do ye.

2 Upon the first *day* of the week let every one of you lay by him in store, as *God* hath prospered him, that there be no gatherings when I come.

3 And when I come, whomsoever ye shall approve by *your* letters, them will I send to bring your liberality unto Jerusalem.

4 And if it be meet that I go also, they shall go with me.

5 Now I will come unto you, when I shall pass through Macedonia: for I do pass through Macedonia.

6 And it may be that I will abide, yea, and winter with you, that ye may bring me on my journey whithersoever I go.

7 For I will not see you now by the way; but I trust to tarry a while with you, if the Lord permit.

8 But I will tarry at Ephesus until Pentecost.

9 For a great door and effectual is opened unto me, and *there are* many adversaries.

10 Now if Timotheus come, see that he may be with you without fear: for he worketh the work of the Lord, as I also *do.*

11 Let no man therefore despise him: but conduct him forth in peace, that he may come unto me: for I look for him with the brethren.

12 As touching *our* brother Apollos, I greatly desired him to come unto you with the brethren: but his will was not at all to come at this time; but he will come when he shall have convenient time.

13 Watch ye, stand fast in the faith, quit you like men, be strong.

14 Let all your things be done with charity.

15 I beseech you, brethren, (ye know the house of Stephanas, that it is the firstfruits of Achaia, and *that* they have addicted themselves to the ministry of the saints,)

16 That ye submit yourselves unto such, and to every one that helpeth with *us*, and laboureth.

17 I am glad of the coming of Stephanas and Fortunatus and Achaicus: for that which was lacking on your part they have supplied.

18 For they have refreshed my spirit and your's: therefore acknowledge ye them that are such.

19 The churches of Asia salute you. Aquila and Priscilla salute you much in the Lord, with the church that is in their house.

20 All the brethren greet you. Greet ye one another with an holy kiss.

21 The salutation of *me* Paul with mine own hand.

22 If any man love not the Lord Jesus Christ, let him be Anathema Maran-atha.

23 The grace of our Lord Jesus Christ *be* with you.

24 My love *be* with you all in Christ Jesus. Amen.

I.V. I CORINTHIANS 16:20.

20 All the brethren greet you. Greet ye one another with **a** holy **salutation.**

1. **Collection for the saints]** See 2 Cor. 8:1-24; 9:1-15.

2. **First day of the week]** Christian worship, as ordained and established by the apostles, was on the first day of the week, the Lord's day. See Rev. 1:9-11.

3. **Your letters]** Something akin to "recommends," or "certificates of ordination," or "ministerial certificates"; documents cer-

tifying to the membership and worthiness of the church members involved.

13. 'Be valiant in the warfare with the world!'

14. See 1 Cor. 13:1-13.

I.V. 20. A holy salutation] See 2 Cor. 13:5-14.

K.J. 22. Let him be Anathema Maranatha] Let him be accursed until the Lord comes.

The Second Epistle of Paul the Apostle to the Corinthians

In First Corinthians, Paul reproved the philosophical and worldly saints in Corinth with sharpness. By the power of the Spirit he warned them to believe sound doctrine and live godly lives. Now he is showing forth an increase of love toward these same church members lest they esteem him to be their enemy. At least he is for the first nine chapters, although for the last four he picks up again some of his blunt and harsh mode of exhortation.

Second Corinthians is not a definitive epistle; it does not analyze and summarize gospel doctrines as such. Instead it applies already known doctrines to the circumstances of the Corinthians, much as an inspired sermon applies the gospel to the congregation in which it is preached.

Yet, wise counselor that he was, Paul wove in sufficient doctrinal data to leave modern readers with a great sense of thanksgiving for the epistle. In it we read, among other things, of how God comforteth and careth for his saints; of the law of reconciliation; that there is no second chance for salvation for the saints; of how God's ministers gain approval; of the true principle of glorying in the Lord; of false apostles and the signs of true apostles; and we learn that Paul, like the three Nephites, was caught up into heaven and heard and saw things beyond mortal comprehension.

GOD COMFORTETH AND CARETH FOR HIS SAINTS

II CORINTHIANS 1:1-24.

1 Paul, an apostle of Jesus Christ by the will of God, and Timothy *our* brother, unto the church of God which is at Corinth, with all the saints which are in all Achaia:

2 Grace *be* to you and peace from God our Father, and *from* the Lord Jesus Christ.

3 Blessed *be* God, even the Father of our Lord Jesus Christ, the Father of mercies, and the God of all comfort;

4 Who comforteth us in all our tribulation, that we may be able to comfort them which are in any trouble, by the comfort wherewith we ourselves are comforted of God.

5 For as the sufferings of Christ abound in us, so our consolation also aboundeth by Christ.

6 And whether we be afflicted, *it is* for your consolation and salvation, which is effectual in the enduring of the same sufferings which we also suffer: or whether we be comforted, *it is* for your consolation and salvation.

7 And our hope of you *is* stedfast, knowing, that as ye are partakers of the sufferings, so *shall ye be* also of the consolation.

8 For we would not, brethren, have you ignorant of our trouble which came to us in Asia, that we were pressed out of measure, above strength, insomuch that we despaired even of life:

9 But we had the sentence of death in ourselves, that we should not trust in ourselves, but in God which raiseth the dead:

10 Who delivered us from so great a death, and doth deliver: in whom we trust that he will yet deliver *us;*

11 Ye also helping together by prayer for us, that for the gift *bestowed* upon us by the means of many persons thanks may be given by many on our behalf.

12 For our rejoicing is this, the testimony of our conscience, that in simplicity and godly sincerity, not with fleshly wisdom, but by the grace of God, we have had our conversation in the world, and more abundantly to youward.

13 For we write none other things unto you, than what ye read or acknowledge; and I trust ye shall acknowledge even to the end;

14 As also ye have acknowledged us in part, that we are your rejoicing, even as ye also *are* our's in the day of the Lord Jesus.

15 And in this confidence I was minded to come unto you before, that ye might have a second benefit;

16 And to pass by you into Macedonia, and to come again out of Macedonia unto you, and of you to be brought on my way toward Judea.

17 When I therefore was thus minded, did I use lightness? or the things that I purpose, do I purpose according to the flesh, that with me there should be yea yea, and nay nay?

18 But *as* God *is* true, our word toward you was not yea and nay.

19 For the Son of God, Jesus Christ, who was preached among you by us, *even* by me and Silvanus and Timotheus, was not yea and nay, but in him was yea.

20 For all the promises of God in him *are* yea, and in him Amen, unto the glory of God by us.

21 Now he which stablisheth us with you in Christ, and hath anointed us, *is* God ;

22 Who hath also sealed us, and given the earnest of the Spirit in our hearts.

23 Moreover I call God for a record upon my soul, that to spare you I came not as yet unto Corinth.

24 Not for that we have dominion over your faith, but are helpers of your joy: for by faith ye stand.

Special spiritual rewards are poured out upon the saints. In the midst of turmoil, war, persecution, suffering — all of the vicissitudes and seeming ills of life — they nonetheless partake of a peace and satisfaction of soul that comes from God, because of Christ, by the power of the Spirit. This comfort, consolation, and peace is for all the saints, not just for apostles and prophets. "The Father of mercies, and the God of all comfort," has a tender and personal solicitude for all of his children. Whenever any of them come unto him, they are assured of peace in this life and eternal life in the world to come.

1. An apostle of Jesus Christ] See Acts 13:50-52; 14:1-7; 1 Cor. 4:1-21. **Saints]** See Philip. 1:1-6.

2. God our Father] "Our Father which art in heaven" (Matt. 6:9), the Father of spirits, the literal Parent of all men.

3. The Father of our Lord Jesus Christ] The Father of the mortal body of the Lord Jesus, he who thus became the Only Begotten Son, the only person conceived and born, with God as his Father, "after the manner of the flesh." (1 Ne. 11:18.) The mere recitation of such a profound and basic truth is sufficient to identify forever the nature and kind of being that God is.

The Father of mercies, and the God of all comfort] Mercy and loving kindness are showered upon all those who love and serve God; from him they receive peace and comfort through "the visitation of the Holy Ghost, which Comforter filleth with hope and perfect love." (Moro. 8:26.)

4-7. Those who suffer for Christ and his Cause, receive from him comfort and consolation which drowns out and swallows up all sorrow and tribulation.

11. Pray for us] Paul and Timothy needed the prayers of the saints; and if apostles and prophets seek strength and comfort through the faith-filled petitions of church members, how much more need have the saints in general for the heaven-borne pleadings of each other!

12. 'We rejoice in the privilege of this mortal probation.'

14. Both the missionary and the convert shall have joy and rejoicing together in that day when the Lord Jesus returns to glorify his saints.

17-20. All the promises of God — as far as the obedient are concerned! — are yea and not nay; that is, to those who love and serve him, his voice is one of peace and mercy, of joy and reward, of salvation and glory and eternal life; it is only to the rebellious that he speaks in the negative, in terms of blood and fire, of destruction and war, of damnation and eternal sorrow.

21. Anointed us] Given us the Holy Ghost.

22. See Eph. 1:13-14.

24. By faith ye stand] After the grace of God as manifest through the sacrifice of his Son, after baptism, after temple marriage, after the Lord offers any blessing to men — still the promised rewards come by individual faith, by personal righteousness, by one man standing alone before his Maker and doing those things which enable him to work out his salvation.

SAINTS LOVE AND FORGIVE ONE ANOTHER

II CORINTHIANS 2:1-17.

1 But I determined this with myself, that I would not come again to you in heaviness.

2 For if I make you sorry, who is he then that maketh me glad, but the same which is made sorry by me?

410

3 And I wrote this same unto you, lest, when I came, I should have sorrow from them of whom I ought to rejoice; having confidence in you all, that my joy is *the joy* of you all.

4 For out of much affliction and anguish of heart I wrote unto you with many tears; not that ye should be grieved, but that ye might know the love which I have more abundantly unto you.

5 But if any have caused grief, he hath not grieved me, but in part: that I may not overcharge you all.

6 Sufficient to such a man *is* this punishment, which *was inflicted* of many.

7 So that contrariwise ye *ought* rather to forgive *him*, and comfort *him*, lest perhaps such a one should be swallowed up with overmuch sorrow.

8 Wherefore I beseech you that ye would confirm *your* love toward him.

9 For to this end also did I write, that I might know the proof of you, whether ye be obedient in all things.

10 To whom ye forgive any thing, I *forgive* also: for if I forgave any thing, to whom I forgave *it*, for your sakes *forgave I it* in the person of Christ;

11 Lest Satan should get an advantage of us: for we are not ignorant of his devices.

12 Furthermore, when I came to Troas to *preach* Christ's gospel, and a door was opened unto me of the Lord,

13 I had no rest in my spirit, because I found not Titus my brother: but taking my leave of them, I went from thence into Macedonia.

14 Now thanks *be* unto God, which always causeth us to triumph in Christ, and maketh manifest the savour of his knowledge by us in every place.

15 For we are unto God a sweet savour of Christ, in them that are saved, and in them that perish:

16 To the one *we are* the savour of death unto death; and to the other the savour of life unto life. And who *is* sufficient for these things?

17 For we are not as many, which corrupt the word of God: but as of sincerity, but as of God, in the sight of God speak we in Christ.

4. Sharp reproof and blunt exhortation, when moved upon by the Spirit, are signs of abundant love for those on whose behalf such a course is taken. It is as with parents who discipline their children as an aid to character building.

411

5-11. However, any so rebuked should be showered with an increase of love, lest enmity and ill will remain in the hearts of the saints. Further, the saints should forgive one another their trespasses in the true spirit of Christian love and forbearance. Speaking of the heartfelt forgiveness needed by the Corinthian and other ancient and modern saints, the Lord said this in our dispensation: "My disciples, in days of old, sought occasion against one another and forgave not one another in their hearts; and for this evil they were afflicted and sorely chastened. Wherefore, I say unto you, that ye ought to forgive one another; for he that forgiveth not his brother his trespasses standeth condemned before the Lord; for there remaineth in him the greater sin. I, the Lord, will forgive whom I will forgive, but of you it is required to forgive all men." (D. & C. 64:8-10.)

Forgiveness] See *Commentary I*, pp. 175-180, 270-276, 421-423, 818-819; *Mormon Doctrine*, 2nd ed., pp. 292-298. **Confession]** See 1 John 1:8-10; 2:1-2. **Repentance]** See Acts 11:1-18.

14. God . . . always causeth us to triumph in Christ] God does not fail; he is the Almighty. His purposes prevail; there are none who can stay his hand. "Therefore, fear not, little flock; do good; let earth and hell combine against you, for if ye are built upon my rock, they cannot prevail." (D. & C. 6:34.)

God . . . maketh manifest the savour of his knowledge by us] 'When the saints breathe the spirit of the gospel, they thereby manifest its beauties to others.' Sacrifices were offered as "a sweet savour before the Lord." (Ex. 29:25.) That is, the taste and smell, showing sacrifices were being offered, symbolized man's conformity to the divine law involved, and were thus pleasing to Deity.

15. We are unto God a sweet savour of Christ] 'We are like Christ when we breathe the same spirit of the gospel which he breathed.' Conversely, when Peter sought to deter Christ from doing the work assigned him, the Savior rebuked him by saying: "Thou savourest not the things that be of God, but those that be of men" (Matt. 16:23), meaning Peter was breathing the spirit of the world and thereby sending its influence forth.

412

16. We are the savour of death unto death; and . . . of life unto life] Those who partake of the spirit breathed by the saints, the spirit of the gospel, the sweet influence that results from obedience to God's laws, gain eternal life; those who reject it inherit eternal death. That is, the gospel is an instrument of life and of death, of life to the obedient, of death to the disobedient.

17. In the sight of God speak we in Christ] 'We swear before God and angels that our words are true.'

GOSPEL GREATER THAN THE LAW OF MOSES

II CORINTHIANS 3:1-18.

1 Do we begin again to commend ourselves? or need we, as some *others*, epistles of commendation to you, or *letters* of commendation from you?

2 Ye are our epistle written in our hearts, known and read of all men:

3 *Forasmuch as ye are* manifestly declared to be the epistle of Christ ministered by us, written not with ink, but with the Spirit of the living God: not in tables of stone, but in fleshy tables of the heart.

4 And such trust have we through Christ to God-ward:

5 Not that we are sufficient of ourselves to think any thing as of ourselves; but our sufficiency *is* of God;

6 Who also hath made us able ministers of the new testament; not of the letter, but of the spirit: for the letter killeth, but the spirit giveth life.

7 But if the ministration of death, written *and* engraven in stones, was glorious, so that the children of Israel could not stedfastly behold the face of Moses for the glory of his countenance; which *glory* was to be done away:

8 How shall not the ministration of the spirit be rather glorious?

9 For if the ministration of condemnation *be* glory, much more doth the ministration of righteousness exceed in glory.

10 For even that which was made glorious had no glory in this respect, by reason of the glory that excelleth.

11 For if that which is done away *was* glorious, much more that which remaineth *is* glorious.

12 Seeing then that we have such hope, we use great plainness of speech:

413

13 And not as Moses, *which* put a vail over his face, that the children of Israel could not stedfastly look to the end of that which is abolished:

14 But t h e i r minds were blinded: for until this day remaineth the same vail untaken away in the reading of the old testament; which *vail* is done away in Christ.

15 But even unto this day, when Moses is read, the vail is upon their heart.

16 Nevertheless when it shall turn to the Lord, the vail shall be taken away.

17 Now the Lord is that Spirit: and where the Spirit of the Lord *is*, there *is* liberty.

18 But we all, with open face beholding as in a glass the glory of the Lord, are changed into the same image from glory to glory, *even* as by the Spirit of the Lord.

I.V. II CORINTHIANS 3:4, 16.

4 And such trust have we through Christ **toward God.**

16 Nevertheless, when **their heart** shall turn to the Lord, the **veil** shall be taken away.

In all parts of the primitive Church — Corinth, Rome, Galatia, everywhere — the need existed to remind the saints that the law of Moses was done away in Christ. Since the gospel went first to the Jews and thereafter to other lineages, there were in all parts of the new kingdom those who had been subject to the old Mosaic system, a system which some of them found it hard to give up fully and without mental reservation.

It is much the same today where congregations of new converts are concerned. These new church members come from the sects of Christendom into the living kingdom of power and glory. Their baptism does not automatically cause them to forget all they have known and believed and perhaps taught. In the very nature of things and almost without being aware of it, some of them still retain fragments of those sectarian vagaries inherited from their fathers.

2-3. In the ultimate sense, the gospel is not written on tablets of stone or in books of scripture, but in the bodies of faithful and obedient persons; the saints are, thus, living epistles of the truth, the books of whose lives are open for all to read.

4. Through Christ to God] "Jesus saith . . . I am the way, the truth, and the life: no man cometh unto the Father, but by me." (John 14:6; D. & C. 132:12.)

4-11. That law which God gave to Moses is not to be taken lightly. True it was a "manifestation of death," in that salvation did not come by the law alone. True it was a "ministration of condemnation," in that those who received it had first rejected the law of God; but it was the most perfect system of religion on earth for a millennium and a half; and it was so designed as to prepare men for the fulness of that gospel truth which Christ brought. Paul's approach here is to say: 'There was glory and honor in the law of Moses, during the time when God reigned through it, but now, through Christ, has come "the glory that excelleth." If the law of Moses "was glorious," how much more so is the gospel of Christ?'

Law of Moses] See Acts 15:1-35; Rom. 7:1-6, 7-25; *Commentary I*, pp. 218-223, 505-507.

6. New testament] 14. Old testament] The new covenant made through Christ and the old covenant made through Moses; the gospel of Christ and the law of Moses.

12-18. After Moses was with God for 40 days in the Holy Mount, his face shone so that Israel could not stand his presence. Accordingly, he put a veil on his face, signifying thereby that Israel was not prepared for the fulness of that glory which is reserved for the saints. (Ex. 34:27-35; D. & C. 84:19-27.) This veil, however, is done away in Christ, so that all who will remove it from their hearts may now receive "the fulness of his glory." (D. & C. 84:24.)

17. Where the Spirit of the Lord is, there is liberty] It is an eternal principle that has existed with God from all eternity that man should be free. God ordained the law of agency in pre-existence so that his spirit children could either follow him or rebel against his laws and go to perdition with Lucifer. Then in this mortal probation man again was given freedom of choice, freedom to gain salvation by obedience or to be damned through disobedience. Since Satan always seeks to destroy the agency of man, he influences churches and governments to deny freedom of worship and to force man to perform acts contrary to the divine will. Governments and churches which curtail or deny man the power to worship God according to the dictates of his own conscience, are not of God; they are not directed by the power of his Spirit; and eventually, in the onrush of that truth which shall prevail, they shall be swept away.

18. 'As a mirror reflects the likeness of a person, so the saints should reflect the image of Christ, and as they progress in obedience and personal righteousness, they attain this image; by the power of the Spirit, they become like Christ.'

GOSPEL LIGHT SHINES ON THE SAINTS

II CORINTHIANS 4:1-7.

1 Therefore seeing we have this ministry, as we have received mercy, we faint not;

2 But have renounced the hidden things of dishonesty, not walking in craftiness, nor handling the word of God deceitfully; but by manifestation of the truth commending ourselves to every man's conscience in the sight of God.

3 But if our gospel be hid, it is hid to them that are lost:

4 In whom the god of this world hath blinded the minds of them which believe not, lest the light of the glorious gospel of Christ, who is the image of God, should shine unto them.

5 For we preach not ourselves, but Christ Jesus the Lord; and ourselves your servants for Jesus' sake.

6 For God, who commanded the light to shine out of darkness, hath shined in our hearts, to *give* the light of the knowledge of the glory of God in the face of Jesus Christ.

7 But we have this treasure in earthen vessels, that the excellency of the power may be of God, and not of us.

1. **We have this ministry]** 'We are legal administrators; God sent us; we present his message.'

2. **Dishonesty]** "Perfect honesty is one of the invarying characteristics exhibited by all who are worthy to be numbered with

the saints of God. Honest persons are fair and truthful in speech, straightforward in their dealings, free from deceit, and above cheating, stealing, misrepresentation, or any other fraudulent action. Honesty is the companion of truth, dishonesty of falsehood; honesty is of God, dishonesty of the devil, for he was a liar from the beginning. (D. & C. 93:52; 2 Ne. 2:18.)" (*Mormon Doctrine*, 2nd ed., pp. 363-364.)

Not walking in craftiness] Not skilfully and cunningly deceiving others, as is common in the world.

Handling the word of God deceitfully] Twisting and perverting the scriptures; preaching false doctrine; proclaiming any doctrine other than the doctrine of Christ. Unless professing ministers have the fulness of the gospel, they are themselves deceived, and they must of necessity practice deception in maintaining their false system of religion.

3-4. All men have sufficient spiritual talent to believe and understand the gospel; but some are deceived, some reject the light, some are lost. Even many "honorable men of the earth" are "blinded by the craftiness of men," and shall attain nothing higher in eternity than a terrestrial inheritance. (D. & C. 76:75.)

4. The god of this world] Satan. This world is the sensual, carnal, and devilish society of men who live on the face of the earth; it is a world that shall continue to exist until Christ comes and the wicked are destroyed, which destruction is, "the end of the world." (Jos. Smith 1:4.)

The glorious gospel of Christ] See Rom. 1:1-17. **Christ, who is the image of God**] Both spiritually and physically; spiritually because he has earned the character, perfections, and attributes of the Father; physically because he is the Only Begotten in the flesh and thereby inherited the bodily likeness and form of his Eternal Parent.

6. The light of gospel truth shines in the hearts of the saints just as truly as the light of the sun dispels darkness in the earth.

MORTAL TRIALS CONTRASTED WITH ETERNAL GLORY

II CORINTHIANS 4:8-18.

8 *We are* troubled on every side, yet not distressed; *we are* perplexed, but not in despair;

9 Persecuted, but not forsaken; cast down, but not destroyed;

10 Always bearing about in the body the dying of the Lord Jesus, that the life also of Jesus might be made manifest in our body.

11 For we which live are alway delivered unto death for Jesus' sake, that the life also of Jesus might be made manifest in our mortal flesh.

12 So then death worketh in us, but life in you.

13 We having the same spirit of faith, according as it is written, I believed, and therefore have I spoken; we also believe, and therefore speak;

14 Knowing that he which raised up the Lord Jesus shall raise up us also by Jesus, and shall present *us* with you.

15 For all things *are* for your sakes, that the abundant grace might through the thanksgiving of many redound to the glory of God.

16 For which cause we faint not; but though our outward man perish, yet the inward *man* is renewed day by day.

17 For o u r light affliction, which is but for a moment, worketh for us a far more exceeding *and* eternal weight of glory;

18 While we look not at the things which are seen, but at the things which are not seen: for the things which are seen *are* temporal; but the things which are not seen *are* eternal.

I.V. II CORINTHIANS 4:12, 15.

12 So then **it worketh death unto us,** but life **unto you.**

15 For **we bear** all things for your sakes, that the abundant grace might, through the thanksgiving of many, redound to the glory of God.

Mortal trials, persecution, suffering, even the laying down of one's life for the Cause of Christ, are as nothing compared to the immortal glory reserved for those who endure all things well. All these things are part of the Lord's program for testing his saints to the full. "I will try you and prove you herewith," he says. "And whoso layeth down his life in my cause, for my name's sake, shall find it again, even life eternal. Therefore, be not afraid of your enemies, for I have decreed in my heart, saith the Lord, that

I will prove you in all things, whether you will abide in my covenant, even unto death, that you may be found worthy. For if ye will not abide in my covenant ye are not worthy of me." (D. & C. 98:12-15.)

8. Despair] "Despair cometh because of iniquity." (Moro. 10:22.)

10-18. The Lord Jesus is our Prototype. As a mortal he suffered all things, even death, and was then raised in immortal glory. If we endure in like manner, we also shall come forth in the resurrection and receive glory and honor with him.

17. A far more exceeding and eternal weight of glory] Exaltation as a result of the continuation of the family unit in eternity. (D. & C. 132:16.) Paul's application of the term to himself is one of a great number of indications that he was married.

Salvation] See 1 Pet. 1:1-16.

SAINTS SEEK TABERNACLES OF IMMORTAL GLORY

II CORINTHIANS 5:1-11.

1 For we know that if our earthly house of *this* tabernacle were dissolved, we have a building of God, an house not made with hands, eternal in the heavens.

2 For in this we groan, earnestly desiring to be clothed upon with our house which is from heaven:

3 If so be that being clothed we shall not be found naked.

4 For we that are in *this* tabernacle do groan, being burdened: not for that we would be unclothed, but clothed upon, that

mortality might be swallowed up of life.

5 Now he that hath wrought us for the selfsame thing *is* God, who also hath given unto us the earnest of the Spirit.

6 Therefore *we are* always confident, knowing that, whilst we are at home in the body, we are absent from the Lord:

7 (For we walk by faith, not by sight:)

8 We are confident, *I say,* and willing rather to be absent from

the body, and to be present with the Lord.

9 Wherefore we labour, that, whether present or absent, we may be accepted of him.

10 For we must all appear before the judgment seat of Christ; that every one may receive the things *done* in *his* body, according to that he hath done, whether *it be* good or bad.

11 Knowing therefore the terror of the Lord, we persuade men;

but we are made manifest unto God; and I trust also are made manifest in your consciences.

I.V. II CORINTHIANS 5:10.

10 For we must all appear before the judgment-seat of Christ, that every one may receive **a reward of the deeds** done in **the** body; **things** according to **what** he hath done, whether good or bad.

1. Our earthly house] Our mortal body, the temporary tabernacle of the spirit.

An house not made with hands, eternal in the heavens] An immortal body, one that houses the spirit eternally and dwells in the realms of glory.

2-4. The saints desire to be raised "in immortality unto eternal life," that is to come forth in the resurrection and be clothed with robes of righteousness. (D. & C. 29:43.)

5. The earnest of the Spirit] See Eph. 1:13-14.

6. We are absent from the Lord] We left the pre-mortal estate and are no longer in the personal presence of the Lord.

7. We walk by faith, not by sight] In the pre-mortal life we were in the presence of God; we saw him and knew the course he had charted for us. Now we are out of his personal presence, no longer remember our association in his household, and are being tested under circumstances where we must accept him and his laws on faith.

10. See Rev. 20:11-15.

Salvation] See 1 Pet. 1:1-16. **Pre-existence]** See Heb. 12:9-10.

GOSPEL RECONCILES MAN TO GOD

II CORINTHIANS 5:12-21.

12 For we commend not ourselves again unto you, but give you occasion to glory on our behalf, that ye may have somewhat to *answer* them which glory in appearance, and not in heart.

13 For whether we be beside ourselves, *it is* to God: or whether we be sober, *it is* for your cause.

14 For the love of Christ constraineth us; because we thus judge, that if one died for all, then were all dead:

15 And *that* he died for all, that they which live should not henceforth live unto themselves, but unto him which died for them, and rose again.

16 Wherefore henceforth know we no man after the flesh: yea, though we have known Christ after the flesh, yet now henceforth know we *him* no more.

17 Therefore if any man *be* in Christ, *he is* a new creature: old things are passed away; behold, all things are become new.

18 And all things *are* of God, who hath reconciled us to himself by Jesus Christ, and hath given to us the ministry of reconciliation;

19 To wit, that God was in Christ, reconciling the world unto himself, not imputing their trespasses unto them; and hath committed unto us the word of reconciliation.

20 Now then we are ambassadors for Christ, as though God did beseech *you* by us: we pray *you* *in* Christ's stead, be ye reconciled to God.

21 For he hath made him *to be* sin for us, who knew no sin; that we might be made the righteousness of God in him.

I.V. II CORINTHIANS 5:13-14, 16-19.

13 **For we bear record that we are not beside ourselves;** for whether **we glory,** it is to God, or whether we be sober, it is for your **sakes.**

14 For the love of Christ constraineth us; because we thus judge, that if one died for all, then **are** all dead;

16 Wherefore, henceforth **live** we **no more** after the flesh; yea, though **we once lived** after the flesh, **yet since we have known Christ,** now henceforth **live** we no more **after the flesh.**

17 Therefore if any man **live** in Christ, he is a new creature; old things are passed away; behold, all things are become new,

18 And **receiveth all the things** of God, who hath reconciled us to himself by Jesus Christ, and

hath given to us the ministry of reconciliation:

19 To wit, that God is in Christ, reconciling the world unto himself, not imputing their trespasses unto them; and hath committed unto us the word of reconciliation.

12. We commend not ourselves] "Let another man praise thee, and not thine own mouth; a stranger, and not thine own lips." (Prov. 27:2.)

Them which glory in appearance, and not in heart] "The Lord seeth not as man seeth; for man looketh on the outward appearance, but the Lord looketh on the heart." (1 Sam. 16:7.)

I.V. 13. We glory] See 2 Cor. 10:1-18; 11:1-11.

I.V. 14:18. Since all men are spiritually dead, Christ died for them all. Those who accept him are born again; they live again spiritually because of the ransoming power of his atonement, and having put on Christ, they no longer live for themselves alone. Once they lived carnal lives; now they are new creatures of the Holy Ghost; once they were children of disobedience; now they are the children of God. Consequently they shall receive and inherit all things in eternity.

17. A new creature] See Rom. 6:1-11.

18-21. Through his fall Adam brought spiritual death into the world; that is, man was cast out of the presence of God and died as pertaining to the things of righteousness or of the Spirit. As a consequence man became carnal, sensual, and devilish by nature and were thereby an enemy of God. (Mosiah 3:19; Alma 42:7-11.) Through his atoning sacrifice Christ brought spiritual life into the world; that is, man was given power to return to the presence of God by receiving the companionship of the Holy Spirit; he was able to become alive as to the things of righteousness or of the Spirit.

Reconciliation is the process of ransoming man from his state of sin and spiritual darkness and of restoring him to a state of harmony and unity with Deity. Through it God and man are no longer enemies. Man, who was once carnal and evil, who lived after the manner of the flesh, becomes a new creature of the Holy

Ghost; he is born again; and, even as a little child, he is alive in Christ. "Reconcile yourselves to the will of God, and not to the will of the devil and the flesh," Jacob taught, "and remember, after ye are reconciled unto God, that it is only in and through the grace of God that ye are saved." (2 Ne. 10:24.)

20. Ambassadors for Christ] Every legal administrator represents and, in his inspired acts, stands in the place and stead of Christ; the ambassador's inspired words and acts then become those of the Lord Jesus himself.

DO SAINTS HAVE A SECOND CHANCE FOR SALVATION?

II CORINTHIANS 6:1-2.

1 We then, *as* workers together *with him*, beseech *you* also that ye receive not the grace of God in vain.

2 (For he saith, I have heard thee in a time accepted, and in the day of salvation have I succoured thee: behold, now *is* the accepted time; behold, now *is* the day of salvation.)

I.V. II CORINTHIANS 6:1-2.

1 We then, as workers together with **Christ,** beseech you also that ye receive not the grace of God in vain.

2 (For he saith, I have heard thee in a time accepted, and in the day of salvation have I succoured thee; behold, now is the day of salvation.)

Whenever the gospel is offered to any person or group, they then have the obligation to believe and obey its doctrines; otherwise, they do not become inheritors of its blessings.

The doctrine of salvation for the dead, great and glorious as it is, does not mean that those who reject the truth, or who disobey their gospel covenants in this life, shall have a second chance to gain salvation by accepting and living the law in the spirit world. Salvation for the dead is for those who die without a knowledge of the gospel and who would have received it, with all their hearts, had it been presented to them in this mortal life.

God's plan is "to save them that believe," when the gospel, "by the foolishness of preaching," is offered to them. (1 Cor. 1:21.)

Those who do not believe and are not baptized are damned. (3 Ne. 11:33-34.) Such is the eternal decree. Jesus, for instance, in his resurrected ministry among the Nephites told them: "Except ye shall keep my commandments, which I have commanded you at this time, ye shall in no case enter into the kingdom of heaven." (3 Ne. 12:20.) To Joseph Smith the Lord said that those who reject the gospel in this life and receive it in the spirit world shall go, not to a celestial, but to a terrestrial kingdom. (D. & C. 76:73-74.) And using some of the same language which Paul here records, Amulek summarized the true doctrine by saying: "Now is the time and the day of your salvation. . . . For behold, this life is the time for men to prepare to meet God; yea, behold the day of this life is the day for men to perform their labors. . . . Do not procrastinate the day of your repentance until the end; for after this day of life, which is given us to prepare for eternity, behold, if we do not improve our time while in this life, then cometh the night of darkness wherein there can be no labor performed." (Alma 34:31-33.)

Salvation for the dead] 1 Pet. 3:18-22; 4:1-6.

HOW GOD'S MINISTERS GAIN HIS APPROVAL

II CORINTHIANS 6:3-10.

3 Giving no offence in any thing, that the ministry be not blamed:

4 But in all *things* approving ourselves as the ministers of God, in much patience, in afflictions, in necessities, in distresses,

5 In stripes, in imprisonments, in tumults, in labours, in watchings, in fastings;

6 By pureness, by knowledge, by long-suffering, by kindness, by the Holy Ghost, by love unfeigned,

7 By the word of truth, by the power of God, by the armour of righteousness on the right hand and on the left,

8 By honour and dishonour, by evil report and good report: as deceivers, and *yet* true;

9 As unknown, and *yet* well known; as dying, and, behold, we live; as chastened, and not killed;

10 As sorrowful, yet alway rejoicing; as poor, yet making many rich; as having nothing, and *yet* possessing all things.

Christ's ministers must be Christ-like. He is the Prototype; he set the perfect example. To the degree his ambassadors are like him, they succeed as he did; wherein they do not measure up to his standard of excellence, they fall short of perfection in their ministry. "What manner of men ought ye to be?" he asked his Nephite disciples, and then answered, "Verily I say unto you, even as I am." (3 Ne. 27:27.)

As to the devotion and godly attributes needed by ministers of Christ, the revealed word commands: "O ye that embark in the service of God, see that ye serve him with all your heart, might, mind and strength, that ye may stand blameless before God at the last day. . . . And faith, hope, charity and love, with an eye single to the glory of God, qualify him for the work. Remember faith, virtue, knowledge, temperance, patience, brotherly kindness, godliness, charity, humility, diligence." (D. & C. 4:2, 5-6.)

Those called to serve in God's earthly kingdom are expected to magnify their callings. This they do by performing in the approved manner whatever service is involved. "Wherefore, now let every man learn his duty, and to act in the office in which he is appointed, in all diligence. He that is slothful shall not be counted worthy to stand, and he that learns not his duty and shows himself not approved shall not be counted worthy to stand." (D. & C. 107:99-100.)

4. **Ministers of God**] Legal administrators who hold the priesthood and are thereby empowered to represent the Lord, doing and saying what he wants done and said for the salvation of his earthly children. All true ministers are in a sense prophets; they have the testimony of Jesus, which is the spirit of prophecy. They all receive revelation, all have the gift of the Holy Ghost, all enjoy the gifts of the Spirit, and all put first in their lives the things of God's kingdom. They are both servants and friends of the Lord, and they act in his place and stead in their inspired ministrations.

6. **By the Holy Ghost**] No man is or can be a minister of Christ unless he has received the gift and enjoys the presentment of the Holy Ghost. It is by this gift that the Lord reveals to each faithful person what he would do and say in any given situ-

ation. Without this revealed knowledge none can represent the Lord with power and authority.

7. By the power of God] The priesthood. No man can be a minister of Christ unless he holds the Aaronic or the Melchizedek Priesthood, for these very orders of divine authority are the commission which Deity gives to his agents to represent him.

8. True ministers are always considered by men to be deceivers and dishonorable, while in fact they are both honorable and true.

10. Making many rich] "Seek not for riches but for wisdom, and behold, the mysteries of God shall be unfolded unto you, and then shall you be made rich. Behold, he that hath eternal life is rich." (D. & C. 6:7.)

Possessing all things] Not in this life, but eventually in eternity. "All things are theirs, whether life or death, or things present, or things to come, all are theirs and they are Christ's, and Christ is God's." (D. & C. 76:59.)

"WHAT CONCORD HATH CHRIST WITH BELIAL?"

II CORINTHIANS 6:11-18.

11 O *ye* Corinthians, our mouth is open unto you, our heart is enlarged.

12 Ye are not straitened in us, but ye are straitened in your own bowels.

13 Now for a recompense in the same, (I speak as unto *my* children,) be ye also enlarged.

14 Be ye not unequally yoked together with unbelievers: for what fellowship hath righteousness with unrighteousness? and what communion hath light with darkness?

15 And what concord hath Christ with Belial? or what part hath he that believeth with an infidel?

16 And what agreement hath the temple of God with idols? for ye are the temple of the living God; as God hath said, I will dwell in them, and walk in *them;* and I will be their God, and they shall be my people.

17 Wherefore come out from among them, and be ye separate, saith the Lord, and touch not the unclean *thing;* and I will receive you,

18 And will be a Father unto you, and ye shall be my sons and daughters, saith the Lord Almighty.

What kind of alliances can the saints make with unbelievers and still find favor in the Lord's eyes? Can they marry out of the Church? Or join secret and oath-bound organizations? Or compromise church standards on moral issues? Can they join the Communist party? Or send their young children to, say, a Catholic school where they will be taught the catechisms of that organization?

What associations can the saints maintain with outsiders without departing from gospel standards? Can they participate in cocktail parties? Publish pornographic literature? Attend indecent plays and movies? Work for institutions whose major purpose is to fight the truth and destroy the influence of the Church?

14-16a. Without legislating on any specific case, in persuasive and powerful language, Paul here proscribes and excoriates improper alliances, affiliations, and associations with the world, leaving to each individual the need to choose the course he personally will follow.

15. Belial] Satan.

16b-18. Paul's usage of three Old Testament scriptures illustrates how an inspired author can paraphrase scriptural passages so as to explain, amplify, and clarify their meaning.

To Israel, by the mouth of Moses, God said: "And I will walk among you, and will be your God, and ye shall be my people" (Lev. 26:12), which Paul interpreted to mean that God, by the power of his Spirit, would dwell in his people.

To latter-day Israel, from the lips of Isaiah, speaking of fleeing from Babylon and gathering to Zion, the Lord said: "Depart ye, depart ye, go ye out from thence, touch no unclean thing; go ye out of the midst of her; be ye clean, that bear the vessels of the Lord" (Isa. 52:11), which Paul applied to the need of the saints in his day to be separate from the world.

Speaking to gathered Israel in latter days, God said through Hosea: "Ye are sons of the living God" (Hos. 1:10), which Paul interpreted to mean that God would be a Father unto Israel, both to her sons and to her daughters.

GODLY SORROW FOR SIN LEADS TO REPENTANCE

II CORINTHIANS 7:1-16.

1 Having therefore these promises, dearly beloved, let us cleanse ourselves from all filthiness of the flesh and spirit, perfecting holiness in the fear of God.

2 Receive us; we have wronged no man, we have corrupted no man, we have defrauded no man.

3 I speak not *this* to condemn *you:* for I have said before, that ye are in our hearts to die and live with *you.*

4 Great *is* my boldness of speech toward you, great *is* my glorying of you: I am filled with comfort, I am exceeding joyful in all our tribulation.

5 For, when we were come into Macedonia, our flesh had no rest, but we were troubled on every side; without *were* fightings, within *were* fears.

6 Nevertheless God, that comforteth those that are cast down, comforted us by the coming of Titus;

7 And not by his coming only, but by the consolation wherewith he was comforted in you, when he told us your earnest desire, your mourning, your fervent mind toward me; so that I rejoiced the more.

8 For though I made you sorry with a letter, I do not repent, though I did repent: for I perceive that the same epistle hath made you sorry, though *it were* but for a season.

9 Now I rejoice, not that ye were made sorry, but that ye sorrowed to repentance: for ye were made sorry after a godly manner, that ye might receive damage by us in nothing.

10 For godly sorrow worketh repentance to salvation not to be repented of: but the sorrow of the world worketh death.

11 For behold this selfsame thing, that ye sorrowed after a godly sort, what carefulness it wrought in you, yea, *what* clearing of yourselves, yea, *what* indignation, yea, *what* fear, yea, *what* vehement desire, yea, *what* zeal, yea, *what* revenge! In all *things* ye have approved yourselves to be clear in this matter.

12 Wherefore, though I wrote unto you, *I did it* not for his cause that had done the wrong, nor for his cause that suffered wrong, but that our care for you in the sight of God might appear unto you.

13 Therefore we were comforted in your comfort: yea, and exceedingly the more joyed we for the joy of Titus because his spirit was refreshed by you all.

14 For if I have boasted any thing to him of you, I am not

ashamed; but as we spake all things to you in truth, even so our boasting, which *I made* before Titus, is found a truth.

15 And his inward affection is more abundant toward you, whilst he remembereth the obedience of you all, how with fear and trembling ye received him.

16 I rejoice therefore that I have confidence in you in all *things.*

1. Filthiness of the flesh and spirit] Is it the body or the spirit that commits sin? In pre-existence it was the spirit only. In this life the spirit is clothed with a tabernacle which is subject to the lusts of the flesh; that is, mortal appetites encourage sin. But the mind of man and the will to act are in the spirit. Hence, body and spirit join in the commission of sin and both become unclean thereby.

Fear of God] Not love of God, but a reverential awe which impels to righteousness lest sore judgments befall.

4. My glorying] See 2 Cor. 10:1-18; 11:1-11.

Tribulation] "As part of their mortal probation the saints are called upon to pass through tribulations, that is to undergo severe afflictions, distress, and deep sorrow. (D. & C. 78:14; 109:5; 112:13; 122:5.) 'In the world ye shall have tribulation,' our Lord said. (John 16:33.)

" 'Tribulation worketh patience,' (Rom. 5:3; 12:12; D. & C. 54:10), and it is only 'through much tribulation' that men may 'enter into the kingdom of God.' (Acts 14:22.) 'He that is faithful in tribulation, the reward of the same is greater in the kingdom of heaven. Ye cannot behold with your natural eyes, for the present time, the design of your God concerning those things which shall come hereafter, and the glory which shall follow after much tribulation. For after much tribulation come the blessings.' (D. & C. 58:2-4; 103:12.) Exalted beings are described in these words: 'These are they which came out of great tribulation, and have washed their robes, and made them white in the blood of the Lamb.' (Rev. 7:14.) The saints glory in tribulation. (Rom. 5:3; D. & C. 127:2.)" (*Mormon Doctrine*, 2nd ed., p. 809.)

7-11. The rebukes and exhortations set forth by Paul in First Corinthians had their intended effect Those saints in Corinth who needed so to do "were made sorry after a godly manner," and as a consequence repented of their sins. Godly sorrow for sin is the first step toward forgiveness for those who have already been baptized and who are thus in the Church. The other steps are abandonment of sin, confession, restitution, and obedience to all gospel standards. (*Mormon Doctrine*, 2nd ed., pp. 292-298.)

10. Godly sorrow] "This includes an honest, heartfelt contrition of soul, a contrition born of a broken heart and a contrite spirit. It presupposes a frank, personal acknowledgment that one's acts have been evil in the sight of Him who is holy. There is no mental reservation in godly sorrow, no feeling that perhaps one's sins are not so gross or serious after all. It is certainly more than regret either because the sin has been brought to light or because some preferential reward or status has been lost because of it." (*Mormon Doctrine*, 2nd ed., p. 292.)

Repentance] See Acts 11:1-18.

SAINTS IMPART OF THEIR SUBSTANCE TO POOR

II CORINTHIANS 8:1-24.

1 Moreover, brethren, we do you to wit of the grace of God bestowed on the churches of Macedonia;

2 How that in a great trial of affliction the abundance of their joy and their d e e p poverty abounded unto the riches of their liberality.

3 For to *their* power, I bear record, yea, and beyond *their* power *they were* willing of themselves;

4 Praying us with much intreaty that we would receive the gift, and *take upon us* the fellowship of the ministering to the saints.

5 And *this they did*, not as we hoped, but first gave their own selves to the Lord, and unto us by the will of God.

6 Insomuch that we desired Titus, that as he had begun, so he would also finish in you the same grace also.

7 Therefore, as ye abound in every *thing*, in faith, and utterance, and knowledge, and *in* all diligence, and *in* your love to us, *see* that ye abound in this grace also.

8 I speak not by commandment, but by occasion of the forwardness of others, and to prove the sincerity of your love.

9 For ye know the grace of our Lord Jesus Christ, that, though he was rich, yet for your sakes he became poor, that ye through his poverty might be rich.

10 And herein I give *my* advice: for this is expedient for you, who have begun before, not only to do, but also to be forward a year ago.

11 Now therefore perform the doing *of it;* that as *there was* a readiness to will, so *there may be* a performance also out of that which ye have.

12 For if there be first a willing mind, *it is* accepted according to that a man hath, *and* not according to that he hath not.

13 For *I mean* not that other men be eased, and ye burdened:

14 But by an equality, *that* now at this time your abundance *may be a supply* for their want, that their abundance also may be *a supply* for your want: that there may be equality:

15 As it is written, He that *had gathered* much had nothing over; and he that *had gathered* little had no lack.

16 But thanks *be* to God, which put the same earnest care into the heart of Titus for you.

17 For indeed he accepted the exhortation; but being more forward, of his own accord he went unto you.

18 And we have sent with him the brother, whose praise *is* in the gospel throughout all the churches;

19 And not *that* only, but who was also chosen of the churches to travel with us with this grace, which is administered by us to the glory of the same Lord, and *declaration of* your ready mind:

20 Avoiding this, that no man should blame us in this abundance which is administered by us:

21 Providing for honest things, not only in the sight of the Lord, but also in the sight of men.

22 And we have sent with them our brother, whom we have oftentimes proved diligent in many things, but now much more diligent, upon the great confidence which *I have* in you.

23 Whether *any do enquire* of Titus, *he is* my partner and fellowhelper concerning you: or our brethren *be enquired of, they are* the messengers of the churches, *and* the glory of Christ.

24 Wherefore show ye to them, and before the churches, the proof of your love, and of our boasting on your behalf.

I.V. II CORINTHIANS 8:1, 5, 22-23.

1 Moreover, brethren, we **would have you to know** of the grace of God bestowed on the churches of Macedonia;

431

5 And this they did, not as we required, but first gave their own selves to the Lord, and unto us by the will of God.

22 And we have sent with them our brother, whom we have proved diligent in many things, but now much more diligent.

23 **Therefore we send him unto you, in consequence of** the great confidence which **we** have in you, **that you will receive the things concerning you, to the glory of** Christ; **whether we send by the hand of Titus, my partner and fellow-laborer, or our brethren, the messengers of the churches.**

Paul and the other ancient brethren set up some kind of a welfare system, geared to the needs and circumstances of the saints in that day, whereby they were privileged to help each other temporally. They thereby were able, in part at least, to keep the covenant, made in the waters of baptism, "to bear one another's burdens." (Mosiah 18:8.) The Macedonian Saints are here being exhorted to send their contributions to their fellow saints in Jerusalem.

Some kind of an arrangement always exists in the Church of God to care for the temporal needs of the poor among them. The welfare plan, in any age, is that part of the gospel which is designed, under the then existing circumstances, to care for the temporal needs of the saints on the basis of gospel principles. Such a system is one of the evidences of the divinity of the Lord's Church. Unless and until members of the Church give freely of their means for the support of their less fortunate brethren, they do not develop those attributes of goodness and godliness which prepare them for a celestial inheritance. (D. & C. 105:5.) **United Order]** See Acts 4:32-37.

In modern times the Lord gave his law on these points in these words: "I, the Lord, stretched out the heavens, and built the earth, my very handiwork; and all things therein are mine. And it is my purpose to provide for my saints, for all things are mine. But it must needs be done in mine own way; and behold this is the way that I, the Lord, have decreed to provide for my saints, that the poor shall be exalted, in that the rich are made low. For the earth is full, and there is enough and to spare; yea, I prepared all things, and have given unto the children of men to be agents unto themselves. Therefore, if any man shall take of the abundance which I have made, and impart not his portion, according to the law of my gospel, unto the poor and the needy, he shall, with the wicked, lift up his eyes in hell, being in torment." (D. & C. 104:14-18.)

7. Those who abound in faith and the attributes of godliness are the ones who impart liberally of their substance for the temporal welfare of their brethren in the kingdom.

9. We speak often of the riches of Christ, meaning the glories and rewards bestowed upon the faithful. "Behold, he that hath eternal life is rich." (D. & C. 6:7.) Paul says these riches grow out of and come because of our Lord's poverty. That is, though he was a God, though he had all power, though with his Father he owned and ruled the universe, yet he forsook the wealth of eternity, became mortal, and by way of contrast, dwelt in temporal poverty, that thereby he might perform the labors whereby many could gain eternal riches.

12. A willing mind] "The Lord requireth the heart and a willing mind." (D. & C. 64:34.)

13-15. All contributions in the Church should be based on ability to pay. The rich pay more tithing than the poor and similarly should give more to succor the needy, to aid the missionary cause, and to build houses of worship. Thus fast offering collections from areas where the saints have in abundance supply the needs of those who for a time and a season are less blessed temporally.

14. Equality] Temporal equality — equality according to a man's circumstances, according to his just needs and wants (D. & C. 51:3; 82:17) — is one of the goals of the gospel. "For, behold, the beasts of the field and the fowls of the air," the Lord says, "and that which cometh of the earth, is ordained for the use of man for food and for raiment, and that he might have in abundance. But it is not given that one man should possess that which is above another, wherefore the world lieth in sin." (D. & C. 49:19-20.)

24. Proof of your love] Love is shown forth or proved by good works. How much do we love our brethren? Proportionately as we serve them. How much do we love the Lord? "If ye love me," he answers, "keep my commandments." (John 14:15.)

433

GOD LOVETH AND REWARDETH A CHEERFUL GIVER

II CORINTHIANS 9:1-15.

1 For as touching the ministering to the saints, it is superfluous for me to write to you:

2 For I know the forwardness of your mind, for which I boast of you to them of Macedonia, that Achaia was ready a year ago; and your zeal hath provoked very many.

3 Yet have I sent the brethren, lest our boasting of you should be in vain in this behalf; that, as I said, ye may be ready:

4 Lest haply if they of Macedonia come with me, and find you unprepared, we (that we say not, ye) should be ashamed in this same confident boasting.

5 Therefore I thought it necessary to exhort the brethren, that they would go before unto you, and make up beforehand your bounty, whereof ye had notice before that the same might be ready, as a *matter of* bounty, and not as *of* covetousness.

6 But this *I say,* He which soweth sparingly shall reap also sparingly; and he which soweth bountifully shall reap also bountifully.

7 Every man according as he purposeth in his heart, *so let him give;* not grudgingly, or of necessity: for God loveth a cheerful giver.

8 And God *is* able to make all grace abound toward you; that ye, always having all sufficiency in all *things,* may abound to every good work:

9 (As it is written, He hath dispersed abroad; he hath given to the poor: his righteousness remaineth for ever.

10 Now he that ministereth seed to the sower both minister bread for *your* food, and multiply your seed sown, and increase the fruits of your righteousness;)

11 Being enriched in every thing to all bountifulness, which causeth through us thanksgiving to God.

12 For the administration of this service not only supplieth the want of the saints, but is abundant also by many thanksgivings unto God;

13 Whiles by the experiment of this ministration they glorify God for your professed subjection unto the gospel of Christ, and for *your* liberal distribution unto them, and unto all *men;*

14 And by their prayer for you, which long after you for the exceeding grace of God in you.

15 Thanks *be* unto God for his unspeakable gift.

Some of the tests incident to man's mortal probation involve his instinctive love for money, his pursuit of riches in general, his desires for the power, influence, and ease that grow out of great wealth. When "he yields to the enticings of the Holy Spirit," however, "and putteth off the natural man and becometh a saint through the atonement of Christ the Lord" (Mosiah 3:19), he then becomes subject to a higher law. Money is no longer his master; it is his servant to do good and work righteousness; he becomes a cheerful giver. **Almsgiving]** See *Commentary I*, pp. 237-238.

"Think of your brethren like unto yourselves," the Nephite Jacob taught, "and be familiar with all and free with your substance, that they may be rich like unto you. But before ye seek for riches, seek ye for the kingdom of God. And after ye have obtained a hope in Christ ye shall obtain riches, if ye seek them; and ye will seek them for the intent to do good — to clothe the naked, and to feed the hungry, and to liberate the captive, and administer relief to the sick and the afflicted." (Jac. 2:17-19.)

6. "There is that scattereth, and yet increaseth. . . . The liberal soul shall be made fat: and he that watereth shall be watered also himself" (Prov. 11:24-25.)

7. Give; not grudgingly] What blessings flow to a grudging giver? In answer Mormon taught: "God hath said a man being evil cannot do that which is good; for if he offereth a gift, or prayeth unto God, except he shall do it with real intent it profiteth him nothing. For behold, it is not counted unto him for righteousness. For behold, if a man being evil giveth a gift, he doeth it grudgingly; wherefore it is counted unto him the same as if he had retained the gift; wherefore he is counted evil before God." (Moro. 7:6-8.)

8-11. Bounteous blessings flow to the liberal saints. God rewardeth his own.

15. His unspeakable gift] What is it? The gift of the Holy Ghost in this life, and eternal life in the world to come; one is the greatest gift obtainable in mortality, the other in immortality.

PAUL GLORIETH IN THE LORD

II CORINTHIANS 10:1-18;
11:1-11.

1 Now I Paul myself beseech you by the meekness and gentleness of Christ, who in presence *am* base among you, but being absent am bold toward you:

2 But I beseech *you*, that I may not be bold when I am present with that confidence, wherewith I think to be bold against some, which think of us as if we walked according to the flesh.

3 For though we walk in the flesh, we do not war after the flesh:

4 (For the weapons of our warfare *are* not carnal, but mighty through God to the pulling down of strong holds;)

5 Casting down imaginations, and every high thing that exalteth itself against the knowledge of God, and bringing into captivity every thought to the obedience of Christ;

6 And having in a readiness to revenge all disobedience, when your obedience is fulfilled.

7 Do ye look on things after the outward appearance? If any man trust to himself that he is Christ's, let him of himself think this again, that, as he *is* Christ's, even so *are* we Christ's.

8 For though I should boast somewhat more of our authority, which the Lord hath given us for edification, and not for your destruction, I should not be ashamed:

9 That I may not seem as if I would terrify you by letters.

10 For *his* letters, say they, *are* weighty and powerful; but *his* bodily presence *is* weak, and *his* speech contemptible.

11 Let such an one think this, that, such as we are in word by letters when we are absent, such *will we be* also in deed when we are present.

12 For we dare not make ourselves of the number, or compare ourselves with some that commend themselves: but they measuring themselves by themselves, and comparing themselves a m o n g themselves, are not wise.

13 But we will not boast of things without *our* measure, but according to the measure of the rule which God hath distributed to us, a measure to reach even unto you.

14 For we stretch not ourselves beyond *our measure*, as though we reached not unto you: for we are come as far as to you also in *preaching* the gospel of Christ:

15 Not boasting of things without *our* measure, *that is*, of other men's labours; but having hope, when your faith is increased, that we shall be enlarged by you according to our rule abundantly,

16 To preach the gospel in the *regions* beyond you, *and* not to boast in another man's line of things made ready to our hand.

17 But he that glorieth, let him glory in the Lord.

18 For not he that commendeth himself is approved, but whom the Lord commendeth.

1 Would to God ye could bear with me a little in *my* folly: and indeed bear with me.

2 For I am jealous over you with godly jealousy: for I have espoused you to one husband, that I may present *you as* a chaste virgin to Christ.

3 But I fear, lest by any means, as the serpent beguiled Eve through his subtilty, so your minds should be corrupted from the simplicity that is in Christ.

4 For if he that cometh preacheth another Jesus, whom we have not preached, or *if ye* receive another spirit, which ye have not received, or another gospel, which ye have not accepted, ye might well bear with *him*.

5 For I suppose I was not a whit behind the very chiefest apostles.

6 But though *I be* rude in speech, yet not in knowledge; but we have been throughly made manifest among you in all things.

7 Have I committed an offence in abasing myself that ye might be exalted, because I have preached to you the gospel of God freely?

8 I robbed other churches, taking wages *of them*, to do you service.

9 And when I was present with you, and wanted, I was chargeable to no man: for that which was lacking to me the brethren which came from Macedonia supplied: and in all *things* I have kept myself from being burdensome unto you, and *so* will I keep *myself*.

10 As the truth of Christ is in me, no man shall stop me of this boasting in the regions of Achaia.

11 Wherefore? because I love you not? God knoweth.

I.V. II CORINTHIANS 11:4.

4 For if he that cometh preacheth another Jesus, whom we have not preached, or if ye receive another spirit, which ye have not received, or another gospel, which ye have not accepted, ye might well bear with **me**.

10:1. The meekness and gentleness of Christ] The meek are the godfearing and the righteous; the gentle are those who shun strife and contention, who teach the gospel in kindness and patience. As the Prototype of all godly attributes, the Lord Jesus, after whom Paul patterned his own life, exemplified these characteristics in perfection. "I am meek and lowly in heart" (Matt. 11:29), is our Lord's own description of himself. And of his mortal ministry, the prophetic pronouncement is: "He shall feed his flock like a shepherd: he shall gather the lambs with his arm, and carry them in his bosom, and shall gently lead those that are with young." (Isa. 40:11.)

3-6. 'Though we are mortal, our weapons in the war with evil come from God who is immortal. By his power we overcome the world and refute that reasoning which does not lead to the true knowledge of God and his laws.'

5. Bringing into captivity every thought] Thoughts are the material from which belief is built, and to be saved men must believe and therefore think the right things. We are, therefore, expected to govern our thoughts. "Let thy thoughts be directed unto the Lord." (Alma. 37:36.) "Let virtue garnish thy thoughts unceasingly." (D. & C. 121:45.) "Our thoughts will also condemn us." (Alma 12:14.)

7. Do ye look on things after the outward appearance?] "The Lord seeth not as a man seeth; for man looketh on the outward appearance, but the Lord looketh on the heart." (1 Sam. 16:7.)

8. Boast] 13. Boast] 15. Boasting] 16. Boast] 17. He that glorieth, let him glory in the Lord] There is a difference between boasting after the manner of the world and glorying in the Lord. One is a form of self-righteous pride, the other a song of praise and thanksgiving to that Holy Being whose mercy endureth forever. The great prophet Ammon, for instance, boasted in righteousness when he made the following statements: "I do not boast in my own strength, nor in my own wisdom; but behold, my joy is full, yea, my heart is brim with joy, and I will rejoice in my God. Yea, I know that I am nothing; as to my strength I am weak; therefore I will not boast of myself, but I will boast of my God, for in his strength I can do all things; yea, behold, many mighty miracles we have wrought in this land, for which we will praise his name forever." Then he recounted the great success that had attended his preaching and that of his brethren, and said: "Therefore, let us glory, yea, we will glory in the Lord; yea, we will rejoice, for our joy is full; yea, we will praise our God forever. Behold, who can glory too much in the Lord? Yea, who can say too much of his great power, and of his mercy, and of his long-suffering towards the children of men?" (Alma 26:11-16.)

11:2. Godly jealousy] Righteous jealousy. "I the Lord thy God am a jealous God." (Ex. 20:5) **One husband]** Christ. **A chaste virgin]** Those saints whom the Bridegroom will embrace when he cometh in the clouds of heaven in all the glory of his Father's kingdom.

3. The simplicity that is in Christ] The gospel of Jesus Christ is plain, pure, simple, easy to be understood. It is not some hidden mystery beyond man's comprehension. Its doctrines are clear to the understanding; its ordinances are easy to identify; its symbolisms are not buried in obscurity. Its God stands revealed and is known to the true worshipers. Mystery, complexity, an incomprehensible and unknowable God — these and all such like are born of apostasy.

4. Preacheth another Jesus] From Paul's day to this, hosts of would-be ministers have and do preach a Jesus of every sort and fashion. One group says he saves all those who merely confess his name with their lips; another that regardless of the deeds done in the flesh there will be a final harmony of all souls with God; another that he was a great moral teacher, but not the literal Son of God; another that he is a spirit essence who has already come again, and who now dwells in the hearts of those who believe; another that all churches are equally true and that it matters not what strait and narrow path men choose to follow, for all roads lead to heaven; and so on and so on and so on. Doctrines and plans of salvation are almost as varied as the number of churches and preachers.

6. Rude in speech] Paul was an orator — apparently a blunt, plain spoken one who taught, praised, and rebuked without hiding his message under the verbiage of linguistic niceties.

439

SATAN SENDS FORTH FALSE APOSTLES

II CORINTHIANS 11:12-15.

12 But what I do, that I will do, that I may cut off occasion from them which desire occasion; that wherein they glory, they may be found even as we.

13 For such *are* false apostles, deceitful workers, transforming themselves into the apostles of Christ.

14 And no marvel; for Satan himself is transformed into an angel of light.

15 Therefore *it is* no great thing if his ministers also be transformed as the ministers of righteousness; whose end shall be according to their works.

Satan imitates the truth. God has a Church and so does the devil. There are false Christs, false prophets, false apostles, false spirits, false ministers. "In relation to the kingdom of God," the Prophet Joseph Smith said, speaking of the Church restored in this dispensation, "the devil always sets up his kingdom at the very same time in opposition to God." Also: "False prophets always arise to oppose the true prophets and they will prophesy so very near the truth that they will deceive almost the very chosen ones." (*Teachings*, p. 365.)

13. False apostles] In the general sense, a true apostle is an especial witness of the Lord's name, one who knows by revelation that Jesus is the Lord. A false apostle is one who pretends to be a teacher and witness of true doctrine without having the requisite personal revelation. In the specific sense, a true apostle is one who has been ordained to that office in the Melchizedek Priesthood and who normally serves as a member of the Council of the Twelve, and who therefore has power and authority to govern the Church. A false apostle is one who professes to have power to govern the affairs of the Church on earth, but does not in fact have the requisite endowment of divine authority.

14. There are true visions and false ones. Angels appear to men and so do devils. Manifestly when a devil appears, he pretends to be an angel and to be delivering a true message from Deity. As Jacob describes it, he "transformeth himself nigh unto an angel of light." (2 Ne. 9:9.) Korihor was one person to whom

440

such an appearance was made. After being struck dumb by the power of God, he wrote this confession: "Behold, the devil hath deceived me; for he appeared unto me in the form of an angel, and said unto me: Go and reclaim this people, for they have all gone astray after an unknown God. And he said unto me: There is no God; yea, and he taught me that which I should say. And I have taught his words; and I taught them because they were pleasing unto the carnal mind; and I taught them, even until I had much success, insomuch that I verily believed that they were true; and for this cause I withstood the truth, even until I have brought this great curse upon me." (Alma 30:53; *Teachings*, pp. 204-205, 214.)

15. His ministers] Satan's ministers. Who are they and how may they be known? Joseph Smith has given us this answer: "If any person should ask me if I were a prophet, I should not deny it, as that would give me the lie; for, according to John, the testimony of Jesus is the spirit of prophecy; therefore, if I profess to be a witness or teacher, and have not the spirit of prophecy, which is the testimony of Jesus, I must be a false witness; but if I be a true teacher and witness, I must possess the spirit of prophecy, and that constitutes a prophet; and any man who says he is a teacher or preacher of righteousness, and denies the spirit of prophecy, is a liar, and the truth is not in him; and by this key false teachers and impostors may be detected." (*Teachings*, p. 269.)

False doctrine] See Gal. 1:1-12.

PAUL GLORIES IN HIS SUFFERINGS FOR CHRIST

II CORINTHIANS 11:16-33.

16 I say again, Let no man think me a fool; if otherwise, yet as a fool receive me, that I may boast myself a little.

17 That which I speak, I speak *it* not after the Lord, but as it were foolishly, in this confidence of boasting.

18 Seeing that many glory after the flesh, I will glory also.

19 For ye suffer fools gladly, seeing ye *yourselves* are wise.

20 For ye suffer, if a man bring you into bondage, if a man devour

you, if a man take *of you,* if a man exalt himself, if a man smite you on the face.

21 I speak as concerning reproach, as though we had been weak. Howbeit whereinsoever any is bold, (I speak foolishly,) I am bold also.

22 Are they Hebrews? so *am* I. Are they Israelites? so *am* I. Are they the seed of Abraham? so *am* I.

23 Are t h e y ministers of Christ? (I speak as a fool) I *am* more; in labours more abundant, in stripes above measure, in prisons more frequent, in deaths oft.

24 Of the Jews five times received I forty *stripes* save one.

25 Thrice was I beaten with rods, once was I stoned, thrice I suffered shipwreck, a night and a day I have been in the deep;

26 *In* journeyings often, *in* perils of waters, *in* perils of robbers, *in* perils by *mine own* countrymen, *in* perils by the heathen, *in* perils in the city, *in* perils in the wilderness, *in* perils in the sea, *in* perils among false brethren;

27 In weariness and painfulness, in watchings often, in hunger and thirst, in fastings often, in cold and nakedness.

28 Beside those things that are without, that which cometh upon me daily, the care of all the churches.

29 Who is weak, and I am not weak? who is offended, and I burn not?

30 If I must needs glory, I will glory of the things which concern mine infirmities.

31 The God and Father of our Lord Jesus Christ, which is blessed for evermore, knoweth that I lie not.

32 In Damascus the governor under Aretas the king kept the city of the Damascenes with a garrison, desirous to apprehend me:

33 And through a window in a basket was I let down by the wall, and escaped his hands.

I.V. II CORINTHIANS 11:23, 29.

23 Are they ministers of Christ? (I speak as a fool.) **so am I;** in **labors** more abundant, in stripes above measure, in prisons more frequent, in deaths oft.

29 Who is weak, and I am not weak? who is offended, and I **anger** not?

Blessed is Paul who was persecuted for righteousness' sake, for his is the kingdom of heaven. Blessed is he because he was reviled and persecuted and men spake all manner of evil against him falsely. Why then should he not rejoice and be exceeding glad? Why should he hesitate to recount his scourgings, stonings, and shipwrecks, suffered while on the Lord's errand? Why not glory in overcoming perils, weariness, pain, cold, and nakedness? Truly the sufferings of the faithful are swallowed up in the glory of Christ's service. (D. & C. 84:80.)

23-33. Persecution and sufferings] See Acts 5:33-42; 14:19-28; 17:1-14; 21:27-39; 22:22-30; 23:1-5; Heb. 11:35b-40.

30. If I must needs glory] See 2 Cor. 10:1-18; 11:1-11.

PAUL CAUGHT UP TO THE THIRD HEAVEN

II CORINTHIANS 12:1-6.

1 It is not expedient for me doubtless to glory. I will come to visions and revelations of the Lord.

2 I knew a man in Christ above fourteen years ago, (whether in the body, I cannot tell; or whether out of the body, I cannot tell: God knoweth;) such an one caught up to the third heaven.

3 And I knew such a man, (whether in the body, or out of the body, I cannot tell: God knoweth;)

4 How that he was caught up into paradise, and heard unspeakable words, which it is not lawful for a man to utter.

5 Of such an one will I glory: yet of myself I will not glory, but in mine infirmities.

6 For though I would desire to glory, I shall not be a fool; for I will say the truth: but *now* I forbear, lest any man should think of me above that which he seeth me *to be*, or *that* he heareth of me.

I.V. II CORINTHIANS 12:6.

6 For though I would desire to glory, I shall not be a fool; for I will say the truth; but now I forbear, lest any man should think of me above that which he seeth **of me,** or that he heareth of me.

1. Visions] "Through supernatural means, by the power of the Holy Ghost, devout persons are permitted to have visions and to see within the veil. They are enabled to see spiritual personages and to view scenes hidden from ordinary sight. These visions are gifts of the Spirit. (Seventh Article of Faith.)

"They come by faith and vanish away when faith dies out. (1 Sam. 3:1; Isa. 29:9-14.) Thus they stand as an evidence of the divinity of the Lord's work in any age. If the Lord is giving visions and revelation to a people, such a group constitutes the people of God. If visions and revelations are not being received by any church or people, then that group is not the Lord's people. By this test the identity of the true Church is known. (Moro. 7:30-38.)

"Actual personages from the unseen world frequently appear to mortals in visions. In the First Vision, the Prophet beheld and conversed with the Father and the Son. (Jos. Smith 2:15-20.) 'The Lord came unto Abram in a vision,' promised him seed (Gen. 15), and made covenant with him. (Gen. 17.) Similarly, 'God spake unto Israel in the visions of the night,' authorizing him 'to go down into Egypt.' (Gen. 46:1-4.) Paul saw the risen Lord in vision (Acts 9:1-9; 26:12-19), even as the weeping women at the empty tomb saw 'a vision of angels' saying their Lord had risen from the dead. (Luke 24:1-23.)

"Moses and Elijah personally appeared on the Mount of Transfiguration where they were seen by Peter, James, and John in vision. (Matt. 17:1-9.) When Moses, Elijah, Elias, and the Lord Jehovah stood before Joseph and Oliver in the Kirtland Temple, they were seen in vision because 'the veil was taken' from their mortal eyes. (D. & C. 110.) On August 12, 1831, on the Missouri River, 'Elder William W. Phelps, in daylight vision, saw the destroyer riding in power upon the face of the waters.' (Heading, D. & C. 61.) An angel came to Amulek 'in a vision' and commanded him to receive Alma. (Alma 8:20.)

"Power is also given to the Lord's prophets to see and converse with heavenly beings in vision, though such divine personages are not at the time in the immediate and personal presence of the one receiving the vision. Being 'overcome with the Spirit,' Lehi, for instance, 'was carried away in a vision, even that he saw the heavens open, and he thought he saw God sitting upon his throne, surrounded with numberless concourses of angels in the attitude of singing and praising their God.' (1 Ne. 1:8.) Joseph Smith and Sidney Rigdon 'beheld the glory of the Son, on the right hand of the Father, and received of his fulness; And saw the holy angels, and them who are sanctified before his throne, worshiping God, and the Lamb, who worship him forever and ever.' (D. & C. 76:20-21.) Stephen saw 'the heavens opened, and the Son of man standing on the right hand of God.' (Acts 7:51-56.) In his glorious vision of the celestial world, given January 21, 1836, the Prophet also saw 'the blazing throne of God, whereon was seated the Father and the Son.' (*Teachings*, p. 107.)

"By visions the Lord reveals past, present, and future events. Nephi saw in vision the destruction of Jerusalem after he and his people had left that wicked city. (2 Ne. 1:4.) Moroni opened to the view of the Prophet the hiding place of the plates in Cumorah. (Jos. Smith 2:42.) Daniel foresaw the great gathering at Adam-ondi-Ahman (Dan. 7:9-14), and Ezekiel saw the resurrection of the house of Israel. (Ezek. 37:1-10.) The kingdoms of glory in the eternal worlds were opened to the view of the Prophet (D. & C. 76); Abraham and Moses beheld the infinite multitude of the Lord's creations (Moses 1; 2; 3; Abra. 3; 4; 5); and Enoch and Abraham saw the host of pre-existent spirits. (Moses 6:36; Abra. 3:22-25.)

"Images, figures, and symbolical representations are often portrayed in visions as means of conveying gospel truths. Lehi and Nephi both learned much by seeing the tree of life, the rod of iron, the straight and narrow path, and so on. (1 Ne. 8; 11.) Peter learned that the gospel was to go to the Gentiles when the Lord showed him the vision of the unclean animals and commanded him to kill and eat. (Acts 10:9-48; 11:1-18.) Paul learned that he should take the message of salvation to Macedonia when he saw in vision a man praying and asking for gospel light. (Acts 16:9-10.) Daniel was informed of the history of nations and kingdoms by the beasts and figures shown him representing those kingdoms. (Dan. 7; 8; 9; 10.) In contrast, John the Revelator saw actual beasts in heaven to establish in his mind the truth that animals are resurrected and dwell in heavenly spheres. (*Teachings*, pp. 289-292.)

"Visions serve the Lord's purposes in preparing men for salvation. By them knowledge is revealed (2 Ne. 4:23), conversions are made (Alma 19:16), the gospel message is spread abroad, the church organization is perfected (D. & C. 107:93), and righteousness is increased in the hearts of men. And visions are to increase and abound in the last days, for the Lord has promised to pour out his 'spirit upon all flesh,' so that 'old men shall dream dreams,' and 'young men shall see visions.' (Joel 2:28-32.)" (*Mormon Doctrine*, 2nd ed., 823-824.)

Revelations] See Acts 11:27-30; 1 Cor. 2:9-16. **Trance]** See Acts 10:9-20.

2-4. Paul and other pillars of spiritual strength have been caught up into heaven and have seen and heard marvelous things which cannot be revealed to the less spiritually talented and indeed can only be comprehended by those who do hear and see.

Joseph Smith said: "Paul ascended into the third heavens, and he could understand the three principle rounds of Jacob's ladder — the telestial, the terrestrial, and the celestial glories or kingdoms, where Paul saw and heard things which were not lawful for him to utter. I could explain a hundred fold more than I ever have of the glories of the kingdoms manifested to me in the vision, were I permitted, and were the people prepared to receive them." (*Teachings*, pp. 304-305.)

After recording that portion of their vision of the three degrees of glory which the Lord wanted published to the world, Joseph Smith and Sidney Rigdon added these inspired words: "But great and marvelous are the works of the Lord, and the mysteries of his kingdom which he showed unto us, which surpass all understanding in glory, and in might, and in dominion; Which he commanded us we should not write while we were yet in the Spirit, and are not lawful for man to utter; Neither is man capable to make them known, for they are only to be seen and understood by the power of the Holy Spirit, which God bestows on those who love him, and purify themselves before him; To whom he grants this privilege of seeing and knowing for themselves; That through the power and manifestation of the Spirit, while in the flesh, they may be able to bear his presence in the world of glory. And to God and the Lamb be glory, and honor, and dominion forever and ever." (D. & C. 76:114-119.)

The three Nephite disciples who were promised that they should never taste of death had similar visions. "The heavens were opened, and they were caught up into heaven, and saw and heard unspeakable things. And it was forbidden them that they should utter; neither was it given unto them power that they could utter the things which they saw and heard; And whether they were in the body or out of the body, they could not tell; for it did seem unto them like a transfiguration of them, that they were changed from his body of flesh into an immortal state, that they could behold the things of God" (3 Ne. 28:13-15.)

2. A man in Christ] Paul himself, as he makes clear in verse seven of this same account.

The third heaven] The celestial kingdom. "Paul saw the third heavens, and I more," the Prophet said. (*Teachings*, p. 301.) **Degrees of glory]** See 1 Cor. 15:35-42a.

4. Caught up into paradise] Paradise is not the third heaven, nor any of the other heavens. Rather it is that part of the spirit world where the righteous go to await the day of their resurrection. (*Mormon Doctrine*, 2nd ed., pp. 554-555.) If our account of Paul's experience is accurately preserved to us, it means that he was caught up to the celestial kingdom and to the paradise of God, a thing which is entirely probable. **Paradise]** See *Commentary I*, pp. 823-825.)

THE LORD GIVES MEN WEAKNESSES

II CORINTHIANS 12:7-10.

7 And lest I should be exalted above measure through the abundance of the revelations, there was given to me a thorn in the flesh, the messenger of Satan to buffet me, lest I should be exalted above measure.

8 For this thing I besought the Lord thrice, that it might depart from me.

9 And he said unto me, My grace is sufficient for thee: for my strength is made perfect in weakness. Most gladly therefore will I rather glory in my infirmities, that the power of Christ may rest upon me.

10 Therefore I take pleasure in infirmities, in reproaches, in necessities, in persecutions, in distress for Christ's sake: for when I am weak, then am I strong.

Weaknesses cause men to rely upon the Lord and to seek his grace and goodness. If all men excelled in all things, would any develop the humility and submissiveness essential to salvation? As shown by Paul's life, even the greatest prophets — for their own benefit and schooling — though strong in the Spirit, are weak in other things. Some have physical infirmities, others are denied financial ability, or are lacking in some desirable personality trait, lest any think of themselves more highly than they ought.

When Moroni complained to the Lord that the Gentiles would criticize the literary weaknesses of the Nephites, the Lord replied: "Fools mock, but they shall mourn; and my grace is sufficient for the meek, that they shall take no advantage of your weakness; And if men come unto me I will show unto them their weakness. I give unto men weakness that they may be humble; and my grace is sufficient for all men that humble themselves before me; for if they humble themselves before me, and have faith in me, then will I make weak things become strong unto them. Behold, I will show unto the Gentiles their weakness and I will show unto them that faith, hope and charity bringeth unto me — the fountain of all righteousness." (Ether 12:26-28.)

7. A thorn in the flesh] Some unnamed physical infirmity, apparently a grievous one from which the Apostle suffered either continuously or recurringly.

Messenger of Satan] Whence come diseases and infirmities? From Satan or some other source? Without any question sickness, distress, and physical incapacity arise because of the laws which God has ordained. Obedience to the laws of health brings health; disobedience to these laws opens the door to disease and deformity. This principle is implicit in the very fact that Deity has given us such revelations as the Word of Wisdom. (D. & C. 89.) If it were otherwise, Satan would smite apostles and prophets, and the good and great in general, with disease and affliction, so that universal anarchy, disability, and plague would reign over all the earth.

On the other hand, the devil uses and delights in diseases and afflictions, and in some cases he has power to impose them, as when "Satan . . . smote Job with sore boils from the sole of his foot unto his crown" (Job 2:7), or when Jesus loosed from her infirmity "a daughter of Abraham, whom," he said, "Satan hath bound, lo, these eighteen years." (Luke 13:11-17; Acts 10:38.)

WHAT ARE THE SIGNS OF AN APOSTLE?

II CORINTHIANS 12:11-21;
13:1-4.

11 I am become a fool in glorying; ye have compelled me: for I ought to have been commended of you: for in nothing am I behind the very chiefest apostles, though I be nothing.

12 Truly the signs of an apostle were wrought among you in all patience, in signs, and wonders, and mighty deeds.

13 For what is it wherein ye were inferior to other churches, except *it be* that I myself was not burdensome to you? forgive me this wrong.

14 Behold, the third time I am ready to come to you; and I will not be burdensome to you: for I seek not your's, but you: for the children ought not to lay up for the parents, but the parents for the children.

15 And I will very gladly spend and be spent for you; though the more abundantly I love you, the less I be loved.

16 But be it so, I did not burden y o u : nevertheless, being crafty, I caught you with guile.

17 Did I make a gain of you by any of them whom I sent unto you?

18 I desired Titus, and with *him* I sent a brother. Did Titus make a gain of you? walked we not in the same spirit? *walked we* not in the same steps?

19 Again, think ye that we excuse ourselves unto you? we speak before God in Christ: but *we do* all things, dearly beloved, for your edifying.

20 For I fear, lest, when I come, I shall not find you such as I would, and *that* I shall be found unto you such as ye would not: lest *there be* debates, envyings, wraths, strifes, backbitings, whisperings, swellings, tumults:

21 *And* lest, when I come again, my God will humble me among you, and *that* I shall bewail many which have sinned already, and have not repented of the uncleanness and fornication and lasciviousness which they have committed.

1 This *is* the third *time* I am coming to you. In the mouth of two or three witnesses shall every word be established.

2 I told you before, and foretell you, as if I were present, the second time; and being absent now I write to them which heretofore have sinned, and to all other, that, if I come again, I will not spare:

3 Since ye seek a proof of Christ speaking in me, which to

449

you-ward is not weak, but is mighty in you.

4 For though he was crucified through weakness, yet he liveth by the power of God. For we also are weak in him, but we shall live with him by the power of God toward you.

12:11. The very chiefest apostles] Those who have the strongest testimonies, to whom God has revealed more of his mind and will, who teach the doctrines of salvation with greater clarity and perfection, who work more miracles, who serve more effectively in God's kingdom on earth. All apostles and prophets are no more equal than are all the elders or all Sunday School teachers. What a man knows and the revelations he receives depend on him, on his diligence and personal righteousness, not on his office or assignment in the Church. **Apostles]** See 1 Cor. 4:1-21.

12. Signs of an apostle] Those miracles, gifts of the Spirit, visions, and revelations which God pours out upon all those who love and serve him. They are healing the sick, casting out devils, raising the dead; they are preaching and teaching and suffering in the Cause of Christ; they are walking uprightly before all men and being adopted into the family of God as his sons, becoming thus joint-heirs with his natural Son. They are precisely the same divine endowments which should rest upon all the elders of the kingdom, upon every person who has received the right to the constant companionship of the Holy Spirit. The Lord's Church is designed to be a kingdom of kings and of priests, a kingdom in which eventually, "They shall teach no more every man his neighbour, and every man his brother, saying, Know the Lord: for they shall all know me, from the least of them unto the greatest of them, saith the Lord." (Jer. 31:34.)

20. Debates] Disputations and contentions about gospel matters. Jesus said: "He that hath the spirit of contention is not of me, but is of the devil, who is the father of contention." (3 Ne. 11:29.)

Envyings] Resentful, grudging, and covetous feelings toward others who are seemingly more fortunate.

Wraths] Exhibitions of violent anger and rage.

Strifes] Altercations, conflicts, fights, emulations.

Backbitings] Instances of slanderous and evil speaking about absent persons.

Whisperings] Instances of gossip, or speaking ill in secret, of conspiring and criticizing.

Swellings] Instances of being puffed up or inflated, as with pride. "Your hearts are not drawn out unto the Lord," was the word of a Lamanite Prophet to his Nephite brethren, "but they do swell with great pride, unto boasting, and unto great swelling, envyings, strifes, malice, persecutions, and murders, and all manner of iniquities." (Hela. 13:22.)

Tumults] Violent outbursts; also, violent agitations of mind or feelings; also, commotions involving multitudes, usually attended by great uproars and much confusion.

21. Fornication] See 1 Cor. 6:9-20.

Lasciviousness] Lustfulness, lewdness, wantonness; acts productive of lewd emotions. True ministers of Christ always "preach against all lyings, and deceivings, and envyings, and strifes, and malice, and revilings, and stealing, robbing, plundering, murdering, committing adultery, and all manner of lasciviousness, crying that these things ought not so to be." (Alma 16:18.)

13:1. Witnesses] See *Commentary I*, pp. 197-200; Acts 10:36-43.

4. He was crucified through weakness] He was able to die because Mary was his mother and from her he inherited the power of mortality.

He liveth by the power of God] He was able to live again because God was his Father and from him he inherited the power of immortality.

"EXAMINE YOURSELVES, WHETHER YE BE IN THE FAITH"

II CORINTHIANS 13:5-14.

5 Examine yourselves, whether ye be in the faith; prove your own selves. Know ye not your own selves, how that Jesus Christ is in you, except ye be reprobates?

6 But I trust that ye shall know that we are not reprobates.

7 Now I pray to God that ye do no evil; not that we should

appear approved, but that ye should do that which is honest, though we be as reprobates.

8 For we can do nothing against the truth, but for the truth.

9 For we are glad, when we are weak, and ye are strong: and this also we wish, *even* your perfection.

10 Therefore I write these things being absent, lest being present I should use sharpness, according to the power which the Lord hath given me to edification, and not to destruction.

11 Finally, brethren, farewell. Be perfect, be of good comfort, be of one mind, live in peace; and the God of love and peace shall be with you.

12 Greet one another with an holy kiss.

13 All the saints salute you.

14 The grace of the Lord Jesus Christ, and the love of God, and the communion of the Holy Ghost, *be* with you all. Amen.

I.V. II CORINTHIANS 13:12.

12 Greet one another with **a** holy **salutation.**

5. Examine yourselves] Do you keep the commandments? Are you sound in doctrine? Do you believe all that God has revealed? Are you receiving revelation, seeing visions, working miracles, enjoying the companionship of the Spirit? Does the gospel live in your life? **Enduring to the end]** See Acts 2:41-47.

Jesus Christ is in you] "We have the mind of Christ." (1 Cor. 2:16.) **How God dwells in us]** See 1 John 4:7-21.

Reprobates] Disobedient, depraved, and unprincipled persons who have departed from the faith and are thereby rejected of God.

8. We can do nothing against the truth] In the eternal sense, nothing we do to fight the truth shall prosper. However plausible and popular error may be, eventually it shall die. Truth only shall prevail.

11. Be perfect] See *Commentary I*, pp. 231-232; Heb. 6:1-3.

Be of one mind] See 1 Cor. 1:1-16.

I.V. 12. A holy salutation] Special sacred salutations of greeting are reserved for those who belong to the family of Jesus Christ, who have taken upon themselves his name, and who are worthy to enter his holy temples. Such are made "in the name of the Lord, with uplifted hands unto the Most High," and are to this effect: "I salute you in the name of the Lord Jesus Christ, in token or remembrance of the everlasting covenant, in which covenant I receive you to fellowship, in a determination that is fixed, immovable, and unchangeable, to be your friend and brother through the grace of God in the bonds of love, to walk in all the commandments of God blameless, in thanksgiving, forever and ever. Amen." Persons unworthy of this sacred greeting have no place in the house of the Lord. (D. & C. 88:119-120, 133-136.)

The Epistle of Paul the Apostle
to the Galatians

All of Paul's epistles are written for the saints of God, for those who belong to the Church, for those who already know the doctrines of salvation, for those who have the gift of the Holy Ghost and are thereby able to interpret and understand the Apostle's teachings.

But they are also written to answer the questions and solve the problems of specific groups of saints. And in the case of the Galatians, the problem is apostasy. These Galatians are Gentile converts. They are now being contaminated by Jewish-Christians who tell them they must also be circumcised and live the law of Moses to be saved. Paul's purpose is to call them back to Christ and his gospel.

Galatians is thus written to people who are losing the true faith, who are adopting false doctrines and ordinances, who are being overcome by the world, who are commingling the dead law of Moses with the living word which is in Christ. Thus, in principle, Galatians is written to the Sectarian world, to those plagued with apostasy, to people who no longer believe the gospel in its purity and perfection.

Consequently we read in it what the Galatians and the sectarians alike must believe and do to be saved. For instance:

That there is only one true gospel, only one plan of salvation, only one way whereby men may be saved, and that is in and through the gospel revealed to and taught by Paul, and all who preach any other gospel shall be accursed;

That salvation does not come by the law of Moses, but is available through Christ and his atoning sacrifice;

455

That God gave the gospel to Abraham 430 years before the days of Moses, that the law of Moses was added because of the transgressions of the people, and was in fact a system of laws and performances to prepare Israel for Christ and the gospel which he would bring again;

That all men who accept and live the gospel become the seed of Abraham, the children of Christ, and the sons of God;

That the saints should stand fast in the faith, crucify the flesh and walk in the Spirit, and bear one another's burdens;

And that those who sow to the flesh shall of the flesh reap corruption, while those who sow to the Spirit shall of the Spirit reap life everlasting.

Galatians is indeed an inspired work of priceless value to those who sincerely seek guidance in spiritual matters!

PREACHERS OF FALSE GOSPELS ARE ACCURSED

GALATIANS 1:1-12.

1 Paul, an apostle, (not of men, neither by man, but by Jesus Christ, and God the Father, who raised him from the dead;)

2 And all the brethren which are with me unto the churches of Galatia:

3 Grace *be* to you and peace from God the Father, and *from* our Lord Jesus Christ,

4 Who gave himself for our sins, that he might deliver us from this present evil world, according to the will of God and our Father:

5 To whom *be* glory for ever and ever. Amen.

6 I marvel that ye are so soon removed from him that called you into the grace of Christ unto another gospel:

7 Which is not another; but there be some that trouble you, and would pervert the gospel of Christ.

8 But though we, or an angel from heaven, preach any other gospel unto you than that which we have preached unto you, let him be accursed.

9 As we said before, so say I now again, If any *man* preach any other gospel unto you than that ye have received, let him be accursed.

10 For do I now persuade men, or God? or do I seek to please men? for if I yet pleased men, I should not be the servant of Christ.

11 But I certify you, brethren, that the gospel which was preached of me is not after man.

12 For I neither received it of man, neither was I taught *it*, but by the revelation of Jesus Christ.

I.V. GALATIANS 1:10.

10 For do I now **please** men, or God? or do I seek to please men? for if I yet pleased men, I should not be the servant of Christ.

1. An apostle . . . by Jesus Christ] Christ chooses his own ministers, be they apostles, or elders, or deacons (John 15:16), and wo unto those who profess to hold ministerial power unless it has in fact come from the Almighty! **Apostles]** See Acts 13:50-52; 14:1-7; 1 Cor. 4:1-21.

3. God the Father, and . . . our Lord Jesus Christ] Two Gods, not one, and wo unto those who wrest the scriptures in futile attempts to sustain false creeds!

4. For our sins] Christ died for our sins on conditions of repentance (D. & C. 18:11-12), and wo unto those who do not accept his gospel and repent of all their sins! (D. & C. 19:4-21.)

According to the will of God] "I came into the world to do the will of my Father, because my Father sent me." (3 Ne. 27:13.)

Our Father] God the Eternal Father, the Father of spirits, the personal Parent of all men in pre-existence.

6-12. Apostasy was rampant among the Galatian Saints. Chiefly they were trying to harmonize their newly found faith with the law of Moses, so as to preserve the laws and ordinances of both the old and the new covenants. It was as though members of the Church today should attempt to harmonize the truths of the restored gospel with the beliefs and practices of the sectarian world.

6. Another gospel] **7. Which is not another]** That there is and can be only one gospel — one Church, one plan of salvation, one true religion — is as self-evident as any truth known to man.

457

There can no more be two true gospels or two true churches than there can be two true and differing scientific facts. Truth is truth. And truth and salvation and the gospel all are ordained of God. They are what they are; and they are not what they are not. Men either have the truths of salvation or they do not; they either possess the gospel, which is the plan of salvation, or they do not. If they have the gospel, it is, in over-all scope and in minutest detail, exactly what Paul had. If any part or portion of their system of religion differs from what the ancient Apostle taught and believed, what they have is in fact a perversion of the true gospel. There is no more sense or reason in saying that two differing churches are both true than in claiming that black and white are both the same color.

The gospel of Christ] Rom. 1:1-17.

8. That which we have preached] 9. That ye have received] What gospel is this? It is the gospel of God concerning his Son, Jesus Christ our Lord; it is that God is the Creator, that Christ is the Redeemer, and that based on his atoning sacrifice, men may be saved by obedience to his laws and ordinances. It is a gospel of faith, repentance, baptism, the receipt of the Holy Ghost, and enduring in righteousness to the end. It is a gospel of priestly power received from God; of apostles, prophets, pastors, teachers, and numerous legal administrators; of miracles, tongues, gifts of the Spirit, revelation, visions. It is the everlasting gospel; the gospel of Adam, Enoch, Noah, and Abraham; of the Nephites and Jaredites; and of Joseph Smith and the Latter-day Saints. It is the same gospel preached by an angel sent from God in heaven to man on earth in modern times. It is the gospel recorded in the Bible, the Book of Mormon, the Doctrine and Covenants, and the Pearl of Great Price. It is the power of God whereby men are saved in his kingdom; and in this day and age it is found only in The Church of Jesus Christ of Latter-day Saints.

Let him be accursed] Who? Anyone in heaven or on earth, in time or eternity, in Paul's day or ours, anyone who preaches any gospel other than the true one. Why? Because there is no salvation in a false religion. There is no saving power in a man-made system of salvation. Man does not have power to create the celestial kingdom any more than he has power to resurrect himself. Religion comes from God. He created it; he ordained it; he established the laws and conditions whereunder salvation may be gained. And any man — whether mortal or immortal, whether man or angel — who preaches any system other than the very one ordained by Deity, leads men astray and keeps them from gaining celestial salvation.

To whom, then, doth the Apostle make reference? Specifically to the false teachers among the Galatians, but in principle to all false teachers, teachers of whom Nephi said, "And all those who preach false doctrines, . . . wo, wo, wo be unto them, saith the Lord God Almighty, for they shall be thrust down to hell!" (2 Ne. 28:15.)

And who is a false teacher, a false minister, a false prophet? Anyone who does not teach the truth, minister the elements of true religion, or prophesy truly of that which is yet to be. It is truth, pure, diamond truth that counts, and nothing else. A true preacher is one who belongs to the true Church, believes the true gospel, holds that priesthood which is in fact the power of God delegated to man on earth, and who receives revelation from the one true Spirit Being who is the Holy Ghost. And wo unto all others for they fall under the eternal law here announced by one who was a legal administrator and who wrote by the power of the Spirit.

False apostles] See 2 Cor. 11:12-15. **False rites]** See 1 Cor. 10:16-33.

10. One of the chief identifying characteristics of the true gospel is that it is not pleasing to the carnal mind; it does not make friends with the world; it does not please worldly people. Those who choose to eat, drink, and be merry, who are unclean and immoral, who are proud and worldly, always find themselves in opposition to the truths of salvation and to the organization which sponsors and teaches them.

11-12. Paul got the gospel in the same way every convert gets it — by personal revelation. No one ever receives the true gospel

459

from man. It is not taught my man's power, but dawns upon true converts, by the power of the Spirit, in the form of personal testimony. Once the spirit of testimony is planted in the heart of a man, the door is open for the revelation of that added light and knowledge which assures an inheritance in the heavens above.

PAUL BELIEVES, IS TAUGHT, PREACHES TO GENTILES

GALATIANS 1:13-24.

13 For ye have heard of my conversation in time past in the Jews' religion, how that beyond measure I persecuted the church of God, and wasted it:

14 And profited in the Jews' religion above many my equals in mine own nation, being more exceedingly zealous of the traditions of my fathers.

15 But when it pleased God, who separated me from my mother's womb, and called *me* by his grace,

16 To reveal his Son in me, that I might preach him among the heathen; immediately I conferred not with flesh and blood:

17 Neither went I up to Jerusalem to them which were apostles before me; but I went into Arabia, and returned again unto Damascus.

18 Then after three years I went up to Jerusalem to see Peter, and abode with him fifteen days.

19 But other of the apostles saw I none, save James the Lord's brother.

20 Now the things which I write unto you, behold, before God, I lie not.

21 Afterwards I came into the regions of Syria and Cilicia;

22 And was unknown by face unto the churches of Judea which were in Christ:

23 But they had heard only, That he which persecuted us in times past now preacheth the faith which once he destroyed.

24 And they glorified God in me.

I.V. GALATIANS 1:24.

24 And they glorified God **on account of** me.

GALATIANS 2:1-10.

1 Then fourteen years after I went up again to Jerusalem with Barnabas, and took Titus with *me* also.

2 And I went up by revelation, and communicated unto them that gospel which I preach among the Gentiles, but privately to them which were of reputation, lest by

any means I should run, or had run, in vain.

3 But neither Titus, who was with me, being a Greek, was compelled to be circumcised:

4 And that because of false brethren unawares brought in, who came in privily to spy out our liberty which we have in Christ Jesus, that they might bring us into bondage:

5 To whom we gave place by subjection, no, not for an hour; that the truth of the gospel might continue with you.

6 But of those who seemed to be somewhat, (whatsoever they were, it maketh no matter to me: God accepteth no man's person:) for they who seemed *to be somewhat* in conference added nothing to me:

7 But contrariwise, when they saw that the gospel of the uncircumcision was committed unto me, as *the gospel* of the circumcision *was* unto Peter;

8 (For he that wrought effectually in Peter to the apostleship of the circumcision, the same was mighty in me toward the Gentiles:)

9 And when James, Cephas, and John, who seemed to be pillars, perceived the grace that was given unto me, they gave to me and Barnabas the right hands of fellowship; that we *should go* unto the heathen, and they unto the circumcision.

10 Only *they would* that we should remember the poor; the same which I also was forward to do.

I.V. GALATIANS 2:4.

4 **Notwithstanding, there were some brought in by false brethren unawares,** who came in privily to spy out out liberty which we have in Christ Jesus, that they might bring us into bondage;

1:13. **My conversation]** My course of conduct. **I persecuted the church of God]** See Acts 8:1b-4. The God involved is Christ in that it is he for whom the Church is named.

15. God . . . called me] See Acts 9:1-9 and 10:19a.

18. I went up to Jerusalem] See Acts 9:19b-31.

24. With Christlike forgiveness the saints accept their former persecutor and rejoice in his conversion.

2:1. I went up again to Jerusalem] Second and third journeys to Jerusalem are recorded in Acts 11:27-30 and Acts 15, this latter one being the occasion when circumcision was considered.

2. I . . . communicated unto them that gospel, which I preach]
He reported to them, probably in detail, what his teachings were;
he did not make known unto them some new gospel which differed
from theirs; both he and they believed and taught the same
eternal truths. He was simply letting his superiors judge the
soundness and truth of his views.

3-5. Paul here utterly refuses to permit the circumcision of
Titus, a Greek, lest he become subject to the law of Moses; later
he acceded to the circumcision of Timothy, a half-Jew, apparently
on the pretense that it was a matter of nationality and not of
religion. (Acts 16:1-15.)

6. Paul was not impressed with the rank and status of the
leading brethren who in fact added nothing to his knowledge and
understanding of the gospel.

7-8. Primarily, Peter taught the gospel to those who were
circumcised, to the Jews in whose flesh was the token of the
covenant God made with Abraham their father. Paul, on the
other hand, went primarily to the uncircumcised Gentiles, those
outside the once favored lineage. Both presented the same saving
truth; but to Peter it was the gospel of the circumcision, because
it grew out of the law of Moses and was for those who had been
circumcised, while to Paul it was the gospel of the uncircumcision
because it offered the same salvation to those who had never been
privileged to have the original blessings of the covenant of circumcision. It was a matter of emphasis and perspective and not
a matter of substance.

9. The right hands of fellowship] Total and complete acceptance as fellow saints, entitled to all of the blessings of the gospel
in this life and the hope of eternal life in the world to come.

SALVATION COMES THROUGH CHRIST, NOT MOSES

GALATIANS 2:11-21.

11 But when Peter was come to
Antioch, I withstood him to the
face, because he was to be blamed.

12 For before that certain came
from James, he did eat with the
Gentiles: but when they were
come, he withdrew and separated

462

himself, fearing them which were of the circumcision.

13 And the other Jews dissembled likewise with him; insomuch that Barnabas also was carried away with their dissimulation.

14 But when I saw that they walked not uprightly according to the truth of the gospel, I said unto Peter before *them* all, If thou, being a Jew, livest after the manner of Gentiles, and not as do the Jews, why compellest thou the Gentiles to live as do the Jews?

15 We *who are* Jews by nature, and not sinners of the Gentiles,

16 Knowing that a man is not justified by the works of the law, but by the faith of Jesus Christ, even we have believed in Jesus Christ, that we might be justified by the faith of Christ, and not by the works of the law: for by the works of the law shall no flesh be justified.

17 But if, while we seek to be justified by Christ, we ourselves also are found sinners, *is* therefore Christ the minister of sin? God forbid.

18 For if I build again the things which I destroyed, I make myself a transgressor.

19 For I through the law am dead to the law, that I might live unto God.

20 I am crucified with Christ: nevertheless I live; yet not I, but Christ liveth in me: and the life which I now live in the flesh, I live by the faith of the Son of God, who loved me, and gave himself for me.

21 I do not frustrate the grace of God: for if righteousness *come* by the law, then Christ is dead in vain.

Peter and Paul — both of whom were apostles, both of whom received revelations, saw angels, and were approved of the Lord, and both of whom shall inherit the fulness of the Father's kingdom — these same righteous and mighty preachers disagreed on a basic matter of church policy. Peter was the President of the Church; Paul, an apostle and Peter's junior in the church heirarchy, was subject to the direction of the chief apostle. But Paul was right and Peter was wrong. Paul stood firm, determined that they should walk "uprightly according to the truth of the gospel"; Peter temporized for fear of offending Jewish semi-converts who still kept the law of Moses.

The issue was not whether the Gentiles should receive the gospel. Peter himself had received the revelation that God was no respecter of persons, and that those of all lineages were now to be heirs of salvation along with the Jews. (Acts 10:21-35.) Further, the heads of the Church, in council assembled, with the Holy Ghost guiding their minds and directing their decisions, had determined that the Gentiles who received the gospel should not be subject to the law of Moses. (Acts 15:1-35.) The Jewish members of the Church, however, had not been able to accept this decision without reservation. They themselves continued to conform to Mosaic performances, and they expected Gentile converts to do likewise. Peter sided with them; Paul publicly withstood the chief apostle and won the debate, as could not otherwise have been the case. Without question, if we had the full account, we would find Peter reversing himself and doing all in his power to get the Jewish saints to believe that the law of Moses was fulfilled in Christ and no longer applied to anyone either Jew or Gentile.

13. Dissimulation] Concealing and disguising true doctrines with false ones; believing doctrines that simulate true ones, that have a semblance of truth but are in fact erroneous.

16. Justified] See Rom. 2:17-29; 3:1-20, 21-31; 4:1-25; 5:1-11.

18. 'If I should build again the law of Moses, which I have already helped destroy, I would be a transgressor.' Or: 'If I should attempt to strengthen and sustain sectarian doctrines, which I have already refuted, I would be a sinner.'

20. I am crucified in Christ] 'Because of Christ and his goodness, I have crucified the man of sin, the lusts of the flesh.' **Christ liveth in me]** 'Hence, being dead to sin, I possess the Spirit of Christ and am like him; my life is a manifestation of his.'

24. The grace of God] See Rom. 4:1-25; Eph. 2:1-10.

If righteousness come by the law, then Christ is dead in vain] 'If men are saved by the law of Moses, then Christ and his atonement are nothing.'

Law of Moses] See Acts 15:1-35.

GOD GAVE THE GOSPEL TO ABRAHAM

GALATIANS 3:1-25.

1 O foolish Galatians who hath bewitched you, that ye should not obey the truth, before whose eyes Jesus Christ hath been evidently set forth, crucified among you?

2 This only would I learn of you, Received ye the Spirit by the works of the law, or by the hearing of faith?

3 Are ye so foolish? having begun in the Spirit, are ye now made perfect by the flesh?

4 Have ye suffered so many things in vain? if *it be* yet in vain.

5 He therefore that ministereth to you the Spirit, and worketh miracles among you, *doeth he it* by the works of the law, or by the hearing of faith?

6 Even as Abraham believed God, and it was accounted to him for righteousness.

7 Know ye therefore that they which are of faith, the same are the children of Abraham.

8 And the scripture, foreseeing that God would justify the heathen through faith, preached before the gospel unto Abraham, *saying,* In thee shall all nations be blessed.

9 So then they which be of faith are blessed with faithful Abraham.

10 For as many as are of the works of the law are under the curse: for it is written, Cursed *is* every one that continueth not in all things which are written in the book of the law to do them.

11 But that no man is justified by the law in the sight of God, *it is* evident: for, The just shall live by faith.

12 And the law is not of faith: but, The man that doeth them shall live in them.

13 Christ hath redeemed us from the curse of the law, being made a curse for us: for it is written, Cursed *is* every one that hangeth on a tree:

14 That the blessing of Abraham might come on the Gentiles through Jesus Christ; that we might receive the promise of the Spirit through faith.

15 Brethren, I speak after the manner of men; Though *it be* but a man's covenant, yet *if it be* confirmed, no man disannulleth, or addeth thereto.

16 Now to Abraham and his seed were the promises made. He saith not, And to seeds, as of many; but as of one, And to thy seed, which is Christ.

17 And this I say, *that* the covenant, that was confirmed before of God in Christ, the law, which was four hundred and thirty years after, cannot disannul, that it should make the promise of none effect.

465

18 For if the inheritance *be* of the law, *it is* no more of promise: but God gave *it* to Abraham by promise.

19 Wherefore then *serveth* the law? It was added because of transgressions, till the seed should come to whom the promise was made; *and it was* ordained by angels in the hand of a mediator.

20 Now a mediator is not *a mediator* of one, but God is one.

21 *Is* the law then against the promises of God? God forbid: for if there had been a law given which could have given life, verily righteousness should have been by the law.

22 But the scripture hath concluded all under sin, that the promise by faith of Jesus Christ might be given to them that believe.

23 But before faith came, we were kept under the law, shut up unto the faith which should afterwards be revealed.

24 Wherefore the law was our schoolmaster *to bring us* unto Christ, that we might be justified by faith.

25 But after that faith is come, we are no longer under a schoolmaster.

I.V. GALATIANS 3:14-15, 19-20, 24.

14 That the blessing of Abraham might come on the Gentiles through Jesus Christ; that **they** might receive the promise of the Spirit through faith.

15 Brethren, I speak after the manner of men; Though it be but a man's covenant, yet **when** it be confirmed, no man disannulleth, or addeth thereto.

19 Wherefore then, **the law was** added because of transgressions, till the seed should come to whom the promise was made **in the law given to Moses, who was ordained by the hand of angels to be a mediator of this first covenant, (the law.)**

20 **Now this mediator was not a mediator of the new covenant; but there is one mediator of the new covenant, who is Christ, as it is written in the law concerning the promises made to Abraham and his seed. Now Christ is the mediator of life; for this is the promise which God made unto Abraham.**

24 Wherefore the law was our schoolmaster **until** Christ, that we might be justified by faith.

God has spoken in successive ages, giving as much saving truth to every people as they are able to bear. Adam, Enoch, Noah, Abraham, and hosts of others, had the fulness of the everlasting gospel, the same gospel restored and established anew by Jesus and his apostles. To Moses and all Israel, God offered this gospel which had blessed and saved men from the beginning, but Israel rejected the offer and refused to live by gospel standards. Accordingly God gave them the law of Moses, the lesser law, the law of carnal commandments, to school and train them for the day when once again they would be able to receive and live that which enables men to enter into the rest of the Lord, which rest is the fulness of his glory. (D. & C. 84:17-27; I.V. Ex. 34:1-2. **Gospel dispensations]** See Eph. 1:9-12.

1-6. Paul upbraids the Galatians for turning from the gospel of Christ back to the performances and rituals of the law of Moses. Through faith in Christ, he says, they had overcome the flesh, received the Holy Ghost, worked miracles, and been accounted righteous before God as was Abraham. Accordingly, he asks: 'What possible benefits can flow to you now by forsaking faith in Christ and returning to the dead performances of a dead law?

7-9. What were the promises of God to Abraham? And to his seed? How do these promises affect the Gentiles, those who are not of the blood of Abraham? To begin with Abraham had a dispensation of the everlasting gospel. His faith was centered in the Lord Jesus Christ who is the Almighty Jehovah. Abraham was baptized, held the holy Melchizedek Priesthood, was married for eternity, and has now gone on to glory and exaltation in the kingdom of God. (D.& C. 132:29-32.) To him Jehovah said: "And I will make of thee a great nation, and I will bless thee above measure, and make thy name great among all nations, and thou shalt be a blessing unto thy seed after thee, that in their hands they shall bear this ministry and Priesthood unto all nations; And I will bless them through thy name; for as many as receive this Gospel shall be called after thy name, and shall be accounted thy seed, and shall rise up and bless thee, as their father; And I will bless them that bless thee, and curse them that curse thee; and in thee (that is, in thy Priesthood) and in thy seed (that is, thy Priesthood), for I give unto thee a promise that this right shall continue in thee, and in thy seed after thee (that is to say, the literal seed, or the seed of the body) shall all the families of the earth be blessed, even with the blessings of the Gospel, which are the blessings of salvation, even of life eternal." (Abra. 2:9-11; Gen. 12:1-3; 17:1-8; 22:15-18.)

7. The children of Abraham] Those who keep the commandments, who live as Abraham lived, who are worthy to be members of his family in celestial exaltation. Among them are hosts of his literal descendants and other hosts of Gentile descent, who, adopted into his household, rise up and bless him as their father.

8. The gospel] See Rom 1:1-17.

10-14. The law of Moses alone cannot save, for salvation is in Christ; hence, the law becomes a curse in that it brings condemnation unless man obeys it in full. "Cursed be he that confirmeth not all the words of this law to do them." (Deut. 27:26.) Since only those who have faith in Christ are spiritually alive, man is not justified by the works of the law alone, for the law came because men rejected faith in Christ and his gospel.

And yet those of old were blessed through the law, in accordance with the decree: "Ye shall therefore keep my statutes, and my judgments: which if a man do, he shall live in them: I am the Lord." (Lev. 18:5.) That is, those of old who kept the law, as for instance the Nephites, gained spiritual life through faith in Christ. Hence Nephi's explanation that, "Notwithstanding we believe in Christ, we keep the law of Moses, and look forward with steadfastness unto Christ, until the law shall be fulfilled. For, for this end was the law given; wherefore the law hath become dead unto us, and we are made alive in Christ because of our faith; yet we keep the law because of the commandments." (2 Ne. 25:24-25.)

But now, Paul continues, Christ hath fulfilled the law of Moses so that we are no longer cursed for failure to obey all of its performances. We have been redeemed from the curse. Since Christ, by hanging on the cross, thus removed the instrument whereby we were cursed, he became as it were a curse for us. And this very thing is symbolized in the law itself, which decrees a curse upon anyone hanged on a tree. (Deut. 21:23.) Thus — that is by fulfilling the law of Moses, and by bringing again the gospel which

Abraham had — Christ has brought the blessings of Abraham to the Gentiles in that they, as adopted members of his family, receive all of the gospel blessings which Abraham himself enjoyed. **Children of the covenant]** See Acts 3:25-26. **Adoption]** See Rom. 11:11-24.

11. No man is justified by the law] See Rom. 2:17-29; 3:1-20.

14. The blessings of Abraham] "Abraham received promises concerning his seed, and of the fruit of his loins — from whose loins ye are, namely, my servant Joseph — which were to continue so long as they were in the world; and as touching Abraham and his seed, out of the world they should continue; both in the world and out of the world should they continue as innumerable as the stars; or, if ye were to count the sand upon the seashore ye could not number them. This promise is yours also, because ye are of Abraham, and the promise was made unto Abraham." (D. & C. 132:30-31.)

These blessings of Abraham were offered first to the literal seed of his body and thereafter to the Gentiles, as Christ explained to the Nephites in these words: "Ye are the children of the prophets; and ye are of the house of Israel; and ye are of the covenant which the Father made with your fathers, saying unto Abraham: And in thy seed shall all the kindreds of the earth be blessed. The Father having raised me up unto you first, and sent me to bless you in turning away every one of you from his iniquities; and this because ye are the children of the covenant — And after that ye were blessed then fulfilleth the Father the covenant which he made with Abraham, saying: In thy seed shall all the kindreds of the earth be blessed — unto the pouring out of the Holy Ghost through me upon the Gentiles." (3 Ne. 20:25-27.) And once a people receive the Holy Ghost they continue to progress in the things of the Spirit until, as with Abraham, all things are theirs.

15-25. When a man makes a valid will (that is, a testament or covenant), so others may inherit from him, no one else can come forward and disannul the document. How much more sure, then, are the promises of God to Abraham whereby his seed shall inherit blessings. Obviously, the law of Moses, which came 430 years after the promises, cannot disannul the eternal decrees of God. Rather the law of Moses was added to prepare rebellious Israel for the time when they could receive again the fulness of the gospel and thereby be entitled to the blessings of Abraham. Moses, the mediator of the old covenant, gave them this lesser law; Jesus, the mediator of the new covenant, has now come, abolishing the old and replacing it with the very thing possessed by Abraham. Christ is the mediator who brings spiritual life, as God revealed to Abraham. If salvation had come by the law of Moses alone, there would have been no need for Christ and his atonement. But as those who had the law were all under sin, Christ came to bear their sins and those of all men on conditions of faith and repentance. Thus the law was a schoolmaster to prepare men for Christ and the gospel, and now that Christ has come there is no longer any need for the law and all of its preparatory rituals.

The law of Moses] See Acts 15:1-35. **Mediator, mediation]** See 1 Tim. 2:1-7.

16. His seed] Specifically, Christ, the preeminent descendant of Abraham; generally, all of the descendants of Abraham who keep the commanmdents, plus those adopted into his lineage, who are thus made heirs with his natural descendants.

17. The covenant] The new and everlasting covenant, which is the gospel, the covenant of salvation which God makes with his children on earth. **The promise]** The blessings which flow from obedience to the gospel law; peace in this life and eternal life in the world to come, including eternal increase and exaltation. (D.& C. 132:29-32.)

19. Added because of transgressions] Israel had the Melchizedek Priesthood, which "administereth the gospel," but "they hardened their hearts," rebelled against God, and were given the Aaronic Priesthood which administers "the preparatory gospel; . . . and the law of carnal commandments." These lesser things were thus added to the greater, or rather the blessings of the greater were taken from them. (D. & C. 84:19-27.)

24. Justified by faith] See Rom. 2:17-29; 3:1-20, 21-31; 4:1-25; 5:1-11.

SAINTS ARE CHILDREN OF GOD BY FAITH

GALATIANS 3:26-29.

26 For ye are all the children of God by faith in Christ Jesus.

27 For as many of you as have been baptized into Christ have put on Christ.

28 There is neither Jew nor Greek, there is neither bond nor free, there is neither male nor female: for ye are all one in Christ Jesus.

29 And if ye *be* Christ's, then are ye Abraham's seed, and heirs according to the promise.

Who are the children of God? Such depends entirely upon the usage of terms and what is meant in a particular situation. Births are of various kinds, and each has its own parents and its own children. To be born does not mean to come into existence out of nothing, but rather to begin a new type of existence, to live again in a changed situation. Birth is the continuation of life under different circumstances.

All men were born in pre-existence as the spirit children of God the Father, meaning that the spirit element which existed from all eternity, and has neither beginning nor end, was organized into spirit children, which children were the offspring of celestial Parents and were thus members of the family of God the Father.

Mortal men are born into mortality, meaning that the spirits from pre-existence come into tabernacles which have been created from the dust of the earth through the normal birth processes. In this case the parents are mortal persons and the family relationship includes the immediate kinsmen.

Those accountable mortals who then believe and obey the gospel are born again; they are born of the Spirit; they become alive to the things of righteousness or of the Spirit. They become members of another family, have new brothers and sisters, and a new Father. They are the sons and daughters of Jesus Christ. They take upon them his name in the waters of baptism and certify anew each time they partake of the sacrament that they have so done; or, more accurately, in the waters of baptism power

471

is given them to become the sons of Christ, which eventuates when they are in fact born of the Spirit and become new creatures of the Holy Ghost.

Thereafter, through celestial marriage, they are adopted into the family of God the Father, becoming his sons and daughters. In this sense they are brothers, not sons, of Christ; they become heirs of God; they are joint-heirs with Christ.

26. Children of God] Sons and daughters of Jesus Christ, adopted members of his family. "Because of the covenant which ye have made ye shall be called the children of Christ, his sons, and his daughters," King Benjamin said, "for behold, this day he hath spiritually begotten you; for ye say that your hearts are changed through faith on his name; therefore, ye are born of him and have become his sons and his daughters. And under this head ye are made free, and there is no other head whereby ye can be made free. There is no other name given whereby salvation cometh." (Mosiah 5:7-8; Rev. 21:7.) This, of course, is one of the ways in which the Son of God becomes the Father, enabling him to say: "I am the Father, I am the light, and the life, and the truth of the world." (Ether 4:12.) See *Commentary I*, pp. 278-281. **Born again]** See 1 John 5:1-5.

27. Baptized into Christ] After announcing Christ's divinity, John wrote: "He came unto his own, and his own received him not. But as many as received him, to them gave he power to become the sons of God, even to them that believe on his name." (John 1:11-12.) Then in modern times that same Lord said he was, "The same which came in the meridian of time unto mine own, and mine own received me not; But to as many as received me, gave I power to become my sons; and even so will I give unto as many as will receive me, power to become my sons. And verily, verily, I say unto you, he that receiveth my gospel receiveth me; and he that receiveth not my gospel receiveth not me. And this is my gospel — repentance and baptism by water, and then cometh the baptism of fire and the Holy Ghost, even the Comforter, which showeth all things, and teacheth the peaceable things of the kingdom." (D. & C. 39:3-6.)

Put on Christ] Take upon oneself the name of Christ, making it the new family name, the new name by which the saints are called. King Benjamin's counsel to those who had entered the covenant of baptism was: "Take upon you the name of Christ, all you that have entered into the covenant with God that ye should be obedient unto the end of your lives. And it shall come to pass that whosoever doeth this shall be found at the right hand of God, for he shall know the name by which he is called; for he shall be called by the name of Christ." (Mosiah 5:8-9.) Men in this day are commanded: "Take upon you the name of Christ, and speak the truth in soberness. And as many as repent and are baptized in my name, which is Jesus Christ, and endure to the end, the same shall be saved. Behold, Jesus Christ is the name which is given of the Father, and there is none other name given whereby man can be saved; Wherefore, all men must take upon them the name which is given of the Father, for in that name shall they be called at the last day; Wherefore, if they know not the name by which they are called, they cannot have place in the kingdom of my Father." (D. & C. 18:21-25.) And each time the saints partake of the sacrament, they certify anew to the Father that they are willing to take upon them the name of his Son. (D. & C. 20:77.)

28. "He inviteth them all to come unto him and partake of his goodness; and he denieth none that come unto him, black and white, bond and free, male and female; and he remembereth the heathen; and all are alike unto God, both Jew and Gentile." (2 Ne. 26:33.)

29. Abraham's seed] See Gal. 3:1-25; *Commentary I*, pp. 458-462. According to the terms and conditions of the covenant of the priesthood, those who magnify their callings in the priesthood become, by adoption, "the seed of Abraham," and have the sure promise of exaltation in the kingdom of God. (D. & C. 84:33-40.)

Heirs according to the promise] See Gal. 3:1-25; 4:1-7.

HOW SAINTS BECOME SONS OF GOD

GALATIANS 4:1-7.

1 Now I say, *That* the heir, as long as he is a child, differeth nothing from a servant, though he be lord of all;

2 But is under tutors and governors until the time appointed of the father.

3 Even so we, when we were children, were in bondage under the elements of the world:

4 But when the fulness of the time was come, God sent forth his Son, made of a woman, made under the law,

5 To redeem them that were under the law, that we might receive the adoption of sons.

6 And because ye are sons, God hath sent forth the Spirit of his Son into your hearts, crying, Abba, Father.

7 Wherefore thou art no more a servant, but a son; and if a son, then an heir of God through Christ.

As men pursue the goal of eternal life, they first enter in at the gate of repentance and baptism, thereby taking upon themselves the name of Christ. They then gain power to become his sons and daughters, to be adopted into his family, to be brethren and sisters in his kingdom. Baptism standing alone does not transform them into family members, but it opens the door to such a blessed relationship; and if men so live as to obtain the Spirit and are in fact born again, then they become members of the Holy Family.

Then, if they press forward with a steadfastness in Christ, keeping the commandments and living by every word that proceedeth forth from the mouth of God, they qualify for celestial marriage, and this gives them power to become the sons of God, meaning the Father. They thus become joint-heirs with Christ who is his natural heir. Those who are sons of God in this sense are the ones who become gods in the world to come. (D. & C. 76:54-60) They have exaltation and godhood because the family unit continues in eternity. (D. & C. 132:19-24.) Celestial marriage standing alone does not transform them into sons of God and make them joint-heirs with Christ, but it opens the door to this greatest of all blessings; and if those involved keep their covenants, they are assured of receiving the promised inheritance. Through Christ and his atoning sacrifice they "are begotten sons and daughters unto God" (D. & C. 76:24), meaning the Father. "And all those who are begotten through me," Christ says, "are partakers" of his glory. (D. & C. 93:22.)

1-5. Israel under the law of Moses was being trained and prepared for the coming of Christ so they could receive the adoption of sons. Similarly: Though we are heirs of God, destined to inherit all that the Father hath (D. & C. 84:38), yet as long as we are in mortality, we are under tutors and governors; we are being schooled and trained and prepared to use our inheritance wisely when it is finally received.

4. His Son, made of a woman] God was his Father; Mary was his mother. **Made under the law]** Christ himself, while dwelling in mortality, was subject to the law of Moses, until such time as he, the giver of the law, had fulfilled and abolished it.

5. The adoption of sons] See *Commentary I,* pp. 73-74.

6. Abba, Father] **7. An heir]** See Rom. 8:14-19.

PAUL CALLS THE GALATIANS BACK TO CHRIST

GALATIANS 4:8-20.

8 Howbeit then, when ye knew not God, ye did service unto them which by nature are no gods.

9 But now, after that ye have known God, or rather are known of God, how turn ye again to the weak and beggarly elements, whereunto ye desire again to be in bondage?

10 Ye observe d a y s , and months, and times, and years.

11 I am afraid of you, lest I have bestowed upon you labour in vain.

12 Brethren, I beseech you, be as I *am;* for I *am* as ye *are:* ye have not injured me at all.

13 Ye know how through infirmity of the flesh I preached the gospel unto you at the first.

14 And my temptation which was in my flesh ye despised not, nor rejected; but received me as

an angel of God, *even* as Christ Jesus.

15 Where is then the blessedness ye spake of? for I bear you record, that, if *it had been* possible, ye would have plucked out your own eyes, and have given them to me.

16 Am I therefore become your enemy, because I tell you the truth?

17 They zealously affect you, *but* not well; yea, they would exclude you, that ye might affect them.

18 But *is is* good to be zealously affected always in *a* good

thing, and not only when I am present with you.

19 My little children, of whom I travail in birth again until Christ be formed in you,

20 I desire to be present with you now, and to change my voice; for I stand in doubt of you.

I.V. GALATIANS 4:12.

12 Brethren, I beseech you to **be perfect as I am perfect; for I am persuaded as ye have a knowledge of me,** ye have not injured me at all **by your sayings.**

8-11. These Galatians had forsaken the world and accepted the truth; now they were leaving the gospel for the practices and rituals of the Mosaic law.

8. Before the Galatians gained the knowledge of God by revelation from the Holy Ghost, they served false gods.

10. The various feasts, fasting periods, and sabbatical years which were part of the worship of ancient Israel.

12. Be as I am] I.V. 12. **Be perfect as I am perfect]** The gospel is designed to lead men to finite perfection in this life and infinite perfection in the life to come, the one is a relative degree of perfection, the other the kind of absolute perfection possessed by Deity. See Heb. 6:1-3. And Paul here testifies that the gospel had worked in his life and that he was what every minister should be — a perfect example.

13-15. When Paul first preached to the Galatians, he was suffering from some physical affliction, and yet they received him with as much deference as though he had been an angel or the Lord himself — which is symptomatic of the way receptive investigators always bear with and rejoice in Christ's ministers.

16-18. Now they esteem him an enemy and follow Jewish teachers, whereas they should have remained true and faithful in his absence as in his presence.

19. I travail in birth again] Paul again suffers anxiety and distress as he labors for the spiritual rebirth of those who once before were born again through his teachings and testimony.

Repentance] See Acts 11:1-8. **Forgiveness]** See 2 Cor. 2:1-17.

PAUL COMPARES THE TWO COVENANTS

GALATIANS 4:21-31.

21 Tell me, ye that desire to be under the law, do ye not hear the law?

22 For it is written, that Abraham had two sons, the one by a bondmaid, the other by a freewoman.

23 But he *who was* of the bondwoman was born after the flesh; but he of the freewoman *was* by promise.

24 Which things are an allegory: for these are the two covenants; the one from the mount Sinai, which gendereth to bondage, which is Agar.

25 For this Agar is mount Sinai in Arabia, and answereth to Jerusalem which now is, and is in bondage with her children.

26 But Jerusalem which is above is free, which is the mother of us all.

27 For it is written, Rejoice, *thou* barren that bearest not; break forth and cry, thou that travailest not: for the desolate hath many more children than she which hath an husband.

28 Now we, brethren, as Isaac was, are the children of promise.

29 But as then he that was born after the flesh persecuted him *that was born* after the Spirit, even so *it is* now.

30 Nevertheless what saith the scripture? Cast out the bondwoman and her son: for the son of the bondwoman shall not be heir with the son of the freewoman.

31 So then, brethren, we are not children of the bondwoman, but of the free.

Paul here uses the life of Abraham as an allegory to dramatize the superiority of the gospel over the law of Moses — a mode of teaching designed to drive his doctrine home anew each time his hearers think of Abraham and his life.

Hagar, the bondwoman, bore Ishmael; and Sarah, the free-woman, brought forth Isaac. Ishmael was born after the flesh, while Isaac, as a child of promise, came forth after the Spirit. Hagar is thus made to represent the old covenant, the law of Moses, the covenant under which men were subject to the bondage of sin; while Sarah symbolizes the new covenant, the gospel, the covenant under which men are made free, free from bondage and sin through Christ.

Mt. Sinai, from whence the law came, and Jerusalem, from whence it is now administered, symbolize the law, and their children are in bondage. But the spiritual Jerusalem, the heavenly city of which the saints shall be citizens, is symbolized by Sarah, and she is the mother of freemen. Sarah, who was so long barren, as our spiritual mother, has now made us all, like Isaac, heirs of promise.

But it is now, as it was then, those born after the flesh war against those born of the Spirit. And as God rejected Ishmael and accepted Isaac, so does he now reject those who cleave to the law of Moses and accept those who turn to Christ.

24. The two covenants] The first is the old covenant, the law of Moses, the law of carnal commandments, the preparatory gospel, the covenant God made with Israel, through Moses, to prepare them for the second. The second is the new covenant, the everlasting covenant, the fulness of the gospel, the covenant God offers to make with all men, through Christ, to prepare them for the fulness of his glory. The old covenant was the lesser law, the new is the higher law. Moses was the mediator of the old covenant, standing between God and his people, pleading their cause, seeking to prepare them for the coming of their Messiah. Jesus is the mediator of the new covenant, standing between God and all men, pleading their cause, seeking to prepare them for that celestial inheritance reserved for the saints.

26. Jerusalem which is above] See Heb. 12:18-24.

'STAND FAST LEST YE FALL FROM GRACE'

GALATIANS 5:1-4.

1 Stand fast therefore in the liberty wherewith Christ hath made us free, and be not entangled again with the yoke of bondage.

2 Behold, I Paul say unto you, that if ye be circumcised, Christ shall profit you nothing.

3 For I testify again to every man that is circumcised, that he is a debtor to do the whole law.

4 Christ is become of no effect unto you, whosoever of you are justified by the law; ye are fallen from grace.

1. Keep the commandments; live the gospel; endure to the end. "Abide ye in the liberty wherewith ye are made free; entangle not yourselves in sin, but let your hands be clean, until the Lord comes." (D. & C. 88:86.) **Enduring to the end]** See Acts 2:41-47.

2-4. Circumcision, as a religious ordinance, is the token and sign certifying belief in, acceptance of, and conformity to the whole Mosaic system, and therefore for the Christians of that day it constituted a rejection of Christ and his gospel which replaced the law. See Acts 15:1-35.

4. Justified by the law] See Rom. 2:17-29; 3:1-20, 21-31; 4:1-25; 5:1-11.

Fallen from grace] Those who keep the commandments, striving to live by every word that proceedeth forth from the mouth of God, find favor in his sight. Their course of conduct is pleasing to him, and they are in a state of grace; that is, because of their personal righteousness Deity pours out his love, mercy, and goodness upon them in bountiful measure. They are guided by the Spirit, have power to work miracles and do good, and frequently taste the good things of the world to come.

To fall from grace is to turn from such a course of obedience so that the goodness of God departs and the former saint is left to his own power and strength. God is no longer pleased with his conduct and no longer pours out upon him special blessings. Thus the Prophet in discussing whether a person who is once in

479

grace is always in grace, or whether having fallen from grace he can return again to that blessed state, says: "If men have received the good word of God, and tasted of the powers of the world to come, if they shall fall away, it is impossible to renew them again, seeing they have crucified the Son of God afresh, and put him to an open shame; so there is a possibility of falling away; you could not be renewed again, and the power of Elijah cannot seal against this sin, for this is a reserve made in the seals and power of the priesthood." (*Teachings*, p. 339.) On the other hand, if a man is not worthy of so great a condemnation, he can repent and attain again his favored state of grace. For all faithful members of the Church, the revealed counsel is: "There is a possibility that man may fall from grace and depart from the living God; Therefore let the church take heed and pray always, lest they fall into temptation; Yea, and even let those who are sanctified take heed also." (D.& C. 20:32-34.) See Heb. 6:4-9; 10:19-39.

Grace] See Rom. 4:1-25.

SEEK FAITH, LOVE, CHRIST, AND THE SPIRIT

GALATIANS 5:5-15.

5 For we through the Spirit wait for the hope of righteousness by faith.

6 For in Jesus Christ neither circumcision availeth any thing, nor uncircumcision; but faith which worketh by love.

7 Ye did run well; who did hinder you that ye should not obey the truth?

8 This persuasion *cometh* not of him that calleth you.

9 A little leaven leaveneth the whole lump.

10 I have confidence in you through the Lord, that ye will be none otherwise minded: but he that troubleth you shall bear his judgment, whosoever he be.

11 And I, brethren, if I yet preach circumcision, why do I yet suffer persecution? then is the offence of the cross ceased.

12 I would they were even cut off which trouble you.

13 For, brethren, ye have been called unto liberty; only *use* not liberty for an occasion to the flesh, but by love serve one another.

14 For all the law is fulfilled in one word, *even* in this; Thou shalt love thy neighbour as thyself.

15 But if ye bite and devour one another, take heed that ye be not consumed one of another.

Seek righteousness — such is the whole aim, desire, and goal of true saints. And righteousness consists in conformity to the laws and ordinances of the gospel, in being submissive to the mind and will of God, in pursuing the course charted by the Son of Righteousness, who thereby became the possessor of all righteousness and thus the inheritor of that eternal life which makes him like his Father. "He who doeth the works of righteousness shall receive his reward, even peace in this world, and eternal life in the world to come." (D. & C. 59:23.) **Saints live in righteousness]** See Eph. 4:17-29.

5. Hope of righteousness] Hope of salvation. "And what is it that ye shall hope for? Behold I say unto you that ye shall have hope through the atonement of Christ and the power of his resurrection, to be raised unto life eternal, and this because of your faith in him according to the promise." (Moro. 7:41.)

6. It is not circumcision and the consequent conformity to the law of Moses that saves, nor is salvation available to the Gentiles through their systems of religion. Salvation is in Christ and comes by faith in his holy name and in no other way.

Faith . . . worketh by love] Love is the motive power underlying all things. The atonement, righteous living, all good things grow out of love — the love of God for his children and the love of his children for each other and their Creator.

7-12. 'You once kept the commandments, why don't you do so now? I, Paul, have not taught doctrines which led you astray, as that circumcision is necessary to salvation. Avoid the influence of false teachers; they shall be condemned and should be excommunicated.'

13. Called unto liberty] Called to the gospel, which is the perfect law of liberty; called to forsake the performances and rituals of the Mosaic system; called to the truth which makes men free, free from the bondage of darkness and sin.

Use not liberty for an occasion to the flesh] Use your Christian liberty properly. "Be wise in the days of your probation; strip yourselves of all uncleanness; ask not, that ye may consume it on your lusts, but ask with a firmness unshaken, that ye will yield to no temptation, but that ye will serve the true and living God." (Morm. 9:28.)

Love] See Rom. 13:8-10; *Commentary I*, pp. 229-230; 725-727; 746-749.

CRUCIFY THE FLESH AND WALK IN THE SPIRIT

GALATIANS 5:16-26.

16 *This* I say then, Walk in the Spirit, and ye shall not fulfil the lust of the flesh.

17 For the flesh lusteth against the Spirit, and the Spirit against the flesh: and these are contrary the one to the other: so that ye cannot do the things that ye would.

18 But if ye be led of the Spirit, ye are not under the law.

19 Now the works of the flesh are manifest, which are *these;* Adultery, fornication, uncleanness, lasciviousness,

20 Idolatry, witchcraft, hatred, variance, emulations, wrath, strife, seditions, heresies,

21 Envyings, murders, drunkenness, revellings, and such like: of the which I tell you before, as I have also told *you* in time past, that they which do such things shall not inherit the kingdom of God.

22 But the fruit of the Spirit is love, joy, peace, longsuffering, gentleness, goodness, faith,

23 M e e k n e s s , temperance: against such there is no law.

24 And they that are Christ's have crucified the flesh with the affections and lusts.

25 If we live in the Spirit, let us also walk in the Spirit.

26 Let us not be desirous of vain glory, provoking one another, envying one another.

In this mortal probation our objective is to follow God and flee from Satan, to overcome the world, to put off the natural man and put on Christ, to bridle our passions, to rise above "the lusts of the flesh and the things of the world," to refrain from "all manner of iniquity" (1 Ne. 22:23) — to crucify the flesh and walk in the Spirit. **Overcome the world]** See Rev. 2:1-7.

16. Walk in the Spirit] Keep the commandments after baptism and thus gain the promised companionship of the Holy Ghost.

17. There is eternal warfare between good and evil, virtue and vice, the saints and the world, the flesh and the Spirit.

18. Or: 'If you are led by the Spirit, you have left the world and become a saint.'

19. Works of the flesh] All unrighteous acts.

Adultery, fornication] See 1 Cor. 6:9-20.

Uncleanness] State of accountable persons whose sins have not been washed away in the waters of baptism, and who are not keeping the commandments so as to walk in the Spirit. "No unclean thing can inherit the kingdom of heaven." (Alma 11:37.)

Lasciviousness] See 2 Cor. 12:11-21; 13:1-4.

20. Idolatry] See 1 Cor. 6:9-20.

Witchcraft] Sorcery; intercourse with evil spirits; a system of false religion wherein mediums or other persons communicate with devils. (*Mormon Doctrine*, 2nd ed., pp. 839-840.)

Hatred] "Hate is the opposite of love; in its full force it is to abhor, abominate, and detest; in lesser degree it is merely to dislike or regard with displeasure. Hatred is a proper and holy emotion when channeled properly. 'Hate the evil, and love the good.' (Amos 5:15.)" (*Mormon Doctrine*, 2nd ed., p. 344.)

Variance] Disagreement on gospel principles; dissension and discord in the Church; unwarranted differences of opinions about the law of the Lord.

Emulations] Envious rivalries born of jealousy and worldly ambitions.

Wrath] Violent anger and rage, often leading to attempts at revenge for real or supposed wrongs.

Strife] Strugglings for superiority; altercations and conflicts.

Seditions] Acts of resistance to either church or governmental authority; stirring up of discontent against either of these authorities.

Heresies] See 1 Cor. 11:16-19.

21. Envyings] Begrudging discontent at the excellence and good fortune of others. "Preach against all lyings, and deceivings, and envyings, and strifes, and malice, and revilings, and stealing, robbing, plundering, murdering, committing adultery, and all manner of lasciviousness, crying that these things ought not so to be." (Alma. 16:18.)

Murders] See 1 John 3:10-18.

Drunkenness] See 1 Cor. 6:9-20.

Revellings] Acts of unseemly merrymaking, carousing, and conviviality.

22. Fruit of the Spirit] Attributes of God.

Love] See Rom. 13:8-10.

Joy] A state of happiness and bliss. "Men are, that they might have joy." (2 Ne. 2:25.)

Peace] Both freedom from war and an inner sense of tranquillity and satisfaction.

Longsuffering] Patient and extended endurance of offenses.

Gentleness] Refinement, gentility, and honorableness.

Goodness] Righteousness, virtue, and excellence.

Faith] See Heb. 11:1-3.

23. Meekness] "The meek are the godfearing and the righteous. They are the ones who willingly conform to the gospel standards, thus submitting their wills to the will of the Lord." (*Mormon Doctrine*, 2nd ed., p. 474.) "Blessed are the meek, for they shall inherit the earth" (3 Ne. 12:5), meaning in that day when celestial beings abide forever on its surface. (D. & C. 88:16-32.)

Temperance] A course of moderation and control of the passions and appetites; also, abstinence from the use of intoxicants.

24. 'The saints have overcome the world.'

25. 'If we are members of the Church, let us be guided by the Holy Ghost.'

26. Vainglory] Excessive pride in one's own accomplishments, abilities, or achievements, as manifest through boasting and vaunting of one's self.

BEAR ONE ANOTHER'S BURDENS

GALATIANS 6:1-6.

1 Brethren, if a man be overtaken in a fault, ye which are spiritual, restore such an one in the spirit of meekness; considering thyself, lest thou also be tempted.

2 Bear ye one another's burdens, and so fulfil the law of Christ.

3 For if a man think himself to be something, when he is nothing, he deceiveth himself.

4 But let every man prove his own work, and then shall he have rejoicing in himself alone, and not in another.

5 For every man shall bear his own burden.

6 Let him that is taught in the word communicate unto him that teacheth in all good things.

1. Christ came to save sinners; the gospel is designed to restore erring saints to grace and perfection; the Lord does not desire the failure, excommunication, and spiritual death of his people. The program of the Church is to restore, renew, and reactivate, to bring all who will come to that full fellowship which leads to eternal life.

2. As members of the family of Christ, church members treat each other as brothers and sisters. One of the express promises made in the waters of baptism is: 'I covenant to bear the burdens of my brethren in the Church, that they may be light.' (Mosiah 18:8.) **Welfare plan]** See Acts 4:32-37.

The law of Christ] The gospel. (D. & C. 88:21.)

4. 'Test yourselves and see if you are keeping the commandments and can therefore rejoice in your own good works.'

5. Men are accountable for their own sins.

6. Communication is a two-way street; both teacher and learner must be enlightened by the Spirit, in which event, "he that preacheth and he that receiveth, understand one another, and both are edified and rejoice together." (D. & C. 50:22.)

'AS YE SOW, SO SHALL YE REAP'

GALATIANS 6:7-18.

7 Be not deceived; God is not mocked: for whatsoever a man soweth, that shall be also reap.

8 For he that soweth to his flesh shall of the flesh reap corruption; but he that soweth to the Spirit shall of the Spirit reap life everlasting.

9 And let us not be weary in well doing: for in due season we shall reap, if we faint not.

10 As we have therefore opportunity, let us do good unto all *men*, especially unto them who are of the household of faith.

11 Ye see how large a letter I have written unto you with mine own hand.

12 As many as desire to make a fair show in the flesh, they constrain you to be circumcised; only lest they should suffer persecution for the cross of Christ.

13 For neither they themselves who are circumcised keep the law; but desire to have you circumcised, that they may glory in your flesh.

14 But God forbid t h a t I should glory, save in the cross of our Lord Jesus Christ, by whom the world is crucified unto me, and I unto the world.

15 For in Christ Jesus neither circumcision availeth any thing, nor uncircumcision, but a new creature.

16 And as many as walk according to this rule, peace *be* on them, and mercy, and upon the Israel of God.

17 From henceforth let no man trouble me: for I bear in my body the marks of the Lord Jesus.

18 Brethren, the grace of our Lord Jesus Christ *be* with your spirit. Amen.

7-10. The law of the harvest! Men (the saints included!) reap what they sow! These Galatians are in the Church; they have received Christ and his gospel; they are Paul's converts; to some extent at least they are in harmony with God and his laws. But salvation does not come to them because they believed, because they once confessed the Lord Jesus with their lips, because of the grace of God alone; they are not justified by faith only, as such is generally understood and taught in modern Christendom.

But in addition to accepting Christ, in addition to baptism and the receipt of the Holy Ghost, they are now required to

486

keep the commandments, to overcome the world, to "press forward with a steadfastness in Christ, having a perfect brightness of hope, and a love of God and of all men." They are now required to feast "upon the word of Christ, and endure to the end." (2 Ne. 31:20.)

Members of the Church who keep the commandments shall be saved; those who disobey them shall not be so blessed. Salvation is not a matter of belief alone, of grace alone, of the cross of Christ only; it is all this coupled with "obedience to the laws and ordinances of the Gospel." (Third Article of Faith.)

8. Corruption] Spiritual death. **Life everlasting]** Eternal life. See 2 Tim. 1:1-12.

9. We shall reap] 'We shall gain eternal life.' **If we faint not]** 'If we endure to the end.'

10. Though the saints, as their strength and circumstances permit, do good to all men, their special obligation is to bless and help their fellow saints, the members of their church-family.

12-14. Those Galatian Saints who advocated and practiced circumcision did so to avoid persecution; they were not in fact attempting to keep the whole law of Moses, of which circumcision was the symbol. But because they were compromising the gospel with the law of Moses, they were not and could not center their whole hearts on Christ and the salvation made possible through his atoning sacrifice.

15. The gospel is for all, Israel of that day who are circumcised and the Gentiles who are not. Salvation, regardless of circumcision, comes to all who accept Christ, are baptized, receive the Holy Ghost, and are born again, becoming new creatures, alive to the things of the Spirit.

16. Peace and mercy are bestowed upon the obedient. (*Mormon Doctrine*, 2nd ed., pp. 483-486.)

17. The marks of the Lord Jesus] The scars in Paul's flesh which testified of his steadfastness in the face of persecution (2 Cor. 11:23-27); also, the holy symbols typifying faith in Christ and his gospel, which are borne by all the faithful.

The Epistle of Paul the Apostle to the Ephesians

Ephesians is an epistle for all the world, for Jew and Gentile, for husband and wife, for parent and child, for master and servant. It was the mind and will of God in Paul's day; it is the voice of inspiration in our day; it is an epistle of universal appeal and application.

Ephesians proclaims the supremacy of God, the glory of his gospel, the dignity and identity of the Church through which salvation is offered to man. It contains some of Paul's best writing, and is a document that deals with fundamentals, with the gospel of God in all its saving glory.

In it, among other things, the Apostle teaches:

That the saints of God are foreordained to receive the gospel with all of its ordinances, glories, and blessings;

That the same gospel had in his day shall be restored in the dispensation of the fulness of times;

That through obedience to the gospel the saints receive the Holy Spirit of Promise and are sealed up unto eternal life;

That God and Christ and the gospel are known only by revelation;

That salvation comes by the grace and goodness of God and is for all men, Jew and Gentile alike;

That the gospel is administered through one true Church, the Church which receives revelation, the Church directed by living apostles and prophets; and

That because of gospel law Christ's people live righteously, perfect their families, and qualify for exaltation.

SAINTS FOREORDAINED TO RECEIVE THE GOSPEL

EPHESIANS 1:1-8.

1 Paul, an apostle of Jesus Christ by the will of God, to the saints which are at Ephesus, and to the faithful in Christ Jesus:

2 Grace *be* to you, and peace, from God our Father, and *from* the Lord Jesus Christ.

3 Blessed *be* the God and Father of our Lord Jesus Christ, who hath blessed us with all spiritual blessings in heavenly *places* in Christ:

4 According as he hath chosen us in him before the foundation of the world, that we should be holy and without blame before him in love:

5 Having predestinated us unto the adoption of children by Jesus Christ to himself, according to the good pleasure of his will,

6 To the praise of the glory of his grace, wherein he hath made up accepted in the beloved.

7 In whom we have redemption through his blood, the forgiveness of sins, according to the riches of his grace;

8 Wherein he hath abounded toward us in all wisdom and prudence;

What blessings are the saints of God foreordained to receive in this life? Paul here lists the following: 1. All spiritual blessings, which of necessity includes the companionship of the Holy Ghost and the gifts of the Spirit in this life, to say nothing of eternal life in the realms ahead; 2. The everlasting gospel; 3. Baptism; 4. Membership in the Church; 5. The gift of the Holy Ghost; 6. Redemption from the spiritual fall, including the remission of sins; and 7. Adoption into the family of God the Father, as sons of God and therefore as joint-heirs with Christ his natural Son. **Foreordination]** See Rom. 8:28-34a.

1. Apostle] See Acts 13:50-52; 14:1-7; 1 Cor. 4:1-21. **Saints]** See Philip. 1:1-26.

2-3. Two Gods, not one! Since true religion centers in a knowledge of the true God, Paul, wisely, begins each of his epistles by talking about the Father and the Son. Only when men know the true and living God, and Jesus Christ whom he hath sent, who also is God, can their worship lead them to eternal life. (John 17:3.)

490

3. All spiritual blessings] Everything which God, in his infinite wisdom and by his grace and goodness, has, through the gospel, showered upon the saints, and more particularly that blessing, eternal life, which shall be enjoyed in heavenly places.

3-4. Thus, the saints came into this world with the promise of eternal life, a promise given them in pre-existence, before the foundation of the world.

4. He] God the Father. **Hath chosen us]** Hath chosen, elected, and foreordained us, his saints. **Before the foundation of the world]** While we were yet in pre-existence. **That we should be holy and without blame before him in love]** That we should receive his gospel and gain membership in his Church and, through baptism of water and the Spirit, have our sins remitted and thus become clean and spotless before him. (3 Ne. 27:19-21.)

5. Having predestinated us] Having foreordained us. **Unto the adoption of children by Jesus Christ to himself]** To be adopted into the family of God the Father, as the sons of God, thus inheriting, receiving, and possessing the fulness of his kingdom, along with his natural born Son Jesus — all of which comes to pass because of Christ's atonement. **Sons of God]** See Gal. 4:1-7. **Joint-heirs with Christ]** See Rom. 8:14-19.

6. He hath . . . us accepted in the beloved] God hath accepted us as his sons along with his Beloved Son.

7. In whom] In Christ. **We have redemption through his blood, the forgiveness of sins]** We are redeemed from the "spiritual fall" and become alive in Christ through repentance and baptism. (D. & C. 29:43-44.)

GOSPEL TO BE RESTORED IN LATTER DAYS

EPHESIANS 1:9-12.

9 Having made known unto us the mystery of his will, according to his good pleasure which he hath purposed in himself:

10 That in the dispensation of the fulness of times he might gather together in one all things in Christ, both which are in heaven, and which are on earth; *even* in him:

491

11 In whom also we have obtained an inheritance, being predestinated according to the purpose of him who worketh all things after the counsel of his own will:

12 That we should be to the praise of his glory, who first trusted in Christ.

The ancient saints understood, Paul here says, two great truths which were and are mysteries to the carnal mind:

1. How God called, elected, and foreordained his chosen saints to receive blessings and honor, purity and perfection, sonship and eternal life in that day; and

2. How he would yet in a future day, a day when all gospel dispensations ran into one, call other chosen ones who also had been foreordained to receive, by the grace of God, these same glorious blessings.

9. Having made known unto us] By revelation the Ephesian Saints knew of the doctrine of foreordination, as it operated in their day and as it would operate in the dispensation of the fulness of times.

The mystery of his will] That which is hidden from the world but is revealed to the saints relative to the plans and purposes of Deity.

10. The everlasting gospel is revealed or dispensed from heaven in various ages, periods, or dispensations. In each of these God speaks, angels minister among men, and the gift of the Holy Ghost is poured out upon the faithful. (Moses 5:58-59.) In each there are legal administrators who hold the higher priesthood, who preach the gospel, work miracles, and perform the ordinances of salvation so they will be binding on earth and in heaven. And in each there are special commissions and endowments that pertain to the age and period involved.

The dispensation of the fulness of times is the dispensation of the fulness of dispensations, it is the time or age of the fulness of times or ages. In other others, it is the dispensation of restoration, the one in which all things possessed and enjoyed in any past age have or shall be given again. This final great dispensation commenced in the Spring of 1820 with the appearance of the Father and the Son to Joseph Smith, to whom also the subsequent revelations came pursuant to which the Church and kingdom of God on earth was once again established. The keys or presiding authority over this final gospel dispensation rested with Peter, James, and John and were by them conferred upon Joseph Smith and Oliver Cowdery in about June of 1829. Thereafter the Lord said that the gospel revealed through Joseph Smith was given "for the last times; and for the fulness of times, in the which," the Lord continued, "I will gather together in one all things, both which are in heaven, and which are on earth." (D. & C. 27:13; 128:18-21; *Mormon Doctrine*, 2nd ed., pp. 200-202.)

Gospel] See Rom. 1:1-17. **Restoration of the gospel]** See Rev. 14:6-7.

11. In whom] In Christ. **We have obtained an inheritance]** We have gained an inheritance in his earthly kingdom, which is the Church, and shall hereafter abide in his heavenly kingdom, which is the celestial kingdom. **Being predestinated]** Being foreordained to inherit such.

SAINTS SEALED BY THE HOLY SPIRIT OF PROMISE

EPHESIANS 1:13-14.

13 In whom ye also *trusted*, after that ye heard the word of truth, the gospel of your salvation: in whom also after that ye believed, ye were sealed with that holy Spirit of promise,

14 Which is the earnest of our inheritance until the redemption of the purchased possession, unto the praise of his glory.

"The Holy Spirit of Promise is the Holy Spirit promised the saints, or in other words the Holy Ghost. This name-title is used in connection with the sealing and ratifying power of the Holy Ghost, that is, the power given him to ratify and approve the righteous acts of men so that those acts will be binding on earth and in heaven. 'All covenants, contracts, bonds, obligations, oaths, vows, performances, connections, associations, or expectations,' must be sealed by the Holy Spirit of Promise, if they are to have 'efficacy, virtue, or force in and after the resurrection from the dead; for all contracts that are not made unto this end have an end when men are dead.' (D. & C. 132:7.)

"To seal is to ratify, to justify, or to approve. Thus an act which is sealed by the Holy Spirit of Promise is one which is ratified by the Holy Ghost; it is one which is approved by the Lord; and the person who has taken the obligation upon himself is justified by the Spirit in the thing he has done. The ratifying seal of approval is put upon an act only if those entering the contract are worthy as a result of personal righteousness to receive the divine approbation. They 'are sealed by the Holy Spirit of promise, which the Father sheds forth upon all those who are just and true.' (D. & C. 76:53.) If they are not just and true and worthy the ratifying seal is withheld. . . .

"Even if a person progresses to that state of near-perfection in which his calling and election is made sure, in which he is 'sealed up unto eternal life' (D. & C. 131:5; 132:18-26), in which he receives 'the promise . . . of eternal life' (D. & C. 88:3-4), in which he is 'sealed up unto the day of redemption' (D. & C. 124:124; Eph. 1:13) — yet with it all, these great promises are secured only if the 'performances' are sealed by the Holy Spirit of Promise." (*Mormon Doctrine*, 2nd ed., pp. 361-362.)

Justification] See Rom. 3:21-31.

13-14. Joseph Smith said that the particular seal placed upon these Ephesian Saints was that their callings and elections had been made sure. (*Teachings*, pp. 149-151.) Theirs was the same promise and assurance given certain worthy persons in this dispensation to whom the Lord said: "I now send upon you another Comforter, even upon you my friends, that it may abide in your hearts, even the Holy Spirit of promise; which other Comforter is the same that I promised unto my disciples, as is recorded in the testimony of John. This Comforter is the promise which I give unto you of eternal life, even the glory of the celestial kingdom; Which glory is that of the church of the Firstborn, even of God, the holiest of all, through Jesus Christ his Son." (D. & C. 88:3-5.)

14. Earnest of our inheritance] Earnest is something of value given to bind a bargain. Here God himself, by giving the ratifying seal of the Spirit, is guaranteeing compliance with his own covenant and promise, the promise of an inheritance of eternal life.

The redemption of the purchased possession] Christ has purchased his saints, that is, those who are his have been "bought with a price" (1 Cor. 6:20), the price being his own "precious blood." (1 Pet. 1:19.) Now, these Ephesian Saints, building upon the foundation of our Lord's atoning sacrifice, have made their callings and elections sure; they have, in effect, worked out their salvation; they have purchased, by good works, an everlasting inheritance with him who purchased them with his blood. (D. & C. 132:26.)

Calling and election made sure] See 2 Pet. 1:1-19.

SAINTS KNOW GOD AND CHRIST BY REVELATION

EPHESIANS 1:15-23.

15 Wherefore I also, after I heard of your faith in the Lord Jesus, and love unto all the saints,

16 Cease not to give thanks for you, making mention of you in my prayers;

17 That the God of our Lord Jesus Christ, the Father of glory, may give unto you the spirit of wisdom a n d revelation in the knowledge of him:

18 The eyes of your understanding being enlightened; that ye may know what is the hope of his calling, and what the riches of the glory of his inheritance in the saints,

19 And what *is* the exceeding greatness of his power to us-ward who believe, according to the working of his mighty power,

20 Which he wrought in Christ, when he raised him from the dead, and set *him* at his own right hand in the heavenly *places*,

21 Far above all principality, and power, and might, and dominion, and every name that is named, not only in this world, but also in that which is to come:

22 And hath put all *things* under his feet, and gave him *to be* the head over all *things* to the church,

23 Which is his body, the fulness of him that filleth all in all.

17. God stands revealed or he remains forever unknown. There is no way to know God but by revelation. He cannot be discovered by science or found in the laboratory. Man may discover his laws and the manifestations he has left of himself. But God himself, our Eternal Father, the holy being who created all things, who governs and upholds the universe, he is known only by revelation and only to those to whom he reveals himself. **God]** See Acts 17:15-34. **Holy Ghost reveals Jesus is the Christ]** See 1 Cor. 12:1-3.

The God of our Lord Jesus Christ] God the Father, our God, the Father of spirits, including Christ's, the same God whom Christ worships and by whose power Christ himself worked out his own salvation and gained the fulness of his Father's kingdom. How apt and reverential, thus, for the risen Lord to say: "I ascend unto my Father, and your Father; and to my God, and your God." (John 20:17.)

18-23. There is no language to describe the grace and goodness of God. No tongue can utter the praise and adoration due him who created us and who then, through the sacrifice of his Son, redeemed us from death and opened the door to us for an inheritance of exaltation in his kingdom. Paul struggles with this problem of proper expression. He speaks of the riches of God's glory; of the exceeding greatness of his power; of Christ ascending above all principalities, powers, mights, and dominions, and above every name and thing that exists on earth and in eternity; of his thereby sitting down on the right hand of God himself; and also of Christ's body, the Church, gaining a like eminence with him, and thus also filling all in all.

But the full significance of all this is beyond mortal comprehension. It can only "be seen and understood by the power of the Holy Spirit, which God bestows on those who love him, and purify themselves before him; To whom he grants this privilege of seeing and knowing for themselves; That through the power and manifestation of the Spirit, while in the flesh, they may be able to bear his presence in the world of glory. And to God and the Lamb be glory, and honor, and dominion forever and ever. Amen." (D. & C. 76:116-119.)

18. The eyes of your understanding being enlightened] 'Your spirit eyes being opened.' Natural things are seen by the natural eye, spiritual things by the spiritual eye. Hence, the account of the Lord's appearance to Joseph Smith and Oliver Cowdery in the Kirtland Temple begins: "The veil was taken from our minds, and the eyes of our understanding were opened. We saw the Lord standing upon the breastwork of the pulpit, before us." (D. & C. 110:1-2.)

21. The faithful saints "shall inherit thrones, kingdoms, principalities, and powers, dominions, all heights and depths." (D. & C. 132:19.) And above them is Christ, who sitteth at the right hand of the Father!

Every name that is named] See Philip. 2:9-11; Acts 4:1-12.

23. The fulness of him that filleth all in all] In the Lectures on Faith, Joseph Smith describes the Father and the Son as "filling all in all" because the Son, having overcome, has "received a fulness of the glory of the Father," and possesses "the same mind with the Father." Then he announces the conclusion to which Paul here only alludes: "And all those who keep his commandments shall grow up from grace to grace, and become heirs of the heavenly kingdom, and joint-heirs with Jesus Christ; possessing the same mind, being transformed into the same image or likeness, even the express image of him who fills all in all; being filled with the fulness of his glory, and become one in him, even as the Father, Son and Holy Spirit are one." (*Lectures on Faith*, pp. 50-51.)

"BY GRACE ARE YE SAVED THROUGH FAITH"

EPHESIANS 2:1-10.

1 And you *hath he quickened*, who were dead in trespasses and sins;

2 Wherein in time past ye walked according to the course of this world, according to the prince of the power of the air, the spirit that now worketh in the children of disobedience:

3 Among whom also we all had our conversation in times past in the lusts of our flesh, fulfilling the desires of the flesh and of the mind; and were by nature the children of wrath, even as others.

4 But God, who is rich in mercy, for his great love wherewith he loved us,

5 Even when we were dead in sins, hath quickened us together with Christ, (by grace ye are saved;)

6 And hath raised *us* up together, and made *us* sit together in heavenly *places* in Christ Jesus:

7 That in the ages to come he might show the exceeding riches of his grace in *his* kindness toward us through Christ Jesus.

8 For by grace are ye saved through faith; and that not of yourselves: *it is* the gift of God:

9 Not of works, lest any man should boast.

10 For we are his workmanship, created in Christ Jesus unto good works, which God hath before ordained that we should walk in them.

Salvation in all its forms, kinds, and degrees comes by the grace of God. That is, because of his love, mercy, and condescension, God our Father ordained the plan and system of salvation which would "bring to pass the immortality and eternal life of man." (Moses 1:39.) Pursuant to this plan he sent his Only Begotten Son into the world to work out the infinite and eternal atoning sacrifice.

Then Our Lord, in turn, also because of his love, mercy, and condescension, performed the appointed labor so that all men are "raised in immortality," and those who believe and obey the gospel law inherit "eternal life." (D. & C. 29:43-44.) The faithful gain a forgiveness of their sins and are reconciled to God because they believe and obey his laws.

Men are thus saved by grace alone, in the sense of being resurrected; they are saved by grace coupled with obedience, in the sense of gaining eternal life. The gospel plan is to save men in the celestial kingdom, and hence Paul teaches salvation by grace through faith, through obedience, through accepting Christ, through keeping the commandments. Thus Nephi writes, "Be reconciled to God; for we know that it is by grace that we are saved, after all we can do" (2 Ne. 25:23), and Moroni records, "Come unto Christ, and be perfected in him, and deny yourselves of all ungodliness; and if ye shall deny yourselves of all ungodliness and love God with all your might, mind and strength, then is his grace sufficient for you, that by his grace ye may be perfect in Christ." (Moro. 10:32.)

Grace] See Rom. 4:1-25. **Justification]** See Rom. 3:21-31. **Falling from grace]** See Heb. 10:19-39.

1. You hath he quickened] 'You are born again; you have received the Holy Ghost; you are alive in Christ; you are members of the Church; you are under covenant to keep the commandments and work the works of righteousness.'

2. Prince of the power of the air] Satan; an idiomatic expression indicating Satan's rule and dominance in "this world," in, as it were, the very air around us.

Children of disobedience] Those who walk after the manner of the world, who are carnal, sensual, and devilish, who are subject to the lusts of the flesh.

3. By nature the children of wrath] Man by nature is subject to the lusts and appetites of mortality and so remains until he crucifies the flesh and becomes a new creature in Christ. "For the natural man is an enemy to God, and has been from the fall of Adam, and will be, forever and ever, unless he yields to the enticings of the Holy Spirit, and putteth off the natural man and becometh a saint through the atonement of Christ the Lord, and becometh as a child, submissive, meek, humble, patient, full of love, willing to submit to all things which the Lord seeth fit to inflict upon him, even as a child doth submit to his father." (Mosiah 3:19.)

4. Mercy . . . love] Elements of grace.

5. When we were dead in sins] 'Before we joined the Church and were baptized for the remission of sins.' **Hath quickened us together with Christ]** 'Hath made us new creatures of the Holy Ghost, so that we are now born again and have become alive in Christ.' **By grace ye are saved]** How else could salvation possibly come? Can man save himself? Can he resurrect himself? Can he create a celestial kingdom and decree his own admission thereto? Salvation must and does originate with God, and if man is to receive it, God must bestow it upon him, which bestowal is a manifestation of grace.

6. In heavenly places] In the celestial kingdom.

8. By grace are ye saved through faith] 'By grace are ye saved through faith in the Lord Jesus Christ, through repentance and baptism for the remission of sins, through receipt of the gift of the Holy Ghost, through keeping the commandments after baptism and thus enduring to the end.' **And that not of yourselves]** No man has power to save himself anymore than he has power to resurrect himself.

9. Not of works] Salvation does not come by the works and performances of the law of Moses, nor by "circumcision," nor by "the law of commandments contained in ordinances" (as Paul specifies in verses 11 and 15), nor does it come by any good works standing alone. No matter how righteous a man might be, no matter how great and extensive his good works, he could not save himself. Salvation is in Christ and comes through his atonement. God through Christ reconciles man to himself. But building on the atonement man must perform the works of righteousness to merit salvation, as verse 10 and the whole passage testify.

10. Good works] Keeping the commandments after baptism. **God hath before ordained that we should walk in them]** 'God fore-ordained the saints to keep the commandments,' a necessary requisite to the receipt of the foreordained promise of eternal life. See Ephesians 1:9-12.

BLOOD OF CHRIST SAVES JEW AND GENTILE ALIKE

EPHESIANS 2:11-18.

11 Wherefore remember, that ye *being* in time past Gentiles in the flesh, who are called Uncircumcision by that which is called the Circumcision in the flesh made by hands;

12 That at that time ye were without Christ, being aliens from the commonwealth of Israel, and strangers from the covenants of promise, having no hope, and without God in the world:

13 But now in Christ Jesus ye who sometimes were far off are made nigh by the blood of Christ.

14 For he is our peace, who hath made both one, and hath

broken down the middle wall of partition *between us;*

15 Having abolished in his flesh the enmity, *even* the law of commandments *contained* in ordinances; for to make in himself of twain one new man, *so* making peace;

16 And that he might reconcile both unto God in one body by the cross, having slain the enmity thereby:

17 And came and preached peace to you which were afar off, and to them that were nigh.

18 For through him we both have access by one Spirit unto the Father.

Of olden times the Jews had the law, the covenants, the promises, and the hope of a coming Messiah, through whose atoning grace salvation would be possible. Also of olden times the Gentiles had none of this knowledge; they were without a true understanding of God and knew nothing of salvation. And such had been the state of these Ephesians.

But now Messiah-Christ has come. The law possessed by the Jews, which pointed every whit to that coming is fulfilled, and hence no longer acts to point men toward salvation. Accordingly, all men now have the same standing before God, and salvation is available to Jew and Gentile alike, through the shedding of the blood of Christ.

Christ has thus made peace between the Jew and Gentile; the two nations have become one in Christ; both are reconciled to God on the same basis, that of Christ's atonement; and both have access to the Father by the same Spirit, the Holy Ghost which is poured out upon the faithful without reference to nationality or kinship. As Nephi expressed it, the Lord God inviteth "all to come unto him and partake of his goodness; and he denieth none that come unto him, black and white, bond and free, male and female; and he remembereth the heathen; and all are alike unto God, both Jew and Gentile." (2 Ne. 26:33.) **Law of Moses]** Acts 15:1-35.

11. Uncircumcision . . . Circumcision] Symbolical names for Gentiles and Jews.

12. Covenants of promise] See Rom. 9:1-33.

Without God in the world] Those who did not belong to the true Church, who had not been baptized and received the gift of the Holy Ghost, who had not been born again, who had not received the knowledge of God by revelation. After making his famous pronouncement that "wickedness never was happiness," Alma said: "All men that are in a state of nature, or I would say, in a carnal state, are in the gall of bitterness and in the bonds of iniquity; they are without God in the world, and they have gone contrary to the nature of God; therefore, they are in a state contrary to the nature of happiness." (Alma 41:11.)

13. The blood of Christ] See Heb. 10:1-18.

14. Middle wall of partition] "Perhaps an allusion to the warning barrier which marked off the Court of the Gentiles from the higher level of the Court of the Women in the Temple. It was death for a Gentile to pass the barrier." (*Dummelow*, p. 962.) Thus, even as that wall, now rejected of God, no longer separated Jews and Gentiles, so no gospel blessings available to the Jews are withheld from the Gentiles.

16. Reconcile both unto God] See 2 Cor. 5:12-21.

GENTILES ARE FELLOW HEIRS WITH ISRAEL

EPHESIANS 2:19-22; 3:1-13.

19 Now therefore ye are no more strangers and foreigners, but fellowcitizens with the saints, and of the household of God;

20 And are built upon the foundation of the apostles and prophets, Jesus Christ himself being the chief corner *stone;*

21 In whom all the building fitly framed together groweth unto an holy temple in the Lord:

22 In whom ye also are builded together for an habitation of God through the Spirit.

1 For this cause I Paul, the prisoner of Jesus Christ for you Gentiles,

2 If ye have heard of the dispensation of the grace of God which is given me to you-ward:

3 How that by revelation he made known unto me the mystery; (as I wrote afore in few words,

4 Whereby, when ye read, ye may understand my knowledge in the mystery of Christ)

5 Which in other ages was not made known unto the sons of men, as it is now revealed unto his holy apostles and prophets by the Spirit;

6 That the Gentiles should be fellowheirs, and of the same body, and partakers of his promise in Christ by the gospel:

7 Whereof I was made a minister, according to the gift of the grace of God given unto me by the effectual working of his power.

8 Unto me, who am less than the least of all saints, is this grace given, that I should preach among the Gentiles the unsearchable riches of Christ;

9 And to make all *men* see what *is* the fellowship of the mystery, which from the beginning of the world hath been hid in God, who created all things by Jesus Christ:

10 To the intent that now unto the principalities and powers in heavenly *places* might be known by the church the manifold wisdom of God,

11 According to the eternal purpose which he purposed in Christ Jesus our Lord:

12 In whom we have boldness and access with confidence by the faith of him.

13 Wherefore I desire that ye faint not at my tribulations for you, which is your glory.

I.V. EPHESIANS 3:1-3.

1 For this cause, I, Paul, **am** the prisoner of Jesus Christ **among** you Gentiles.

2 **For** the dispensation of the grace of God which is given me to you-ward;

3 **As ye have heard** that by revelation he made known unto me the mystery of Christ; as I wrote before in few words;

In Paul's day we see the change from the more perfect family Church to the less perfect world Church. From Adam to Christ, God operated through chosen families; since then the chosen seed has been swallowed up in the hosts and nations of men. Adam and his descendants had the gospel and the Church; they were governed in both civic and ecclesiastical matters by the patriarchal system. When any branch of Adam's family apostatized, Deity still left his civic and ecclesiastical government with selected family groups. In due course Abraham and his seed were chosen out of all mankind to possess the fulness of the Lord's law. Then the family of Israel, for a millennium and a half, was favored and chosen above all others.

But now there is to be a new era, an era in which God sends the gospel to all the world, and every creature is to hear it in due course. True the family concept is to be preserved, and those who receive the gospel are to be adopted into the family of Israel as fellow heirs with those who inherited the right to the gospel because of blood lineage. But civic government is to pass from a patriarchal system to a national system, and only the spiritual blessings of the patriarchal order are to be retained. The Church itself is no longer to be a family Church. Now we are to have a world Church.

Israel] See Acts 1:1-8. **Gentiles]** See Acts 10:21-35. **Gospel gifts to Gentiles]** See Rom. 15:8-33.

2:19. Strangers and foreigners] Nonmembers of the Church, members of other kingdoms than the Lord's. **Fellowcitizens with the saints]** Members of the Church, citizens in the kingdom of God on earth. **Household of God]** Those who dwell together as brethren under one roof, the roof of the gospel.

20. Christ established his Church upon the rock of revelation. (See *Commentary I*, pp. 380-390.) Apostles and prophets, as the revelators of God's will to the Church, are therefore the foundation upon which the whole structure of revealed religion rests. Unless a Church has apostles and prophets who receive revelation from the Lord and who hold the keys of the kingdom of God on earth, it is not the Lord's Church. **Apostles]** See 1 Cor. 4:1-21.

20-22. In the true Church, Christ is the chief cornerstone, the apostles and prophets are the foundation, other officers and members are fitly framed into the structure, and the building itself become a holy temple where God dwells by the power of his Spirit.

22. Habitation of God] God dwells in the true Church in that his Spirit is there. Where the Spirit of God is not, there the true Church is not.

3:2. Dispensation of the grace of God] An outpouring, by direct revelation to an individual, of knowledge of the grace and goodness of God in making salvation available through Jesus Christ.

3. The mystery . . . 5. Is now revealed] What mystery? That the gospel in former ages was reserved primarily for the members of certain families, but that now it is to go to all the world.

5-6. Though prophets in former ages had known that the gospel would go to the Gentiles, this knowledge was now coming with greater clarity and perfection to the living apostles and prophets in the Church. Similarly, though ancient prophets knew of the restoration of the gospel in latter-days, inspired persons in the Church today have a more perfect knowledge of what is actually taking place as part of that restoration because they are participants in it.

8. The unsearchable riches of Christ] The incomprehensible and thus inexplorable blessings available because of Christ and his atoning sacrifice, including those things "which surpass all understanding in glory, and in might, and in dominion." (D. & C. 76:114.)

9-10. 'Now that the gospel is going to the Gentiles, everyone can see that it is for all men, while those who accept it shall also know of heavenly things.'

LOVE CHRIST AND GAIN FULNESS OF GOD

EPHESIANS 3:14-21.

14 For this cause I bow my knees unto the Father of our Lord Jesus Christ,

15 Of whom the whole family in heaven and earth is named,

16 That he would grant you, according to the riches of his glory, to be strengthened with might by his Spirit in the inner man;

17 That Christ may dwell in your hearts by faith; that ye, being rooted and grounded in love,

18 May be able to comprehend with all saints what *is* the breadth, and length, and depth, and height;

19 And to know the love of Christ, which passeth knowledge, that ye might be filled with all the fulness of God.

20 Now unto him that is able to do exceeding abundantly above all that we ask or think, according to the power that worketh in us,

21 Unto him *be* glory in the church by Christ Jesus throughout all ages, world without end. Amen.

14. Prayers are made to God the Father.

15. Family in heaven] God the Father has a family in heaven. Indeed he is the Father because he has children, spirit offspring, progeny born in his family.

16. Always, invariably, and everlastingly the chief and foremost prayer of righteous persons is that they may have the Spirit of the Lord. When the Nephite Twelve "prayed to the Father in the name of Jesus, . . . They did pray for that which they most desired; and they desired that the Holy Ghost should be given unto them." (3 Ne. 19:8-9.)

17-19. Those who love Christ, and signify the same by keeping his commandments, advance and progress until they gain the fulness of the Father — until they know what he knows; possess the character, perfections and attributes embodied in him; have all power, might, and dominion, as he does; and thereby fulfil the command to be perfect even as he is perfect. (Matt. 5:48; D. & C. 93:1-22; 132:19-24.) See Col. 2:1-9.

IS THERE MORE THAN ONE TRUE CHURCH?

EPHESIANS 4:1-6.

1 I therefore, the prisoner of the Lord, beseech you that ye walk worthy of the vocation wherewith ye are called,

2 With all lowliness and meekness, with longsuffering, forbearing one another in love;

3 Endeavouring to keep the unity of the Spirit in the bond of peace.

4 *There is* one body, and one Spirit, even as ye are called in one hope of your calling;

5 One Lord, one faith, one baptism,

6 One God and Father of all, who *is* above all, and through all, and in you all.

I.V. EPHESIANS 4:4.

4 **In** one body, and one Spirit, even as ye are called in one hope of your calling;

There is no more self-evident truth in this world, there is nothing in all eternity more obvious than that there is and can be only one true Church. A true Church does not create itself any more than man creates God, or resurrects himself, or establishes for himself a celestial heaven. All churches may be false, but only one can be true, simply because religion comes from God, and God is not the author of confusion.

Truth is only one thing, and every truth is in harmony with every other truth. If one church proclaims that God is an exalted Man and another says he is an incorporeal spirit essence; if one church teaches that baptism is essential to salvation and another considers it of no importance whatever; if one church says salvation consists in the continuation of the family unit in eternity and another affirms there is no marrying or giving in marriage in heaven; and so on and so on, through a thousand gospel doctrines, something is wrong with somebody's religious views.

Just as there is only one true science, or one true mathematics, so there is one true God, one true Church, one true gospel, one true baptism, one true celestial marriage, and on and on. When the Lord restored the gospel and set up his Church in modern times, naming it The Church of Jesus Christ of Latter-day Saints, by his own voice he described it as, "the only true and living church upon the face of the whole earth." (D. & C. 1:30.) In contrast, all other churches are man-made, which accords with the instruction given the Prophet in the First Vision that he "must join none of them, for they were all wrong." (Jos. Smith 2:19.)

1. Vocation wherewith ye are called] Living the gospel, seeking righteousness, pursuing truth, these are vocations, not avocations; they are the true occupations and businesses of the saints, as distinguished from their temporal pursuits and businesses, which are of lesser importance.

2. Meekness] See Gal. 5:16-26.

3. Where the Spirit of the Lord is, there is unity! And peace!

4. One body] One true Church — not many. **One Spirit]** One true Holy Ghost — not many. **One hope of your calling]** One true eternal life for which the saints hope — not many.

5. One Lord] One true Christ — not many. **One faith]** One true religion, one true plan of salvation, one true gospel, one true

507

redeeming sacrifice, one course back to the presence of God — not many. **One baptism]** One true ordinance whereby sins are remitted and repentant sinners are started out on the strait and narrow path that leads to eternal life — not many.

6. One God and Father of all] One Supreme Deity, one Father of spirits — not many. **Who is above all, and through all, and in you all]** Whose influence, because he is God above all, is everywhere. "God who sitteth upon this throne . . . comprehendeth all things, and all things are before him, and all things are round about him; and he is above all things, and in all things, and is through all things, and is round about all things; and all things are by him, and of him, even God, forever and ever." (D. & C. 88:13, 41.)

WHAT ORGANIZATION EXISTS IN CHRIST'S CHURCH?

EPHESIANS 4:7-16.

7 But unto every one of us is given grace according to the measure of the gift of Christ.

8 Wherefore he saith, When he ascended up on high, he led captivity captive, and gave gifts unto men.

9 (Now that he ascended, what is it but that he also descended first into the lower parts of the earth?

10 He that descended is the same also that ascended up far above all heavens, that he might fill all things.)

11 And he gave some, apostles; and some, prophets; and some, evangelists; and some, pastors and teachers;

12 For the perfecting of the saints, for the work of the ministry, for the edifying of the body of Christ:

13 Till we all come in the unity of the faith, and of the knowledge of the Son of God, unto a perfect man, unto the measure of the stature of the fulness of Christ:

14 That we *henceforth* be no more children, tossed to and fro, and carried about with every wind of doctrine, by the sleight of men, *and* cunning craftiness, whereby they lie in wait to deceive;

15 But speaking the truth in love, may grow up into him in all things, which is the head, *even* Christ:

16 From whom the whole body fitly joined together and compacted by that which every joint supplieth, according to the effectual working in the measure of every

part, maketh increase of the body unto the edifying of itself in love.

I.V. EPHESIANS 4:10, 13.

10 He who descended, is the same also who ascended up into heaven, to glorify him who reigneth over all heavens, that he might fill all things.)

13 Till we, **in the unity of the faith, all come** to the knowledge of the Son of God, unto a perfect man, unto the measure of the stature of the fulness of Christ;

Proper church organization is one of the essential, identifying characteristics of the true Church. God establishes his own Church, the only true and living Church upon the face of the whole earth; and he puts into it those offices which please him. Here Paul names the officers, specifies their duties, and designates the time during which they shall remain in the true Church.

The officers: Apostles, prophets, patriarchs, and so on — and where these are not, the true Church is not.

Their duties: To perfect the saints, to edify church members, to minister as Christ did — and where this course is not pursued, there is no true Church.

Period during which these officers are to remain in the Church: Until every living soul on earth is converted, knows God, and is seeking to be like Christ and have exaltation — and where any church does away with these officers before this specified millennial state has been reached, there the true Church is not.

7-11. 'All men receive blessings from the Lord, of one degree or kind or another, according to the prophetic promise that when he overcame death and ascended again to heaven, he would give gifts unto men. Among these gifts are the officers of his Church who guide men to salvation.'

8. He led captivity captive] He overcame death; all men were the captives of death until Christ captured the captivator and made death subject to him, or, as the Psalm from which Paul is quoting continues to say, "He that is our God is the God of salvation; and unto God the Lord belong the issues from death." (Ps. 68:20.)

And gave gifts unto men] Gave immortality to all men as a free gift; made available the gift of eternal life on certain conditions; and also gave an infinite variety of good things to all men, conferring blessings upon them according to their needs and circumstances.

9-10. 'Christ descended from heaven to live on earth, to undergo his own mortal probation, and to work out the infinite and eternal atonement; he even descended into the spirit prison where he preached to the captive spirits. But now he has ascended into heaven to glorify his Father who is God above all.'

10. All heavens] There are many heavens, with God the Father supreme over them all. **Fill all things**] See Eph. 4:1-6.

11. Apostles] See 1 Cor. 4:1-21. **Prophets**] See Rev. 19:9b-10.

Evangelists] "An evangelist is a patriarch even the oldest man of the blood of Joseph or of the seed of Abraham. Wherever the Church of Christ is established in the earth, there should be a patriarch for the benefit of the posterity of the saints, as it was with Jacob in giving his patriarchal blessing unto his sons." (*Teachings*, p. 151.)

Pastors] Shepherds of the flock; those appointed to feed and care for the Lord's sheep, such as bishops and stake presidents. **Teachers**] See 1 Tim. 1:1-11.

12. For the perfecting of the saints] The saints cannot be perfected and therefore cannot be saved unless living apostles and prophets minister among them. Why? Because apostles and prophets are the ones to whom the doctrines of salvation are revealed, and, as holders of the keys of the kingdom, they are the ones appointed to perform or authorize the performance of the ordinances of salvation.

For the work of the ministry] There can be no true ministry of Christ on earth unless it is headed and directed by apostles and prophets. Why? Because these highly favored officers in God's earthly kingdom hold those keys and powers pursuant to which all things are done in the Church and without which nothing can be performed so as to be binding on earth and in heaven.

For the edifying of the body of Christ] Without living apostles and prophets the members of the Church would not be enlightened from on high or taught what the Lord would have them know. Why? Because they make known the true doctrines of salvation; and they confer or authorize the conferral of the Holy Ghost, without whose enlightening power none can comprehend the things of pure religion.

13. The unity of the faith] That state when all men on earth believe alike and conform to the same standards of conduct. Such a blessed day — a day when "the earth shall be full of the knowledge of the Lord, as the waters cover the sea" (Isa. 11:9) — shall not come until after Christ has commenced his millennial reign.

A perfect man] A saved and exalted being, one who has eternal perfection, who is "perfect, even as your Father which is in heaven is perfect" (Matt. 5:48), who, like Christ when he rose from the dead, receives "All power . . . in heaven and in earth." (Matt. 28:18; *Mormon Doctrine*, 2nd ed., pp. 567-568.)

The measure of the stature of the fulness of Christ] The status of glory and exaltation enjoyed by Christ himself. The whole plan of salvation is designed to enable men to become like God. Those who gain infinite perfection shall be like Christ and he is like the Father. (3 Ne. 28:10.) As Joseph Smith said: "Salvation consists in the glory, authority, majesty, power and dominion which Jehovah possesses and in nothing else; and no being can possess it but himself or one like him." (*Lectures on Faith*, pp. 63-67.)

Fulness of Christ] Fulness of the Father. Christ "received a fulness of the glory of the Father; And he received all power, both in heaven and on earth, and the glory of the Father was with him, for he dwelt in him." (D. & C. 93:16-17.)

14. 'Unless there are apostles and prophets to guide God's Church, its members, being thus without revelation from on high, and driven by the winds of doubt and uncertainty, are soon drowned in the sea of apostasy.'

15. 'But with apostles and prophets, the saints, being thus guided by God, increase in spiritual things until they become like Christ their Head.'

16. 'For it is through Christ that the whole body of the Church is able so to function that all its members are edified and prepared for salvation.'

CHRIST'S PEOPLE LIVE RIGHTEOUSLY

EPHESIANS 4:17-29.

17 This I say therefore, and testify in the Lord, that ye henceforth walk not as other Gentiles walk, in the vanity of their mind,

18 Having the understanding darkened, being alienated from the life of God through the ignorance that is in them, because of the blindness of their heart:

19 Who being past feeling have given themselves over unto lasciviousness, to work all uncleanness with greediness.

20 But ye have not so learned Christ;

21 If so be that ye have heard him, and have been taught by him, as the truth is in Jesus:

22 That ye put off concerning the former conversation the old man, which is corrupt according to the deceitful lusts;

23 And be renewed in the spirit of your mind;

24 And that ye put on the new man, which after God is created in righteousness and true holiness.

25 Wherefore putting away lying, speak every man truth with his neighbour: for we are members one of another.

26 Be ye angry, and sin not: let not the sun go down upon your wrath:

27 Neither give place to the devil.

28 Let him that stole steal no more: but rather let him labour, working with *his* hands the thing which is good, that he may have to give to him that needeth.

29 Let no corrupt communication proceed out of your mouth, but that which is good to the use of edifying, that it may minister grace unto the hearers.

I.V. EPHESIANS 4:21-23, 26, 28.

21 If so be that ye have **learned** him, and have been taught by him, as the truth is in Jesus;

22 **And now I speak unto you** concerning the former conversation, **by exhortation, that ye put off** the old man, which is corrupt according to the deceitful lusts;

23 And be renewed in the **mind of the Spirit;**

26 **Can ye be angry, and not sin?** let not the sun go down upon your wrath;

28 Let him that stole steal no more; but rather let him **labor,** working with his hands **for** the things which **are** good, that he may have to give to him that needeth.

Let not the saints of God continue to walk after the manner of the world! Those who have learned of Christ and his laws, who have turned from sin to righteousness, who have crucified the old man of sin and are now new creatures of the Holy Ghost — let them not give place again to the devil!

19. Lasciviousness] See 2 Cor. 12:21.

22. Conversation] Manner of life.

The old man] "The natural man" who "is an enemy to God." (Mosiah 3:19.) **24. The new man]** The man who has been born again, who has become a new creature of the Holy Ghost. (Mosiah 27:24-26.)

Righteousness] See Gal. 5:5-15.

SAINTS SEALED UP UNTO THE DAY OF REDEMPTION

EPHESIANS 4:30.

30 And grieve not the holy Spirit of God, whereby ye are sealed unto the day of redemption.

Those saints who keep the commandments, who overcome the world, who are faithful in all things, who are married in the temple, who live by every word that proceedeth forth from the mouth of God, have their calling and election made sure. "They are sealed by the Holy Spirit of promise . . . unto the day of redemption." (D. & C. 132:26.)

Holy Spirit of Promise] See Eph. 1:13-14.

Calling and election sure] See 2 Pet. 1:1-19.

Patriarchal blessings] See Heb. 11:17-22.

WALK UPRIGHTLY AS CHILDREN OF LIGHT

EPHESIANS 4:31-32; 5:1-21.

31 Let all bitterness, and wrath, and anger, and clamour, and evil speaking, be put away from you, with all malice:

32 And be ye kind one to another, tenderhearted, forgiving one another, even as God for Christ's sake hath forgiven you.

1 Be ye therefore followers of God, as dear children;

2 And walk in love, as Christ also hath loved us, and hath given himself for us an offering and a sacrifice to God for a sweetsmelling savour.

3 But fornication, and all uncleanness, or covetousness, let it not be once named among you, as becometh saints;

4 Neither filthiness, nor foolish talking, nor jesting, which are not convenient: but rather giving of thanks.

5 For this ye know, that no whoremonger, nor unclean person, nor covetous man, who is an idolater, hath any inheritance in the kingdom of Christ and of God.

6 Let no man deceive you with vain words: for because of these things cometh the wrath of God upon the children of disobedience.

7 Be not ye therefore partakers with them.

8 For ye were sometimes darkness, but now *are ye* light in the Lord: walk as children of light:

9 (For the fruit of the Spirit *is* in all goodness and righteousness and truth;)

10 Proving what is acceptable unto the Lord.

11 And have no fellowship with the unfruitful works of darkness, but rather reprove *them.*

12 For it is a shame even to speak of those things which are done of them in secret.

13 But all things that are reproved are made manifest by the light: for whatsoever doth make manifest is light.

14 Wherefore he saith, Awake thou that sleepest, and arise from the dead, and Christ shall give thee light.

15 See then that ye walk circumspectly, not as fools, but as wise,

16 Redeeming the time, because the days are evil.

17 Wherefore be ye not unwise, but understanding what the will of the Lord *is.*

18 And be not drunk with wine, wherein is excess; but be filled with the Spirit;

19 Speaking to yourselves in psalms and hymns and spiritual

songs, singing and making melody in your heart to the Lord;

20 Giving thanks always for all things unto God and the Father in the name of our Lord Jesus Christ;

21 Submitting yourselves one to another in the fear of God.

Ethical principles, godly conduct, personal righteousness, everything that is good and right — all such grow out of the gospel.

Exhortations to walk in the light, to pursue a course leading to celestial peace, to keep the commandments — all such bear fruit when men know the doctrines of Christ.

If there were no God, no gospel, no eternal life, men might as well eat, drink, be merry, and let lust and passion rule.

But there is a God; he has ordained a gospel of salvation; the saints were foreordained to receive the plan of salvation; they are sealed by the Holy Spirit of Promise; salvation does come by grace through faith; the blood of Christ does save, redeem, and justify; the Gentiles are fellow heirs with Israel; there is one true Church; apostles and prophets guide its destiny and give revelation to the saints and to the world — all of which Paul has already told the Ephesians with power and in plainness.

Building on this foundation — a foundation of God and his gospel — Paul is now continuing his mighty exhortations, exhortations that change the lives of men who believe in Christ and his gospel.

4:31. Bitterness] Caustic and acrimonious attitudes; feelings of harshness or cruelty toward others.

Wrath] See Gal. 5:16-26.

Anger] "As with nearly all strong emotions or passions, anger is manifest both in righteousness and in unrighteousness. Always there is a sense of displeasure attending it, and usually this is accompanied by a feeling of antagonism, excited by a sense of injury or insult.

"Righteous anger is an attribute of Deity. His anger is everlastingly kindled against the wicked. (D. & C. 1:13; 5:8; 60:2; 63:11,

32; 84:24.) Similarly, an inspired man might speak or act in righteous anger, as when Moses broke the tablets upon which the Ten Commandments were written, or as when our Lord drove the money changers from the temple." (*Mormon Doctrine*, 2nd ed., p. 37.)

Clamour] A vocal and violent outcry giving vent to discontent.

Evil speaking] False, corrupt, wicked, degrading, profane, or belittling words spoken about persons or things.

Malice] Ill will or enmity of heart toward others; feelings of dislike which are deep seated and unreasonable and which take pleasure in seeing others suffer.

32. Tenderhearted] Compassionate; easily moved to love, sorrow, or pity.

God for Christ's sake hath forgiven you] Forgiveness comes from the Father, because of Christ's atonement, to those who obey the gospel.

5:1. Be . . . followers of God] 'Walk in the paths he walked in, obey the laws he obeyed, do the things he did, until you become "perfect, even as your Father which is in heaven is perfect" (Matt. 5:48), until you become like him and have exaltation with him.' God is the great prototype; Jesus is next. "What did Jesus do? 'Why; I do the things I saw my Father do. . . . My Father worked out his kingdom with fear and trembling, and I must do the same.' . . . So that Jesus treads in the tracks of his Father." (*Teachings*, pp. 347-348.)

Dear children] Sons of God, adopted members of the family of God the Father, sons who are joint-heirs with Christ and who are thus followers of God because they tread in the tracks of Jesus.

2. Christ . . . a sacrifice to God for a sweetsmelling savour] Even as each sacrifice offered anciently, as it prefigured the coming sacrifice of the Lamb of God, was "a sweet savour . . . unto the Lord" (Ex. 29:18), so was Christ's offering of himself a pleasing thing to God. The sweet smell of the burning sacrifices in Israel symbolized the pleasing blessings flowing from our Lord's personal offering.

3. Fornication] See 1 Cor. 6:9-20.

Uncleanness] Moral filthiness, obscenity, or unchastity; any unholy or impure practice, as masturbation.

Covetousness] See 1 Cor. 6:9-20.

4. Filthiness] Obscenity, or any form of moral corruption or transgression.

Foolish talking] Talk of fools, as conversation without depth or substance which makes light of the plan of salvation and sacred things.

Jesting] Not something said in banter or raillery which is not to be taken seriously, as is our current definition. But, as the original Greek word indicates, a form of discourse "which turns about and adapts itself, without regard to principle, to the shifting circumstances of the moment, and to the varying moods of those with whom it may deal." (*Jamieson*, p. 353.) However, the true saints are expected to maintain a sound and balanced sobriety in harmony with the command: "Cast away your idle thoughts and your excess of laughter far from you." (D. & C. 88:69.)

5. Whoremonger] A whoremaster, that is, one given to whoring, a lecher.

Covetous . . . idolater] See 1 Cor. 6:9-20.

6. Children of disobedience] See Eph. 2:1-10.

8. Children of light] The saints who have come out of the darkness of the world into the marvelous light of the gospel.

14. Paul is either quoting a lost scripture or giving a paraphrasing interpretation to Isaiah 60:1. "Arise, shine; for thy light is come, and the glory of the Lord is risen upon thee."

16. Redeeming the time] Buying up or making wise use of the time.

18. Be not drunk with wine] "Inasmuch as any man drinketh wine or strong drink among you, behold it is not good, neither meet in the sight of your Father." (D. & C. 89:5.)

Be filled with the Spirit] 'Gain the constant companionship of the Holy Ghost.'

Obedience] See Jas. 1:22-25.

HUSBANDS AND WIVES: LOVE EACH OTHER

EPHESIANS 5:22-33.

22 Wives, submit yourselves unto your own husbands, as unto the Lord.

23 For the husband is the head of the wife, even as Christ is the head of the church: and he is the saviour of the body.

24 Therefore as the church is subject unto Christ, so *let* the wives *be* to their own husbands in every thing.

25 Husbands, love your wives, even as Christ also loved the church, and gave himself for it;

26 That he might sanctify and cleanse it with the washing of water by the word,

27 That he might present it to himself a glorious church, not having spot, or wrinkle, or any such thing; but that it should be holy and without blemish.

28 So ought men to love their wives as their own bodies. He that loveth his wife loveth himself.

29 For no man ever yet hated his own flesh! but nourisheth and cherisheth it, even as the Lord the church:

30 For we are members of his body, of his flesh, and of his bones.

31 For this cause shall a man leave his father and mother, and shall be joined unto his wife, and they two shall be one flesh.

32 This is a great mystery: but I speak concerning Christ and the church.

33 Nevertheless let every one of you in particular so love his wife even as himself; and the wife *see* that she reverence *her* husband.

Marriage and love are eternal. Those who continue in the married state in eternity have exaltation and possess the attributes of godliness. They then love each other with a perfect and abiding love. And the marriage status, here in mortality, is the schooling, preparatory state in which love may grow and blossom into that fulness of joy and perfection which can come only when body and spirit are inseparably connected in immortality. (D. & C. 93:33-34.)

Hence, Paul, using Christ as his pattern, here teaches: Christ has taken the Church as his bride; he is married to that body of true believers who have become saints; they are "members of his body, of his flesh, and of his bones." He loves them, gave himself for them, and cleansed and sanctified them; he will perfect and glorify them so they shall dwell with him eternally in holiness and exaltation. He is their Savior.

And so it is in the true order of matrimony. A man marries a wife "for time and for all eternity" (D. & C. 132:18); those so married are separate from all others; she is now his, he is hers, and they become one flesh; they are no longer twain but have one body. Those who receive "all the ordinances of the house of the Lord," must get them "in the same way that Jesus Christ obtained" them (*Teachings*, p. 308), thus following the pattern of Christ their Head. They must then love their wives, sacrifice for their well-being and salvation, and guide them in holiness until they are cleansed, sanctified, and perfected, until they are prepared for exaltation in that glorious heaven where the family unit continues. Husbands thus become in effect the saviors of their wives (and their families!), and these in turn are called to bestow reverence and respect upon the heads of their eternal family units. Truly, in Paul's language, "This is a great mystery," as least until men's minds are opened by the power of the Spirit.

Marriage] See 1 Cor. 7:1-24. **Love]** See Rom. 13:8-10.

22. As unto the Lord] In the patriarchal order of celestial marriage, the husband is the eternal and everlasting head of the wife; he is the Lord's agent and representative, holding the fulness of the holy Melchizedek Priesthood; accordingly, he is the proper recipient of respect from his eternal companion, "Even as Sara obeyed Abraham, calling him lord." (1 Pet. 3:6.) And Abraham — acting in the true spirit of Christ, and setting the pattern for all who should thereafter enter into that same order of enduring matrimony — showered like appreciation and respect upon Sarah.

23. The husband is the head] Marriage is a partnership, but there is a senior partner. God set man to lead, to preside, to be the last word. Woman is obligated to conform, to obey, to be in subjection to the will of the husband, as long as his rulership is exercised in righteousness.

25. Husbands, love your wives] "Thou shalt love thy wife with all thy heart, and shalt cleave unto her and none else." (D. & C. 42:22.)

26. The washing of water by the word] Baptism is called "the washing of regeneration" (Titus 3:5), and it is the way nonmembers of the Church gain the Holy Spirit, by whose power they are cleansed and sanctified. But Paul is here speaking of how the Lord sanctifies "the church," those who have already received the washing of regeneration. It would appear, thus, that he well may have had reference to those "washings" which the Lord says are performed only "in a house which you have built to my name" (D. & C. 124:37-40), and with reference to which he commanded: "Sanctify yourselves; yea, purify your hearts, and cleanse your hands and your feet before me, that I may make you clean; That I may testify unto your Father, and your God, and my God, that you are clean from the blood of this wicked generation." (D. & C. 88:74-75.)

27. As the Lord perfects and glorifies his Church, so husbands are expected to lead their wives to perfection, glory, and exaltation.

28-33. Since husbands and wives have become one flesh, for husbands to love their wives is to love themselves, for their wives are as their own bodies.

PARENTS TO TEACH; CHILDREN TO OBEY

EPHESIANS 6:1-4.

1 Children, obey your parents in the Lord: for this is right.

2 Honour t h y father a n d mother; which is the first commandment with promise;

3 That it may be well with thee, and thou mayest live long on the earth.

4 And, ye fathers, provoke not your children to wrath: but bring them up in the nurture and admonition of the Lord.

When the Father of spirits entrusts his spirit children to the care and custody of mortal parents, he does so upon the most explicit and positive conditions. For instance:

Parents are commanded to "bring up" their children "in light and truth." (D. & C. 93:40.) They are to teach them the plan of salvation (Moses 6:57-60), and the whole law of the whole gospel. (Deut. 6:4-9.) Theirs is the specific obligation to "teach their children to pray, and to walk uprightly before the Lord," as also "to understand the doctrine of repentance, faith in Christ the Son of the living God, and of baptism and the gift of the Holy Ghost by the laying on of the hands, when eight years old." (D. & C. 68:25-28.)

Indeed, parents are to care for their children in all things both temporal and spiritual. As King Benjamin counseled: "Ye will not suffer your children that they go hungry, or naked; neither will ye suffer that they transgress the laws of God, and fight and quarrel one with another, and serve the devil, who is the master of sin, or who is the evil spirit which hath been spoken of by our fathers, he being an enemy to all righteousness. But ye will teach them to walk in the ways of truth and soberness; ye will teach them to love one another, and to serve one another." (Mosiah 4:14-15.)

And children come into mortality with the inborn requirement, planted in their souls by that very Being who gave them birth as spirits, to honor their parents and to obey their counsel in righteousness.

1. **In the Lord]** In righteousness.

3. **Live long on the earth]** God's promise to Israel was that if they honored their parents, their days would be long upon the land which he gave them. (Ex. 20:12.) That is, by obedience the land of promise was to be theirs from generation to generation, and in fact they were scattered for rebellion and for apostasy from those truths handed down from their fathers. But Paul here interprets the promise as a personal one. Obedient and faithful children are to have long lives upon the earth. That is, in the generality of instances, temporal life is prolonged by obedience to gospel laws; but, more particularly and in the ultimate sense, those who are godfearing and righteous — meaning the meek —

shall live upon the earth again in its final or celestial state. (D. & C. 88:16-20.)

4. In the priesthood-led home, where the family is eternal and the Spirit of the Lord dwells, parents represent the Lord in giving counsel and admonition to their children.

SERVANTS AND MASTERS JUDGED BY SAME LAW

EPHESIANS 6:5-9.

5 Servants, be obedient to them that are *your* masters according to the flesh, with fear and trembling, in singleness of your heart, as unto Christ;

6 Not with eyeservice, as menpleasers; but as the servants of Christ, doing the will of God from the heart;

7 With good will doing service, as to the Lord, and not to men:

8 Knowing t h a t whatsoever good thing any man doeth, the same shall he receive of the Lord, whether *he be* bond or free.

9 And, ye masters, do the same things u n t o them, forbearing threatening: knowing that your Master also is in heaven: neither is there respect of persons with him.

Masters and slaves, kings and peasants, lords and vassals, all men, regardless of rank, caste, or social and economic status are saved on the same terms and conditions. Every man shall be stripped of all rank and worldly honor in that "day when the Lord shall come to recompense unto every man according to his work, and measure to every man according to the measure which he has measured to his fellow man." (D. & C. 1:10.)

5-8. These servants were slaves. The social structure which kept them in bondage was outside the power of the Ephesian Saints to change or overthrow. Paul thus has no alternative but to recognize their state and counsel them how to live under it. Slavery as such is in fact abhorrent to gospel standards. "It is not right," the Lord says, "that any man should be in bondage one to another." (D. & C. 101:79.)

6. Doing the will of God] Keeping the commandments. **7. Doing service]** Laboring honestly and diligently. **As to the Lord]** Service rendered others should be performed as though for the Lord.

"PUT ON THE WHOLE ARMOUR OF GOD"

EPHESIANS 6:10-24.

10 Finally, my brethren, be strong in the Lord, and in the power of his might.

11 Put on the whole armour of God, that ye may be able to stand against the wiles of the devil.

12 For we wrestle not against flesh and blood, but against principalities, against powers, against the rulers of the darkness of this world, against spiritual wickedness in high *places*.

13 Wherefore take unto you the whole armour of God, that ye may be able to withstand in the evil day, and having done all, to stand.

14 Stand therefore, having your loins girt about with truth, and having on the breastplate of righteousness;

15 And your feet shod with the preparation of the gospel of peace;

16 Above all, taking the shield of faith, wherewith ye shall be able to quench all the fiery darts of the wicked.

17 And take the helmet of salvation, and the sword of the Spirit, which is the word of God:

18 Praying always with all prayer and supplication in the Spirit, and watching thereunto with all perseverance and supplication for all saints;

19 And for me, that utterance may be given unto me, that I may open my mouth boldly, to make known the mystery of the gospel,

20 For which I am an ambassador in bonds: that therein I may speak boldly, as I ought to speak.

21 But that ye also may know my affairs, *and* how I do, Tychicus, a beloved brother and faithful minister in the Lord, shall make known to you all things:

22 Whom I have sent unto you for the same purpose, that ye might know our affairs, and *that* he might comfort your hearts.

23 Peace *be* to the brethren, and love with faith, from God the Father and the Lord Jesus Christ.

24 Grace *be* with all them that love our Lord Jesus Christ in sincerity. Amen.

Our mortal probation is a war, a continuation of the war in heaven(Rev. 12:7-17), a war against the world, against evil, against Satan. And there are no neutrals; all men are for the Lord or they are against him; they either serve under his banner or they live after the manner of the world and are in the bondage of sin. The only way for the Christian soldiers to come off victorious is to put on the whole armor of God. Paul did, and as his life drew to a close he was able to affirm, "I have fought a good fight, . . . I have kept the faith." (2 Tim. 4:7.) King Mosiah did likewise and after he had "gone the way of all the earth," Alma the younger was able to say of him that he had "warred a good warfare" because he had walked "uprightly before God." (Alma 1:1.)

11-18. To the saints of latter-days the Lord himself revealed, in these words, the same. truths previously given, by the power of his Spirit, to his ancient Apostle: "Lift up your hearts and rejoice, and gird up your loins, and take upon you my whole armor, that ye may be able to withstand the evil day, having done all, that ye may be able to stand. Stand, therefore, having your loins girt about with truth, having on the breastplate of righteousness, and your feet shod with the preparation of the gospel of peace, which I have sent mine angels to commit unto you; Taking the shield of faith wherewith ye shall be able to quench all the fiery darts of the wicked; And take the helmet of salvation, and the sword of my Spirit, which I will pour out upon you, and my word which I reveal unto you, and be agreed as touching all things whatsoever ye ask of me, and be faithful until I come, and ye shall be caught up, that where I am ye shall be also." (D. & C. 27:15-18.)

19. The mystery of the gospel] The gospel and all things pertaining to it are beyond human comprehension unless and until men's souls are touched by the Spirit of God. True religion is a thing of the Spirit, not of the intellect; and it can only be known and understood by the power of the Spirit. To the carnal mind it is and ever shall be a mystery.

The Epistle of Paul the Apostle to the Philippians

"This epistle is a letter of friendship, full of affection, confidence, good counsel and good cheer. It is the happiest of St. Paul's writings, for the Philippians were the dearest of his children in the faith. . . . It is a classic of spiritual autobiography. St. Paul writes here at his ease; he makes those spontaneous disclosures of the inner self which only the tenderest sympathy can elicit. . . . Philippians reveals the spring of his inward peace and strength. It admits us to St. Paul's prison meditations and communings with his Master. We watch his spirit ripening through the autumn hours when patience fulfilled in him its perfect work." (*Dummelow*, p. 969.)

But Philippians is more than a window into the life and soul of Paul. Though he is not under the necessity of correcting or rebuking his "children in the faith," he does assume the parental prerogative to remind them of some glorious gospel concepts. Without going into detail, as he does in Romans or Hebrews, he alludes to and comments briefly about the equality of the Father and the Son, the greatness of Christ, and the personal obligation of man to pursue salvation. He speaks of martyrdom, of sacrifice, of example and devotion, and of various Christian virtues.

Philippians is not a mighty dissertation, one to shake the earth or serve as a guidepost to Christendom, but it is a sweet and refined statement into which a number of gospel doctrines are woven. And our Bible is greatly enriched by its presence there.

WHAT CHRIST SHALL WE PREACH?

PHILIPPIANS 1:1-26.

1 Paul and Timotheus, the servants of Jesus Christ, to all the saints in Christ Jesus which are at Philippi, with the bishops and deacons:

2 Grace *be* u n t o you, and peace, from God our Father, and *from* the Lord Jesus Christ.

3 I thank my God upon every remembrance of you,

4 Always in every prayer of mine for you all making request with joy,

5 For your fellowship in the gospel from the first day until now;

6 Being confident of this very thing, that he which hath begun a good work in you will perform *it* until the day of Jesus Christ:

7 Even as it is meet for me to think this of you all, because I have you in my heart; inasmuch as both in my bonds, and in the defence and confirmation of the gospel, ye all are partakers of my grace.

8 For God is my record, how greatly I long after you all in the bowels of Jesus Christ.

9 And this I pray, that your love may abound yet more and more in knowledge and *in* all judgment;

10 That ye may approve things that are excellent; that ye may be sincere and without offence till the day of Christ;

11 Being filled with the fruits of righteousness, which are by Jesus Christ, unto the glory and praise of God.

12 But I would ye should understand, brethren, that the things *which happened* unto me have fallen out rather unto the furtherance of the gospel;

13 So that my bonds in Christ are manifest in all the palace, and in all other *places;*

14 And many of the brethren in the Lord, waxing confident by my bonds, are much more bold to speak the word without fear.

15 Some indeed preach Christ even of envy and strife; and some also of good will:

16 The one preach Christ of contention, not sincerely, supposing to add affliction to my bonds:

17 But the other of love, knowing that I am set for the defence of the gospel.

18 What then? notwithstanding, every way, whether in pretence, or in truth, Christ is preached; and I therein do rejoice, yea, and will rejoice.

19 For I know that this shall turn to my salvation through your prayer, and the supply of the Spirit of Jesus Christ,

20 According to my earnest expectation and *my* hope, that in nothing I shall be ashamed, but *that* with all boldness, as always, *so* now also Christ shall be magnified in my body, whether *it be* by life, or by death.

21 For to me to live *is* Christ, and to die *is* gain.

22 But if I live in the flesh, this *is* the fruit of my labour: yet what I shall choose I wot not.

23 For I am in a strait betwixt two, having a desire to depart, and to be with Christ; which is far better:

24 Nevertheless to abide in the flesh *is* more needful for you.

25 And having this confidence, I know that I shall abide and continue with you all for your furtherance and joy of faith;

26 That your rejoicing may be more abundant in Jesus Christ for me by my coming to you again.

I.V. PHILIPPIANS 1:4, 21-22, 26.

4 Always in every prayer of mine, for **the steadfastness of** you all, making request with joy,

21 But if I live in the flesh, **ye are** the fruit of my labor. Yet what I shall choose I **know** not.

22 **For me to live, is to do the will of Christ; and to die, is my gain.**

26 That your rejoicing **with me** may be more abundant in Jesus Christ, **for** my coming to you again.

---

1. Saints] "Faithful members of the Church and kingdom of God on earth are called saints (1 Ne. 14:12, 14; Acts 9:32, 41; Eph. 1:1), a title signifying that they have been cleansed by baptism and are pure and clean before the Lord. (2 Ne. 9:18.) Ancient Israel, for instance, consisted of a 'congregation of saints' (Ps. 149:1), and the term is one of the most frequently used designations of the Lord's people. Paul, in speaking of the Second Coming of our Lord, pointedly recorded that the true believers in the last days would be called saints, for Christ 'shall come to be glorified in his saints, and to be admired in all them that believe.' (2 Thess. 1:10.) The only true saints in this day are thus members of The Church of Jesus Christ of Latter-day Saints. Saints are named nearly 40 times in the Old Testament, over 60 times in the New Testament, about 30 times in the Book of Mormon, and over 70 times in the Doctrine and Covenants.

"The plan of salvation consists in putting off 'the natural man,' who 'is an enemy to God,' and in becoming 'a saint through the atonement of Christ the Lord.' Saints are 'submissive, meek, hum-

527

ble, patient, full of love, willing to submit to all things which the Lord seeth fit to inflict upon' them. (Mosiah 3:19.)

"The saints from the beginning on down who had preceded our Lord in death were with him in his resurrection. (Matt. 27:51-53; Hela. 14:25; 3 Ne. 23:9-11; D. & C. 133:53-55.) Saints who have lived since then will be resurrected in the coming first resurrection (D. & C. 43:18), will be with Christ in the great events incident to his Second Coming (1 Thess. 3:13; Jude 14; D. & C. 133:56), and finally 'all the saints shall dwell with God.' (Moro. 8:26.)" (*Mormon Doctrine*, 2nd ed., p. 667.)

Bishops] See 1 Tim. 3:1-7. **Deacons]** See 1 Tim. 3:8-13.

6. The day of Jesus Christ] The day of judgment by Jesus Christ, into whose hands "the Father . . . hath committed all judgment." (John 5:22.)

9. As with mercy, justice, faith and all of the attributes of godliness, love is gained by obedience to law. Though all men, in and out of the Church, possess and bestow it in varying degrees, yet the saints are to seek it "more and more," by conformity to those laws upon which its receipt is predicated.

12-14. The Lord's hand is in all things; he governs and controls the spread and triumph of his gospel; persecution, imprisonment, war, and world conditions of every sort are used by him for his purposes — for the spread of truth, for the testing of his saints, for the ultimate salvation of all who will be saved.

15-18. Christ is many things. He is a God of vengeance to the wicked, of loving kindness to his saints. He is a Man of War on one occasion, a Prince of Peace on another. His message is death to the wicked, life to the righteous. His voice is one of condemnation to some, of praise to others. Who then is the Christ whom his servants should preach? Obviously there is only one way for any preachers to know what perspective to take on any given occasion, and that is to receive revelation from Christ by the power of the Holy Ghost. There is no other way to say what he would say if he personally were the Preacher, which is the same thing as saying what he wants said in any given situation. When this spirit of inspiration is lost, the end result is apostasy, with professing ministers choosing their own fields of emphasis, thus preaching conflicting gospels, and crying, "Lo, here is Christ," and "Lo, there," as is the case in the sectarian world today.

19. Spirit of Jesus Christ] The Light of Christ. See Jas. 1:17-21.

20-26. Paul did not fear death. As with others who have fought the good fight and overcome the world, he desired to be relieved of the burdens of mortality and rest in the paradise of God; yet his sense of duty caused him to know his ministry here was not over, that though his own salvation was assured, he must remain in the flesh and work further for the salvation of his fellow saints.

20. Christ shall be magnified in my body] 'The greatness and glory of Christ shall be known because I keep the commandments and stand as a living witness of him.'

BE OF ONE SPIRIT AND ONE MIND

PHILIPPIANS 1:27-30; 2:1-4.

27 Only let your conversation be as it becometh the gospel of Christ: that whether I come and see you, or else be absent, I may hear of your affairs, that ye stand fast in one spirit, with one mind striving together for the faith of the gospel;

28 And in nothing terrified by your adversaries: which is to them an evident token of perdition, but to you of salvation, and that of God.

29 For unto you it is given in the behalf of Christ, not only to believe on him, but also to suffer for his sake;

30 Having the same conflict which ye saw in me, and now hear *to be* in me.

1 If *there be* therefore any consolation in Christ, if any comfort of love, if any fellowship of the Spirit, if any bowels and mercies,

2 Fulfil ye my joy, that ye be likeminded, having the same love, *being* of one accord, of one mind.

3 *Let* nothing *be done* through strife or vainglory; but in lowliness of mind let each esteem other better than themselves.

4 Look not every man on his own things, but every man also on the things of others.

I.V. PHILIPPIANS 1:27-28, 30.

27 **Therefore** let your conversation be as it becometh the gospel of Christ; that whether I come and see you, or else be absent, I may hear of your affairs, that ye stand fast in one spirit, with one mind striving together for the faith of the gospel;

28 And in nothing terrified by your adversaries, **who reject the gospel, which bringeth on them destruction; but you who receive the gospel, salvation;** and that of God.

30 Having the same conflict which ye saw in me, and now **know** to be in me.

27. Let your conversation be as it becometh the gospel of Christ] 'Let your conduct conform to gospel standards; keep the commandments.' **Stand fast in one spirit]** 'Each of you exemplify the same spirit of love, of charity, of mercy, of godliness.' **With one mind]** 'Believing the same truths, thinking the same thoughts, having the same hopes.' **Striving together for the faith of the gospel]** 'Laboring to gain that power (faith) which comes from gospel obedience.'

Unity] See 1 Cor. 1:1-16. **Mind of Christ]** See 1 Cor. 2:9-16.

29. In the behalf of Christ, . . . to suffer] When the saints suffer persecution for righteousness' sake, they stand in the place and stead of Christ and are receiving what the ungodly would heap upon the Son of God were he personally present.

1-2. 'If you have found consolation in Christ, if you have gained comfort in his love, if you have fellowship with the Holy Ghost, if you have tasted the mercy of God, then exemplify that unity which becometh the saints of God.'

3. Strife . . . vainglory] See Gal. 5:16-26. **Let each esteem other better than themselves]** "Let every man esteem his brother as himself. . . . Be one; and if ye are not one ye are not mine." (D. & C. 38:24-27.)

HOW THE FATHER AND THE SON ARE EQUAL

PHILIPPIANS 2:5-8.

5 Let this mind be in you, which was also in Christ Jesus:

6 Who, being in the form of God, thought it not robbery to be equal with God:

7 But made himself of no reputation, and took upon him the form of a servant, and was made in the likeness of men:

8 And being found in fashion as a man, he humbled himself, and became obedient unto death, even the death of the cross.

While speaking of the sheep of his fold, our Lord propounded two great truths about the Godhead: 1. That his Father is above all; that he is, thus, the supreme ruler of the universe; and 2. That he and his Father are one. (John 10:28-30; 3 Ne. 28:10.) In the Upper Room, after the introduction of the sacramental ordinance, Jesus said: "My Father is greater than I." (John 14:28.) And after his resurrection, our Lord again acclaimed the divine supremacy of the Father, calling him, "My God, and your God." (John 20:17.) That is, Christ is subject to and in fact worships the Father, as all his fellowmen are commanded to do.

Wherein, then, lies our Lord's equality with his God and our God? Is it not in that Jesus, crowned now himself with exaltation, has received from the Father all knowledge, all truth, all wisdom, and all power? Is it not in the same sense that all of the sons of God, as joint-heirs with Christ, shall receive all that the Father hath? (D. & C. 76:54-60; 84:38; 132:20.) Is it not in that, treading in the tracks of the Father, those who are adopted as his sons gain exaltation of their own? (*Teachings*, pp. 347-348.) See *Commentary I*, pp. 741-743.

God] See Acts 17:15-34.

5-6. President Lorenzo Snow, early in his ministry, received by direct, personal revelation the knowledge that (in the Prophet Joseph Smith's language), "God himself was once as we are now, and is an exalted man, and sits enthroned in yonder heavens," and that men "have got to learn how to be Gods . . . the same as all Gods have done before." (*Teachings*, pp. 345-346.) After this glorious doctrine had been taught by the Prophet, President Snow felt free to teach it also and to summarize it in couplet form by saying:

As man now is, God once was;

As God now is, man may be.

In amplifying the thought in this couplet, in direct response to Paul's declaration in these verses, and referring also to 1 John 3:1-3, President Snow penned this reply to the Apostle of old:

Dear Brother:

> Hast thou not been unwisely bold,
> Man's destiny to thus unfold?
> To raise, promote such high desire,
> Such vast ambition thus inspire?

> Still, 'tis no phantom that we trace
> Man's ultimatum in life's race;
> This royal path has long been trod
> By righteous men, each now a God:

> As Abra'm, Isaac, Jacob, too,
> First babes, then men — to gods they grew.
> As man now is, our God once was;
> As now God is, so man may be, —
> Which doth unfold man's destiny.

> For John declares: When Christ we see
> Like unto him we'll truly be.
> And he who has this hope within,
> Will purify himself from sin.

> Who keep this object grand in view,
> To folly, sin, will bid adieu,
> Nor wallow in the mire anew;

> Nor ever seek to carve his name
> High on the shaft of worldly fame;
> But here his ultimatum trace:
> The head of all his spirit-race.

> Ah, well: that taught by you, dear Paul,
> 'Though much amazed, we see it all;
> Our Father God, has ope'd our eyes,
> We cannot view it otherwise.

> The boy, like to his father grown,
> Has but attained unto his own;

To grow to sire from state of son,
Is not 'gainst Nature's course to run.

A son of God, like God to be,
Would not be robbing Deity;
And he who has this hope within,
Will purify himself from sin.

You're right, St. John, supremely right:
Whoe'er essays to climb this height,
Will cleanse himself of sin entire —
Or else 'twere needless to aspire.

(Lorenzo Snow, *Improvement Era*, vol. 22,
pp. 660-661, June, 1919.)

7-8. Christ is the source of salvation for all men; through him immortality and eternal life come. But he also had to work out his own salvation, to serve in mortality, to humble himself before the Father, to keep the commandments, to endure to the end.

EVERY KNEE SHALL BOW, EVERY TONGUE CONFESS

PHILIPPIANS 2:9-11.

9 Wherefore God also hath highly exalted him, and given him a name which is above every name:

10 That at the name of Jesus every knee should bow, of *things* in heaven, and *things* in earth, and *things* under the earth;

11 And *that* every tongue should confess that Jesus Christ *is* Lord, to the glory of God the Father.

No tongue can tell, no pen can write, no man can utter, no human mind can conceive of the glory, majesty, might, power, and dominion that is Christ's. He is the Lord God Almighty, the Creator of heaven and earth and all that in them is, the Eternal Jehovah, the Holy One of Israel, the Savior and Redeemer. He made the earth; salvation comes by him; his atoning sacrifice is infinite and eternal.

"Hear, O ye heavens, and give ear, O earth, and rejoice ye inhabitants thereof, for the Lord is God, and beside him there is no Savior. Great is his wisdom, marvelous are his ways, and the extent of his doings none can find out. His purposes fail not, neither are there any who can stay his hand. From eternity to eternity he is the same, and his years never fail." (D. & C. 76:1-4.)

Since Christ is the Savior, since all things pertaining to life and salvation center in him, since he is God — it follows that all men must turn to him and his gospel for salvation, and that in his own due time he shall receive the worship and adoration of all men. Indeed, to all men, by the mouth of Isaiah, Israel's Jehovah said: "Look unto me, and be ye saved, all the ends of the earth: for I am God, and there is none else. I have sworn by myself, the word is gone out of my mouth in righteousness, and shall not return, That unto me every knee shall bow, every tongue shall swear." (Isa. 45:22-23.)

How appropriate, then, for Paul, knowing that the Lord Jesus was the Lord Jehovah, to apply Isaiah's pronouncement to Christ. And how appropriate also for Christ himself to say to Joseph Smith that when he "shall have subdued all enemies under his feet, . . . Then shall he be crowned with the crown of his glory, to sit on the throne of his power to reign forever and ever"; and to add, speaking of the telestial hosts, whose numbers shall be "as the stars in the firmament of heaven, or as the sand upon the sea-shore," that "These are they who are cast down to hell and suffer the wrath of Almighty God, until the fulness of times, when Christ shall have subdued all enemies under his feet, and shall have perfected his work; When he shall deliver up the kingdom, and present it unto the Father, spotless, saying: I have overcome and have trodden the wine-press alone, even the wine-press of the fierceness of the wrath of Almighty God. Then shall he be crowned with the crown of his glory, to sit on the throne of his power to reign forever and ever. But behold, and lo, we saw the glory and the inhabitants of the telestial world, that they were as innumerable as the stars in the firmament of heaven, or as the sand upon the seashore; And heard the voice of the Lord saying: These all shall bow the knee, and every tongue shall confess to him who sits upon the throne forever and ever." (D. & C. 76:106-110.)

Salvation comes because of Christ] See Acts 4:1-12.

"WORK OUT YOUR OWN SALVATION"

PHILIPPIANS 2:12-16.

12 Wherefore, my beloved, as ye have always obeyed, not as in my presence only, but now much more in my absence, work out your own salvation with fear and trembling.

13 For it is God which worketh in you both to will and to do of *his* good pleasure.

14 Do all things without murmurings and disputings:

15 That ye may be blameless and harmless, the sons of God, without rebuke, in the midst of a crooked a n d perverse nation, among whom ye shine as lights in the world;

16 Holding forth the word of life; that I may rejoice in the day of Christ, that I have not run in vain, neither laboured in vain.

Salvation comes by the grace of God, in that because of his love, mercy, and condescension, he sent his Only Begotten Son to work out the infinite and eternal atonement. This atonement brings immortality to all and offers those who believe and obey an inheritance in the kingdom of God. This celestial inheritance, itself also available because of God's grace, must be earned. It is reserved for those who live the gospel law. "We believe that through the Atonement of Christ, all mankind may be saved, by obedience to the laws and ordinances of the Gospel." (Third Article of Faith.)

Nephi said that the gate to the "straight and narrow path which leads to eternal life" is repentance and baptism. Then he asked: "After ye have gotten into this straight and narrow path, I would ask if all is done?" That is, what must men do to be saved after baptism, after belief in Christ, after joining the Church? Nephi answers: "Ye must press forward with a steadfastness in Christ, having a perfect brightness of hope, and a love of God and of all men. Wherefore, if ye shall press forward, feasting upon the word of Christ, and endure to the end, behold, thus saith the Father: Ye shall have eternal life. And now, behold, my beloved brethren, this is the way; and there is none other way nor name given under heaven whereby man can be saved in the kingdom of God." (2 Ne. 31:17-21.)

Salvation] See 1 Pet. 1:1-16.

535

14. Murmurings] Grumblings, complaints. **Disputings]** Controversial discussions, quarrels.

15. Sons of god] See Gal. 3:26-29; 4:1-7.

A crooked and perverse nation] A dishonest, devious, obstinate nation which has forsaken true principles. The Lord describes our modern generation in the same way. (D. & C. 34:6.)

PAUL FACES MARTYRDOM WITH JOY

PHILIPPIANS 2:17-30.

17 Yea, and if I be offered upon the sacrifice and service of your faith, I joy, and rejoice with you all.

18 For the same cause also do ye joy, and rejoice with me.

19 But I trust in the Lord Jesus to send Timotheus shortly unto you, that I also may be of good comfort, when I know your state.

20 For I have no man likeminded, who will naturally care for your state.

21 For all seek their own, not the things which are Jesus Christ's.

22 But ye know the proof of him, that, as a son with the father, he hath served with me in the gospel.

23 Him therefore I hope to send presently, so soon as I shall see how it will go with me.

24 But I trust in the Lord that I also myself shall come shortly.

25 Yet I supposed it necessary to send to you Epaphroditus, my brother, and companion in labour, and fellowsoldier, but your messenger, and he that ministered to my wants.

26 For he longed after you all, and was full of heaviness, because that ye had heard that he had been sick.

27 For indeed he was sick nigh unto death: but God had mercy on him; and not on him only, but on me also, lest I should have sorrow upon sorrow.

28 I sent him therefore the more carefully, that, when ye see him again, ye may rejoice, and that I may be the less sorrowful.

29 Receive him therefore in the Lord with all gladness; and hold such in reputation:

30 Because for the work of Christ he was nigh unto death, not regarding his life, to supply your lack of service toward me.

I.V. PHILIPPIANS 2:17.

17 Yea, and if I be offered **a** sacrifice **upon the service** of your faith, I joy, and rejoice with you all.

There is always the human element in church administration. Some of Christ's ministers serve well, others poorly, and some decline calls to service, even for personal and selfish reasons. Sickness and disease plague the saints as well as the world. Thus, Timothy was faithful; Epaphroditus incurred serious illness while engaged in his appointed missionary work; and some who should have responded to gospel calls preferred to pursue their own interests rather than "the things which are Jesus Christ's."

17. If I be offered] Martyrdom in the Cause of Christ carries the assured reward of eternal life. (D. & C. 98:13.)

Martyrdom] See Rev. 6:9-11.

PAUL SACRIFICES ALL THINGS FOR CHRIST

PHILIPPIANS 3:1-12.

1 Finally, my brethren, rejoice in the Lord. To write the same things to you, to me indeed *is* not grievous, but for you *it is* safe.

2 Beware of dogs, beware of evil workers, beware of the concision.

3 For we are the circumcision, which worship God in the spirit, and rejoice in Christ Jesus, and have no confidence in the flesh.

4 Though I might also have confidence in the flesh. If any other man thinketh that he hath whereof he might trust in the flesh, I more:

5 Circumcised the eighth day, of the stock of Israel, *of* the tribe of Benjamin, an Hebrew of the Hebrews; as touching the law, a Pharisee;

6 Concerning zeal, persecuting the church; touching the right-eousness which is in the law, blameless.

7 But what things were gain to me, those I counted loss for Christ.

8 Yea doubtless, and I count all things *but* loss for the excellency of the knowledge of Christ Jesus my Lord: for whom I have suffered the loss of all things, and do count them *but* dung, that I may win Christ,

9 And be found in him, not having mine own righteousness, which is of the law, but that which is through the faith of Christ, the righteousness which is of God by faith:

10 That I may know him, and the power of his resurrection, and the fellowship of his sufferings, being made conformable unto his death;

11 If by any means I might attain unto the resurrection of the dead.

12 Not as though I had already attained, either were already perfect: but I follow after, if that I may apprehend that for which also I am apprehended of Christ Jesus.

I.V. PHILIPPIANS 3:11.

11 If by any means I might attain unto the resurrection of the **just.**

"Sacrifice is the crowning test of the gospel. Men are tried and tested in this mortal probation to see if they will put first in their lives the things of the kingdom of God. (Matt. 6:33.) To gain eternal life, they must be willing, if called upon, to sacrifice all things for the gospel. 'If thou wilt be perfect,' Jesus said to the rich young man, 'go and sell that thou hast, and give to the poor, and thou shalt have treasure in heaven: and come and follow me.'

"Hearing this injunction, Peter said: 'Behold, we have forsaken all, and followed thee; what shall we have therefore?' To this query our Lord replied: 'Every one that hath forsaken houses, or brethren, or sisters, or father, or mother, or wife, or children, or lands, for my name's sake, shall receive an hundredfold, and shall inherit everlasting life.' (Matt. 19:16-29; D. & C. 132:55.)

"Joseph Smith taught the law of sacrifice in these words: 'For a man to lay down his all, his character and reputation, his honor, and applause, his good name among men, his houses, his lands, his brothers and sisters, his wife and children, and even his own life — counting all things but filth and dross for the excellency of the knowledge of Jesus Christ — requires more than mere belief or supposition that he is doing the will of God; but actual knowledge, realizing that, when these sufferings are ended, he will enter into eternal rest, and be a partaker of the glory of God. . . .

" 'A religion that does not require the sacrifice of all things never has power sufficient to produce the faith necessary [to lead] unto life and salvation; for, from the first existence of man, the faith necessary unto the enjoyment of life and salvation never could be obtained without the sacrifice of all earthly things. It was through this sacrifice, and this only, that God has ordained that men should enjoy eternal life; and it is through the medium of the sacrifice of all earthly things that men do actually know that they are doing the things that are well pleasing in the sight of God. When a man has offered in sacrifice all that he has for the truth's sake, not even withholding his life, and believing before God that he has been called to make this sacrifice because he seeks to do his will, he does know, most assuredly, that God does and will accept his sacrifice and offering, and that he has not, nor will not seek his face in vain. Under these circumstances, then, he can obtain the faith necessary for him to lay hold on eternal life.

" 'It is vain for persons to fancy to themselves that they are heirs with those, or can be heirs with them, who have offered their all in sacrifice, and by this means obtained faith in God and favor with him so as to obtain eternal life, unless they, in like manner, offer unto him the same sacrifice, and through that offering obtain the knowledge that they are accepted of him. . . .

" 'From the days of righteous Abel to the present time, the knowledge that men have that they are accepted in the sight of God is obtained by offering sacrifice. . . .

" 'Those, then, who make the sacrifice, will have the testimony that their course is pleasing in the sight of God; and those who have this testimony will have faith to lay hold on eternal life; and will be enabled, through faith, to endure unto the end, and receive the crown that is laid up for them that love the appearing of our Lord Jesus Christ. But those who do not make the sacrifice cannot enjoy this faith, because men are dependent upon this sacrifice in order to obtain this faith: therefore, they cannot lay hold upon eternal life, because the revelations of God do not guarantee unto them the authority so to do, and without this guarantee faith could not exist.' (*Lectures on Faith*, pp. 58-60.)" (*Mormon Doctrine*, 2nd ed., pp. 663-664.)

Law of sacrifice] See Heb. 8:1-5.

1. Rejoice in the Lord] See 2 Cor. 10:1-18; 11:1-11. **Write the same things]** Paul is now going to repeat what he has written or said to the Philippians before.

2-3. Beware of Jewish circumcision, which presupposes acceptance of the whole law of Moses and the rejection of Christ, and is in fact nothing more than the cutting of the flesh. Remember the true circumcision is of the spirit and includes acceptance of Christ and his gospel.' The reasoning is that those who accepted the true circumcision anciently possessed the same spirit of worship as do those who now accept Christ and his gospel.

2. Beware of dogs, . . . evil workers, . . . the concision] Those who advocate circumcision as a saving ordinance. They are as dogs who rage against the truth and seek to devour the saints. **The concision]** The cutting (mutilation) of the flesh by circumcision; such a cutting, the Apostle teaches, has no more saving virtue than any mutilation of the body.

3. Circumcision] See Acts 15:1-35.

4-12. If salvation came by the Jewish formula — by birth in Israel, by circumcision of the flesh, by blameless conformity to Mosaic law and ritual, by the common practice of persecuting the Church — then Paul had few peers. But, rather, he says, he has forsaken all this to gain Christ. He no longer has the supposed righteousness that comes from Mosaic obedience, but now strives for the true righteousness which flows from faith in Christ.

8-11. Having sacrificed all for Christ, Paul is now ready to suffer and die as his Lord had done, that he might thereby gain a part in the resurrection of the just.

TRUE MINISTERS SET EXAMPLES OF RIGHTEOUSNESS

PHILIPPIANS 3:13-21.

13 Brethren, I count not myself to have apprehended: but *this* one thing I *do*, forgetting those things which are behind, and reaching forth unto those things which are before,

14 I press toward the mark for the prize of the high calling of God in Christ Jesus.

15 Let us therefore, as many as be perfect, be thus minded: and if in any thing ye be otherwise minded, God shall reveal even this unto you.

16 Nevertheless, whereto we have already attained, let us walk by the same rule, let us mind the same thing.

17 Brethren, be followers together of me, and mark them which walk so as ye have us for an ensample.

18 (For many walk, of whom I have told you often, and now tell you even weeping, *that they are* the enemies of the cross of Christ:

19 Whose end *is* destruction, whose God *is their* belly, and *whose* glory *is* in their shame, who mind earthly things.)

20 For our conversation is in heaven; from whence also we look for the Saviour, the Lord Jesus Christ:

21 Who shall change our vile body, that it may be fashioned like unto his glorious body, according to the working whereby he is able even to subdue all things unto himself.

I.V. PHILIPPIANS 3:18-19.

18 (For many walk, of whom I have told you often, and now tell you even weeping, as the enemies of the cross of Christ;

19 Whose end is destruction, whose God is their belly, and who glory in their shame, who mind earthly things.)

14. I press toward the mark] 'I press forward with a steadfastness in Christ. I endure to the end. I keep the commandments after baptism. I do the works of righteousness. I work out my salvation.' **The prize]** Eternal life.

16-17. All saints should seek salvation in the same way Paul does.

17. Be followers . . . of me] As with Christ so with his ministers, those who stand in his place and stead in administering life and salvation to men, all are exemplars. How many souls have been saved because a righteous man has been able to say, with Christ, "Follow thou me." (2 Ne. 31:10.)

19. Whose God is their belly] They honor sensual appetite, which is symbolic of the appetites and passions of the flesh, like a god.

20. Our conversation is in heaven] 'Our citizenship is in heaven; as citizens of the kingdom of God on earth, we are preparing for eternal citizenship in his kingdom in heaven.'

21. Our vile body] 'Our corruptible, mortal body.' **His glorious body]** 'His celestial, immortal body.'

Righteousness] See Gal. 5:5-15.

"STAND FAST IN THE LORD"

PHILIPPIANS 4:1-7.

1 Therefore, my brethren dearly beloved and longer for, my joy and crown, so stand fast in the Lord, *my* dearly beloved.

2 I beseech Euodias, and beseech Syntyche, that they be of the same mind in the Lord.

3 And I intreat thee also, true yokefellow, help those women

which laboured with me in the gospel, with Clement also, and *with* other my fellowlabourers, whose names *are* in the book of life.

4 Rejoice in the Lord alway: *and* again I say, Rejoice.

5 Let y o u r moderation be known unto all men. The Lord *is* at hand.

6 Be careful for nothing; but in every thing by prayer and supplication with thanksgiving let

your requests be made known unto God.

7 And the peace of God, which passeth all understanding, shall keep y o u r hearts and minds through Christ Jesus.

I.V. PHILIPPIANS 4:6.

6 Be **afflicted** for nothing; but in everything by prayer and supplication with thanksgiving let your requests be made known unto God.

Paul's recurring, repetitious, and never ending counsel to the saints is: Keep the commandments, live the gospel, obey the law, stand fast in the faith. It is: "He who doeth the works of righteousness shall receive his reward, even peace in this world, and eternal life in the world to come." (D. & C. 59:23.)

Enduring to the end] See Acts 2:41-47.

2. **Be of the same mind]** See 1 Cor. 1:1-16.

3. **The book of life]** See Rev. 20:11-15.

4. **Rejoice in the Lord]** See 2 Cor. 10:1-18; 11:1-11.

6. **Prayer]** 1 John 3:19-24.

"WE BELIEVE IN BEING HONEST, TRUE, CHASTE"

PHILIPPIANS 4:8-23.

8 Finally, brethren, whatsoever things are true, whatsoever things *are* honest, whatsoever things *are* just, whatsoever things *are* pure, whatsoever things *are* lovely, whatsoever things *are* of good report; if *there be* any virtue, and if *there*

be any praise, think on these things.

9 Those things, which ye have both learned, and received, and heard, and seen in me, do: and the God of peace shall be with you.

10 But I rejoiced in the Lord greatly, that now at the last your

care of me hath flourished again; wherein ye were also careful, but ye lacked opportunity.

11 Not that I speak in respect of want: for I have learned, in whatsoever state I am, *therewith* to be content.

12 I know both how to be abased, and I know how to abound: every where and in all things I am instructed both to be full and to be hungry, both to abound and to suffer need.

13 I can do all things through Christ which strengtheneth me.

14 Notwithstanding ye have well done, that ye did communicate with my affliction.

15 Now ye Philippians know also, that in the beginning of the gospel, when I departed from Macedonia, no church communicated with me as concerning giving and receiving, but ye only.

16 For even in Thessalonica ye sent once and again unto my necessity.

17 Not because I desire a gift: but I desire fruit that may abound to your account.

18 But I have all, and abound: I am full, having received of Epaphroditus the things *which were sent* from you, an odour of a sweet smell, a sacrifice acceptable, well-pleasing to God.

19 But my God shall supply all your need according to his riches in glory by Christ Jesus.

20 Now unto God and our Father *be* glory for ever and ever. Amen.

21 Salute every saint in Christ Jesus. The brethren which are with me greet you.

22 All the saints salute you, chiefly they that are of Caesar's household.

23 The grace of our Lord Jesus Christ *be* with you all. Amen.

8. The gospel embraces all truth. Every good thing comes from God. If the world has any edifying principle, any sound practice, any true doctrine, it is automatically accepted by the true Church. Converts to the Church never forsake anything they believe which is good and true; they simply gain the added light and knowledge which God has given by revelation to his servants the prophets. Thus we find Joseph Smith, building upon the concept here given by Paul, saying: "We believe in being honest, true, chaste, benevolent, virtuous, and in doing good to all men; indeed, we may say that we follow the admonition of Paul — We believe all things, we hope all things, we have endured many things, and hope to be able to endure all things. [1 Cor.

13:7.] If there is anything virtuous, lovely, or of good report or praiseworthy, we seek after these things." (Thirteenth Article of Faith.)

Christian conduct and virtues] See 1 Pet. 3:8-17.

11-13. Paul's concern was his ministry, not his worldly possessions.

18. The gift of the Philippians to Paul was a gift to the Lord and was pleasing in Deity's sight.

End of Volume Two